Richard R. Ryan

THE ORIGINAL NEW TESTAMENT

THE ORIGINAL NEW TESTAMENT

Edited and Translated from the Greek by
the Jewish Historian of Christian Beginnings

HUGH J. SCHONFIELD

Harper & Row, Publishers, San Francisco

Cambridge, Hagerstown, New York, Philadelphia
London, Mexico City, São Paulo, Singapore, Sydney

FIRST US EDITION

ISBN 0–06–250776–1
LC 85–42792

85 86 87 88 89 10 9 8 7 6 5 4 3 2 1

Contents

Palestine at the time of Jesus Christ

SYRIA

ABILENE

● **Damascus**

● **Sidon**

● Sarepta

P H O E N I C I A

● **Tyre**

● **Caesarea Philippi**

ITUREA

Jordan

The Great

Sea

TRACHONITIS

● Ptolemais

Chorazin

Capernaum

Bethsaida-Julius

GALILEE

Bethsaida

G A U L A N I T I S

B A T A N E A

● Raphana

Magdala

Sepphoris ●

Tiberias

Sea of Galilee

Nazareth ●

Cana

● Hippos

● Canatha

● Nain

● Gadara

AURANITIS

DECAPOLIS

● Scythopolis

● Dium

Caesarea ●

● Pella

SAMARIA

● Aenon

● Gerasa

Samaria ●

P l a i n   o f   S h a r o n

Apollonia ●

Shechem ● ● Salim

PEREA

Joppa ●

● Antipatris

● Ephraim

● Philadelphia

● Lydda

J U D E A

● Nicopolis

Jericho ●

Jamnia ●

Emmaus

Jerusalem

Bethany-beyond-Jordan

Azotus ●

Bethlehem ●

Ascalon ●

Herodium ●

● Machaerus

Hebron ●

Gaza ●

Engedi ●

Dead Sea

Masada ●

I D U M E A

Beersheba ●

Tetrarchy of Philip

Tetrarchy of Herod Antipas

0   Miles   30

Preface

The term 'Original' in the title of this version of the New Testament documents is intended to convey that it aims at giving back their contents to the modern world in the meaning intended by the writers, and at the same time to represent as closely as possible the original structures. Necessarily, since these writings represent conditions and ideas current in the Mediterranean area some two thousand years ago, the accompaniment of explanatory studies, notes and references has been essential, indeed indispensable.

Historically the documents are of major importance, not only for what they tell us of the Christian movement itself, but also for their reflection of many aspects of the social, political and religious life of the period, both among the Jews and in the Graeco-Roman world. As contemporary, or very near contemporary accounts they are singularly revealing, and in certain respects the information they furnish is obtainable from no other source; and it is therefore high time such a version was available, which did not seek to serve any theological or polemical aim.

Of course, the chief claim of the New Testament on our attention is that it offers us a great deal of the 'inside story' of Christian beginnings, and especially of the part played by Jesus in the character of the Christ (the Jewish Messiah). Many of the documents are letters, and what makes them so fresh and stimulating is that they were written almost on the spur of the moment, with no thought of general publication, in emotional reaction to internal needs and situations.

The language in which these documents have come down to us is Greek, not for the most part the polished Greek of polite and educated society, but more the commercial and domestic Greek of the multi-national Near East, sometimes even Yiddish-Greek, as colourful in imagery and metaphor as it is often careless in grammatical construction. Behind some texts are Hebrew and Aramaic sources. How can one convey the atmosphere of these records to the reader who is forced to depend on a translation? And more importantly, how can one persuade him to listen again to a tale he has probably heard so many times before, and convince him that he never has heard the whole story and the true story?

So many people already know all about the New Testament, or believe they do. Has it not been translated a number of times, read and studied for centuries? Is there not widespread familiarity with its language and contents? Yes, of course. Only let us consider this New Testament that is so well known. It is the volume held by Christians to be divinely inspired, the second part of the Holy Bible. It is a work of religious authority, read for devotional and doctrinal purposes. The translation of it, even in the very latest versions, has been almost exclusively the work of Christian theologians and conforms to an ecclesiastical pattern. A great deal of its terminology is the verbal currency of the Christian Faith, as this had become stereotyped in the course of a long tradition.

It is perfectly right and proper that the Church should have its authoritative versions of its sacred books. There must be some norm to sustain the common life of the Church in faith and worship. There can be improvement in accuracy of rendering on the basis of fresh evidence, and within limits the diction and presentation can be modernised. But the purpose of such versions obviously excludes any fundamental reassessment of ideas and values, any high-spirited kicking over of the ecclesiastical traces.

The reader of the Greek obviously enjoys many advantages. He can appreciate differences in style and literary quality. He can detect influences and the use of sources. He can more readily grasp the mood and feelings of the writers, sympathise with their difficulties in expressing themselves, or admire the facility and beauty of their compositions. It is the responsibility of the translator to be the medium by which as much of the character and quality of the documents can be achieved in a readable and realistic manner. This is difficult enough where only a single author is concerned. Manifestly it is much harder when the translator has to deal with a number of strongly individual writers. He may not, to do his job properly, employ a uniform style throughout. He must endeavour to vary it appropriately as the actor his voice and gestures. He must not be afraid of the unliterary phrase and the colloquialism, when much of what he is translating is unliterary and colloquial.

It was felt to be desirable not to employ familiar ecclesiastical terms where these could be avoided, since the use of them would give the impression that they were peculiarly Christian. This relates to such words as 'baptism' (immersion), 'church' (community), 'apostle' (envoy), 'bishop' (supervisor), and 'deacon' (administrator), but also sometimes to words like 'salvation', 'righteousness', 'faith', and 'grace', which occasionally do not accurately represent the sense of the original. Many Greek words have different meanings, according to the context in which they occur, or are interpreting Hebrew words, and it would be quite wrong always to translate them by the same English expression. Some very telling composite words like *oligopistos* cannot effectively be rendered by a single word in English, and one has to do one's best with a phrase like 'feeble in faith'.

While in general modern speech has been employed, the older English has been kept for the language of prayer, and here and there to retain the flavour of an orientalism. As regards proper names, these are as a rule given in their most familiar form, whether they relate to Old or New Testament personalities, thus Isaiah and Elijah, not Esias and Elias. But there are exceptions, especially where the termination of the name either in Hebrew or Greek has reference to God, thus Zechariah, not Zacharias, father of John the Baptist, and Timotheus, not Timothy. Place names have mostly been retained in the form best known, e.g. Capernaum instead of the more accurate Kefar-Nahum.

In tackling the New Testament texts a certain abandon and lack of refinement is imperative. The records in the original simply do not read as they are reproduced to serve the spiritual needs of the Christian Faith. As I have indicated, there is a diversity of style, often an absence of literary grace. There is passionate fervour as well as gentleness and moderation, sarcasm as well as courtesy, both beauty and ugliness. The translator has to endeavour to be as many persons as his strongly individualistic authors with their diverse characters and abilities. What we have been accustomed to reading is largely an idealised interpretation created by the various schools of Christian faith and piety. Set beside these hallowed versions the Original New Testament is an Epstein among the Old Masters, which may shock and even antagonise traditionalists before it comes to be understood and appreciated.

There must be no intention, of course, wilfully to run counter to cherished belief. But equally, consideration of the possible consequences must not induce the editor and translator to sacrifice literary and religious integrity. These venerable documents cannot rightly be comprehended unless they are related to the life and thoughts of their period. Especially is this the case with Jewish matters with which the New Testament is continually concerned. The present version is, so far as I am aware, the first to give the Jewish sources their proper place in elucidating the text of the New Testament.

I have sought to approach these records objectively, as if they had recently been recovered from a cave in the Holy Land or from beneath the sands in Egypt, and had never previously been given to the public. This has been my attitude of mind, though naturally I have availed myself of a host of scholarly authorities. But one cannot become intimate with people solely through study and learning: there must be sympathy, feeling and association. Otherwise one may misunderstand and misinterpret. For this reason, so far as the New Testament writers are concerned, I have spent to the best of my competence a great many years, more than half a lifetime, in their company and climate of ideas, so that I might represent them more faithfully and enable the first century of our era to speak directly to the twentieth.

It is now thirty years since I brought out on a limited scale the pioneer version of what I described as the Authentic New Testament, because it was a version authentic in accent and atmosphere that I was striving to reproduce. It received very high commendation from scholars and Church dignitaries. In the meantime knowledge has increased by so much and so many fresh sources of information have come to light, that revisions have been necessitated, not only in the translation itself but more particularly in the references to sources and background information, and in the chronology of events. I myself have been occupied with more researches published from time to time.

There is, I believe, a much greater interest in the real meaning and significance of the New Testament than there used to be. It is of course for Christians God's Revelation. I have been very mindful of that, and I am sure it will be evident that I have handled the text in no materialistic spirit and without any polemical purpose; and if I shall have offended or distressed anyone I am deeply sorry. But the New Testament also represents one of mankind's pregnant yesterdays, and merits the widest reading also by non-Christians. Here, then, are the circumstances of a Movement, and the terms of a Message, which nineteen centuries ago sought to communicate Faith, Hope and Love to a world which is still so sadly in need of all three.

It may be fitting in the special circumstances for the writer not to conclude with his own words, or with the words either of a Jewish or Christian authority, when he might be accused either of prejudice or flattery, but rather with the words not particularly gracious of a Christian scholar, George Sale, presenting his English version of the *Quran*, the Scriptures of Islam. "Having therefore undertaken a new translation, I have endeavoured to do the original impartial justice; not having, to the best of my knowledge, represented it, in any one instance, either better or worse than it really is."

H.J.S.

Introduction

For nearly eighteen centuries the volume known as the New Testament has formed the second division of the Holy Bible, the part of it relating to a Jew called Jesus (Yeshua) and his followers. He had believed himself to be the Messiah his people were anxiously awaiting, and many who subscribed to this conviction spread the word about him to his coreligionists in many parts of the Roman Empire. The message had largely to be communicated in the *lingua franca* of the Empire, which was Greek; and the designation *Christos* was employed to represent the Messiah (God's anointed), an idea alien to the Hellenes.

Initially, the proclamation was made in the synagogues of the Diaspora which were attended by many non-Jews attracted by the teaching about One invisible God, and the simplicity of Jewish worship. Their responsiveness to the dramatic tidings led certain of the envoys ('apostles'), notably a Jew called Saul (afterwards Paul), to proclaim the message directly to Gentiles. As a consequence there sprang up in different areas small groups of those who came to be known as Christians.

In the course of these developments need was soon found for documents. The activities of Paul in particular were creating a number of communities, mainly in Asia Minor and Greece, and he had need to maintain contact with them by letter, to instruct and encourage them, and to deal with various situations which arose. At this time no long period of history was anticipated before the climax of the Ages took place, when Jesus was expected to return from his lodgment in heaven to inaugurate his kingdom which would last a thousand years. But time passed, and his advent did not materialise. The initial envoys were speedily becoming extinct, largely because the Roman authorities were executing them as revolutionaries and prophets of doom, bent on ill-wishing and overthrowing the Empire. This conviction increased after the outbreak of the Jewish revolt in AD 68. But already before this the Great Fire of Rome had happened in the reign of the Emperor Nero, and had been attributed to the Christians.

The first official collection of documents to be made consisted of a number of Paul's letters, mostly addressed to leading communities. The collection served to share Paul's thinking and experiences, and also to counter the influence of teachers opposed to his views, some of whom had gone to the length of forging letters in his name.

Another documentary development reflected the public life and teaching of Jesus in his Messianic capacity. The books produced came to be known as *Gospels* because they recorded the 'Good News' of the Messiah's advent. They arose in two ways, firstly as a result of the activities of Peter, a Galilean fisherman who had been a close friend and follower of Jesus. According to early tradition, Peter visited the Christian groups in several countries to relate what he could recall of Jesus; but since he had to speak in Aramaic he required an interpreter. A young man, John Mark of Jerusalem, served him in this capacity, and afterwards wrote down what he could remember of what Jesus had said and done. But later, when he came to put these things in a book, he did not know with many of them the order in which they had occurred. Nevertheless, *Mark's Gospel* was to serve as a model for others.

A circumstance which may have contributed to the composition of *Mark's Gospel* was the publication of *The Jewish War* by Flavius Josephus. It was written in Greek and had a very wide circulation around AD 75. The work had dealt in considerable detail with the period in which Jesus had been active; but it made no mention of him. This could be damaging to the Christian propaganda, and made it of consequence that a biographical account of Jesus should become available.

The second cause which contributed to the writing of *Gospels* was the circulation of instruction documents which could readily be carried by those who proclaimed the Good News. Traditionally there were two such documents. One was a collection of passages from the Old Testament (the Hebrew Bible) held to demonstrate that Jesus was truly the predicted Messiah, with interpretations in terms of his experiences. The recovery of the Dead Sea Scrolls composed by the sect of Essenes before the time of Jesus has positively illustrated the manner in which this type of prophetic exegesis was conducted. The other document was a collection of sayings by or attributed to Jesus. Again we have illustrations of this kind of production in the compilation of sayings of the early Jewish rabbis, and in the *Gospel of Thomas* found in Egypt.

No copies of these originally Hebrew works have yet come to light; but they provided much of the non-Marcan material we find in the *Gospels* attributed to Matthew and Luke, more notably in *Matthew*. Reflecting the contents of the first document we have the citation of a number of Old Testament texts with their interpreted fulfilment in relation to Jesus. The second comes out most prominently in the Sermon on the Mount, which is a compendium of sayings. What is particularly to be noted in *Matthew* is their Hebraic character, including typical Hebrew parallelisms. We note that the Greek translator or scribe has made an occasional slip.

The Introduction to *Luke's Gospel* conveys that when this work was composed many *Gospels* were already in existence. This was quite natural as Christian communities in various parts of the Roman Empire would have their own, often reflecting something of the local environment of conditions and beliefs. Some tended to be quite alien and far-fetched, as we can perceive from fragments of several of the uncanonical *Gospels* which have survived in manuscript or quotations.

We have already made reference to Josephus. His works in Greek were an exciting phenomenon for the Christians, and Luke drew a good deal of his inspiration from them as we shall illustrate in the Preface to his *Gospel*. Another Jewish writer of the first century who greatly influenced the Christians was Philo of Alexandria. *John's Gospel* has Philonic concepts in it, and a particular fan of Philo was the author of the *Epistle to the Hebrews* who may have been a certain Apollos of Alexandria, who became a Christian through converts of Paul.

The choice of the four *Gospels* which are in the New Testament was held in the second century to be due partly to a respectable derivation, and partly as being representative of the Roman Empire itself: *Mark* the West, *Matthew* the South, *Luke* the North, and *John* the East. But we may believe that the choice was also influenced by the fact that these *Gospels* were relatively less exotic and more straightforward. Already by the second century there were a variety of off-shoots of Christianity promulgated by different teachers, such as Marcion and Cerinthus, and the Gnostics. Some were responsible for new Gospels. If the Four had not been made 'official' the Christian Church might well have disintegrated. More information will be found in the Prefaces to my translation of the Four. None of these was composed in the Holy Land. The considered view of the present editor is that *Mark* was composed in Italy, *Matthew* in Egypt, *Luke* in Greece, and *John* in Asia Minor.

We have to see the New Testament not as a planned volume in the sense that a number of individuals were invited to become

contributors, but as a compendium of the positions representative of what were regarded as being the most reliable traditions
of Jesus and his early followers, and which could exert a
unifying influence. In this last connection were included the
Acts of the Apostles and the *Second Epistle of Peter*, which aimed at
reconciling the conflicting positions of Peter and Paul, and to
convey that the granting of Christian status to Gentiles without
obligation to observe the Laws of Moses had the assent of the
Christian leadership, if not the approval. The ruling of the
Jerusalem Council did not in fact do what Paul wanted. It was
prepared to acknowledge Paul's converts as brethren under the
Messiah, provided they worshipped the One God and observed
the 'Laws of Noah' applicable to the righteous of all nations. But
they would not be regarded as part of Israel unless they became
naturalised Israelites upon whom the laws of Israel were
binding. Much of Paul's argument in his Letters was concerned
with his contention that converts from the Gentiles had become
Israelites by faith in the Messiah, and were covered by Jesus
having perfectly kept the Law. The circumstances have largely
been misinterpreted by the Church.

But there was a related aspect of the controversy. Peter had
represented the position of a human Jesus who had fulfilled the
Messianic Hope of Israel, while Paul was more concerned with a
mystical Messiah, whose appearance on earth was essential as
the Second Adam, but was subordinate to his transcendent
sovereignty of the universe, which anyone could acknowledge
by grace, and thus become united with him. The Pauline
position was more intellectual, and in certain respects related to
that of the chief contributor to the Fourth *Gospel*, who claimed
for the human Jesus that when he was in the world he had
exhibited the qualities of the Heavenly Messiah (the Son of Man)
portrayed by the Essenes and the mystics among the Pharisees.
Paul was finished with the human Jesus, and in all his letters
cites only one saying of his.

It is unfortunate that the account of Jesus produced by the
body of his Jewish followers in the Near East did not get into the
New Testament. Consequently, for the most part, Christians
have been denied access to highly relevant information affecting
their beliefs. The *Gospel* of these Jewish believers in Jesus as
Messiah had been composed in Hebrew, but it was known
anciently to the eastern division of the Gentile Church, and also
to Jewish scholars in the Holy Land. A copy had been in the
Christian Library at Caesarea, assembled by one called Pamphi-
lus. The erudite Jerome had translated a version into Latin, of

which some quotations have been preserved in his writings; and the Church Father Origen knew it well. There are certain Gospel MSS which have marginal notes from 'the Jewish'. Some instances of what could be read in the *Gospel of the Hebrews* will be given in the footnotes to the present translation.

According to early tradition the Mother Community of followers of Jesus was based in Jerusalem, under the leadership of his personal disciples, and headed by his brother next in age James (Jacob). James was a saintly personality, adored as their champion by the Jewish populace of Jerusalem. He was done to death at the instigation of the autocratic chief priest Annas the Younger, as Josephus recorded in his *Jewish Antiquities*. Annas was himself murdered in the course of the Jewish revolt.

Just before the outbreak of the war with the Romans, in AD 67, a number of members of the Jewish Christian Community – informed it is said by a revelation – under the leadership of Simeon, a first cousin of Jesus, went to Syria where there were numerous Essenes. The exiles were ruled for half a century by relations of Jesus, known as 'the Heirs'; but they failed to regain authority over the Christians at large, who now, being predominantly Gentiles, were inclined to antisemitism, especially after the disastrous ending of the Jewish Revolt, and still more the second revolt in the reign of Hadrian (in AD 132–135), when Simon Bar-Cochba had claimed the Messiahship.

The story of Christian beginnings has commonly been related with little reference to or comprehension of its Jewish aspects, the early history of the Nazoreans (Jewish Christians). An exception in the fourth century was the *Ecclesiastical History* of Eusebius of Caesarea. The omission is understandable in so far as it could have had an adverse effect on the Church's doctrines as they were to develop. But it is a deprivation which resulted in a one-sided and very inaccurate viewpoint, with horrifying consequences so far as the Jews of Europe were concerned. Jesus was made not only a stranger to his brethren, but their mortal foe seeking their extermination. It is only now, and especially since the creation of the State of Israel, that Jesus is being given back to his own people.

The dejudaising of Jesus was appreciably to affect both the Christian Faith, as in the Church's Creeds, and the comprehension of the New Testament, since it was responsible for a good deal of mistranslation and misinterpretation of the text. There still remain in the text itself a few wilful falsifications, rather more of them in the translations.

In honesty this has to be said and will be demonstrated in the translation and notes, but always mindful of the fact that for many millions the New Testament is part of the divinely inspired Word of God. In whatever sense this may be held to be true, it is not the case that the documents were dictated by spirit communication, as often depicted in churches. None of the manuscripts we have are the originals, or can be demonstrated to be the exact copies of originals. And there are a number of textual differences in the Greek manuscripts and in early translations like the Old Latin and Old Syriac. The authors themselves are frequently in disagreement with one another, in their ideas and convictions, and in the matters they record.

We will be turning to such issues shortly. But we have also to say here how extraordinarily 'alive' this collection of writings is. Here is the expression of primitive Christianity 'with the lid off'. Not only do we have the emotionally charged traditions relating to the person and experiences of Jesus: his story related as a kind of cosmic drama. We have the clashes and disputes of his devotees, their convictions, adventures and enterprises.

From whatever point of view the circumstances may now be regarded, Christianity was an extraordinary historical phenomenon. The native climate of its thought and teaching was that of pietistic and prophetic Judaism, attaching itself to an extraordinary ideology, the Messianic, and to a man believed to embody its fulfilment. But it drew also upon the mysticism and mythology of the non-Jewish world, fusing the longing and expectations of a sick and superstitious age in its own apocalyptic crucible, and generating in the process a white heat of fanatical zeal and anticipation. The electrifying Message, the Good News, spread madly, eagerly, like a raging fire, challenging the greatest aggregation of human power and authority the world had ever seen, and insisting on its replacement by the peaceful and benign new order of the Kingdom of God.

Because of its character there is every reason, especially in this day and age, to reveal the New Testament in its natural meaning and as a product of the time in which its contents were created, without over-concentration on doctrine and dogma. Certainly these writings have much to teach us, especially about ourselves. As someone has said: the Bible is not so much about Man's theology, as about God's anthropology.

The books of the New Testament are so much a product of their own period and varying environment that a translation without appropriate explanatory notes and references is an invitation to error on the part of the reader. This has been fully recognised by modern scholars in preparing their versions of antique literature of the Graeco-Roman period.

For the New Testament the translator has not only to be at home in Greek and Hebrew, he has to be informed of contemporary history, secular and religious, and of a whole library of relevant literature of the general period. The sources include many Jewish documents, ponderously labelled Apocrypha and Pseudepigrapha, known to and utilised by the New Testament authors, certain of the texts being regarded by the Christians as sacred writings in addition to the Old Testament, such as the Book of *Enoch* and the *Testaments of the Twelve Patriarchs*. A number of these works have only become generally accessible in the present century. An index of all ancient authorities involved or consulted will be found at the end of this publication.

The Period Atmosphere

The age that extended some four hundred years, roughly between 200 BC and AD 200, was extraordinarily prolific in literary expression. Men's minds were alert to a sense of history, to new knowledge of the meaning of life, to both spiritual and scientific pursuits and discoveries. There was an eager interchange of ideas, much questioning of positions both social and political; and in the background there was a brooding sense of climax, as if the peak of human destiny would soon be reached. Was there to be extinction, or was there something beyond? Inevitably prophets, astrologers and soothsayers flourished, and mystics of many kinds. Charlatanry reaped rich rewards. There was much syncretism of faiths and ideologies. The reader may feel that this is holding up a mirror to the contemporary world scene, and the two ages do have much in common.

The wise student of the New Testament will seek to inform himself fully of the prevailing circumstances, and seek as far as possible to comprehend them on a very broad front. Especially must he aim at a comprehension of Messianism as a driving force that made the world scene intelligible and purposeful.

Looking back to the first century it can be seen that Romanism was in the nature of an alternative to Messianism in that it was inspired by a sense of mission. The poet Virgil had written:

'Others, no doubt, will better mould the bronze
To the semblance of soft breathing, draw from marble
The living countenance; and others plead
With greater eloquence, or learn to measure
Better than we the pathway of the heaven,

The risings of the stars; remember, Roman,
To rule the people under law, to establish
The way of peace, to battle down the haughty,
To spare the meek. Our fine arts, these, forever.'[1]

But Romanism elected under the Caesars to assert a right to
dominate and control rather than to serve, and this gave
Christianity an opening. The clash between the two became
inevitable, in a kind of rivalry. But the issues were not clear cut,
since there was also something of domination in the Christian
programme. The conflict was at a level far more human than
divine, despite the claims to heavenly guidance on both sides.
The Christians saw the Messiah as God's representative at the
head of a new World Order, which would overthrow the Empire
with violence. The Romans saw Caesar as no less exalted. The
Emperor Augustus, around the time that Jesus was born, had
been addressed in an inscription as: "Jupiter, who holds from
Jupiter his father the title of Liberator, Master of Europe and
Asia, Star of all Greece, who lifts himself up with the glory of
Great Jupiter, Saviour."

At first the Romans had got on very well with the Jews: they
had much in common. In the Roman dominions the Jews had
enjoyed a measure of autonomy in the cities in which they
congregated, and their religious laws and practices had been
respected. An edict of Dolabella to the Ephesians stated: "I do
therefore grant them a freedom from going into the army, as the
former prefects have done, and permit them to use the customs
of their forefathers, in assembling together for sacred and
religious purposes, as their law requires, and for collecting
oblations necessary for sacrifices; and, my will is, that you write
this to the several cities under your jurisdiction." Another edict,
of Lucius Antonius, to the Sardinians, affirms: "Those Jews that
are our fellow-citizens of Rome, came to me and demonstrated
that they had an assembly of their own, according to the laws of
their forefathers, and this from the beginning, as also a place of
their own, wherein they determined their suits and controversies with one another. Upon their petition, therefore to
me, that these might be lawful to them, I gave order that these
their privileges be preserved, and they be permitted to do
accordingly."[2] At Miletus the Jews even had their own seats in
the theatre. One row was inscribed, "Place of the Jews, who are

---

[1] Virgil, *Aenid* VI, tr. C. Day Lewis.
[2] See Josephus, *Antiquities*, XIV.223ff.

also called God-fearing."[3]

But Roman imperialism was to change things, especially in relation to the Jews in their homeland, which was brought under Roman control as part of the Province of Syria. The assumption of divinity by Augustus made the introduction of the imperial tribute to be levied on the Jews intolerable for multitudes. Judas of Galilee raised the standard of revolt with the slogan "No Ruler but God". The party of Zealots for the Torah was born, and Messianic fervour was intensified. Relations rapidly deteriorated, and a further impulse to antagonism developed when the mad emperor Gaius Caligula sought to have a gold statue of himself set up for worship in the Temple at Jerusalem. The Antichrist was now revealed as one who would seat himself in God's Temple claiming to be God (*II Thess* 2:4).

In the middle of the first century AD the Christians could not readily be distinguished from the Jewish Zealots. Indeed many of them were Zealots (*Acts* 21:20). The Emperor Claudius, who succeeded Caligula, found it imperative to write to the Jews of Alexandria warning them not to entertain itinerant Jews from Syria, if they did not wish to be treated as abettors of "a pest which threatens the whole world". More drastically he ordered the expulsion of (foreign) Jews from Rome, "who were continually making disturbances at the instigation of Chrestus"[4] (ie engaging in Messianic agitation). Dio Cassius says that Claudius closed the synagogues at Rome,[5] as a consequence of Messianic propaganda, which included preaching the Gospel.

Many of the Jews in the Roman Provinces were themselves alarmed at the arrival of these Zealots, which imperilled their own security, if it was believed that they were parties to this subversive propaganda. Paul and his companion Silas were taken to be two of these agitators by the Jews of Thessalonica. In self-protection they denounced them, informing the politarchs that "these subverters of the civilized world (the Roman Empire) have now reached here . . . and they are all actively opposed to the imperial decrees, saying there is another king, one Jesus".[6]

---

[3] A. Deissmann, *Light from the Ancient East*, p 446.
[4] Suetonius, Claudius, xxv, *Lives of the Caesars*. The proper name Chrestus was often used in place of the unfamiliar Christus. Once in the New Testament itself by a scribal slip we have the reverse *christos* read for *chrestos* (*Phil* 1:21). And see *Acts* 18:2.
[5] Dio Cassius *Hist.* xl.6.
[6] *Acts* 17:6–7.

Paul was later indicted before the procurator Felix at Caesarea as a "plague-carrier, a fomentor of revolt among all the Jews of the Empire, a ringleader of the Nazarene sect".[7]

It has to be mentioned that one of the causes why in the Empire fewer and fewer Jews joined the Christian communities was their composition. Many members were slaves without rights, who found a haven, and some of the dregs of society were attracted by the promise of divine pardon. The Christians came to be distinguished both from the Jews and the Gentiles. They were credited, not without some cause, with horrible practices at their love-feasts, and stigmatised as "enemies of the human race".[8] They multiplied none the less, offering salvation from sin and hope of eternal life by identification with Christ in his death, burial and resurrection, a mystery understandable by those acquainted with the mystery cults of the period, especially that of Mithras. Unlike other associations and cults, which had costly rights of initiation, no slave was barred from the Community of Christ: he enjoyed equal rights. Inevitably, therefore, the slave and the social misfit, the pervert and the outcast, gravitated towards the Movement, causing a great deal of trouble within, and getting the Christians a bad name without. Salvation was theirs "without money, and without price" and a position of favour and comfort when Jesus should return to the earth.

The apostle Paul, who had chiefly been responsible for this development was terribly distressed by the unexpected interpretation of his principle of "liberty from the Law, in Christ". From the Jewish Christian side, and from the more sober Christians, horror at these developments was expressed in open letters sent out in the names of Jude and Peter (*II Peter*).

The Environment of Jesus

We return now to the homeland of Jesus and to the circumstances of his time. As imagined in the atmosphere of the Christian Sunday School we have a Jesus touring the peaceful countryside preaching and healing, and in Jewish terms a Wonder-Rabbi, almost totally unconcerned with the contemporary political and social circumstances. Such views are completely unrealistic, and do Jesus the gravest injustice. How could a man who believed he was his people's Messiah be unconcerned

[7] *Acts* 24:5.
[8] Tacitus, *Annals*, xv:44.

with their desperate plight? In fact the *Gospels*, especially *Matthew* and *Luke*, are very eloquent about the situation when we read them in conjunction with the works of Josephus and other sources.

The Jewish homeland had been taken over by the Romans in AD 6 after the deposition of Archelaus for misgovernment. A procurator was appointed for Judea, but Galilee was allowed to continue under an heir of Herod the Great, Herod Antipas, yet only as a puppet. The whole country was subject to the Legate of Syria, whose seat was at Antioch, and thus Roman rule effectively prevailed everywhere, but more positively in Judea where a Roman procurator, based at the seaport of Caesarea, was in charge. Following a period of comparative quiet the Jewish people were made more positively conscious of Roman domination when Pontius Pilate was made Procurator of Judea in AD 26. And he meant to show these Jews that they were no longer masters in their own house. Even the Jewish high priests were being appointed by the Romans, and to a considerable extent were collaborators with the regime upon which their position depended. Some had given bribes to obtain office, and were regarded as traitors to Israel. These were the functionaries who acted against Jesus, while the Jewish populace was on his side.[9]

Under these conditions many patriotic Jews had been made outlaws, and were forced to live by violence and highway robbery. Many fishermen on the Sea of Galilee were hand in glove with the rebels,[10] and sometimes acted as a link between the outlaws and their secret sympathisers.

Let us glance briefly at the contemporary circumstances referred to in the *Gospels*. A man who could not pay his lord the exorbitant dues demanded was liable to be sold with his wife and children to defray the debt (*Mt* 18:25). The poor widow, whose little livelihood has been taken away, has to deal with an unjust judge who fears neither God nor man, and she has no other means of redress than her importunity (*Lk* 18:1–5). Burglary and brigandage are common crimes (*Mt* 6:19, 24:23, *Lk* 10:30), while the rich man, hated for his hardness, goes off to enjoy himself abroad, leaving his underlings to amass money for him in the best way they can in his absence (*Lk* 12:16–21). The

---

[9] *Mark* 14:1–2.

[10] One at least of the Twelve Apostles was a Zealot, and some carried daggers, including Peter. Jesus quoted concerning himself. "He was classed with outlaws" (*Lk* 22:35–38; *Jn* 18:10).

plutocrat feasts sumptuously in his villa, caring nothing for the beggar covered with sores lying at his gates (*Lk* 16:19–31). The self-satisfied capitalist decides to retire on his gains (*Lk* 12:16–21). In a mental stupor by reason of their privations the common people follow any benefactor about like dogs (*Mt* 9:23–25, 15:30–31). False prophets trade on the people's misery (*Mt* 7:15–16). On signs of open disaffection the forces of the occupying power cut down the people in cold blood, even when engaged in worship (*Lk* 12:1–2). Reformers and patriotic preachers are arrested, and more often than not executed (*Mt* 10:16–39). Faithful souls run grave risks in giving such persons shelter (*Mt* 10:16–39). Spies and informers abound, and mingle with the crowds waiting to catch some word of antagonism to the authorities (*Mt* 13:9–13), or ask pointed questions involving political issues (*Mt* 15:15–21). The authorities are in continual fear of popular risings (*Mt* 26:5).

All these things and more came within the observation and experience of Jesus. Galilee was seething with unrest. Beggary had multiplied to an inconceivable extent even in a country where the mendicant was a familiar figure. Robbery with violence was so common that the courts had difficulty in dealing with the cases. Disease was rampant. A physician visiting the small towns and villages could not hope to cope with the number of nerve-cases; the blind, the deaf, the dumb, lepers, epileptics and paralytics, many owing their sufferings to the political and economic conditions. Women were hysterical, men frightened at shadows. The land was ridden by a great fear of the Evil One and his demons, believed to be working against the redemption of Israel. Superstition and religiosity flourished. There were those who gave themselves up to agonised prayer and severe fasting, and poor souls who ran wild and naked in the waste places and sheltered in tombs and in the rocks.

A system of spying on the meetings of citizens had been introduced by Herod the Great, and was still being operated. When Jesus spoke of the coming Kingdom of God, not a heavenly realm in the sky but a new age on earth, this was a dangerous theme. He was forced to speak in parables so that his message would not readily be intelligible to his audience, signalling what he was doing with the words: "Let him who can catch my meaning do so." Similarly, until he was ready to reveal himself as Messiah at Jerusalem he adopted the synonym of the mystics and referred to himself as the Son of Man, which would not convey to the masses and to government spies that he claimed to be king of the Jews (*Jn* 12:34). If Jesus had not taken these precautions his ministry would have abruptly ended when it had just begun, since any claim to be king in any part of the Roman Empire without the authority of Caesar was an act of high treason. It was for the crime of claiming to be king of the Jews that Jesus was crucified, as specified in the placard nailed to his cross.

Jesus was a master of repartee, and a quick and clever thinker, as he showed when put on the spot at Jerusalem by barbed questions. It was the time when the detested Roman tribute had come round again for payment (it was levied every fourteen years). "Are we to pay the Roman tax?" they asked him. He asked to be shown a Roman coin, a *denarius*, and said, "Whose is this portrait and inscription?" It is to be noted that like a Zealot he would not handle the coin himself which credited Caesar with divinity. Then said he, "Render to Caesar what is Caesar's, and to God what is God's." No official could take offence at this answer, as it was the custom when entering the Temple to exchange foreign coins for those of the Sanctuary which bore no heathen image and legend. They would understand that Jews should respect the two allegiances, the secular and the religious. But the Zealots would know that for loyal Jews the only Ruler was God, and consequently the second part of the saying cancelled the first. These were times of crisis for Israel, for multitudes the last great crisis, when God must surely intervene. And as if to confirm expectation there had suddenly appeared from the wilderness the figure of a man wearing the garment of a prophet of old. The voice of John the Baptist rang out with urgency and authority. For Jesus himself it had been a signal verifying that he was the Messiah, and throughout his brief career he upheld that status with insight and dignity.

Jesus packed into his teaching all that he felt was of real import for the spiritual and material welfare of his people in their hour of great need, following here in the steps of pious teachers, the Chasidim. In the work called *Testaments of the Twelve Patriarchs* it was written: "Unless you keep yourselves from the spirit of lying and of anger and love, truth and long-suffering, you shall perish. For anger is blindness, and does not permit one to see the face of any man with truth."[11] And again, "For the spirit of hatred works with Satan, through hastiness of spirit, in all things to men's death; but the spirit of love works with the Law of God in long-suffering to the salvation of men."[12] The

---

[11] *Test. Dan.* ii:1–2.
[12] *Test. Gad*, iv:7.

Chasidim had insisted that oaths were not required, and that
'Yes' or 'No' should be as binding as any oath. All swearing
indirectly countenanced idolatry.

Into the brief compass of the Sermon on the Mount is packed
all that Jesus felt was of real import in those grim and critical
times. He cleared away the shifting sands and got down to
bed-rock, enunciating those abiding principles upon which
alone the Community of the Kingdom of God could be securely
founded. But as the months went by he knew ever more clearly
that he would be, indeed must be, the victim of the forces
governing 'this world', but remaining firm in his conviction that
this was the only way to attain 'that world', the Kingdom of God
finally established among men. Thus at the last, knowing what
must happen to him there, Jesus "turned firmly towards
Jerusalem".

It is a Roman author, even if he may be guilty of some
prejudice, who has supplied what may be regarded both as a
justification of the Sermon on the Mount and a commentary on
the ultimate consequences for Jesus himself.

"Among the calamities of that black period," writes the
historian Tacitus, "the most trying grievance was the degenerate spirit, with which the first men in the Senate submitted to the
drudgery of becoming common informers; some without a
blush in the face of day; and others by clandestine artifices. The
contagion was epidemic. Near relations, aliens in blood, friends
and strangers, known and unknown, were, without distinction,
all involved in one common danger. The act recently committed,
and the tale revived, were equally destructive. Words alone
were sufficient; whether spoken in the forum, or amidst the
pleasures of the table . . . Informers struggled, as it were in a
race, who should be the first to ruin his man; some to secure
themselves; the greater part infected by the general corruption
of the times."[13]

Only in AD 28, contemporary with the time of Jesus, in the
calends of January, Sabinus, an eminent Roman knight, had
been seized in Rome, and dragged through the streets to
summary execution on a feast day. The general murmur was:
"Will there never be a day unpolluted with blood? Amidst the
rites and ceremonies of a season sacred to religion, when all
business is at a standstill, and the use of profane words is by law
prohibited, we hear the clank of chains; we see the halter, and
the murder of a fellow-citizen. The innovation, monstrous as it

---

[13] Tacit. *Annals*, Bk. VI. vii.

is, is a deliberate act, the policy of Tiberius. He means to make cruelty systematic. By this unheard-of outrage he gives public notice to the magistrates, that on the first day of the year they are to open, not only the temples and the altars, but also the dungeons and the charnel-house."[14]

And this was in Rome itself, not in captive Judea! So what hope was there for the popularly acclaimed king of the Jews on the feast of the first month of the Jewish national year, if he was charged with 'blasphemy' against divine Caesar, this same Tiberius, before the arrogant Jew-hating Roman who administered Judea for his despotic master?

The New Testament Text

In the foregoing pages we have endeavoured to indicate, mainly in the social and political sphere, how closely in touch were the writers of the New Testament documents with the thought and circumstances of their time, whether in the Holy Land or in other parts of the Roman Empire.

But it is not alone in references and allusions that these records reflect their time and are of their time. They belong to it, as we have partly shown, in atmosphere, and in the realm of ideas, though it is only in our day that knowledge has begun to pile up which discloses what were the precise elements in Judaism which gave rise to Christianity. We can now see relationships where previously there were assumed to be antitheses. This should be salutary both for Jews and Christians, and in fact has already begun to promote a better understanding between them.

The Jewishness that is present almost everywhere in the Greek New Testament is truly remarkable. It comes out in hundreds of small points. Many of these have been recognised by scholars; but there are some which previously have escaped general Christian notice. Of particular interest and significance are the liturgical elements, the Jewish construction of prayers, the delight in benedictions and doxologies. There are both direct and indirect references, not only to rites and ceremonies connected with the Temple and Synagogue, but also to some of the most ancient Hebrew prayers and praises, such as the *Kaddish*, which still have a place in the *Authorised Jewish Prayer Book*. It is needful for the translator to be fully informed on these matters. To give only a single instance of the importance of

[14] Tacitus, *Annals*, Bk. IV. lxx.

consulting Jewish liturgical sources, we should never have had the expression "and on earth peace" in the angelic doxology in *Luke* 2:14 had this been done by previous translators. The "glory" is to God above and below, in the highest and on earth, the "peace" is to men of good will, or better, to men who please him.

There are rectifications of the text itself suggested by a knowledge of Hebrew and Aramaic. Many of these have to be made conjecturally, but in several instances the evidence is quite overwhelming that the original translator into Greek has misunderstood or made a slip in his rendering. Also in translation there have been lost certain plays on words and poetic parallelisms. The reader is invited to be conscious of the notes, and to digest them. Some parts of the text are themselves commentaries, interpretations and explanations, especially in the case of the *Gospels*. These have been excerpted and printed at the foot of the page, and are indicated by letters of the alphabet. The editor's notes have been placed below these, and beneath a rule across the page, and are indicated by numerals.

For some fifteen hundred years the New Testament documents were hand-written by scribes, and mistakes could thus be made by carelessness and inattentiveness on the part of the copyists. One such slip has already been noted where *christos* has been read instead of *chrestos* in *Phil* 2:21. Paul had not said "For me to live is Christ, and to die is gain". What he had said was, "It is useful (*chrestos*) for me to live, and an advantage to die . . . and I hardly know which to choose. I am in a quandary between the two". Such errors could more readily occur in uncial texts, that is those written entirely in capitals, and not even spaces between words. But there could also be small additions and alterations made in the interest of changed Christian doctrine especially around the third century when an 'orthodoxy' was being established.

The text of the New Testament on which this translation is based is what is called a critical text, arrived at by a painstaking study of the more important copies and versions of the different books made for the most part, but not exclusively, between the second and fifth centuries. No individual manuscript is followed completely, and there are some which have preserved venerable and interesting readings which may reflect a genuine tradition. It may be accepted with confidence that we have at our command the New Testament substantially as the writings contained in it could be read within a century of their composition.

There were no chapters and verses in the manuscripts. The chapters now in use were adopted in the thirteenth century and the verse divisions as late as the sixteenth century. Their value was to assist reading and reference, but they are in no sense authoritative. In the present version they have been indicated in the margin, and employed for reference in the footnotes, for purposes of study and comparison. The absence in the manuscripts of the divisions with which we are familiar does not mean, however, that the documents had no structure. In several instances it has been possible to ascertain the plan upon which the book was constructed originally. In such cases, as far as was practicable, that plan has been reproduced. For example, the *Gospel of Mark* is made up of a series of short episodes, which have been numbered. The *Gospel of Matthew* is in five books with sub-sections, together with a Prologue and Epilogue. *John*, which combines the work of two individuals, exhibits, as regards one of these, traces of a series of clearly defined sections. The *Revelation* consists of two books, also with a Prologue and Epilogue, each book containing a series of visions to which the present editor has given descriptive titles. In other documents, eg *Luke–Acts*, chapters have been introduced according to the sense, while letters have only been broken up into suitable paragraphs.

In addition to these changes in presentation designed to bring out the character of each document, elements of documents have wherever possible been distinguished, notably in the case of Paul's letters to the community at Corinth, where the original four letters have been restored, partially and conjecturally, out of the two into which they had become combined. In respect of the *Gospel of John*, apart from problems relating to authorship discussed in the preface to the translation, passages in the nature of comment have had to be treated as such and placed at the foot of the page. This makes things much clearer.

The order in which the books appear in the ecclesiastical versions is not an order of publication, but largely of type and to an extent of authority: *Gospels, Acts, Epistles, Revelation*. But in arranging the elements for general and intelligent reading, certain changes in order are obviously desirable, first to keep together those documents which are in some way associated, and second to give some consideration to chronological sequence. Commonsense requires that the *Gospel of John* should not be sandwiched between the two parts of Luke's work, the *Gospel* and *Acts*. Nor should the *Gospel of John* be separated from the *Letters of John*. Equally a rational editing of Paul's letters requires that they be placed as far as possible in chronological order. *Romans* was only placed first because of the predominance of the Roman Church.

Chronology

Since the aim of this version was to retain the New Testament documents within the framework of their period and setting, questions of chronology could not be ignored. Archaeological discoveries in the present century have made it more practicable to date accurately, or more reliably the sequence of events in the Christian story down to the end of the first century, and a Chronological Table has accordingly been provided.

But it has to be recognised that the dating of events in the life of Jesus cannot be treated so positively. The chief reason for this is the two different accounts of his birth given in the *Gospels* of *Matthew* and *Luke*. They cannot be reconciled despite the noble efforts of staunch Christian scholars. *Matthew* makes Jesus to have been born around 7–6 BC, some two years before the death of Herod the Great, while *Luke* claims he was born at the time of the institution of the Roman Census under Quirinius as legate of Syria, AD 6–7. Early Christian tradition would seem to favour *Matthew* rather than *Luke*. The latter seems to have been influenced by the need to establish that though Jesus resided in Galilee he still qualified as Messiah by having been born in Bethlehem of Judaea, David's city. His parents had come from Galilee to the ancestral home just prior to his birth, because under the census regulations now introduced in the Jewish homeland they were required to register there.

However, the present editor in his capacity as historian, believes that there can be greater certainty in dating the crucifixion of Jesus in the year AD 36, subsequent to the execution of John the Baptist in AD 35. Jesus would then have been 42–43 when he died, consistent with *John* 8:57 where the people say to him, "You are not yet fifty". The problem, so far as the general reader is concerned, should be regarded as not finally resolved.

A complete index of the ancient authorities cited, with an explanation of abbreviations employed, will be found at the end of the volume. In two instances modern sources of information have been utilised, (JE) *Jewish Encyclopaedia* (Funk and Wagnalls) and (AJP) *Authorised (Jewish) Daily Prayer Book* (Eyre and Spottiswoode). The writer has been indebted to the works of a host of scholars; but it would have been out of place in a work primarily intended for popular reading to load the pages with all the acknowledgments that would have had to be listed.

Quite deliberately the notes have been restricted to furnishing such information as might be of material use and interest to the Bible student, without being too academic. There has been no intention to provide a full-scale commentary, only to convey an impression of the native atmosphere and climate of ideas and the quality and sense of the varied documents. For parallel passages in the Gospels explanatory notes have not usually been repeated; but cross-referencing has been supplied.

In a personal capacity I am most deeply grateful to the eminent authorities who have done me the honour to read and comment so favourably on my undertaking. It will represent what they have in common if I quote Prof. Robert M. Grant of The Federated Theological Faculty, The University of Chicago, who wrote: "The New Testament needs translating in every generation, and Schonfield has made a fresh version which really comes alive. His work provides a much-needed bridge between Judaism and Christianity."

It remains to add a footnote on theology, since both the translation and the interpretation of the text are in a number of places affected by it. Christians have understood what they read in terms of the major credal statements of the fourth century, whereas the present version could only have in view the doctrines of the first century in the forms expressed variously in the *Gospels* and the Pauline Epistles.

It is only lately that it has been possible to appreciate the influence of the Christology of pietistic Judaism, with its 'as above so below' imagination. Here the redemption would be effected by the Heavenly Messiah the archetypal Son of Man, incarnating in the Earthly Messiah. The fusion is represented in a number of sayings attributed to Jesus, notably in the story of his transfiguration. The imagination of the Christ Above is particularly set out in a work known as the *Similitudes of Enoch*, advancing from the Son of Man image in the Biblical book of *Daniel*.

Non-Jewish converts to Christianity understood such teachings only with difficulty since the Messianic concept was alien to them. They could more clearly understand that the Christ as king was Son of God as the Roman emperor was Son of Jupiter, worshipped as such, and the ruler of Egypt was son of the god Re.

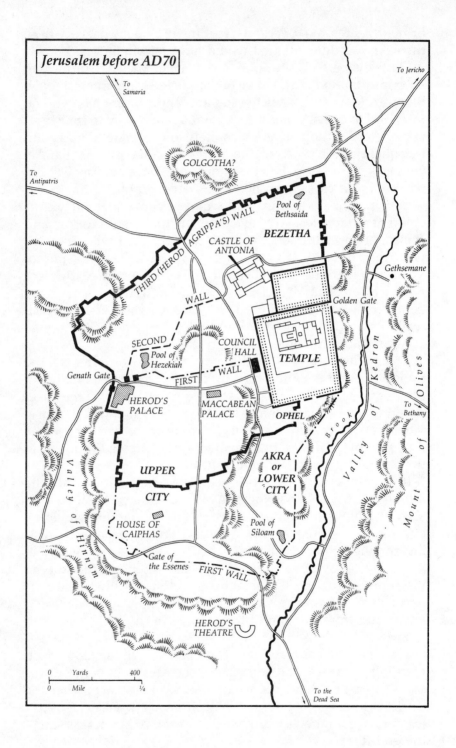

Jerusalem before AD 70

MARK

The Recollections of Peter

Preface to Mark

What is at present the oldest extant account of the career of Jesus is that which is attributed to a certain John of Jerusalem, who bore the Latin name of Mark (Marcus). He is mentioned in the *Acts* and in the letter known as *I Peter*. Having been chosen as assistant to Paul and Barnabas he accompanied them on an initial tour to proclaim the Messiahship of Jesus. But he appears to have taken offence that Paul should speak on this theme in front of the heathen Roman governor of Cyprus, Sergius Paulus, and he returned home. Later he travelled with Peter, acting, according to tradition, as his interpreter, since Peter's Greek was inadequate.

We are informed by an inquiring second-century writer, Papias of Hierapolis, that Mark kept notes of what Peter related in his addresses of things said and done by Jesus, and these ultimately formed the substance of his *Gospel*. But Papias also explains that Mark was not attempting "an orderly narrative", since he was unclear about the actual sequence of events and in some instances what sayings of Jesus belonged to particular occasions.

The tradition agrees with the character of our work, organised into a book from a collection of notes of what Peter had said. The *Gospel* is composed of a series of episodes set down with great economy of words and without literary polish. The author has an extraordinary fondness for the Greek word *euthys*, 'at once', 'directly', 'immediately', often used like the colloquial '*next thing* he was running down the road', which conveys the sense of reported speech rather than literary composition. It is this unaffectedness and conversational tone that constitutes much of the charm of the book, and tends to confirm that substantially it is the reminiscences of Peter we are reading. Some words of Jesus are even left in the original Aramaic, as Peter would have quoted them.

The *Gospel* was probably composed in Italy, the last area of Peter's activities and where he died; but according to Church historians Mark later went to Egypt. The date of the book is perhaps around AD 75–80.

Mark was designed for the non-Jewish reader, as is evident from the text, though Jewish forms of expression often occur as one would expect from a Jewish writer reflecting a Jewish speaker. The book also furnishes comments and some notes explaining Jewish customs or translating Aramaic and Hebrew words. It is impossible to say whether these were made by the author or added by a very early copyist. In conformity with the plan of the present version such notes and comments are printed immediately below the text and are indicated by letters of the alphabet, while the translator's own notes are printed in smaller type below a rule and are indicated by numerals.

Section xxxvi (*Mark* 13) probably reflects a short document in the nature of a revelation by Jesus to the Jerusalem Church, which tradition says was received shortly before the Jewish war with the Romans. Its inclusion suggests that *Mark* was not composed until after the war.

We cannot tell to what extent the text was changed in small details by later copyists, but it has long been known that the end of *Mark* is defective. The book breaks off in the middle of a sentence, and we do not know why. The present ending was tacked on to complete the work and is not part of the original.

From a letter by the second century Church Father Clement of Alexandria, discovered by Morton Smith at the Mar Saba monastery, a longer text of *Mark* had once existed which contained esoteric information. This 'secret gospel' was not put into circulation. It contained a version of the Lazarus story, which is not in *Mark* as we have it, and it is quite possible that the ascription of the book to Mark was due to the fact of his association with Egypt. There is very little mysticism in canonical *Mark*.

The Good News of Jesus Christ

Mark's Version

Introduction

1.1　The Good News of Jesus Christ[1] began as stated in Isaiah the prophet,

> *Lo, I send my messenger before you,*
> *To pave the way for you.*
> *A voice cries out in the wilderness,*
> *"Make ready the Lord's road!*
> *Put his highways in order!"*[2]

John the Baptist[3] appeared in the wilderness, proclaiming a penitential immersion for forgiveness of sins; 5 and the whole Judean countryside and all the inhabitants of Jerusalem flocked to him, and were immersed by him in the River Jordan as they confessed their sins.

John wore camel-hair clothing with a leather girdle round his waist, and his diet was locusts and wild honey. He announced further, "After me will come one who is mightier than me, whose sandal-straps I am not fit to stoop down and untie. I have immersed you in water, but he will immerse you in holy Spirit."

i

Now it was at this time that Jesus came from Nazareth 10 in Galilee, and was immersed by John in the Jordan. No

---

1 Strictly Jesus should be described as *the* Christ (ie the Messiah), but in writing for non-Jews unfamiliar with the term Messiah (the anointed one) the definite article was dropped.
2 *Mal* 3:1 is combined with *Isa* 40:3.
3 The Immerser or Dipper.

sooner, however, had he come up from the water than he saw the skies part and the Spirit like a dove descending to him, while a voice came from the skies, "You are my dear son. I am very pleased with you"

At once the Spirit drove him out into the wilderness; and he remained in the wilderness for forty days, tested there by Satan. He was among the wild beasts, and the angels took care of him.

ii

After John had been arrested, Jesus went to Galilee,
15 proclaiming God's News[4] and declaring, "The appointed time has come, and the Kingdom of God[5] is at hand. Repent, and believe the News!"

As he went along the shore of the Sea of Galilee he saw Simon, and Simon's brother Andrew, casting a net into the sea.[a]

Jesus said to them, "Follow me, and I will make you fishers of men."

They immediately abandoned their nets and joined him.

A little further on Jesus saw James[6] the son of Zebedee and his brother John. They were in the boat repairing
20 their nets. Directly he called them they left their father Zebedee in the boat with the hired hands and set off with him.

iii

They made their way to Capernaum,[7] and there on the sabbaths Jesus went into the synagogue and taught. They were astounded at his teaching; for he taught with authority and not like the scribes.[8]

a They were fishermen.

---

4 Here, as in most other places, it seemed best to render *Evangelion* as 'News' *par excellence*.
5 The time when God will be acknowledged by the world as the supreme ruler.
6 Substitute in the English fashion for the name Jacob.
7 Kfar-Nahum, 'Village of Nahum'.
8 Synagogues were also community centres for discussion and education. Jesus spoke without citing various spiritual authorities in support of his views.

Now in their synagogue there was a man possessed by a foul spirit, and it screamed out, "What do you want with us, Jesus the Nazarene? Have you come to destroy us? I know who you are, the Holy One of God!"

25   "Be quiet!"[9] Jesus rebuked it, "and come out of him."

Then the foul spirit convulsed the man, and with a sharp cry came out of him.

They were all amazed, so much so that they questioned one another, "What does this mean? Is it a new teaching? He even commands the foul spirits with authority, and they obey him!"

At once the report of him spread in all directions throughout the whole region of Galilee.

iv

Jesus left the synagogue and went immediately with James and John to the home of Simon and Andrew.
30   Simon's mother-in-law was laid up with a fever, and they at once told him about her. Going to her he raised her up, taking her by the hand; and the fever left her, and she waited on them.

When evening came, and the sun had set,[10] the people brought him all who were ill and those who were demon-possessed. Indeed, the whole town was assembled at the door. Jesus cured those who were afflicted with various complaints and expelled many demons, but he would not let the demons speak because they knew him to be the Messiah.

35   Having risen early while it was still quite dark, Jesus went out and made for the open country, and there prayed. But Simon and his friends were close behind, and when they found him they said to him, "Everyone is looking for you."

"Let us go elsewhere," he said, "to the neighbouring towns, that I may speak there also. That is why I came away."

So he set off, preaching in their synagogues all over Galilee, and expelling the demons.

9 (And see v34.) The demons identified Jesus as the Messiah, the king of the Jews. To claim to be a king in a Roman province was high treasor. against Caesar. If Jesus had allowed himself to be so addressed he would promptly have been arrested and executed. This is why he did not do so until the close of his activities, first disclosing who he was secretly, to his closest disciples, and later publicly by riding into Jerusalem as king.
10 Signifying the end of the sabbath.

v

40   Now a leper came to him begging him on his knees, "If only you will you can make me clean."

With deep pity Jesus put out his hand and touched him, saying, "I do will it. Be cleansed!"

At once the leprosy was gone from him, and he was clean again.

Jesus immediately sent him away, giving him strict instructions, "Be sure you tell no one. Go instead and show yourself to the priest and offer for your cleansing what Moses prescribed as evidence for them."[11]

45   But when the man left he blurted it all out and broad-cast the fact, so that it became impossible for Jesus to enter a town openly. He was forced to stay outside in the open country; and there they came to him from every quarter.

vi

2.1   When Jesus again entered Capernaum some time afterwards the report went round: "He is back." And so many people collected that there was no more room, not even at the door. And he gave them his message.

One party arrived bringing him a paralysed man carried by four bearers. Unable to get near him because of the crush they dismantled the roof directly above him, and when they had cleared a space they let down the mattress on which the paralysed man was lying.

5   Seeing what faith they had, Jesus said to the paralytic, "Son, your sins are forgiven you."

There were some of the scribes there, sitting and debating in their minds, "What is this he is saying? He blasphemes. Who but One, God himself, can forgive sins?"

Sensing at once that this was what they were arguing among themselves, Jesus said to them, "Why are you debating these things in your minds? Which is easier, to tell the paralytic, 'Your sins are forgiven you', or to say to

10   him, 'Rise, pick up your mattress and walk'? But that you

---

11 See *Lev* 14, and cf *Deut* 4:44.

may know that the Son of Man[12] is entitled to forgive sins on earth" – he addressed the paralytic – "To you I say, rise, pick up your mattress, and go to your home."

He rose, and immediately picking up his mattress went out in front of them all; so that they were all astounded and praised God,[13] for, they said, "we have never seen the like of this".

vii

Jesus went again to the seashore, and the whole crowd came to him there, and he taught them.

As he went along he saw Levi the son of Alphaeus seated at the customs-station,[14] and said to him, "Follow me!"

Levi rose and followed him, and then invited him to
15　dine at his house. And many tax-collectors and sinners[15] sat down to dine with Jesus and his disciples.[a]

The Pharisee scribes, observing that Jesus ate with sinners and tax-collectors, said to his disciples, "How can he eat with tax-collectors and sinners?"[15]

Jesus heard this and said to them, "It is not the healthy who need a doctor: it is those who are ill. I have not come to call pious people, but sinners."

Now the disciples of John[16] and of the Pharisees were observing a fast.[17] Jesus was asked, "Why is it that the disciples of John and the disciples of the Pharisees are fasting while your disciples are not fasting?"

a　A number of them had joined him.

12　'Son of Man' had messianic significance for the Jewish mystics. See *Dan* 8:13–14. The theme was developed in the *Book of Enoch*. But for the Jewish masses it did not have this special implication: it simply meant 'a man', a human being. See *John* 12:34. The term thus gave Jesus anonymity while still relating himself to the Messianic.

13　Formulae of praise to God were prescribed for recitation suited to various occasions, such as on witnessing a marvel, as here. The actual words are given in *Matthew*. See p 73 n 8.

14　As a trading post Capernaum had a customs-station.

15　'Sinners' here means Jews who live like Gentiles not observing the dietary and other laws. They were regarded with Jewish collectors of the Roman imposts as outside the pale of decent society.

16　ie the Baptist.

17　The Pharisees fasted on Mondays and Thursdays.

Jesus replied, "Is it customary for the bridal party[18] to
20 fast while the bridegroom is with them?[a] The time will
come when the bridegroom will have taken his
departure: that will be the time for them to fast.

"No one sews a patch of newly made cloth on an old
cloak. If he does, it will drag the stuff apart – the new
from the old – and the tear will be made worse. Nor does
anyone pour new wine into old wine-skins. If he does,
the wine will burst the skins, and both wine and skins
will be lost."

viii

Jesus happened to take his way on the sabbath
through the standing corn, and his disciples plucked the
ears as they went along. "Look!" the Pharisees said to
him, "Why are they doing what is not permitted on the
sabbath?"
25   "Have you never read," Jesus answered, "what David
did when need arose and he and his companions were
hungry, how he went into the house of God[b] and ate the
loaves of the Presence,[c] and even gave some to his men?
The sabbath was made for man's sake," he pointed out,
"not man for the sabbath's sake."[d][19]
3.1   When next he went to the synagogue there was a man
there with a withered hand. They waited expectantly to
see whether he would cure him on the sabbath, so that
they could bring a charge against him.

"Come up to the front," he invited the man with the
withered hand.

Then he said to them, "Is it permitted on the sabbath to
do good or to do harm, to save life or to destroy it?"

They remained silent.
5   When he had looked angrily around at them, visibly
hurt by their callousness, he said to the man, "Stretch
out your hand!"

a For the period the bridegroom is with them it is not customary to
fast.
b Abiathar was then high priest. (According to I *Sam* 21 the priest was
Ahimelech. *Tr.*)
c Which only the priests were allowed to eat.
d So the Son of Man is master even of the sabbath.

---

18 Lit "children of the bridal bower" (Heb. idiom).
19 This was also the Rabbinical teaching. There was another comparable
saying, "The world was made only for the sake of Israel."

He stretched it out, and his hand was restored.

Thereupon the Pharisees left and immediately conferred with the Herodians[20] about Jesus, how they might destroy him.

ix

Jesus with his disciples withdrew to the sea,[21] and a vast concourse from Galilee followed him. From Judea and Jerusalem too great numbers came to him when they learnt of his activities, and from Idumea, from beyond Jordan, and from the region of Tyre and Sidon.[22]

He told his disciples to hurry forward the preparation
10 of a small ship for him because of the throng, in case they should mob him.[a] Meanwhile he climbed the hill, and summoned those he wanted, and they came to him. Of these he appointed twelve, whom he termed envoys, to be associated with him, so that he could send them out to
15 preach with power to expel demons.

He appointed as the twelve, Peter,[b] James the son of Zebedee and his brother John,[c] Andrew, Philip, Bartholemew, Matthew, Thomas, James the son of Alphaeus, Thaddaeus, Simon the Zealot,[23] and Judas Iscariot.[d]

a For he had cured many, causing all who were afflicted with diseases to fling themselves on him to touch him. And the foul spirits, when they detected him, assailed him with the cry, "You are the Son of God",[24] though he insisted that they should not reveal his identity.

b Meaning 'Rock', the name he gave Simon.

c He gave them the nickname *Boanerges*, which means 'Tempestuous' (Lit. Aram. 'sons of the storm-wind'. *Tr*.)

d Who actually betrayed him.[25]

---

20 The Party supporting the Herodian rulers, who would be hostile to any Davidic claimant to the throne, and indeed to anyone with a popular following who could be politically dangerous, such as John the Baptist whom Herod Antipas arrested in Galilee.

21 ie the Sea of Galilee.

22 Many came from all parts of the country.

23 Lit 'Kananean', Aram. *Qana*, one of the Zealots, the extreme militant patriotic party: cf *Lk* 6:15.

24 Rulers were invested with divine sonship. Thus Pharaoh was 'Son of Ra' and Caesar was 'Son of Jupiter'. 'Son of God' was used of Jewish kings in an adoptionist sense, see *Ps* 2 and II *Sam* 7:13–14, and thus the Messiah as king of Israel was so designated (*Mt* 16:15–18, 26:63).

25 "Betrayed him." Heb. *hisgir-otho* (or *hiskir-otho*), a very early word-play on the name Iscarioth, which actually represents Sicariotes, member of the anti-Roman Jewish terrorists who carried curved daggers (sicars) under their robes.

x

20   When Jesus returned home the crowd reassembled, so that it became impossible for them even to take their meals.

On hearing what was going on, his relations came to take charge of him. "He must be out of his mind," they said. But when the scribes from Jerusalem came down, their view was: "He is possessed by Beelzebul. He expels demons by the chief of the demons."

Calling the scribes to him Jesus addressed them in
25   proverbs. "How can Satan expel Satan?" he inquired. "If a kingdom is at odds with itself that kingdom cannot endure. And if any household is at odds with itself that household cannot endure. So if Satan takes action against himself, and is divided, he cannot endure. That is the end of him. On the other hand no one can enter the Strong One's abode to loot his possessions before he has first bound the Strong One. Only then can he loot his abode.

"I tell you positively,[26] men will be forgiven everything; their crimes, and every slanderous thing they may have spoken: but there can never be forgiveness for the man who slanders the holy Spirit: he has committed a permanent crime."[a]

30   At this juncture his mother and brothers arrived, and standing outside sent to call him. There was a crowd seated round him, but they managed to tell him, "Please, your mother and brothers are outside asking for you."

"What do you mean, my mother and brothers?" he replied. Looking around the circle seated about him, he said, "Here are my mother and brothers. Whoever does the will of God is my brother and sister and mother."

xi

4.1   Once more Jesus taught beside the sea, and such a vast crowd collected that he went on board a ship moored in the shallows, while all the crowd stood on shore at the water's edge.

---

a They had said, "He is possessed by a foul spirit."

---

26 Lit "Amen". Jesus constantly employed this emphatic Hebrew word, which the Greek has not translated.

He taught them a great many things by similes. "Now listen," he said as he taught. "The sower went to sow. As he sowed, some seed fell by the wayside and the birds came and ate it up. Other seed fell on stony ground where there was not much soil, and sprouted rapidly because the soil had little depth. But when the sun came up it was parched, and because it had no root it withered. Other seed fell among thistles, and the thistles sprang up and choked it, and it produced no fruit. Still other seed fell in good soil and produced fruit, having sprung up and grown tall, yielding thirtyfold, sixtyfold, and even a hundredfold." He concluded, "Let him who can catch my meaning do so."[27]

10　When they were on their own, his associates, including the twelve, asked him to explain the simile.

Then he said to them, "You are entitled to know the secret of the Kingdom of God, but for those outside[28] everything is expressed in similes, that

> *They may see indeed, but not perceive,*
> *And hear indeed, yet not understand,*
> *Lest they turn again and be forgiven.*[29]

"Does this simile convey nothing to you?" he asked. "How then will you grasp the implication of my other similes?

15　"The sower sows the Message. There are those who are 'by the wayside' where the Message is sown; and no sooner have they heard it than along comes Satan and pecks out the Message that is sown for them. Then there are those who are like the seed sown on stony ground. No sooner have they heard the Message than they accept it joyfully; but having no root in themselves they are short-lived, and so when trouble or persecution arises because of the Message they are immediately put off. Then there are the 'sown among thistles' kind of people. These are they who really heed the Message; but the constant economic struggle, the lure of getting rich, and

---

27　Lit "Whoever has ears to hear, let him hear."
28　Those who do not belong to the elect, who are those 'on the inside'. The theme of the Kingdom of God was politically dangerous. Spies and informers mixed with the crowd listening for subversive words. Jesus, therefore, deliberately used similes when referring to the Kingdom of God, the Messianic Age.
29　*Isa* 6:9–10.

the cravings that come for all sorts of other things, choke
20   the Message, and it becomes unfruitful. Finally there are
the 'sown in good soil' kind of people. These are they
who hear the Message, welcome it, and produce fruit,
thirtyfold, sixtyfold, and even a hundredfold."

Then he said to them, "Is a lamp brought in to be put
under a measuring-bowl or beneath a bed? Is it not for
setting on the lampstand? Nothing is hidden that is
meant to be disclosed, neither is anything concealed that
is meant to be brought to light. Whoever can catch my
meaning let him do so.

"Mark this," he added. "It is the measure you give that
25   will be measured out to you,[30] and added to you. He who
has will get more, while he who has not will be deprived
even of what he has."

Then he said, "The Kingdom of God is as if a man were
to scatter grain on the soil, and to sleep and wake, day in
and day out, with the grain sprouting and shooting up
he knows not how. For the earth produces fruit by its
own agency, first the blade, then the ear, and finally the
full wheat in the ear. But when the grain is ripe, he at
once employs the sickle; for it is harvest time.

30   "How can we best illustrate the Kingdom of God?" he
continued. "By what simile shall we depict it? As a grain
of mustard seed, perhaps, which when it is sown is the
most minute of seeds. Yet once sown it shoots up and
becomes taller than any other herb, and produces large
branches, so that the birds of the air nestle in its shade."

By many such similes he gave his message to the
people, so far as they were capable of grasping it. He did
not address them, however, except by simile; but
privately he made everything clear to his disciples.[31]

xii

35   That same day when evening came Jesus said to them,
"Let us cross to the farther shore."

So when they had dismissed the crowd they took him
along in the ship on which he was, while other ships
accompanied him. But a severe squall of wind arose, and

30 A current proverb, meaning here "You will be enlightened according to
your lights".
31 This paragraph is perhaps a scribe's comment.

the waves flooded into the ship, so that it was already
awash. He himself was asleep on the mat in the stern.

So they woke him, and said to him, "Teacher, don't
you care that we are perishing?"

When he was roused, he rebuked the wind and said to
the sea, "Hush! Be still!" Then the wind died away and
40 there was a great calm. "Why are you so cowardly?" he
said to them. "Have you no faith?"

Then they were terribly afraid, and said to one
another, "Who can he be, that both the wind and the sea
obey him?"

xiii

5.1   So they came to the other side of the sea, to the land of
the Gerasenes.[32] As soon as he had landed from the ship
there came to meet him from the cemetery a man possessed by a foul spirit, who made his home in the tombs.
It had been found impossible to confine him even with
chains; for the man had often been confined with fetters
and chains, and had torn off the chains and forced the
5   fetters. No one now had the power to restrain him. Night
and day he was in the tombs or in the hills shrieking and
gashing himself with stones.

Seeing Jesus from a distance he ran and prostrated
himself before him screaming out, "What do you want
with me, Jesus, Son of God Most High? Do you swear to
God not to torture me?"[a]

Jesus asked the spirit, "What is your name?"

"My name is Legion," it replied. "There are many of
10 us." And it begged him repeatedly not to send them out
of the country.

Now on the hill there a large herd of swine was
feeding. So the spirits begged, "Send us into the swine.
Please let us enter them."

Jesus yielded to their entreaty,[33] and when the foul
spirits had come out they entered the swine, and the
herd, two thousand strong, dashed down the steep
slope into the sea, and were drowned.

a He had said, "Come out of the man, you foul spirit."

---

32 Some MSS read "Gadarenes".
33 As for Jews swine were unclean animals it was deemed justifiable for Jesus
to transfer the foul spirits to them.

The herdsmen ran off and told their tale to town and farm, and everyone went to see what had happened.

15   When they came to Jesus and looked at the demoniac, now seated, clothed and sane, they took alarm. Those who had been witnesses described to them what had happened to the demoniac and about the swine, and they begged Jesus to leave their territory.

As he was going on to the boat, the demoniac begged to come with him. He would not permit this, however, but told him, "Go back to your own people, and tell them what the Lord has done for you, and how he has taken pity on you."

20   But he went away and started to proclaim in the Decapolis[34] what Jesus had done for him; and everyone marvelled.

xiv

No sooner had Jesus recrossed by boat to the other side and set foot on shore than a great crowd gathered round him. The president of one of the synagogues came, a man called Jair, and when he saw him he fell at his feet with the moving entreaty, "My small daughter is near her end, but if you will only come and lay your hand on her she will be spared and live."

Jesus set off with him. The crowd followed, pressing him closely.

25   There was a woman who had suffered twelve years with a flow of blood. She had undergone a variety of treatments from numerous doctors, and had exhausted her resources without obtaining any benefit: on the contrary, she had got worse. Having heard what was being said about Jesus she came up behind him in the crowd and touched his cloak, for she said, "If I can only touch his clothes I shall get better."[35]

At once her flow of blood stopped at its source, and she was physically conscious that she was cured of her

---

34   Territory embracing ten confederate Greek cities mainly east of the Jordan: Gadara, Scythopolis, Hippos, Damascus, Canatha, Pella, Gerasa, Philadelphia, Dium and Raphana (Pliny, *Nat. Hist.* v:18).

35   She had actually touched the sacred fringe worn by Jews on their robes (*Mt* 9:20, *Lk* 8:44). This is an indication that *Mark* was designed for non-Jews with whom the allusion would not have registered. Jewish words and customs are usually explained. See *Num* 15:38–40 and note 43.

30　complaint. Jesus also was immediately aware that power had been drawn from him, and he turned round in the crowd and asked, "Who touched my clothes?"

"You can see how the crowd has been pressing you," said his disciples, "and you ask, 'Who touched me?'"

But he went on looking around to discover who had done it.

Then the woman, fearful and trembling, knowing what had happened to her, came forward and fell down before him and told him the whole truth.

"Daughter," he said to her, "your faith has cured you. Go in peace, and be free of your complaint."

35　Hardly had he finished speaking when word came from the president's house, telling him, "Your daughter has died; why trouble the teacher further?"

But Jesus, hearing the message delivered, said to the president, "Don't be afraid, simply trust."

He would not allow anyone to accompany him now except Peter and James, and James's brother John. When they reached the president's house he was confronted with a scene of uproar with much weeping and wailing, and as he went in he said to them,[36] "What are you howling for and making such a din? The child is not

40　dead, only sleeping." But they jeered at him.

When he had got rid of them all, he took the girl's father and mother and his companions and entered the girl's room. Taking her hand he said, *"Talitha, koum!"*[a]

The little girl rose directly and walked about.[b] At this the parents were quite overcome with emotion. Jesus gave them strict orders to keep the matter to themselves, and told them to give the child some nourishment.

XV

6.1　On leaving there Jesus went to his native place, and his disciples accompanied him. When the sabbath came he taught in the synagogue, and the congregation was astounded as they listened, and said, "Where does he get all this? How has he obtained this wisdom and these

a　This means when translated, 'Wake up little girl, I tell you.'
b　She was twelve years old.

36　The professional mourners who attended on such occasions.

various powers manifested by him? Isn't he the carpenter, the son of Mary, brother of James, Joses, Juda and Simon? Aren't his sisters still resident here?" And they were affronted at him.

Then Jesus said to them, "Is it not a fact that a prophet is only unhonoured in his native place, among his own kin, and in his own home?"

5   He was unable to perform a single miracle there, except to lay his hand on a few sick folk and cure them. He was amazed at their lack of faith.

So he toured the surrounding villages teaching. Then, summoning the twelve, he sent them out in pairs, and gave them authority over foul spirits. He instructed them to take nothing on their journeys but a staff, no food, no wallet, no money, to wear sandals and to carry no spare tunic.[37]

10   "Wherever you lodge," he told them, "make that your quarters until you leave again. Any place where they will not welcome you, or even listen to you, when you resume your journey shake the dust from under your feet as evidence to them."

Setting out, therefore, they called on the people to repent, expelled many demons, and anointed with oil many sick folk and cured them.

xvi

Now King Herod[38] heard of Jesus, for his name had become famous, and he said, "John the Baptist has risen from the dead; that is why miracles are effected by him."

15   Others declared he was Elijah, still others that he was a prophet like one of the prophets of old. But when Herod heard of him he said, "It is John whom I beheaded: he has risen again."

It was Herod who had been responsible for arresting John and confining him in a fortress[39] on account of Herodias, his brother Philip's wife, because he had married her. John had told Herod, "It is illegal for you to

---

37 The Jewish brotherhood of Essenes travelled in this way. See Josephus, *Jewish War* II:124–127.

38 Herod Antipas was tetrarch of Galilee, and only by courtesy could he be called king.

39 Machaerus, east of the Dead Sea, on the Nabataean border. See Josephus, *Antiquities*, XVIII:109–119.

have your brother's wife." So Herodias bore him a
20 grudge, and wanted to have him executed. But this she
could not accomplish, for Herod was in awe of John,
knowing him to be a saintly and holy man. He observed
him closely, and was much affected by hearing him, and
was very ready to listen to him.

An opportune day came for Herodias when Herod
gave his anniversary banquet to his nobles, commanders, and the leading Galileans. The daughter of this
Herodias came in and danced and charmed Herod and
the assembled guests.

"Ask whatever you like and it is yours," the king said
to the maiden. Indeed he swore to her, "Whatever you
ask is yours, even if it is half my kingdom."[40]

When she went out she said to her mother, "What
shall I ask for?"

"The head of John the Baptist," her mother replied.
25 At once she hastened to the king and said, "I want you
to give me here and now on a platter the head of John the
Baptist."

The king was greatly upset, but because of his oaths
and the guests he could not refuse her. So he immediately sent his executioner with orders to bring John's
head. The man went off and beheaded John in the
fortress, and brought his head on a platter and handed it
to the maiden, and she gave it to her mother.

When John's disciples heard what had happened they
came and fetched his body and laid it in a tomb.

xvii

30 Now the envoys rejoined Jesus and reported to him
everything they had done and taught. And he said to
them, "Come away to the country by yourselves and rest
awhile."[a]

So they set off for the country by boat; but they were
noticed and recognised by many, who ran round the lake
in a body on foot from all the towns and arrived ahead of
them.

a There were many people coming and going, and not even a place to
eat.

40 cf *Esth* 5:3.

On stepping ashore Jesus was confronted with a vast crowd, and was filled with compassion for them, for they were like shepherdless sheep; and he taught them at some length.

35   It was already getting late when his disciples approached him and said, "This place is open country and it is now late. Dismiss the people that they may go off to the surrounding hamlets and villages and buy themselves something to eat."

"Why do you not give them food yourselves?" he replied.

They protested, "Are we to go off and buy two hundred dinars'[41] worth of bread to feed them with?"

"How many loaves have you?" he inquired. "Go and find out."

"Five," they said on investigating, "and two fish."

He told them to get all the people to sit down in

40   parties, and they squatted in groups of hundreds and fifties. Taking the five loaves and the two fish Jesus looked up to heaven, recited the blessing, broke the bread into small pieces, and gave them to his disciples to distribute, and shared out the two fishes to everyone. They all ate and were satisfied, and they collected twelve basketfuls of crumbs and fragments of fish. No less than five thousand men had partaken of the loaves.

45   Jesus next insisted that his disciples embark in the boat and cross in advance to Bethsaida[42] while he dismissed the crowd. When he had said good-bye to them he went off to the hill to pray. The boat was well out to sea when evening came, while he was alone on the shore. Observing them labouring at their oars, for they had the wind against them, he came to them towards dawn walking on the sea, and made as if to pass them by. But seeing him

50   walking on the sea they thought he was a ghost and cried out.[a] At once he spoke to them and said, "It's all right! It's me. Don't be alarmed."

When he got into the boat with them the wind died down. They were in a great state; for they gave no

a They all saw him and were terrified.

---

41 A dinar represented the Roman denarius, a coin of small value.
42 A fishing village at the north end of the Sea of Galilee, not far from Capernaum.

thought to what had happened in the case of the loaves: their minds were obtuse.

On completing the crossing they came to land at Gennesaret and moored there. But no sooner were they
55 out of the boat than the people recognised Jesus and ran round the whole district, and started to bring those who were ill on mattresses to where they heard he was. And no matter where he went, into village, town, or hamlet, they laid the infirm in the open streets where they begged him to let them touch the tassel of his cloak,[43] and whoever succeeded in touching it recovered.

xviii

7.1   Now the Pharisees betook themselves to Jesus with certain of the scribes coming from Jerusalem, and they observed some of his disciples eating their meal with
5   soiled hands.[a] So they asked him, "Why do your disciples not act in accordance with the tradition of the elders? Why do they eat with soiled hands?"

Jesus replied, "Well did Isaiah prophesy of you hypocrites, as it is stated:

> *Here is a people that pays me lip-service,*
> *But their minds are far removed from me.*
> *It is useless for them to worship me*
> *While teaching as doctrines injunctions of men.*[44]

Neglecting God's commandments you cling to human traditions.

"No doubt you are right," he continued, "to set aside God's commandment if you have to keep your own
10   tradition. For Moses said, 'Honour your father and

a That is to say unwashed. The Pharisees, and indeed all Jews, adhering to the tradition of the elders, never eat before washing the whole hand. They do not eat what comes from the market until they have soused it in water, and there is a great deal more they have to do, rinsing cups, bowls and dishes.

---

43 See note 35 above. The blue thread in the fringe on male garments was obligatory. Today it is worn on a special four-cornered undergarment and in synagogue on the prayer-shawl. In synagogue it is customary to touch the scroll of the Law with it when carried in procession. That Jesus wore this fringe indicates his observance of the Law.

44 *Isa* 29:13.

mother,'[45] and 'he who speaks ill of father or mother shall surely die.'[46] But you declare, 'If anyone says to father or mother, Whatever of mine might benefit you is *korban*,[a] he is released from obligation to provide for his father or mother.'[47] Thus you nullify the word of God by the tradition you have transmitted. You do other things of the same sort."

Summoning the crowd to him once more, he said to them, "Listen to me, all of you, and mark what I say.
15   Nothing external to a man can soil him by entering him: it is only what emanates from a man that soils him."

When he had gone indoors away from the crowd his disciples questioned him about this saying.

"Are you so dense?" he said. "Do you not realise that everything external that enters a man cannot soil him, because it enters his stomach, not his mind, and is
20   evacuated in the toilet.[b] It is what emanates from a man that soils him," he continued. "It is from inside, from a man's mind, that evil designs proceed, impurity, thieving, murder, adultery, covetousness, roguery, deceit, lewdness, envy, slander, arrogance and folly. All these evil things emanate from within and they soil a man."

xix

Setting out from there Jesus went away to the borders of Tyre and Sidon.[48] Entering a house, he did not wish his presence to be known; but he could not escape notice.
25   In fact at once a woman who had heard about him, and whose daughter was possessed by a foul spirit, came and threw herself at his feet,[c] and entreated him to expel the

---

a Meaning 'a votive gift'.
b He thus pronounced every kind of food clean. (Actually he did nothing of the kind. *Tr.*)
c The woman was a Greek, in origin a Syrophoenician.

---

45 *Exod* 20:12.
46 *Exod* 21:17.
47 A man was obligated to maintain his parents, and yet by a 'rash vow' of his property to God he might seem to escape his obligation, his vow of *korban* becoming in effect a curse on his parents.
48 Some MSS omit "and Sidon".

"The children must be fed first,"[49] he told her. "It is not proper to take the children's food and throw it to puppies."

"Quite so, sir," she replied. "Yet the puppies under the table eat the scraps the children drop."

"Because you have said that," he said, "go your way: you will find the demon has gone from your daughter."

30 When she arrived home she found the child lying in bed and the demon gone.

xx

Leaving the borders of Tyre, Jesus made his way via Sidon to the Sea of Galilee, along the frontier of the Decapolis.[50]

They brought to him a deaf man with an impediment in his speech, and begged him to lay his hand on him. So he took him aside out of the crowd and inserted his fingers in his ears. Then spitting, he touched his tongue,[51] and looking up to heaven heaved a sigh, and 35 said to the man, *"Ephphatha!"*[a] And his ears were opened, and the constriction on his tongue was freed, and he could speak properly.

He gave them orders to say nothing about it; but as explicitly as he had ordered them the more decidedly did they proclaim it. And the people were astounded beyond measure, and exclaimed, "He[52] has done everything well", and, "He makes the deaf hear and the dumb speak."[53]

xxi

8.1 At that time again, the crowd being so great, and

a This means 'Open up!'

---

49 The mission of Jesus as Messiah was to his own people, for it was their mission when repentant to bring the nations to God. This is why he did not go outside the borders of Israel, and instructed his disciples not to do so (*Mt* 10:5–6).
50 See above n 34.
51 ie with the saliva.
52 "He" refers here to God. The people said the blessing customarily recited on hearing good news: "Blessed is He who is good and the doer of good" (*Berach* 9:2). See above p 9 n 13.
53 *Exod* 5:11.

having nothing to eat, Jesus summoned his disciples and said to them, "I am deeply concerned about the people. For three days now they have remained with me with nothing to eat, and if I send them home starving they will collapse on the way, and some of them have come a long distance."

His disciples answered, "Where in this open country is anyone going to get bread enough to feed these people?"

5   "How many loaves have you?" he asked.

"Seven," they said.

Jesus then instructed the crowd to sit down, and taking the seven loaves he gave thanks, broke the bread, and handed it to his disciples to distribute; and they distributed it to the people. They also had a few small fish, over which he recited the blessing, and told them to distribute these as well. So the people ate and were satisfied, and they took up seven hampers of the fragments left over. There were about four thousand people.

10   After dismissing them, Jesus at once went on board ship and left for the region of Dalmanutha.

xxii

The Pharisees there came forward to question him, trying to trap him, inviting him to furnish a sign from Heaven.

With a deep sigh Jesus said, "Why does this generation require a sign? I say positively, this generation will get no sign."

Upon this he left them, and re-embarking crossed to the other side.

Now the disciples had neglected to take bread, and
15   had no more than a single loaf with them on board. Then he advised them, "Be on your guard against the leaven of the Pharisees and of Herod!"

They argued among themselves, "Is this because we have no bread?"

Realising this, he said to them, "What are you arguing about? That you have no bread? Haven't you yet grasped or understood? Are your wits so dull? Have you lost the use of your eyes and ears? Don't you remember when I broke the five loaves for the five thousand? How many basketfuls of fragments did you take up?"

"Twelve," they told him.

20   "And the seven for the four thousand? How many hampers of fragments did you take up?"

"Seven," they told him.

Then he said, "Do you still not understand?"

xxiii

They now came to Bethsaida. There they brought to him a blind man and begged him to touch him. He took the blind man's hand and led him outside the village. And when he had spat on his eyes he laid his hands on him and inquired, "Do you see anything?"

He screwed up his eyes and said, "I can distinguish people now, because they look as if trees were walking about."

25   Once more Jesus laid his hands on his eyes. The man stared, and his sight adjusted itself, and he could see everything distinctly. Then Jesus sent him home saying, "Do not even go into the village."

xxiv

Jesus with his disciples went next to the villages belonging to Caesarea-Philippi, and on the way he asked his disciples, "Whom do people say I am?"

"John the Baptist," they replied. "Though others say Elijah, or one of the other prophets."

"And whom do you say I am?" he asked them.

Peter answered, "You are the Messiah."

30   He gave them strict injunctions to tell this to no one.[54]

Jesus now taught them that the Son of Man must undergo much suffering and be rejected by the elders, head priests and scribes, and be killed, and rise again three days later. He stated the fact plainly; but Peter took him up on it, and remonstrated with him. Then Jesus turned, and with his eye on his disciples reproved Peter, and said, "Follow me, *satan*![55] Yours is the human viewpoint, not God's."

Then he summoned the crowd as well as his disciples

---

54 Otherwise under Roman law the government would have arrested him for rebellion.

55 Peter was acting in opposition as a *satan*, an 'adversary'. Others render, "Get behind me, Satan."

and said to them: "Whoever will follow me must be utterly reckless and ready for execution in joining me;[56]

35   for whoever would preserve his life will lose it, while he who loses his life for me and the News will preserve it. How will it benefit a man to gain the whole world if his life is forfeit? What can a man offer in barter for his life? Whoever, therefore, is disdainful of me and of my words in this adulterous and reprobate generation will find the Son of Man disdainful of him when he comes in his Father's glory with the holy angels.

9.1   "I tell you positively," he continued, "there are some standing here now who will not experience death before they see the Kingdom of God instituted with power."

xxv

Six days later Jesus took as companions Peter, James and John, and led them up a high mountain entirely by themselves. In their presence he was transformed, and his robes became more dazzlingly white than any fuller on earth could bleach them. Then Moses and Elijah appeared to them, and entered into conversation with

5   Jesus. Peter could not help saying, "Rabbi, how fortunate we are to be here! Now let us make three bowers, one for you, one for Moses, and one for Elijah."[a]

Then a cloud came, casting a shadow over them, and a voice spoke out of the cloud, "He is my dear son. Hearken to him."

Suddenly on looking around they no longer saw anyone with them but Jesus himself.

As they descended the mountain he gave them instructions not to relate what they had seen to anyone

10   before the Son of Man had risen from the dead. So they kept the matter to themselves, only debating what this rising from the dead could mean. All they asked him was, "Why do the scribes say, 'First of all Elijah must come'?"

He answered, "If Elijah is to come first to put everything right,[57] how comes it to be stated of the Son of Man

a   He had no idea what to say: they were all so frightened.

---

56   Lit "Let him disown himself and take up his own cross." Death by crucifixion was primarily for crimes against the state. The condemned often carried their cross to the place of execution.

57   *Mal* 4:5–6.

that he is to undergo much suffering and be treated with contempt?[58] I am telling you differently, that Elijah has in fact come, and they have done what they would with him, just as it is stated of him."[59]

xxvi

When he rejoined his disciples he saw a great crowd
15   round them and scribes debating with them. At once the crowd, surprised to see him, rushed forward to greet him. So he inquired, "What are you debating with my disciples?"

One of the crowd replied, "Teacher, I have brought you my son, who is possessed by a dumb spirit. Wherever he is when the seizure takes him, it hurls him to the ground, and he foams and grinds his teeth. It is wearing him out. I tried to get your disciples to expel it, but they had not the power."

"O faithless generation!" Jesus exclaimed. "How long must I be with you? How long must I put up with you? Bring him to me."

20   So they brought him to Jesus. On seeing him, the spirit at once threw the boy into a fit, and falling to the ground he rolled about foaming.

Jesus asked his father, "How long has he been like this?"

"From infancy," he said. "It has often thrown him into fire and into water to make away with him. If there is anything you can do, please help us and take pity on us."

"'Anything you can do'?" echoed Jesus. "Everything can be done for one who believes."

The child's father at once cried out, "I do believe! Only assist my lack of faith."

25   When Jesus saw the crowd swiftly converging he laid his injunctions on the foul spirit. "You deaf and dumb spirit," he said to it, "I order you to come out of him and never enter him again."

After shrieking and convulsing him violently it went out, leaving the boy like a corpse. Indeed the majority of those present said, "He's dead." But Jesus, taking him by the hand, raised him, and he stood up.

---

58 cf *Ps* 21; *Isa* 53.
59 cf *I Ki* 19:2,10. In *Mt* 17:13 Jesus is thought to have been alluding to the execution of John the Baptist.

When Jesus had gone indoors his disciples asked him privately, "Why couldn't we expel it?"

Jesus told them, "This type can be got out in no other way than by prayer."[60]

xxvii

30   On leaving there they travelled through Galilee, but Jesus did not want the fact publicised, since he was teaching his disciples and telling them, "The Son of Man will be handed over to the authorities, and they will kill him, but three days after he has been killed he will rise again."

They did not understand what he meant, however, and were afraid to ask him.

Then they reached Capernaum. As soon as he was inside the house Jesus asked them, "What were you arguing about on the way?"

They were speechless; for what they had been arguing with each other about on the way was which of them would be greatest.

35   When he had sat down he called the twelve and said to them, "Whoever wants to be chief must be the lowliest of all and the servant of all."

Then taking a child he stood him before them, and putting his arm around him told them, "Whoever receives a child like this on my behalf receives me, and whoever receives me does not so much receive me as him who sent me."

John said to him, "Teacher, we saw someone expelling demons in your name, but we stopped him because he does not belong to our company."

"You did wrong to stop him," Jesus told him, "for no one who exercises power in my name can readily revile

40   me. For whoever is not against us is on our side.

"Whoever refreshes you with a cup of water because you belong to the Messiah, I tell you truly, he will not lose his reward. But whoever gives one of these humblest of believers in me grounds for complaint, it would be much better for him to have a millstone hung round his neck and to be thrown into the sea. So if your hand gives ground for complaint, cut it off. It is better for

60 Some MSS add "and fasting".

you to enter Life[61] maimed than with two hands to have
45 to go to Gehenna.[a] And if your foot gives you grounds
for complaint, cut it off. It is better for you to enter Life
crippled than with two feet to be thrown into Gehenna.
And if your eye gives you grounds for complaint, pluck it
out. It is better for you to enter the Kingdom of God one-
eyed than with two eyes to be thrown into Gehenna.[b]
50 Salt is an excellent thing, but if the salt becomes insipid
how shall its tang be restored? Keep your keenness,[62] but
be at peace with one another."

xxviii

10.1   When he left there, Jesus went to the borders of Judea
and Transjordan, and again the crowds resorted to him,
and again as was his practice he taught them.
    There were also Pharisees who came to trap him,
asking him if it was right for a man to divorce his wife.
    "What did Moses command you?" he answered.
    They told him, "Moses allowed a deed of severance to
be written, and in this way to divorce her."[63]
5   "Because of your callousness he wrote that commandment for you," Jesus told them. "But from the beginning
of creation 'He made them male and female. For this
reason a man shall leave his father and mother, and the
two shall be one flesh.'[64] So then they are two no longer,
but one flesh, so let no one sever what God has united."
10   When they were indoors again his disciples asked him
about this, and he said to them, "Whoever divorces his
wife and marries another commits adultery against his
true wife,[65] and should she divorce her husband and

a To the unquenchable fire. (Symbolised by the burning rubbish
dumps of Ge-Hinnom, in the valley outside Jerusalem. *Tr*.)
b Where their worm never dies and the fire never goes out (*Isa* 66:24.
Tr.); for each will be preserved[66] by fire.

---

61 Short for 'the life of the messianic era', the Kingdom of God on earth,
when the righteous will have acquired immortality.
62 Lit "Have salt in yourselves."
63 *Deut* 24:1.
64 *Gen* 1:27, 2:24.
65 This was the view of the Essenes and John the Baptist, which was why
John denounced Herod Antipas. See *Mt* 14:3–4.
66 Lit 'salted' (cured), explaining the previous words. Some MSS add, "And
every sacrifice shall be salted with salt" (*Lev* 2:13), finding difficulty with
the sense and wrongly attributing the comment to Jesus because of what
follows.

marry another she too commits adultery."

The people brought him their children to touch, but the disciples reproved them. Jesus was displeased when he saw it, and said to them, "Let the children come to me. Do not stop them. The Kingdom of God is composed
15   of such as they. I tell you positively, whoever does not accept the Kingdom of God like a child can never enter it."

Gathering the children in his arms he blessed them, laying his hand on each.[67]

xxix

When Jesus again took the road there was a man who ran forward and kneeling before him asked him, "Good Teacher, what must I do to share in the Messianic Era?"[68]

"Why do you address me as good?" Jesus said. "None is good but one, God himself. Surely you know the commandments, 'Commit no murder, commit no adultery, commit no theft, bear no false witness, do not defraud, honour your father and mother'?"[69]
20   "I have truly kept all these from my youth, Teacher," he told him.

Jesus regarded him with affection, and said to him, "You have one thing more to do. Go and sell all you possess and give to the poor, and you will have treasure in heaven. Then come and join me."

He was dejected at this, and went away distressed, for he owned considerable property.

As Jesus gazed after him he said to his disciples, "How hard it is for those with means to enter the Kingdom of God!"

The disciples were greatly surprised at his words. But Jesus repeated, "Children," he said, "how hard it is to
25   enter the Kingdom of God! It is easier for a camel to pass through the eye of a needle[70] than for a rich man to enter the Kingdom of God."

"How then can anyone be saved?" they said in

---

67 Blessing was conferred by laying the right hand on the recipient's head.
68 Lit 'to inherit eternal life', ie at the resurrection of the just. Just before Jesus the Rabbi Hillel had said, "He who has acquired for himself things of the Law has acquired for himself life in the world to come" (*Aboth*, 2:8).
69 *Exod* 20.
70 A proverbial saying, meaning to achieve the impossible. It is otherwise found in ancient Jewish literature with the substitution of 'elephant' for 'camel'.

amazement.

Jesus looked at them and replied, "Humanly it is impossible; but not to God. To God everything is possible."

Peter spoke up, "What about us? We have given up everything to follow you."

Jesus said, "I tell you for a fact, there is not one who has given up house or brothers or sisters or mother or father or children or lands for my sake and the News 30 without expecting, as well as persecution, to receive here and now a hundred times as much – houses, brothers, sisters, mothers, children and lands, and eternal life in the Messianic Era. But many who would be chief will be lowest, and the lowest will be chief."[71]

xxx

They were now on their way up to Jerusalem, and Jesus was preceding them, when they took alarm, and those who followed became afraid. So once more Jesus called the twelve to his side and told them what was going to happen to him. "See," he said, "we are on the way up to Jerusalem, and the Son of Man will be handed over to the head priests and scribes. They will condemn him to death and hand him over to the Gentiles, who will make sport of him, flog him, and kill him; yet three days later he will be raised up."

35   Then James and John, the two sons of Zebedee, came to him and said, "Teacher, there is something we want you to do for us."

"What is it you want me to do for you?" he inquired.

They told him, "Grant us when you attain your state[72] to be seated one on your right and the other on your left."

"You have no idea what you are asking," Jesus said to them. "Can you drink from the same cup as myself, or experience the immersion I shall undergo?"

"We can," they replied.

Jesus told them, "You shall indeed drink the same cup as myself, and experience the immersion I undergo; but 40 to sit on my right or on my left is not mine to grant: that is for those for whom it is reserved."

71 Lit "Many that are first shall be last; and the last first."
72 Lit "in your state (or glory)".

When the ten heard of this they were furious with James and John. So Jesus summoned them to him and said to them, "You know that those who are regarded as rulers among the Gentiles lord it over them, and their notables wield authority over them. It shall not be so with you. Rather if anyone would be of note among you, let him be your servant, and if anyone would be chief 45 among you, let him be everyone's slave; for even the Son of Man did not come to be served, but to serve, and to give his life as a ransom for many."

xxxi

So they came to Jericho. As Jesus was leaving Jericho with his disciples and a considerable crowd, Bar-Timaeus,[a] a blind beggar, was seated by the roadside. Hearing it was Jesus the Nazarene, he called out, "Pity me, Son of David,[73] Jesus!"

Many insisted he should be silent, but he only cried out the more, "Pity me, Son of David!"

Jesus stood still. "Call him," he said.

So they called the blind man. "Take heart," they told him. "Get up, he's calling you."

50 He threw aside his cloak, leapt to his feet, and went to Jesus.

"What can I do for you?" Jesus inquired.

"Rabboni, if only I may see again," said the blind man.

Jesus said to him, "Go your way, your faith has cured you."

At once he could see again, and joined Jesus on the road.

11.1 As they neared Jerusalem at Bethphage[74] and Bethany[75] by the Mount of Olives, Jesus sent two of his disciples with the instructions, "Go to the village there, and as soon as you have entered it you will find a foal tethered, never previously ridden by anyone. Untie him and bring him here. Should anyone ask you, 'What are

a The son of Timaeus.

---

73 By addressing Jesus as 'Son of David', the beggar was publicly identifying him as King of the Jews, the Messiah, a dangerous thing politically. Previously Jesus had silenced anyone who did so; but not this time.
74 Beth-page, Place of Unripe Figs.
75 Beth-th'ena, Place of a Figtree, or perhaps Beth-hine.

you up to?' say, 'The Master needs him. Then he will at once send him back here.' "

5 They went off and found a foal tethered by a doorway in the open on the outskirts, and untied him. When some of those standing there said to them, "What are you up to, untying the foal?" they replied as Jesus had told them, and they let them have him. They brought the foal to Jesus and laid their cloaks on him, and he mounted him. Many spread their cloaks on the road, others spread rushes cut from the fields, while those in front and those

10 behind cried, "Hosanna![76] Blessed is he who comes in the Lord's name! Blessed is the coming kingdom of our father David! *Hosanna* in the heavenly heights!"[77]

xxxii

So Jesus entered the Temple at Jerusalem. But after looking about at everything[a] he left for Bethany with the twelve.

The following day, when they were coming away from Bethany, Jesus was hungry. Seeing in the distance a fig tree in leaf he made for it in hope of finding fruit on it.[b] But when he reached it he found nothing but leaves. Thereupon he said to it, "Let no one eat fruit of you again for ever!"[c]

15 Then they came to Jerusalem. On entering the Temple Jesus ejected those who bought and sold in the Temple, and overturned the tables of the moneychangers and the stalls of the pigeon-dealers, and would not allow anyone to carry gear through the Temple.[78] And he taught, "Is it not stated, 'My house shall be known as a place of prayer for all nations'?[79] You have turned it into a robbers' den."[80]

a It was already late in the day.
b Actually it was not the season for figs.
c His disciples heard him say it.

76 'Aid us now!' followed by words from *Ps* 118:25–6, last of the festival psalms (113–118) known as the *Hallel* (Praise).
77 cf *Job* 25:2.
78 The outer court of the Temple, known as the Court of the Gentiles, was used for the sale of sacrificial birds and beasts and for the exchange of heathen coinage for that of the Sanctuary. Because the chief priests benefitted from the mart the people called it Annas's Bazaar.
79 *Isa* 56:7.
80 *Jer* 7:11.

This came to the attention of the head priests and scribes, and they discussed how to destroy him; for they were in fear of him, because all the people were greatly impressed by his teaching. But when evening came he and his disciples left the city.

20   As they passed by in the morning they saw the fig tree withered from its roots. Recalling what had happened, Peter said to Jesus, "Look, Rabbi! The fig tree you cursed has withered."

Jesus replied, "Have faith in God. I tell you positively, if anyone should say to this hill, 'Go and hurl yourself into the sea,' and should have not the slightest doubt, but fully believe that what he says will happen, he will bring it about. That is why I tell you, whatever it may be you pray for or ask for, believe that you will obtain it and

25   you will have it. And let all of you when you stand in prayer forgive, if you have something against anyone, that your heavenly Father may also forgive you your failings."

xxxiii

So they came once more to Jerusalem. While Jesus was walking in the Temple the head priests and scribes with the elders approached him and said, "By what right are you acting in this way, and who gave you the right to do so?"

Jesus replied, "Let me ask you one question, and when you have answered it I in turn will tell you by what

30   right I am acting in this way. Was John's rite of immersion of divine or human origin? Answer me that."

They debated among themselves, "If we say, 'of divine origin', he will say, 'Why then did you not believe him?' But if we say, 'of human origin –'." There they feared the people, who all held John to have been a prophet. So they answered, "We cannot tell."

"In that case," said Jesus, "I do not have to tell you by what right I am acting in this way."

12.1   Then he proceeded to speak to them in similes. "There was once a man who planted a vineyard,[81] and surrounded it with a hedge, excavating a vat, and erecting a watch-tower. Then he leased it to cultivators and went

81 cf *Isa* 5:1–7.

abroad. In due course he sent a retainer to the cultivators to receive his share of the vineyard's produce. But they seized and beat him, and sent him away empty-handed.

5 So he sent to them again, another retainer this time. They set on this one and treated him shamefully. He sent yet another. Him they killed. So with many more, whom they either flogged or put to death.[82] There still remained his own dear son. Finally he sent him to them saying, 'They must respect my son.' But those cultivators said to themselves, 'Here is the heir. Come on! We have only to kill him and the estate will be ours.' So they did kill him, and threw him outside the vineyard. How will the owner of the vineyard act? He will come and destroy those cultivators and lease the vineyard to others. You do not

10 seem to have read the Scripture,

> *The stone which the builders rejected*
> *has become the coping-stone.*
> *This is the Lord's doing,*
> *and is marvellous in our eyes."*[83]

Then they considered arresting him, but feared the people; for they realised that he had directed the simile against themselves. So they left him and went away.

xxxiv

Now they sent some of the Pharisees and Herodians to trap him in speech. When they came they said to him, "Teacher, we are aware of your sincerity and impartiality, for you are not influenced by outward appearance, but teach the way of God honestly. Is it right

15 or not, to pay the census-tax to Caesar? Should we pay it, or not pay?"[84]

Marking their dissimulation, however, Jesus said to them, "Why are you trying to catch me? Bring me a dinar[85] to look at."

---

82 cf II *Chron* 36:15–16.
83 *Ps* 118:22–3.
84 The Roman census for tax was taken every fourteen years. A census had been taken in the year 34–35 and was now due for payment. This helps to date the dialogue in the Spring of AD 36.
85 The Roman denarius, bearing an inscription crediting Caesar with divinity. See Introduction p xxvii.

They brought him one. Then he said to them, "Whose is this portrait and inscription?"

"Caesar's," they told him."

"In that case," said Jesus, "render to Caesar what is Caesar's . . . and to God what is God's."

They were amazed at him.

Then Sadducees*ᵃ* came to him, and they put it to him, "Teacher, Moses laid it down for us that if anyone's brother dies and leaves a wife but no children, he should marry his brother's wife to raise a family for his brother.[86]

20   Once there were seven brothers. The first married and died childless. Then the second married his widow, and also left no family. It was the same with the third. Indeed all the seven left no family, and finally the woman herself died.[87] In the resurrection, of which of them will she be the wife, since all seven were married to her?"

Jesus said to them, "Surely your error is due to
25   ignorance of the Scriptures and of the power of God. For when the resurrection of the dead takes place there will be no marrying or giving in marriage: they will be like the angels in heaven. But in confirmation that the dead are raised, you must have read in the book of Moses about the bush, where God spoke to Moses saying, 'I am the God of Abraham, and the God of Isaac, and the God of Jacob.'[88] He is not the God of the dead, but of the living. You are greatly in error."

Having listened to their questions, one of the scribes approached him, appreciating how well Jesus had answered them. He asked him, "Which is the supreme commandment?"

Jesus replied, "The supreme commandment is, 'Hear,
30   O Israel, the Lord is our God, the Lord is one. And you are to love the Lord your God with your whole heart, with your whole soul, with your whole mind, and your whole might.'[89] The next is, 'You are to love your neighbour as yourself.'[90] No other commandment is

a Those who say that there is no resurrection.

---

86 *Deut* 25:5–6.
87 cf the story of the seven brothers martyred with their mother in the Antiochian persecution (II *Macc* 7:1–41), which concludes, "And finally after her sons the mother died."
88 *Exod* 3:2–6.
89 *Deut* 6:4–5.
90 *Lev* 19:18.

greater than these."

The scribe said to him, "Excellent, Teacher! As you rightly say, he is One, and there is no other beside him, and to love him with all one's understanding and with all one's might, and to love one's neighbour as oneself, is of far more consequence than all the burnt-offerings and sacrifices."

Then Jesus, finding him speak so intelligently, said to him, "You are not far from the Kingdom of God."

No one ventured to question him further.

XXXV

35   Now Jesus asked as he taught in the Temple, "Why do the scribes declare that the Messiah is to be the son of David? Did not David himself say by inspiration,[91]

The Lord said to my lord, 'Sit on my right
Till I set your enemies beneath your feet.'[92]

Since David himself calls him 'Lord', how then is he his son?"[93]

The vast crowd listened to him with pleasure. In the course of his teaching he said, "Beware of those scribes who love to parade in uniform, to be saluted in the market-places, to have the chief seats in the synagogues, and the best places at the festal banquets. They are the
40 people who prey on widows,[94] and for pretext pray at great length. There is a still longer sentence in store for them."

As he sat opposite the treasury he watched how the crowd threw coins into the treasury,[95] and many rich people threw in a great deal. Then there came one poor widow and threw in two lepta.[a] On this he summoned his disciples and said to them, "I tell you positively, that

a Which amounts to a farthing (Lit quadrantes *Tr.*).

---

91 Lit "by the holy Spirit."
92 *Ps* 110:1.
93 The psalm is called 'A Psalm of David'. So in saying "my lord" he was deemed to be alluding to the Messiah as his superior, even though he would be his descendant.
94 Lit "devour widows' homes".
95 ie into the donation chests. There were thirteen of these in the Temple court, shaped like inverted trumpets for protection against theft, each one labelled with the purpose for which the fund was employed.

poor widow has thrown in more than all the others who have thrown money into the treasury. All of them have given out of their affluence, but she out of her penury has given all she has, her entire means."

xxxvi

13.1   As Jesus was leaving the Temple one of his disciples said to him, "Look, Teacher, what magnificent stones and buildings these are!"

Jesus replied, "You see these great buildings? There will not be left here one stone upon another that is not thrown down."

As he sat on the Mount of Olives opposite the Temple, Peter, James, John and Andrew, asked him privately, "Tell us when this will happen, and what sign there will be when all this is to take place."

5   Jesus proceeded to tell them. "Take care," he said, "that no one misleads you. Many will come using my title,[96] saying, 'I am he', and will deceive many. But when you hear of wars and rumours of wars do not be perturbed. This is bound to happen; but it is not the End[97] yet. For nation will rise against nation and king-dom against kingdom. There will be earthquakes in various places; there will be famines. These are the beginnings of the pangs.[98]

"But watch out for yourselves. They will hand you over to sanhedrins, and flog you in synagogues, and you will be brought before governors and kings on my
10   account, as a testimony to them; for the News must first be proclaimed to all the nations. Now when they bring you up for examination do not be concerned in advance with what you are going to say. Say what comes to you at the time; for it will not be you who speak but the holy Spirit. Brother will then betray brother to death, and the father his son, and children will rise up against their

---

96 Lit "claiming to be me."
97 The end of the present world order (*Dan* 12:13).
98 Known as 'The Pangs of Messiah' (the birth pangs of the Messianic Era). The whole of section xxxvi, which has been called the Little Apocalypse, may reflect a revelation traditionally said to have been given to the Christian community just prior to the Jewish war with Rome (AD 67–70) on account of which many fled to the north-east under the leadership of Simeon, son of Cleophas, a first cousin of Jesus. A fuller version is given in *Matthew* (see pp 109–111).

parents and be the cause of their death. You will be universally detested on my account, but he who is steadfast to the end will be saved.

"When, however, you see the 'abomination of desolation'[99] standing where it should not,[a] then let those who
15 are in Judea flee to the hills. Let not him who is on the house-top go down or enter inside to fetch anything from his house; and let not him who is in the field turn back to fetch his cloak. Woe, indeed, to pregnant women and nursing mothers in those days! Pray that it may not be winter; for those days will bring such misery as there has never been the like from the beginning of the world
20 God created until that time, nor ever shall be again. If the Lord did not limit those days not a single human being would survive; but for the sake of his elect, whom he has chosen, those days will be limited.

"Then should anyone say to you, 'Look, here is the Messiah!' or 'There he is!' do not credit it, for false messiahs and false prophets will arise, and will exhibit signs and wonders to lead the elect astray if possible. Be on your guard! I have warned you beforehand. But when those days come, after that misery, the sun will be
25 eclipsed, the moon will not shed its lustre, the stars will fall from heaven, and the planets will reel.[100] Then the Son of Man will be seen coming in the clouds[101] with great pomp and splendour, and then he will dispatch the angels to gather up the elect from the four winds, from farthest earth to farthest heaven.[102]

"Take an illustration from the fig tree. When its branch is tender and the leaves sprout you know that the summer[103] is near. So you, when you see all this happen,
30 will know that it (the end) is near, at the very doors. I tell you positively, this generation will not pass away before all this takes place. Heaven and earth will pass away, but

---

a Let the reader take note (or, 'work this out', *Tr.*).

---

99 *Dan* 9:27, 12:11.
100 Lit "the powers (or influences) of heaven", *Isa* 13:10, 24:4. And see below
p 110.
101 *Dan* 7:13.
102 *Zech* 2:6; *Deut* 30:4.
103 In an old Hebrew MS of *Matthew* a play is indicated on the words *qa'its* (summer fruit) and *gets* (the end), *Amos* 8:1–2. Perhaps to imitate this the Greek has 'at the doors' (*thyrais*) following upon 'summer' (*theros*).

my words will never pass away.*ᵃ* Be watchful! Be
vigilant! For you do not know when the time will be.

"It is like a man absent from home, who has vacated
his house and left his servants in charge, assigning to
each his duties, and has instructed the doorman to keep
35   on the alert. Be alert, therefore, for you do not know
when the master of the house will come, in the evening,
at midnight, at cock-crow, or in the morning,[104] in case
coming suddenly he should find you sleeping. What I
say to you I say to all, be alert!"

xxxvii

14.1   Now the Passover and the Feast of Unleavened
Bread[105] were two days away, and the head priests and
scribes were discussing how they could arrest Jesus by
stealth and execute him. "It can't be at the festival," they
said, "or there may be a popular outbreak."

While Jesus was at Bethany dining at the house of
Simon the leper, there came a woman with an alabaster
flask of pure oil of nard, a most costly perfume, which
she opened and poured over his head. But there were
some there who waxed indignant. "What good has been
5   done by this waste of oil? That oil could well have been
sold for more than three hundred dinars to be given to
the poor." And they berated her.

"Leave her alone," Jesus said. "Why do you scold her?
She has done me a good turn. You always have the poor
with you, and you can show them a kindness whenever
you wish. But you will not always have me. She has done
her best: she has anticipated the anointing of my body for
burial. I tell you positively, wherever the News shall be
proclaimed throughout the world, what she has done
will also be related to commemorate her."

10   Then Judas Iscariot, one of the twelve, went off to the
head priests to betray Jesus to them. When they heard

---

a   But none can tell when that day or hour will be, neither the angels in
heaven, nor the Son, only the Father. (This comment was needed
since evidently the time indicated had already expired when the
Gospel was composed. *Tr.*)

---

104 Jewish day was sunset to sunset, with night divided into four watches,
thus these times, 9 pm, 12 pm, 3 am and 6 am.
105 See *Exod* 12.

what he had to say they were delighted and promised him money. So he set himself to find out how he might conveniently betray him.

xxxviii

On the first day of the Feast of Unleavened Bread, when they sacrifice the passover,[106] the disciples of Jesus said to him, "Where do you wish us to make ready for you to eat the passover?"

He then dispatched two of his disciples[107] and told them, "Go into the city, where a man will meet you carrying a water-pot. Follow him, and wherever he enters say to the owner of that house, 'The Teacher says, which guest-room am I to have to eat the passover with
15 my disciples?' He will then show you a large upstairs dining-room ready laid out.[108] There prepare for us."

So the disciples went off to the city and found everything turn out as he had told them; and they made ready the passover.

When evening came he arrived wth the twelve. As they reclined and ate Jesus said, "I tell you positively, one of you eating with me will betray me."

Deeply distressed, one after another said to him, "Not me, surely?"

20 "It is one of the twelve[109] dipping in the dish with me,"[110] he told them. "Though the Son of Man goes the way that is written of him, woe, none the less, to the one by whom the Son of Man is betrayed. Better for him had he never been born."

As they were eating he took the bread, and reciting the blessing broke it and gave it to them,[111] and said, "Take it: it signifies my body." Then taking a cup and giving thanks he handed it to them, and all of them drank from

---

106 ie the paschal lamb.
107 *Luke* (22:8) says that the two were Peter and John.
108 There is a mystery about these secret arrangements which Jesus had evidently made with the owner of the house some time in advance whom he must have greatly trusted, and whose identity is not disclosed. But see *Jn* 13:23, 19:27–7, below p 515 n 4 and p 527.
109 This could imply that there was at least one other present with Jesus beside the twelve, namely the owner of the house, who would in fact be the chief participant next to Jesus, the one called in *John* 'the dear disciple' (See *Jn* 13:23).
110 In the Passover ceremony (*seder*) the dipping was of bitter herbs.
111 The bread was unleavened bread.

it, and he said to them, "It signifies my 'blood of the
25   covenant' poured out for many. I tell you positively, I
will not again drink of the fruit of the vine[112] till the day
when I drink it new in the Kingdom of God."

After the hymn-singing[113] they went out to the Mount
of Olives. Then Jesus said to them, "All of you will waver
in your loyalty, for it is stated, 'I will strike at the
shepherd, and the sheep will be scattered.'[114] But after I
have been raised up I will precede you to Galilee."

Peter told him, "Even if everyone else wavers, I shall
not."
30   Jesus replied, "I tell you positively, today – this very
night indeed – before the cock crows twice you yourself
will disown me three times."

But he insisted, "Even if I have to die with you I will
never disown you."

So said they all.

xxxix

When they came to a spot called Gethsemane[115] Jesus
said to his disciples, "Stay here while I pray." Then he
took Peter, James and John along with him. He was
restless and depressed, and said to them, "I am in very
low spirits.[116] Stay here and keep watch."
35   Going a bit further Jesus fell upon the ground and
prayed that if it were possible the crisis might pass him
by. "*Abba*,"[a] he said, "to thee everything is possible. Let
this cup pass me by. Yet let it not be as I wish, but what
thou wishest."

When he came back he found them sleeping, and said
to Peter, "Are you asleep, Simon? Could you not manage
to stay awake a single hour? Be vigilant and prayerful, or
you may find yourself tempted. The spirit is willing
enough, but the flesh is frail."

a   "Father" (in Aramaic).

---

112   Jesus had recited the blessing over the wine in these terms: "Blessed art
thou, O Lord our God, King of the Universe, creator of the fruit of the
vine."
113   The 'Hallel' psalms (*Ps* 113–118).
114   *Zech* 13:7.
115   Ge-shemanim, 'the fertile valley' (*Isa* 28:1).
116   Lit "My soul is very sad, even to death."

He went away again and prayed the same prayer.
40 Returning once more he again found them asleep; for their eyes were heavy and they could hardly speak to him. When he came the third time he said to them, "Are you going on sleeping and taking your rest? That's enough! The time has come. Look, the Son of Man is betrayed into the hands of sinners! Come, let us be going. See, my betrayer approaches!"

He was still speaking when Judas, one of the twelve, came, and with him a force armed with swords and clubs[117] dispatched by the head priests, scribes and elders. The betrayer of Jesus had arranged the following signal with them, "The one I embrace is the man you
45 want; seize him and take him away securely." So directly he arrived he approached Jesus with "Rabbi!" and embraced him warmly. Then they laid hands on Jesus and seized him; but one of the bystanders[118] drew his sword and struck the high priest's servant, severing his ear.

Jesus said to them, "Have you come out as after a brigand[119] with swords and clubs to apprehend me? I was with you daily in the Temple teaching, and you did not arrest me there, so that the Scriptures should be fulfilled."

50 Everyone then deserted him and fled. One youth did follow close behind him clad only in a linen wrap. They seized him; but abandoning the linen wrap he fled away naked.[120]

xl

Now they led Jesus away to the high priest, and there were assembled all the chief priests and the elders and scribes. Peter had followed at a distance as far as the

---

117 Evidently considerable resistance was expected. The force was mixed, consisting of some troops and the Temple police. The latter were armed with clubs, as weapons were not allowed to be carried in the Temple.
118 *John*, however, says it was Peter.
119 Members of the Jewish Resistance were so described. At this period the antisemitic Roman governor Pontius Pilate, by his harsh actions, had greatly stimulated the spirit of revolt. It requires to be understood that the Jewish officals, in civil matters, were agents of the Roman government.
120 The youth is not identified, as we would expect. There must have been a reason for referring to him. A guess might be that he was the young John Mark of Jerusalem, author of the book. See *Acts* 12:12.

entrance hall of the high priest's residence, and seated himself with those in attendance and warmed himself by the fire.

55   The head priests and the entire Sanhedrin sought evidence against Jesus on which to condemn him to death; but they failed to find it. Though many gave false testimony against him their testimonies did not agree. Then some came forward and testified falsely against him, "We have heard him say, 'I will pull down this man-made Sanctuary, and in three days I will build another that is not man-made.' "[121] But even so their testimonies did not agree.

60   On this the high priest rose in person to ask Jesus: "Have you no answer to make to these charges?"

But he was silent and made no reply.

So the high priest addressed him again, "You are the Messiah are you not, the son of the Blessed One?"

"Yes I am," Jesus replied. "And you shall see the Son of Man installed in the seat of authority,[122] and coming with the clouds of Heaven."

Then the high priest tore his tunic[123] and cried, "What further evidence do we need? You have heard the traitorous confession.[124] What is your verdict?"

Unanimously[125] they judged him deserving of the
65   death penalty. Some of them spat on him, and covered his face and struck him saying, "Prophesy!" Even the attendants cuffed him.

Meanwhile, as Peter was below in the hall, one of the maidservants of the high priest came by, and noticing Peter warming himself she looked at him intently and said, "Of course, you were with the Nazarene, with that Jesus."

But he flatly denied it. "I don't know him," he said, "and I don't know what you are talking about." He went

---

121 Accusing Jesus of the capital crime of practising wizardry. See *Lev* 20:27. The charge had of course no clear foundation. But according to *John* Jesus had said, "Demolish this temple, and in three days I will raise it up" (*Jn* 2:19).

122 Lit "on the right hand of power" (cf *Dan* 7:13–14).

123 An action expressing grief, customary with mourners.

124 Claiming to be the Messiah, king of the Jews, was a capital crime; in Roman law, not Jewish, high treason against divine Caesar, *Lk* 23:2; Tacitus *Annals* Bk IV:70, Bk VI:7, *Acts* 17:6–7. And see the Introduction, pp xxvi–xxvii.

125 A note in *Luke* 23:51 says that Joseph of Arimathea, a member of the Sanhedrin, had not assented.

out into the courtyard, and the cock crew.[126]

But the maid, noticing him again, said to the bystanders, "He's one of them."

70   Again he denied it. But shortly after, the bystanders said to Peter, "You certainly are one of them. You're a Galilean."[127]

He cursed and swore, "I don't know this man you're talking about."

Immediately the cock crowed a second time. Then Peter recalled what Jesus had told him, "Before the cock crows twice you will disown me three times." As it came home to him he wept.

xli

15.1   Directly morning came, after the head priests had conferred with the elders and scribes, the entire Sanhedrin in fact, they had Jesus manacled and led him away and handed him over to Pilate.[128]

Then Pilate asked him, "Are you king of the Jews?"

"As you say," he replied.

The head priests then indicted him in full.[129]

"Have you no defence to make?" Pilate asked him again. "You hear all the charges they bring against you."

5   But to Pilate's surprise Jesus made no further response.

It was customary at this festival for Pilate to release to the people any one prisoner for whom they asked clemency. Now there was one called Bar-Abbas[130] imprisoned with other insurgents who had committed murder during the rising.[131] So the crowd came round and required him to follow his usual practice. Pilate

---

126 "And the cock crew." A number of MSS omit these words.
127 Some MSS add, "Your accent gives you away." The Galileans were noted for slurring their gutterals. cf *Acts* 2:7.
128 Pontius Pilate, Roman governor of Judea, AD 26–36.
129 See *Lk* 23:2.
130 Alternatively referred to as Bar-Rabban.
131 Perhaps that which occurred when Pilate appropriated the sacred funds to build an aqueduct. See Jos. *Jewish War* II:175–177 and cf *Lk* 13:1. On verses 5–15 see notes to *Mt* 27, notes 15 and 16.

replied, "Do you want me to release the king of the Jews?"[a]

10   The head priests, however, persuaded the crowd to prefer Bar-Abbas to be released to them. Pilate put it to them, "What then am I to do with him you call king of the Jews?"

"Crucify him!" they cried.

"But what crime has he committed?" Pilate asked.

They only shouted the more, "Crucify him!"

15   So Pilate, anxious to appease the crowd, released Bar-Abbas to them, and after having Jesus flogged, handed him over to be crucified.

xlii

The soldiers marched Jesus outside the court,[b] and summoned the whole cohort. Then they arrayed him in scarlet, and when they had plaited it they invested him with a victor's wreath made of thorn, and saluted him with, "Hail, king of the Jews!" They also struck him on the head with a cane, and spat at him, and bent their knees in homage to him.

20   After they had mocked him, they stripped off the scarlet and dressed him in his own clothes and marched him away to be crucified. They requisitioned a passer-by, one Simon the Cyrenian,[c][132] who was coming in from the country, to carry his cross.

When they had brought Jesus to the place Golgotha[d] they offered him wine impregnated with myrrh; but he refused it. Then they crucified him, and shared out his clothes among themselves, throwing dice to decide who should have what.

25   It was nine o'clock[133] in the morning when they crucified him. The wording of the charge which had been

a He realized it was out of malice that the head priests had handed him over.
b That is to say, the praetorium.
c He was the father of Alexander and Rufus (persons presumably known to the Christians. *Tr.*)
d This means when translated 'Place of a Skull' (the Aramaic should read *Golgoltha. Tr.*)

---

132 Cyrenaica was west of Egypt and had a large Jewish community.
133 The third hour by Jewish reckoning, as given in the text.

written out was "The King of the Jews".[134] With him they crucified two brigands, one on his right and the other on his left.[135] And all who went that way vilified him, nodding their heads and saying, "Hi, you, who can pull
30 down the Sanctuary and build it in three days, save yourself and come down from the cross!"

The head priests also, with the scribes, derided him, and said, "He delivered others, but cannot save himself. Let the Messiah, the king of Israel, come down now from the cross that we may see and believe." Even those who were crucified with him reviled him.

When midday came there was darkness over the whole landscape until three o'clock. Then at three o'clock Jesus called out, "*Eloi, Eloi, lama sabachthani?*"[a]
35 Some of the bystanders hearing this said, "Hark, he is calling Elijah!" Someone ran to saturate a sponge with vinegar, spiked it on a cane and offered it to him to drink, saying, "Quiet! Let us see if Elijah will come to take him down."

But Jesus, giving a piercing cry, expired; and the curtain of the Sanctuary was ripped in two from top to bottom.

When the centurion who stood opposite him saw that he had expired, he said, "Truly, this man was son of a god!"[136]
40 There were also some women there looking on at a distance. Among them were Mary of Magdala, Mary the mother of the younger James and of Joses, and Salome. These had followed Jesus in Galilee and looked after him; but there were others as well who had come up with him to Jerusalem.

xliii

When evening came, since it was the preparation day,[b]

---

a This means when translated 'My God, my God, why hast thou abandoned me' (*Ps* 22:1 in Aramaic. *Tr.*)

b That is to say, the day before the sabbath.

---

134 *Matthew* and *John* claim that 'Jesus the Nazarene' was also in the wording of the charge.

135 Some MSS add here: "And the scripture was fulfilled which reads, 'He was reckoned with the transgressors'" (*Isa* 53:12). This was perhaps initially a comment (written in the margin).

136 *Lk* has "A true man if ever there was one" (*Lk* 23:47).

Joseph of Arimathea,[137] a distinguished councillor, arrived, who was also himself awaiting the Kingdom of God. He ventured to go to Pilate and ask for the body of Jesus. Pilate was surprised that he had died so quickly, and having sent for the centurion asked if he was already

45   dead. When the centurion confirmed it, Pilate granted Joseph the corpse. After purchasing a linen winding-sheet Joseph took Jesus down, swathed him in the linen, and laid him in a tomb quarried out of the rock: he then rolled a boulder against the entrance of the tomb. Mary of Magdala and Mary mother of Joses observed where he was laid.

16.1   When the sabbath was ended, Mary of Magdala, Mary mother of James, and Salome, brought spices in order to go and anoint him. And very early in the morning of the day after the sabbath they came to the tomb as soon as the sun was up. "Who is going to roll away the boulder for us from the entrance of the tomb?" they asked themselves. But when they came to look they saw that the boulder had been rolled aside.[a]

5   On entering the tomb they were startled to see a young man sitting on the right side clad in a flowing white robe.[138] "Do not be alarmed," he said to them. "You are looking for Jesus the Nazarene who was crucified. He has risen. He is not here. Look, here is the place where he was laid. Go now and tell his disciples, and Peter particularly, he is preceding you to Galilee. You will see him there just as he told you."

They fled from the tomb, for they were trembling and unnerved. And they said nothing to anyone, for they were afraid . . .

(*Here the text breaks off abruptly. The standard ending*[139] *was supplied by a later copyist and reads as follows:*)

[Having risen early on the morning after the sabbath, Jesus appeared in the first instance to Mary of Magdala

10   from whom he had expelled seven demons. She then

---

a It was very massive.

---

137 Arimathea. In Hebrew Ramathaim.
138 This was the kind of garment worn by the Essenes.
139 The supplied ending largely reflects information found in *Matthew* and *Luke–Acts*. A much shorter form is extant. It is not known how much of the original text is missing, or for what reason.

went and informed those who had been with him, who were mourning and weeping. When they heard he was alive and that she had seen him they did not credit it. But later on he appeared to two of them in another guise while they were out walking on their way into the country. They too came and told the others; yet still they did not credit it. Afterwards while they were dining he appeared to the eleven and reproached them for their disbelief and obtuseness in failing to credit those who

15 had seen him when he had risen from the dead."Travel the world over," he told them, "and proclaim the News to all creation. Whoever believes and is immersed will be saved, but whoever does not believe will be condemned. And these signs shall attend those who have believed: they shall expel demons in my name; they shall speak in tongues; they shall take up snakes; if they drink anything poisonous it will not harm them; and they shall lay hands on the sick and cure them."

So then the Lord Jesus, after he had spoken to them,
20 was taken up to heaven and sat at God's right hand. But they set off and preached everywhere, the Lord working with them and confirming the Message by the signs that authenticated it.]

MATTHEW

The Maxims of the Master

Preface to Matthew

Matthew, as we learn, was a Jew employed at Capernaum in Galilee as a collector of government imposts. His real name would seem to have been Levi the son of Alphaeus, and he could have been the brother of James the son of Alphaeus. Both were among the twelve envoys of Jesus.

According to tradition the missionary activities of the envoys developed in the reign of the Emperor Cladius (AD 41–54). When they set out they were equipped with two short documents for which Matthew was said to have been responsible. One was a collection of passages from the Old Testament claimed to have been fulfilled by Jesus (cf *Luke* 24:27). This was in five divisions like the Books of Moses. The other document was an anthology of the sayings and teachings of Jesus. These documents of course were in Hebrew, and had to be translated into Greek. The *Gospel of Matthew* as we have it was so called because in addition to the *Gospel of Mark* it made use of both these sources not now extant, and the resultant work was also in five books with a prologue and epilogue. This structure has been represented in the present translation. The Sermon on the Mount reflects much of the teaching document. There are other elements in *Matthew* to which reference will be found in the notes.

The Hebrew contents of *Matthew* fostered a later belief that this *Gospel* had originally been written in Hebrew, and some would confound it with an Aramaic work known as the *Gospel of the Hebrews*, of which some quotations have survived. There are also evidences that *Matthew* was translated into Hebrew, and these help us in places to recover the Hebrew of the two source documents, and so to correct the Greek.

Matthew, as we have it, probably originated in Egypt around about AD 90. There was a large Jewish population there, especially in Alexandria, the city created by Alexander the Great, who had settled many Jews there, and Egypt later became a place of refuge for others escaping from Palestine. It was, perhaps, as a tribute to Egptian hospitality that the story was created of the flight of the parents of Jesus to Egypt to save their infant son from the sword of Herod. A Greek-speaking Hellenic–Jewish culture was to develop in the country, which in the first century AD was notably represented by Philo of Alexandria. Mark's final sphere of evangelization had been Egypt, and in modern times there was found there part of a collection of sayings of Jesus, largely unknown previously.

Our present *Matthew* is thus a curious blend of materials and views, Jewish and non-Jewish. The style of the writing naturally varies with that of the sources employed. But the strong Hebraic tone in many places can be misleading. It requires close examination to determine that the author of the work as it stands was not himself a Jew. He was no mere compiler, and left his own impress on the book, notably in his treatment of the *Markan* material, and in his heightening of miraculous elements. In places he doubles the number of persons cured, for example two Gadarene demoniacs and two blind men at Jericho. He also makes Jesus use two donkeys to ride into Jerusalem, not understanding Hebrew poetic parallelism.

After the Jewish revolt against the Romans in AD 67–70 anti-Jewish feeling was intensified in Gentile circles, and this unfortunately embraced Greek-speaking Christians, who became anxious to reject – as their Messianism might convey – that they were involved in Anti-Roman activities. Hence the hostile attitude to Jews and Judaism in this Gospel, especially in connection with the crucifixion of Jesus, and this in spite of the inclusion of sources very strongly Jewish in character as with the Sermon on the Mount. Some indications of a comparatively late date are references to the destruction of Jerusalem in AD 70, to the status of the Church and to Church discipline, to the delay in the Second Advent, and the evidences of persecution by the Roman authorities, as well as such language as *Matthew* 28:15. The Sermon itself appears largely to reflect a collection of sayings where the circumstances that gave rise to them were unknown.

The Good News of Jesus Christ

Matthew's Version

i

1.1   The ancestral scroll[1] of Jesus Christ, son of David, son
of Abraham.
Abraham begot Isaac:
Isaac begot Jacob:
Jacob begot Judah and his brothers:
Judah begot Pharez and Zarah by Tamar:
Pharez begot Hezron:
Hezron begot Ram:
Ram begot Amminadab:
Amminadab begot Nahshon:
Nahshon begot Salmon:
5   Salmon begot Boaz by Rahab:
Boaz begot Obed by Ruth:
Obed begot Jesse.
Jesse begot King David.

David begot Solomon by Uriah's wife:
Solomon begot Rehoboam:
Rehoboam begot Abijam:
Abijam begot Asa:
Asa begot Jehoshaphat:
Jehoshaphat begot Joram:
Joram begot Uzziah:
Uzziah begot Jotham:

---

1 This scroll may derive from records circulated by the *Desposynoi*, 'Heirs', as
the surviving relations of Jesus were called. "These coming from the Jewish
villages of Nazara and Cochaba to other parts of the country set out the
foregoing genealogy from the chronicles" (Jul. Afric., *Letter to Aristides*,
quoted by Euseb. *Eccl. Hist*. Bk I ch 7). The record was evidently originally
in Hebrew.

Jotham begot Ahaz:
Ahaz begot Hezekiah:
10   Hezekiah begot Menasseh:
Menassah begot Ammon:
Ammon begot Josiah:
Josiah begot Jeconiah and his brothers about the time
    of the Babylonian Exile.

During the Babylonian Exile
Jeconiah begot Shealtiel:
Shealtiel begot Zerubbabel:
Zerubbabel begot Abiud:
Abiud begot [Abner:[2]
Abner begot] Eliakim:
Eliakim begot Azzur:
Azzur begot Zadok:
Zadok begot Achim:
Achim begot Elihud:
15   Elihud begot Eleazar:
Eleazar begot Matthan:
Matthan begot Jacob:
Jacob begot Joseph the husband of Mary, who begot[3]
    Jesus styled Christ.

Thus there were fourteen[4] generations in all from
Abraham to David, fourteen generations from David to
the Babylonian Exile, and fourteen generations from the
Babylonian Exile to the Messiah.

ii

The birth of the Messiah came about in this way. His
mother Mary had become betrothed to Joseph; but
before they could be wed she was found to be with child
by the Holy Spirit. Joseph her husband being a devout
man, yet unwilling to disgrace her in public, wished to
20   divorce her quietly. But while he was thinking the matter
over an angel of the Lord appeared to him in a dream and

2 Restored from an old Hebrew MS (Du.Tillet) in the Paris National Library.
  Likeness in Heb of the name Abner (*Abiner*, I Sam 14:50) to the preceding
  name Abiud (*Abiur*, Sin Syr.) doubtless caused the omission by a careless
  scribe. Without it the third group has only thirteen names, instead of
  fourteen.
3 Following the Sinaitic Syriac text.
4 The number is artificial and obtained by omissions. It has been suggested
  that the three groups correspond to the three letters of the name David in
  Heb. (DVD), the numerical value of which is 14.

said, "Joseph, son of David, do not be afraid to accept Mary as your wife, for the child she has conceived is by the holy Spirit. She will bear you[5] a son whom you are to name Jesus; for he will save[6] his people from their sins"[a7]

When Joseph woke he acted as the angel of the Lord bade him, and accepted his wife; but he had no intercourse with her until she had borne a son, whom he named Jesus.

iii

2.1   Now when Jesus was born in Judean Bethlehem in the reign of King Herod[9], magi[10] from the East arrived in Jerusalem inquiring, "Where is he who is born to be king of the Jews, for we in the East have seen his star and have come to pay him homage?"

King Herod was greatly agitated[11] when he heard this, and all Jerusalem as well; and convening all the head priests and learned representatives of the people[12] he asked to be informed where the Messiah would be born.

5   "In Judean Bethlehem," they told him, "for it is so stated by the prophet,

> *And you, Bethlehem, country of Judah,*
> *are not least among the leaders of Judah;*
> *For from you shall arise the prince,*
> *who shall shepherd my people Israel.*"[13]

Then Herod sent for the magi privately, and obtained

a   All this transpired to fulfil what the Lord had announced by the prophet saying, "See, the maiden is with child, and shall bear a son, whom they shall call Immanuel"[8], which means when translated, "God is with us".

---

5 So the text of Sin. Syr.

6 Heb *yoshia*, reflected in the name *Yeshua* (Gr. Jesus).

7 "Sins". The original source word was probably "enemies" (cf *Lk* 1:71). The nativity story in *Matthew* owes much to the contemporary legends of the birth of Moses. See Jos. *Antiq*. II. 205–223.

8 *Isa* 7:14.

9 Herod the Great was king of Judea 37–4 BC.

10 Magi, strictly Persian priests of the Zoroastrian faith, but also sages credited with astrological and occult knowledge.

11 Heb *y'cherad*, possibly a word-play on the name Herod. He was in great fear of plotters against his life and throne.

12 Lit "scribes of the people". Herod summoned the full Sanhedrin consisting of the Sadducean hierarchy and Pharisee scribes.

13 *Mic* 5:2.

from them the exact date at which the star had appeared. Then he sent them to Bethlehem and said, "Go and make exhaustive inquiries for the child; and directly you have discovered him send me word that I too may come and pay him homage".

When they had heard the king they set out, and the star which they had seen in the East led them on until it came and stood still directly above where the child was.

10   Seeing the star they rejoiced greatly, and entering the house they saw the child with his mother Mary. Prostrating themselves before him they opened their baggage and presented their gifts to him, gold, frankincense and myrrh. But being apprised in a dream that they should not return to Herod they travelled back to their own country by a different route.

No sooner had they taken their departure than an angel of the Lord appeared in a dream to Joseph and said, "Rouse yourself, and take the child and his mother and escape to Egypt, and stay there until I tell you; for Herod will attempt to kill the child". On waking, therefore, he took the child and his mother by night and

15   departed for Egypt, and remained there until Herod's death.*a*

When Herod realised that he had been duped by the magi he flew into a passion, and had all the boys killed in Bethlehem and in its entire vicinity who were two years old or under, going by the time he had ascertained from the magi.*b*

Once Herod was dead, however, the angel of the Lord

20   appeared in a dream to Joseph in Egypt and said, "Rouse yourself and take the child and his mother and journey to

---

a This was to fulfil what the Lord had announced by the prophet, saying, "Out of Egypt have I called my son."[14]

b Then was fulfilled what was announced by the prophet Jeremiah saying,

A sound was heard in Ramah,
Lamentation and bitter weeping,
Rachel weeping for her children,
Inconsolable for their loss.[15]

---

14 *Hos* 11:1.
15 *Jer* 31:15. Rachel, wife of the Patriarch Jacob, was buried near Bethlehem (*Gen* 35:19).

the land of Israel; for those who tried to take the child's life are dead." On waking, therefore, he took the child and his mother and went to the land of Israel. But learning that Archelaus was ruling Judea in his father Herod's stead he was afraid to go there; and being warned in a dream he travelled on to the district of Galilee, and settled in a town called Nazareth.[a]

---

a Then was fulfilled what was announced by the prophets, "He shall be called Nazorean."[16]

---

16 There is no exact OT reference for this quotation. It may be that by a Hebrew word-play the town Nazara is linked with the Hebrew word *zara* ('the seed' of promise, the Messiah) looking back to *Gen* 21:12, lit "(In Isaac) shall be called (to thee) seed (*zara*)". See *Rom* 9:7; *Heb* 11:18; *Gal* 3:16. The play is also on the word Nazirite, cf *Exod* 13:2 with *Judg* 13:5 and I *Sam* 1:20. A Nazirite was one dedicated or under a special vow to God. Cf also *netzer* (the branch), *Isa* 11:1.

Book 1

3.1   At this period John the Baptist made his appearance, proclaiming in the wilderness of Judea, "Repent, for the Kingdom of Heaven[1] is at hand!"

This was he whom the prophet Isaiah announced when he said,

A voice cries out in the wilderness,
'Make ready the Lord's road!
Put his highways in order!'[2]

John wore clothing of camel hair with a leather girdle round his waist, and he lived on locusts and wild honey.

5   Then Jerusalem, and all Judea, and all the vicinity of Jordan, flocked to him, and were immersed by him in the River Jordan as they confessed their sins.

Observing many of the Pharisees and Sadducees coming for immersion John said to them, "Vipers' brood, who warned you to escape from the coming Wrath? Well then, produce fruit consistent with repentance, and content yourselves no longer with saying, 'We have Abraham as our father,' for I tell you that from these

10   stones[3] God can supply Abraham with sons. Already the axe is laid to the root of the trees. Any tree that fails to produce good fruit will be cut down and cast into the fire. I am only immersing you in water in token of repentance. But after me comes one mightier than myself whose sandals I am not fit to carry: he will immerse you in holy Spirit and fire. His winnowing-shovel is in his hand, and he will thoroughly cleanse his threshing-floor, gathering the wheat into his granary, but burning up the chaff with unquenchable fire."

1 Among pious Jews 'Heaven' was employed as a substitute for the word 'God' to avoid the risk of taking God's name in vain. Thus a Jewish source is indicated.
2 *Isa* 40:3.
3 Reproducing the play on words in Hebrew, *abanim* (stones) and *banim* (sons).

Then Jesus arrived at the Jordan from Galilee to be immersed by John. But John stopped him and said, "I need to be immersed by you, and do you come to me?"

15 Jesus replied, "Never mind that. It is of more consequence that one should do one's whole duty."

So John let him have his way.

[When Jesus was immersed a bright light played upon the water, so that all who had come there were afraid.][4] After his immersion Jesus at once rose up from the water, and lo, the skies were parted, and he saw the Spirit of God descend like a dove alighting on him, while a voice from the skies declared, "This is my dear son with whom I am well satisfied."

ii

4.1 Then Jesus was led by the Spirit into the wilderness to be tempted by the Devil. After fasting for forty days and forty nights[5] he was starving. So when the tempter came he said to him, "If you are son of God tell these stones to become loaves."

To this Jesus replied, "It is stated, 'Not by bread alone shall a man live, but by every utterance that proceeds from the mouth of God.' "[6]

5 Then the Devil took him to the holy city and set him on a turret of the Temple, and said to him, "If you are son of God throw yourself down, for it is stated,

> *He shall charge his angels on your behalf,*
> *And with their hands they shall support you,*
> *Lest you strike your foot against a stone."*[7]

Jesus answered, "It is also stated, 'You are not to put the Lord your God to the proof.' "[8]

Next the Devil took him off to a lofty mountain, and showed him all the kingdoms of the world and their splendour, and said to him, "I will give you all of these if you will fall down and do me homage."

10 Then Jesus said to him, "Begone Satan! It is stated, 'You are to do homage to the Lord your God, and be

4 This is in the Hebrew Gospel and some Old Latin MSS.
5 The time Moses was on the mountain. See *Exod* 24:18 etc.
6 *Deut* 8:3.
7 *Ps* 91:11–12.
8 *Deut* 6:16.

subject to him alone.' "[9]

Thereupon the Devil left him and angels came and attended to his needs.

iii

When Jesus learnt that John had been arrested[10] he returned to Galilee; but abandoning Nazareth he made his home at Capernaum, which is beside the sea[11] on the
15   Zebulon–Naphtali border.[a]

From that time Jesus began to proclaim, "Repent, for the Kingdom of Heaven is at hand!"

As he walked by the Sea of Galilee Jesus saw two brothers who were fishermen, Simon called Peter and his brother Andrew. "Follow me," he said to them, "and I will make you fishers of men."
20   Forthwith they abandoned their nets and followed him.

Farther on he saw two other brothers, James the son of Zebedee and his brother John. They were in the boat with their father Zebedee mending their nets. When he called them they too at once left the boat and their father and followed him.

Then Jesus toured Galilee teaching in their synagogues, proclaiming the News of the Kingdom, and curing every kind of disease and ailment among the people. Report of him spread throughout Syria,[13] and

---

a Thereby was fulfilled what was announced by the Prophet Isaiah,

Lands of Zebulon and Naphtali,
The sea road, beyond the Jordan,
Galilee of the Gentiles.
The people who sat in darkness
Saw great light;
And those who sat in deepest gloom,
To them light has arisen.[12]

---

9 *Deut* 6:13.
10 To avert a revolt in Galilee while going to war with the Arabs, Herod Antipas, ruler of Galilee, arrested John and took him with him as a precaution.
11 ie the Sea of Galilee.
12 *Isa* 9:1–2.
13 The Old Hebrew has the more likely reading "among all the people" (*haam*) later changed to *aram* (Syria). See Euseb. *Eccl. Hist.* 1:13; *Letter of Abgar, Prince of Edessa.*

they brought to him all who were ill, afflicted with various diseases and pains, or demon-possessed (epi-
25 leptics and paralytics); and he cured them. And many people followed him from Gaililee, the Decapolis, Jerusalem, Judea, and from beyond Jordan.

iv

5.1 Now when Jesus saw the crowds he ascended the hillside, and when he had sat down his disciples gathered round him, and he began to teach them.

"How fortunate are the oppressed in spirit," he said, "for theirs is the Kingdom of Heaven!

"How fortunate are those who grieve, for they shall be comforted!

5 "How fortunate are the gentle, for they shall inherit the land!

"How fortunate for those who hunger and thirst for justice, for they shall be satisfied!

"How fortunate are those with pure minds, for they shall see God!

"How fortunate are the peacemakers, for they shall be called sons of God![14]

10 "How fortunate are those who are persecuted in the cause of justice, for theirs is the kingdom of Heaven!

"How fortunate are you when they revile you, and persecute you, and speak every kind of evil of you falsely because of me! Rejoice and be glad, for your heavenly reward is great; for so did they persecute the prophets who were before you.

"You are the salt of the earth. But if the salt becomes insipid by what means can its tang be restored? It is then good for nothing but to be thrown out for men to trample underfoot.

"You are the light of the world. A city that is perched
15 on the brow of a hill cannot be hidden. Neither is a lamp lit to be placed under a measuring-bowl: it is placed on a lampstand, to give light to all who are in the house. So let your light shine in the sight of men, that they observe your good conduct and praise your heavenly Father.

"Do not imagine that I have come to abrogate the Law

---

14 Solomon, whose name means Peaceable, was the first king of Israel to be called 'son of God'.

and the prophets: I have not come to abrogate them but to give effect to them. I tell you positively, until heaven and earth passs away not one iota, not a single stroke, shall be removed from the Law until it has completely been put into effect. So whoever would relax the most insignificant of commandments, and teach men so, shall be treated as insignificant in the Kingdom of Heaven. But whoever both observes and teaches them shall be treated

20 as of consequence in the Kingdom of Heaven. I tell you, therefore, unless your devoutness exceeds that of the scribes and Pharisees, you will never enter the Kingdom of Heaven.

"You have heard how those of old were told, 'You shall not commit murder.'[15] Those who commit murder are liable to the death penalty. But I tell you that whoever is enraged with his brother is liable to the death penalty, whoever calls his brother 'Raka'[16] is liable to punishment by the Sanhedrin, and whoever calls him 'Morē'[17] is liable to be doomed to blazing Gehenna. So if you bring your offering to the altar, and there recall that your brother has something against you, leave your offering before the altar. First make your peace with your brother, and then come and present your offering.

25   "Come to terms with your opponent quickly while you and he are on the way to court, in case your opponent turns you over to the judge, and the judge in turn to the executive officer, and you are thrown into jail. I tell you positively, you will not get out again until you have paid up the last farthing.

"You have heard how it was declared, 'You shall not commit adultery.'[18] But I tell you, whoever stares lustfully at a woman has already committed adultery with her in his mind. If, therefore, your right eye gives cause for complaint, pluck it out and cast it from you. It is more advantageous for you to be disfigured than that your

30 body intact should be cast into Gehenna. Or if your right hand gives cause for complaint cut it off and cast it from you. It is more advantageous for you to be maimed than that your body intact should go into Gehenna.

---

15 *Exod* 20:13. The reader is referred to the Introduction for additional matter explanatory of the Sermon on the Mount.
16 Aram. meaning scoundrel.
17 Aram. meaning rebel against God.
18 *Exod* 20:14.

"It was also declared, 'Whoever divorces his wife must give her a deed of severance.'[19] But I tell you, whoever discards his wife, except on grounds of adultery, makes her commit adultery; and whoever then marries her commits adultery.

"Further you have heard how those of old were told, 'You are not to swear falsely, but pay to the Lord what you vow.'[20] But I tell you, use no oath at all, neither by
35 heaven, since it is God's throne, nor by the earth, since it is his footstool, nor by Jerusalem, since it is the city of the Great King. Do not even swear by your head, since you are powerless to whiten a single hair or to turn it black again. Confine yourself, therefore, to plain Yes or No. Anything beyond that is wrong.[21]

"You have heard how it was declared, 'An eye for an eye, and a tooth for a tooth.'[22] But I tell you, do not offer resistance to wrong.[23] Whoever hits you on the right side
40 of your jaw, turn the other side to him. Whoever would go to law to take away your tunic, let him have your cloak as well. Whoever would compel you to go one mile, go with him even two.[24] Give to him who asks you, and from him who would borrow from you do not turn away.

"You have heard how it was declared, 'You are to love your neighbour, but hate your enemy.'[25] But I tell you, love your enemies, pray for those who persecute you,
45 that you may become sons of your heavenly Father, who makes his sun rise on the bad and the good alike, and showers rain on the just and the unjust. For if you only love those who love you, what reward have you? Do not even tax-collectors[26] do this? And if you only have regard for your brothers, what do you do more than others? Do not the Gentiles do the same? So you must be perfect as your heavenly Father is perfect.

19 *Deut* 24:1.
20 *Deut* 5:11 with 23:23.
21 This agrees with the Essenes. "Any word of theirs has more force than an oath; swearing they avoid, regarding it as worse than perjury" (Jos. *Jewish War* II.135).
22 *Exod* 21:24.
23 Galilee was a centre of the Jewish Resistance.
24 Forced impressment by troops to carry their baggage.
25 *Lev* 19:18. The second part of the saying is not in the OT but is in line with Essene teaching "to love all the Children of Light and hate all the Children of Darkness" (*Manual of Discipline*).
26 Collectors of the alien regime's imposts.

6.1   "Be sure you do not let people see you perform your charitable actions. If you do you will have no reward from your heavenly Father. So when you bestow alms do not blare it out in advance like the hypocrites do in the synagogues and streets to court public esteem. I tell you for a fact, they are receiving their reward in full. But you, when you bestow alms, do not let your left hand know what your right hand is doing; so that your alms are in secret, and your Father who sees in secret will reward you.

5   "Similarly when you pray, do not be like the hypocrites, who love to stand praying in the synagogues and at street corners so that people may see them.[27] I tell you positively, they are receiving their reward in full. But you, when you pray, enter your inner apartment and close the door, and pray to your Father who is in secret, and your Father who sees in secret will reward you. Further, when you pray, do not uselessly repeat yourself as the Gentiles do,[28] for they imagine that by constant repetition they will gain attention. Do not imitate them, therefore, since your Father knows what your needs are before you ask him.

"Pray rather in this way, 'Our heavenly Father, may
10   thy Name be sanctified, thy Kingdom established, thy will be obeyed on earth as it is in heaven. Give us to-day our needful food, and forgive us our failings,[29] as we too forgive those who have failed us. And do not put temptation in our way, but shield us from harm.'[30] For if you forgive people their failures your heavenly Father will
15   forgive you; but if you do not forgive people their failures neither will your heavenly Father forgive yours.

"And when you fast do not be like the long-faced hypocrites, who mar their looks so that it may be evident to people that they are fasting. I tell you positively, they are receiving their reward in full. But you, when you fast,

---

27 Jews commonly stood when reciting their prayers.
28 It was the pagan custom to emphasise petitions and invocations by crying out the same words several times. Cf *I Ki* 18:26.
29 A formula of absolution from rash vows and promises (*Kol Nidrei*) was recited by Jews on the eve of the Fast Day of Atonement. 'Failings', or obligations, is used in this sense, confirmed by the following reference to fasting.
30 Or, "rescue us from the Evil One". The whole prayer is an epitome of the Jewish morning prayers, with especial reference to the ancient Aramaic prayer known as the *Kaddish*.

anoint your head and bathe your face, so that you do not appear to people to be fasting, only to your Father who is in secret, and your Father who sees in secret will reward you.

"Lay up for yourselves no store on earth, where locust-grub and moth destroy, and where thieves break
20 in and steal. Rather lay up for yourselves store in heaven, where neither locust-grub nor moth destroys, and where no thieves break in and steal. For 'where your hoard is your heart is.'[31]

"The eye is the lamp of the body. If therefore your sight is sound your whole body will be radiant; but if your sight is bad your whole body will be in gloom.[32] If then the light that is in you is gloom, how deep the gloom!

"No one can serve two masters, for either he will hate the one and love the other, or else he will be devoted to the one and despise the other. You cannot serve both God and mammon.[33]

25 "Therefore I tell you, do not vex yourselves about what you are to eat or drink, or how your body is to be clad. Is not the soul of more consequence than food, and the body than clothing? See the birds of the air. They neither sow nor reap, nor gather into granaries, yet your heavenly Father feeds them. Are you not of more value than they? Which of you by mental effort can add a span to his height? Why then are you worried about your clothes? Study the wild irises, how they shoot up. They neither toil nor spin; yet I tell you that not even Solomon
30 in full regalia was arrayed like one of these. So if God thus attires the wild plant, which blooms to-day and to-morrow is thrown into the oven, shall he not much more clothe you, you feeble in faith? Be anxious then no longer, saying, 'What are you to eat, or drink?' or 'What are you to wear?' With such matters the Gentiles concern themselves. So make God's Kingdom and your duty to him your first concern, and all these things will be added to you. Do not worry about to-morrow. Let to-morrow

31 "Store on earth . . . in heaven", a current saying, as is also the quotation.
32 Double meaning. If your outlook is generous your whole personality will be radiant, if envious it will be gloomy.
33 Mammon, ie wealth, commonly called 'the false mammon'.

worry about itself. 'One day's trouble at a time is enough.'[34]

v

7.1 "Do not judge, and you will not be judged.
Do not condemn, and you will not be condemned.[35]
For the judgment you make will be made on you,
And the measure you use will be used for you.

"How is it you can see the speck in your brother's eye but cannot detect the plank that is in your own eye?[36] How can you say to your brother, 'Permit me to extract the speck from your eye,' while all the time there is a
5 plank in your own? Hypocrite! First extract the plank from your own eye, and then you will see clearly to extract the speck from your brother's eye.

"Do not offer gems[37] to the dogs,
    or they may turn and rend you;
Nor strew your pearls before pigs,[38]
    or they may trample them underfoot.

"Ask, and you will be given.
Seek, and you will find.
Knock, and you will be admitted.
For he who asks will receive,
And he who seeks will find,
And he who knocks will be admitted.

"Which of you will give his son a stone if he asks for
10 bread, or a snake if he asks for fish? If you then, bad as you are, know how to give good gifts to your children, how much more shall your heavenly Father give what is good to those who ask him. Therefore, in whatever way you would have people treat you, treat them the same; for this sums up the Law and the prophets.[39]

34 Current proverb.
35 Restored from the Old Hebrew, and so restoring the parallelism of the 1st and 3rd, 2nd and 4th lines. *Lk* 6:37.
36 Based on a current saying. See *Baba Bathra*, 15b, *Arachin.*, 16b. 'Speck' may be read 'splinter'.
37 The Greek has 'a holy thing', but the underlying Hebrew word has also the sense of bright, sparkling. Cf *Lam* 4:1, "precious stones".
38 The lost parallelism is restored by a transposition of the lines. "Dogs . . . pigs" were derogatory terms for pagans. Cf *Mt* 15:26; *Phil* 3:2.
39 The famous Rabbi Hillel (died *c* AD 10) had taught to this effect, and his dictum could have been known to Jesus.

"Enter by the narrow gate; for wide is the gate and spacious the way that leads to Destruction,[40] and many there are who enter by it. But narrow is the gate and constricted the way that leads to Life, and few there are who find it.

15 "Beware of false prophets, who come to you in sheep's fleeces,[41] but underneath they are ravening wolves. You will recognise them by their fruits. Are grape-clusters picked from thorns, or figs from brambles? So every good tree produces good fruit, while every harmful tree produces harmful fruit. A good tree cannot bear harmful fruit, neither can a harmful tree produce good fruit. Every tree that does not produce good fruit is cut down

20 and cast into the fire.[42] So by their fruits you will recognise them.[43]

"Not everyone who hails me as 'Lord, lord!' will enter the Kingdom of Heaven, only those who do the will of my heavenly Father. Many will say to me at that time, 'Lord, lord, have we not prophesied in your name, expelled demons in your name, and in your name performed many miracles?' But then I shall tell them plainly, 'I have never authorised you. Be off with you, you illegal practitioners!'[44]

"Whoever, therefore, hears these sayings of mine and carries them out will be like a prudent man who built his

25 house on rock. The torrent poured down, the floods came, the tempest blew, and beat against that house; but it did not fall, for it was founded on rock. Everyone, however, who hears these sayings of mine and fails to carry them out will be like a stupid man who built his house on sand. The torrent poured down, the floods came, the tempest blew, and beat against that house; and down it fell, and heavy was its collapse."

As Jesus came to the end of his discourse the people

---

40 Representing the Heb. *Abaddon* (the Abyss of Doom) opposed to Life (the resurrection life of the just in the Messianic Age).
41 cf *Zech* 13:4.
42 cf the Baptist's words in *Mt* 3:10.
43 cf a current proverb, "A gourd, a gourd, is known by its branch".
44 But cf *Lk* 6:46. The last part of the Sermon may indicate that in fact it was a collection of sayings circulating among followers of Jesus as a distinct document.

were amazed at his teaching, for he taught them as one with authority, and not as their scribes.[45]

---

45 Jesus spoke as a teacher in his own right, while the scribes were accustomed to quote authorities for the views they expressed. The impression seems intentionally to be conveyed of the Messiah as a second Moses delivering to his people the even more exacting demands of the Kingdom of God.

Book II

i

8.1   When Jesus came down from the hill great crowds followed him. Now there came a leper and prostrated himself before him, saying, "Sir, if you will you can make me clean."

Then Jesus put out his hand and touched him and said, "I do will it. Be clean!"

At once he was cleansed of his leprosy, and Jesus said to him, "See that you tell no one. But go and show yourself to the priest, and present the offering Moses prescribed as evidence to them."[1]

5   As Jesus entered Capernaum a centurion approached him and said, "Sir, my orderly is lying at home paralysed, suffering terribly."

"I will come and cure him," Jesus said to him.

But the centurion replied, "Sir, I am no fit person for you to come under my roof. Simply command it and my orderly will recover. I am a man under orders myself, and soldiers are under my orders.[2] I have only to say to one 'Go', and he goes, and to another 'Come', and he comes, and to my servant 'Do this', and he does it."

10   When Jesus heard this he was astonished and said to those who were following him, "Not in all Israel have I found faith like this. I tell you that many from the East and the West shall come and recline[3] with Abraham, Isaac and Jacob in the Kingdom of Heaven, while the sons of the Kingdom[4] will be ejected into the darkness outside where there will be wailing and grinding of teeth."

Then Jesus said to the centurion, "Go! As you have believed, so let it be for you."

At that very hour the orderly was cured.

On entering Peter's house Jesus saw his mother-in-law
15   who had been laid up with fever. He took her by the

---

1 See *Lev* 14.
2 See note to parallel passage in *Lk* 7.
3 At the Messianic banquet of the just.
4 The natural heirs, Israelites.

hand and the fever left her, and she got up and waited upon him.

When evening came many demoniacs were brought to him, and he expelled the spirits by a command, and cured all who were ill.[a]

ii

When Jesus saw the crowd about him he gave orders to cross over to the farther shore. Then one of the scribes approached him and said, "Teacher, I will follow you wherever you go."

20   "The foxes have lairs," Jesus replied, "the birds of the air have nests, but the Son of Man has not a floor[5] on which he may lay his head."

Another disciple said to him, "Sir, give me leave first to bury my father."

"Follow me," Jesus told him, "and leave the dead to bury their dead."

Then he went on board ship and his disciples accompanied him. While on the sea a great squall arose, so that the ship was swamped by the waves. But he lay

25   sleeping. So his disciples came and roused him and said, "Save us, sir, we are lost!"

"What cowards you are, you feeble in faith!" he answered.

Then he rose and rebuked the winds and the sea, and a great calm ensued. The men were amazed and said, "Whoever is he, that even the winds and the sea obey him?"

When Jesus reached the Gadarene country on the farther shore he was met by two demoniacs coming out of the tombs. So highly dangerous were they that no one would venture to take that road.

"What do you want with us, Son of God?" they shrieked. "Have you come to torture us before the time?"

30   Some way off from where they were a herd of many swine were feeding. So the demons in the man begged

---

a Thereby was fulfilled what was announced by the prophet Isaiah, "Himself took our infirmities and bore our diseases."[b]

---

5 Following the Old Hebrew.
6 *Isa* 53:4.

him, "If you are going to expel us send us into the herd of swine."

"Be gone!" he told them.

So on coming out of the men they went into the swine, and the whole herd made a wild dash down the bank into the sea, and perished in the water. The herdsmen fled and made off to the town[7] and told their tale, and also about the demoniacs. At this the entire city made for Jesus in a body, and when they reached him they
9.1 entreated him to leave their territory. So reembarking he crossed over and came once more to his own town.

Here there was a paralytic brought to him prostrate on a mattress. Then Jesus, seeing the faith of the bearers, said to the paralytic, "Courage, son! Your sins are forgiven you."

Some of the scribes present said to themselves, "He speaks profanely."

Reading their thoughts Jesus said, "Why do you har-
5 bour evil thoughts? Which is easier, to say, 'Your sins are forgiven you' or to say, 'Rise and walk'? But so that you may know that the Son of Man is entitled on earth to forgive sins" – he said to the paralytic, "Rise, pick up your mattress, and go to your home!"

When the people saw this they were afraid, and praised God who had conferred such power on mortal men.[8]

iii

As Jesus continued on his way he saw a man called Matthew seated at the customs-station, and said to him, "Follow me!"

He rose and followed him.
10 When Jesus sat down to dine in the house many tax-collectors and sinners[9] also came and dined with Jesus and his disciples. Now when the Pharisees saw this they said to his disciples, "How comes it that your teacher eats with tax-collectors and sinners?"

7 Gadara was a Greek city of the Decapolis. A herd of swine would not have been kept by Jews. Unclean spirits into unclean animals.

8 Forms of benediction existed for recital on various occasions. The form used here was probably, "Blessed is he who has given of his power to flesh and blood".

9 See *Mk* p 9, n 15.

Jesus overheard this and replied, "It is not the healthy who need a doctor, it is those who are ill. So go and study what this means, 'Compassion is what I desire, not sacrifice.'[10] I have not come to call religious people, only sinners."

Then the disciples of John approached him and asked, "How comes it that we and the Pharisees fast while your disciples do not fast?"

15 Jesus replied, "Does the bridal party[11] grieve while they have the bridegroom with them? The time will come when the bridegroom will have taken his leave: that will be the time for them to fast. No one sews a patch of new cloth on an old cloak, for he only drags the material from the cloak and the tear is made worse. Nor does anyone pour new wine into old wine-skins. If he does, the skins will be split, the wine will be spilt, and the skins spoilt. No, one pours new wine into new wine-skins and both remain intact."

While he was telling them these things a certain official approached and prostrated himself before him and said, "My daughter has just passed away; but if you will come and lay your hands on her she will live."

Jesus rose and followed him, accompanied by his disciples.

20 Now a woman who had suffered twelve years with a haemorrhage came up behind and touched the fringe[12] of his cloak, for she said to herself, "If only I can touch his cloak I shall get well."

But Jesus turned round and saw her and said, "Courage, daughter! Your faith has cured you."

From that moment the woman was cured.

When Jesus entered the official's residence and saw the pipers and professional dirge-makers he said, "Be off! The little girl is not dead, only sleeping."

25 They jeered at him. But when the crowd had been ejected he went in and took her by the hand, and the little girl rose up. The tale of this spread throughout that country.

10 *Hos* 6:6.
11 See *Mk* p 10, n 18.
12 See *Mk* p 16, n 35.

iv

When Jesus continued on his way two blind men followed crying, "Pity us, Son of David!"

As he entered the house the blind men came up to him, and Jesus said, "Do you believe I can do this?"

"Yes, sir," they answered.

Then he touched their eyes and said, "Let it be to you according to your faith."

30 And their eyes were opened. "No one is to know of this," he warned them. But when they went away they spread the tale throughout that region.

As they left there was brought to him a dumb demoniac, and when the demon was expelled the mute spoke. The people were amazed and said, "Nothing like this has been seen in Israel."[a]

35 So Jesus toured all the towns and villages, teaching in their synagogues and proclaiming the News of the Kingdom, and curing every kind of disease and infirmity.

v

When Jesus saw the crowds he was filled with compassion for them, for they were weary and dejected like sheep which have no shepherd. Then he said to his disciples, "The harvest is indeed plentiful, but the labourers are few. Beseech the Harvest-master to send out labourers to gather in his harvest."

10.1 Then summoning his twelve disciples he gave them power over foul spirits to enable them to expel them and to cure every kind of disease and infirmity.

These are the names of the twelve envoys. First there was Simon (called Peter) and his brother Andrew, then James the son of Zebedee and his brother John, Philip and Bartholomew,[13] Thomas and the tax-collector Matthew, James the son of Alphaeus and Thaddaeus, Simon the Zealot and Judas the Iscariot,[14] who in fact betrayed him.

---

a But the Pharisees said, "It is by the chief of the demons that he casts out demons."

---

13 Bar-Tolmai, probably 'Son of Ptolemy' in Aramaic.
14 See *Mk* 3, p 11, n 25.

5   These twelve Jesus dispatched with the following
instructions: "Keep away from Gentile centres, and do
not enter any Samaritan town. Go instead to the lost
sheep of the house of Israel.[15] As you travel proclaim,
'The Kingdom of Heaven is at hand.' Cure the ailing,
raise the dead, cleanse the lepers, expel the demons. You
have received without payment, so give without payment. Take neither gold, nor silver, nor copper in your
10   belts, nor a wallet for the road, nor two tunics, nor shoes,
nor a staff; for 'the labourer deserves his keep.'[16] When
you enter a town or village inquire first who in it is
worthy, and stay there until you leave again. When you
enter a household give it greeting,[17] and if the household
is worthy let your peace come upon it; but if it is not
worthy let your peace return to you. If anyone will not
welcome you or listen to what you have to say, when you
leave that house or town shake off the dust from your
15   feet. I tell you for a fact, it will be more tolerable for the
people of Sodom and Gomorrah in the Day of Judgment
than for that town.

"See, I am sending you as sheep among wolves, so be
as subtle as serpents yet simple as doves. Watch out for
the authorities, for they will hand you over to the
sanhedrins and flog you in their synagogues, and you
will be brought before governors and kings on my
account as a testimony to them and to the Gentiles. But
when they arraign you do not concern yourselves with
the manner or matter of your speech, for it will come to
20   you at the time what you are to say; for it will not really be
you speaking but the Spirit of your Father speaking
through you. Then brother will betray brother to death,
and the father his son, and children will rise up against
their parents to compass their death. You will be universally detested on my account. But he who is constant to
the end will be preserved.[18] I tell you for a fact, you will

15 The function of the Messiah, as king of Israel, was to redeem his own
people, so that his nation would redeem the nations.
16 Of the Essenes it was said: "They carry nothing whatever with them on
their journeys, except arms as a protection against brigands . . . They do
not change their garments or shoes until they are torn to shreds or worn
threadbare with age" (Jos. *Jewish War* II.125–126).
17 In the form, "Peace be with this house".
18 The speech of Jesus has been amplified as a guide to Christian envoys
setting out in the reign of Claudius to convey the News to other lands.

not have exhausted the cities of Israel before the Son of
Man arrives.

25 "The disciple is not superior to his teacher, nor the
servant to his master. Let it suffice for the disciple to be
deemed equal to his teacher, and the servant to his
master. If they have called the owner of the house
Beelzebul,[19] how much more those of his household?
You have no cause to fear them therefore, for nothing is
covered up that shall not be disclosed, nor hidden away
that shall not be made known. What I tell you in the dark
speak out in broad daylight, and what you hear in a
whisper shout from the housetops.[20] Have no fear of
those who kill the body, but can by no means kill the
soul. Fear him instead[21] who can destroy both soul and
body in Gehenna. Are not two sparrows sold for an
assar?[22] Yet not one of them shall fall to earth without
30 your Father's consent. As for yourselves, every hair of
your heads is counted. So have no fear, you are of more
consequence than many sparrows. Whoever, therefore,
identifies himself with me before the authorities, I too
will identify myself with him before my heavenly Father.

35 "Do not imagine I have come to bring peace to the
earth.[23] I have not come to bring peace but a dagger. For I
have come 'to set a man against his father, and the
daughter against her mother, and the daughter-in-law
against her mother-in-law: a man's enemies will be those
of his own household'.[24] He who holds father or mother
dearer than he is not worthy of me, and he who holds
son or daughter dearer than me is not worthy of me. And
he who does not shoulder his cross[25] and follow me is not
worthy of me.

40 "He who gains his life will lose it; but he who is ready
to lose his life will gain it. He who welcomes you
welcomes me, and he who welcomes me welcomes him
who sent me. He who welcomes a prophet as a prophet
will reap a prophet's reward, and he who welcomes a

19 Baal-zebul, Prince of the demons.
20 Jesus was opposed to secret doctrines revealed only to grades of initiates, as
with the Essenes.
21 ie God himself.
22 A coin of very small value.
23 The Messiah was expected to bring peace. cf *Isa* 9:6–7; 11:1–9.
24 *Mic* 7:6.
25 See *Mk* 8:34, p 26, n 56.

just man as a just man will reap a just man's reward;[26] and he who refreshes the humblest believer, if only with a cup of cold water, as a disciple, I tell you truly, he shall not lack his reward."

11.1   When Jesus had finished instructing his twelve disciples he went elsewhere to teach and preach in their various towns.

---

26 There will be a reward for those who do not accept Jesus as the Messiah, but only as a prophet or just man.

Book III

When John in prison came to hear of the Messiah's activities he sent by his disciples to ask Jesus, "Are you the Destined One, or are we to await someone else?"

Jesus answered, "Go back and inform John of what
5 you hear and see. The blind receive sight, the lame walk, the lepers are cleansed, the dead are raised, and the poor are given the Good News.[1] Fortunate is he who has no misgivings about me."

When they had left, Jesus spoke to the crowds about John. "What did you go out into the wilderness to see, a cane[2] shaken by the wind? Or did you go out to see something else, a man clad in soft draperies?[3] Surely those who wear soft draperies are found in kings' palaces. What then did you go out for, to see a prophet? Yes, I
10 tell you, and much more than a prophet. He it is of whom it is stated, 'See, I will send my messenger before you, to pave the way for you.'[4] I tell you truly, among all of women born there has never arisen a greater than John the Baptist,[5] yet the most insignificant person in the Kingdom of Heaven is greater than he. From John the Baptist until now, however, the Kingdom of Heaven is under pressure, and the violent seize upon it;[6] for all the prophets and the Law prophesied up to John, and if you are willing to accept it, he is Elijah who was to come.[7]
15 Whoever can catch my meaning let him do so.

"How shall I describe this generation? It is like children squatting in the market place, who call out to their

---

1 cf *Isa* 35:5; 61:1.
2 Double meaning, playing on the Heb *qaneh* (a reed) and *qana* (a Zealot), ie "a Zealot swayed by passion". The Zealot militants were responsible for the revolt against the Romans of AD 67–70.
3 Metaphorically, 'a man surrounded with flatteries,' another double meaning.
4 *Mal* 3:1.
5 *Deut* 34:10.
6 Again a reference to militant freedom-fighters very prominent in Galilee.
7 cf *Mal* 4:5. The Elijah prophecy is the last word of the Heb. OT division of the Law and the Prophets.

playmates, 'We've played you a jig, but you haven't danced. We've played a dirge, but you haven't lamented.' For John came neither eating nor drinking, and they say, 'He is demon-possessed.' The Son of Man came both eating and drinking, and they say, 'There you are, a glutton and a drunkard, an associate of tax-collectors and sinners.' Yet, 'wisdom is vindicated by her works.' "[8]

20   Then Jesus began to reproach the towns in which his powers had chiefly been displayed, because they had failed to repent.

"Woe to you, Chorazin! Woe to you, Bethsaida! For had the miracles been performed in Tyre and Sidon that have been performed in you they would long since have repented in sackcloth and ashes. Further, I tell you, it will be more tolerable for Tyre and Sidon in the Day of Judgment than for you. As for you, Capernaum, are you not raised up to heaven? You will surely be razed to hell.[9] For had the miracles been performed in Sodom that have been performed in you it would have lasted to this day. Further, I tell you, it will be more tolerable for the land of Sodom in the Day of Judgment than for you."

25   It was on this occasion that Jesus said, "I bow to thy will, Father, Lord of heaven and earth, because thou hast hidden these things from the wise and prudent, and disclosed them to babes. Even so, Father, for so it seemed good in thy sight.

"Everything has been made over to me by my Father, yet no one esteems the Son except the Father. Neither does anyone esteem the Father except the Son, and he to whom the Son chooses to reveal him. Come to me, all you who are weary and overburdened, and I will relieve you. Take my yoke upon you, and learn from me; for I am gentle and of a quiet disposition, and you will get relief;[10]

30   for my yoke does not chafe and my load is light."[11]

ii

12.1   At this time Jesus proceeded on the sabbath through the standing corn, and his disciples, being hungry, began to pick the ears of corn and eat. Observing this, the Pharisees said to him, "Look, your disciples are doing what is not allowed on the sabbath."

8 cf *Wisd. Sol.* 8:6–7.
9 cf *Isa* 14:13–15: 'raised . . . razed' preserving the alliteration in the Old Hebrew.
10 *Jer* 6:16.
11 cf *Ecclus* 51:23–27.

"Have you not read," Jesus replied, "what David did when he was hungry, and his men as well, how he entered God's house and ate the loaves of the Presence, which were forbidden both to him and his men to eat,[12]
5   and were for the priests alone? Or have you not read in the Law that on the sabbath the priests in the Sanctuary violate the sabbath and are guiltless?[13] I tell you, what is greater than the Sanctuary is here. If you had known what the text means, 'Compassion is what I desire, not sacrifice',[14] you would not have condemned the guiltless; for the Son of Man is master of the sabbath."
10   When he left there he went into their synagogue, and there was a man there with a withered hand. They asked him, so that they could bring a charge against him, "Is it permissible to cure on the sabbath?"[15]

Jesus replied, "Which of you with a single sheep will not take hold of it and lift it out if it should fall into a pit on the sabbath? Is not a man of more account than a sheep? Therefore it is entirely permissible to do good on the sabbath."

Then he said to the man, "Stretch out your hand!"

He stretched it out, and it was restored as sound as the other.

Then the Pharisees went out and consulted about him, how best to destroy him.
15   When Jesus knew of this he left there. Many followed him, and he cured them all, but insisted that they should not publicise him.[a]

a This was to fulfil what was announced by the prophet Isaiah saying,

Here is my servant, whom I have chosen,
My dear one, of whom I am so proud!
I have put my Spirit upon him:
He shall dispense justice to the nations.
He will neither wrangle nor shout;
No one will hear his voice in the streets.
A crushed reed he will not break off;
A smouldering wick he will not snuff out;
Till he triumphantly vindicates justice,
And nations confide in his name.[16]

---

12 *I Sam* 21:2–6.
13 *Num* 28:9–10. Servile work in the Temple did not count as such.
14 *Hos* 6:6.
15 This would be a very fanatical group, since Judaism permitted healing on the sabbath.
16 *Isa* 63:1–4 (adapted).

iii

Now there was brought to Jesus a blind and dumb demoniac, and he cured him, so that the dumb could both speak and see. And all the people were amazed and said, "Surely he is the Son of David."[17]

On hearing this the Pharisees said, "He only expels demons with the aid of Beelzebul the chief of the demons."

25   Knowing what was in their minds, Jesus said to them, "Every kingdom in conflict with itself cannot endure. If then Satan expels Satan he is in conflict with himself. How then can his kingdom endure? So if I expel demons by Beelzebul, by whom do your sons expel them? So they shall be your judges. But if I expel demons by the Spirit of God then the Kingdom of God has caught you unawares. For how can anyone enter the Strong One's[18] abode and plunder his possessions without first binding the Strong One? Then he can loot his abode.

30   "Whoever is not with me is against me, and whoever does not gather with me scatters. I tell you, therefore, every folly and insult will be forgiven men, but insult of the Spirit will not be forgiven. Anyone who says a word against the Son of Man will be forgiven, but if he speaks against the holy Spirit he will get no forgiveness either in this world or in the one to come. Either make the tree good and its fruit good, or make the tree harmful and its fruit harmful; for 'the tree is known by its fruit'.

"Vipers' brood! How, evil as you are, can you say anything good? For 'what the mind is stored with the

35   mouth speaks.' The good man from his good store gives out good, while the evil man from his evil store gives out evil. I tell you, men will be called to account at the Day of Judgment for every idle remark they make, for 'it will be your words which right you and your words which ruin you.'"

Some of the scribes and Pharisees then said, "Teacher, we wish to see a sign from you."

Jesus replied, "An evil and adulterous generation requires a sign, does it! Well, it will get no sign except

40   that of the prophet Jonah. For just as Jonah was three days and three nights in the maw of the sea-monster, so

17 ie the Messiah.
18 ie the Devil.

will the Son of Man be three days and three nights in the heart of the earth. The men of Nineveh will rise up at the Judgment, and this generation with them, and they will damn it; for they repented at the preaching of Jonah, and what is of more consequence than Jonah is here. The Queen of the South will rise up at the Judgment, and this generation with her, and she will damn it; for she came from the earth's extremities to hear the wisdom of Solomon, and what is of more consequence than Solomon is here.

"As soon as the foul spirit has left a man it wanders through arid wastes seeking refreshment and finding none. Then it decides, 'I'll go back to my old home.' When it gets there it finds it untenanted, swept clean,
45 and tidied up. Then it sets off and secures seven other spirits more noxious than itself, and in they go to live there. So the last state of that man is worse than the first. So will it be with this evil generation."

He was still addressing the crowds when his mother and brothers stood outside wishing to speak with him. But he put it to the man who informed him, "Who is my mother, and who are my brothers?" Then indicating his disciples he added, "See, here are my mother and
50 brothers. Whoever does the will of my heavenly Father is my brother and sister and mother."

iv

13.1   That day Jesus left the house and sat down on the seashore; and great crowds gathered about him, so that he had to go on board a boat and sit in it while the crowds stood on the shore.

He spoke at great length to them in similes, as for instance: "The sower went out to sow; and as he sowed some seed fell by the wayside where the birds came and
5 picked it up. Other seed fell on stony ground where there was not much soil; and at once it sprouted because the soil had little depth. But when the sun was up it was parched and withered away for lack of root. Other seed fell among thistles, and the thistles shot up and stifled it. Other seed fell on good soil, and yielded a crop, a hundredfold, sixtyfold, or thirtyfold. Let him who can catch my meaning do so."

10   Then the disciples approached and said to him, "Why are you speaking to them in similes?"[19]

Jesus replied, "Because you are entitled to know the secrets of the Kingdom of God, but they are not entitled; for whoever has will get more, and will have a surplus, while he who has not will be deprived even of what he has. That is why I am speaking to them in similes, so that though seeing they do not really see, and though hearing they do not really hear or comprehend. In them is fulfilled the prophesy of Isaiah,

> *You shall hear indeed, but fail to grasp.*
> *You shall see indeed, but fail to perceive.*
15 > *For the mind of this people is dense,*
> *And their ears are hard of hearing,*
> *And their eyes they have fast closed,*
> *In case they should see with their eyes,*
> *And hear with their ears,*
> *And comprehend with their minds,*
> *And turn again, when I must heal them.*[20]

But how fortunate are your eyes, because they do see, and your ears, because they do hear! I tell you positively, many prophets and just men have longed to see what you are seeing, but have missed seeing it, and to hear what you are hearing, but have missed hearing it. Listen then to the simile of the sower.

"Whoever hears the Message of the Kingdom, and fails to comprehend it, along comes the Evil One and promptly picks out what has been sown in his mind. This
20 is he who had the wayside sowing. As for him who had the sowing in stony ground, he it is who hears the Message, and at once accepts it with joy; but having no root in himself he does not last long. So when trial or persecution comes upon him on account of the Message he is at once put off. As for him who had the sowing among thistles, he it is who heeds the Message, but worldly cares and the lure of riches stifle the Message, and he becomes unfruitful. But he who had the sowing

---

19 Jesus was forced to do so because of government spies and informers in the crowds in those days seeking to catch some subversive statement against the Roman regime, when he would have been arrested like John the Baptist and others. The theme of the coming of the Kingdom of God was a dangerous topic, favoured by the Zealot Galileans.
20 *Isa* 6:9–10.

in good soil is he who hears the Message and grasps it, and who bears fruit, and yields a hundredfold, or sixty-fold, or thirtyfold."

He offered them a further simile. "The Kingdom of Heaven may be represented as a man who sowed good
25 seed in his field. But while the labourers slept his enemy came and sowed weeds[21] among the wheat and went away. So when the blade sprouted and bore fruit the weeds were revealed. Then the owner's servants approached and said, 'Sir, didn't you sow good seed in your field? Where do these weeds come from?'

"'Some enemy has done this,' he told them.

"'Do you want us to go and root them out?' they asked him.

"'No,' he replied, 'for in rooting out the weeds you
30 may uproot the wheat as well. Let both grow together until harvest; and at harvest time I will tell the reapers, Root out the weeds first and bind them in bundles for burning, but gather the wheat into my granary.'"

He offered them a further simile. "The Kingdom of Heaven may be represented as a grain of mustard-seed which a man took and planted in his field. It is indeed the smallest of seeds, but when it has grown it is taller than other plants, and reaches tree height,[22] so that the birds of the air come and nest in its branches."

He added another simile, "The Kingdom of Heaven may be represented as leaven which a woman took and buried in three seahs[23] of flour until the whole was leavened."

34 Jesus addressed these things to the people in similes, and except by simile he said nothing to them.[a]

v

Then Jesus dismissed the people and went home. There his disciples approached him and said, "Explain to

a Thereby was fulfilled what was announced by the prophet, "I will open my mouth in proverbs: I will voice things concealed since creation."[24]

21 Wheatlike weeds (Heb. *zunin*, Gr. *zizania*), probably darnel.
22 Around three metres.
23 Three seahs made one ephah, rather more than a bushel.
24 *Ps* 78:2.

us the simile of the weeds in the field."

So he told them, "He who sowed the good seed is the Son of Man. The field is the world. The good seed represents the sons of the Kingdom. The weeds represent the son of the Evil One, while the enemy who sowed them is the Devil himself. The harvest is the Consummation of the Age, and the reapers are the
40 angels. Just as the weeds are rooted out and burnt, so will it be at the Consummation of the Age. The Son of Man will send out his angels, and they will root out of his kingdom all subversive elements, and those who behave lawlessly, and cast them into the fiery furnace, where there will be wailing and grinding of teeth. Then shall the just beam forth like the sun in their Father's Kingdom. Let him who can catch my meaning do so.

"The Kingdom of Heaven may be represented as a treasure buried in a field, which a man found there and hid again. In his delight he goes and sells all he possesses to buy that field.
45 "Alternatively, the Kingdom of Heaven may be represented as a merchant seeking fine pearls. Finding one magnificent specimen, he goes off and disposes of all his stock and buys it.

"The Kingdom of Heaven may again be represented as a drag-net cast into the sea and gathering up fish of every kind, which when filled they hauled on to the beach, and sitting down sorted out the good into crates and threw the bad away. It will be like that at the Consummation of the Age. The angels will go out and separate the wicked
50 from the just and cast them into the fiery furnace, where there will be wailing and grinding of teeth.

"Have you grasped all this?"

"Yes," they told him.

Then he said to them, "Thus every scribe well-versed in the Kingdom of Heaven may be represented as a householder who produced from his store things new and old."

On concluding these similes Jesus left there, and coming to his native town he taught them in their synagogue. They were astounded, and said, "How has
55 he come by this wisdom and these powers? Isn't he the carpenter's son? Isn't his mother called Mary, and his brothers James, Joseph, Simon and Judas? Aren't all his sisters living here?" And they were affronted at him.

"No prophet is unhonoured," Jesus told them, "except in his native town and his own home."

He did not perform many miracles there because of their disbelief.

Book IV

i

14.1   At this time Herod the tetrarch heard tell of Jesus, and said to his attendants, "It is John the Baptist. He has risen from the dead. That is why miracles are effected by him."

Herod had arrested John, bound and imprisoned him, on account of Herodias his brother Philip's wife. John
5   had told him, "It is illegal for you to have her."[1] But though ready to kill him, Herod feared the populace who regarded John as a prophet.

Now on the anniversary of Herod's accession the daughter of Herodias danced before the company, and so charmed Herod that he promised with an oath to give her whatever she asked. Prompted by her mother she said, "Give me here and now on a platter the head of John the Baptist."

Unhappy as the king was, because of his oath and the
10   assembled guests he ordered it to be given her, and sent to the prison and had John executed, and his head brought on a dish and given to the girl, and she took it to her mother.

John's disciples came and fetched his corpse and buried it, and then went and informed Jesus.

When Jesus heard the news he withdrew from there by ship to seclusion in the wilderness. But the people learning of this followed him on foot from the towns. So on arriving he found a vast crowd, and was moved with
15   compassion for them, and cured their sick. When evening came his disciples approached him and said, "This is open country, and it is already late. Dismiss the people that they may go off to the villages and buy themselves food."

"There is no need for them to go," Jesus told them. "Give them something to eat yourselves."

"All we have here," they protested, "is five loaves and two fish."

---

1 Herod was already married to the daughter of the Nabatean monarch Haretath, and according to the Essenes (*Temple Scroll*) it was not lawful to take a second wife while the first was still living.

"Bring them to me," he said.

Then Jesus ordered the people to sit down on the grass, and taking the five loaves and the two fish he looked up to heaven, gave thanks, broke the bread and handed it to his disciples, and they to the people.

20 Everyone ate and was satisfied; and they took up twelve basketfuls of the fragments left over. Of those who had partaken the men alone numbered about five thousand apart from women and children.

Then he insisted that his disciples take ship and precede him to the other side while he dismissed the people. Having done so, he made a solitary ascent of the mountain to pray. When it got late he was still there alone. The ship by now was a considerable distance[2] from land, lashed by the waves, for the wind was contrary.

25 In the fourth watch of the night[3] he came towards them walking on the sea.[4] When the disciples saw him walking on the sea they were terrified and said, "It's a malignant spirit!"[5] and cried out in fear.

But at once Jesus spoke to them. "Courage!" he called out. "It is I. There's nothing to be afraid of."

Then Peter called back, "If it really is you, Master, bid me come to you on the water."

"Come!" he said.

So Peter climbed overboard, and walked on the water,
30 and went towards Jesus. But facing the wind he was afraid, and, beginning to sink, cried out, "Save me, Master!"

Jesus immediately stretched out his hand and caught hold of him, and said to him, "Feeble in faith! Why did you doubt?"

When he got into the ship the wind dropped. Then those who were in the ship prostrated themselves before him and said, "Truly you are God's Son."

Having crossed over they came to the Gennesaret
35 country, and when the local populace became aware of his presence they sent round the whole vicinity, and

2 Gr. 'several furlongs' (nearly a mile).
3 The fourth watch was from 3–6 am.
4 The text certainly intends a miracle here; but it is to be noted that the Hebrew *al* can mean 'by' as well as 'on'.
5 Heb *mazziq*. Such spirits were believed to haunt the lake. The Greek has "phantom" or "apparition".

brought him all who were ill, requesting him that they might simply touch the fringe of his cloak, and all those who did touch it recovered.

ii

15.1   Then Pharisees and scribes from Jerusalem came to Jesus and asked, "How is it that your disciples fail to conform to the tradition of the elders, for they do not wash their hands when they eat food?"

Jesus replied, "And how is it that you fail to conform to the commandments of God through your tradition? For God said, 'Honour your father and mother', and 'he that

5   curses father or mother shall surely die.'[6] Yet you say, 'Should a man say to father or mother, let it be a votive gift whatever of mine may benefit you,[7] he is not to honour his father or mother.' Thus you have nullified the word of God through your tradition. Hypocrites! Isaiah did well to prophesy of you,

> *Here is a people that pays me lip-service,*
> *But their minds are far away from me.*
> *It is useless for them to worship me*
> *While teaching as doctrine devices of men.''*[8]

10   He summoned the people and said to them, "Attend and understand! It is not what enters the mouth that soils a man; it is what comes out of the mouth that soils a man."

Then the disciples approached and said to him, "Do you realise that the Pharisees were affronted on hearing that pronouncement?"

Jesus answered, "Every plant not watered by my heavenly Father will be uprooted. Never mind them. They are blind guides of the blind; and if one blind man guides another both of them will fall into the ditch."

15   "Explain this simile to us", urged Peter.

"Is it possible you still don't understand?" he said. "Don't you realise that whatever enters the mouth finds its way to the stomach and is evacuated in the toilet? But what issues from the mouth emanates from the mind,

6 *Exod* 20:12; 21:17.
7 See above p 22, n 47.
8 *Isa* 29:13.

and it is this that soils a man. For from the mind spring evil suggestions, murders, adulteries, immoralities, rob-
20 beries, false testimonies, slanders. These are the things that soil a man. But eating with unwashed hands does not soil a man."

Leaving there Jesus departed for the borders of Tyre and Sidon. A Canaanite woman from those parts came out crying, "Pity me, Son of David, sir! My daughter is terribly demon-possessed."

But he gave her no reply.

So his disciples approached and begged him, "Do get rid of her, for she keeps crying after us."

"I have only been sent to the lost sheep of the house of Israel," he answered.

25 Then she came forward and prostrated herself and said, "Do help me, sir!"

He replied, "It is not fair to take the children's food and throw it to puppies."[9]

"Quite so, sir", she said. "But even puppies may eat the scraps that fall from their masters' table."

Then Jesus said to her, "Madam, you have great faith. Let it be as you wish."

From that moment her daughter was cured.

iii

Crossing over from there Jesus proceeded along the shore of Galilee, and climbed the hill and sat down there.
30 And great crowds came to him bringing with them the lame, the blind, the dumb, and many others, and laid them at his feet, and he cured them; so that the people were amazed when they witnessed the dumb speaking, the lame walking, and the blind seeing, and they praised the God of Israel.

Then Jesus summoned his disciples and said, "I am full of compassion for the people, for they have stayed with me three days and have nothing to eat. I would not dismiss them fasting or they may collapse on the way."

His disciples said to him, "Where in this open country are we to find enough bread to satisfy such a crowd?"

"How much bread have you?" he asked.

"Seven loaves," they said, "and some small fish."

9 See p 68, n 38.

35   Then Jesus ordered the crowd to sit on the ground, and taking the seven loaves and the fish he gave thanks, broke and distributed the food to the disciples, and they to the people. And everyone ate and was satisfied, and they took up seven hampers full of what was left over of the pieces. No less than four thousand men had eaten not counting women and children.

Jesus then dismissed the people and went on board ship, and came to the borders of Magadan.

16.1   Now the Pharisees and Sadducees came to trap him with the request that he would show them a sign from Heaven. But he answered,[10] "An evil and adulterous generation wants a sign, does it? Well, it will get no sign except that of Jonah."

With that he left them and went away.

5   When the disciples arrived at the farther shore they had forgotten to bring bread. So Jesus said to them, "Be careful to avoid the leaven of the Pharisees and Sadducees."

They argued among themselves, "But we didn't bring any bread?"

Perceiving this Jesus said, "What are you arguing about, you feeble in faith, that you have no bread? Have you no sense or recollection of the five loaves with the

10   five thousand and how many baskets you took up, or of the seven loaves with the four thousand and how many hampers you took up? How can you possibly fail to understand that I was not referring to bread as such when I told you to avoid the leaven of the Pharisees and Sadducees?"

Then it dawned on them that he did not mean that they should avoid leaven in the sense of bread, but the teaching of the Pharisees and Sadducees.

iv

On reaching the vicinity of Caesarea-Philippi[11] Jesus asked his disciples, "Whom do people say the Son of Man is?"

10 Some MSS insert: "When it is evening, you say, 'It will be fine weather, for the sky is red.' And in the morning, 'It will be bad weather, for the sky is red and overcast.' You know how to discern the aspect of the sky, but not the Signs of the Times."

11 Formerly Paneas, at the springs of the River Jordan. Herod Philip had enlarged it and changed its name in honour of the Roman emperor.

"Some say John the Baptist," they replied, "others Elijah, others Jeremiah[12] or some other prophet."

15   "What about you?" he said to them. "Whom do you say I am?"

Simon Peter answered, "You are the Messiah, the Son of the Living God."

"How fortunate you are, impulsive[13] Simon!" Jesus said to him. "No mortal disclosed this to you: it was my heavenly Father. And so I tell you, since you are Peter,[14] upon that rock I will found my Community, and the gates of hell shall not prevail against it. To you I will give the keys of the Kingdom of Heaven. Whatever you prohibit[15] on earth shall be prohibited in heaven, and whatever you permit on earth shall be permitted in heaven."[16]

20   Then he firmly impressed on the disciples that they should tell no one that he was the Messiah.

From then onwards Jesus began to show his disciples how essential it was for him to go to Jerusalem, and there suffer many things at the hands of the elders, head priests and scribes, and be put to death, and rise again on the third day.

Peter caught hold of him and objected strongly, "God forbid, Master! Nothing of the sort shall happen to you."

But he turned on Peter and said, "Get behind me, *satan!*[17] You affront me; for yours is the human viewpoint, not God's."

Then Jesus said to his disciples, "Whoever would follow me must be utterly reckless, and shoulder his
25   cross[18] and follow me. For whoever would preserve his life will lose it, but whoever loses his life on account of me will gain it. What benefit has a man if he wins the whole world if his life is forfeit? What substitute for his life can a man offer? Very soon the Son of Man will come in his Father's state with his angels, and then he will

---

12 Jeremiah was a favourite prophet with Jewish nationalists and Essenes.
13 Lit *Baryona*, not perhaps 'Son of Jona' but Aram. word meaning unrestrained. Those who lost self-control and became openly hostile to Rome were known as *barjonim*.
14 Gr. *petros*, rock, Simon's nickname.
15 'Prohibit . . . permit'. Lit 'bind . . . loose', terms applied to rulings on the application of the religious code to conduct.
16 ie 'Your ruling (for or against) shall be the accepted ruling.'
17 See above, *Mk* 8:33, p 25.
18 See above, note to *Mk* 8:34, p 26.

reward each one according to his deeds. I tell you for a fact, there are some standing here who will not experience death before they see the Son of Man inaugurate his Kingdom."

17.1   Six days later Jesus took as companions Peter, James and his brother John, and led them up a high mountain entirely by themselves. In their presence he was transformed, and his face shone like the sun and his robes became bright as the light. Suddenly Moses and Elijah appeared to them conversing with him.

Peter could not help saying, "Master, how good it is that we should be here! If you wish I will make three bowers, one for you, one for Moses, and one for Elijah."

5   He was still speaking when a bright cloud cast a shadow over them, and a voice spoke out of the cloud, "This is my dear son, with whom I am well satisfied. Listen to him."

When the disciples heard this they fell on their faces and were terribly afraid. But Jesus approached them and reassured them saying, "Rise, there is nothing to fear."

As they descended the mountain Jesus charged them, "Say nothing of the vision to anyone until the Son of Man has risen from the dead."

10   The disciples asked him, "Why do the scribes say that first of all Elijah must come?"

"Elijah must indeed come," Jesus replied, "and effect a general reconciliation.[19] But I tell you, Elijah has come already, but they did not recognise him and did what they would with him. So too will the Son of Man suffer at their hands."

Then the disciples realised that he was speaking to them about John the Baptist.

When they reached the crowd a man approached him
15   and fell on his knees before him and said, "Take pity on my son, sir, he has bad attacks of epilepsy. Frequently he falls into the fire and into the water. So I brought him to your disciples, but they were quite unable to cure him."

Jesus answered, "Faithless and perverse generation! How long must I be with you? How long must I bear with you? Bring him here to me."

Then Jesus reprimanded the demon and it came out of him. And the boy was cured from that hour.

19 *Mal* 4:5–6.

Later the disciples approached Jesus privately and said, "Why could we not expel it?"

20 "Because of your feeble faith," Jesus told them. "I tell you positively, had you but faith as minute as a grain of mustard seed you could say to this mountain, 'Remove from here to there', and it would remove. Nothing would be beyond your capacity."

v

While they were assembling in Galilee[20] Jesus said to them, "The Son of Man is going to be betrayed into the hands of the authorities, and they will put him to death, but the third day he will be raised up."

They were deeply distressed.

When they reached Capernaum collectors of the half-shekel[21] approached Peter and said, "Your teacher pays the half-shekel, doesn't he?"

25 "Of course", he replied.

But when they reached the house Jesus took him up, saying, "What do you think, Simon? Upon whom do earthly kings levy tribute and poll-tax, their own sons or others?" When he replied, "Upon others", Jesus rejoined, "In that case sons are immune. But in case we should upset them, go down to the sea, cast the baited net, and take the first fish that is brought up. Open its mouth and you will find a shekel.[22] Take that and give it to them for us both."

18.1 On that occasion the disciples approached Jesus and asked, "Who will be greatest in the Kingdom of Heaven?"

He called a child to him and stood him in front of them and said, "I tell you positively, unless you change and become childlike you will never enter the Kingdom of Heaven. Whoever therefore is as unassuming as this child will be the greatest in the Kingdom of Heaven.

5 Whoever welcomes one such child on my account welcomes me. But whoever upsets any humble member

---

20 For the pilgrimage to Jerusalem for the Passover.
21 Gr. *didrachma*, the Temple tax obligatory for Jews (*Exod* 30:11–16). On Adar 15 (12th month in the Jewish calendar, about March, 30 days before the Passover) the money-changers' tables were set up in the provinces, and on Adar 25 in the Temple. See *Shekal* 1:3.
22 Gr. *stater*.

who believes in me, it would be better for him to have a millstone hung round his neck and to be thrown into the depth of the sea.

10   "Woe to the world because of grievances! Grievances are inevitable. Yet woe to the man responsible for the grievance! So if your hand or foot gives you grounds for complaint cut it off and cast it from you. It is better for you to enter Life[23] maimed or crippled than with your two hands or feet to be flung into the Everlasting Fire. Or if it is your eye that gives you grounds for complaint pluck it out and cast it from you. It is better for you to enter Life one-eyed than with two eyes to be flung into blazing Gehenna. So take care not to despise any humble members, for I tell you, their angels in heaven[24] are continually in the presence of my heavenly Father.

"What do you think? If a man has a hundred sheep and one of them strays, will he not leave the ninety-nine on the mountainside, and set off to seek the stray? And if he finds its, I tell you positively, he will rejoice over it more than over the ninety-nine that did not stray. So it is not my heavenly Father's will that one of these humble members should be lost.

15   "If then your brother errs, go and reprove him between him and you alone. If he listens to you, you have won back your brother. But if he fails to listen, take with you one witness[25] or two, for 'by the confirmation of two or three witnesses every matter shall be decided'.[26] If he pays no attention to them, speak to the community. If he pays no attention to the community, treat him as a Gentile or a tax-collector.[27] I tell you positively, whatever you prohibit on earth shall be prohibited in heaven.[28] I will go further, and say, that if any two of you agree among yourselves on earth about anything for which you need to ask, my heavenly Father will undertake it for

20   you, for 'in every place where two or three are assembled

---

23 The resurrection life of the Messianic Age.
24 In Jewish belief of those days every individual was represented in heaven by his personal angel.
25 Gr. 'one or two more', the translator from the Hebrew having misread the Heb. *ed* (witness) as *od* (more).
26 *Deut* 19:15.
27 See above p 9 n 15.
28 See p 93 n 15.

in my name I am there among them.' "[29]

Then Peter approached and said, "Master, how often should I forgive my brother when he wrongs me, seven times?"

Jesus replied, "Not seven times, I tell you, but seventy-seven times. For this reason the Kingdom of God may be represented as a king who decided to go over his revenues with his servants. When he began to take account there was brought to him one who owed
25   him ten thousand minas.[30] As he was unable to pay, his lord ordered that he be sold, with his wife and children and all his belongings, and that payment be made. Then the servant fell down and begged him, 'Only be patient with me and I will repay everything.' So the master of that servant took pity on him, released him, and remitted his debt. That servant, however, when he went out encountered one of his fellow servants who owed him a hundred dinars,[31] and took him by the throat saying, 'Pay what you owe me.' Then his fellow servant fell down and appealed to him, 'Only be patient with me and
30   I will repay you.' But he would not have it, and went instead and threw him into prison until he should repay the debt. When his fellow servants were aware of what had happened they were highly indignant, and reported the circumstances in full to their lord. So his lord summoned him and said to him, 'Vile slave! I remitted the whole of your debt to me because you begged me. It was your business to take pity on your fellow servant as I took pity on you.' Then his enraged lord handed him over to the torturers until he should have paid back the whole
35   debt. Just so will my heavenly Father treat you if any of you does not freely forgive his brother."

19.1   When Jesus had concluded this discourse he crossed over from Galilee and came to the borders of Judea beyond Jordan.[32] Great crowds followed him, and he cured them there.

---

29 "My name" ie God's name. The exact source is unknown, but cf *Exod* 20:24 and *I Chron* 7:14–16. Jewish teachers took the same view (*Aboth* 3:2–6), where *Mal* 3:16 is cited to show that God's presence is with two, and *Exod* 20:24 to show that he is even with one person.
30 Equal to about £40,000. The Greek text has "talents".
31 About £4.
32 Taking the Perean route from Galilee to Jerusalem east of the Jordan and within the territory of Herod Antipas, thus avoiding Samaria, whose hostile inhabitants sometimes attacked Jewish pilgrim bands.

Book V

i

Now the Pharisees approached Jesus to trap him saying, "Is it permissible to divorce one's wife on every ground?"

"Have you never read", Jesus replied, "that he who created mankind initially made them male and female,[1] and said, 'For this cause a man shall leave father and mother and cleave to his wife, and the two shall become one flesh'?[2] So they are no longer two but one flesh. Therefore, whom God has united man cannot sever."[3]

They persisted, "Why then did Moses instruct to give her a deed of severance and so to divorce her if she did not please him?"[4]

"Moses gave you leave to divorce your wives because of your callousness", he told them, "but that was not the original intention. Whoever divorces his wife, I tell you, except for adultery, and marries another, himself commits adultery."

10 The disciples put it to him, "If that is how a man stands with his wife it is not advisable to marry."

"It is not everyone who can go as far as this," he said, "only those to whom it is given. For there are eunuchs who have been so from birth, and there are eunuchs who have been made so by human agency, and there are eunuchs who have made themselves so for the Kingdom of Heaven's sake. Whoever can go so far let him do so."[5]

15 Then children were brought to him for him to lay his hand on them and offer a prayer. But the disciples rebuked them. Jesus said, "Let the children alone, and do not hinder them from coming to me, for the Kingdom of Heaven is composed of such as they." And he laid his hand on them, and proceeded on his way.

1 *Gen* 1:27.
2 Ibid 2:24.
3 The view of the Essenes and Baptists.
4 *Deut* 24:1, following the Old Hebrew.
5 Jesus is made to endorse here the pagan practice of continence by religious devotees, which the early Christians adopted in countries like Egypt.

Now a certain personage came to him and said, "Teacher, what good must I do to acquire Eternal Life?"

Jesus said to him, "Why do you ask me of the good? There is but One who is good. But if you desire to enter into Life keep the commandments."

"Commandments to what effect?" he asked.

Jesus said, "You are not to commit murder, you are to commit adultery, you are not to steal, you are not to bear false testimony, honour your father and mother,[6] and you are to love your neighbour as yourself."[7]

20 The youth said to him, "I have carefully observed all these. What else is there?"

"If you wish to be complete", Jesus replied, "go and sell your property and distribute the proceeds to the poor. Then come and join me."[8]

When the youth heard this he went away dejected, for he had very considerable possessions.

Then Jesus said to his disciples, "I tell you for a fact, the rich have a hard struggle to enter the Kingdom of Heaven.[9] I would even say that it is easier for a camel to go through the eye of a needle than for a rich man to enter the Kingdom of God."

25 The disciples were amazed at hearing this and said, "Who then can be saved?"

Jesus looked at them intently and replied, "Humanly speaking no one can, but to God everything is possible."[10]

Peter spoke up, "Here have we sacrificed everything to join you. How shall we fare?"

"I tell you positively", Jesus replied, "in the Reborn World,[11] when the Son of Man takes his seat on his

6 *Exod* 20:12–16.
7 *Lev* 19:18.
8 The early Christians, like the Essenes, handed over all their possessions to the Community, which bore the name of 'the Poor'. The interpretation of poor people in general represents a more ethical position.
9 The ancient Gospel of the Hebrews adds, "But the rich man began to scratch his head, and it did not please him. So the Master said to him, 'How can you say, I have carried out the law and the prophets, since it is stated in the law, you are to love your neighbour as yourself, and there are many of your brethren, sons of Abraham, clad with dung, dying of hunger, and your home is full of many good things, and nothing at all goes out of it to them?'"
10 cf *Gen* 18:4; *Jer* 32:17.
11 'A current expression for the Messianic Era. See *Isa* 65:17f.

throne of state, you too shall be seated on twelve thrones governing the twelve tribes of Israel. And everyone who has sacrificed home, or brother, or sister, or father, or mother, or children, or lands, on my account will receive

30   ever so much more and inherit Eternal Life. But many first will be last and the last first.

20.1   "The Kingdom of Heaven may indeed be likened to a householder who went out very early in the morning to hire labourers for his vineyard. And when he had contracted with the labourers for a rate of a dinar a day he sent them into his vineyard. He went out again at nine o'clock and saw others standing in the market place unemployed. To them he said, 'You too go into my vineyard and I will treat you fairly.' So they went along.

5   He went out again about midday and about three o'clock and acted in the same way. Around five o'clock he again went out and found still others standing about, and said to them, 'How is it you come to be standing the whole day unemployed?' They told him, 'Because no one has hired us.' He said to them, 'You too go into my vineyard.' When evening came the owner of the vineyard said to his steward, 'Call the labourers and pay them their wages, starting with the last and ending with the first.' When the five o'clock men came they each

10   received a dinar. But when the first came they expected to receive more, but they equally received a dinar. So on getting it they grumbled at the householder, 'These last have only worked an hour, and you gave them the same as us who have borne the burden of the day and the heat.' He answered their spokesman, 'I am not wronging you, my friend. Didn't you contract with me for a dinar rate? So take what is yours, and be off. I propose to give

15   these last the same as you. Can't I do as I please with my own money? Or are you envious because I am generous?' So the last shall be first and the first last."

ii

As he was about to go up to Jerusalem Jesus drew his twelve disciples aside privately, and told them as they went along, "See, we are going up to Jerusalem, and the Son of Man will be betrayed to the head priests and scribes, and they will sentence him to death, and hand him over to the Gentiles to be mocked and flogged and crucified,[12] but the third day he will be raised up."

20   Then the mother of Zebedee's sons approached him taking her sons with her. And having prostrated herself she desired to make a request.

"What is your wish?" he said to her.

She answered, "Declare that these two sons of mine shall sit one on your right hand and the other on your left in your Kingdom."

"You have no idea what you are all asking", Jesus replied. "Can you drink the cup I am going to drink?"

"We can", they told him.

"You will certainly drink my cup", he said to them, "but as for sitting on my right and on my left, that does not rest with me: it is for those designated by my Father."

When the ten learnt of this they were highly indignant
25 with the two brothers. So Jesus summoned them and said, "You are aware that the rulers of the Gentiles lord it over them, and their officials tyrannise them. It shall not be so with you. Whoever would be accounted great let him be your attendant, and who ever would be chief let him be your servant; just as the Son of Man did not come to be served but to serve, and to give his life in ransom for many."

Now as they were leaving Jericho a great crowd fol-
30 lowed him. And two blind men were there sitting at the roadside. When they heard that Jesus was passing they cried out, "Pity us, Son of David, sir!"

The crowd tried to silence them, but they only cried out the more, "Pity us, Son of David, sir!"[13]

Then Jesus stopped, and called them saying, "What can I do for you?"

"Sir," they said, "that our eyes may be opened."

So Jesus had compassion on them and touched their eyes, and at once they regained their sight and followed him.

21.1   When they were close to Jerusalem, and had reached Bethphage by the Mount of Olives, Jesus sent forward two of his disciples and told them, "Go to the village

---

12 The author seems not to have been aware that at this period the Jewish Court did not have power to pass a death sentence, or he has ignored the fact. See *Lk* 23:1, *Jn* 18:31.

13 Such an expression was politically dangerous under Roman rule since it was a claim to kingship.

before you, and at once you will find an ass tethered with a foal at her side. Untie them, and bring them to me.[14] If anyone questions you say, 'The Master needs them', and he will send them forthwith.'"[a]

So the disciples went forward and followed Jesus's instructions, and brought the ass and the foal. Then they placed their cloaks on them, and seated him on them, while the crowd spread their cloaks on the road, and others cut down branches from the trees and strewed them on the road. Then the people, both those who preceded him and those who followed, cried out,

"Hosanna, Son of David!
Blessed be he who comes in the name of the Lord.[15]
Hosanna in the heavenly heights!"

10   As he entered Jerusalem the whole city was in commotion saying, "Who is it?"

To this the people responded, "It is the prophet Jesus from Nazareth in Galilee."

Jesus went into the Temple, and drove out all who were buying and selling in the Temple, and overturned the tables of the moneychangers and the stalls of the pigeon-dealers, and told them, "It is written, 'My house shall be called a house of prayer',[17] but you have made it a robbers' den."[18]

Blind and lame people came to him in the Temple and
15   he cured them. Seeing the wonders he performed and the boys calling out in the Temple, "Hosanna, Son of David!", the head priests and the scribes were indignant, and said to him, "Do you hear what they are saying?"

"Of course", Jesus replied. "Have you never read,

a   This happened to fulfil what was announced by the prophet, saying,

5   *Inform the daughter of Zion,*
   'See, your king comes to you,
   Gentle and mounted on an ass,
   And the foal of a beast of burden.'[16]

---

14 The author inclines to stress circumstances by doubling, ie two blind men, an ass with a foal, etc.
15 *Ps* 118:25–26.
16 *Zech* 9:9.
17 *Isa* 56:7.
18 *Jer* 7:11.

'You have trained the lips of babes and sucklings to utter praise'?"[19]

At that he left them and went outside the city of Bethany and lodged there.

Early in the morning as Jesus was returning to the city he was hungry, and noticing a solitary fig tree by the roadside he went towards it; but finding on it nothing but leaves he said to it, "Let there be no more fruit on you for ever!"

The fig tree withered away on the spot.

20 Seeing this the disciples were amazed and exclaimed, "How has the fig tree withered away on the spot?"

"I tell you positively", Jesus said, "if you have faith and never doubt, you will not only do what has been done to the fig tree, but if you say no less to this hill, 'Be uprooted, and be cast into the sea!' it will take place. And indeed whatever you ask for in prayer, if you believe you will receive it."

When he enterd the Temple the head priests and elders of the people approached him as he was teaching and said, "By what authority do you do this, and who furnished you with that authority?"

Jesus answered, "Let me ask you one question myself, and if you answer me I too will tell you by what authority

25 I do this. Was John's rite of immersion of divine or of human inspiration?"

They discussed the question together saying, "If we say, 'of divine inspiration', he will say, 'Why then did you not believe him?' But if we say, 'of human inspiration', we are afraid of the crowd, for they all regard John as a prophet."[20] So they answered, "We cannot tell."

So Jesus in turn said, "In that case neither will I tell you by what authority I do this. But give me your opinion. There was a man who had two sons. He approached the first and said, 'My boy, go and work in my vineyard to-

30 day.' He replied, 'Very well, sir,' but he did not go. Then he approached the second with the same request. 'I don't want to,' he answered, but later he changd his mind and went. Which of the two carried out his father's wishes?"

"The latter", they replied.

19 *Ps* 8:2.
20 The forces of Herod Antipas had just been defeated by the Nabataeans, and the people were saying this was because he had executed the Baptist. See Jos. *Antiq.* XVIII:119.

Jesus said to them, "I tell you for a fact, the tax-collectors and harlots will precede you into the Kingdom of God. For John came to you as in duty bound, and you did not believe him; but the tax-collectors and harlots believed him, and you when you saw this did not even change your minds later and believe in him.

"Now listen to another simile.[21] There was a house-holder who planted a vineyard, erected a fence round it, and dug a winepress, built a watch-tower, and let it out to growers to cultivate, and then went abroad. When the vintage season approached he dispatched his servants to
35   the growers to receive his share of the produce. But the growers seized his servants, beat one, killed another, and stoned a third. So he sent another batch of servants more numerous than before; but they treated them the same way. Finally he sent his son, saying, 'They are bound to respect my son.' But when they saw the son the growers said to themselves, 'Here is the heir! Come on, let us kill him and possess ourselves of his inheritance!' So they seized him, dragged him outside the vineyard,
40   and killed him. When the owner of the vineyard comes what will he do to those growers?"

They said to him, "He will make a dreadful end of those wicked men, and let out the vineyard to growers who will render him the fruits in due season."

"Have you never read in the Scriptures," Jesus said, " 'The stone which the builders rejected has become the coping-stone. This is the Lord's doing and is marvellous in our eyes?'[22] Therefore, I tell you, the kingdom of God will be taken from you and given to a nation which yields its fruits. [Whoever falls on this stone will be crushed, and whoever it falls on will be pulverised.]"[23]
45   When the head priests and Pharisees heard his similes they realised he was referring to them. They were anxious to arrest him, but they were afraid of the people who regarded him as a prophet.

22.1   One more simile Jesus addressed to them. "The Kingdom of Heaven", he said, "may be represented as a king who gave a wedding for his son, and dispatched his servants to invite the guests to the wedding; but they

21 Inspired by *Isa* 5:1–8.
22 *Ps* 118:22.
23 The words within brackets are omitted by some MSS, and are of doubtful authenticity.

would not come. So he dispatched more servants, saying
'Tell the guests my banquet[24] is fully prepared, my oxen
and geese are roasted, everything is ready and waiting.
5   Please come to the wedding.' But disregarding the invitation some went elsewhere, one to his farm, another to
his trading, and others laid hold of his servants and ill-
treated and killed them. So the king was enraged, and
sent his troops, and exterminated those murderers, and
set their city on fire.[25] Then he said to his servants,
'Though the wedding is ready, the guests were unworthy. Now go out into the thoroughfares, and invite to
10   the wedding whoever you come across.' So the servants
went out into the roads and collected all the people they
could find, good and bad alike, and the bridal banquet
was supplied with company. When the king came in to
view the company he noticed one man was not in
wedding attire and said to him, 'Friend, how did you
gain admission without wedding attire?' He was speechless. Then the king said to the servants, 'Bind him hand
and foot and eject him into the darkness outside, where
there will be wailing and grinding of teeth.' For many are
invited, but few are selected.''
15   Then the Pharisees went away and formulated a plan
to trap him in speech. They dispatched some of their
disciples together with the Herodians to say, "Teacher,
we are well aware of your sincerity, and that you are not
influenced by anyone, for you pay no regard to personalities. Give us your opinion therefore. Is it permissible to pay the census-tax to Caesar or not?"
But Jesus detected their evil intention and replied,
"Why do you tempt me, you hypocrites? Show me a coin
of the tax."
They tendered him a dinar.
20   Then he said to them, "Whose is this portrait and
inscription?"
"Caesar's", they answered.
"Render then to Caesar what is Caesar's", he told
them, "and to God what is God's."
They were amazed when they heard this, and left him
and went away.
That same day Sadducees, who say there will be no

---

24 The Messianic Banquet of the righteous in the Kingdom of God.
25 This alludes to the destruction of Jerusalem by the Romans in AD 70. See
   Jos. *Jewish War*, VI:281–282.

resurrection, came to him and questioned him as follows: "Teacher, Moses said, 'If a man dies and leaves no children his brother shall take his widow in marriage and
25 continue his brother's line."'[26] Now there were seven brothers among us. The first married, and dying without issue left his wife to his brother. The same thing happened to the second and third, and to all the seven. Finally the woman herself died. In the resurrection to which of the seven will the woman belong, for they all had her in turn?"

Jesus replied, "You are in error, knowing neither the
30 Scriptures nor the power of God; for in the resurrection they do not marry or give in marriage: they are like the angels in heaven. As to the resurrection of the dead, have you not read what God announced to you saying, 'I am the God of Abraham, the God of Isaac, and the God of Jacob'?[27] He is not God of the dead but God of the living."

When the people heard this they marvelled at his teaching.

On hearing that Jesus had silenced the Sadducees the
35 Pharisees took stock of the situation. Then one of them, a lawyer, posed a question to tempt him, "Teacher, which is the supreme commandment in the Law?"

He told him, "'You are to love the Lord your God with all your heart, and with all your soul, and with all your capacity.'[28] This is the first and foremost commandment. There is a second that matches it. 'You are to love your
40 neighbour as yourself.'[29] On these two commandments hinge the entire Law and the prophets."

While the Pharisees were assembled Jesus in turn asked them, "What is your view of the Messiah? Whose son is he?"

"David's", they replied.

"Why then", he said, "does David under inspiration call him 'lord', saying,

> *The Lord said to my lord, 'Sit at my right hand*
> *Until I lay your enemies beneath your feet?'[30]*

---

26 See *Deut* 25:5.
27 *Exod* 3:6.
28 *Deut* 6:5.
29 *Lev* 19:18.
30 *Ps* 110:1.

45 If David calls him 'lord', how can he be his son?"[31]

No one volunteered an answer, nor from that time forward did anyone venture to question him further.

23.1 Then Jesus addressed the people and his disciples. "The scribes and Pharisees", he said, "sit in Moses' seat. Execute and observe, therefore, whatever they tell you; but do not act as they do, for they preach but fail to practice. They pack up heavy bales and load them on men's shoulders, but they have no wish to lift a finger to 5 carry them themselves. And all their actions are performed for public notice: they broaden their phylacteries and enlarge their fringes.[32] They love the most prominent places at banquets, and the principal seats in the synagogues, to be greeted in the markets, and to be addressed by people as Rabbi. But you are not to be called Rabbi, for you have but one Teacher, and all of you are brothers. Neither are you to call anyone Father on 10 earth, for you have but one heavenly Father. Nor are you to be called Instructor, for your only instructor is the Messiah. The greatest of you shall be your servant; for whoever exalts himself shall be abased, while he who abases himself shall be exalted.

"Woe to you, hypocritical scribes and Pharisees! You obstruct people's way to the Kingdom of Heaven. You neither go in yourselves, nor allow those who are going in to enter.

15 "Woe to you, hypocritical scribes and Pharisees! You traverse sea and land to make a single proselyte, and when he is gained you make him twice the son of Gehenna that you are.[33]

"Woe to you blind guides! You say, 'Whoever swears by the Temple it does not signify, but whoever swears by the gold of the Temple is bound by his oath.' You fools and blind! Which is superior, the gold or the Temple that consecrates the gold? You also say, 'Whoever swears by the altar it does not signify, but whoever swears by the offering on it is bound by his oath.' You blind! Which is superior, the offering or the altar which consecrates the 20 offering? Whoever swears by the altar swears not only by it but by everything on it. And whoever swears by the Temple swears not only by it but by everything con-

---

31 See n 93 to *Mk* 12:37.
32 See *Deut* 6:8; 22:12.
33 ie as reprobate as you are.

tained in it. And whoever swears by heaven swears not only by the throne of God[34] but by him who sits upon it.

"Woe to you, hypocritical scribes and Pharisees! You tithe mint and dill and cummin, but overlook the graver matters of the Law, justice, mercy and honesty. These are the things you should have attended to without neglecting the others. You blind guides! You strain out a gnat and gulp down a camel.

25   "Woe to you, hypocritical scribes and Pharisees! You are much like whitewashed tombs, which appear fair outside, but inside are full of dead men's bones and everything foul. So you too seem righteous to people outwardly, but inwardly you are saturated with hypocrisy and lawlessness.

30   "Woe to you, hypocritical scribes and Pharisees. You build the tombs of the prophets and ornament the monuments of the just, and say, 'Had we lived in our fathers' time we should not have been their accomplices in shedding the blood of the prophets.' So you testify of yourselves that you are the sons of those who slaughtered the prophets. Fill up, then, the measure of your fathers. Serpents, vipers' brood! How can you escape the doom of Gehenna? Therefore,

35   *See, I send you prophets, sages and scribes!*
Some of them you will kill and crucify,
And some you will flog in your synagogues,
And persecute from city to city;
That on you may come all the just blood shed on earth
From the blood of Abel the righteous
To the blood of Zechariah the son of Berechiah,
Whom you slew between the sanctuary and altar.[35]

"I tell you for a fact, all this shall befall this generation.

Jerusalem, Jerusalem! Killer of prophets,
And stoner of those who are sent to her!
How oft would I have gathered your children,
As the mother bird her brood 'neath her wings?
But you would not have it so.
See, your house is left to you desolate![36]

34 cf *Isa* 66:1.
35 The source of the quotation in this late form is unknown. A shorter version in *Lk* 11:49–50 is attributed to the 'Wisdom of God', cf *II Chron* 36:14–15. The Zechariah referred to was actually the son of Jehoiada (*II Chron* 24:20–21).
36 cf *Jubilees*, 23:14.

"So I say to you, on no account will you see me from this time forward until you say, 'Blessed is he who comes in the name of the Lord.' "[37]

24.1   Leaving the Temple Jesus went his way. But his disciples approached to point out to him the buildings of the Temple. "Do you see all these?" he said to them. "I tell you positively, there will not be left here one stone upon another that will not be thrown down."

iv[38]

As Jesus sat on the Mount of Olives his disciples approached him privately and said, "Tell us when these things will happen, and when will be the sign of your advent and of the Consummation of the Age?"

Jesus answered them, "Take care that no one deceives
5   you. For many claiming to be me will come saying, 'I am the Messiah', and will deceive many. Inevitably you will hear of wars and rumours of wars. Do not be alarmed. This is bound to happen, but it does not mean that the End has come. For nation shall be roused against nation, and kingdom against kingdom, and there will be famines and earthquakes in various places; but these are only the beginning of the Pangs.[39] Later they will subject you to torture and will kill you, and you will be detested by all
10   nations on my account. Then many will turn traitor and betray one another and hate one another, and many false prophets will arise and mislead many, and through the increase of lawlessness many will cool in their attachment.[40] But he that is constant to the end will be saved. And this News of the Kingdom shall be proclaimed world-wide as a testimony to all nations. Only then will the End come.
15   "When, therefore, you see the 'Abomination of Desolation' announced by the prophet Daniel[41] stand in the holy place,[a] then let those who are in Judea escape to

a Let the reader understand the allusion.

---

37 See *Ps* 118:26.
38 There follows what has been called the Little Apocalypse; cf *Mk* 13. It reflects and explains delay in the Second Advent; cf *II Pet*. This was troubling Christians after the Fall of Jerusalem in AD 70.
39 The birth-pangs of the Messianic Age.
40 cf Jos. *Jewish War*, II:13:258–260.
41 *Dan* 9:27; 12:11.

the mountains, and let him who is on the housetop not go down to remove anything from his house, and let him who is in the field not turn back to fetch his coat. Woe to pregnant women and nursing mothers in those days!
20   You must pray that your flight will not be in winter or on the sabbath, for there will be great affliction then such as there has never been since the world began down to the present time, nor ever will be again. If that period had not been shortened not a single human being would be preserved; but for the Elect's sake that period will be shortened.

"Then if anyone tells you, 'Look, here is the Messiah!' or 'There he is!' do not credit it; for false messiahs and false prophets will arise and exhibit great signs and
25   wonders, so as to deceive even the Elect if possible. See, I have told you beforehand. So if anyone says to you, 'He is in the wilderness', do not go out. If he says, 'He is behind closed doors', do not credit it. For as the lightning flashes from the east and is visible to the bounds of the west so will be the advent of the Son of Man. 'Where the carcase is, there the vultures flock.'[42]

"Immediately after the affliction of those days,

Eclipsed shall be the sun,
And the moon no more her lustre sheds,
Out of heaven the stars shall fall:
The heavenly bodies shall be shaken.[43]

30   "And then shall appear in heaven the sign of the Son of Man, and then shall all the tribes of earth mourn,[44] when they see the Son of Man coming in the clouds of heaven[45] with great pomp and state. And he will dispatch his angels with a loud trumpet blast to gather up his Elect from the four winds,[46] from one extremity of heaven to the other.[47]

"Now learn a lesson from the fig tree. When its branch has become tender and the leaves sprout you know that summer is at hand. So you, when you see all this, will

42 cf *Job* 39:30.
43 *Isa* 13:10; 34:4.
44 *Zech* 12:10.
45 *Dan* 7:13.
46 *Zech* 2:6.
47 cf *Deut* 30:4.

know that it[48] is at hand, at the very doors. I tell you
truly, this generation will by no means pass away before
35 all these things take place. Heaven and earth will pass
away, but my words will not pass away. Yet no one
knows the exact day and hour, neither the angels in
heaven, nor the Son, only the Father. For as it was in the
time of Noah so will be the advent of the Son of Man. Just
as at that time before the Flood they were eating and
drinking, marrying and giving in marriage, until the day
Noah entered the ark, and knew nothing until the deluge
came and swept them all away, so will be the advent of
40 the Son of Man. Then two men will be in a field, one will
be taken and one left behind. Two women will be
grinding at the mill, one will be taken and one left
behind. So be alert, for you do not know on what day
your Master will come. But realise this, if the householder had known in which watch the thief would come
he would have been on the alert and not allowed his
house to be broken into. So you too be ready, for at an
unexpected hour the Son of Man will come.

45 "Who, then, is that loyal and prudent servant whom
his master has put in charge of his staff to cater for them
regularly? Fortunate is that servant whom his master at
his coming finds so engaged. I tell you truly, he will
entrust him with all his possessions. But if he is a bad
servant, who says to himself, 'My master is detained',
and begins to strike his fellow servants and to eat and
50 drink with drunkards, the master of that servant will
arrive on a day he does not expect, and at an hour he
does not anticipate, and will take him by surprise and
assign his place with the hypocrites. There will be wailing and grinding of teeth."

v

25.1 "The Kingdom of Heaven may then be compared to
ten maidens, who took their lamps and went out to meet
the bridegroom. Five of them were foolish and five were
prudent. The foolish ones took their lamps, but took no
oil with them, while the prudent took oil in the con-
5 tainers with their lamps. When the bridegroom was
detained all of them dozed off and fell asleep. In the

---

48 For the play on words in Hebrew here see above *Mk* 14:28–29, n 103.

middle of the night, however, there came a shout, 'The bridegroom is coming! Go out to meet him.' Then all those maidens rose and trimmed their lamps. The foolish then said to the prudent, 'Give us some of your oil, for our lamps are going out.' But the prudent replied, 'We cannot, or there may not be enough for us and you. You

10   had better go to the dealers and buy what you need.' But while they were away buying the bridegroom arrived, and those who were ready went in with him to the wedding, and the doors were shut. Later the rest of the maidens came and said, 'Sir, sir, let us in!' But he answered, 'I tell you truly, I don't know you.' Be alert, therefore, for you do not know either the day or the hour.

"It is like a man travelling abroad, who summoned his personal servants and entrusted them with his property.

15   To one he gave five talents, to another two, and to another one, to each according to his individual capacity, and so went abroad. Forthwith he who had received the five talents went and traded with them and made a further five talents profit. He who had received two made a profit of two talents. But he who had received one talent went and dug a hole and buried his master's money.

"A long time after, the master of those servants

20   returned and went over the accounts with them. Then he who had received the five talents presented himself and produced the additional five talents and said, 'Master, you entrusted me with five talents, see, I have gained a further five talents.' His master said to him, 'Excellent, my worthy and loyal servant! You have been reliable in minor matters, I will put you in charge of major affairs. Enjoy your master's prosperity.' Then he who had the two talents presented himself and said, 'Master, you entrusted me with two talents, see, I have gained a further two talents.' His master said to him, 'Excellent, my worthy and loyal servant! You have been reliable in minor matters, I will put you in charge of major affairs. Enjoy your master's prosperity.' Then he who had received the one talent presented himself and said, 'Master, I knew you to be a hard man, reaping where you have not sown, and gathering where you have not

25   scattered; so I was afraid and went and buried your talent in the ground. See, here is what is yours.' Then his

master replied, 'You worthless and unenterprising
servant! You knew that I reap where I have not sown,
and gather where I have not scattered. You ought to have
placed my money on the exchange, so that on my return I
should have had back my capital with interest. Take the
talent from him and give it to the one with ten talents. For
to him who has, more shall be given, and he shall have a
surplus, but from him who has not, even what he does
30 have shall be taken away. As for the unprofitable
servant, eject him into the darkness outside, where there
will be wailing and grinding of teeth.'

"When the Son of Man comes in state with all the
angels with him he will sit on his throne of state, and all
nations will be ranged before him. And he will separate
one from another as a shepherd separates the sheep from
the goats. The sheep he will place on his right and the
goats on his left. Then the king will say to those on his
right, 'Come, my Father's blessed ones, inherit the king-
35 dom prepared for you from the creation of the world. For
I was hungry and you fed me, thirsty and you refreshed
me, a stranger and you entertained me, naked and you
clothed me, ailing and you cared for me, in prison and
you visited me.'[49] Then the just nations will reply, 'Lord,
when did we see you hungry and fed you, or thirsty and
refreshed you; when did we see you a stranger and
entertained you, or naked and clothed you; when did we
see you ailing, or in prison, and visited you?' Then the
40 king will answer them, 'I tell you truly, in so far as you
did it to one of these humble brothers of mine you did it
to me.' Then he will say to those on the left, 'Depart from
me, you cursed ones, to the Everlasting Fire prepared for
the Devil and his angels. For I was hungry and you did
not feed me, thirsty and you did not refresh me, a
stranger and you did not entertain me, naked and you
did not clothe me, ailing and in prison and you did not
care for me.' Then they in turn will reply, 'Lord, when
did we see you hungry, or thirsty, or a stranger, or
naked, or ailing, or in prison, and did not serve your
45 need?' He will answer, 'I tell you truly, in so far as you
did not do it to one of these lowliest ones you did not do it

49 The language derives from *Test. XII Patriarchs, Test. Joseph* 1:3–7, where the
Patriarch Joseph refers in similar language to God's dealings with him in
Egypt.

to me.' So these nations will go away to Eternal Punishment, but the just nations to Eternal Life."

26.1   When Jesus had concluded this discourse he said to his disciples, "You know that the Passover is in two days' time, and the Son of Man will be handed over for crucifixion."

Epilogue

i

Now the head priests and elders of the people assembled at the residence of the high priest, who was called Caiaphas, and they deliberated how they might secure
5 Jesus by a trap and kill him. But they decided, "Not on the festival, or there may be a popular outbreak."

While Jesus was at Bethany at the house of Simon the leper a woman approached him with an alabaster flask of costly oil which she poured on his head as he reclined at table. But when the disciples saw this they were indignant and said, "What sense is there in such waste? It could have been sold for a considerable sum and the money distributed to the poor."

10 When Jesus was aware of this he said to them, "Why do you upbraid the woman? It is a very kind action she has performed for me. You have the poor always with you, but you will not always have me. By diffusing this oil over my body she has performed my burial rites. I tell you positively, wherever this News is proclaimed throughout the world what she has done will also be related to commemorate her."

Then one of the twelve, called Judas Iscariot, went off
15 to the head priests and said, "How much will you give me to hand him over to you?"

They made a compact with him for thirty pieces of silver, and from then on he sought a convenient opportunity to betray him.

ii

On the first day of the Feast of Unleavened Bread the disciples approached Jesus and said, "Where do you wish us to prepare for you to eat the passover?"[1]

---

1 ie the paschal lamb.

"Go into the city," he told them, "to so-and-so,[2] and say to him, 'The Teacher says, my time is at hand. I and my disciples will keep the Passover at your house.'"

So the disciples carried out Jesus' instructions and prepared the passover.

20   When evening came he reclined at table with the twelve. As they were eating he said, "I tell you for a fact, one of you will betray me."

They were deeply distressed, and each of them started to protest, "Surely it is not me, Master?"

"He who dips his hand in the dish with me", he replied, "he is the one who will betray me. The Son of Man is certainly going the way that was written of him, yet woe to that man by whom the Son of Man is betrayed. Better for that man had he never been born."

25   Then Judas, who did betray him, answered, "Surely it is not me, Rabbi?"

He said to him, "So you have said."

As they were eating Jesus took bread, recited the blessing, broke it, and gave it to his disciples, and said, "Take, eat, this signifies my body."

Then he took the cup, gave thanks, and passed it to them saying, "Drink from it, all of you, for this signifies my 'blood of the covenant'[3] poured out for many in forgiveness of sins. I tell you, from now on I will by no means drink of this fruit of the vine[4] until the day comes when I drink it new with you in my Father's Kingdom."

30   After the hymn-singing they went to the Mount of Olives.[5] Jesus said to them, "All of you will waver in your loyalty to me to-night, for it is stated, 'Strike at the shepherd and the sheep of the flock will be scattered.'[6] But when I have been raised up I will precede you to Galilee."

Peter replied, "If they all waver in their loyalty to you, I will never waver."

2 The name of the greatly trusted owner of the house is nowhere given; but it may be deduced that it was the 'Dear Disciple' of the Fourth Gospel, connected with the ruling priestly family but a disciple of the Baptist. See *John's Gospel.*

3 *Exod* 24:8.

4 A phrase from the blessing over the fourth obligatory cup of wine in the Passover service, where mention is made of the consolation of Israel in the Messianic Era.

5 On the east of Jerusalem.

6 *Zech* 13:7.

"I tell you for a fact", Jesus said to him, "this very night before cock-crow you will disown me three times."

35   "Even if it means dying with you", declared Peter, "I will never disown you."

So said all the disciples.

Then Jesus arrived with them at a place called Gethsemane[7] and said to the disciples, "You stay here while I go over there to pray." He took with him Peter and the two sons of Zebedee: he felt miserable and depressed. "I am in very low spirits",[8] he said to them. "Stay here and keep watch with me."

Then he went on a little way and fell on his face in prayer saying, "Father, if possible let this cup pass by me, though not as I will, but as thou wilt."

40   He returned to his disciples and found them sleeping, and said to Peter, "Could you not manage to watch with me for a single hour? Be vigilant and prayerful, or you may find yourselves tempted. The spirit is willing enough, but the flesh is frail."

He went away a second time and prayed, "Father, if it is not possible for this cup to pass by me without my drinking it, be it as thou wilt."

Coming once more to his disciples he found them asleep, for their eyes were heavy. So he left them again and went away, and prayed a third time, repeating the same prayer.

45   Then he came back to his disciples and said to them, "Are you going on sleeping and taking your rest? See, the hour is at hand for the Son of Man to be delivered into the hands of sinners. Rise and let us be going. My betrayer approaches."

He was still speaking when Judas, one of the twelve, came, and with him a large crowd armed with swords and clubs, dispatched by the head priests and elders of the people. His betrayer had given them a signal saying, "The one I embrace, that is he. Seize him." At once he approached Jesus and cried, "Greetings, Rabbi!" and embraced him.

50   "Friend, attend to your business." Jesus said to him.

Then they approached and laid hold of Jesus and seized him. At this, one of those with Jesus dropped his

7 In Hebrew *Ge-shemanim*, the Fertile Valley. *Isa* 28:1.
8 Lit "My soul is very sad, even to death."

hand to his sword, drew it, and struck the high priest's servant, severing his ear. Jesus said to him, "Put up your sword, for all who draw the sword shall die by the sword. Do you imagine that I could not appeal to my Father and he would immediately send to my aid full twelve legions of angels? But then how would the Scriptures be fulfilled that this is what must happen?"

55   Thereupon Jesus said to the crowd, "Have you come out to capture me with swords and clubs as if I were a brigand? I sat daily in the Temple teaching and you never arrested me; but all this has come about that the writings of the prophets should be fulfilled."

Then all the disciples deserted him and fled. Those who had arrested Jesus marched him off to the high priest Caiaphas, where the scribes and elders were assembled. Peter had followed him at a distance as far as the high priest's courtyard, and going inside he sat down with the retainers to await the outcome.

Now the high priest and the whole Sanhedrin sought false evidence against Jesus on which they could con-
60   demn him to death; but they failed to obtain it, though many false witnesses came forward who said, "He stated, 'I can pull down God's Sanctuary, and rebuild it in three days.'"

Then the high priest rose and said to him, "Do you make no defence to these charges they bring against you?"

But Jesus was silent.

Then the high priest said to him, "I put you on oath by the Living God to tell us whether you are the Messiah, the Son of God."

"So you have said," Jesus replied. "I will only tell you this; hereafter you will see the Son of Man seated on the right hand of Power and coming with the clouds of heaven."[9]

65   Then the high priest tore his tunic and cried, "He has blasphemed.[10] What further need have we of witnesses? You have just heard his traitorous confession. What is your verdict?"

"He is liable to the death penalty", they answered.

Then they spat on his face and struck him, crying as they

9 *Ps* 110:1; *Dan* 7:13.
10 See above p 44, n 124.

cuffed him, "Prophesy to us, you Messiah! Who hit you?"

Meanwhile Peter had been sitting outside in the courtyard. One of the maidservants approached him and said, "Surely you were with Jesus the Galilean?"

70   But he denied it before them all and said, "I don't know what you are talking about."

As he was going out of the gateway, however, another girl saw him and said to those who were there, "He was with Jesus the Nazarene."

Again he denied with an oath, "I don't know the man."

A little later the bystanders approached and said to Peter, "Of course you're one of them. Your accent gives you away completely."[11]

Then he began to curse and swear, "I don't know the man."

75   Immediately the cock crowed and Peter recalled how Jesus had said, "Before cock-crow you will disown me three times." And he went outside and wept bitterly.

iii

27.1   When morning came all the head priests and elders of the people deliberated how to contrive the death of Jesus. Having manacled him they marched him off and handed him over to Pilate the governor.

Then Judas the betrayer, seeing him condemned, was filled with remorse and returned the thirty pieces of silver to the head priests and elders saying, "I have sinned in betraying innocent blood."

"How does that affect us?" they said. "It is your concern."

5   So he flung the silver into the Temple,[12] and withdrew, and went away and hanged himself.[13] But the head priests took out the silver and said, "It is not proper for it to be cast into the sacred funds since it is blood money." After consultation they bought Potter's Field

---

11 The Galilean dialect was distinctive, slurring the gutterals.
12 ie into the offertory chests, one of which was for the purchase of sin-offerings.
13 A different version of the death of Judas is given in *Acts* 1:18–19.

with it as a burial place for aliens, and this is how it got

10   the name of Bloody Field, which it still bears.[a]

Now Jesus stood before the governor, and the governor interrogated him. "Are you king of the Jews?" he asked.

"As you say", Jesus replied.

But when he was indicted by the head priests and elders he made no reply.

Then Pilate said to him, "Do you not hear how many things they are charging you with?"

But he gave him no reply whatever, so that the governor was greatly astonished.

15   At the festival it was the governor's practice to release to the populace any one prisoner they might choose. There was at this time in custody a noted prisoner called Bar-Abbas. So when the people assembled for the purpose Pilate said to them, "Whom do you wish me to release to you, Bar-Abbas or Jesus styled Christ?" He knew they had handed him over out of malice.[15]

When he had taken his place on the judgment seat his wife sent him a message saying, "Do nothing to that good man, for I have had a very bad time today dreaming

20   about him." But the head priests and elders won over the people to ask for Bar-Abbas and destroy Jesus. So when the governor said to them, "Which of the two do you want me to release to you?" they answered, "Bar-Abbas."

Pilate then said to them, "And what shall I do with Jesus styled Christ?"[16]

a   This was to fulfil what was announced by the Prophet Jeremiah, saying,

> So they took the thirty pieces of silver,
> The price of him who was valued,
> Whom they assessed of the children of Israel,
> And gave them for the potter's field
> As the Lord had instructed me.[14]

---

14 See *Jer* 32:61 and *Zech* 11:12–13.

15 The custom referred to is otherwise unknown. No Jewish crowd could have been present since the arrest of Jesus had been made secretly at night so that the people should be in ignorance of it. The only crowd could have been the retainers of the chief priests, many of them non-Jews.

16 Since the charge against Jesus was of high treason against Rome in claiming to be king of the Jews without the emperor's authorisation, Pilate could never ask such a question. See *Lk* 23:2. Pilate acts here contrary both to the responsibility of his office and to his personal character.

Unanimously they cried, "Let him be crucified!"

"But what crime has he committed?" he asked.

But they shouted persistently, "Let him be crucified!"

When Pilate saw there was nothing further he could do without exciting even more of a tumult, he took water and rinsed his hands in the sight of the people saying, "I am innocent of this man's blood. It is your concern."

25   To this all the people responded, "His blood be on us and our children!"

So he released Bar-Abbas to them, and had Jesus flogged and handed him over for crucifixion.

Then the governor's soldiers took Jesus into the praetorium and gathered the whole cohort round him. Having stripped him they draped him in a scarlet cloak, and when they had plaited a victor's wreath out of thorn they set it on his head, and put a cane in his right hand, and bending the knee to him they mocked him, saying

30   "Hail, king of the Jews!" Then spitting on him they took the cane and struck him on the head. When they had sufficiently derided him they stripped him of the cloak and reclad him in his own clothes and marched him off to be crucified.

As they went out they found a man of Cyrene called Simon and forced him to carry the cross. When they came to the place called Golgotha – which is to say 'Skull Place' – they gave him a drink of wine mixed with gall;

35   but when he had tasted it he refused to drink it. After crucifying him they portioned out his clothes and threw dice for them, and sitting down they kept guard over him there. They also set over his head the charge against him in these terms: "This is Jesus, the King of the Jews."

Then two brigands were crucified with him, one on his right and the other on his left. And all who passed by

40   vilified him, shaking their heads and saying, "You who can pull down the Temple and rebuild it in three days, save yourself. If you are the son of God come down from the cross."

The head priests with the scribes and elders similarly derided him and said, "He saved others, but cannot save himself. He is king of Israel, so let him come down from the cross and we will believe in him. He relied on God: let him rescue him if he wants him,[17] for he said, 'I am the

17 cf *Ps* 22:7–8, and above, previous paragraph.

Son of God.'"

Even the brigands, who were crucified with him, reviled him.

45　　Now from noon there was darkness over the whole land until three o'clock. Then about three o'clock Jesus uttered a loud cry saying, *Eloi, Eloi, lema sabachthani!* – which means, "My God, my God, why have you deserted me?"[18] Some of those standing there, hearing this, said, "He is calling Elijah."

At once one of them ran and fetched a sponge, saturated it with vinegar, and spiking it on a cane held it out to him to drink. But the rest said, "Leave him alone, and we shall see if Elijah will come to save him."

50　　But Jesus gave another loud cry, and expired.

At this, the curtain of the Sanctuary was ripped in two from top to bottom, the earth shook, the rocks were riven, the tombs sprang open and many bodies of the saints laid to rest were raised, and, issuing from their tombs after his resurrection, entered the holy city and were plainly seen by many people.[19]

The centurion and his men who had been guarding Jesus, seeing the earthquake and other disturbances, were greatly frightened and exclaimed, "Undoubtedly

55　he was God's son!" Many women were also there looking on from a distance. They were those who had followed Jesus from Galilee attending to his needs. Among them was Mary of Magdala, Mary the mother of James and Joseph, and the mother of Zebedee's sons.

When evening came a wealthy man from Arimathea called Joseph, himself a disciple of Jesus, personally approached Pilate and asked for the body of Jesus. Then Pilate gave orders for it to be given to him. So Joseph received the body, wrapped it in a clean linen sheet,

60　deposited it in his new rock-cut tomb, and after rolling a heavy boulder across the mouth of the tomb went away. But Mary of Magdala and the other Mary were there sitting opposite the burial place.

---

18 *Ps* 22:1 in Aramaic. The Old Hebrew has *Lama shekachtani* ('why have you forgotten me' *Ps* 62:9).

19 These signs are drawn from current belief of what would happen on the Day of Judgment.

iv

Next day, which was the day following the preparation day, the head priests and Pharisees went together to Pilate and said, "Sir, we recall how that impostor while alive said, 'After three days I shall be raised up.' Give orders, therefore, for the burial place to be secured until the third day has passed, in case his disciples should come and steal him and then tell the people he has risen from the dead. The final imposture would then be worse than the original one."

65   Pilate said to them, "You have your force.[20] Maintain as much security as you like."

So they went away and secured the tomb, and placed a police cordon round the boulder.

28.1   When the sabbath was over, as the day after the sabbath began to dawn, Mary of Magdala and the other Mary came to inspect the burial place. Now there had been a great earthquake, for an angel of the Lord descended from heaven, and approached and rolled aside the boulder and sat on it. His appearance was like lightning and his clothing white as snow. The guards shook with terror at him and became as dead men.[21]

5   Then the angel addressed the women and said, "Do not be alarmed. I know you are looking for Jesus who was crucified. He is no longer here. He has been raised up exactly as he said. Come and look at the place where he lay. Now go quickly and tell his disciples, 'He has been raised from the dead, and is preceding you to Galilee. You will see him there.' My message is delivered."

So they left the tomb quickly with mingled fear and excessive joy, and ran to inform his disciples. Just then Jesus came to meet them and said "Peace be with you."[22]

They approached and grasped his feet, and prostrated
10   themselves before him. "Do not be alarmed", Jesus said. "Go and tell my brothers that they are to go to Galilee and will see me there."

As they resumed their way, some of the police went into the city to inform the head priests of everything that had happened. And when these had consulted with the elders they gave the guards a considerable sum of

---

20 The civil force under the authority of the Sanhedrin, Gr *custodia.*
21 The embellishments are peculiar to *Matthew.*
22 Following the Old Hebrew. The Greek has 'Hail!'

money, telling them, "You are to say, 'His disciples came by night and stole him while we slept.' And if the governor hears of it, we will win him over and exonerate you."

15   So they took the money and acted as they had been primed. And this is the version that is still current among the Jews.[23]

v

The eleven disciples went away to Galilee to the mountain which Jesus had arranged with them. When they saw him they prostrated themselves, though they were somewhat uncertain. But Jesus approached and spoke to them and said, "I have received complete authority in heaven and earth. Go, therefore, and make disciples of all the Gentiles, immersing them in the name

20 of the Father, and the Son, and the hóly Spirit, teaching them to observe whatever I have commanded you. I shall indeed be constantly at your side until the Consummation of the Age."

---

23 This would appear to be the end of the Gospel. What follows, from the nature of what is said, would then be a later addition.

LUKE

A History of Christian Beginnings

Part I

How the Good News came to Israel

Preface to Luke

It is most unfortunate that the ecclesiastical arrangement of the New Testament documents should have separated the *Acts of the Apostles* from *Luke*, since it represents Part II of a single work constituting a history of Christian beginnings. As such, not only is this important in a literary sense: it is intimately related to questions of date and authorship.

The way the Gospel opens, and various elements in it and in the *Acts*, convey that the work is quite a late composition, around the close of the first century AD. It aims positively at putting the Christian story in its historical setting and presenting that story as a whole. The clashes and conflicts of the period before the Fall of Jerusalem in AD 70 are toned down, between the followers of Jesus and the followers of John the Baptist, between the Judaeo-Christians and Graeco-Christians, Petrine factions and Pauline factions. The Roman persecutors of the Church are presented in as favourable a light as possible.

The Church needed such a composition to help secure toleration by the Roman Government after the persecutions in the reign of the Emperor Domitian (died AD 96). It needed it also in face of a growing Christian sectarianism intensified by the failure of the anticipated Second Advent of Jesus to materialise (see *I* and *II Peter*, notably *II Peter* 3).

But what had inspired the author to invest his work with the trappings of historical events and personages? The answer may well be found in the publication in the latter part of the first century of the books of the Jewish historian and apologist Flavius Josephus. These books had much to tell of Palestine in the time of Christ and the Early Christians. One of them was a work *Against Apion*, a somewhat antisemitic Alexandrian intellectual. This was in two parts, and not only so, it is the only one of Josephus's compositions to open by addressing itself to a patron, the "most excellent Epaphroditus". *Luke* adopted this structure for his own work, directed to "the most excellent Theophilus". The name means God-lover.

Luke found the writings of Josephus of great service to him, as will be indicated in the notes. They enabled him to give his story more of a period atmosphere. This does not mean that he did not carry out researches to the extent that was practicable, and the factor which may have caused the attribution of the work to the "Dear Doctor Luke" of Paul's letters (*Col* 4:14, *II Tim* 4:11; *Philem* 24) may have been access to the diary document relating to Paul's later movements (see *Acts* 16:9–18; 20:4–21:19, 27:1–16). This source could have been Doctor Luke's composition.

Our author, whoever he was, clearly had more problems with the story of Jesus than with that of the Early Church, especially in relation to the birth and childhood of Jesus. Here, as in one or two other places, *Luke* had to turn to the Old Testament for aid. He was helped by the birth stories of Samson and Samuel (in the Greek LXX text), and even by Josephus' autobiography, as regards a childhood incident.

Luke was fully prepared to requisition whatever might contribute to his purpose, and in his time this would not be regarded as at all reprehensible. So because the Messiah was expected to come from Bethlehem in Judea *Luke* had to show that Jesus was born there, though his parent's home was in Galilee. He either did not know or disregarded the story in *Matthew*. Luke was able to seize on the device of the first Roman census in Judea, reported by Josephus, which had been so hateful to the Jews, to have Joseph with his wife great with child travel from Galilee to Bethlehem, the city of David, to register. It was of no concern to *Luke* that this census had been taken in AD 6–7, and not in the reign of King Herod, who had died in 4 BC.

Essentially what *Luke* seeks to communicate is first of all a sense of realism, the conviction that the mysterious things which are part and parcel of the Christian heritage do not belong to the realm of fable. The second thing he sets himself to achieve is one of reconciliation of rival and conflicting elements. A typical case in point is *Luke*'s unique presentation of the mother of Jesus and the mother of John the Baptist as cousins, so that their sons are related and almost of the same age. While noting and recognising the devices *Luke* employs, we have to read his work with a sympathetic consciousness of his constructive intentions. He does provide more of a whole picture than any of his contemporaries, and thus may be said to justify his opening statement.

Certainly *Luke*'s composition is the most literary in construction, and the most effective in narration.

The Good News of Jesus Christ

Luke's Version

Foreword

1.1   Since it is the case that many have endeavoured to draw up an account of those matters held by us to be fact, exactly as they transmitted them to us who initially were the eyewitnesses and bearers of the Message, I have thought fit myself, as I have conducted a thorough investigation of all the circumstances from their beginnings, to set them down for you consecutively, most excellent Theophilus, that you may appreciate how well-founded are the things of which you have been informed.

Chapter I[1]

5   In the reign of Herod king of Judea there was a priest called Zechariah, of the course of Abijah,[2] who had a wife of the dughters of Aaron called Elizabeth. They were both devout persons before God, carrying out all the Lord's commandments and enactments scrupulously. They were childless, however, as Elizabeth was barren, and they were now both of them well advanced in years.

An incident occurred while he was officiating as priest before God during the turn of his course. In accordance with priestly custom the duty fell to him of burning 10   incense on going into the Lord's Sanctuary, and the great mass of the people were outside praying at the time of

---

1 Much in this chapter would seem to be derived from Nativity legends composed by followers of John the Baptist. These were also appropriated by Christians to create a *Gospel of the Nativity of Mary*, still extant.
2 *I Chron* 24:10. That of Abijah was the eighth course of priests.

the incense-burning. It was then that there appeared to him an angel of the Lord standing on the right of the altar of incense.

Zechariah was greatly startled at seeing him, and overcome with fear. But the angel said to him, "Do not be afraid, Zechariah, for your petition has been granted, and your wife Elizabeth will bear you a son. You must call him John. He will be your joy and delight, and many
15 will rejoice at his birth. He will be a great man before the Lord, and must not drink wine or intoxicants,[3] and will be filled with holy Spirit from the moment he leaves his mother's womb. Many of the children of Israel will he turn to the Lord their God. He will go before him in the spirit and capacity of Elijah, 'to turn the hearts of the fathers to the children',[4] and the disobedient into exemplary characters, to provide the Lord with a people fully prepared."

"How am I to know this?" Zechariah said to the angel, "I am myself an old man, and my wife is well advanced in years."

"I am Gabriel", the angel replied, "the one who stands before God, and I have been sent to speak to you and
20 convey this news to you. But now you will be dumb and unable to speak until the time when all this comes about, because you have failed to believe my words which will be accomplished in due course."

In the meantime the people were waiting for Zechariah, and were surprised at the length of time he remained in the Sanctuary. When he did come out he could not speak to them, and they realised that he had seen a vision in the Sanctuary by the way he was gesticulating to them while remaining speechless.

He went home as soon as his term of duty was completed, and it was after this that his wife Elizabeth conceived. She kept herself in seclusion for five months
25 saying, "This is what the Lord has done for me when he determined to remove my disgrace among men."

During her sixth month the angel Gabriel was sent by God to a town of Galilee called Nazareth, to a maiden betrothed to a man named Joseph, of the house of David. The maiden's name was Mary. On entering her home he

3 John was to be a Nazirite and thus also unshaven and unshorn.
4 *Mal* 4:6.

said, "Greeting, highly favoured one!⁵ The Lord be with you."

30 She was greatly perturbed by his language, and concerned at what this greeting might imply. But the angel said to her, "Do not be alarmed, Mary. You have found favour with God. You will conceive in your womb and have a son,⁶ whom you are to call Jesus. He will be a great man, and be termed 'Son of the Most High', and the Lord God will give him the throne of his ancestor David. He will reign over the house of Jacob for ever, and his sovereignty shall be without end."⁷

Mary said to the angel, "How can this come about, since I am unwed?"

35 "The holy Spirit will pass over you, and the power of the Most High will overshadow you", replied the angel. "That is why the child that is born will be called 'Holy', 'Son of God'. See, there is your relative Elizabeth, even she has conceived a son in her old age, and the one who was barren is in her sixth month. Nothing whatever is impossible to God."

"I am the Lord's maidservant", said Mary. "Let it be to me as you say."

Then the angel left her.

40 Mary made immediate preparations, and travelled in haste to the hill country to a town of Judah,⁸ where she visited Zechariah's house and greeted Elizabeth. No sooner did Elizabeth hear Mary's greeting than the unborn babe jumped in her womb. And Elizabeth was inspired by the holy Spirit and cried out, "Blest are you among women, and blessed is the fruit of your womb! How comes it that I am honoured by a visit from the mother of my lord? For as soon as your greeting sounded in my ears the unborn babe in my womb jumped for joy.

45 And happy is she who has believed that what has been told her by the Lord will be accomplished."

---

5 The expression can be taken in rather a coarse sense, which would explain Mary's alarm.

6 cf *Judg* 13:3–5 (LXX).

7 *Isa* 9:7.

8 The followers of John the Baptist claimed that he had been born in David's city of Bethlehem. So our author carefully avoids giving the town's name.

Then she sang:[9]

> *My soul magnifies the Lord,*
> *My spirit exults in God my saviour;*
> *For he has marked his servant's disgrace.*
> *All ages will call me happy henceforward;*
> *For the Mighty One has wrought marvels for me,*
> *And holy is his name.*
> 50   *Generation by generation his mercy is shown*
> *To those who revere him.*
> *He has employed the power of his arm;*
> *He has scattered the proud in their purpose:*
> *He has deposed tyrants from their thrones,*
> *And exalted those of low degree.*
> *He has filled the hungry with good fare,*
> *And men of means he has sent away empty.*
> *He has aided his servant Israel,*
> *Mindful of mercy*
> 55   *(As he told our fathers he would be)*
> *To Abraham and his offspring for ever.*[10]

Mary stayed with her for about three months and then returned home.[11]

When the time came for Elizabeth's delivery she gave birth to a son. And when her neighbours and relations heard that the Lord had magnified his mercy to her they rejoiced with her, and on the eighth day they duly attended the boy's circumcision, proposing to name him
60   Zechariah after his father. But the mother intervened. "No", she said, "he is to be called John."[12]

"None of your relations bears that name", they said to her.

They invited his father by signs to indicate what he wanted him called. Having motioned for a tablet he wrote, "His name is John." They were all amazed. Instantly his mouth and tongue were freed of impedi-
65   ment and he spoke, blessing God. Fear fell on all his neighbours, and all these events were widely reported

9 The poem was subsequently transferred to Mary by simply adding her name, though the text makes it clear that the singer is Elizabeth.

10 cf *Jubilees* 25:17. In this pre-Christian work songs are put into the mouths of Rebecca and Isaac of the same order as those attributed here to Elizabeth and Zechariah. See *Jub* 25:15–23; 31:15–20.

11 Our author did not wish to allow Mary to remain with Elizabeth until John was born, as he might then be held to be superior to Jesus.

12 Meaning 'The Lord is compassionate'.

throughout the Judean highlands. Everyone who heard kept them in mind saying, "What is this child going to be, for clearly the Lord's hand is with him?"

Now his father Zechariah was inspired by the holy Spirit and prophesied as follows:

Blessed be the Lord God of Israel,
For he has visited and ransomed his people,
And raised up for us a means of deliverance[13]
Out of the house of his servant David,
70 *As he said by his holy prophets of old;*
Deliverance from our foes and all who hate us,
To maintain his mercy to our fathers,
And to call to mind his holy covenant,
The oath which he swore to our father Abraham,
Assuring that fearlessly, freed from foes,
We should worship him all our days
75 *Purely and piously in his presence.*
And you, child, shall be called "Prophet of the Highest";
For you shall precede the Lord to pave his road,
To give intelligence of deliverance to his people,
Through the tender mercies of our God
Whereby a sunbeam from above reached to us,
Lighting those in gloom and grim shadow,[14]
Directing our feet to a path of safety.

80 The child grew and developed strength of character, and lived in the wilderness until the time of his appearance to Israel.

Chapter II

2.1 At that time a decree was issued by Augustus Caesar to conduct a census of the whole Empire.[a] Everyone went to be registered, each to his own town. So Joseph

a This census was first carried out when Quirinius[1] was legate of Syria.[2]

---

13 Lit 'a horn of deliverance'.
14 See *Isa* 9:2.
1 Publius Sulpicius Quirinius, d AD 21 See Tacit. *Annals* III.48.
2 In AD 6–7. See Jos. *Antiq.* XVIII.1:1. Matthew claims that Jesus was born towards the close of the reign of Herod the Great, d 4 BC. Matthew also claims that Joseph and Mary only settled in Galilee after the birth of Jesus, not before.

went up from Galilee, from the town of Nazareth, to Judea, to David's town called Bethlehem, because he
5 was of the family and lineage of David, there to be registered with Mary his betrothed, who was in an advanced state of pregnancy. The time for her delivery actually came while they were there, and she bore her firstborn son, wrapped him round and laid him in a cattle-trough as they had no place in the inn.

There were shepherds in the same district camped out in the open keeping watch over their flock by night. And an angel of the Lord appeared to them, and the glory of the Lord shone around them; and they were terrified.
10 But the angel said, "Do not be afraid. I bring you word of a great joy which will be shared by all the people, that to-day in David's town a deliverer has been born to you, none other than the Lord Messiah. Here is your proof. You will find a baby wrapped round and lying in a cattle-trough."

Suddenly there was with the angel a concourse of the heavenly host praising God, and singing,

Glory be to God on high and on earth:
Peace be to men who please him.[3]

15 No sooner had the angels left them and returned to heaven than the shepherds said to one another. "Let us by all means go to Bethlehem and see this thing that has happened, of which the Lord has told us."

Hurrying off, they came and found Mary and Joseph, and the baby lying in the cattle-trough. Having seen them, they made known what had been told them about the boy, and all those who heard were amazed at what was told them by the shepherds. But Mary took note of
20 these things, turning them over in her mind. Then the shepherds went back where they came from, glorifying and praising God for everything they had heard and seen, which was exactly as they had been told.

When the requisite eight days had elapsed for circumcising him the boy was given the name Jesus,[4] as called by the angel before he was conceived in the womb.

---

3 In the Temple liturgy the *Kedushah* (Sanctification) expressed the song of the heavenly host in the words of *Isa* 6:3 and *Ezek* 3:12. In the Jewish liturgy we find: "He who makes peace in his high places, may he bestow peace on us and on all Israel" (see *Kaddish* prayer, AJP p 78).

4 In Hebrew, Joshua. *Heb* 4:8.

Later, when the days of her purification were over in accordance with the Law of Moses, they took him to Jerusalem to present him to the Lord,[a] and to offer sacrifice as stated in the law of the Lord, "a pair of turtle-doves or two young pigeons."[5]

25 Now there was a man in Jerusalem named Simeon, a devout man, who awaited the Consolation of Israel,[6] one on whom the holy Spirit rested.[7] It had been conveyed to him by the holy Spirit that he would not die before he had seen the Lord's Anointed. He was led by the Spirit to the Temple; and when the parents brought in the child Jesus to follow the regulations of the Law with regard to him, he took him in his own arms and blessed God, saying, "Now dismiss thy servant in peace, O Lord,
30 according to thy word, for mine eyes have seen thy deliverance, which thou hast provided in the presence of all the peoples, a beacon-light to the Gentiles,[8] a glory to thy people Israel."

Both the father and mother of Jesus were amazed at this statement about him. Simeon blessed them, and said to his mother Mary, "He is put here for the fall and rising
35 again of many in Israel, as a disputed proof – even you will be torn with uncertainty[9] – by which the reasoning of many minds will be disclosed."

Then there was Hannah, a prophetess, daughter of Phanuel, of the tribe of Asher. She had attained a great age, having had seven years of married life from maidenhood, and then had remained a widow for eighty-four years. She never left the Temple now, worshipping there with fasting and prayer night and day. Happening to be by at that moment she praised God aloud, and spoke about the child to all who awaited the liberation of Jerusalem.

When the parents of Jesus had carried out everything required by the Law of the Lord, they returned to Galilee
40 to their own town of Nazareth. There the child grew and

a As it is written in the Law of the Lord, "Every male child that is the beginning of motherhood shall be consecrated to the Lord."[10]

5 *Lev* 12:8.
6 The Messiah's deliverance of Israel.
7 Someone inspired.
8 cf *Isa* 11:10.
9 Lit "a sword shall cleave your soul" (cf *Mark* 3:21, 31).
10 cf *Exod* 13:2.

developed a keen intelligence, being gifted by God.

Now his parents made an annual journey to Jerusalem for the Passover festival. When he was twelve they had gone up as usual for the festival; but when they were on the point of returning, having completed the prescribed period,[11] the boy Jesus lingered in Jerusalem, and his parents were unaware of it. Assuming him to be with the party they had completed a day's journey before they searched for him among their relations and acquain-

45   tances. Failing to find him they turned back to Jerusalem to hunt for him there. It was three days later that they discovered him in the Temple, sitting among the teachers, listening to them and asking them questions, with everyone who heard him amazed at his comprehension and by his answers.[12] They had a shock when they saw him, and his mother said to him, "why have you treated us like this, boy? Here have your father and I been searching anxiously for you."

"Why did you search for me?" he said to them. "Didn't you know I was bound to be occupied with my Father's affairs?"

50   They could not make sense of what he said to them. However, he came away and went back to Nazareth, and behaved obediently towards them; but his mother stored all these things in her mind.

So Jesus advanced in age and intelligence, and in favour with God and man.[13]

Chapter III

3.1   During the fifteenth year of the reign of Tiberius Caesar,[1] when Pontius Pilate was governor of Judea and Herod was tetrarch of Galilee, while his brother Philip was tetrarch of the Iturean Trachonitis region, and Lysanias was tetrarch of Abilene, in the course of the high priesthood of Annas and Caiaphas, divine utterance took possession of John the son of Zechariah in the wilderness. He went over the whole Jordan area

11 The seven days of the festival.
12 cf Josephus, *Life*, ii.
13 Quoted from *I Samuel* 2:26.

1 If dated from Tiberius' shared sovereignty with Augustus this could be AD 26.

proclaiming an immersion in penitence for the forgiveness of sins, as it is stated in the book of the sayings of the prophet Isaiah,

> *A voice cries out in the wilderness*
> *'Make ready the Lord's road:*
> *Put his highways in order!*
> 5 *Let every crevasse be filled in,*
> *And every hill and hump reduced.*
> *Let the twists be straightened,*
> *And the rough places smoothed;*
> *That all flesh may see God's deliverance.'*[2]

Accordingly, he said to the crowds coming to him for immersion, "Vipers' brood! Who warned you to flee from the coming Wrath? Produce fruit, then, consistent with repentance, and refrain from saying to yourselves, 'We have Abraham as our father', for I tell you that from these stones[3] God can supply Abraham with sons. Already the axe is laid to the root of the trees. Any tree, therefore, that fails to produce good fruit will be cut down and cast into the fire."

10 The crowds asked him, "What are we to do then?"

"Whoever has two coats", he replied, "let him share with the man who has none. And whoever has a store of food let him do likewise."

Even tax-collectors came to be immersed, and said to him, "What should we do, master?"

He told them, "Exact no more than the amount fixed for you."[4]

Men in the army also asked him, "What about us? What are we to do?"

"Never use brutality or threats of false charges,"[5] he told them, "but be content with your pay and keep."

15 As the people were agog, with everyone wondering in their minds about John, whether he could be the Messiah, John settled the matter for everyone by saying, "I am certainly immersing you in water, but a mightier than

---

2 *Isa* 11:3–5. The physical changes described seem to be understood as applying to human character.

3 Stones – sons. Imitating the play on words in Hebrew.

4 Tax-collectors were often able to keep any sums they could extort in excess of the sum due under assessment. Hence the people's hatred of them.

5 Soldiers, largely mercenaries, were given to terrorism as a means of supplementing their low pay.

I is coming, whose sandal-strap I am not fit to untie: he will immerse you in holy Spirit and fire. His winnowing-shovel is in his hand to thoroughly cleanse his floor, and gather the wheat into his granary; but he will burn up the chaff with unquenchable fire."

Thus, with many another appeal, did he give his message to the people. But Herod the tetrarch, because he was reproved by John about his brother's wife Herodias,[6] and for all the misdeeds Herod had commit-

20   ted, crowned all his other wrongs by imprisoning John in a fortress.[7]

Now when all the people had been immersed and Jesus too had been immersed and was praying, the sky opened and the holy Spirit descended upon him in bodily form like a dove, while there came a voice from heaven, "You are my dear son: this day I have begotten you."[8]

(Jesus was now about thirty years of age,[9] being, as was understood, the son of Joseph – the son of Eli – the son of Matthat – the son of Levi – the son of Melchi[10] – the

25   son of Jannai – the son of Joseph – the son of Mattathias – the son of Amos – the son of Nahum – the son of Chesli – the son of Naggai – the son of Mahath – the son of Mattathias – the son of Shimei – the son of Josech – the son of Resa[11] – the son of Zerubbabel – the son of Shealtiel[12] – the son of Neri – the son of Melchi – the son of Addi – the son of Kosam – the son of Elmadan – the son of Er – the son of Jesus – the son of Eliezer – the son of

30   Jorim[13] – the son of Matthat – the son of Levi – the son of

---

6 John, following Essene teaching, had denounced Herod for marrying Herodias while his wife, daughter of Aretas king of Arabia, was still living. In the Essene view this was fornication. See Jos. *Antiq.* XVIII.109ff; *Bk. of Zadok* 7.

7 In the fortress of Machaerus. See Jos. *Antiq.* XVIII.119.

8 *Ps* 2:7. This seems to have been the original here.

9 John was imprisoned around AD 35. If Jesus was born, according to *Luke*, in AD 6, at the time of the census, he could now be twenty-nine. There was another census in AD 34–35.

10 There is some evidence that the names of Matthat and Melchi got transposed. Julius Africanus (3rd cent.) makes Melchi the half-brother of Matthan (*Mt* genealogy), married to his widow Estha. Some traditions suggest that Mary was the granddaughter of Matthan on the side of his father Joachim, and they agree that Matthan and Melchi were brothers. This would make Mary mother of Jesus to be also of Davidic descent.

11 Or Rephaiah.

12 Or Salathiel.

13 Or Jehoram.

Simeon – the son of Judah – the son of Joseph – the son of Onan – the son of Eliakim – the son of Melea – the son of Menna[14] – the son of Mattatha – the son of Nathan – the son of David – the son of Jesse – the son of Obed – the son of Boaz – the son of Salmon – the son of Nahshon – the son of Aminadab – the son of Aram – the son of Hezron – the son of Perez – the son of Judah – the son of Jacob – the son of Isaac – the son of Abraham – the son of

35 Terah – the son of Nahor – the son of Serug – the son of Reu – the son of Peleg – the son of Eber – the son of Shelah – the son of Cainan – the son of Arphaxad – the son of Shem – the son of Noah – the son of Lemech – the son of Methuselah – the son of Enoch – the son of Jared – the son of Mehalalel – the son of Kenan – the son of Enosh – the son of Jared – the son of Mehalalel – the son of Kenan – the son of Enosh – the son of Seth – the son of Adam – the son of God.)[15]

4.1 Jesus returned from the Jordan inspired, and was led by the Spirit into the wilderness where he was tempted by the Devil for forty days.[16] He ate nothing during this period, and when it was ended he was starving. So the Devil said to him, "If you are the son of God, why don't you tell this stone to become bread?"

Jesus replied, "Because it is stated, 'Man is not to live by bread alone.'"[17]

5 Then he carried him off to show him all the kingdoms of the Empire[18] in an instant of time. "I will make you master of all this, with all their resources," said the Devil, "because it is given wholly into my power, and I can confer it on whom I please. You have only to pay me homage and it shall be yours."

"It is stated", Jesus replied, " 'You are to pay homage to the Lord your God and to worship him alone.' "[19]

14 Or Menahem.

15 The genealogy traces the descent of Jesus from David through his son Nathan, while *Matthew* traces it through Solomon. The section has been placed between brackets as being possibly an addition, since it seems to break the continuity of the text.

16 A symbolic period. The temptation follows the baptism quite naturally since it was held that the Messianic qualifications (*Isa* 9:6–7) had been conferred on Jesus by the descent of the Spirit.

17 *Deut* 8:3.

18 Lit 'the inhabited world', often used of the Roman Empire.

19 *Deut* 6:13.

Next he took him to Jerusalem, and stationed him on a turret of the Temple, and said to him, "If you are the Son

10 of God throw yourself down from here. For it is stated, 'He will instruct his angels about you to take care of you. They shall cradle you on their hands in case you should strike a foot against a stone.' "[20]

Jesus replied, "It is stated, 'You are not to put the Lord your God to the test.' "[21]

Having fully completed his tempting the Devil left him for the time being.

Jesus returned to Galilee as a powerful preacher, and

15 was the talk of the whole district. When he taught in their synagogues everyone applauded him.[22]

Then he came to Nazareth where he had grown up, and went into the synagogue, as he habitually did on the sabbath days, and stood up to read. The scroll of the prophet Isaiah was handed to him, and having opened the book he found the place where it was written,

The spirit of the Lord is on me,
By which means he has anointed me,
To give good news to the wretched.
He has sent me to proclaim
Release to the prisoners,
The light of day for those denied it;[23]
To set broken men at liberty,
To proclaim the Lord's amnesty year.[24]

20 After reading the passage he rolled up the scroll, returned it to the assistant, and sat down. The eyes of everyone in the synagogue were turned on him.

"To-day in your hearing this scripture is accomplished," he began his address.

He carried his audience with him, spellbound by the cheering words that fell from his lips. "Can this be Joseph's son?" they said.

He went on, "No doubt you will quote to me the proverb, 'Doctor cure yourself!' All that we have heard you have done at Capernaum[25] do here in your home

20 *Ps* 91:11–12.
21 *Deut* 6:16.
22 The Hebrew equivalent of 'Bravo' was used by the congregation at the end of a good preacher's discourse.
23 Those incarcerated in dungeons.
24 AD 26–27 was a Sabbatical year.
25 Details of this visit to Capernaum are not given.

town. I tell you truly, no prophet is accepted in his native
25 place. I must plainly point out to you that there were
many widows in Israel in Elijah's time, when heaven was
shut for three-and-a-half years and the whole country
suffered a severe famine, but Elijah was sent to none of
them except a widow woman of Sidonian Sarepta. There
were also many lepers in Israel when Elisha was prophet, but none of them was cleansed except Naaman the
Syrian."

On hearing this everyone in the synagogue was out-
raged,[26] and rose up to eject him from the town. They
hustled him to the brow of the hill on which their town
30 was built with the intention of hurling him down. But he
extricated himself from them and went away.

He came down to the Galilean town of Capernaum,
and taught there on the sabbaths; and they were
astonished at his teaching because his message had the
force of authority.

In that synagogue there was a man possessed by a foul
demon, which screamed out, "Ai! What do you want
with us, Jesus the Nazarene? Have you come to destroy
us? I know who you are, the holy one of God!"
35 Jesus rebuked it. "Be quiet", he said, "and come out of
him."

When the demon had hurled the man out in front it
went out of him without doing him any injury.

They were all overcome with amazement, and turned
to one another saying, "What can it mean? He commands foul spirits with power and authority, and they
come out!" The whole district was set talking about him.

Rising from the synagogue he went to Simon's[27]
house. Simon's mother-in-law was in a high fever, and
they told him about her. Standing over her he rebuked
the fever and it left her. So she got up at once and waited
on them.
40 As the sun set all who had those who were ailing with
various complaints brought them to him, and he laid his
hands on each of them and cured them. From many of

---

26 The Syrians were mortal enemies of the Galileans. Thus it would be most
offensive to them that Jesus should instance how two Syrians had been
preferred to all Israel. See Jos. *Antiq.* XIV.159
27 Reference is not made to the call of Simon, though it was in *Luke's* source
(*Mk* 1:16), and comes in very abruptly here like the reference to Capernaum
(above n 25).

them demons came out crying, "You are the son of God!" But rebuking them he would not let them speak, because they knew him to be the Messiah.

Going out at daybreak he set off into the country. But the crowds went in search of him, and when they came up with him they hemmed him in so that he should not leave them.

"There are other towns as well", he told them, "where I must proclaim the Kingdom of God. It was for that purpose I was sent."

So he preached in the various synagogues of Judea.[28]

Chapter IV

5.1   Now it happened, with the crowd pressing heavily upon him to hear God's message, that Jesus stood beside Lake Gennesaret. And he noticed two boats drawn up by the lake, but the fishermen had got out of them to clean their nets. Going on board one of them, which was Simon's, he asked him to put out a little from the land, and sitting down he taught the crowd from the boat.

When he had finished speaking, he said to Simon, "Now put out into deep water, and let down your nets for a catch."

5   "We've toiled all night long, chief, and caught nothing," Simon replied, "but if you say so I will lower the nets."

Having done this they enclosed a large shoal of fish, and their nets broke. They made signs to their partners in the other boat to come to their assistance. So they came and filled both the boats to sinking point.

When he saw this Simon Peter[1] fell at Jesus's knees saying, "Leave me, sir, for I am a sinful man!"[a]

10   James and John, the sons of Zebedee, who were Simon's associates, echoed his words.

"Don't be afraid", Jesus told Simon. "From now on your job will be catching men alive."

a He was overcome with amazement, as were those with him, at the haul of fish they had caught.

---

28 Some MSS correct to Galilee. But *Luke* appears to think of all Jewish territory in Palestine as Judea. See below *Lk* 23:5, *Acts* 1:8.

1 Simon had not yet been nicknamed Peter. See *Lk* 6:14.

When they had brought their boats to land they abandoned everything and followed him.

In one of the towns he visited there was a man covered with leprosy. When he saw Jesus he fell on his face entreating him, "Sir, you can cleanse me if only you will."

Stretching out his hand he touched him saying, "I do will it. Be cleansed!"

At once his leprosy left him. He ordered him to tell no one, but to go and show himself to the priest, and offer for his cleansing what Moses prescribed as evidence to them.[2] Yet more than ever the word got around concerning him, and crowds gathered to hear him and to be cured of their complaints. But Jesus retired to the open country to engage in prayer.

It happened one day when he was teaching that there were Pharisees and doctors of the Law sitting there, who had come from various Galilean villages, and from Judea and Jerusalem. He was exercising the Lord's curative power. Just then some men arrived bringing on a mattress a man who was paralysed. They tried to bring him in to lay him before Jesus; but, unable to find a way to get him through the crowd they mounted to the top of the house and lowered him on a mattress through the tiling[3] directly in front of Jesus. Seeing what faith they had he said, "Man, your sins are forgiven."

The scribes and Pharisees started arguing, "Who is this who talks blasphemously? Who but God alone can forgive sins?"

Jesus was aware of their discussion and said to them, "What are you debating in your minds? Which is easier, to say 'Your sins are forgiven', or to say, 'Rise and walk'? But that you may know that the Son of Man is entitled to forgive sins on earth" – he addressed the paralytic – "to you I say, rise, pick up your mattress, and go to your home!"

At once he stood up before them, picked up his bed, and went to his home praising God. They were all astounded, and praised God, murmuring fearfully, "We have seen extraordinary things to-day."

2 See *Lev* 14.
3 *Lk* substitutes a tiled roof for the flat roof (*Mk* 2:4) as this was more familiar where he was writing.

When he went out later he noticed a tax-collector called Levi seated at the customs-station, and said to him, "Follow me!" Leaving everything he got up and followed him.

Then Levi gave a big reception for him at his house, with a large company of tax-collectors and others dining
30   with them. The Pharisees and their scribes voiced their protests to Jesus's disciples, "Why do you eat and drink with tax-collectors and sinners?" they said.

It was Jesus who answered them, "It is not the healthy who need a doctor, but those who are ill. I have not come to summon religious people, but sinners, to repentance."

They said, "John's[4] disciples fast regularly and say the prescribed prayers, exactly like the Pharisees, but yours eat and drink."

"You cannot expect the bridal party to fast while the
35   bridegroom is with them", Jesus told them. "The time will come when the bridegroom will have taken leave of them: that will be the time for them to fast."

He added this illustration. "No one puts a piece torn from a new cloak on an old one. If he does, not only does he tear the new, but the piece from the new is out of keeping with the old. Neither does anyone pour new wine into old wine-skins. If he does, the new wine splits the wine-skins, and is spilt itself, and the skins are destroyed. No, new wine is poured into new wine-skins. Nor does anyone want new wine after drinking the old. 'You can't beat the old', he says."[5]

6.1   Now on the sabbath he happened to take his way through the standing corn, and his disciples picked and ate the ears, rubbing them between their hands. But some of the Pharisees said, "Why are you doing what is not allowed on the sabbath?"

Jesus answered them, "Have you never read what David did when he and his companions were hungry, how he went into the house of God and took the loaves of the Presence and ate them, and shared them with his companions, loaves which only the priests were allowed
5   to eat?"[6] Then he added, "The Son of Man is master of

4 ie the Baptist.
5 Both the form and point of the illustration differ from *Mark*'s version (Mk 2:21–22).
6 See *I Sam* 21:1–6.

the sabbath."[7]

When he went to the synagogue to teach on another sabbath there was a man there whose right hand was withered. The scribes and the Pharisees watched him closely to see whether he would cure on the sabbath, so that they could obtain evidence on which to accuse him. Knowing what was in their minds, he said to the man with the withered hand, "Rise, and come up in front."

He stood up and came forward.

Then Jesus said to them, "I put it to you, which is the right thing on the sabbath, well-doing or evil-doing,
10   saving life or destroying it?"[8] Having looked around at them all, he said to the man, "Stretch out your hand." He did so, and his hand was restored. They were furious and talked together of what they could do to Jesus.

Chapter V

Now at that time Jesus went off to the hill to pray, and was all night long in prayer to God. When it was day he called his disciples, and chose twelve of them, whom he termed envoys. There was Simon, whom he named Peter, and his brother Andrew, James and John, Philip
15   and Bartholomew, Matthew and Thomas, James son of Alphaeus and Simon called the Zealot, Judas son of James and Judas Iscariot, who turned traitor.

Descending with them he stood on a level space with a large body of his disciples, and a mass of the people drawn from all over Judea, from Jerusalem, and from the seaboard of Tyre and Sidon, who had come to hear him and to be cured of their diseases; and those who were troubled with foul spirits were given relief. Indeed, the whole crowd tried to touch him, because power emanated from him and cured everyone.

20   Then looking at his disciples he said, "How fortunate are you poor! Yours is the Kingdom of God. How fortunate are you who hunger now! You shall be satisfied. How fortunate are you who weep now! You shall laugh. How fortunate are you when men detest

7 Codex D inserts: "The same day, observing someone working on the sabbath, he told him, 'My man, if you know what you are doing you are blessed, but if you do not know you are accursed and a violator of the Law.'"
8 These sentiments expressed by Jesus were held by eminent Pharisees.

you, and when they ostracise you, vilify you, and stigmatise all of your kind as bad on the Son of Man's account![1] Rejoice when that happens, and jump for joy, for rich is your recompense in heaven. Their forefathers treated the prophets exactly the same.

"But woe to you rich! You have had your good cheer. Woe to you who have had your fill now! You shall go hungry. Woe to you who laugh now! You shall mourn and weep.[2] Woe to you when all men speak well of you! Their forefathers treated the false prophets exactly the same.

"To all of you who are listening I say, love your enemies, treat well those who hate you, bless those who curse you, pray for those who abuse you. To him who hits you on the right side of the jaw offer him the other as well, and from him who takes your tunic do not withhold your cloak also. Give to all who ask you, and from him who takes your belongings do not demand them back. As you would have people treat you, treat them the same way.

"If you only love those who love you, what virtue is that of yours? Even the sinners love those who love them. And if you treat well those who treat you well, what virtue is that of yours? Even the sinners do that. And if you lend to those from whom you expect to receive, what virtue is that of yours? Sinners lend to sinners on a reciprocal basis. Rather love your enemies and treat them well, and lend without expectation of return. Then you will have a rich recompense, and be sons of the Most High, who is kind to the ungrateful and evil. Be as compassionate as your Father is compassionate.

"Refrain from judging, and you will not be judged. Refrain from condemning, and you will not be condemned. Acquit, and you will be acquitted. Give, and it will be given you. Good measure, pressed down, shaken together, and brimming over, they will tip into your lap: for the measure you use will be used for you."

He also addressed them in proverbs.

---

1 cf *Testaments of the XII Patriarchs* (*Test. Judah*, 25:4). The author has in mind the persecution of Christians in the latter part of the 1st cent AD and alters his source accordingly.

2 cf *Enoch* 94–96.

"Can a blind man guide a blind man? Will not both tumble into the ditch?

40 "The disciple is not superior to his teacher; but when fully trained he has the standing of his teacher.

"How is it you can see the splinter in your brother's eye, but cannot detect the plank in your own eye? How can you say to your brother, 'Allow me to extract the splinter from your eye', when you fail to see the plank in your own? Hypocrite! First extract the plank from your own eye, and then you will see clearly to extract the splinter from your brother's eye.

"No good tree produces harmful fruit, nor yet does a harmful tree produce good fruit. By its own fruit, therefore, will each tree be recognised.

"They do not pick figs from thorns, nor do they gather 45 grape bunches from brambles. The good man from his mind's good store gives out good, while the evil man from his evil store gives out evil; for what his mind is stocked with his mouth speaks.

"Why do you call me 'Master, Master!' and do not do what I say? I will show you what a man is like who comes to me and listens to my sayings and carries them out. He is like a man building a house, who dug deep down and laid his foundations on rock. When a flood came and the torrent dashed against that house, it failed to shake it because it was solidly built. But whoever has heard my sayings and has not carried them out is like a man who built his house on the surface without a foundation.[3] When the torrent dashed against it it immediately collapsed, and great was the ruin of that house."

7.1 When he had completed all he had to say for the benefit of the people he went to Capernaum. There a centurion's servant, whom he greatly prized, had reached the crisis of a serious illness. Having heard about Jesus he dispatched elders of the Jews to him, begging him to come and see his servant safely through. When they reached Jesus they earnestly entreated him, saying, 5 "He deserves to be granted this request; for he loves our people, and had the synagogue built for us himself."

So Jesus went with them. But he had not gone far,

---

3 *Luke* sometimes adapts the wording of his source to suit conditions familiar to his readers. In this instance he changes the comparison with a house built on sand.

being still some distance from the house, when the centurion sent friends to him to say, "Sir, do not inconvenience yourself. I am no fit person for you to come under my roof. Neither for the same reason did I regard myself as worthy to come and see you. Simply command it, and my orderly will be cured. For even I am a man subject to authority,[4] with soldiers under me. I say to one, 'Go', and he goes, and to another, 'Come', and he comes, and to my servant, 'Do this', and he does it."

Jesus was amazed at hearing this, and turning to the crowd that followed him he said, "I tell you, not even in Israel have I found faith like this."

10   When those who had been sent had returned to the house they found the servant better.

The next day he went to a town called Nain,[5] and his disciples with a large crowd accompanied him. As he approached the gate of the town a dead man was being carried out, the only child of his widowed mother;[6] and a crowd from the town was with her. On seeing her the Master took pity on her, and said to her, "Please don't cry."

Advancing, he touched the coffin, and the bearers halted. Then he said, "Young man, I bid you wake!"[7]

15   The young man sat up and began to speak; and he restored him to his mother.

Everyone was seized with fear, and praised God saying, "A great prophet has risen among us", and "God has visited his people."

The saying about him was spread everywhere in Judea as well as throughout the vicinity.

Chapter VI

To John his disciples brought word of all these events, and calling to him a certain two of his disciples he sent them to the Master to ask, "Are you the Destined One, or should we expect someone else?"

---

4 cf the words of the good Roman legate Petronius who helped the Jews when the Emperor Caligula wanted to set up his statue in the Temple at Jerusalem. Josephus quotes him as saying, "For I am under authority as well as you" (Josephus, *Jewish War*, II.195).
5 More correctly Naim.
6 cf Elijah's healing of the son of the widow of Zarephath (*I Ki* 17). She is referred to in *Lk* 4:26.
7 cf *Mk* 5:41.

20   When they reached him the men said, "John the Baptist has sent us to you to ask, 'Are you the Destined One, or should we expect someone else?' "

He was engaged at the time in curing many of diseases, plagues, and evil spirits, and blessing with sight many who were blind. This was the answer he gave them. "Go and tell John what you have seen and heard, the blind see again, the lame walk, the lepers are cleansed, the deaf hear, the dead are awakened, the poor are given good news; and fortunate is he who has no misgivings about me."

25   When John's messengers had left he began to speak to the crowds about John. "What did you go out into the wilderness to look at, a cane shaken by the wind? Or did you go out to see something else, a man enveloped in soft draperies?[1] Surely those who possess fine and delicate clothing are to be found in palaces. What then did you go out to see, a prophet? Yes, I tell you, and much more than a prophet. He it is of whom it was stated, 'See, I will send my messenger before you, to pave the way for you.'[2] I tell you, none born of woman is greater than John, yet the most insignificant in the Kingdom of God is greater than he."

All the people, even the tax-collectors, as they listened declared God just, having undergone John's rite of
30   immersion. But the Pharisees and doctors of the Law had disregarded God's wishes as it affected themselves in not being immersed by him.

"To what shall I compare the men of this generation?" Jesus continued. "What are they like? They are like children squatting in the market-place, calling out to each other,

'We've played you a jig, but you haven't danced.
We've played a dirge, but you haven't mourned.'

"For John the Baptist came neither eating bread nor drinking wine, and you say, 'He is demon-possessed.' The Son of Man came both eating and drinking, and you say, 'There you are, a glutton and a drunkard, an associ-
35   ate of tax-collectors and sinners.' Yet 'Wisdom is vindicated by all her children.' "[3]

1 "Cane – draperies," see note to *Mt* 11:7–8 (Bk III:1).
2 *Mal* 3:1.
3 cf *Wisd. Sol.* 8:6–7.

One of the Pharisees was anxious for him to dine with him. So he entered the Pharisee's house and reclined at table. Now there was a woman in the town known to be a sinner. When she learnt that he was a guest at the Pharisee's house she brought an alabaster flask of perfume and stood behind at his feet weeping,[4] bathing his feet with her tears, and drying them with her hair. Then she caressed his feet and anointed them with the perfume. Seeing this, the Pharisee who was entertaining Jesus said to himself, "If he were a prophet he would be aware what kind of woman she is who is touching him: he would know she is a sinner."

40   Then Jesus turned to him and said, "There is something I wish to say to you, Simon."

"By all means, teacher", he replied.

"There were two debtors of a certain moneylender. One owed him five hundred dinars and the other fifty. Neither of them being able to pay he showed them both consideration. Which of them, then, will have most regard for him?"

"I assume", answered Simon, "the one to whom he showed most consideration."

"You have judged rightly", he told him.

Then turning to the woman he said to Simon, "You see this woman? When I entered your house you gave me no water for my feet, but she has bathed my feet with her 45   tears, and dried them with her hair. You gave me no kiss, but she, ever since she came in, has not left off caressing my feet. You did not anoint my head with oil, but she has anointed my feet with perfume. For that very reason, I tell you, her many sins are forgiven, because she showed respect. But one to whom there has been little to be forgiven shows slight respect.

"Your sins are forgiven", he told her.

The other guests said to themselves, "Who does he think he is that he even forgives sins?"

50   But he told the woman, "Your faith has saved you. Go in peace."

8.1   Thereafter he made a personal tour of every town and village, preaching and giving out the news of the Kingdom of God. The twelve went with him, and certain women whom he had cured of evil spirits and various

---

4 Diners reclined round a table on couches with their feet pointed outwards.

ailments. There was Mary, called Magdalene,[5] from whom seven demons had come out, and Johanna wife of Chuza, Herod's chancellor, Susanna, and many others, who attended to his needs with their means.

When a large crowd had gathered, drawn to him from the various towns, he addressed them in similes.

5 "The sower went out to sow his seed, and as he sowed, some fell by the roadside and was trampled on, and the birds of the air ate it up. Other seed fell on the rock, and when it sprouted withered away from lack of moisture. Other seed fell among thistles, and the thistles sprang up with it and stifled it. Other seed fell on good soil, sprouted, and yielded a hundredfold crop." When he had said this he added distinctly, "Let him who can catch my meaning do so."[6]

His disciples, however, asked him what the simile meant.

10 "It is your privilege to know the secrets of the Kingdom of God," he said, "but for the others they are expressed in similes, that 'while they see they may not perceive, and while they hear they may not understand.'[7]

"Here is the meaning of this simile. The seed is God's Message, and those by the roadside are those who, having heard it, along comes the Devil and plucks the Message out of their hearts, in case they should believe it and be saved. Those on the rock are those who welcome the Message with joy when they hear it, but these have no root: they believe for a while, but when the testing time comes they shrink away. What fell among thistles means those who have heard, but get themselves stifled with cares and riches and the pleasures of life, and never

15 ripen. What fell on good soil means those who have heard the Message with a good and honest heart, possess themselves of it and bear fruit sturdily.

"No one lights a lamp to conceal it in a jar or put it under a bed: he sets it on a lampstand that those who enter may see the light. All this, then, is not concealed so as to remain undetected, nor hidden away that it should

5 From the town of Magdala.
6 On themes like the Kingdom of God with political implications Jesus resorted to crypticism because of government spies and informers in the audience. *Luke* fudges this. But see note to *Mk* 4:11 (note 28).
7 *Isa* 6:9.

not be known and brought into the open. So listen very carefully; for to him who has shall be given, but from him who has not even what he seems to have shall be taken away."

20 Then his mother and brothers came to him, but they could not get to him because of the crowd. He was informed, "Your mother and brothers are standing outside wishing to see you."

"My mother and brothers", he replied, "are those who hear God's Message and carry it out."

One day both he and his disciples went on board ship, and he said to them, "Let us cross to the other side of the lake."

So they put to sea. But as they sailed he fell asleep.

Then a heavy squall of wind swept down on the lake, so that they were being swamped and in great danger. They went and woke him crying, "Chief, chief, we are lost!"

When he was awake he rebuked wind and wave, and 25 they ceased and were calm. "Where is your faith?" he said to them.

Fearful and astounded they said to one another, "Who can he be that commands both the winds and the water and they obey him?"

They came to shore in the country of the Gerasenes, which lies opposite Galilee. No sooner had he landed than he was met by a man of their city who was demon-possessed. For a considerable time he had worn no clothes, and lived not in a house but in the tombs. Shrieking out directly he saw Jesus, he fell down before him crying loudly, "What do you want with me, Jesus, son of the most high God? Please do not torture me!"

That was because he had ordered the foul spirit to leave the man; for it had frequently seized him in its clutches, and he had been bound protectively with chains and fetters. But he had snapped his bonds, and had been driven by the demon into the wilderness.

30 Jesus asked him, "What is your name?"

"Legion", he replied, for a horde of demons had entered him. They begged him not to order them off to the Abyss.

Now there was a herd of a sufficient number of swine feeding on the hillside, and they begged him to give them permission to enter these. So he gave them permission. Abandoning the man the demons entered the swine and the herd made a wild dash down the slope into the lake and were drowned.

35 When they saw what had happened the herdsmen ran off and told their tale to town and farm; and the people went to see what had happened and came to Jesus. There they found the man from whom the demons had gone out seated clothed and sane at Jesus's feet, and they were afraid. But those who had been onlookers informed them how the demon-possessed man had been cured. Nevertheless the whole population of the Gerasene district asked him to leave them, for they were in the grip of mortal fear. So going on board ship he took his departure, though the man from whom the demons had gone out begged to come with him. He sent him away, however, saying, "Return home, and relate all that God has done for you."

But he went away and proclaimed all over the city all that Jesus had done for him.

40 On Jesus's return the crowd gave him a hearty welcome, for they were on the look-out for him. Then came a man called Jair, president of the synagogue, and fell at Jesus's feet begging him to come to his house as his only daughter, aged about twelve, was dying. As he was taking him there the crowds hemmed him in tightly. One woman, who had a haemorrhage for twelve years which no one had been able to cure, managed to reach him from behind and touch the fringe of his cloak, and instantly her haemorrhage ceased.

45 "Who touched me?" exclaimed Jesus.

When everyone disclaimed responsibility Peter said, "The whole crowd is pressing and crushing you."

"Someone did touch me", Jesus persisted, "for I can feel that power has been drawn from me."

Seeing that she had not escaped notice the woman came forward trembling, and prostrating herself before him declared in front of all the people why she had touched him and how she was instantly cured.

"Daughter", he told her, "your faith has cured you. Go in peace."

While he was still speaking someone came for the president of the synagogue to say, "Your daughter has died. Do not trouble the teacher further."

50 But Jesus, overhearing it, told him, "Don't be afraid.

Simply believe, and she will be spared."

On reaching the house he would allow none to enter but Peter, John and James, and the child's father and mother. Everyone was weeping and mourning for her. "Do not weep", he said. "She is not dead, only asleep."

But they jeered at him, aware that she was dead. He, however, took her by the hand and cried out, "Wake up, child!" And her spirit returned, and she rose instantly, and he ordered food to be given her. Her parents were transported with joy; but he insisted that they should tell no one what had happened.

Chapter VII

9.1   When Jesus had called the twelve together he gave them power and authority over all demons, as well as to cure diseases. Then he dispatched them to proclaim the Kingdom of God, as well as to heal. "Take nothing with you on your travels," he told them, "neither staff, nor wallet, nor food, nor money, not even two tunics. At whatever house you enter stay there until you have to leave again. Where they will not receive you, when you leave that town shake off the dust from your feet as a testimony to them."

So on their departure they went from village to village proclaiming the News and effecting cures everywhere.

Now Herod the tetrarch heard of all these occurrences, and was quite at a loss, as it was being said by some that John had risen from the dead, by others that Elijah had appeared, and by others that one of the prophets of old had come to life. Herod said, "I have beheaded John.[1] Who then can this be of whom I hear such things?" And he endeavoured to see him.

10   When the envoys returned they related to Jesus everything they had done. Receiving them back, he quietly withdrew to a town called Bethsaida. But the populace, becoming aware of it, followed him, and welcoming them he spoke to them of the Kingdom of God and cured those who stood in need of healing.

As the day declined the twelve approached him and said, "Dismiss the crowd that they may go to the

---

1 Considering the author's interest in historical circumstances it is surprising that he omitted the details of John's death.

neighbouring villages and farms and get accommodation and procure provisions, for here we are in open country."

"You feed them yourselves", he replied.

"But we have no more than five loaves and two fish", they said. "Unless you expect us to go and buy food for all these people?"[a]

"Get them seated in parties of about fifty", he told his disciples.

15 So they did this and sat everybody down. Then taking the five loaves and two fish he looked up to heaven, said a blessing for them, broke, and handed them to his disciples to give out to the people. They all ate and were satisfied, and twelve basketfuls were picked up of the fragments they left over.

Once when he was praying alone his disciples joined him, and he asked them, "Who do people say I am?"

"John the Baptist", they replied, "though others say Elijah, and others one of the prophets of old come to life."

20 "And you," he said, "who do you say I am?"

"You are God's Anointed", Peter answered.

He gave them strict instructions to tell no one this,[2] declaring that the Son of Man must endure much suffering, and be rejected by the elders, head priests and scribes, and be killed, and be raised again on the third day.

Publicly he said, "Whoever would follow me must be truly reckless, and take up his cross daily and follow me. For whoever would preserve his life will lose it; but

25 whoever loses his life for me will preserve it. For how will it benefit a man to have gained the whole world and to perish or forfeit himself? Whoever, therefore, is disdainful of me and of my words will find the Son of Man disdainful of him when he comes in his own and the Father's glory, and that of the holy angels. I tell you positively, there are some standing here now who will not experience death before they see the Kingdom of God."

a There were about five thousand men.

---

2 Since it would make Jesus liable to immediate arrest by the Romans for claiming kingship without authorisation.

Some eight days after he had said this he took with him Peter, John and James, and ascended the mountain to pray. As he was praying the appearance of his face changed and his clothing turned to a dazzling white.

30 And now two men were conversing with him. These were Moses and Elijah, who appeared in glory and discussed his exodus[3] which he was soon to solemnise at Jerusalem. Peter and his companions were weighed down with sleep, but they became wide awake when they saw his splendour and the two men standing with him. Then as these were vanishing Peter said to Jesus, "Chief, how fortunate we are to be here! Now let us erect three bowers, one for you, one for Moses, and one for Elijah", not realising what he was saying.

As he was speaking there came a cloud, and cast a shadow over them, and they grew fearful as they entered

35 the cloud. Then a voice spoke out of the cloud, "He is my chosen son. Listen to him."

When the voice finished Jesus was found to be alone.

They kept silent at the time, and said nothing to anyone of what they had seen.

The next day a considerable crowd met him when they came down from the mountain. One man in the crowd cried out, "Do take a look at my son, teacher. He is all I have, and there is a spirit that seizes him, and he will suddenly cry out; and it convulses him accompanied by foaming at the mouth, and leaves him with such diffi-

40 culty as to shatter him completely. I begged your disciples to expel it, but they were quite unable to do so."

"O faithless and perverse generation!" Jesus replied. "How long must I be with you? How long must I bear with you? Bring your son here."

But even as he came forward the demon threw him down and convulsed him. Jesus, however, rebuked the foul spirit, and cured the lad, and restored him to his father. All were amazed at God's superlative power.

While everyone was wondering about all he was doing, he said to his disciples, "Get this clear, the Son of Man is to be delivered into the hands of the authorities."

---

3 The Passover commemorated the Exodus of Israel from Egypt. It would appear that the Crucifixion was interpreted as that of Israel (Jesus) from Egypt (Jerusalem). See *Rev* 11:6, where again the two witnesses would seem to represent Moses and Elijah. Jesus here has the glory of the heavenly Son of Man whom the Essenes identified as the Messiah Above. See *Bk of Enoch*.

45 But they did not catch his meaning, and were prevented from grasping it; and they were afraid to ask him for an explanation. A dispute, however, arose between them as to which of them would be greatest. Then Jesus, realising what was going on in their minds, took a small boy and placing him at his side said to them, "Whoever accepts this little boy for my sake accepts me and whoever accepts me accepts him who sent me. So it is the most unassuming of you all who will be great."

John said, "Chief, we saw someone expelling demons in your name, but we stopped him because he does not belong to our company."

50 "Do not stop him," Jesus told him, "for he who is not against you is on your side."

Chapter VIII

Now when the time was due for him to be taken up, Jesus turned firmly towards Jerusalem, and sent messengers ahead of him. As they went forward they entered a Samaritan village to make preparations for him. But the people would not make him welcome because he was set on going to Jerusalem. When his disciples James and John saw this they said, "Master, will you have us invoke fire to descend from heaven to consume them, as Elijah
55 did?" But he turned and rebuked them,[1] and they went on to another village.

As they were travelling along the road a man said to them, "I will follow you wherever you go."

"The foxes have lairs", Jesus told him, "and the birds of the air have nests, but the Son of Man has no place where he may lay his head."

To another he said, "Follow me." But he answered, "First give me leave to go and bury my father."

60 "Leave the dead to bury their own dead", said Jesus, "while you go and proclaim the Kingdom of God."

There was yet another who said, "I will join you, sir, but first give me leave to say good-bye to those at home."

"No one who sets his hand to the plough and looks

---

1 *II Ki* 1:10. Some MSS add: "and said, 'You do not realise the kind of spirit you represent. The Son of Man has not come to destroy men's lives but to preserve them.' "

backward is of any use to the Kingdom of God", Jesus told him.

10.1   Later the Master nominated seventy others, and sent them ahead of him in pairs to every town and village he intended to visit. "The harvest is plentiful", he advised them, "but the labourers are few. Entreat the Harvest-master to furnish adequate labour for his harvest.

"Now go! I am sending you like lambs into the midst of wolves. Carry no purse, no pack, no shoes. Do not stop
5   to speak to anyone on the road. When you are about to enter a house say first, 'Peace be on this house.' If the occupier is peaceable your peace will rest upon him; but if he is otherwise it will revert to you. Stay in the one house, eating and drinking what they provide; for 'the workman is entitled to his wages'.[2] Don't go wandering from house to house. Equally, when you have entered a town where you are welcomed, eat what they offer you and cure the sick people in it, and tell them, 'For you the
10   Kingdom of God is at hand.' But when you enter a town where you are not welcomed, announce in its public highways, 'We will take nothing from your town. We wipe ourselves clean even of the particles of dust that stick to our feet. But you may as well know that the Kingdom of God is at hand.' I tell you, when that day comes it will be more tolerable for Sodom than for that town.

"Woe to you, Chorazin! Woe to you Bethsaida! For if the miracles had been performed in Tyre and Sidon[3] that have been performed in you they would long since have repented in sackcloth and ashes. However, when the Judgement comes it will be more tolerable for Tyre and
15   Sidon than for you. You too, Capernaum! Will you be raised to heaven? No, you will be brought down to hell.

"Whoever gives heed to you gives heed to me, and whoever ignores you ignores me. And whoever ignores me ignores him who sent me."

The seventy returned delighted. "Master", they said, "in your name even the demons obey us."

Jesus told them, "I saw Satan fall like lightning from heaven. I have indeed invested you with power to stamp on snakes and scorpions,[4] and on every minion of the

2 A current proverb.
3 Cities of the Gentiles where Jesus did not preach.
4 *Ps* 91:13.

20 Enemy; and nothing whatever shall harm you. Nevertheless, do not rejoice simply because the spirits are subject to you: rather rejoice that your names are registered in heaven."

Moved to ecstasy by the holy Spirit at that moment, he exclaimed, "I acknowledge unto thee, Father, Lord of heaven and earth, that thou hast hidden these matters from the sage and the prudent and hast disclosed them to babes. Even so, Father, for so it seemed good in thy sight. Everything has been made over to me by my Father, yet no one esteems the Son except the Father, nor the Father except the Son, and he to whom the Son chooses to reveal him."

Then turning to his disciples exclusively he said, "How fortunate are the eyes that see what you see! I can tell you that many prophets and kings have wanted to see what you see, but have not seen it, and to hear what you hear, but have not heard it."

25 Now a certain lawyer rose to test him saying, "Teacher, what am I to do to inherit Eternal Life?"[5]

Jesus replied, "What is stated in the Law? What do you read there?"

He said, "You are to love the Lord your God with your whole heart, and your whole soul, with your whole strength, and with your whole mind, and your neighbour as yourself."[6]

"You have answered correctly", Jesus told him. "Do that, and you will live."

But wanting to make quite certain he said to Jesus, "But what is meant by my 'neighbour'?"

30 In answer Jesus said, "There was a man who went down from Jerusalem to Jericho and was waylaid by robbers,[7] who stripped him and beat him and made off, leaving him half dead. Now a priest happened to be taking that road, and seeing him there gave him a wide berth.[8] It was the same with a Levite who came to the place, and seeing him gave him a wide berth. But a

---

5 The reader should note how *Luke* often brings in incidents and sayings of Jesus out of their true context because he is anxious to include them somewhere. cf *Mt* 22:35–40.
6 *Deut* 6:5 with *Lev* 19:18.
7 Travellers were very liable to be attacked in the wild and precipitous country through which the Jerusalem–Jericho road passed.
8 To avoid the ritual defilement caused by contact with a corpse.

travelling Samaritan came upon him, and moved to pity at seeing him, approached him and bandaged his wounds, pouring on oil and wine. Then laying him across his own beast he conveyed him to a hostelry and

35 took care of him. When departing on the morrow he gave two dinars to the host with the injunction, 'Take care of him well, and I will reimburse you for any additional expense on my return journey.' Which of these three, do you think, acted as neighbour to the man waylaid by robbers?"

"The one who treated him compassionately", he replied.

"Go then", said Jesus, "and act in the same way."

As they journeyed on he entered a certain village,[9] and a woman there called Martha welcomed him to her home. She had a sister called Mary,[10] who seated herself

40 at the Master's feet to listen to his discourse. But Martha was preoccupied with her various duties. Pausing beside him she said, "Master, aren't you concerned that my sister should let me do all the waiting myself? Please tell her to give me a hand."

"Martha, Martha," the Master replied, "you are anxious and distracted about many things, when only one is essential. Mary has selected that important function, and she shall not be deprived of it."

11.1 When he was engaged in prayer at one place, one of his disciples said to him as he finished, "Master, teach us a prayer just as John taught his disciples."[11]

"Whenever you pray," he told them, "say, 'Father, let thy name be sanctified, let thy Kingdom be inaugurated. Give us daily our needful food; and forgive us our sins, for we ourselves forgive everyone obligated to us. And do not bring us into temptation.'

5 "Take any of you who has a friend," he continued, "and you go to him in the middle of the night and say,

---

9 *Luke* does not identify this village with Bethany, close to Jerusalem, or omits the name because the reference to Martha and Mary is premature in his account. cf *Lk* 19:29.

10 Mary of Bethany should not be confused with Mary of Magdala, or either of them with the harlot who anointed the feet of Jesus. Traditions were confused about someone who anointed his head and someone who anointed his feet. Who did what cannot now be established.

11 From here until the end of Chapter X (*Lk* 18), much teaching material is introduced for which the author had not found a suitable place earlier in his book. It brings the narrative to a halt.

'Please lend me three loaves, for a friend of mine has arrived unexpectedly at my place, and I have nothing to offer him.' But his friends answered from within, 'Don't bother me. The door is already bolted, and my family and I are all in bed. I cannot get up and give you anything.' I tell you, if he will not get up to give him anything because he is his friend, yet because of his very importunity he will bestir himself to give him as much as ever he wants. So I say to you, ask and you will be given, seek and you will find, knock and you will obtain entry.

10   For whoever asks receives, the seeker finds, and for the one who knocks the door is opened.

"Take any father among you, if his son asks for fish will he give him a snake instead of fish? Or if he asks for an egg will he give him a scorpion? If you, then, bad as you are, know you must give good gifts to your children, how much more will your heavenly Father give holy Spirit to those who ask him?"

He was once expelling a dumb demon; and when the demon had gone out the dumb man spoke. The crowds
15   were amazed, but some of them said, "It is by Beelzebul the chief of the demons he expels the demons." Others, to tempt him, wanted him to furnish a sign from Heaven. But knowing their thoughts he told them, "Every kingdom divided against itself is brought to ruin, and house topples on house. So if Satan is divided against himself, how will his kingdom endure? For you say it is by Beelzebul I expel the demons. If then it is by Beelzebul I expel the demons, by whom do your children expel
20   them? Therefore they shall be your judges. But if I expel the demons by the finger of God then the Kingdom of God has caught you unawares.

"When the Strong One, fully armed, guards his own place his property is safe. But when a mightier than he comes along and conquers him, he secures the armour on which he relied and distributes his spoils. Whoever is not on my side opposes me, and whoever is not gathering with me scatters. When the foul spirit leaves a man it traverses arid zones seeking relief and finding none.
25   Then it decides, 'I will go back to my old home.' When it gets there it finds it swept clean and tidied up. Then it sets off and procures seven other spirits more noxious than itself, and in they go and live there; so the last state of that man is worse than the first."

As he said this a woman in the crowd raised her voice and called out, "Blessed is the womb that bore you and the breasts you have sucked!"

"No", he said, "Blessed are those who listen to God's Message and obey it."

To the crowd, now grown dense he said, "This present generation is an evil generation. It requires proof, but no
30   proof will be given it except that of Jonah; for just as Jonah was a proof to the Ninevites, so will the Son of Man be to this generation. The Queen of the South will rise up at the Judgement with the men of this generation, and will damn them; for she came from the lower hemisphere to listen to the wisdom of Solomon, and what is of more consequence than Solomon is here.

"No one lights a lamp to put it in a cupboard or under a measuring-bowl, but on a lampstand, so that those who come in may see the light. Your eye is the lamp of your body. When your sight is sound your whole body will be radiant; but when it is bad your whole body will be in
35   gloom. See to it, then, that the light that is in you does not become darkness. So if your whole body is radiant, with no trace of gloom, it will be lit up as completely as when the lamp illuminates you with its light."

When he had spoken thus far, a Pharisee invited him to lunch with him. He accepted, and took his place at table. The Pharisee was rather surprised when he observed that he did not wash first before lunch. But the Master said to him, "You know, you Pharisees are at pains to clean the outside of cups and plates, while your
40   insides are full of rapacity and chicanery. What stupid people you are! Did not he who made the outside also make the inside? Bestow what you have hoarded in charity, and then you will have everything clean right through.

"But woe to you Pharisees! You tithe mint and rue and all kinds of herbs, and pass over justice and the love of God. These are the things you should have attended to without neglecting the others.

"Woe to you Pharisees! You love the chief stall in the synagogues, and salutations in the market-places. Woe to you, because you are like hidden graves, of which those who walk over them are unaware."[12]

---

12 Thus accidentally becoming defiled by contact.

45   One of the lawyers broke in here. "Teacher," he said to him, "by talking like that you are castigating us as well."

"Yes, and woe to you too, you lawyers!" Jesus replied. "You load men with insupportable burdens, but you will not move a finger to move these burdens yourselves. Woe to you, because you build tombs for the prophets your ancestors killed. Thus you both testify to and express your approval of the deeds of your ancestors, because they did the killing while you do the tomb-building. That is why the Wisdom of God states: 'I will send them prophets and envoys, and some of them they will kill, and persecute others, that this generation may

50   be answerable for the blood of all the prophets which has been shed since the foundation of the world, from the blood of Abel to the blood of Zechariah who perished between the altar and the house.'[13] Yes, I tell you, this generation shall be answerable for it.

"Woe to you lawyers! You have taken away the key of knowledge. You will not enter yourselves, and you prevent others entering."

As he was about to leave, the scribes and Pharisees badgered and plied him with questions on many issues, lying in wait to pounce on something he might say.

12.1   Meanwhile as the crowd massed in its thousands, so that they trod on one another, he had this to say to his disciples first of all, "Be on your guard against the leaven of the Pharisees, namely their hypocrisy; for there is nothing covered up that shall not be revealed, or secret that shall not be known. Whatever you may say under the cloak of darkness will be heard in broad daylight, and whatever you may whisper behind closed doors will be shouted from the housetops.

"To you my friends I say, don't be afraid of those who

5   can do no more than kill the body. If you would know whom to fear, fear him who after killing can cast into Gehenna. Are not five sparrows sold for two assars?[14] Yet not one of them escapes God's memory. The very hairs of your head are all counted. You have nothing to fear. You are of more consequence than many sparrows.

"I tell you, whoever identifies himself with me before men, the Son of Man will also identify himself with him

10   before God's angels. But whoever repudiates me before

13 See note to *Mt* 24:29–36 (*Mt* Bk V n 36).
14 Assar, a small coin serving as a penny.

men will be repudiated before God's angels. Whoever says a word against the Son of Man will be forgiven, but slander of the holy Spirit will not be forgiven. And when they bring you before synagogues, rulers and authorities, do not concern yourselves with the manner of your defence, or what you are to say; for the holy Spirit will instruct you at the time what you should say."

Here one of the crowd called out to him, "Teacher, tell my brother he must share our inheritance with me."

"Man", he replied, "who constituted me a judge or arbitrator over you?"

15   Then he addressed them all. "Be sure you guard yourselves from greed of every kind, because one's life is not assured by the extent of what one possesses."

He told a story to explain this to them. "A certain rich man's lands were very productive. So he debated with himself, 'What am I going to do, with insufficient space to store my crops? I have it,' he said, 'I will pull down my barns and build larger ones. There I can store my grain and all other fruits of my good fortune. Then I can say to my soul, Soul, you have an ample fortune laid by for many a year. Now take your ease, eat, drink, and enjoy

20   yourself.' But God said to him, 'You foolish fellow, this very night your soul will be demanded from you. Whose, then, will be all you have accumulated?' That is the position of the man who hoards for himself but fails to become rich where God is concerned."

Then he spoke directly to his disciples. "That is why I tell you, do not vex your souls about what you are to eat, nor how your bodies are to be clothed; for the soul is more important than food, and the body than clothing. Look at the crows. They neither sow nor reap: they have neither storehouse nor barn. Yet God feeds them. Of

25   how much greater consequence are you than birds? And which of you by mental effort can add an ell to his height? If you cannot do what is least, why worry about the rest? Study the wild irises, how they shoot up. They neither toil nor spin. Yet I tell you that not even Solomon in full regalia was arrayed like one of these. If God thus attires the wild plant that blooms to-day and to-morrow is thrown into the oven, shall he not much more clothe you, you feeble in faith? So do not be concerned with what you are to eat and drink, or get yourselves in a

30   state, for with all these matters the nations of the world

concern themselves. Your Father knows perfectly well that you need them. Concern yourselves with his Kingdom, and all these things will be added to you.

"Never fear, little flock. Your Father is pleased to give you the Kingdom. Sell your possessions and bestow the proceeds in charity. Provide yourselves with wallets that never wear out, treasure never failing in heaven, where the thief never comes nor locust-grub ruins; for 'where your hoard is your heart is.'

35 "Let your belts be on and your lamps lit, and you yourselves like men awaiting their master's return from his wedding; so that when he arrives and knocks they may open the door to him immediately. Fortunate are those servants whom their master finds on the alert when he arrives. I tell you for a fact, he will put on an apron, seat them at table, and come forward himself to wait on them. And whether it is in the second watch or the third that he comes, fortunate are they. But you can appreciate this, if the householder had known the time the thief would come, he would have been on the alert

40 and not allowed his house to be broken into. So be ready yourselves, for the Son of Man will come when you least expect him."

Then Peter asked, "Master, are you using this illustration for our benefit, or does it apply to everybody?"

The Master replied, "Who can be meant by the faithful and prudent steward whom his master has put in charge of his staff to distribute their rations regularly? Fortunate is that servant whom his master on arrival finds so doing! I tell you for a fact, he will put him on charge of all his

45 possessions however, that servant should say to himself, 'My master is postponing coming', and begins to beat the men and women servants, and to eat and drink and get drunk, the master of that servant will turn up one day when least expected, at a time he does not dream of, and surprise him suddenly, and treat him as a disloyal person. That servant who knew his master's wishes will be flogged heavily, while the servant who was ignorant, but acted in a way that deserved a beating, will be flogged lightly. From him to whom much is given much is expected, and from him to whom much is entrusted much more is required.[15]

15 This group of sayings is directed to the time when many had given up hope of a Second Advent and were behaving badly.

"I have come to start a fire on earth, and how I wish it
50   were already blazing! I have an immersion to undergo,
and how anxious I am to get it over! You think I have
come to give the earth peace. That is not so, I tell you. It is
dissension I bring; for from now on five people in one
house will be at odds, three ranged against two, and two
against three, father opposed to son, and son to father,
mother against daughter, and daughter against mother,
mother-in-law   against   her   daughter-in-law,   and
daughter-in-law against her mother-in-law."[16]

Then he spoke to the crowds. "When you see it
clouding over from the west you say at once, 'There's
55   rain on the way.' And so it proves. And when the south
wind blows you say, 'There's a hot spell coming.' And so
it proves. Well, you forecasters, you can assess the
aspects of earth and sky, how is it that you fail to assess
the significance of the time?

"Why do you not judge what is the best course for
yourselves? Thus when you go with your opponent
before the magistrate, you should be at pains while on
the way to get free of his clutches, in case he hauls you
before the judge, and the judge hands you over to the
debt-collector, and the debt-collector throws you into
jail. I tell you, you won't get out again until you have
paid up the very last lepton."[17]

13.1   At this juncture some people arrived to inform him
about the Galileans whose blood Pilate had mingled with
that of their sacrifices.[18]

"Do you imagine", he replied, "that these Galileans
were worse sinners than all the other Galileans because
they suffered in this way? That is not so, I tell you. But
unless you repent you will all similarly perish. Or those
eighteen who were killed when the tower at Siloam fell
on them,[19] do you imagine that they deserved this fate
5   more than all the other inhabitants of Jerusalem? That is
not so, I tell you, but unless you repent you will all perish
as they did."

Then he told this story. "A man had a fig tree growing

16 The Messiah was expected to bring peace on earth, but the delayed coming
of the Kingdom of God had bred strife and dissension among the followers
of Jesus at an early date.
17 The term 'cent' can be substituted.
18 See note to *Mk* 15:7, n 131.
19 This incident is not recorded by Jósephus.

in his vineyard, and he came in quest of fruit on it, but
found none. 'For three years now,' he told the gardener,
'I have come in quest of fruit on this fig tree, but I have
never found any. Chop it down. Why should it take up
ground-space?' 'Let it be for this year, sir,' replied the
gardener, 'to give me a chance to dig round it and
manure it. If it should bear fruit next year – well, you can
still chop it down if it doesn't.'"

10   When he was teaching in one of the synagogues on the
sabbath there was a woman there who had been possessed by a spirit of infirmity for eighteen years. She was
bent double, and without power to draw herself upright.
On seeing her, Jesus called her to him and said to her,
"Madam, you are freed from your infirmity", and laid
his hand on her. At once she became erect, and praised
God.

Displeased that Jesus cured on the sabbath, the
president of the synagogue said to the congregation,
"There are six days set aside for work, so come and be
cured on those, but not on the sabbath day."

15   "You hypocrites!" Jesus said to him. "Does not each of
you on the sabbath loose his ox or his ass from its stall
and lead it away to drink? But this woman, apparently,
because she is a daughter of Abraham, whom Satan has
bound all these eighteen years, ought not to be loosed
from her bonds on the sabbath day?"

When he put it this way all who opposed him were
heartily ashamed, and the whole congregation rejoiced
at his remarkable accomplishments. He said therefore,
"How shall I represent the Kingdom of God, and to what
shall I compare it? It is like a grain of mustard-seed which
a man took and sowed it in his garden. There it grew and
became a tree, and the birds of the air nested in its
branches."

20   Again he said, "To what shall I compare the Kingdom
of God? It is like leaven, which a woman took and buried
in three measures of flour until the whole was
leavened."

Thus, teaching as he travelled, Jesus passed through
town after town and village after village, ever proceeding
steadily towards Jerusalem.

One man said to him, "Sir, will there be only a few
saved?"

"Strive to enter by the narrow gate", Jesus told them.

"Many, I tell you, will attempt to enter but will not
25   succeed. Once the master of the house has got up and
closed the door, you will be left outside banging at the
door crying, 'Sir, let us in!' But he will reply, 'I'm sorry,
but you are total strangers to me.' Then you will protest,
'We have eaten and drunk with you, and you have
taught in our streets.' But he will repeat, 'You are
complete strangers to me. Be off, you rogues!' There will
be howling and grinding of teeth then, when you see
Abraham, Isaac and Jacob, and all the prophets in the
30   Kingdom of God, though some who are in the lowliest
place will be foremost and some of the foremost will be
lowest."

At this juncture some Pharisees came to warn him,
"Leave here and get away, for Herod[20] is out to kill you."

"Go and tell that fox", he replied, "I propose to expel
demons and perform cures to-day and to-morrow, and
conclude my work on the third day. But it is essential that
I continue to-day, to-morrow, and the next day, for it will
never do for a prophet to perish outside Jerusalem.

"Jerusalem, Jerusalem, slayer of prophets and stoner
of those sent to her! How often would I have gathered
your children together like a bird her brood 'neath her
35   wings! But you would not have it. Your house is now left
to yourselves; for you will not see me again, I tell you,
until you say, 'Blessed is he who comes in the name of
the Lord.' "[21]

Chapter IX

14.1   One sabbath when Jesus went to dine at the house of
one of the leading Pharisees the company watched him
intently. Just in front of him was a man suffering from
dropsy. So Jesus asked the lawyers and Pharisees
present, "Do you permit curing on the sabbath, or not?"

They made no response. So he cured the man and
5   dismissed him. Then he said to them, "Should an ass or
ox fall into a cistern,[1] which one of you will not at once
extricate it on the sabbath day?" They were quite unable

---

20 Herod Antipas, ruler of Galilee.
21 *Ps* 118:26. See *Mt* 23:37–39, above p 109.

1 The illustration is purposely chosen to link up with the nature of dropsy, a
gathering of water fluid.

to dispute this.

Then he pointed a moral for the company in general, having noted how they chose the best places at table. "When you are invited by someone to a wedding," he told them, "don't take the best seat, in case the host has invited a more esteemed guest than yourself, and having asked both you and him, he has to come to you and say, 'Would you mind giving up this place?' Then, to your

10   discomfort, you will have to move lower down. Instead, when you are invited, occupy a low place; so that when your host comes he may say to you, 'Do go up higher, friend.' That will confer a distinction on you in the eyes of your fellow-guests. For everyone who elevates himself will be abased, while he who abases himself will be elevated."

Then he addressed himself to his host. "When you give a luncheon or dinner, do not ask either your friends, your brothers, your relations, or your rich neighbours, in case they too invite you back, and you get your favour returned. Rather, when you give a reception, invite the poor, the crippled, the lame, and the blind. Then you will be blessed, because they cannot return your favour, and you will be repaid at the resurrection of the righteous."

15   On hearing this one of the guests said to him, "He will be a most fortunate man who banquets in the Kingdom of God."

"There was once a man", Jesus told him, "who gave a great banquet, and invited many people. At the time fixed for the banquet he dispatched his servant to the guests with the message, 'Your presence is requested, as all preparations are complete.' But they all excused themselves. 'I have bought a piece of land,' the first replied, 'and it is essential that I should inspect it. I do beg you to excuse me.' Another said, 'I have bought five yoke of oxen, and I am about to try them out. I do beg you

20   to excuse me.' Another said, 'I have just got married, so am unable to come.' So the servant presented himself and reported all this to his master. Then the master of the house was furious, and said to his servant, 'Go out at once into the streets and lanes of the town, and bring in the poor, the crippled, the blind, and the lame.' The servant reported, 'Master, your instructions have been followed, and there is still room.' So the master told his

servant, 'Go out into the highways and suburbs, and compel the people to come, that my house may be filled. I tell you, not a man of those who were invited will even taste my banquet.' "

25   Now there was a vast crowd travelling along with him, and turning to them he said, "If anyone comes to me and does not hate his father and mother, wife and children, brothers and sisters, yes and himself as well, he cannot be a disciple of mine. Anyone who does not shoulder his own cross and follow me cannot be a disciple of mine. For which of you desiring to build a tower does not sit down first and work out the cost to make sure he has enough to complete it, in case having laid the foundations and being powerless to complete the work, all the

30   onlookers should jeer at him and say, 'He started to build, but was powerless to complete'? Or what king on his way to engage in battle with another king does not sit down first and take counsel, whether with a force of ten thousand it is practicable to encounter one who is advancing against him with twenty thousand? Or whether, if it is not, while he is still at a distance, he should send an embassy to sue for peace? So then, whoever of you does not turn his back on all he calls his own cannot be a disciple of mine. Salt is indeed good, but if the salt becomes insipid, how may its tang be restored? As soil or manure it is useless. They can only throw it outside. Let him who can catch my meaning do so."

15.1   The tax-collectors and sinners habitually drew near to listen to him. This led the Pharisees and scribes to complain, "He entertains sinners and eats with them."

So Jesus used this illustration to them. "Which of you men with a hundred sheep, if he loses one of them, will not leave the ninety-nine in the open and go after the lost

5   one until he finds it? And when he does find it, will he not joyfully lay it across his shoulders, and reaching home call together his friends and neighbours crying, 'Congratulate me, I have found my lost sheep'? Just so, I tell you, there will be more joy in heaven over one repentant sinner than over ninety-nine righteous people who have no need of repentance. Or which of you women with ten drachmas, if she loses a single drachma,[2] will not light a lamp and search diligently till

---

2 A small Greek silver coin.

she finds it? And when she does find it, will she not call together her friends and neighbours crying, 'Congratu-
10 late me, I have found my lost drachma'? Just so, I tell you, there will be joy in the presence of God's angels over one repentant sinner.

"There was once a man who had two sons", he continued. "The younger of them said to his father, 'Father, please give me the share of your fortune that will come to me.' So he divided his estate between them.

"Some time afterwards the younger son sold up and travelled to a distant land, and there dissipated his fortune in loose living. When he had run through the lot a severe famine afflicted that country, and he began to
15 feel the pinch. So he took service with a citizen of that country, who gave him a job on his farm feeding swine; and he longed to cram himself with the pods the pigs were eating, but no one gave him any. Then it came over him, 'There are all those employees of my father's with more food than they can possibly eat, while here I am starving to death. I will get up and go to my father and tell him, "Father, I have sinned against Heaven and in your sight, and no longer deserve to be called your son.
20 Treat me as one of your employees."' So he got up and went to his father.

"But while he was still a good way off his father saw him, and yearning with pity ran and threw himself on his neck and kissed him. Then the son said to him, 'Father, I have sinned against Heaven and in your sight, and no longer deserve to be called your son . . .'

"But his father called to his servants, 'Hurry! Fetch my best robe and put it on him, and give him a ring for his hand, and shoes for his feet. Have the fattened calf slaughtered, and let us eat it up and enjoy ourselves; for this son of mine was dead and is alive again, he was lost and is found.' So they set about merry-making.
25 "Now his elder brother was in the field at the time; and as he approached the house on his way back he heard music and dancing, and called to one of the lads to inquire what it was all about. 'Your brother has come', he told him, 'and your father has slaughtered the fattened calf, because he has got him home safe and sound.' He was so angry he would not go in. His father came out to beseech him, but he answered, 'Here have I served you all these years and never once disobeyed your orders,

and you have never given me even a kid to enjoy myself
30   with my friends. But no sooner does this son of yours
come, having squandered your estate with harlots, than
you slaughter the fattened calf for him.'

" 'But son,' he said to him, 'you are constantly with
me, and all that I have is yours. Surely we should make
merry and rejoice because this brother of yours was dead
and is alive again, and was lost and is found?' "

16.1   Jesus also told his disciples, "There was once a
wealthy man who had an agent who was accused to him
of dissipating his resources. So he sent for him and said
to him, 'What is all this I hear about you? Give in the
account of your management, for it is out of the question
to keep you on as agent.'

" 'Whatever am I going to do', the agent said to
himself, 'now that my master is discharging me from my
position? I am quite unfit for manual labour, and I am
ashamed to beg. I know what I'll do, so that when I am
deprived of the management the tenants will welcome
me to their homes.'

5   "So he sent for every single one of those who stood in
his master's debt.

" 'How much do you owe my master?' he asked the
first.

" 'A hundred baths[3] of oil,' he replied.

" 'Take the contract,' he told him, 'and sit down
quickly and substitute fifty.'

" 'And how much do you owe?' he asked another.

" 'A hundred kors[4] of wheat,' he replied.

" 'Take the contract and substitute eighty,' he told
him.

"The master applauded the unsatisfactory agent for
his smartness; for the children of this world[5] in their
generation are smarter than the children of Light.[6] So
secure yourselves friends, I tell you, independent of the
false mammon,[7] so that when this fails[8] they will
welcome you to the Eternal Abodes.

10   "He who is reliable with a little is equally reliable with
a great deal. But he who is unsatisfactory in minor

---

3 One *bath* equals about nine gallons.
4 One *kor* equals about ten bushels.
5 People in general, not the Elect.
6 See p 65 n 25.
7 Delusive material wealth.
8 Or "when you quit (this life)", an alternative reading.

matters is unsatisfactory in major ones. If, therefore, you have not proved reliable with the false mammon, who will entrust you with the true? And if you have not proved reliable with what is another's who will give you what is your own? No man-servant can serve two masters. Either he will detest the one and love the other, or he will be devoted to the one and despise the other. You cannot serve both God and mammon."

15   Listening to all this, the Pharisees being avaricious sneered at him. "You are the people who vindicate yourselves in the sight of men," Jesus told them, "but God knows your hearts. For what rates high with men is an abomination in the sight of God. Until John's time there were the Law and the prophets; but since then the Kingdom of God is proclaimed and everyone forces his way into it. Yet it is easier for heaven and earth to pass away than for a single item of the Law to lapse.

"Everyone who divorces his wife and marries another commits adultery, and whoever marries a divorced woman commits adultery.

20   "There was once a rich man, who entertained lavishly every day robed in purple and fine linen. There was also a beggar named Lazarus, who was covered with ulcers, laid at his door and longing to make a meal of the scraps from the rich man's table. Instead of that the dogs came and licked his sores.

"In due course the beggar died and was borne by the angels to the lap of Abraham.[9] The rich man also died and was buried. And in Hades, being in torment, he raised his eyes and from a distance saw Abraham with Lazarus in his lap, and cried out, 'Father Abraham, take pity on me and send Lazarus to dip the tip of his finger in water and cool my tongue, for I am suffering agonies in this flame.'

25   "'My child,' replied Abraham, 'recall that you received your good fortune during your lifetime, while Lazarus for his part had evil fortune. But here and now he is comforted while you suffer agonies. And quite apart from that a huge chasm yawns between us and all of you, which prevents those who may wish to do so from crossing to you from this side, or crossing from your side to us.'

9 ie to Paradise.

" 'I beg you then, father,' he said, 'to send him to my father's house – for I have five[10] brothers – that he may give them solemn warning, in case they too should come to this place of torment.'

" 'They have Moses and the prophets,' said Abraham. 'Let them heed them.'

30   " 'Oh no, Father Abraham,' he replied. 'But if someone should come to them from the dead they will repent.'

" 'If they do not heed Moses and the prophets,' he told him, 'neither will they be convinced if someone should rise from the dead.' ' '

17.1   Then he said to his disciples, "Causes of stumbling are bound to come, yet woe to him by whom they come. It would be better for him to have an upper millstone hung round his neck and to be flung into the sea than to upset one of these little ones. Be on your guard. If your brother sins, admonish him; and if he is contrite, forgive him. Even if he wrongs you seven times in a day, and seven times makes amends to you and says, 'I'm sorry', forgive him."

5   "Give us faith", said the envoys to the Master.

"If you have faith no bigger than a grain of mustard-seed," the Master told them, "you could say to this mulberry tree, 'Be uprooted and replanted in the sea!' and it would obey you.

"Which of you with a man doing the ploughing or herding says to him when he returns from the field, 'Come along and sit down'? Doesn't he say to him instead, 'Get my dinner ready and tidy yourself up, and wait on me until I have eaten and drunk. You can eat and drink yourself later'? Is he grateful to his servant for

10   carrying out his orders? So with you, when you have carried out all your instructions, say, 'We are mere menials. We have simply done our duty.' "

Chapter X

In the course of his journey to Jerusalem Jesus had to pass through Samaria and Galilee.[1] As he entered one

---

10 "Five" perhaps because of the Five Books of Moses.

1 Geographically this reference to Galilee is out of place, since travelling south Jesus had already passed through Samaria. But the author's Markan source had located the healing of a leper in Galilee (*Mk* 1:44).

village he was met by ten men who were lepers. They stood at a distance and hailed him, "Your lordship Jesus, take pity on us!"

When he saw their condition he said to them, "Go and show yourselves to the priests."[2] And as they went on their way they were cleansed.

15   One of them, finding himself cured, turned back praising God aloud, and fell on his face at Jesus's feet thanking him; and he was a Samaritan.

"Surely there were ten cleansed", Jesus commented. "Where are the other nine? Have none of them come back to give God praise except this foreigner? Rise up and go your way", he told him. "Your faith has saved you."

20   Now being asked by the Pharisees when the Kingdom of God would be manifested, he replied, "The Kingdom of God will not come by keeping a sharp look-out for it. Neither is it going to be said, 'Here it is!' or 'There it is!' – for the Kingdom of God is right beside you."

To his disciples he said, "The time will come when you will passionately long to see a single day of the Era of the Son of Man, and will not see it. They will tell you, 'There he is!' or 'Here he is!' But do not stir or hurry off; for as the lightning flashes across the sky so will be the Son of Man when his day comes. First, however, he must suffer

25 greatly and be rejected by this generation.

"And just as it was in Noah's time, so will it be in the time of the Son of Man. They ate, they drank, they married and were given in marriage, until the day Noah entered the Ark, and the deluge came and destroyed them all. Similarly, just as it was in Lot's time: they ate, they drank, they bought and sold, planted and built. But on the very day when Lot left Sodom it rained fire and

30 sulphur from heaven and destroyed them all. So will it be on the day the Son of Man is revealed.

"On that day let no one who is on the housetop with his things in his house go down to fetch anything, and let no one who is in the field turn to glance back. Remember Lot's wife. Whoever attempts to preserve his life will lose it, and whoever loses it will assure its survival. I tell you, there will be two men in one bed that night; the one will

35 be taken and the other left behind. There will be two

2 See *Lev* 14:2.

women together grinding; the one will be taken and the other left behind."

"Where, Master?" they asked him.

"Where the carcase is the vultures will flock", he replied.

18.1   Then he told a story to illustrate how essential it was to be constant in prayer and not to slacken. "There was once a judge in a certain town, who neither revered God nor respected man. And there was a widow in the same town who was always coming before him crying, 'Protect me from my persecutor!' For some time he would not, but later he said to himself, 'Though I neither revere
5   God nor respect man, yet because this widow keeps pestering me I will give her protection, or eventually with her coming she will completely wear me out.'

"Listen", said the Master, "to what this false judge says. And shall not God give satisfaction to his Elect, who cry to him day and night? Will he forbear in their case? I tell you he will give them satisfaction speedily. Nevertheless, when the Son of Man comes will he find faith on earth?"

He also told the following story to some who were convinced of their own righteousness and were contemptuous of others.

10   "Two men went up to the Temple to pray. One was a Pharisee and the other a tax-collector. The Pharisee stood and prayed for his own gratification to this effect, 'I give thee thanks, O God, that I am not like the generality of men, grasping, dishonest, adulterers, or even like this tax-collector here. I fast twice a week,[3] I pay tithe on all my increase.'[4] But the tax-collector stood at a distance, unwilling even to raise his eyes to heaven, and beat his breast saying, 'O God, be reconciled to me a sinner!' I tell you this man went down to his house exonerated rather than the other. For everyone who exalts himself shall be abased, while he who abases himself will be exalted."

15   When they also brought their infants to him to fondle, the disciples, observing this, reproved them. But Jesus summoned them and said, "Let the little children come to me, do not prevent them; for the Kingdom of God is

---

3 On Mondays and Thursdays.

4 It is believed that the Pharisees came into existence originally as an association pledged to separate the tithes required by the Mosaic Law.

composed of such as they. I tell you for a fact, whoever does not accept the Kingdom of God like a little child will never enter it."

One of the rulers then asked him, "Good Teacher, what must I do to inherit Eternal Life?"[5]

"Why do you call me good?" said Jesus. "There is
20   none good but One, God himself. You know the commandments: 'Do not commit adultery, do not murder, do not steal, do not bear false witness, honour your father and mother.'"

"I have kept all these from my youth", he replied.

When Jesus heard this he told him, "That leaves only one thing more for you to do: sell everything you possess and distribute the proceeds to the poor and you will have treasure in heaven. Then come and join me."

He became very dejected at hearing this, for he was extremely wealthy.

When Jesus saw this he said, "What a hard struggle it
25   is for those with means to get into the Kingdom of God! It is easier for a camel to pass through the eye of a needle than for a rich man to enter the Kingdom of God."

Those who were listening said, "Who then can be saved?"

"What is impossible to man is possible to God", he replied.

"Here are we", said Peter, "we have left all we possess to follow you."

"I tell you for a fact", he said to them, "there is no one who has left house, or wife, or brothers, or parents, or
30   children, for the sake of the Kingdom of God, who will not receive many times more in the present time and Eternal Life in the Age to Come."

Getting the twelve together, he said to them, "Look, we are now going up to Jerusalem, and all those things which have been written by the prophets of the Son of Man will have their fulfilment; for he will be handed over to the Gentiles, mocked, ill-used and spat upon, and when they have flogged him they will kill him; but the third day he will be raised up."

But they understood nothing of this. The matter was hidden from them, and they failed to grasp the purport of what was said.

---

5 See above p 30 n 68 (*Mk* 10:17).

35   Now as Jesus approached Jericho a certain blind man sat by the roadside begging. Hearing the crowd go by he asked them what was going on. They told him that Jesus the Nazarene was passing. So he cried out, "Jesus, Son of David, pity me!"

Those who were in front insisted that he be silent.[6] But he only cried out the more, "Son of David, pity me!"

40   Jesus stood still and ordered him to be brought to him. When he had approached he asked him, "What can I do for you?"

"Sir," he said, "I want to see again."

"Then regain your sight,"[7] Jesus told him. "Your faith has saved you."

Instantly he recovered his sight and followed him praising God. And all the people who saw it extolled God.

19.1   On entering the town Jesus passed through Jericho. Now there was a man there called Zacchaeus, who was the chief tax-collector and extremely well off. He was most anxious to catch a glimpse of Jesus; but being of small stature he could not manage it on account of the crowd. So running on ahead he clambered up a sycamore-fig tree so that he could see Jesus; for he was bound to pass that way.

5   As Jesus reached the spot he looked up and said to him, "Hurry up and come down, Zacchaeus. I have to stay at your house to-day."

Descending hastily he welcomed Jesus with joy; but all the onlookers murmured, "He's gone to be the guest of a man well-known to be a sinner."

But standing there Zacchaeus told the Master, "Half of my possessions, sir, I will give to the poor, and if I have extorted anything from anyone I will repay four times as much."

"Salvation has come to this house to-day," Jesus said

---

6 They were concerned to silence the man because he was in fact acclaiming Jesus as king of the Jews of the line of David, in violation of Caesar's sovereignty over Judea at this time. Such dangerous language could condemn Jesus to death for high treason against Rome. Jesus knew this, and refused to rebuke the man. Consequently the crowd was now expecting the Kingdom of God (the Messianic Age) to commence.

7 The Jewish historian Josephus had claimed that the Roman emperor Vespasian was the Messiah, because he had been proclaimed emperor on Jewish soil (*Jewish War* vi.312–314). Consistent with this, Vespasian healed a blind man and a lame one (Suet. *Vespasian* vii, Tacit. *History*, Bk iv:81).

10   to him, "since here too is a son of Abraham. For the Son of Man came to seek and to save what was lost."

To everything they had already heard Jesus added this simile because of his proximity to Jerusalem, and because they had the idea that the Kingdom of God would be instituted forthwith.[8] So he said, "There was a certain exalted personage, who set off for a distant land to obtain for himself a crown, and return. Calling ten of his servants he gave them ten minas, and said to them, 'Look after my interests until I return.'

"But his countrymen hated him, and sent a deputation after him to say, 'We do not want this man to reign over us.'[9]

15   "When he had returned, having gained the crown, he directed that those servants to whom he had given the money should be summoned to his presence that he might learn the result of their transactions. Then came the first and said, 'Sir, your mina has earned ten minas.'

"'Fine, you excellent servant,' he replied. 'Since you have proved trustworthy in a small matter, take charge of ten cities.'

"Then came the second and said, 'Your mina, sir, has made five minas.' He told him similarly, 'You take charge of five cities.'

20   "Then another came and said, 'Sir, here is your mina, which I have kept tucked away in a handkerchief. I was afraid of you, because you are a harsh man, lifting what you never laid down, and reaping where you never sowed.'

"'I will convict you out of your own mouth, you rascally servant,' he exclaimed. 'You knew I was a harsh man, lifting what I never laid down, and reaping what I never sowed. Why, then, did you not invest my money, so that when I came I could get it back with interest?' Then he said to his henchmen, 'Take the mina from him and give it to the one with ten minas.'

25   "'But sir,' they said, 'he already has ten minas.'

"'I tell you,' he replied, 'that to everyone who has, more shall be given; but from him who has not, even

---

8 See n 6 above.

9 *Lk*'s version of the story told in *Mt* 25:14–30 seems to have been influenced by the history of Archelaus, Herod the Great's successor, who went to Rome to be confirmed in the kingship by Augustus. His people also sent a deputation to oppose him (Jos. *Jewish War*, II.vi.:80–95).

what he has shall be taken away. As for these enemies of mine, who did not want me to reign over them, bring them here and slay them in my presence.' "

Having told this story Jesus resumed his progress, ascending towards Jerusalem.[10]

As he approached Bethphage and Bethany towards the hill called the Mount of Olives he dispatched two of
30 his disciples saying, "Go to the village ahead of you, and as you enter it you will find a colt tethered which no one has ridden previously. Untie him and lead him here. And if anyone says to you, 'Why are you untying him?' just say, 'The Master needs him.' "

Going off, those who had been sent found it turn out exactly as they had been told. As they were untying the colt his owners said to them, "Why are you untying the
35 colt?" And they replied, "The Master needs him." So they brought the colt to Jesus, and throwing their cloaks across its back mounted Jesus on it, and as he moved off they spread their cloaks on the road.

When Jesus reached the descent of the Mount of Olives the whole company of his disciples broke into joyful cries of praise to God for all the wonders they had witnessed, saying,

"Blessed be the king, who comes in the name of the Lord. Peace be in heaven, and glory be on high."[11]

Some of the Pharisees in the crowd said to him, "Teacher, reprimand your disciples."
40 But he answered, "I tell you, if they are silent the stones will cry out."

Viewing the city as he approached, Jesus wept over it, saying, "Oh, if only you realised at this moment what is for your welfare! But, alas, it is concealed from your sight. For a time is coming for you when your enemies will surround you with palisades, encircle and hem you in on all sides, and stamp you into the dust and your children with you.[12] They will not leave in you one stone upon another, because you failed to realise the time of your visitation."

10 The road ascends very steeply from Jericho, which lies about 1,200 ft below sea-level, to Jerusalem, 2,900 ft above sea level.
11 *Lk* has changed the wording here, apparently to relate it to the song of the heavenly host at the Nativity. cf above p 133.
12 The words here attributed to Jesus reflect the circumstances of the siege and capture of Jerusalem as related by Josephus.

45   Then he entered the Temple, and began to eject those who sold there, telling them, "It is stated, 'My house shall be called a house of prayer',[13] but you have made it a robbers' den."[14]

He taught daily in the Temple, while the head priests and scribes sought to destroy him, and even the leaders of the people. But they could not determine how to effect this because the people stuck close to him to listen to him.

Chapter XI

20.1   One day while Jesus was teaching in the Temple and proclaiming the News, the head priests and scribes accompanied by the elders came up to him and said, "Tell us by what authority you are acting in this way, and who gave you this authority?"

He replied, "I too have something to ask you. Will you tell me, was John's right of immersion of divine or human inspiration?"[1]

5   They discussed the matter among themselves to the effect that, "If we say, 'of divine inspiration', he will say, 'Why then did you not believe him?' But if we say, 'of human inspiration', all the people will stone us, for they are convinced that John was a prophet."[2] So they answered that they did not know its source.

So Jesus said to them, "Neither will I tell you what authority I have for acting as I do."

He then told the following story.[3] "A man planted a vineyard and let it out to cultivators, and went abroad for

10   a time. But when the vintage season came he dispatched a servant to the cultivators for them to give him his share of the vineyard's produce. But the cultivators thrashed him and sent him away empty-handed. The owner then sent another servant; but they thrashed him as well, and after treating him shamefully sent him away. He sent yet a third, and they went so far as to wound this one, and

---

13 *Isa* 61:7.
14 *Jer* 7:11.

1 Lit "Of Heaven or of men."
2 The people believed that the defeat of Herod Antipas by the Nabataeans was a divine punishment for his execution of the Baptist (Jos. *Antiq.* XVIII.119).
3 Perhaps inspired by *Isa* 5:1–9.

threw him out. Then the owner of the vineyard said, 'What am I to do? I will send my dear son. Surely they will respect him.' But when the cultivators saw him they argued to themselves, 'Here is the heir. Let us kill him,
15   that the inheritance may be ours.' So they threw him outside the vineyard and killed him. What then will the owner of the vineyard do to them? He will come and destroy those cultivators and give the vineyard to others."

When they heard this they said, "God forbid!"

Looking straight at them he inquired, "What then does this scripture mean, 'The stone which the builders rejected has become the coping stone'?[4] Whoever falls on that stone will be crushed, while whoever it falls upon will be pulverised."

The scribes and head priests dearly wished they could lay hands on him at that moment, but they were afraid of the people; for they knew perfectly well that this illustra-
20   tion was directed at them. Keeping him under close observation, however, they planted spies masquerading as pious persons to catch him out on some expression of his, so that they could obtain grounds for handing him over to the secular power and the governor's authority. These men questioned him, "Teacher", they said, "we are aware that you speak and teach with complete candour, and make no personal distinctions, but teach the way of God in sincerity. Is it permissible or not to pay tribute to Caesar?"[5]

Detecting their trickery, he said to them, "Show me a dinar.[6] Whose portrait and inscription does it bear?"

"Caesar's", they answered.
25   "In that case render to Caesar what is Caesar's and to God what is God's."[7]

So they failed to catch him out before the people on this point, and being amazed at his reply they were silent.

Then some of the Sadducees came to him, those who say there is no resurrection, and questioned him as

---

4 *Ps* 118:22.
5 The Jewish Zealots strongly opposed on religious grounds, as well as patriotic, the institution by the Romans of the periodic tribute arrived at by census-taking. See Josephus.
6 Like the Zealots Jesus would not handle the heathen coin himself.
7 The Zealot slogan was 'No ruler but God' (see Jos. *Antiq*.XVIII.23).

follows. "Teacher, Moses laid down for us that should a man's married brother die childless he should marry his brother's wife so as to continue his brother's line.[8] Now there were seven brothers. The first took a wife and died 30 childless, then the second and the third, and similarly all seven married her, but died and left no children. Finally the woman herself died. In the resurrection, then, of which of them will the woman be the wife, for all seven were married to her?"

Jesus answered, "The children of this world marry and 35 are given in marriage, but those who are deemed worthy to attain That World[9] and the resurrection of the dead neither marry nor are given in marriage. Neither are they any longer subject to death: they are equal to the angels and are sons of God, having become so by resurrection. But that the dead will be raised Moses indicates quite clearly at the bush, where he calls the Lord 'the God of Abraham, of Isaac, and of Jacob'.[10] He is not God of the dead, but of the living; for all are alive to God."[11]

Some of the scribes then remarked,[12] "Teacher, you 40 have put that very well." They did not venture to ask him anything further.

But he said to them, "Why is the Messiah said to be the son of David? For David himself says in the Book of Psalms, 'The Lord said to my lord, Sit at my right hand until I make your enemies your footstool.' Since David calls him lord, how can he be his son?"[13]

45 Then in the hearing of all the people he said to his disciples, "Beware of those scribes who like to parade in long robes, and love to be saluted in the markets, to have the chief stalls in the synagogues, and the best places at the festal banquets. They are the people who prey on widows, and for pretense pray at great length. There is a still longer sentence in store for them."

21.1 Glancing up he saw the rich throwing their gifts into the treasury-chests.[14] He also saw one very poor widow

---

8 *Deut* 25:5–6.
9 The coming Messianic Age.
10 *Exod* 3:2–6.
11 The comment may be a scribe's note. cf *Rom* 6:15.
12 These would be Pharisees who believed in resurrection.
13 *Ps* 110:7. Since the Book of Psalms stands in the name of David, it is assumed that he was the speaker. But many of the Psalms were written by others, and "my lord" could refer to David or Solomon.
14 See above p 37, n 95.

throw in two lepta, and said, "I tell you truly, that poor widow has thrown in more than all the others; for all of them have thrown in their gifts out of their affluence, while she, out of her penury, has thrown in all the means she possessed."

5   When some spoke of the Temple, how it was adorned with magnificent stones and votive gifts,[15] he said, "You see all this? The time will come when there will not be left here one stone on another that is not thrown down."

Then they asked him, "Teacher, when will this actually happen, and what indication will there be when it is going to happen?"

"Take care that you are not deceived", he replied, "for many will come claiming to be me,[16] saying, 'I am he,' and 'The time has come.' Do not go after them. Then when you hear of wars and disorders do not get excited, for these have to come first, but the End will not follow

10   immediately. Nation will be roused against nation, and kingdom against kingdom", he informed them. "There will be great earthquakes with famine and pestilence in various places, appalling spectacles also, and awful signs from heaven.[17] But before all this they will lay hands on you and persecute you, handing you over to synagogues and prisons, dragging you before kings and governors on my account. This will serve you as evidence. Fix in your minds, therefore, not to rehearse beforehand what

15   you will say in your defence, for I will give you words and wisdom which none of your persecutors will be able to resist or refute. You will be betrayed by parents and brothers, relations and friends: they will be responsible for the death of some of you; and you will be universally detested on my account. Yet not a hair of your heads shall perish. By your constancy win your lives.

20   "Then when you see Jerusalem ringed with armies be certain that its devastation is at hand. Then let those who are in Judea flee to the hills, and those who are inside the city take their departure, and let those who are in the

15 The Temple had been rebuilt on a lavish scale by Herod the Great. Many eminent foreigners made votive gifts.

16 ie the Messiah. Josephus refers to such false messiahs in the first century AD. The conviction was strong at this time that the Messianic Age was about to commence.

17 Josephus relates some of the prodigies and heavenly signs that preceded the war with the Romans and the fall of Jerusalem. See Jos. *Jewish War*, VI.288–310.

country not enter it; for these are the Days of Retribution in fulfilment of all that the Scriptures have stated.[18] Alas for pregnant women and nursing mothers in those days, for there will be great distress on earth and terror for this people! They will fall by the edge of the sword and be carried away captive to all nations; and Jerusalem will remain under Gentile domination until the Era of the

25   Gentiles has ended.[19] That moment will be marked by signs in the sun, the moon and the stars, and on earth by nations haggard with utter helplessness at the pounding of sea and billow, men chill with fear and foreboding of what is overtaking the existing order; for the planets will totter. And they they shall see the Son of Man coming in cloud with great pomp and splendour.[20] When these things begin to happen emerge from your retreat and lift up your heads, for your deliverance is at hand."

Then he gave them an illustration. "Take the fig tree
30   and all the trees.[21] Once you see they have sprouted you are well aware that summer is close at hand. So when you see these things happen you will be no less aware that the Kingdom of God is at hand. I tell you positively, this generation will not pass away before all this takes place. Heaven and earth will pass away, but my words shall not pass away.

"But take care that your minds are not enfeebled by over-indulgence, drunkenness, or worldly pleasures, so
35   that that day catches you unexpectedly like a trap; for inevitably it will spring upon all who dwell on the face of the earth.[22] So keep awake, pray constantly, that you may succeed in escaping all those things that are about to happen, and to stand in the presence of the Son of Man."

Now during the day Jesus was in the Temple teaching, but at night he went out and camped on the hill called the

18 cf *Hos* 9:7; *Dan* 9:26. In obedience to a revelation they had received the Jewish Christians are said to have taken refuge near Pella, beyond the Jordan. cf *Rev* 12:14.
19 cf *Rev* 11:2.
20 *Bk of Enoch*, 62; *Dan* 7:13.
21 The words "and all the trees" are added because the author or scribe did not grasp Jesus's play on the Hebrew words for 'summer fruit' and 'end'. See p 31, n 103.
22 *Isa* 24:17, and see *I Thess* 5:2–8.

Mount of Olives;[23] and all the people came early to the Temple to listen to him.

Chapter XII

22.1   The Feast of Unleavened Bread, called Passover, was at hand, and the head priests and scribes were seeking a way to kill Jesus, for they feared the people. Then Satan entered Judas called Iscariot, who was one of the twelve, and he went off to confer with the head priests and officers on the best way of handing him over to them.
5   They were overjoyed and agreed to give him money, while he gave his solemn assurances and sought a convenient opportunity to deliver him to them when away from the crowd.

Then came the day of unleavened bread when the passover has to be sacrificed, and Jesus sent Peter and John, saying, "Go and prepare for us to eat the passover."

"Where do you wish us to make preparation?" they inquired.

10   "As you enter the city," he told them, "a man will meet you carrying a water-pot. Follow him into the house he enters, and say to the master of the house, 'The Teacher asks you, which guest-room am I to have to eat the passover with my disciples?' He will then show you a large upstairs dining-room ready laid out. There prepare."

Setting off they found everything turn out just as he told them, and they prepared the passover. Then when the time came he took his place in company with the
15   envoys. "I have greatly longed to eat this passover with you before I suffer," he said to them, "for I tell you I will not eat another until its fulfilment in the Kingdom of God."

Taking the cup, he said after giving thanks, "Take it, and share it between you. I tell you, from now on I will not drink of the fruit of the vine till the Kingdom of God is inaugurated."

Then taking bread, after giving thanks he broke and

---

23 At the season of the Passover Jerusalem was so crowded with pilgrims that thousands had to camp outside the city. This was an advantage to Jesus, since inside the city there was greater risk at night of his seizure or assassination. At night, of course, the city gates were closed.

gave it to them saying, "This signifies my body which is given for you. Do this in commemoration of me."

20 Similarly he gave them the cup after the meal saying, "This is the new covenant in my blood, which is poured out for you.[1] Moreover, the hand of my betrayer lies here on the table with mine. The Son of Man indeed goes his appointed way, yet alas for that man by whom he is betrayed."

They began to speculate as to which of them would be likely to do such a thing. They also began to argue over which of them should be considered greatest.

25 But Jesus intervened. "The kings of the Gentiles lord it over them", he said, "and their chief authorities are termed 'Benefactors'. It is otherwise with you. Let the greatest among you be as the least, and the one who issues orders as the one who receives them. Which is greater, the one who sits at table or the one who serves? Surely it is the one who is seated. Yet I am among you as one who serves. You are those who have stayed with me through all my trials, and just as my Father has promised

30 me his Kingdom, so do I now promise you that you will eat and drink at my table in my Kingdom; and you shall sit on thrones governing the twelve tribes of Israel.

"Simon, Simon, Satan has begged to have you that he may prise you loose like husks from the grain. But I have prayed that your loyalty may not fail, and on your restoration you must confirm your brothers."

"In your cause, Master," he replied, "I am ready to go to prison and to death too."

But he said, "I tell you for a fact, Peter, the cock will not crow to-day before you have denied three times that you know me."

35 Then to all of them he said, "When I sent you out without purse, or wallet, or sandals, did you go short of anything?"

"No, nothing", they answered.

"Yet now", he said, "whoever has a purse let him take it, and a wallet as well, and whoever has no dagger let him sell his cloak and buy one. For I tell you that this scripture will have its accomplishment in me, 'He was classed with outlaws'.[2] Yes, indeed, whatever has

1 The language in this paragraph could have been influenced by *I Cor.* 11:24–25.
2 *Isa* 53:12.

reference to me will have its fulfilment."

"Here are two daggers, Master", they said.

"That will do", he told them.

40 Taking his departure he went as usual to the Mount of Olives, and his disciples followed him. When he reached the spot he said to them, "Pray that you are not put to the test." Then he withdrew about a stone's throw from them, and knelt down and prayed, "O Father, if it be thy will let this cup pass me by. Yet not my will but thine be done."

Then an angel appeared to him strengthening him. And being in agony he prayed more fervently, his sweat falling to the ground like splashes of blood.

45 On rising from prayer he came to his disciples and found them sleeping from grief, and said to them, "Why are you sleeping? Be up, and at your prayers, or you may find yourselves tempted."

He was still speaking when a crowd came in sight, with the one of the twelve called Judas at their head.[3] Approaching Jesus he embraced him. Jesus said to him, "Judas, do you betray the Son of Man with a kiss?"

Those surrounding Jesus, seeing what was going to happen, cried, "Master, shall we strike with the sword?"

50 One of them did strike the high priest's servant and severed his right ear.

"Leave this to me", Jesus replied, and touching the ear healed him.

Then Jesus addressed those who had taken action against him, the head priests, officials of the Temple, and elders, "Have you come out against a brigand with swords and clubs?[4] While I was with you daily in the Temple you never laid hands on me. But now is your time, when darkness reigns."

Seizing him they conveyed him to the high priest's

55 residence, while Peter followed at a distance. There they made up a fire in the courtyard, and when they sat down Peter sat with them. One of the servant girls seeing him seated there before the blaze gave him a keen look, and then announced, "This man was with them too."

But he denied it, "I don't know him, woman."

---

3 The author forgot to mention that Judas had left his companions.
4 Weapons were not allowed in the Temple courts. So the police there carried clubs.

After a while someone else who saw him declared, "Of course you are one of them."

"I am not", Peter declared.

When about another hour had elapsed another man stated with conviction, "Certainly he was with them. He's a Galilean."

60 "I don't know what you are talking about", replied Peter.

Just then, before he had finished speaking, the cock crowed. The Master turned and looked at Peter; and Peter recalled the remark the Master had made to him, "This very day before the cock crows you will deny me three times." Going outside he wept bitterly.

Now the men who had charge of Jesus made sport of him, striking him while blindfolded, and then demand-65 ing, "Come on, prophesy! Who was it hit you?" And they addressed many other insulting remarks to him.

When it was daylight, the senate of the people, head priests and scribes, assembled and conducted him to their Sanhedrin, urging him, "If you are the Messiah, tell us."

But he replied, "Even if I do tell you, you will not believe, nor will you answer if I ask you a question. But hereafter the Son of Man will be seated at the right hand of the power of God."

70 "Are you then the son of God?" they all inquired.

"I am, as you say", he told them.

Then they said, "What further evidence do we need? We have heard his own confession."

23.1 With that the whole assembly rose and brought him before Pilate and proceeded to accuse him as follows: "We have found this man subverting our nation, forbidding the payment of tribute to Caesar, and claiming to be Messiah, a king."

"Are you the king of the Jews?" Pilate asked him.

"As you say", he replied.

Pilate told the head priests and the crowd, "I can find nothing criminal in the man."[5]

5 But they pressed their charges saying, "He rouses the people, teaching all over Judea,[6] beginning with Galilee

5 The author is at fault here. Pilate would know perfectly well that the charge against Jesus, to which he had confessed, was one of high treason against Caesar under Roman law.

6 See p 142 n 13.

and ending up here."

When Pilate heard that, he inquired whether the man was a Galilean, and learning that he belonged to Herod's jurisdiction he turned him over to Herod, who was at Jerusalem at this time. Herod was greatly delighted at seeing Jesus, for he had wanted to see him for a long time. From reports about him he hoped to witness some miracle performed by him. So he interrogated him at considerable length. Jesus, however, made no response.

10   But the head priests and scribes stood there and vehemently accused him.

Once Herod with his men had had their sport with him and mocked him, he returned him to Pilate, after arraying him in magnificent robes. That day Herod and Pilate became friends with one another, for previously they had been at enmity.[7]

Pilate now summoned the head priests, rulers and people,[8] and said to them, "You have brought this man before me accused of subverting the people. After examining him in your presence I found nothing crimi-

15   nal such as you charged him with. Neither did Herod, for he has sent him back to us. You see, therefore, that he has done nothing to deserve death. Consequently I shall chastise him and release him."

But the entire concourse yelled, "Away with him! Release Bar-Abbas to us!"[a]

20   Once more Pilate, wanting to release Jesus, addressed them. But they only clamoured the more, "Crucify him, crucify him!"

A third time he spoke to them. "But what crime has he committed? I have found nothing in him to merit death. Consequently I shall chastise him and release him."

But they bellowed their insistent demand for him to be crucified, and their clamour prevailed. Pilate gave the

25   judgment they called for. He released the man thrown into prison for riot and murder, for whom they had

---

a This was a man who had been thrown into prison for participation in a riot in the city and for murder.

---

7 See *Lk* 13:1, p 166. The cause of enmity between Herod and Pilate could have been that Pilate had massacred some of Herod's Galilean subjects.

8 The people would not have been present on the night of the Passover, and were in any case on the side of Jesus.

asked, and surrendered Jesus to their will.[9]

As they marched him off they seized a certain Simon, a Cyrenian, coming from the country, and laid the cross on him for him to carry it behind Jesus. A great concourse of people followed him, and women who beat their breasts and bewailed him. Turning to them Jesus said, "Daughters of Jerusalem, do not weep for me, but rather for yourselves and your children; for the time is coming when they will say, 'Fortunate are the barren, and the wombs that have never borne, and the breasts that have

30   never suckled!' Then will they cry to the mountains, 'Topple on us,' and to the hills, 'Cover us.'[10] For if this is what they do with green wood, what will happen to the dry?"

They brought two other malefactors to be executed with him.

When they reached the place called Skull they crucified him there, with the malefactors one on his right and the other on his left. [But Jesus said, "O Father, forgive them. They do not know what they are doing."][11] And they distributed his clothes by drawing lots.

35   The people stood there looking on, while their rulers sneered, "He saved others, let him save himself if he is God's Anointed, the Chosen One. The soldiers also mocked him, coming to him and offering him vinegar with the jeer, "Save yourself, if you are king of the Jews."[a] Even one of the hanged malefactors reviled him, "Aren't you the Messiah? Then save yourself and us."

40   But the other malefactor rebuked him. "Have you lost all fear of God because you have been given an identical sentence? In our case it was justified, for we have only got our deserts; but he has committed no felony." Then he said, "Spare me a thought, Jesus, when you inaugurate your kingdom."

"I tell you for a fact", Jesus replied, "this very day you will be with me in Paradise."

By this time it was about noon, and there was darkness

---

a   The notice over him was in these terms, "The King of the Jews".

---

9 Pilate here acts contrary to his known character and in contradiction of Roman law which he was obliged to enforce.

10 *Hos* 10:8, and cf *Rev* 6:16.

11 The insertion breaks the sequence. cf *Acts* 7:60. James the brother of Jesus is said to have used these words when executed (Hegesippus, *Memoirs*).

45   over the whole land until three o'clock due to an eclipse of the sun; and the curtain of the Sanctuary was split down the middle. Then Jesus cried with a loud voice, "Father, into thy hands I commit my spirit."[12] So saying he expired.

When the centurion saw what had happened he praised God saying, "A true man if ever there was one!" And all the people who had gathered for the spectacle, when they observed what had happened turned away beating their breasts [saying, "Woe to us! What has been done to-day? Woe for our sins, for the desolation of Jerusalem has drawn near."][13]

All the acquaintances of Jesus and the women who had followed him from Galilee were standing at a distance looking on.

50   Now there was a man called Joseph, a member of the Council, a good man and true,[a] from Arimathea, a town of Judea, one who awaited the Kingdom of God. Approaching Pilate he requested the body of Jesus, and taking it down, wrapped it in linen, and deposited it in a rock-cut tomb where no one had previously been buried. It was the day of preparation, and the sabbath had

55   almost begun. The women, those who had come from Gailee with Jesus, followed behind, and took note of the tomb and how the body was laid, and went away to prepare spices and ointments.

24.1   They were inactive on the sabbath as the commandment required; but at early dawn of the day after the sabbath they went to the tomb carrying the spices they had prepared. There they found the boulder rolled aside from the tomb, but when they entered it they did not find the body. While they were puzzling over this, suddenly

5   two men stood beside them in dazzling robes. As the women bent their faces to the ground with fear, they said to them, "Why do you seek the living among the dead? Remember how he told you while still in Galilee that the Son of Man must be betrayed into the hands of sinful men, and be crucified, and be raised up on the third day." Then they recalled those words of his, and return-

a He had been no party to their design and action.

---

12 Ps 31:5.
13 Reading preserved in the Old Latin, and partly in the Curetonian Syriac text.

ing from the tomb reported all this to the eleven and the others.

10   There were Mary of Magdala, Johanna, Mary mother of James, and the other women with them, who told this to the envoys. But what they said seemed to them completely fantastic, and they would not believe them. [But Peter got up and ran to the tomb, and peering in saw only the linen wrappings, and he went home wondering what had happened.][14]

That same day, however, two of the Envoys were making their way to a village nearly seven miles from Jerusalem called Emmaus, and talking to each other of all

15   these circumstances. They were deep in conversation and discussion when Jesus himself came up with them and walked beside them; but their eyes were kept from recognising him.

"What is all this you are debating with each other as you walk?" he said to them.

They stood abashed.

Then one of them called Cleopas[15] answered, "Are you such an isolated stranger in Jerusalem that you do not know what has been going on there these days?"

"What, for instance?" he inquired.

"Why, about Jesus the Nazarene," they said, "a prophet mighty in word and deed in the sight of God and all

20   the people, and how our head priests and rulers had sentence of death passed on him and crucified him. We were expecting him to be the one destined to deliver Israel. But there it is, it is now the third day since all this happened, though some women connected with us gave us a shock. They were at the tomb very early, and not only did not find his body, but came and told us also that they had seen a vision of angels, who declared he was alive. So some of our company went to the tomb, and found it just as the women said, but they did not see him."

25   Then Jesus said to them, "You fools, so slow-witted in grasping all that the prophets have declared! Did not the Messiah have to suffer in this way before attaining his

---

14 Possibly, but not certainly, an interpolation. cf *Jn* 20:1–4.

15 Tradition makes Cleopas the brother of Joseph, and therefore an uncle of Jesus. The one with him could then be his son Simeon, who became head of the Jewish Christians after the fall of Jerusalem and lived to be more than a hundred years of age.

glory?" And he proceeded from Moses and the various prophets to explain to them in all the Scriptures what related to himself.

They were now approaching the village for which they were bound, and he gave the impression he was going farther. But they pressed him saying, "Do stay with us. It's getting towards evening and daylight is going fast." So he stayed with them.

30   Then when he sat down with them to eat he took the bread, recited the blessing, broke it, and handed it to them. Now their eyes were opened and they recognised him; and he vanished from their sight. Then they said to each other, "Did not our hearts glow as he talked to us on the road, and as he expounded the Scriptures to us?"

Instantly they rose to return to Jerusalem, and found the eleven and their associates gathered there, who informed them that the Master had indeed risen and had

35   appeared to Simon. Then they described their own experiences on the road, and how they recognised him when he broke the bread.

No sooner had they told their story[16] than Jesus stood before them and said, "Peace be with you." Startled and terrified, they believed they were seeing a ghost. But he said to them, "Why are you alarmed, and what puts this idea into your heads? See my hands and my feet, that it is indeed I myself. Feel me and see. A ghost does not have

· 40   flesh and bones as you see I have." So saying, he showed them his hands and feet.

As they were still incredulous from joy and amazement, he said to them, "Have you anything to eat handy?"

They offered him a piece of grilled fish. He accepted it and ate it in front of them. Then he said to them, "I used these very words to you when I was with you, 'Everything that is written of me in the Law of Moses, and in the prophets and Psalms, must be fulfilled.' "

45   Then he explained to them the implication of the Scriptures[17] and told them, "Thus it is written, for the

---

16 Plutarch (*Lives*) relates a resurrection and ascension story of Romulus, founder of Rome, which may be compared.
17 The manner of such explanations can be apprehended now from the Commentaries of the Essenes in the Dead Sea Scrolls.

Messiah to suffer and be raised from the dead the third day, and for repentance to be proclaimed in his name to all nations for the forgiveness of their sins. Starting with Jerusalem, you are to testify to these matters. Be sure I shall send what the Father promised you. Stay in the city until you are invested with power from on high."

50   Then he led them as far as Bethany, and lifting his hands blessed them. And as he blessed them he parted from them and was borne up to heaven. And they, when they had paid him homage, returned to Jerusalem full of joy, and were habitually in the Temple, blessing God.

LUKE

A History of Christian Beginnings

Part II

How the Good News came to the Gentiles
(Acts of the Envoys)

Preface to the Acts

In this sequel to his account of the life and teaching of Jesus, the author tells the story of the growth and expansion of the Messianic Community. His canvas now embraces a great part of the Roman Empire. His principal task was to show how it came about that so many non-Jews throughout the Empire had become followers of Jesus, and in this context to placate the authorities on behalf of the Christians by a narrative that makes it clear that they have no political or subversive designs and in general have been treated with fairness and friendliness by Roman officials. When the author was writing Christianity was a proscribed religion officially regarded, and with good reason, as hostile to Rome. To profess Christianity was therefore a capital crime.

The author also continues to be concerned to play down the conflicts within the Movement, especially between the Jewish and non-Jewish elements. The hero of the book is Paul, self-styled envoy to the Gentiles, himself a Roman citizen. The author brings him at the end to Rome, after he had appealed to Caesar in order to escape certain death through the charges against him of the Sadducean hierarchy at Jerusalem. In the book Paul is left with that appeal still to be heard, enjoying at Rome full liberty of speech and access to his friends. It would have defeated the author's purpose if Paul's execution by the Romans had been related. "And so we came to Rome" rather marks the climax of Christian achievement.

The title *Acts of the Envoys*, not original, is therefore somewhat misleading. Of the Twelve only Peter plays any considerable part in the story, and chiefly in connection with the "opening of the door of faith to Gentiles". The early scenes and events in Palestine are carefully chosen and arranged with an eye to the main object of the work, and leave great and tantalising gaps, which other available sources permit us as yet to cover only sketchily. The side of the story relating to the Jewish adherents of Jesus as Messiah is inadequately represented. But what we are given – if examined carefully – is of much historical importance. It is particularly of consequence to appreciate that

Christianity in its inception was not a new religion: it was a Movement of Messianic Judaism. At its head, as a kind of regent, was Jacob, the next younger brother of Jesus, more familiar to English readers as James. Since the recovery of the Dead Sea Scrolls we now know that the Christian organisation at this time was largely derived from that of the Essenes. Paul was thus responsible to the Council set up at Jerusalem, and required to report periodically on his activities, especially at the annual festival of Pentecost.

The narrative flows more smoothly than with the *Gospel*, and affords us an intimate and often dramatic glimpse of life and conditions in many lands in the first century AD. Some minor errors which can be detected serve to bring more strongly into relief the general authenticity of atmosphere. The style and phraseology of much of the first half of the book suggest some dependence on Hebrew or Aramaic sources. In the second half, and of particular worth, is the use of a contemporary 'diary' document in the first person plural. This may have been the work of Doctor Luke, and helped to associate his name with the whole narrative.

The Acts of the Envoys
Luke (Part Two)

Foreword

1.1   In my previous treatise, Theophilus, I covered every-thing that Jesus did and taught down to the time when, having instructed by the holy Spirit the envoys he had chosen, he was taken on high. To those envoys he had shown himself alive after he had suffered, by many conclusive proofs, being seen by them over a period of forty days, during which he spoke of matters relating to the Kingdom of God. While in their company he ordered them not to leave Jerusalem,[1] but to await "what the
5   Father promised, which you have heard from me. For John immersed in water, but you shall be immersed in holy Spirit very shortly."

As they were going along together they asked him, "Master, are you going to restore the kingdom to Israel at this time?"

"It is not for you to know times and seasons", he replied. "These are matters which the Father has reserved exclusively for himself.[2] But you will be given power when the holy Spirit comes upon you, and will be my witnesses in Jerusalem, and throughout Judea and Samaria, and to the ends of the earth."

When he had said this, while they looked on, he was
10   borne on high, and a cloud blotted him from view. As they strained their eyes skywards after his going, two men in white robes appeared suddenly beside them, who said, "Why are you Galileans staring at the sky?

---

1 The other Gospels convey that the disciples returned to Galilee where they would meet Jesus. Luke seems to be stressing the importance of Jerusalem as the Messianic seat of government.
2 Since Jesus had not returned to deliver Israel when the *Acts* was written the time is deliberately made vague.

This Jesus who has been taken from you to heaven will return in exactly the same way as you have seen him go."[3]

Then they returned to Jerusalem from the hill called the Mount of Olives.[a]

When they got back they went upstairs to the upper part of the house where they were staying, they being Peter, John, James and Andrew, Philip and Thomas, Bartholomew and Matthew, James son of Alphaeus, Simon the Zealot, and Judas son of James. These all by common consent were regular in attendance at prayers,[4] with the women, with Mary mother of Jesus, and with his brothers.

Chapter I

15   At this time Peter stood up before the brothers[a] and said, "Brothers, it was inevitable that the scripture should be fulfilled which the holy Spirit declared beforehand by the mouth of David, regarding Judas who acted as guide to those who arrested Jesus, for he was of our

20   number and appointed by choice to our function.[b] For it is written in the book of Psalms, 'Let his villa be desolate, and let no one dwell in it', and, 'Let another take over his charge.'[1] It is therefore essential that of the men associated with us during the whole course of the coming and going of the Lord Jesus among us, from the immersion by John to the day he was taken from us, one of them should be a witness with us to his resurrection."

a It is close to Jerusalem, only a sabbath day's walk away. (About half a mile. *Tr.*)

---

3 cf *Dan* 7:13; *Rev* 1:7.
4 The three Jewish sessions of morning, afternoon and evening prayers.

a There was a gathering of about a hundred and twenty persons in all.
b This Judas acquired a plot of ground with his ill-gotten gains, and having pitched forward gashed open his middle and his intestines gushed out.[2] The fact became known to all the inhabitants of Jerusalem, so that that plot got the name in their language of Haceldama (Aram. *Chaquel-dema*), which means 'Bloody Patch'.

---

1 *Ps* 69:25 with *Ps* 109:8.
2 cf *Book of Ahikar* 7:38; Papias, *Exposition of the Dominical Oracles*, Bk IV, quoted by Apollinarius.

There were two nominations, Joseph surnamed Bar-Sabbas, called Justus,[3] and Matthias.

Then they prayed, "Thou, O Lord, who knowest the hearts of all, do thou declare which of these two thou

25   hast chosen to take the place in this ministry and envoy-ship left vacant by Judas when he went to his own place."

So they held a ballot, and the vote went to Matthias; and he was elected to office in association with the eleven envoys.

2.1   At the completion of the Pentecostal period[4] they were all together in the same place, when suddenly there came a whistling out of the sky as of a tearing furious blast of wind that filled the whole house where they were sitting, and forking tongues as if of fire were seen by them which settled on each of them.[5] And all of them became ecstatic,[6] and began speaking in various tongues as the Spirit gave them articulation.

5   Now there were resident in Jerusalem pious Jews from every nation under the skies.[7] When this noise came the greater part gathered together and could not make it out, because each one of them heard them speaking his own language. Mystified and amazed they said, "Aren't all these speakers Gaileans? How is it then that we each hear our native language? Parthians, Medes, Elamites, natives of Mesopotamia, Edessa[8] and Cappadocia, Pon-

10   tus, Asia, Phrygia and Pamphylia, Egypt and the parts of Libya around Cyrene, foreigners domiciled in Rome (both Jews and proselytes), Cretans, and Arabians,[9] we hear them proclaiming in our own tongues the great attributes of God!"

---

3 Meaning 'the Pious'.
4 When they had counted to the 50th day after Passover (*Lev.* 23:15).
5 The description answers to the wind called *khamsin*, which blows at this season of the year (*Ps* 29:5–8), though the manifestation here conveys a psychic experience.
6 Lit "filled with the holy Spirit".
7 Most of these would be pilgrims to Jerusalem for the festivals of Passover and Pentecost.
8 Both context and sense show that the reading 'Judea' here must be wrong. A scribal misreading of Edessa (*Hadditha*) has been assumed, which comes appropriately geographically between Mesopotamia and Cappadocia. On the evangelisation of Edessa see Euseb. *Eccl. Hist.* 1:13.
9 The list has 12 divisions, those associated between commas counting as one, corresponding to the 12 envoys.

They were indeed mystified and bewildered, asking each other, "What can this possibly mean?" But some said scornfully, "They're full of new wine."

Then Peter, standing up with the eleven, raised his voice and told them bluntly, "Jews[10] and residents in

15   Jerusalem all, get this clear, and heed what I say. These men are not drunk as you imagine: it is only nine in the morning. On the contrary, this represents what was stated by the Prophet Joel:

> 'Then in those Closing Days,' God says,
> 'I will pour out my Spirit on all flesh,
> And your sons and daughters will prophesy;
> Your young men shall see visions,
> And your old men dream dreams.
> Even on my menservants and maidservants
> Will I pour my Spirit,
> And they will prophesy.
> I will show portents in the skies above,
> And signs on the earth beneath,
> Blood and fire and fumes of smoke.'
20
> The sun will be turned to darkness,
> And the moon will become blood red.
> Ere that great and awful Day of the Lord comes.
> Then all who invoke the Lord's name will be saved.[11]

"Listen to this, Israelites! It concerns Jesus the Nazarene, a man proved to you to be from God by the miracles, signs and wonders, which God performed by him among you, as you yourselves know. This man, delivered up by God's deliberate intention and fore-knowledge, you killed by having non-Jews[12] nail him up. But God raised him, having loosed the grip of death; for

25   it was not possible for him to be held by it. David indeed, personating him, says,

> I kept the Lord steadfastly in view;
> For he is at my right hand lest I be shaken.
> So my heart is cheered and my tongue is glad:
> My very flesh will continue confident.

---

10 'Jews' (ie Judeans), not a reference to religion.
11 *Joel* 2:28–32. Josephus notes the appearance of various heavenly prodigies in the first century AD interpreted by seers as signs of the Last Times.
12 Lit "the hands of those without law" (the Law of Moses).

For you will not relinquish my soul to Hell,[13]
Nor will you allow your holy one to see decay.
You have acquainted me with the ways of life:
You will fill me with joy by your presence.[14]

"Brothers, one can speak to you quite frankly about
the patriarch David. There is no question that he died
and was buried, and we have his tomb to this very day.[15]

30 Being then a prophet, and knowing that God had sworn
to him by oath that he would seat one of his descendants
on his throne,[16] he spoke with foresight of the Messiah's
resurrection, that neither would he be relinquished to
Hell, nor would his flesh see decay. God has raised this
Jesus, a fact of which we are all witnesses. Being then
exalted to God's right hand, and obtaining from the
Father the promise of the holy Spirit, he has poured out
what you now see and hear. David did not ascend to
heaven, for he says himself,

The Lord said to my lord, 'Sit at my right hand
35 *Till I make your foes a footstool 'neath your feet.'*[17]

"Let the whole house of Israel know positively that
God has made this Jesus whom you have crucified both
Lord and Messiah."[18]

As they listened they were cut to the quick, and said to
Peter and the rest of the envoys, "Oh brothers, what are
we to do?"

"Repent," Peter told them, "and let each of you be
immersed for the forgiveness of your sins in the name of
Messiah Jesus, and you will receive the gift of the holy
Spirit. For the promise is for you and your children, and
for as many of those outside Israel[19] as the Lord our God
shall call."

40 In many other ways did he beg and entreat them,
"Save yourselves from this perverse generation."

Then all those who accepted his message were

13 Hades, *Sheol*, here personifying the grave.
14 *Ps* 16:8–11.
15 See Josephus, *Antiq.* XVI.179.
16 *Ps* 132:11.
17 *Ps* 110:1.
18 The reader should appreciate that in those days such speeches were
composed by the author of the work, a Gentile, in language which he
deemed appropriate. Peter's hearers had not crucified Jesus.
19 Lit "those far off" (*Isa* 57:19). cf *Eph* 2:17.

immersed; and that day about three thousand persons were recruited. They were regular in attending the instruction of the envoys and the communal gathering with the breaking of bread and prayers. Every individual was awed, and many signs and wonders occurred through the envoys. All the believers collectively held

45 everything in common.[20] They sold their goods and possessions and distributed the proceeds to all according to individual need. By common consent also they were regular in daily attendance at the Temple, and breaking their bread at home took their meals with gladness and simplicity of mind, praising God and enjoying popular favour. Every single day the Lord added to those who were being saved.[21]

Chapter II

3.1 Once when Peter and John were going up to the Temple for the afternoon service at three o'clock, a man lame from birth was carried there. He was deposited daily by the entrance of the Temple called the Golden Gate[1] to solicit alms from those passing into the Temple. Seeing Peter and John about to enter the Temple he asked for alms from them. Peter looked at him, and so

5 did John, and said, "Rely on us." So he reached out to them, expecting to receive something from them.

"I have no silver or gold, "Peter told him, "but what I have I will give you. In the name of Jesus Christ the Nazarene, walk!" And he took him by the hand and raised him up.

Immediately his feet and ankles acquired strength, and he sprang upright and walked about, and entered the Temple with them, walking and skipping and praising God.

20 Candidates to join the Essene community were required to hand over all their possessions.
21 Pentecost, the chief Essene festival, was particularly the festival of first fruits. Being saved meant being spared in the judgments which would fall on sinners when the Kingdom of God would be established on earth.

1 The eastern gate of polished Corinthian bronze which was exceptionally magnificent (Jos. *Jewish War*, V. 201).

10   All the people saw him walking and praising God, and recognising him as the man who used to sit begging at the Golden Gate of the Temple, they were amazed and greatly excited at what had happened to him. As he kept close to Peter and John, all the people rushed to them in the portico called after Solomon.[2] There Peter addressed them as follows:

"Israelites, why are you surprised at this? Why do you stare at us as if by our own power or piety we had made this man walk? The God of Abraham, Isaac and Jacob, the God of our fathers, has honoured his servant Jesus, whom you handed over and disowned before Pilate when he had decided to release him.[3] Yes, you disowned the holy and just one, and demanded that a murderer be

15   granted you. You put to death the Fount[4] of Life, whom God raised from the dead, as we are witnesses; and by virtue of his name this man whom you see and know has been set on his feet. It is his name and the confidence it inspires which has given him his soundness of limb in the presence of you all.

"Well, brothers, I know you acted in ignorance, just as your rulers did, and God thus fulfilled what he had previously announced by the mouth of all his prophets, that the Messiah should suffer. Repent then, and turn again, that your sins may be blotted out, and that times

20   of relief[5] may come from the presence of the Lord, and he may send Jesus your[6] foreordained Messiah, whom heaven must harbour till the Era of Restoration of which God spoke by the mouth of his holy prophets of old. Moses truly said, 'The Lord God will raise up for you from your brothers a prophet like myself. You must heed whatever he tells you, and whoever fails to attend to that prophet will be cut off from the people.'[7] In fact all the prophets, from Samuel onwards, who have at any time spoken, have announced these times.

25   "You are the sons of the prophets and of the covenant[8] which God made with our fathers, saying to Abraham,

---

2 On the porticoes see Jos. *Jewish War*, V. 191–192.
3 *Lk* 23:13–16.
4 The means or instrument of life in the Messianic Age. cf *Rev* 2:10.
5 cf *Esth* 4:14.
6 Peter is made to speak as a non-Jew, which of course the author was.
7 *Deut* 18:15, 18–19.
8 Heb. idiom, Son of the Covenant, ie a Jew.

'In your offspring all families of the earth shall be blest.'[9]
To you first, God, having raised up his servant, has sent
him to bless you by turning every one of you from your
evil ways."

4.1   While they were addressing the people, the head
priests, the captain of the Temple guard, and the Sadducees, came upon them, incensed at their teaching the
people and proclaiming with reference to Jesus the resurrection of the dead.[10] They arrested them and remanded
them in custody until the following day; for it was
already evening. But many of those who heard the
Message believed, and the number of men now totalled
about five thousand.

5   Next day their[11] rulers, with the elders and scribes,
met in Jerusalem,[a] and having called the prisoners before
them, demanded, "By what kind of power or name have
you done this?"

Then Peter under inspiration replied, "Rulers of the
people and elders, if we are being interrogated to-day
regarding the benefit conferred on a cripple, by what
10   means he has been made sound, let it be known to you
all, and to the whole house of Israel, that it is by the name
of Jesus Christ the Nazarene whom you crucified, whom
God raised from the dead. It is by this means that this
man stands before you well and strong. This is the stone
rejected by you builders, which has become the coping-
stone.[12] Deliverance by any other name there is none; for
in all the world no other name has been provided by
which we should be delivered."

Remarking the eloquence of Peter and John, and noting that they were common uneducated men, they were
amazed. As they recognized them for associates of Jesus,
and seeing the man had been cured standing there with
15   them, they could make no rejoinder. Having ordered
them to withdraw from the Sanhedrin they put their

---

a Those who attended included the high priest Annas, Caiaphas,
John, Alexander, and as many as were of the rank of head priests.

---

9 *Gen* 12:3; 22:18.
10 It was no crime to preach the resurrection of the dead, a doctrine accepted
by most Jews, though not by the Sadducees.
11 See n 6 above.
12 See *Ps* 118:22.

heads together saying, "What are we going to do with these men? It is patent that a significant sign has occurred through them for all the inhabitants of Jerusalem, and there is no denying it. But that it may not obtain even wider circulation among the people, let us intimidate them by threats never to use this name again to anyone ." So calling them in they gave them stringent orders neither to mention Jesus nor to teach in his name.

Peter and John replied, however, "You must be the judges whether it is right in God's sight to heed you in preference to God. So far as we are concerned we cannot refrain from speaking of what we have seen and heard."

20

After subjecting them to further threats they let them go, finding no safe way of punishing them on account of the people, because they all praised God for what had happened; for the man was over forty years of age on whom this curative sign had been performed.

On their release they went to their own friends and reported to them what the head priests and elders had said. When they heard it they cried aloud to God with one accord, "Lord of the universe, thou who didst make heaven and earth, the sea and all that is therein, thou art he who didst say through the holy Spirit by the mouth of our father David thy servant:

25

> *Wherefore did the heathen rage,*
> *And the peoples meditate vain things?*
> *The kings of the earth ranged themselves,*
> *And the rulers joined forces together,*
> *Against the Lord and his Anointed.*[13]

For assuredly in this city they joined forces together against thy devoted servant Jesus, whom thou didst anoint, both Herod and Pontius Pilate, with the Gentiles and people of Israel[14] to accomplish whatever thy hand and will had determined beforehand should be done.

"And now, Lord, regard their threatenings, and grant to thy servants to declare thy Message with all eloquence, with the stretching forth of thy hand to heal,

30

---

13 *Ps* 2:1–2.
14 This is a rhetorical statement, since in fact the Jewish people, as the records show, had had no responsibility for the death of Jesus: they were in fact on his side (*Mk* 14:2; *Mt* 26:5), which was why the authorities were forced to arrest Jesus secretly.

and with signs and wonders to be performed through the name of thy devoted servant Jesus."

When they had offered their petition the place where they were assembled was shaken, and they all became ecstatic and declared God's message eloquently.

Chapter III

The mass of believers were united heart and soul, and not one claimed any of his possessions as his own. Everything to them was common property. With telling effect the envoys of the Lord Jesus recounted the evidence of his resurrection, and indeed intense fervour animated them all. Neither was any of them in want; for all those who owned lands or houses sold them and 35 brought the price they realised and laid it at the feet of the envoys: it was then distributed to each according to need. For instance, Joseph a Levite, by birth a Cypriot, who was given the name of Barnabas[a] by the envoys, sold a farm he had and brought the money and laid it at the feet of the envoys. On the other hand, a man called Ananias with his wife Sapphira sold a property and kept back part of the proceeds with his wife's connivance, and bringing only a proportion laid that at the feet of the envoys.

5.1   "Ananias," Peter said to him, "however did Satan possess you to make you play the holy Spirit false and keep back part of the proceeds of the land? While you had it wasn't it your own? And when you disposed of it wasn't the money under your own control? Whatever made you do it? You have not lied to men, but to God."[1]

5   On hearing this Ananias fell dead, and great fear took hold of all who had listened. The young men rose and covered him up, and carried him out and buried him.

Some three hours later his wife came in unaware of

---

a Translated it means 'Son of Encouragement' (ie the Encourager, contraction of Bar-Nadabas. Ed.).

---

1 The *Community Rule* of the Essenes provides that if anyone has lied in matters of property, "he shall be excluded from the pure Meal of the Many, and do penance with respect to a quarter of his food" (ch 7). There was no death penalty.

what had happened. "Tell me," Peter said to her, "did you sell the land for such a figure?"

"Yes", she replied, "that was the figure."

"Whatever made you conspire together to try the Lord's Spirit?" Peter demanded. "There at the door are the footsteps of those who have been burying your husband: they will carry you out too."

10 Instantly she fell at his feet and expired. When the young men entered they found her dead, and carrying her out buried her beside her husband.

Great awe seized the whole community as well as those who had heard all this.[a]

15 Now by the hands of the envoys many signs and wonders were performed among the people, so that they even brought the ailing out into the streets and laid them on couches and mattresses, that when Peter came by at least his shadow might fall across some of them. The concourse of those bringing the ailing and people afflicted with foul spirits even came from towns all round Jerusalem, and every one of them was cured.

Then the high priest rose in a towering passion with all his associates,[b] and arrested the envoys and lodged them in the public jail. But during the night an angel of the Lord opened the prison doors, let them out, and said, 20 "Go and stand in the Temple, and declare to the people everything that concerns this Life."[2]

On hearing this the envoys entered the Temple first thing in the morning and taught there.

When the high priest and his associates arrived they convened the Sanhedrin and the entire Senate[3] of the children of Israel, and sent to the jail to fetch the envoys. But when the officers got there they did not find them in the prison. So they returned and reported, "We found the jail securely shut and the warders on duty at the

---

a They were all by common consent in Solomon's portico. But none of the others dared adhere to them, though the people extolled them. Yet more believers did come over to the Master, a number both of men and women.

b They were of the Sadducean party.

---

2 A Hebraism, lit "all the words of this Life", how to obtain the promise of Eternal Life in the Messianic Age.

3 The Great Sanhedrin, not merely the council of the hierarchy, the Lesser Sanhedrin, which dealt only with religious issues.

doors, but on gaining admittance we found no one inside."

When the captain of the Temple guard and the head priests heard this they were quite at a loss how it could have happened. Then someone came and informed them, "The men you put in prison are actually standing in the Temple teaching the people."

25

So the captain of the Temple guard went with his officers and brought them, but without using force, for they were afraid they might be stoned by the people.

When the envoys were before the Sanhedrin the high priest asked them, "Did we not give you strict orders not to teach in this name? Yet here have you filled Jerusalem with your teaching and want to make us answerable for this man's blood."

30

Peter replied for the envoys, "We owe a higher obedience to God than to man. The God of our fathers raised Jesus, for whose hanging on a gibbet[4] you were directly responsible. God has elevated him to his right hand as Founder and Deliverer to afford Israel repentance and forgiveness of sins. We are witnesses to this fact, and so is the holy Spirit which God has bestowed on those who obey him."

When they heard this they were cut to the quick and wanted to execute them. But a Pharisee called Gamaliel,[5] a teacher of the Law respected by the entire people, rose in the Sanhedrin and ordered the men to be taken outside for a while.

35

Then he said to the assembly, "Israelites, be very careful before you carry out your intentions regarding these men. Some time ago Theudas started up,[6] claiming to be someone of consequence. To him about four hundred men attached themselves. He was killed, and all his followers scattered and brought to nothing. Later, Judas the Galilean started up at the time of the census,[7] and drew people after him. He too was killed, and all his followers dispersed. So I say to you, therefore, stand

---

4 Crucifixion not being a Jewish form of punishment there was no Hebrew or Aramaic word for it.

5 Rabbani Gamaliel, grandson of the famous Hillel.

6 Jos. *Antiq.* XX.97–98, dates the activity of Theudas much later than that of Judas of Galilee, later even than the time at which Gamaliel here makes this speech.

7 See *Lk* 2:1 and Jos. *Jewish War*, II.118.

aside from these men and leave them alone, in case you may be found in conflict with God. If their design or action is of human inspiration it will fizzle out, but if it is of divine inspiration you cannot suppress them."

40   Persuaded by him, they recalled the envoys, had them flogged, and after ordering them not to speak in the name of Jesus set them at liberty.

They left the presence of the Sanhedrin rejoicing that they had been thought worthy to suffer dishonour for the name; and daily in the Temple and at home they never ceased to teach and to proclaim Jesus as Messiah.

Chapter IV

6.1   At that period, when the number of disciples had substantially increased, there was a murmuring of the foreign Jews against the native Jews[1] because their widows were discriminated against in the daily distribution. The twelve called a general meeting of the disciples and said, "It is not satisfactory that we should neglect God's Message to look after tables.[2] So, brothers, recommend from among yourselves seven men of sympathy and sense who have your confidence, and we will appoint them for this function, while we concentrate on prayer and the requirements of the Message."

5   The suggestion met with the approval of the entire company, and they selected Stephen, a man of great faith and insight, together with Philip, Prochorus, Nikanor, Timon, Parmenas,[3] and Nikolaus a proselyte from Antioch. These they presented to the envoys, who after prayer ordained them.

God's Message spread, and the number of disciples in Jerusalem was greatly augmented. Quite a considerable body of the priests gave their allegiance.[4]

Stephen, full of fervour and power, performed great

---

1 Gr "Hellenists against Hebrews".
2 Or perhaps "act as bankers". The Envoys had been receiving and distributing funds. Moneychangers were called 'table-men'.
3 Most of these would have been Greek-speaking Jews, as their names suggest.
4 The headquarters of the Movement was on the fringe of the area where the priests were domiciled.

signs and wonders among the people. However, some persons arose belonging to the synagogue known as that of the Libyans,[5] Cyrenians and Alexandrians, and to the
10 synagogue of those from Cilicia and Asia. But they were unable to resist the sense and conviction with which he spoke. So they primed men to say, "We have heard him use insulting language about Moses, and even about God", and they roused both the people and the elders and scribes. Then setting upon him they seized him and brought him before the Sanhedrin, and produced false witnesses who stated, "This man never stops denouncing this Holy Place[6] and the Law; for we have heard him say that Jesus the Nazarene will destroy this Place and change the customs handed down to us by Moses."

7.1   Then all who sat in the Sanhedrin bent their gaze on him, and saw a countenance as open as that of an angel. "Is all this true?" asked the high priest.

"Listen, brothers and fathers", Stephen replied. "The God of glory appeared to our father Abraham when he was in Mesopotamia, prior to his residence in Harran, and said to him, 'Leave your country and kindred, and go to the land I will show you.'[7] So he left the country of the Chaldeans and made his home in Harran. Later, after his father's death, God removed him from the land in
5 which you now live. But he gave him no inheritance in it, not even a foot[8] of territory, though he had promised, when he had no child, to give it to him as a possession and his descendants after him.[9] God also declared that his descendants would be aliens in a foreign land, where they would be enslaved and ill-treated for four hundred years; but 'the nation to which they are enslaved I will judge',[10] God said, 'and afterwards they shall go out and worship me in this place.'[11] And God gave him the covenant of circumcision.

"So Abraham begot Isaac, and circumcised him on the eighth day, and Isaac begot Jacob, and Jacob the twelve

---

5 Accepting the emendation *Libystinon* for *Libertinon* (freedmen). Jews from different lands and trades had their own synagogues in Jerusalem. Here those from N. Africa and Asia Minor are distinguished.

6 ie the Temple.

7 *Gen* 12:1.

8 Lit "step of a foot", *Deut* 2:5.

9 *Gen* 17:8.

10 *Gen* 15:13–14.

11 *Exod* 3:12.

Patriarchs.[12] And the Patriarchs out of jealousy sold
10 Joseph to Egypt; but God was with him, and brought him
out of all his troubles, and gave him wit and wisdom in
audience with Pharaoh king of Egypt and of all his
household.

"Now a famine and great affliction affected the whole
of Egypt and Canaan, and our fathers could find no
fodder. But Jacob having heard there was corn in Egypt
dispatched our fathers on a first mission. On the second
occasion Joseph made himself known to his brothers,
and Joseph's kinship was disclosed to Pharaoh. Then
Joseph sent and invited his father Jacob and all his
relations to come to him, seventy-five persons in all; and
15 Jacob went down to Egypt. There he and our fathers
ended their days, and were carried to Shechem, and laid
to rest in the sepulchre Abraham had purchased for a
sum of money from the sons of Hamor at Shechem.

"As the promised time approached which God had
sworn to Abraham, the people increased and multiplied
in Egypt until another king reigned over Egypt, who had
no knowledge of Joseph. He got the better of our race,
and ill-used our fathers, by forcing them to expose their
20 infants so as to cause the race to die out. It was at this
period that Moses was born, a lovely child, who was
nurtured for three months in his father's house. And
when he was exposed, Pharaoh's daughter picked him
up and reared him as her own son. Moses was trained in
all the wisdom of the Egyptians and was mighty in
speech and action.

"When he had reached the age of forty he had an
inclination to take a look at his brothers of the children of
Israel. Seeing one of them being injured, he defended
him, and avenged the man who had been bludgeoned by
25 striking down the Egyptian. He imagined that his
brothers would realise that God was going to deliver
them through his instrumentality; but they did not
realise it. The next day, indeed, coming across two of
them fighting, he intervened to make peace, saying,
'You are brothers. Why do you harm each other?' But the
one who was injuring his fellow pushed him aside and
said, 'Who constituted you our ruler and adjudicator?

12 A favourite book of the 1st cent. BC, used by Christians, was entitled
Testaments of the XII Patriarchs. See above p 113 n 50. The book is available,
and in English.

Perhaps you would like to kill me as you did the Egyptian yesterday?'[13] Upon this Moses fled, and became an alien in the land of Midian, where he begot two sons.

30   "At the expiry of his fortieth year an angel appeared to him in the wilderness of Mount Sinai in the flame of a burning thorn-bush, and Moses was amazed at the spectacle. As he went forward to inspect it the voice of the Lord came to him saying, 'I am the God of your fathers, the God of Abraham, Isaac and Jacob.' Then Moses trembled and dared not investigate. And the Lord said to him, 'Remove your sandals, for the place on which you stand is holy ground. I have indeed seen the ill-treatment of my people in Egypt, and I have heard their groans, and have come down to set them free. So
35   now come, I am going to send you to Egypt.'[14] This Moses whom they rejected saying, 'Who constituted you ruler and adjudicator?' God sent to them as ruler and redeemer with the aid of the angel who appeared to him in the bush. He brought them out, performing signs and wonders in Egypt, and at the Red Sea, and in the wilderness for forty years.[15]

"It was this Moses who said to the children of Israel, 'God will raise up for you from your brothers a prophet like myself.'[16] He it was who at the assembly in the wilderness acted as intermediary between the angel who spoke to him on Mount Sinai and our fathers, and who received vital pronouncements[17] to give us. But our fathers did not want to submit to him, and put him from
40   them, turning back in their minds to Egypt, telling Aaron, 'Make us gods to march at our head, for we do not know what has become of this Moses who brought us out of the land of Egypt.'[18] They made themselves a calf at this time, and celebrated a sacrifice to an idol, and rejoiced over what their hands had made. So God turned from them and gave them over to the worship of the host of heaven, as it is stated in the Book of the Prophets,[19]

---

13 *Exod* 2:13–14.
14 *Exod* 3:6–10.
15 cf *Assumpt. Mos.* 3:11. To this point the speech follows the lines of the recital of the Exodus given at the *Seder* (Passover Eve Service).
16 *Deut* 18:15.
17 Or 'Oracles' (*Logia*).
18 *Exod* 32:1.
19 The 12 Minor Prophets (*Hosea* to *Malachi*) forming one book.

'Was it to me you offered victims and sacrifices
Those forty years in the desert, house of Israel?
It was the shrine of Moloch you bore along,
And the star of the god Rompha,
Those images you made for your worship:
So will I remove you beyond Babylon.'[20]

"Yet our fathers had the Tent of Testimony in the
wilderness, as God had ordained, telling Moses to make
45 it according to the design[21] he had seen. Our fathers who
succeeded them brought it in with Joshua to the territory
possessed by the nations whom God drove out before
our fathers. So it remained to the time of David, who
found favour in God's sight, and promised to find a
habitation for the God of Jacob. It was Solomon who built
a house for God; though the Most High does not dwell in
edifices, as the prophet says,

'The heaven is my throne,
And the earth my footstool.
What sort of house will you build me?'
Says the Lord,
'Or on what spot am I to rest?
50   Did not my hand make all these things?'[22]

"You[23] stiffnecked and uncircumcised in heart and
ears, you are always in opposition to the holy Spirit! As it
was with your fathers, so it is with you. Which of the
prophets did your fathers not persecute? And which of
those did they not kill, who proclaimed in advance the
coming of the Just One whose betrayers and murderers
you have now become, you who received the Law as an
angelic compact, but have not kept it?"

When the members of the court heard this they were
55 cut to the quick and ground their teeth at him. Stephen,
inspired, gazed fixedly heavenwards and saw the divine
glory, and Jesus stationed at God's right hand. "Look!"

20 *Amos* 5:25–27.
21 The same words are used for 'tent' and 'pattern' as for 'shrine' and 'images'
in the quotation from *Amos*.
22 *Isa* 66:1–2.
23 In this paragraph, as in 7:4, the author, who was not a Jew, seems to have
been unable to avoid using the second person in the speech he has given
Stephen, who of course as a Jew himself would have said 'we' and 'our'.

he cried. "I see heaven wide open and the Son of Man standing at God's right hand."[24]

Shouting out, they stopped their ears, and rushing at Stephen by common consent they hustled him outside the city and stoned him. The witnesses[25] deposited their cloaks at the feet of a young man called Saul, and Stephen's execution had Saul's full approval.[a]

8.1   That same day there broke out a violent persecution of the community at Jerusalem, and except for the envoys they were all dispersed over the countries of Judea and Samaria. Pious men interred Stephen, and made great lamentation for him. Meanwhile Saul ravaged the community, entering house after house and dragging off both men and women to prison.

Those who were dispersed went far afield proclaiming
5   the Message. Philip, however, went down to the capital of Samaria[26] and proclaimed the Messiah to them. The populace paid the closest attention to what Philip had to say, listening with one accord to his words, and noting the signs he performed.[b] There was indeed much rejoicing in that city.

Now a man called Simon had been in that city previously, practising magic and turning the heads of the Samaritan people, claiming to be someone of conse-
10   quence. High and low alike had given heed to him saying, "He is that divine power called the Great Power." He had so taken them in with his magical arts that they had adhered to him for quite a time. But when they believed Philip's preaching about the Kingdom of God and the name of Jesus Christ they underwent immersion, both men and women. Even Simon himself believed, and after his immersion dogged the steps of Philip, observing with utter astonishment both the signs and the remarkable miracles that took place.

---

a So they stoned Stephen, while he appealed, "Lord Jesus, receive my spirit." Bending his knees he cried aloud, "Lord, count not this sin against them," and so saying fell asleep.
b For many possessed by foul spirits had them come out of them shrieking, and many paralytics and lame people were cured.

---

24 In the first century AD the Christians did not identify Jesus with God, or believe in a Trinity.
25 Who were obliged to cast the first stone.
26 Then called Sebaste.

When the envoys at Jerusalem heard that Samaria had welcomed God's Message they sent Peter and John to 15 them. On coming down these prayed that they might receive holy Spirit.[a] Then they laid their hands on them and they received holy Spirit.

When Simon saw that the Spirit was bestowed through the imposition of hands by the envoys he offered them money saying, "Give me this power too, so that whoever I place my hands on may receive holy Spirit."

20 "May your silver and yourself go to perdition!" Peter said to him, "for imagining that God's gift could be acquired for money. You have no part or lot in this business, for your heart is not right in God's sight. So repent of your wickedness, and beg God that what your brain has hatched may be forgiven you; for I perceive you are a sac of venom and the essence of malevolence."

"Do please entreat the Lord for me", Simon replied, "that not a thing of what you have said may befall me!"

25 When the envoys had testified and given the Master's Message they returned to Jerusalem after proclaiming the News to many Samaritan villages. But an angel of the Lord spoke to Philip saying, "Rise and go south along the road that runs from Jerusalem to Gaza."[b]

So he rose and set off, and thus came upon a Ethiopian eunuch holding high office under Kandace queen of the Ethiopians,[c] who had been to worship at Jerusalem and was now returning seated in his chariot reading the prophet Isaiah.

"Go and join that chariot", the Spirit prompted Philip. 30 When he ran forward he heard him reading the prophet Isaiah, and said, "Do you understand what you are reading?"

"However can I", he replied, "unless someone explains it to me?" He begged Philip to get up and sit beside him. The portion of Scripture he was reading was this,

> *He was led as a sheep to the slaughter,*
> *And as a lamb before its shearers is mute,*
> *So he opens not his mouth.*

---

a So far it had not fallen on any of them: they had only reached the stage of being immersed in the name of the Lord Jesus.
b The road is desert.
c He was actually her Lord Treasurer.

In his humility his judgment is taken away.
His generation who shall describe;
For his life is taken from the earth?[27]

So the eunuch said to Philip, "Of whom, may I ask, is the prophet saying this, of himself or of someone else?"

35   Speaking up, Philip began from the scripture to proclaim Jesus to him.

As they continued along the road they came to water. "Look, water!" cried the eunuch. "What is to prevent my being immersed?"[28]

He ordered the chariot to stop, and they both stepped down into the water, Philip and the eunuch, and he immersed him.

When they rose from the water the Spirit of the Lord snatched Philip away, and the eunuch joyfully resuming

40   his journey never saw him again. But Philip found himself at Azotus,[29] and passing through proclaimed the News in every town until he reached Caesarea.[30]

Chapter V

9.1   In the meantime Saul, still giving vent to dire threats against the disciples of the Master, went to the high priest and begged him for letters to Damascus, for the synagogues there, so that should he find any of this persuasion, whether men or women, he could bring them in bonds to Jerusalem as prisoners.[1]

As he neared Damascus in the course of his journey, suddenly a light from heaven blinded him, and falling to the ground he heard a voice saying to him, "Saul, Saul, why are you hunting me?"

---

27 Isa 53:7–8 (LXX).
28 Some MSS insert: "Philip said, 'You may if you believe with all your heart.' And he replied and said, 'I believe that Jesus Christ is the Son of God.'"
29 Otherwise Ashdod on the coastal plain.
30 Travelling north, touching Lydda, Joppa, and other places which Peter visited later (9:32). Caesarea was the seat of the Roman governor of Judea and Samaria.

1 No explanation is given as to why Saul should travel as far afield as Damascus in quest of believers in Jesus. From the Dead Sea Scrolls and Rabbinical sources, however, we learn that the area was a place of refuge for Jewish sectarians and persecuted people. In this region the True Teacher of the Essenes had proclaimed his 'New Covenant'.

5   "Who are you, lord?" he asked.

"I am Jesus, whom you are hunting.[2] Now rise, and go into the city, and you will be told what to do."

Saul's companions stood there speechless, hearing the voice but seeing no one.

When Saul rose from the ground, and had opened his eyes, his sight had gone. So they led him by the hand, and conducted him to Damascus. For three days he was unable to see, and neither ate nor drank.

10   Now there was a disciple in Damascus called Ananias, and the Master said to him in a vision, "Ananias!"

"Here I am, Master", he replied.

"Rise", said the Master, "and go to the street called Straight Cut, and inquire at the house of Judas for Saul called the Tarsian. He is praying there, and has beheld a man called Ananias coming and laying his hands on him so that he may regain his sight."

"But Master", Ananias answered, "I have heard of this man from many people, how much harm he has done your saints at Jerusalem. And now he is here with authority from the head priests to apprehend all who invoke your name."

15   "Go nevertheless", the Master told him, "for he is my chosen instrument to uphold my name before nations and kings and the children of Israel. I will give him to understand how much he must suffer for my sake."

So Ananias set off and went to the house, and laying his hand upon him said, "Brother Saul, the Master – Jesus who appeared to you on the road as you came – has sent me, that you may regain your sight and receive spiritual illumination."

At once something like scales fell from his eyes, and he could see again. Rising, he was immersed, and taking nourishment was strengthened.

Saul remained some time with the Damascus dis-
20 ciples[3] and forthwith proclaimed Jesus in the synagogues as Son of God. All who listened were amazed and said, "Isn't he the man who at Jerusalem was so bent on the destruction of those who invoked this name that he

---

2 Some MSS insert: "It is hard for you, kicking against the goad."
3 The writer either was not aware of, or chose to ignore, Paul's statement (*Gal* 1:17) that he went to Arabia and returned later to Damascus. During this period he had "an excess of revelation" (*II Cor* 12:7).

came here expressly to conduct them as prisoners to the head priests?''

But Saul became increasingly skilful, and completely discomfited the Jewish inhabitants of Damascus, proving that here indeed is the Messiah.

When things had gone on like this for some time the Jews plotted to kill him; but the plot was disclosed to Saul. They even kept a watch on the gates day and night 25 to kill him. The disciples, however, took him by night and lowered him down the wall in a basket.[4]

On arriving at Jerusalem Saul attempted to join the disciples.[5] But they were all afraid of him and refused to credit that he was a disciple. Barnabas got in touch with him, however, and brought him to the envoys, and described to them how Saul had seen the Master on the road, and how he had spoken to him, and how at Damascus he had argued eloquently on behalf of Jesus. So then he was free to come and go with them at Jerusalem, and spoke eloquently on behalf of the Master, 30 particularly engaging the Hellenic Jews in debate. But when the brothers became aware that these had designs on his life they brought him down to Caesarea and sent him away to Tarsus.

The Community throughout Judea, Galilee, and Samaria now enjoyed peace. Founded upon and motivated by the fear of the Lord and the exhortation of the holy Spirit it grew ever larger.

Chapter VI

In the course of his visits to every section of the Community Peter duly came down to the saints living at Lydda. There he found a man called Aeneas, who had been bed-ridden with paralysis for eight years.

---

4 When Paul's escape was contrived, Damascus was governed by an ethnarch appointed by Haretath king of Nabataean Arabia (*II Cor* 11:32). This is an important date clue, since Damascus was temporarily returned to Nabataean rule, by the Roman emperor Gaius Caligula in AD 37. It reverted to the Romans on the death of Haretath (Harith IV) in AD 40.
5 Paul (Saul) says (*Gal* 1:17–19) that he made no such attempt. The only persons he saw at Jerusalem were Peter and James the brother of Jesus.

"Jesus Christ cures you, Aeneas", Peter said to him. "Rise up, and make your bed."

35 At once he got up; and all who lived at Lydda and Sharon saw him, and they came over to the Master.

In Joppa there was a female disciple called Tabitha.[a] She was noted for her charitable actions and gifts. At this time she was taken ill and died, and having washed her corpse they laid her in the women's apartment upstairs. Lydda was close to Joppa,[1] so the disciples, learning that Peter was there sent two men to him with the request, "Please come to us as quickly as you can."

So Peter rose and accompanied them. When he arrived at Joppa they took him upstairs, and all the widows stood there with him weeping and displaying the tunics and cloaks Dorcas had made while she was with them.

40 Putting them all outside, Peter went down on his knees and prayed. Then turning to the corpse he said, "Tabitha, rise!"

She opened her eyes, and seeing Peter, sat up. After assisting her to rise he called in the saints and widows and presented her to them alive. This became known throughout Joppa, and many believed in the Master.

Peter stayed on for some time at Joppa with a certain Simon the tanner.

10.1 Now at Caesarea there was a man called Cornelius, a centurion of the cohort known as Italica,[3] pious and revering God[4] with all his family, one who gave a great deal in charity to the people and looked continually to God.

About three o'clock[5] one afternoon he saw distinctly in a vision an angel of God coming and saying to him, "Cornelius!"

Staring at him fearfully he replied, "What is it, lord?"

"Your prayers and charitable actions have come up for
5 remembrance before God", he told him. "So now send to

---

a Known as Dorcas, by translation[2] (ie into Greek).

---

1 In the Jewish War with the Romans both Lydda and Joppa were destroyed by the Romans.
2 The name means 'gazelle'.
3 ie the Italian Cohort.
4 A Gentile who believed in the One God, but had not become a full proselyte to Judaism.
5 The time of afternoon prayer.

Joppa with an invitation to one Simon known as Peter. He is lodging with Simon the tanner, whose house is by the sea."

When the angel who spoke to him had vanished, Cornelius summoned two of his retainers and a pious soldier who was devoted to him, explained everything to them, and dispatched them to Joppa.

Next day, while they were still on the road and approaching the city, Peter went up on the roof about noon to pray. He was feeling rather hungry and wanted his meal. While they were preparing it he fell into a trance, and saw heaven opened and a kind of bag let down like a huge sail-cloth, lowered to the ground by the four corners.[6] In this were a variety of quadrupeds, creeping things of the earth and birds of the air. "Rise, Peter, kill and eat!" came a voice to him. "On no account, Lord", said Peter, "I have never eaten anything impure[7] or unclean." A second time the voice came to him, "What God has cleansed you are not to treat as impure." This happened three times, and then the bag was drawn up to heaven.

While Peter was struggling in his own mind for an explanation of the vision he had seen, the men sent by Cornelius had been inquiring for Simon's house, and now stood at the gate calling out to learn if the Simon known as Peter lodged there.

Peter was still pondering over the vision when the Spirit said, "There are three[8] men looking for you. Rise and go down and set off with them without hesitation, for I have sent them."

Then Peter went down and told the men, "I am the one you want. What can I do for you?"

They told him, "Centurion Cornelius, a religious and godfearing man, well-respected by the whole Jewish nation, was advised by a holy angel to send for you to come to his house to hear things you would have to say."

So he invited them in and put them up, and the next day he rose and went with them accompanied by some of the brothers from Joppa. The following day they reached Caesarea. There Cornelius was awaiting them, and had

6 The vision could have reflected the scene of loading and unloading in Joppa harbour.
7 See *Lev* 5:2; 11:46–47.
8 Some MSS omit the figure.

25 invited his relations and intimate friends. Directly Peter entered he came forward and prostrated himself at his feet. But Peter raised him and said, "Please stand up. I am just an ordinary human being."

Conversing with him he went in, and found a number of persons assembled. "You are well aware", Peter said to them, "that it is quite against the rules for a Jew to associate with or visit someone of another race. But God has shown me that I must not regard any man as impure or unclean. That is why I came when I was sent for without raising any objection. Please tell me, then, the reason you sent for me."[9]

30 "About this time four days ago," Cornelius replied, "about three in the afternoon, I was praying in my house, when a man stood beside me in shining robes and said, 'Cornelius, your prayer has been heard, and your charitable actions have been mentioned before God. Send therefore to Joppa, and call for Simon known as Peter who lodges at the house of Simon the tanner by the sea.' Now here we all are in God's presence to listen to everything the Lord has bid you say."

Then Peter proceeded to speak as follows. "Now
35 indeed I realise that God makes no distinctions, but in every race the man who reveres him and acts charitably is accepted by him.

"You know the Message that God, who is Lord of all, sent to the children of Israel, proclaiming peace by Jesus Christ. That announcement, taking its rise from Galilee after the immersion which John proclaimed, spread throughout Judea, telling of Jesus of Nazareth, whom God anointed with holy Spirit[10] and power, who went about doing good and curing all who were in the Devil's clutches; for God was with him. We are witnesses to everything he did in the land of the Jews and in Jerusalem. But they killed him and hanged him on a

9 Peter would have been well aware of the injunction given by Jesus to the twelve that they were not to go to the Gentiles (*Mt* 10:5). Our author omits this injunction (*Lk* 9:2) and supplementary statements were appended to *Matthew* and *Mark* rescinding it. If it had been known that Jesus had ultimately told his followers to evangelise Gentiles, this would surely have been quoted, and the elaborate Cornelius story would have been quite unnecessary. Evidently *Luke* was quite unaware of the words attributed to Jesus after his resurrection.

10 For the early Christians Jesus had become the Messiah (the Christ), ie the Anointed One, at his baptism by the Spirit of God coming upon him.

40   gibbet. This man God raised on the third day, and granted a sight of him, not to all the people but to witnesses previously selected by God, namely ourselves, who ate and drank with him after his resurrection from the dead. He then commanded us to preach to the people and solemnly declare that he is the man appointed by God as judge of the living and the dead.[11] All the prophets testify to this, that every one who puts his trust in him will receive forgiveness of sins for his sake."

While he was delivering this speech the holy Spirit fell
45   on all those who were listening to the Message. The believers from the Circumcision[12] who had accompanied Peter were amazed that the gift of the holy Spirit was poured out on Gentiles as well; for they heard them speaking in tongues and magnifying God.

Then Peter challenged, "Dare anyone refuse water for the immersion of these people who have received the holy Spirit just as we did?"

So he ordered that they should be immersed in the name of Jesus Christ. Afterwards they begged him to stay a few days.

11.1   Now the envoys and brothers resident throughout Judea heard that the Gentiles had also accepted God's Message. So when Peter went up to Jerusalem the believers of the Circumcision joined issue with him saying, "You visited men who were uncircumcised and ate with them."

Then Peter related to them the whole sequence of
5   events. "I was in the town of Joppa", he told them, "engaged in prayer, when in a trance I saw a vision, a kind of bag like a huge sail-cloth, lowered from heaven by the four corners right to me. Peering into it, I clearly distinguished and saw the quadrupeds of the earth, wild beasts, creeping things, and the birds of the air. I also heard a voice saying to me, 'Rise, Peter, kill and eat.' I replied, 'On no account, Lord, for nothing impure or unclean has ever passed my lips.' The voice came from heaven a second time, 'What God has cleansed you are

11 In this speech, as in so many other places, the author of *Luke–Acts*, as *Matthew* and *Mark*, represents Jesus as wholly human. The doctrine of the deity of Jesus, and that of the Trinity, was quite unknown to the early Christians. His status was that of Messiah, the ultimate king of Israel.

12 Jews are thus distinguished from Gentiles (the Uncircumcised) corresponding to the Hebrew 'a son of the Covenant' and 'a non-son of the Covenant'.

10   not to treat as impure.' Three times this happened, and then the whole was drawn up again to heaven. At that very moment three men had arrived at the house where I was staying, sent to me from Caesarea; and the Spirit told me to accompany them without hesitation.

"These six brothers went with me, and we entered the man's house. He informed me that he had seen an angel in his house, standing there telling him, 'Send to Joppa to Simon known as Peter, who has that to tell you by

15   which you will be saved, you and all your house.' As I proceeded to speak, the holy Spirit fell on them just as it did on us in the first place, and I was reminded of the Master's words, 'John immersed in water, but you will be immersed in holy Spirit.'[13] If, therefore, God was giving them the identical gift he gave us when we believed in the Lord Jesus Christ, was I someone who could impede God?"

When they listened to this explanation they were satisfied, and praised God saying, "So to the Gentiles too God has granted repentance that they should live."[14]

Chapter VII

Now those who were dispersed as a result of the persecution that broke out over Stephen, travelled as far as Phoenicia, Cyprus and Antioch,[1] proclaiming the

20   Message to none but Jews.[2] Some of them were Cypriots and Cyrenians, who when they came to Antioch declared the Message to Greeks as well, proclaiming the Lord Jesus. The Lord's hand was with them, and a great number believed and came over to the Master.

When the news about them reached the ears of the Jerusalem Community they dispatched Barnabas[3] to Antioch. Having arrived and seen the evidence of God's

---

13 See *Acts* 1:9.
14 Lit "to Life", a Hebraism. They recited a benediction of God for bestowing on Gentiles a share in the Messianic Kingdom. cf the dictum of R. Joshua ben Hananiah (c AD 100): "The righteous of all nations have a share in the World to Come (the Messianic Age)."

1 In Syria on the Orontes, seat of the Roman legate of Syria.
2 See above p 225 n 9.
3 Himself a Cypriot, above p 210.

mercy he was delighted, and encouraged them all with firm resolve to remain loyal to the Master; for he was a good man, of great spirituality and faith. A substantial

25   body was now associated with the Master. So Barnabas set off for Tarsus in quest of Paul, and when he had found him he brought him to Antioch. For a whole year they were jointly entertained by the community and instructed a considerable number of people. It was at Antioch too that the disciples first received[4] the designation of *Christiani*.[5]

Now at this period prophets came down from Jerusalem to Antioch. One of them called Agabus rose and indicated[6] under inspiration that a severe famine would soon afflict the whole Empire.[a] Thereupon the disciples determined, as the means of each of them permitted, to send a contributon for the benefit of the

30   brothers resident in Judea. This they carried out, forwarding it to the elders by Barnabas and Saul.

12.1   It was about this time that King Herod[7] launched a savage attack on certain members of the Community. He beheaded James the brother of John, and finding that this pleased the Jews he proceeded to apprehend Peter, whom he imprisoned on arrest,[b] setting four squads of four soldiers to guard him,[8] purposing to bring him before the people after the Passover.

5   So Peter was held in custody, while prayer to God on his behalf was offered assiduously by the Community.

The very night before Herod was going to bring him up for trial, Peter was sleeping between two soldiers chained to them both,[9] while warders posted at the entrance guarded the prison. Suddenly, however, an angel of the Lord stood by him, and a light shone in the cell. Tapping Peter on the side, he roused him and said,

---

a It came in the reign of Claudius. (In AD 46. *Ed.*)
b The festival of Unleavened Bread was then in progress.

---

4 Or "first gave themselves".
5 ie Messianists, a coined Greek word with a Latin ending.
6 By some symbolic action. See below *Acts* 21:10–11.
7 Herod Agrippa I, a grandson of Herod the Great, made king of Judea by Claudius in AD 41. He did everything possible to cultivate Jewish good opinion in religious matters, but died in AD 44.
8 An indication of the political importance of the prisoner.
9 Lit "bound with two chains".

"Get up quickly!" And his chains fell away from his wrists.

"Fasten your girdle, and strap on your sandals", said the angel. And Peter obeyed.

"Now wrap your cloak round you and follow me", he told him.

10 He followed him out, and had no idea that what the angel had done had really happened: he imagined he was seeing a vision. When they had passed through the inner and outer prison[10] they came to the iron gate leading to the city, which opened for them of its own accord. They went out, and had gone the length of one street when the angel suddenly left him.

"Now", said Peter when he had recovered himself. "I know for certain that the Lord has sent his angel to extricate me from Herod's clutches and every expectation of the Judeans."[11]

Convinced of this, he went to the house of Mary mother of John known as Mark, where a number were assembled at prayer. Knocking at the street door, a maid called Rhoda came to answer it. Recognising Peter's voice, she was too excited to open the gate, and ran to tell them that Peter was standing at the gate.

15 "Nonsense", they said. But she insisted it was true. "It must be his angel[12] then", they said.

Peter meanwhile kept on knocking. And when they did open up and saw him they were astounded. Waving his hand for silence, he described to them how the Lord had brought him out of the prison, and added, "Give James[13] and the brothers the news." Then he left and went elsewhere.

When morning came there was no little commotion among the soldiers as to what had become of Peter. When Herod sent for him, and he was not to be found, after interrogating the guards he ordered their execu-

---

10 Lit "the first guard, then the second".

11 As in many other places *Judaioi* here means inhabitants of Judea as distinct from Galilee, and is not a reference to religion.

12 In ancient Jewish belief each person had his own angelic counterpart. Similarly it could be conceived, as in the NT, that there could be a heavenly counterpart of the Messiah (the Son of Man) and of Jerusalem and the Temple.

13 James (Jacob) the brother of Jesus next in age, and now titular head of all followers of Jesus.

tion. Then he went down from Judea to Caesarea and took up his residence there.[14]

20   Now Herod was greatly incensed with the Tyrians and Sidonians. So they waited on him by common consent, and having secured the good offices of Blastus the king's chamberlain they sued for peace, dependant as their country was on the royal domains for food supplies. So on a day appointed, Herod in full regalia seated himself in state and made them a speech.

The deputation greeted this with acclamation. "It is the voice of a god, not of a man!"[15] they cried.

Instantly an angel of the Lord struck him down, because he did not give God the praise, and being eaten by worms he expired.

But God's Message progressed and spread widely.

Chapter VIII

25   Meanwhile Barnabas and Saul, having fulfilled their mission, returned from Jerusalem taking John known as Mark with them.

13.1   Now there were at Antioch with the community there both prophets and teachers. There was Barnabas, and Simeon nicknamed Niger,[1] Lucius a Cyrenian, Menahem a foster-brother of Herod the tetrarch, and Saul. As they were performing their religious rites and fasting, the holy Spirit said, "Set apart for me Barnabas and Saul for the task I have assigned to them."

So when they had all fasted and prayed they laid their hands upon them and let them go. Thus commissioned by the holy Spirit they came down to Seleucia,[2] and from

5   there sailed to Cyprus. Landing at Salamis they proclaimed God's Message in the Jewish synagogues, with

---

14 Caesarea had a mixed Jewish and non-Jewish population, and the king evidently felt safer there from what he believed was the plotting against him of Jewish extremists.

15 In those days rulers were regarded by non-Jews as having divine status, which was why Christians from the Gentiles came to hold this of Jesus, who as Messiah was king of the Jews. Among the Jews the term son of God was not employed in a literal sense, which would have compromised the Divine Unity.

1 ie 'the Black'.
2 The port of Antioch.

John acting as their attendant.

Having traversed the whole island to Paphos, they encountered a magus, a Jewish false prophet, called Bar-Jesus, who was in the retinue of the proconsul Sergius Paulus, a man of insight. The proconsul summoned Barnabas and Saul, desiring to hear God's Message. But Elymas, the magus,[a] opposed them, trying to divert the proconsul from the faith. But Saul, otherwise Paul,[3] in an inspired state, glared at him and said, "You crafty parasite, Devil's spawn, enemy of everything straightforward! Must you for ever be making crooked the direct ways of the Lord? See, the Lord's hand is upon you. Blind shall you be, getting no sight of the sun for a season."

10

At once there fell on him a mist and a darkness, and he groped about for someone to lead him by the hand. Then the proconsul, seeing what had happened, believed, overwhelmingly impressed by the Master's teaching.

Taking passage from Paphos those associated with Saul reached Perga in Pamphylia. There John parted company with them and returned to Jerusalem,[4] while they travelled on from Perga and arrived at Pisidian Antioch, where they attended the synagogue on the sabbath day and took their seats. After the reading of the Law and the Prophets the wardens of the synagogue sent them a message, "Brothers, if there is any word of encouragement you would like to address to the congregation, please speak."

15

Then Paul rose, and waving his hand for silence said, "Fellow Israelites, and you who revere God,[5] give me your attention.

"The God of this people Israel chose our fathers and raised up the people when they sojourned in Egypt, and brought them out with a high arm,[6] and sustained[7] them

a For so his appellation is to be translated.[8]

---

3 Saul was a Roman citizen. He may have been nicknamed Paulus because he was small of stature: the name means 'small'. He appears to have decided to employ it after his meeting with the proconsul L. Sergius Paulus.
4 The reason for his abrupt departure is not indicated. But it was resented by Paul. See *Acts* 16:37–38.
5 Gentile monotheists who attended Jewish worship.
6 *Deut* 26:8.
7 *Deut* 1:31 (LXX), reading *trophophoreo* for *tropophoreo*.
8 The author or commentator supposes Elymas to mean magus. cf the Arabic *Alim*, a sage.

for some forty years in the wilderness. Having subju-
gated seven nations in the land of Canaan, he gave Israel
possession of their land for about four hundred and fifty
20   years. After the subjugation he gave them judges down
to the Prophet Samuel. Then they asked for a king, and
God gave them Saul the son of Kish, a man of the tribe of
Benjamin, for forty years. Then in his stead he raised up
David as their king, of whom he testified, 'I have found
David the son of Jesse a man after my own heart, who
will carry out my wishes.'[9] From his descendants, as he
promised, 'he raised up for Israel a deliverer',[10] namely
Jesus, John having first proclaimed to all the people of
Israel an immersion in penitence before Jesus came on
25   the scene. Towards the end of his public career John
declared, 'I am not the one you suppose me to be. But
after me there will come one whose sandals I am
unworthy to untie.'[11]

"Brothers, sons of Abraham's race, and those here
with you who revere God, to us now comes the Message
of deliverance. For the inhabitants of Jerusalem and their
rulers, having failed to appreciate it and the utterances of
the prophets read every sabbath, by condemning him
have fulfilled them. Having discovered nothing that
merited death, they none the less begged Pilate that he
should be killed. After completing everything written of
him, they took him down from the gibbet and laid him in
30   a tomb. But God raised him from the dead, when he was
seen on a number of occasions by those who had come
with him from Galilee to Jerusalem, who are now his
witnesses to the people.

"Thus we are able to announce to you that the promise
God made he has carried out for us their children by
having raised up Jesus, just as in the second Psalm it is
stated, 'You are my son, to-day I have begotten you.'[12]
As to God's raising him from the dead, never more to
return to decay, he has stated this, 'I will bestow on you
35   the benefits assured to David,'[13] relating to what he had

---

9 *I Sam* 13:14.
10 cf the *Amidah* (18 *Benedictions*), *Bened.* 1, "who rememberest the pious deeds
of the fathers, and in love will bring a redeemer to their children's children"
(AJP p 44). This prayer formed part of the service.
11 See *Lk* 3:15–16.
12 *Ps* 2:7.
13 *Isa* 55:3 (LXX).

said elsewhere, 'You will not let your beneficiary see decay.'[14] David, indeed, having complied with God's wishes in his own generation, slept and was gathered to his fathers, and experienced decay. But he whom God raised up did not experience decay.

"Be it known to you, therefore, brothers, that through this man forgiveness of sins is proffered you, and by him all who believe are exonerated from everything in respect of which you could not be exonerated by the Law
40 of Moses. Take heed, then, that there does not befall you what was stated in the prophets,[15]

> *Look, you despisers, marvel and vanish away;*
> *For I will perform a miracle in your days*
> *You will never credit if one relates it to you.'*[16]

As Paul and Barnabas were leaving, the wardens invited them to address the congregation on the same subject the following sabbath. When the people came out of synagogue, many of the Jews and God-fearing Gentiles followed the envoys, who conversed with them, and urged them to retain God's favour.

On the ensuing sabbath nearly the whole town was
45 assembled to hear God's Message. When the Jews saw the crowds, however, they were filled with envy and spoke in opposition to Paul's statements, and became abusive. So Paul and Barnabas bluntly told them, "It was essential initially to proclaim God's Message to you; but since you spurn it and do not deem yourselves worthy of Eternal Life, perforce we turn to the Gentiles. The Lord has instructed us to this effect,

> *I have set you as a light to the Gentiles,*
> *To serve for salvation to the ends of the earth.*[17]

When the Gentiles heard this they rejoiced and praised God's word; and those who were meant for Eternal Life believed.[18] So the Lord's Message was
50 spread throughout the region. But the Jews worked

---

14 *Ps* 16:10 (LXX), 'benefits . . . beneficiary' playing on the Greek '*ta hosia . . . ton hosion.*'
15 The Book of the 12 Minor Prophets.
16 *Hab* 1:5.
17 *Isa* 49:6.
18 Only a predestined number of Gentiles, it was believed, would share in the Messianic Kingdom.

upon the proselytes among the influential ladies[19] and upon the leading townsmen, and roused hostility against Paul and Barnabas; and they expelled them from their borders. The envoys shook the dust from their feet in protest, and went to Iconium; but they left the disciples joyful and inspired.

14.1   In Iconium similarly they went to the Jewish synagogues and spoke to the same effect, with the result that both Jews and a considerable number of Greeks believed. They therefore spent some time there, speaking boldly for the Master, who confirmed his gracious Message by permitting signs and wonders to be performed though their instrumentality. But the unconvinced Jews agitated and poisoned the minds of the Gentiles against the brothers. The townsfolk were divided, some taking the side of the Jews, others siding

5   with the envoys. So when a concerted attack was made by the Gentiles and the Jews with their rulers to mob and stone the envoys, they were apprised of it, and escaped to the cities of Lycaonia, to Lystra and Derbe and the neighbouring district, where they resumed their preaching.

At Lystra there sat a man impotent in his feet. Lame from birth, he had never been able to walk. He was one of those who listened to Paul speaking. Paul noticed him, and observing that he had the faith to be cured he

10   said to him sharply, "Get to your feet!" The man sprang up and walked.

When the populace saw what Paul had done they shouted in the Lycaonian tongue, "The gods have come down to us in human form." Barnabas they called Zeus, and Paul Hermes, because he was the spokesman.[20] Thereupon the priest of Zeus-more-ancient-than-the city[21] brought oxen and garlands to the gates, proposing with the populace to offer sacrifice. But learning of this the envoys Barnabas and Paul, rending their garments,

15   rushed into the crowd crying, "Men, what are you about? We are the same kind of human beings as yourselves, preaching to you to turn from these errors to the

---

19 Judaism is known to have made a great appeal to these.
20 Hermes (Mercury) messenger of the gods.
21 Lit "Zeus (in being) before the city", his temple having been there prior to the city's foundation.

Living God, who made heaven and earth, and the sea, and all they contain. In bygone ages he let all the nations go their own way. Yet even so, by his beneficence, he did not leave himself unattested, giving you rain from heaven and fruitful seasons, satisfying your hearts with food and good cheer."[22] But even by saying this they with difficulty prevented the people from sacrificing to them.

Then there came Jews from Antioch and Iconium, and incited the populace to violence; and having stoned Paul they dragged him outside the town believing him to be

20   dead. But when the disciples had surrounded him he picked himself up and went into the town. The next day he set off with Barnabas for Derbe. After giving that town the News, and making a number of disciples, they turned back to Lystra, Iconium and Antioch, confirming the disciples, encouraging them to maintain their allegiance, and telling them, "We have to enter the Kingdom of God by the hard road."[23]

When they had ordained elders for them in each community, and had prayed with fasting, they committed them to the keeping of the Lord in whom they had put their trust.

25   Traversing Pisidia, they reached Pamphylia, and after delivering the Message at Perga came down to Attaleia. From there they sailed for Antioch, from which city they had been commended to God's mercy for the mission they had now accomplished. Calling the community together on their arrival, they reported all that God had done for them, and how he had opened the door of faith to the Gentiles. They stayed on there with the disciples for a considerable time.

Chapter IX

15.1   Now certain persons came down from Judea[1] and instructed the brothers, "Unless you are circumcised in

---

22 cf *Deut* 11:14. Paul's words here reflect passages in the Jewish festival grace before and after meals, where God is praised as "the doer of good to all".

23 Lit "through many trials." Quoted by Prochorus, *Acts of John*, as a saying of Jesus.

1 The author does not wish to state that these emissaries actually came from James the brother of Jesus (*Gal* 2:12).

conformity with the Mosaic ordinance you cannot be saved." And when there arose no small conflict and controversy with them on the part of Paul and Barnabas, it was decided that Paul and Barnabas with some others of the community should go up to the envoys and elders at Jerusalem about this question. Forwarded on their way by the community, they went through Phoenicia and Samaria giving out the news of the turning of the Gentiles to God to the great joy of the brothers.

5   On arrival at Jerusalem they were welcomed by the community, and by the envoys and elders, and reported all that God had done for them. But some of the Pharisee party raised objections and said, "It is essential to circumcise them and charge them to observe the Mosaic Law."[2] The envoys and elders duly met to deliberate on the matter. After there had been much argument, Peter rose and addressed them.

"You are aware, brothers", he said, "that in the early days of our association God chose that through my agency the Gentiles should hear the Message of the Good News and believe it. God, who knows the heart, testified to their sincerity, giving them the holy Spirit equally with ourselves, and making no distinction of allegiance between us and them when purifying their

10   hearts. Why then do you now try God, clamping a yoke on the necks of these disciples which neither our ancestors nor ourselves could manage to bear? Rather is it by the mercy of the Lord Jesus that we trust to be saved as they do."[3]

The entire company preserved silence, and listened while Barnabas and Saul described the signs and wonders God had performed through them among the Gentiles.

When they had finished James[4] summed up. "Brothers", he said, "please give me your attention. Symeon has narrated exactly what God contemplated originally, the taking from among the Gentiles of a

2 Assuming that these Gentiles, who had now given their allegiance to the Messiah as king of Israel, were on that account to be regarded as Israelites and therefore subject to the laws of Israel.

3 The speech is, of course, the composition of the non-Jewish author, as the sentiments convey. The real circumstances are conveyed by Paul in his letter to the Galatians (*Gal* 2:11–14).

4 The brother of Jesus was head of the Council, at this time governing all Christians.

15 people to bear his name. With this the sayings of the prophets are in complete accord, as it is stated:

> Thereafter I will return,
> And re-erect the fallen tent of David.
> I will re-erect its wreckage and set it upright;
> That the rest of mankind[5] may seek the Lord
> Even all the Gentiles by whom my name is invoked,
> Says the Lord, who makes this known from of old.[6]

"Consequently my verdict is, that those of the Gentiles
20 who turn to God be not molested, but that we write to them to abstain from whatever is polluted by idols, from sexual impurity, from eating strangled animals, and from blood.[7] For Moses from ancient times has had his preachers in every town, being publicly read in the synagogues every sabbath."

Then the envoys and elders, and the entire convocation, resolved to select certain of their number and send them to Antioch with Paul and Barnabas, namely Judas called Bar-Sabbas and Silas, prominent men among the
25 brothers, to convey the following letter:

"The envoys and elders, your brothers, present their compliments to the brothers from the Gentiles in Antioch, Syria and Cilicia.

Since it has come to our attention that some of our number, to whom we gave no such instructions, have been confusing you with their statements, unsettling your minds, it was unanimously resolved to send you special delegates along with our good friends Barnabas and Paul who have so devoted themselves to the cause of our Lord Jesus Christ. Accordingly we have commissioned Judas and Silas, who will confirm our decision verbally.

It was resolved by the holy Spirit and ourselves to impose on you no greater burden than these essential things, to abstain from what is dedicated to idols, from blood, from eating strangled animals, and from sexual

---

5 Reading *Adam* for *Edom*. At this time Edom was a term applied by Jews to the Roman Empire, representing the habitable world.
6 *Amos* 9:11–12 (loosely quoted).
7 Part of the so-called Laws of Noah applicable to the righteous of all nations, and by practice of which a Gentile became a 'stranger *within* the gate' (friend and brother), but not a fellow-Israelite.

impurity. If you keep strictly to this you will be quite in order.

> Farewell."

30   When the envoys were dismissed they went down to Antioch, and having called the membership together they handed over the letter. On reading it they rejoiced at the cheering news. Judas, and Silas also, both of whom were prophets, greatly encouraged the brothers by their words and gave them confidence.

In due course the brothers let them go with their good
35   wishes to those who had sent them. But Paul and Barnabas stayed on at Antioch teaching and preaching the Lord's Message in association with many others.

Chapter X

After some time Paul said to Barnabas, "Let us go back and see how the brothers are faring in all those cities where we proclaimed the Lord's Message."

Barnabas was anxious to take John known as Mark too. But Paul did not think fit to take along one who had deserted them on reaching Pamphylia, and had not shared in the mission. Friction resulted, so that they parted company. Barnabas, taking Mark with him, sailed
40   for Cyprus, while Paul, choosing Silas, left with the brothers' commendation to the Lord's favour, and travelled through Syria and Cilicia confirming the communities.

16.1   In due course they reached Derbe and Lystra. There they met a disciple called Timotheus, son of a believing Jewish woman and a Greek father, very well spoken of by the brothers at Lystra and Iconium. Paul wanted him to go with him, and had him circumcised because of the Jews in those parts; for they all knew his father was a Greek.

As they passed through the cities they delivered the stipulations for the communities to observe which had been decided upon by the envoys and elders at
5   Jerusalem. Thus the communities were strengthened in their allegiance and increased in membership daily.

The envoys now traversed Phrygia and the Galatian region, being debarred by the holy Spirit from delivering the Message in Asia. Coming then in line with Mysia they attempted to travel into Bithynia[1]; but the spirit of Jesus did not permit them. So on reaching Mysia they came down to Troas.[2] There a vision appeared to Paul: it was a certain man of Macedon,[3] standing and appealing to him, "Cross over to Macedonia and aid us."

10   [4]"In accordance with the vision Paul had seen we at once endeavoured to get to Macedonia, deducing that God had summoned us to proclaim the News to them. Putting to sea from Troas, therefore, we ran a straight course to Samothrace, and the day following to Neapolis, and thence to Philippi, which is the top-ranking city of Macedonia, a Roman colony. We spent some time in the city, and on the sabbath day we went outside the gate to the river bank where we had reason to believe there was a Jewish oratory.[5] There we sat down and spoke to the women who attended it. There was one woman who listened called Lydia, a worship-per of God, of the city of Thyatira, who was in the purple cloth trade. The Lord opened her mind to

15   receive what Paul said, and when she was immersed with her household she begged, 'If you are satisfied of my loyalty to the Master you must come and stay with me.' We were absolutely forced to accept.

"Once as we were going to the oratory a slave-girl possessed by an oracular spirit[6] met us, who made her masters a good living by fortune-telling. She persisted in following Paul and ourselves crying, 'These men are servants of the Most High God, who tell you the way of salvation.' For several days she carried on like this, until in desperation Paul turned round and told the spirit, 'In the name of Jesus Christ I order you to leave her!' Out it went that very instant."[7]

When her masters saw that their prospect of gain was

---

1 Mysia lay to their west, Bithynia north and north-west.
2 The port of Alexandria-Troas (Trojan Alexandria).
3 Some definite person seems to be indicated, the most probable being the famous Philip of Macedon, father of Alexander the Great, known as 'the Man of Macedon' (Horace, Bk III, Ode 16).
4 Here begins the first of the notebook extracts used by the author. If Luke wrote them it would suggest that he joined the envoys at Troas.
5 In Hebrew *Bet-tefilah* (Gr *Proseuche*), a prayer centre.
6 Lit "a pythonic spirit", associated with ventriloquism.
7 The extract seems to extend further, but as this is not certain the indentation has been confined to what is written in the first person plural.

20   gone, they seized Paul and Silas and dragged them to the magistrates' court, and brought them before the praetors. "These men", they said, "Jews of course, are making serious trouble for this city of ours, advocating practices which as Romans we are not permitted to entertain, much less engage in."

The crowd was solidly against the envoys; so the praetors gave orders to have them stripped and beaten with rods. When numerous strokes had been given them, they threw them into prison, cautioning the jailer to guard them securely. Having had a warning like that, he threw them into the inner prison, and secured their feet in stocks.

25   Around midnight Paul and Silas were at prayer praising God, with the other prisoners listening to them, when all of a sudden there was such a great earthquake as to shake the foundations of the jail. Immediately all the doors sprang ajar, and the fetters of all the prisoners were freed. Roused from his sleep, and seeing the doors of the prison standing open, the jailer drew his sword, and was about to kill himself thinking the prisoners had escaped, when Paul shouted, "Don't harm yourself! We are all here." Calling for lights he burst in, and all of a

30   tremble fell down before Paul and Silas. Taking them outside he said, "Oh sirs, what must I do to assure my safety?"

"Put your trust in the Lord Jesus", they said, "and both you and your family will be preserved."

Then they gave him and his family God's Message. He took immediate care of them at that time of night, bathed their stripes, and was himself immersed and all connected with him. Conducting them to his house he set food before them, and rejoiced with all his family in their new found faith in God.

35   When morning came the praetors sent lictors with the message, "Release those men." The jailer broke this news to Paul. "The praetors have sent word that you are to be released. So now you are quite free to go."

But Paul sent word back to them, "After flogging us in public uncondemned, men who are Romans of course,[8], they threw us into prison. Now they are throwing us out

---

8 Echoing the sneer 'Jews of course' (of verse 20). Paul, and evidently Silas, held Roman citizenship.

again secretly. Oh no! Let them come officially and fetch us out."

The lictors reported these words to the praetors, who were dismayed when they heard they were Romans. Hurrying to the prison, they entreated them, and bringing them out begged them to leave the city.

40   On coming out of the prison they went to Lydia's house, and having seen and encouraged the brothers they took their departure.

17.1   Following the road through Amphipolis and Apollonia they came to Thessalonica, where there was a Jewish synagogue. As was Paul's custom they went in, and for three successive sabbaths they discoursed from the Scriptures, expounding them, and explaining how the Messiah had to suffer and to rise again from the dead, and that "this Jesus I am telling you about is the Messiah."[9]

Some of them were convinced and adhered to Paul and Silas, with a large number of Greek proselytes and

5   not a few influential ladies. But the Jews in their jealousy got hold of some worthless loafers, and forming a mob set the town in an uproar. They concentrated on Jason's house with the intention of bringing the envoys before the court; but failing to find them they dragged Jason and some other brothers before the politarchs,[10] clamouring that "these subverters of the Empire[11] have now reached here, and Jason has harboured them. All of them are violators of Caesar's decrees, and declare there is another king, one Jesus."[12] They alarmed the people and the politarchs when they heard this; but after taking sureties from Jason and the others they let them go.

10   At once the brothers sent away Paul and Silas by night to Beroea, where on arrival they went straight to the Jewish synagogue. The Jews there were more civil than those at Thessalonica: they received the Message with every consideration, examining the Scriptures daily to ascertain whether it was correct. Consequently many of

9 See *I Thess* 2:2.
10 The city prefects.
11 Lit "Of the (civilized) world."
12 The envoys were ignorantly or deliberately confounded with the Jewish nationalist agitators, who at this period were visiting the Jewish communities in various parts of the Empire in order to foster revolt against Rome. See Suetonius, *Claud.* xxv; Dio Cass. *Rom. Hist.* lx:6; and the *Letter of Claudius to the Alexandrians.*

them believed, and not a few ladies and gentlemen of quality.

When the Jews of Thessalonica were aware that God's Message was being proclaimed by Paul at Beroea as well, they came there too to sway and stir up the populace. At once the brothers sent Paul away to the coast, though

15   Silas and Timotheus stayed on at Beroea. Those who were escorting Paul accompanied him as far as Athens, and there left him, taking back his instructions to Silas and Timotheus to rejoin him as quickly as they could.

While Paul waited for them at Athens his spirit flared up within him when he saw how the city was idol-ridden. Therefore he held forth in the synagogue to the Jews and proselytes, and daily in the market-place to those who happened to be by. There certain of the Epicurean and Stoic philosophers encountered him. "What is this garbage-picker driving at?" said some. To which others replied, "He seems to be a propagator of foreign divinities."[a] So they took him along and brought him before the Areopagus[13] with the request, "May we be informed of the nature of the new doctrine you are

20   preaching? You are bringing some very queer notions to our attention, and consequently we should much like to know precisely what they mean."[b]

So Paul, standing before the Areopagus, spoke as follows:

"Athenians, I cannot help but notice how intensely religious you are. For as I went about and looked at your various objects of worship I even came across a pedestal[14] on which was inscribed, 'To a God Unknown.' It is he with whom I am acquainting you, the One you unwittingly revere.

"The God who made the universe and everything in it, being as he is Lord of heaven and earth, does not reside

25   in artificial temples, nor is he tended by human hands as though he stood in need of anything, since he is the giver

a This was because he was proclaiming Jesus and the Resurrection.[15]
b All Athenians and the foreign residents enjoy nothing better than retailing or listening to the latest notion.

---

13 The Council of Public Morals and Welfare.
14 Or 'altar'.
15 They took the Resurrection (*Anastasis*) to be a female divinity.

of life, breath and substance to all.[16] From one man he produced every section of the human race which occupies the entire surface of the earth, and fixed the exact dimensions and boundaries of their settlement,[17] that they should seek after God; for if they would grope for him they would find him, for in fact he is not far from each one of us. Indeed, 'by him we live, and move, and have our being' as some of your own poets have also stated, 'for we are truly his offspring.'[18] Being then God's offspring, we ought not to conceive the Divine nature as capable of representation in gold, silver, or stone, modelled by art and human ingenuity.

30　　　"The ages of ignorance, however, God overlooked; but now he calls upon all mankind everywhere to repent, since he has set a day on which he will judge the world with justice[19] by the man[20] he has appointed, furnishing everyone with concrete proof of this by raising him from the dead."

When they heard of the resurrection of the dead some scoffed, while others said, "Perhaps you will tell us about this some other time."

So Paul left their presence. But some joined him and believed, including Dionysius the Areopagite, a woman called Damaris, and a few others.

Chapter XI

18.1　　　After this Paul left Athens and went to Corinth. There he came across a Jew called Aquila, a native of Pontus, who had recently come from Rome with his wife Priscilla because Claudius had decreed the banishment of all Jews from Rome.[1] Paul got to know them, and because he was of the same trade he stayed with them and they worked

16 cf Jewish Grace after meals (AJP).
17 cf *Deut* 32:8.
18 From the opening lines of the *Phenomena* of Aratus of Cilicia. See also Cleanthes, *Hymn to Zeus*.
19 At the dawn of the Messianic Age.
20 Jesus, in the Messianic capacity of Son of Man.

1 See p 241 n 12. It appears that the Emperor Claudius expelled all foreign Jews from Rome because of Messianic agitation. See Suetonius, *Claud.* xxv, Dio Cass. *Rom. Hist.* lx:6. The date was c AD 50.

together.[a] Every sabbath he discoursed in the synagogue, and convinced both Jews and Greeks.

5   When Silas and Timotheus came down from Macedonia Paul was deeply engaged with the Message, adducing evidence to the Jews that Jesus was the Messiah. But when they ranged themselves against him, and became abusive, he shook out his clothes, and told them, "Your blood be on your own heads! I am guiltless. From now on I go to the Gentiles."

So he changed his venue, and went to the house of a proselyte called Titus Justus,[2] which adjoined the synagogue. But Crispus,[3] president of the synagogue, believed in the Master, as did his whole family, and many of the Corinthians who listened believed and were immersed. The Master told Paul in a vision of the night,

10   "Do not be afraid. Speak out and do not be silent; for I am with you, and no one shall inflict any injury on you; for I have many people in this city."[4] So he settled down for a year and a half teaching them God's message.

During Gallio's term as proconsul of Achaia,[5] however, the Jews took common action against Paul, and brought him before the tribunal saying, "This man is seducing the people to become proselytes without reference[6] to Jewish Law."

As Paul was about to reply, Gallio said to the Jews, "If this was a matter of misdemeanour or criminal offence,

15   Jews, I would quite properly sustain your cause.[7] But if it is a question of esteem and reputations, and of law as it concerns yourselves, that is your affair. I would rather not be a judge of such things." And he barred them from the tribunal.[8]

Then all those present seized Sosthenes, president of the synagogue, and beat him in front of the tribunal; but Gallio had no responsibility for this.

---

a   They were tentmakers by trade.

---

2 Gentiles who became full proselytes to Judaism, *Ger-zedek*, often on conversion took the appellation Zedek (Lat. Justus).

3 See *I Cor.* 1:4.

4 Paul wrote more letters to the community at Corinth than to any other.

5 L. Junius Gallio, brother of Seneca. He was Proconsul of Achaia, July 51–June 52 AD.

6 Or "contrary to".

7 ie allow you to plead.

8 ie refused their case a hearing.

Paul stayed on for some time, and then, saying good-bye to the brothers sailed for Syria accompanied by Priscilla and Aquila, having his head shaved at Cenchreae as he was under a vow.[9] When they reached Ephesus Paul left them there, and going by himself into the synagogue he discoursed to the Jews. They begged him to make a longer stay, but he declined, bidding them farewell and saying, "I must by all means keep the approaching festival at Jerusalem.[10] But, God willing, I will return to you."

He set sail from Ephesus, and on arrival at Caesarea went up to Jerusalem to pay his respects to the Community. Then he went down to Antioch, and after allowing himself a certain time there[11] he left again, covering successively the Galatian region and Phrygia, confirming all the disciples.

Meanwhile there arrived at Ephesus a Jew called Apollos, a native of Alexandria, a learned man well-versed in the Scriptures.[12] He had some knowledge of the Faith of the Master, and being an enthusiast he spoke and taught very much to the point the matters relating to Jesus, though acquainted only with John's rite of immersion. He spoke very boldly in the synagogue, and Priscilla and Aquila having listened to him made friends with him and explained God's way to him more exactly. And when he wished to cross over to Achia, the brothers, who were very taken with him, wrote to the disciples to make him welcome. On his coming he proved a valuable ally to those who by God's mercy had believed; for he confuted the Jews most forcefully by common consent, demonstrating from the Scriptures that Jesus was the Messiah.

19.1 Now while Apollos was at Corinth Paul came to Ephesus[13] by the up-country route and found some

20

25

---

9 Some hold that it was Aquila who was under a vow.

10 Some MSS omit. The Christians would seem to have followed the Essenes in reporting on their activities at the feast of Pentecost to their Supreme Council. Paul had to make his report. There is some evidence of condensation at this part of the narrative.

11 It is considered probable that Paul's letter to the Galatian communities was written at this time.

12 Presumably the Messianic interpretation of the Scriptures. It is possible that Apollos was the author of the *Epistle to the Hebrews,* which makes much use of the writings of the philosopher Philo of Alexandria.

13 Ephesus was the capital of the Roman province of Asia. Its temple of Artemis (Diana) was one of the wonders of the world. See next chapter.

disciples there. "Did you receive holy Spirit when you believed?" he asked them.

"We have heard nothing of any holy Spirit", they told him.

"In what connexion, then, were you immersed?" he said.

"In connexion with John's immersion."

"John carried out a rite of immersion as an indication of repentance," said Paul, "telling the people they were to put their trust in the one who would come after him, namely in Jesus."

5   On hearing this they were immersed in the name of the Lord Jesus. And when Paul had laid his hands on them the holy Spirit took possession of them, and they spoke in tongues and prophesied.[a]

Then Paul entered the synagogue, and over a period of three months he spoke out boldly, arguing and persuading about the Kingdom of God. But when some remained obstinate and unconvinced, disparaging the Faith[14] before the congregation, he parted company with them and took the disciples away, continuing his dis-
10   courses daily in the lecture hall of Tyrannus.[15] This went on for two years; so that all who lived in Asia, Jews and Greeks alike, heard the Master's message. God effected extraordinary miracles through Paul's instrumentality, so that even handkerchiefs and loincloths[16] were taken away for the sick after physical contact with him, and by this means they were freed from their diseases and the evil spirits left them.

Then certain Jewish travelling exorcists attempted to use the name of the Lord Jesus on those possessed by evil spirits, saying, "I adjure you by Jesus whom Paul pro-
15   claims!"[b] But the evil spirit replied, "I know Jesus, and I

---

a There were about twelve men in all.

b They were[17] sons of a certain Skeva, a Jewish head priest, who did this.

---

14 Lit "that Way" or "persuasion"? See 19:23 n 1.

15 Cod. D. adds, "from eleven to four".

16 Greek words of Latin origin, 'suderia' and 'semicinctia'.

17 Omitting 'seven' before 'sons' since evidently there were only two. The name Skeva may have suggested the number seven (Heb. *sheva*).

am familiar with Paul, but who do you think you are?"
And the man in whom the evil spirit dwelt leapt on them
and overpowered them both, so that they fled from that
house lacerated and with their clothes in ribbons. This
became known to all the inhabitants of Ephesus, Jews
and Greeks alike, and they were seized with fear, the
name of the Lord Jesus was magnified. Many of those
who believed came and confessed, and made a clean
breast of their practices. Several who were practitioners
of magic made a bonfire of their books in the sight of all.[18]
The value was computed, and was found to come to fifty
thousand pieces of silver.

20   Thus did the Master's Message powerfully extend and
prevail.

Chapter XII

At this stage of affairs Paul formed the intention of
travelling to Jerusalem via Macedonia and Achaia, saying, "When I have been there I must also visit Rome." So
he despatched two of his assistants, Timotheus and
Erastus, to Macedonia, while he stayed for a time in Asia.

Just at this period there was a serious disturbance over
the Faith.[1] It was due to a certain Demetrius, a
silversmith, who provided a good living for his crafts-
25   men making shrines of Artemis. Calling them together,
and others engaged in similar employment, he addressed them as follows:

"Men, you fully appreciate that our livelihood
depends on this employment. You will also have
observed and noted that this fellow Paul with his persua-
sions has affected a whole lot of people, not only of
Ephesus but of pretty well all Asia, saying that what
human hands have made are no gods at all. This means
not only that we run a grave risk of loss of reputation, but
also that the temple of the great goddess Artemis, whom
all Asia and the Empire reveres, will count for nothing
and her sway will be ended."

18 Ephesus was known as the home of magic (Ephesian Scripts). All kinds of
magical texts and conjurations, largely in Hebrew and Chaldean scripts,
were sold to the superstitious Greeks.

1 "That Way" or "persuasion". Not implying a new religion.

When they heard this they got wildly excited and yelled, "Up with Artemis of the Ephesians!"

The city was filled with confusion, and by common consent they rushed to the theatre, carrying along with them the Macedonians Gaius and Aristarchus, Paul's
30   travelling companions. Paul would have gone in there to the people, but the disciples would not let him. Some of the Asiarchs[2] too, who were his friends, sent him word begging him to keep out of the theatre. Some there were shouting one thing and some another; for the assembly was completely confused, the majority not having the slightest idea for what cause they had congregated. Among all the crowd they decided it must have to do with Alexander, because the Jews were pushing him forward. Alexander then waved his hand for silence, anxious to defend himself to the people. But no sooner were they aware that he was a Jew than they broke into a chorus of yelling for some two hours on end, "Up with Artemis of the Ephesians!"
35   When the city recorder had got the crowd calmed down he said, "Ephesians, where is there a single individual who does not know the city of the Ephesians as custodian of the temple of mighty Artemis, and of the heaven-sent statue?[3] Since these facts are indisputable, you ought to keep calm and do nothing outrageous; for you have brought these men here who are neither sacrilegious nor insulters of your goddess. If, therefore, Demetrius and the craftsmen with him have a grievance against anyone, the courts are open and there are pro-consuls: let them mutually prefer their charges. If you wish to take the matter further, it will be dealt with in the
40   assembly provided by law. For we run the risk of being accused of riot over to-day's uncalled for proceedings; for we cannot offer the slightest justification for this concourse."[4] With this he dismissed the assembly.
20.1   When the general commotion had subsided, Paul sent for the disciples, and having exhorted them and said farewell he left for Macedonia. Travelling through those districts he addressed to the brothers many words of

---

2 Prominent men elected to office as presidents and patrons of the festivals and games, also exercising some priestly functions in connexion with the cult of Rome and the Emperor.
3 Apparently a meteoric stone having some resemblance to a woman.
4 Or 'mass meeting'.

cheer, and so reached Greece, where he spent three months. But when a treacherous design was formed against him by the Jews, as he was about to embark for Syria, he decided to return via Macedonia.

[5]"In attendance on Paul were Sopater son of Pyrrhus of Beroea, Aristarchus and Secundus of the Thessalonians, Gaius of Derbe and Timotheus, and Tychicus and Trophimus of Asia. These going on ahead awaited us at Troas.

"After the festival of Unleavened Bread we sailed from Philippi, and in five weeks' time we reached them at Troas, where we spent a week. Then on the day after the sabbath, when we were together for the communal meal, Paul discoursed to them prior to setting off on the morrow, and prolonged his address until midnight.

"There were a number of lamps burning in the upstairs room where we were gathered, so a youth called Eutychus sat in the window.[6] As Paul's discourse went on and on, he grew drowsy and fell fast asleep. Drooping in his sleep he fell three floors down, and was picked up for dead. Paul went down, and threw himself upon him, and taking him in his embrace said, 'Do not lament. He is still alive.' He went upstairs again, broke bread, ate, carried on conversation for quite a time until dawn, and was then leaving, when the lad was carried in conscious, and they were enormously relieved.

"We ourselves having gone on ahead to the ship, sailed for Assos, with the intention of taking Paul on board there in accordance with his instructions. He proposed himself to travel overland. When he met us at Assos we embarked him and came on to Mitylene, and from there set sail and arrived the following day off Chios. The day after we hove to at Samos, and on the next day reached Miletus. This was because Paul had decided to sail past Ephesus, so that he would not have to linger in Asia; for he was anxious if at all possible to reach Jerusalem by Pentecost. From

5 The notebook extracts are resumed here at Philippi, the city where the previous extract ended (above p 239).
6 Because of the smoke and fumes from the oil lamps. Windows were unglazed.

Miletus he sent to Ephesus, however, to summon the elders of the community. When they arrived he addressed them as follows:

"You are well aware how I have constantly acted in your interests ever since I first set foot in Asia, serving the Master with all humility and tears, and with the trials that came my way through the hostile schemes of the
20   Jews.[7] I have never concealed anything that might be of benefit to you, whether in preaching to you or teaching you, both in public and private, most earnestly entreating Jews and Greeks alike to turn to God and have faith in Jesus our Master.

"Well, now I feel constrained to go to Jerusalem, not knowing what I shall have to face there. I only know that in city after city the holy Spirit has solemnly assured me that imprisonment and severe trials await me. But I set no value whatever on life for myself, only that I may finish my course and the commission I received from the Lord Jesus to witness expressly to the News of God's mercy.
25   "I know full well that all of you among whom I have gone, proclaiming the Kingdom of God, will never see my face again. See to it that you tend the Master's community, which he has acquired with his own blood[8]. I know that after I have gone home grievous[9] wolves will
30   get in among you who will not spare the flock; and even from yourselves men will arise talking twistedly to draw away disciples. So be on your guard, remembering that night and day for three years on end I never ceased tearfully warning each one of you.

"Now I commit you to God and to the Message of his mercy, which can fortify you and give you inheritance among all who are sanctified. I have coveted no one's silver, gold, or belongings. You are well aware that these

---

7 Actually the Jewish hostility was in self-defence. The missionary activities of the Messianists was confused with the – also Messianic – propaganda of the militant Zealots in Judea, who at this time were seeking to turn the Provincial Jews against Rome. These Jews were loyal to Rome, which gave them civic and religious protection, and feared the effects of Christian propaganda. Paul, with his mysticism, did not understand or realise this. See *Acts* 24:5.

8 Or read, "God's community, which he has acquired with the blood of his own."

9 Gr *Baris*, also meaning influential.

35 hands have provided for my own needs and those of my associates. I have given you a complete demonstration how thus by your own toil you should assist the incapacitated, bearing in mind those words uttered by the Lord Jesus, 'It is a finer thing to give than to get.'"[10]

When he finished speaking he knelt down with them all and prayed. A fit of weeping seized them, and they fell on Paul's neck and embraced him, grieving most over what he had said, that they were never going to see his face again. Then they escorted him to the ship.

21.1 "When we sailed, after tearing ourselves away from them, we came on a straight course to Cos, the next day to Rhodes, and then to Patara. Finding a ship bound for Phoenicia, we went on board and sailed with her. After sighting Cyprus, and leaving it on our left, we sailed on to Syria and coasted down to Tyre; for there the ship was to discharge her cargo. Having located the disciples we stayed there a week; though they warned Paul by the Spirit not to go on to

5 Jerusalem. We left, however, when our time was up, and were escorted on our way by them all, with their wives and children, until we were outside the town. Then after kneeling in prayer on the beach we said good-bye to one another; and we went on board while they returned home.

"Completing the voyage from Tyre we arrived at Ptolemais. We paid our respects to the brothers and remained a day with them; but on the next we left for Caesarea, where we went to the house of the evangelist Philip[a] and stayed with him. He had four maiden

10 daughters who were prophetesses. In the course of our lengthy stay a prophet called Agabus[11] came down from Judea and visited us. Taking Paul's girdle he bound his own hands and feet and declared, 'Thus says the holy Spirit, the man to whom this girdle belongs the Jews in Jerusalem will bind, and deliver him into the hands of the Gentiles.'

a One of the seven (ie the seven administrators). (See *Acts* 6:5).

10 One of the 'Maxims of the Master' not in our present *Gospels*.
11 He predicted the great famine (*Acts* 11:28).

"When we heard this, both we and the local disciples begged Paul not to go up to Jerusalem. But he replied, 'Why do you cry so, and weaken my resolve? For the sake of the Lord Jesus I am quite ready not only to be bound but even to die at Jerusalem.'

"Failing to persuade him, we gave it up and said, 'The Lord's will be done.'

15   "Some days later we made our arrangements to go up to Jerusalem. Several of the disciples from Caesarea went along with us to conduct us to Mnason, a Cypriot, one of the earliest disciples, with whom we would obtain lodging. Having duly reached Jerusalem, the brothers gave us a most friendly welcome. The next day Paul and ourselves had an audience with James.[12] All the elders were present. And when we had paid our respects to them, Paul gave a full description of all God had done among the Gentiles by his agency."[13]

Chapter XIII

20   When the elders had listened to what Paul had to say they praised God, and then said to him, "You must take into consideration, brother, how many ten thousands there are of Jews who have believed. Naturally they are staunch upholders of the Law.[1] But they have been informed about you that you teach all the Jews in Gentile lands to apostasize from Moses, telling them not to circumcise their children or conform to the customs.[2] What is this going to mean? They are bound to learn of your arrival. Here then is what you must do. We have four men under a mutual vow. Take over these men and undergo purification with them and pay their offering costs so that they can shave their heads. Everyone will then realise that there is no foundation whatever for

---

12 ie James the brother of Jesus, head of all Christians.
13 The notebook extract appears to end at this point since the first person plural is not longer employed. But a long further extract begins at *Acts* 27:1 (below ch XV).

1 ie by acknowledging Jesus as Messianic king his Jewish followers had not changed their religion.
2 Actually Paul had done nothing of the kind.

what they have been informed about you, and that on the contrary you yourself conform to and observe the
25 Law. So far as Gentiles who have believed are concerned, we have communicated our decision that they should avoid what is dedicated to idols, blood, eating strangled animals, and sexual impurity."[3]

Then Paul the very next day took over the men, and being purified with them entered the Sanctuary, giving notice of when the completion of the purifactory period would take place on which the sacrifice should be offered for each one of them.[4]

When the seven days were almost up some Jews of Asia caught sight of him in the Sanctuary and roused all the people, crying as they seized him, "Help, Israelites! Here is the fellow who goes around turning everyone everywhere against our people, and the Law, and this Place. He has even brought Greeks into the Sanctuary and desecrated this Holy Place."[a][5]

30 The whole city was set in uproar, and the people came rushing together. Those who had seized Paul dragged him outside the Sanctuary, and at once the gates were closed. They were attempting to kill him when word reached the military tribune that all Jerusalem was seething.[6] Instantly he took troops and centurions and ran down to them, and as soon as they saw the tribune and the troops they stopped striking Paul.

Coming up, the tribune took him in charge, and ordered him to be bound with two chains, and inquired who he was and what he had been up to. Some of the crowd said one thing and some another; and as he could not discover the truth because of the commotion he
35 ordered Paul to be conveyed into the fort. When the steps were reached it was found that he had to be lifted

---

a They had previously seen Trophimus the Ephesian in the city with him, and imagined Paul had brought him into the Sanctuary.

---

3 See *Acts* 15.

4 The men had taken a Nazirite vow, from which Paul assisted in their absolution. See *Num* 6; Mishnah, *Naz*. 2:3.

5 Gentiles were forbidden to enter the Temple proper. An inscription in Greek, Latin and Hebrew warned: "No stranger is to enter the balustrade round the Temple and enclosure. Whoever is caught will be responsible for his own death, which will ensue."

6 Whatever went on in the Temple area was under observation from Fort Antonia which had a Roman garrison and access to the Temple courtyard.

up them by the soldiers because of the pressure of the crowd; for the mass of the people surged close behind yelling, "Away with him!"

When they were about to enter the fort, Paul said to the tribune, "May I have a word with you?"

"Do you speak Greek?" he replied. "Aren't you then the Egyptian who recently started an insurrection[7] and led those four thousand sicarii[8] out into the wilderness?"

"I am actually a Jew", said Paul, "from Tarsus in Cilicia, a citizen of no insignificant city. Please allow me to address the people."

40 Receiving permission, Paul stood at the top of the steps and waved his hand for silence. When there was sufficient quiet he addressed them in the Hebrew language, "Brothers and fathers, give me a chance to explain myself to you." Hearing him speak to them in Hebrew they quietened down still more.

22.1 "I am a Jew born in Tarsus of Cilicia", Paul continued, "but brought up in this city at the feet of Gamaliel,[9] strictly trained in our ancestral Law, being zealous on God's behalf, just as all of you here are. I was one who hunted down this persuasion[10] to the death, binding and

5 delivering to prison men and women alike, as the high priest and the whole Sanhedrin[11] can bear me out; for they furnished me with the letters to the brothers at Damascus with which I travelled to bring those who had gone there in bonds to Jerusalem for punishment.

"Now on my journey, when I was nearing Damascus, suddenly about noon a dazzling light from heaven flashed around me. I fell prone, and heard a voice saying to me, 'Saul, Saul, why are you hunting me?'

"'Who are you, lord?' I answered. 'I am Jesus the Nazarene whom you are hunting,' he replied. Those who accompanied me saw the light, but they did not

10 hear the voice of the one who spoke to me. Then I said, 'What am I to do, lord?' The Master told me, 'Rise, and go

---

7 This pseudo-messiah or prophet is credited by Josephus with 30,000 followers. He planned to enter Jerusalem and overpower the Roman garrison; but he was defeated and escaped with a few of his men. (See Jos. *Jewish War*, II. 261–263.)

8 Lit "assassins", who were active at this time.

9 Rabbani Gamaliel (*Acts* 5:34).

10 Lit "way".

11 Lit Gr. 'Presbytery' (a Council of Elders).

to Damascus, and there you will be told exactly what has been assigned you to do.'

"As I was sightless from the brilliance of that light, I had to be led by the hand into Damascus by those who were with me. But Ananias, a man meticulous according to the Law and highly respected by all the local Jews, came to me, and standing there said, 'Brother Saul, regain your sight!' And there I was looking at him that very instant. Then he said, 'The God of our fathers has designated you to know his will, to see that Just One,[12]

15   and to hear his very voice, that you may be a witness to everyone of what you have seen and heard. So now what keeps you? Rise, and be immersed, and wash away your sins as you invoke his name.'

"When I had returned to Jerusalem, and was engaged in prayer in the Sanctuary, in trance I saw Jesus saying to me, 'Hurry, get out of Jerusalem quickly, for they will not tolerate your testimony to me!' 'But Master,' I protested, 'they know for a fact that it was I who in synagogue after synagogue imprisoned and bound those who believe in

20   you; and when the blood of your witness Stephen was shed, I was the one who stood there approvingly and took charge of the cloaks of those who killed him.' But his answer was, 'Go, for I am sending you to the benighted Gentiles.' "[13]

Up to this point they listened to him, but then they cried out, "Away with this fellow from the earth! He's not fit to live."

As they shouted, and tore their clothes, and flung dust in the air,[14] the tribune ordered him to be taken into the fort and examined by flogging, to discover the reason

25   why they were so vociferous against him. As they were making him fast with straps, Paul said to the centurion in charge, "Is it right for you to flog one who is a Roman and uncondemned?"

When he heard this the centurion went to the tribune and reported it. "What do you propose to do?" he asked. The man is a Roman citizen."

Going along, the tribune said to Paul, "Tell me, are you a Roman?"

---

12 A designation comparable to the Essene 'Teacher of Righteousness,' or 'Justice.'
13 Or 'the Gentiles afar off'.
14 As a mourning for the dead.

"Yes", he replied.

"I had to pay a pretty penny for my citizenship", said the tribune.

"But I had it by birth", said Paul.

Those who going to interrogate him at once stood away from him; and even the tribune was uneasy when he was aware that he was a Roman, and that he had been responsible for binding him.

30　　The next day, concerned to get at the truth of why Paul was denounced by the Jews, the tribune freed him, and requested the high priest and the full Sanhedrin to meet, and brought Paul down to confront them. Paul peered at[15] the Sanhedrin and said, "Brothers, I have lived with a perfectly clear conscience before God to this day."

23.1　　Here the High Priest Ananias[16] ordered those who stood beside Paul to strike him on the mouth.

Then Paul said to him, "God will strike you, you whitewashed wall. Do you sit there to judge me in accordance with the Law, and illegally order me to be struck?"

Those who stood beside him cried, "Do you abuse God's high priest?"

5　　"I did not know he was the high priest, brothers", Paul said, "for it is stated, 'You must not speak evil of the ruler of your people.'"[17]

When Paul was aware that one part of the Sanhedrin were Sadducees and that the others were Pharisees, he cried out, "Brothers, I am a Pharisee of Pharisee stock. I am being judged for the expectation of the resurrection of the dead."

By saying this he set the Pharisees at loggerheads with the Sadducees, and there was a split in the assembly. For the Sadducees say there is no resurrection, nor any angel or spirit, while the Pharisees affirm both propositions. A first-class row ensued, with some of the Pharisee scribes hotly contending, "We find nothing criminal in this

10　　man. If a spirit has spoken to him, or an angel. . ." The conflict here became so furious that the tribune, afraid lest Paul would get torn to pieces, ordered a company

---

15 Or 'looked straight at'. 'Peering' has been used because the context suggests that Paul had only a blurred impression of the white-robed person presiding, and suffered from defective vision.

16 Ananias son of Nedebaeus (Jos. *Antiq*.XX.103). He was murdered in AD 66.

17 *Exod* 22:28.

down to extricate him from them and escort him back into the fort.

The following night the Master stood beside him and said, "Courage! As you have pleaded my cause in Jerusalem, so must you testify in Rome also."

When day came some of the Jews made a compact, and took an oath neither to eat nor drink until they had killed Paul. There were more than forty who were parties to this conspiracy.[18] These going to the high priest and elders said, "We have taken a most solemn oath to taste nothing until we have killed Paul. You should therefore, with the Sanhedrin, represent to the tribune that he should bring him down to you as you propose to investigate his case more thoroughly, while we will be in wait to kill him before he reaches here."

Paul's sister's son, who was close by, heard about the ambush, and went into the fort and informed Paul. Paul then called one of the centurions and said, "Take this young man to the tribune. He has something to tell him." So he took him along to the tribune and said, "The prisoner Paul sent for me, and asked me to bring this young man to you as he has something to tell you."

The tribune then took him by the arm, and retiring with him in private inquired, "What is that you have to say to me?"

"Some of the Jews",[19] he said, "have agreed to ask you to bring Paul down to the Sanhedrin to-morrow as they propose to go into his case more thoroughly. But you must not consent, for more than forty of their men will be lying in wait for him. They have taken an oath not to eat or drink till they have killed him. And now they are in readiness awaiting your assurances."

The tribune then dismissed the youth, cautioning him "not to tell a soul what you have disclosed to me." Next, having summoned two of his centurions, he issued instructions, "Have two hundred men ready to go to Caesarea, also seventy cavalry and two hundred light infantry, this evening at nine o'clock sharp. And have a baggage train brought round to convey Paul[20] safely to

---

18 Probably these were members of the fanatical nationalist party of the time.
19 The young man would have used some other word. But the author is writing for non-Jewish Christians.
20 The tribune would probably have said 'the prisoner' (see n 19 above).

25   the Governor Felix." He also wrote a letter to this effect:

> "Claudius Lysias presents his compliments to His Excellency the Governor Felix.
>
> "This man had been apprehended by the Jews, and they were about to kill him, when I arrived with a force and extricated him. On learning he was a Roman, and wishing to ascertain the reason he was being accused by them, I brought him down to their Sanhedrin. There I found him to be accused of questions affecting their law, but not of anything meriting death or
30   imprisonment. On information received of there being a plot against this man, I have at once sent him to you, and likewise advised his accusers to lay before you their charges against him."

Then in accordance with their instructions the soldiers took Paul and escorted him by night to Antipatris. But the next day they returned to the fort, leaving the cavalry to go forward with Paul. On reaching Caesarea[21] they delivered the letter to the governor, and also surrendered Paul to him. When the governor had read the letter he asked Paul from which Province he came, and
35   being told it was Cilicia he said, "I will hear you as soon as your accusers arrive", and remanded him in custody in Herod's praetorium.

24.1   Five days later the high priest Ananias came down with some of the elders and an advocate Tertullus. These laid information against Paul with the governor.

When Paul had been summoned, Tertullus opened the case for his accusers as follows:

"Thanks to you, Your Excellency Felix, profound peace is our lot and law and order has been restored to our nation under your wise guidance.[22] This we freely and fully acknowledge with deep gratitude. In order not to weary you unduly, therefore, I beg for your consideration in putting our case wth the utmost brevity.
5   "We have found this man a plague-carrier, a fomentor of revolt among all the Jews of the Empire, a ringleader of the Nazarene sect.[23] When we apprehended him he was

---

21 The seat of the Roman governor.
22 Felix had ruthlessly suppressed the Jewish patriotic revolutionaries. On his character and activities see Jos. *Antiq.* XX.160–161; Tacit. *Annals*, XII.liv.
23 The Messianists (Christians) were regarded as part of the Jewish patriotic movement opposed to and seeking to overthrow the Roman regime in Israel. And not without reason. See p 241, n 12; p 243, n 1.

also attempting to desecrate the Sanctuary,[24] as you can ascertain for yourself by investigating these several charges we bring against him."

The Jews concurred, affirming that the facts were as stated.

10   Then at a nod from the governor Paul made his reply.

"Knowing that you have had many years' experience in governing our nation I speak in my own defence with every confidence, since you can ascertain that barely twelve days have elapsed since I went up to worship at Jerusalem. They neither found me in the Sanctuary arguing with anyone, nor haranguing a crowd either in the synagogues or up and down the city. They can offer no shred of evidence to support the charges they now bring against me.

"I will admit to you that I serve the God of our fathers in accordance with the persuasion[25] which they term a sect, believing whatever has been recorded in the Law
15   and the Prophets, and having hope in God – which indeed they themselves share – that there will be a resurrection of the just and also of the unjust. Because of this I am personally at pains always to have a clear conscience towards God and man.

"Now after an interval of several years I arrived to make charitable gifts to my nation, and also to offer sacrifices, engaged in which activities some Jews of Asia found me in the Sanctuary when I had undergone purification, with no sign of a crowd or commotion. They should have been here before you to accuse me if there
20   had been anything against me. As they are not, let those who are here speak of what wrongdoing they discovered when I stood before the Sanhedrin, or about the one thing I cried out as I stood among them, 'Concerning the resurrection of the dead I am being judged by you to-day!'"

Here Felix, who had very accurate knowledge of the Way, adjourned the proceedings, saying, "When Tribune Lysias gets down I will decide your case."

While instructing the centurion to hold Paul, he was to permit him his liberty, and not to prevent his own people looking after him.

---

24 As quoted in the Authorised Version, some MSS add the words from the last clause of verse 6 to the first clause of verse 8, here omitted.
25 ie 'the Way'.

Shortly after this Felix was again in Caesarea with his wife Drusilla,[26] who was a Jewess, and sending for Paul

25   listened to him on the subject of faith in Christ Jesus. As he discoursed about righteousness, self-control, and the coming Judgment, Felix became uncomfortable and said, "You had better go now. When I have time to spare I'll call for you again."

He rather hoped that Paul would make him a gift of money, which was why he sent for him fairly frequently and conversed with him. But when two years had passed Felix was succeeded by Porcius Festus. Anxious to stand well with the Jews, Felix left Paul still a prisoner.

Chapter XIV

25.1   Three days after his entry into the Province Festus went up from Caesarea to Jerusalem. There the head priests and leading Jews made representations to him against Paul, and begged the favour of having him sent to Jerusalem, intending to ambush and kill him on the way. But Festus replied that he was having Paul kept at Caesarea as he himself would be going there very soon.

5   "Any of you who care to do so," he said, "can accompany me down and bring your charges against him if the man has done something monstrous."

When Festus had spent some eight or ten days with them he went down to Caesarea, and the day following took his seat on the tribunal and ordered Paul to be brought in. As soon as he was present, the Jews who had come down from Jerusalem surrounded him, preferring many serious charges which they could not substantiate. Paul's reply was, "I have committed no offence against Jewish law, nor against the Sanctuary, nor against Caesar."

Festus, anxious to stand well with the Jews, said to Paul, "Are you willing to go up to Jerusalem to be tried before me there regarding these matters?"

10   Paul replied, "I am standing now at Caesar's tribunal,

26 She was a sister of Agrippa II, and left her husband Azizus king of Emessa to marry Felix. She was noted for her beauty. See Jos. *Antiq.* XX.141–142.

where I should be tried. I have not injured Jews, as you can see quite plainly. If I am at fault and have done something that merits death I am not trying to beg myself off from dying. But if there is no foundation for these charges they bring against me, no one is entitled to gratify them. I appeal to Caesar."

Then Festus, after conferring with the Council, answered, "You have appealed to Caesar. To Caesar you must go."

Shortly after, King Agrippa[1] and Berenice arrived at Caesarea to pay their respects to Festus. When they had been there a few days Festus broached the subject of Paul to the king. "We have a man here", he said, "left a prisoner by Felix, against whom the head priests and elders made representations to me when I was in Jerusalem. They asked for his condemnation; but I told them it was not customary in the case of Roman citizens to grant any individual such a favour before the accused had had an opportunity to face his accusers and offer his defence to the charge. Consequently, when they came here with me, without any delay I took my seat next day on the tribunal, and ordered the man to be produced. But when his accusers stood forward they did not bring against him a single charge of any of the crimes I had supposed. They only had against him certain questions affecting their own religion, and a certain Jesus who had died, and whom Paul affirmed was alive. As I was quite out of my depth with an investigation dealing with such matters, I asked him whether he would go to Jerusalem and be tried there. But when Paul appealed for his case to be reserved for the verdict of Augustus,[2] I ordered his remand until I could send him to Caesar."

"I should rather like to hear the man myself", said Agrippa to Festus.

"You shall hear him to-morrow", he replied.

The next day Agrippa and Berenice came in full state, and entered the audience chamber accompanied by the military commanders and the city notables. Festus ordered Paul to be brought in.

Festus then spoke. "King Agrippa, and all who have

1 Son of Agrippa I, given the kingdom of Chalcis by Claudius. Berenice was his sister, afterwards mistress of Titus, son of the Emperor Vespasian.
2 A title of the emperor like 'His Majesty'.

honoured us with their presence. Here you find a man for whom I have had the whole pack of Jews down on me both in Jerusalem and here, yelping that he ought not to
25   live any longer. But when I was aware that he had really done nothing meriting death, and when he appealed to Augustus, I decided to send him. I find myself, however, with nothing definite to write to our lord. I have therefore brought him before you, and especially before you, King Agrippa, so that after this examination I might know what to write; for it seems senseless to me to be sending a prisoner without at the same time specifying the charge against him.''

26.1   Then Agrippa said to Paul, ''You have our leave to speak for yourself.''

So Paul extended his arm and began his defence.

''I count myself fortunate, King Agrippa, that it is before you to-day that I am to answer all the charges Jews have brought against me, particularly because I know you to be so well-versed in all Jewish customs and questions. I beg you, therefore to accord me a patient hearing.

''With my early life, which was spent entirely among my own nation at Jerusalem, Jews are fully familiar.
5   Being acquainted with my antecedents they could testify, if they would, that I lived in accordance with the strictest sect of our faith, as a Pharisee.[3]

''So here I stand trial for that Hope,[4] which was God's own promise to our fathers, and to which by their devotional zeal night and day our twelve tribes expect to attain. It is for harbouring this very Hope, Sire, that Jews are accusing me. Why should one regard it as incredible that God raises the dead? I used myself to think it necessary to act in utmost opposition to the authority of
10   Jesus the Nazarene, which moreover I did in Jerusalem, and locked up many of the saints in prison with the warrant I had from the head priests. When they were sent to their death I pressed the vote against them, and had them punished repeatedly in all the synagogues, and compelled them to revile Jesus. Being mad with them beyond measure I even hunted them to towns across the border.

3 cf Jos. *Life*, ii, on Josephus's early training as a Pharisee.
4 The Messianic Hope of the Redemption of Israel and the institution of the Kingdom of God on earth.

"Travelling while so engaged to Damascus, with a warrant and commission from the head priests, I saw, Sire, while on the road at midday, a light from heaven stronger than the sun's glare shining about me and those who accompanied me. We all fell to the ground, and then I heard a voice saying to me in Hebrew, 'Saul, Saul, why do you hunt me? You only hurt yourself kicking against the goad.' 'Who are you, lord?' I asked. The Master said, 'I am Jesus whom you are hunting. Get up now, and stand on your feet. I have appeared to you personally to take you in training as my assistant, and as witness that you have seen me, and of what I shall make clear to you later. I am setting you apart from your people, and from the Gentiles to whom I am going to send you, to give them the power of distinction, that they may turn from darkness towards the light, and from the authority of Satan to God; that they may receive forgiveness of their sins and inheritance with the sanctified by their loyalty to me.'

"There could be no question, King Agrippa, of disobeying the heavenly vision, and accordingly, to those in Damascus first, then to the inhabitants of Jerusalem, the whole country of Judea, and afterwards to the Gentiles, I preached repentance and turning to God, and the performance of deeds indicative of repentance. As a consequence the Jews seized me in the Sanctuary and attempted to murder me. Aided, however, by God's providence, I continue to stand – just as I am doing at this moment – witnessing to high and low, uttering no single word beyond what the prophets foretold would happen, yes, and Moses himself, that the Messiah would suffer, that he would be the first to rise from the dead, and thereafter bring light to our people and to the Gentiles."

When he had reached this part of his defence, Festus interjected, "You are raving, Paul! All this study has disturbed your reason."

"I am not mad, Your Excellency Festus", Paul rejoined. "I am speaking plainly matters of fact and sense; for the king, before whom I can express myself freely, well understands these things. I am persuaded that none of them has escaped his notice, for they were not done in a corner.

"King Agrippa, do you believe the prophets? Of course you do."

Said Agrippa to Paul, "In next-to-no-time you will be persuading me to turn Christian."

"I pray God", Paul replied, "that whether in next-to-no-time or a long time, not only you but all who hear me today will become as I am, except for these chains."

30 Then the king rose, followed by the governor, Berenice, and the assembled company. When they had withdrawn they discussed the matter among themselves. "The man has done nothing", they agreed, "to deserve death or imprisonment."

"He could have been released", said Agrippa to Festus, "had he not appealed to Caesar."

Chapter XV[1]

27.1 "When it was decided we should sail for Italy, they entrusted Paul and some other prisoners to a centurion called Julius of the Augustan[2] cohort. Going on board a ship of Adramyttium which was due to sail, calling at the Asiatic ports, we put to sea. Aristarchus,[3] a Macedonian of Thessalonica, accompanied us.

"The next day but one we touched at Sidon, Julius treating Paul very decently, liberating him on parole to visit his friends to benefit by their attentions. Putting to sea again, we ran under the lee of Cyprus because of

5 adverse winds, and driving on through the sea of Cilicia and Pamphylia we made the port of Myra in Lycia. There our centurion found an Alexandrian boat[4] bound for Italy, and transferred us to her. For some days, battling against the wind, we made poor progress, and with difficulty reached a point off Cnidus, and had to sail under the lee of Crete off Cape Salmone. We had a hard job to weather it and reach a place called Fair Havens, next to which was the town of Lasea.

"After being held up here for a considerable time, and navigation having become very risky because the

---

1 Almost the whole of this chapter is from the notebook source.
2 Gr. *Sebastes*. Either Augustan, or even Samaritan. The city of Samaria had had its name changed to Sebaste in honour of Augustus Caesar.
3 He had come with Paul from Philippi. See notebook quote p 249.
4 One of the Alexandrian grain ships, as appears further on.

Fast Day[5] had already gone by, Paul advised them,
10   'Gentlemen, it is my conviction that the voyage will
bring strain and stress not only to cargo and vessel but
to ourselves as well.' But the centurion preferred to
follow the advice of the navigator and the captain
rather than Paul's recommendation. The harbour was
by nature unsuitable for lying up, so the majority
favoured putting to sea again and having a good try to
reach and lie up at Phoenix, a harbour of Crete facing
south-west and north-west. So when a moderate wind
from the south sprang up they weighed anchor hug-
ging the coast of Crete, thinking they would achieve
their object.

"But not long after there swept down from the
15   island a violent norther[6] known as Euraclyon. When it
caught the ship, and finding ourselves unable to turn
her into the wind, we let her drive along. Running
under the lee of a small island called Clauda, we
struggled hard to haul in the ship's boat; and when it
was aboard they brought into commission their cable
supports to undergird the vessel. Then, apprehensive
of being thrown on the Syrtis quicksands,[7] they let
down sail and drifted.

"Next day, as we were in great distress, they cleared
the decks, and the day following we threw the ship's
20   gear overboard with our own hands. For days on end
neither sun nor stars were visible, while the storm
raged with unabated fury and all remaining hope that
we should be saved was abandoned. Then, when food
was running short, Paul stood before them and said,
'You should have taken my advice, gentlemen, and
never put out from Crete, and let yourselves in for this
storm and stress. But as things are now, my advice to
you is to take heart, for not one life will be lost, only the
ship. For last night there stood by me an angel of the
God whose I am and whom I serve, saying, "Never
fear, Paul, you must stand before Caesar. And see,
25   God has given you all those who sail with you." So
courage, gentlemen, for I have faith in God that it will

---

5 The Day of Atonement, 10th of the 7th month Tishri of the Jewish year,
falling in October.
6 Lit "a typhonic wind" (typhoon).
7 North of Libya.

turn out exactly as I have been told. But we are to be cast on an island.'

"The fourteenth night of our drift across the Adriatic,[8] around midnight, the sailors had the impression they were approaching land. When they took soundings they found twenty fathoms, and sounding again after a short interval they found fifteen fathoms. Fearing we should be cast on a rocky coast, they let go four anchors by the stern, and longed for daylight. But some of the sailors tried to abandon the ship, and they were lowering a boat into the sea, on the pretext that they were going to lay anchors from the bow, when Paul said to the centurion and his men, 'If they don't stay on board there is no chance of your being saved.' Then the soldiers hacked away the boat's hawsers, and let her fall away.

"While they waited for daybreak Paul encouraged them to take some food, saying, 'This will be the fourteenth day you have been constantly on the alert and gone without your meals, never taking a bite. I beg you, therefore, to take some nourishment, for this will contribute to your preservation. In no case will a hair of your heads be lost.' Having said this, he took bread and gave thanks to God before them all, broke it and began to eat. At this they all cheered up and followed his example. All told we were about seventy-six souls on board. Then when they had eaten sufficient food they lightened the ship by throwing out the grain[9] into the sea.

"When day came they did not recognise the coast; but they perceived a creek with a sandy shore on which they determined if they could to beach the vessel. Casting off the anchors fore and aft, they left them in the sea, and at the same time loosing the lashings of the rudders and hoisting the foresail to the breeze they held for the shore. Chancing on a place where two seas met, they ran the ship aground. Here the forepart stuck fast and held firm, while the stern went to pieces under the shock.

"The soldiers were for killing the prisoners in case any of them should swim off and escape. But the

8 Then including the central Mediterranean.
9 The boat was a grain ship.

centurion, determined to save Paul, vetoed their suggestion, and ordered those who could swim to jump for it first and get to land, while the rest followed, some on planks and others on any other pieces of the ship that were handy. In this way all came safely to shore.

28.1   "It was not until we had recovered that we found out that the island was called Melita.[10] The natives treated us with uncommon civility, for they kindled a fire and made us comfortable because of the drenching and the cold. Paul had been collecting an armful of sticks, and was engaged in laying them on the fire, when a viper drawn out by the heat fastened itself on his hand. Seeing the creature hanging from his hand, the natives said to one another, 'He must be a murderer, whom Justice will not allow to live, even

5   though he has safely escaped the sea.' However, he shook off the creature into the fire and suffered no ill effects, though they fully expected him to swell up or suddenly drop dead. After waiting for some time and seeing nothing out of the ordinary happen to him they changed their minds and said he must be a god.

"Hereabouts was the estate of the chief commissioner of the island, called Poplius,[11] who received us and very kindly provided lodging for three days. The father of Poplius was laid up with an attack of fever and dysentery. Paul went to his room, and after praying laid his hands on him and cured him. The consequence was that others on the island who had

10   ailments came and were cured. They not only loaded us with handsome presents, but furnished the requisite stores.

"Three months later we embarked in an Alexandrian ship displaying the emblem of the Dioscuri[12] that had wintered at the island. Putting in at Syracuse we stayed there three days, and from there by tacking we reached Rhegium. A day later we had the advantage of a south wind which wafted us in two more days to

10 Now called Malta.
11 Possibly the Greek name Popilius, but more likely the Latin name Publius.
12 The heavenly twins Castor and Pollux.

Puteoli,[13] where we found brothers who invited us to spend a week with them.

15   "And so we came to Rome. From there the brothers, who had heard all about us, had come to meet us as far as Market Appii and Three Taverns, and Paul when he saw them thanked God and took courage. When we had entered Rome[14] Paul was allowed to occupy a private lodging with the soldier who acted as his guard."[15]

When three days had passed Paul summoned the heads of Jewish community, and when they had assembled he addressed them as follows:

"You see in me, brothers, a prisoner from Jerusalem, who though he has done nothing against our people or our ancestral customs was handed over to the Romans. When they had examined me they proposed to release me, as there was nothing whatever against me to warrant a death sentence. But when some of the Jews[16] opposed this I was forced to appeal to Caesar, though not because I have any grounds of complaint against my

20   nation. My reason for asking you here is to see you and speak with you, because it is for the sake of the Hope of Israel[17] I wear this chain."

"We have received no communication about you from Judea," they told him, "neither have any of the brothers arrived to report to us or advise us of anything to your detriment. But we would appreciate hearing from you what your opinions are, for all we know for certain about this sect is that everywhere it is disparaged."

Having fixed a date with him, most of them turned up at his lodging. To these he earnestly expounded the Kingdom of God, persuading them about Jesus from the Law of Moses and from the Prophets from early morning until evening. Some were convinced by what he said, but

25   others did not credit it. On this note of discord among

---

13 cf the somewhat similar voyage and shipwreck of the historian Josephus when Felix was governor of Judea (*Life* 13–15).

14 Omitting the gloss, "the centurion handed the prisoners over to the camp commander, but . . ."

15 The notebook 'we' extracts would seem to end here.

16 Again showing that the book was for Gentile readers. Paul, speaking to Jews, would have said 'our people'.

17 The Messianic Hope.

themselves they took their leave, with Paul saying this parting word, "Rightly did the holy Spirit say to your[18] fathers by the Prophet Isaiah,

> *Go to this people, and tell them,*
> *You will hear indeed, but not comprehend.*
> *You will see indeed, but not perceive.*
> *For the mind of this people is obtuse;*
> *Their ears have grown hard of hearing,*
> *And their eyes they have fast closed,*
> *In case they should see with their eyes,*
> *And hear with their ears,*
> *And turn again, and I should heal them.*[19]

"You had better know this, that God's salvation has been sent to the Gentiles. They certainly will listen to it."[20]

30   Paul resided two full years in his own rented apartment, and welcomed all who visited him there, proclaiming the Kingdom of God, and teaching all about the Lord Jesus Christ with unrestricted freedom of speech.[21]

---

18 See note 16.
19 *Isa* 6:9–10.
20 Omitting the gloss (verse 29): "When he said this the Jews took their departure, arguing heatedly among themselves."
21 The last paragraph may well be a later copyist's or commentator's addition.

THE LETTERS OF PAUL OF TARSUS

First Series

Letters on Active Service

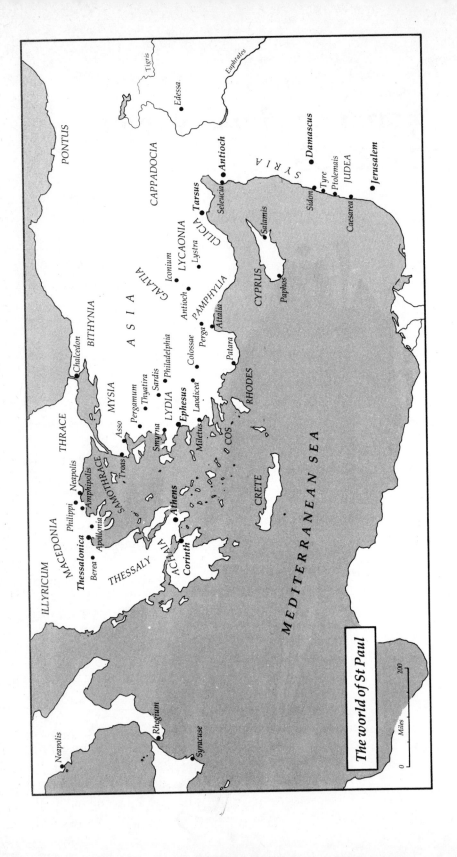

The world of St Paul

Preface to Paul's Letters
(First Series)

The *Acts of the Envoys* is the indispensable introduction to the letters of Paul, though later in date. Without the outline of Paul's career which it provides we should largely be unaware when or in what circumstances the envoy to the Gentiles visited various cities and countries. Many passages in the correspondence would be obscure, and we should find great difficulty in arranging the letters in chronological order and determining their approximate dates. As it is, we can be fairly sure of our ground in editing the letters, and this is of the utmost importance, as the letters in turn, as first hand and also the earliest Christian documents at present known, enable us to test the general historical accuracy of the *Acts*. We can see by comparison that in the *Acts* much has been toned down and omitted, especially in relation to internal controversies. Paul, writing on the spur of the moment to particular communities of believers, is singularly revealing of the actual state of Christian affairs in the eastern part of the Roman Empire. Here is no idealised picture, but a frank and sometimes scathing disclosure of situations and conditions.

As we discover the largely unpromising material – the dregs of society – of which the communities were often composed, and apprehend what pain and anxiety were given to the man chiefly responsible for their creation, we cannot but feel tremendous admiration for Paul's vision and courage, dedication and organising ability. Paul lives in his letters, and from them, if we are equipped with his Jewish skills, we may get to know him more intimately than any other New Testament character. We may not always be in sympathy with him. We may find him rather puritanical and dogmatic, his ideas often strange, his illustrations far-fetched, his arguments involved and hard to follow; but in every mood he is stimulating and challenging.

Paul's correspondence is admittedly difficult to translate. There are several reasons for this. For the most part he dictated to secretaries, partly because he had weak eyesight, and often at odd times; and this allowed him to let his thoughts follow bypaths before returning to his main theme, or alternatively to proceed at a great pace, piling clause on clause in a sentence which seemed as if it would be interminable. The different amanuenses have some responsibility for the uneven result and construction; but Paul was often dictating under strong emotion. He had the further difficulty of trying to convert peculiarly Jewish ideas into Greek terms, which sometimes meant using Greek words in other than their normal connotation, thus creating a kind of *lingua Christiana*. His mind was cast in a rabbinical mould: he had studied under a noted Pharisee rabbi. Thus his thoughts were filled with Jewish concepts, expressions and phrases, Biblical, liturgical and mystical, which were alien to the majority of his readers, and have largely remained so to their successors down to the present day.

Without Paul's peculiar equipment one may easily misunderstand him and misrepresent him, especially in theological matters. This the Church Fathers and subsequent exponents of Christianity did most effectively. Paul as a student had gravitated towards Pharisee occult and mystical lore, which in many respects was close to that of the Essenes. He himself had mystical experiences, stimulated – as some believe – by some form of epilepsy to which he was prone. He largely moved in the realm of the spirit, unconscious of the agony of the Jewish people seeking salvation from Roman rule. He himself had the privilege of Roman citizenship and was at home in a Greek-speaking environment. It had taken possession of him that he was the Messianic envoy to the Gentiles preparing the way for the imminent return of the Son of Man from heaven to raise the dead and set up his terrestrial kingdom. He claimed for his non-Jewish converts that by accepting the king of Israel they had become Israelites, and their sins were covered by the Messiah's sinlessness. Related to this was the doctrine of the organic relationship between the Christ and his Community (his body). This was also demanded in the interests of unity and morality. For Paul the ascended Jesus was identified with the heavenly Son of Man of the Jewish mystics, who was now the mediator between God and mankind, the Second Adam. He had no thought of Jesus as incarnate deity, or the Second Person of a Trinity. Christianity as a new religion did not exist in Paul's time; but almost inevitably the pagans who joined the Movement would give rise to it, which Paul failed to foresee.

In presenting the letters they have been divided into two groups, those written in the course of Paul's propagandist activities as the Messianic King's special envoy, and those written while a prisoner at Rome. As far as practicable they have been placed – as they should be – in chronological order, with the approximate dates and places where written. They largely feature the running conflict between Paul and the envoys of the central Christian authority in Jerusalem, some of whom had been personally appointed by Jesus in his lifetime, now headed by James (Jacob) the brother of Jesus, with Peter and John. These were concerned for a loyal and united Christian Israel, observant of the Laws given to Israel as a qualification for functioning as "a kingdom of priests and a holy nation". Consequently they sought to influence the communities Paul had founded to impress this upon them. The conflict that arose was only partially solved by permitting the Gentile believers to hold a secondary citizenship, as "proselytes of the gate" coming under the Laws of Noah and not those of Moses. Paul would not tolerate this. He hit back particularly in his letter to the communities of Galatia.

But the letters speak of other problems. At Thessalonica there were many who expected the immediate return of Jesus, and as a consequence had abandoned their occupations. The Corinthian believers presented Paul with numerous questions on various subjects. He had also to deal with the besetting Greek vices of factiousness and immorality. Evidently four letters were written to the Corinthian community, later compressed into two; and it is easier to follow the arguments if the original structure and order is tentatively restored.

The letter to the believers at Rome is of a different character. Paul had not visited this community, and had had no hand in founding it. Substantially its membership was Jewish. The *Acts* conceals the fact of its existence, and makes the Jews of Rome ignorant of its local activities. Paul used the notification of his plan to come to Rome on his way to Spain as a means of acquainting the community with his teaching as it affected both Jews and Gentiles, and his language is much more circumspect, even though he is amplifying to an extent the arguments used in the letter to the Galatians. The document forms a fitting conclusion to the First Series as a carefully reasoned statement of Paul's beliefs and convictions, boldly introduced by the challenging assertion that he is an envoy of one greater than Caesar, charged with procuring the submission of all nations to the authority of his lord and master.

To the Community at Thessalonica (1)

(Probably written from Corinth about AD 51)

1.1   Paul, Silvanus and Timotheus, to the community of Thessalonians in God the Father and the Lord Jesus Christ. May peace and prosperity be yours.

We invariably thank God for all of you, making mention of you in our prayers, continually remembering in the presence of God our Father the intensity of your faith, the ardour of your love, and the constancy of your hope in the Lord Jesus Christ.

I[1] know, brothers dear to God, how truly chosen you
5   are, because my News came to you not merely with speech, but with power, with inspiration, and with strong conviction; even as *you* know the kind of man I was with you for your sakes. You became imitators of me, and of the Master, welcoming the Message in circumstances of great difficulty with fervent joy,[2] so that you became an example to all the believers in Macedonia and Achaia. For from you the Master's Message resounded not only throughout Macedonia and Achaia, but indeed far and wide your faith in God has penetrated, so that there is no need for me to speak of it. The people of those parts themselves tell of the effect of my visit to you, how you turned from idols to serve the
10   Living and True God, and to await his Son from heaven, whom he raised from the dead, Jesus our rescuer from the coming Wrath.

---

1 Paul continues to use the first person plural as he writes in the names of himself and his colleagues. But here and in his other letters the singular has been substituted where Paul's personal views and experiences are referred to.

2 Lit "joy of holy Spirit".

2.1   You yourselves know, brothers, that my visit to you was by no means ineffective. Though I had previously suffered and been ill-treated, as you are aware, at Philippi,[3] I made bold in God with a great effort to give you God's News.[4] My appeal to you was without imposture or impure motives, neither did I use guile. I spoke as one approved by God as worthy to be entrusted with the News, not as one who seeks to please men, but God who

5   tries my heart.[5] For I was never in speech a flatterer, as you know, nor one with covetous designs, God is my witness, nor one who seeks human commendation, neither from you nor anyone else, though entitled to be of consequence as an envoy of Christ. Rather was I very tender with you, as if I was a foster-mother nursing her own children. Thus yearning over you, I was delighted to impart to you not only God's News but my very life, so dear had you become to me.

Only call to mind, brothers, my toil and drudgery. Night and day I laboured so as not to be a burden to you

10   in any way while proclaiming God's News. You are witnesses, and God also, how correctly, honourably and blamelessly I acted towards you believers, just as you know how I exhorted, encouraged and charged every single one of you, as a father his own children, to behave worthy of God who has invited you to share his sovereignty and state.

I do indeed thank God constantly for this, that on acceptance of God's Message as you heard it from me, you welcomed it not as a human message, but for what it truly is – God's Message, which is certainly operative in you believers. For, brothers, you became counterparts of the communities of God in Judea which are in Christ Jesus; for you yourselves have suffered similarly from

15   your own countrymen as they from the Judeans, who put to death the Lord Jesus and the prophets, and hounded me out, who incur God's displeasure, setting themselves against everyone, hindering me from speaking to the Gentiles that they might be saved and so filling up in every way the measure of their sins. Thus "Wrath to the full has fallen on them."[6]

3 See above pp 239–240.
4 See p 240.
5 cf *Prov* 17:3.
6 *Test. XII Patr.* (*Test. Levi* 6:11).

But though separated from you for a while, brothers, in presence not in mind, I have been exceedingly anxious and greatly longing to see your faces. Consequently I, Paul, wanted personally to visit you time and again, but Satan put difficulties in my way. For what, if not you, is my hope or joy or proud crown in presence of our Lord

20 Jesus at his coming? It is you who are my glory and my joy.

3.1 So when I could bear it no longer, I was content to be left at Athens alone,[7] while I sent Timotheus, our brother and God's agent for the News of Christ, to sustain and encourage you in your faith, that none of you should wilt under these trials. You know yourselves that we are put here for this purpose; and further when I was with you I forewarned you, as you know, "we are bound to have

5 trouble", exactly as it turned out. So, as I say, being unable to bear it any longer, I sent to learn the state of your faith, in case the Tempter had tempted you, and my toil had been in vain.

But now, when Timotheus returned to me from visiting you, and gave me the good news of your loyalty and love, and that you always have a pleasant recollection of me and long to see me, as I to see you, this consoled me as far as you are concerned for all my anguish and distress. Now indeed I live again, since you stand fast in the Master. How can I sufficiently thank God on your account for all the happiness I enjoy because of you in the

10 presence of our God! Night and day I supplicate beyond all bounds that I may be permitted to see your faces and make good any deficiencies. May God himself, our Father, and our Lord Jesus make it practicable for me to come to you!

The Lord make you increase and abound in love for one another and for all others, as my love goes out to you, so as to lift up your hearts blameless[8] in holiness in the presence of God our Father at the coming of our Lord Jesus with all his saints.[9]

4.1 Further, brothers, I entreat and appeal to you in the Lord Jesus, that as you have received from me the

---

7 See above p 242.
8 As the offering was elevated in the Sanctuary.
9 Here as everywhere in Paul's letters Jesus is distinguished from God.

manner in which you should conduct yourselves and be pleasing to God – as indeed you do conduct yourselves – so should you do better still. You know I gave you certain instructions on behalf of the Lord Jesus. Doing the will of God implies your consecration, that you keep clear of immorality, that each of you knows how to possess his

5 own mate[10] in purity and with respect; not swayed by lust like the Gentiles who do not know God,[11] that there be no meddling with or coveting what belongs to your brother;[12] for the Lord will avenge anything of that sort as I warned and solemnly told you. God has not called us to impurity but to consecration. Accordingly, whoever disregards this breaks faith not with men but with God, who has given us his Spirit which is holy.

As regards brotherly affection there is no need for me to write to you, for you yourselves are taught by God to

10 love one another; and you do indeed practise it towards all the brothers throughout Macedonia. But I appeal to you, brothers, to do better still, and to make a real effort to be quiet and mind your own business. Labour with your hands, as I have instructed you, that you may comport yourselves with dignity towards those outside,[13] and require no one's assistance.[14]

Now I do not want you to be ignorant, brothers, about those who are laid to rest, that you do not grieve like those who are without hope. For if we believe that Jesus died and rose again, so do we also that God, by means of

15 Jesus, will bring back those who are laid to rest. I tell you this by the word of the Lord, that we who are alive and survive till the coming of the Master will not forestall those who are laid to rest. The Master will himself descend from heaven with a cry of command, with archangelic voice and divine trumpet-blast, and the dead in Christ will rise first. Next we who are alive and survive will be caught up with them by clouds to meet the Master in the air; and so shall we be ever with the Master. Cheer one another, therefore, with this information.

5.1 As regards dates and times, brothers, there is no need

10 Or 'his own person'.
11 cf *Ps* 79:6.
12 The 10th Commandment, *Exod* 20:17.
13 See p 13, n 28.
14 Some Thessalonian believers, expecting the speedy return of Jesus, were neglecting their employment. See *Thess* (2).

for me to write to you, for you yourselves know perfectly well that the Day of the Lord will come like a thief in the night.[15] Just when they are saying, "A peaceful night, and all's well", then suddenly destruction will be upon them like pangs on a pregnant woman, and they will have no chance of escape.[16] But you, brothers, are not in darkness, that the Day should catch you like a thief; for

5   all of you are Children of the Light[17] and beings of the day. We do not belong to the night or to darkness.

Well then, let us not slumber like others, but be wakeful and sober. For those who slumber slumber at night, and those who are drunkards are drunk at night. But let us who belong to the day be sober, clad in the corselet of faith and love, and helmeted with the hope of deliverance. For God has not destined us to Wrath, but to be preserved for Deliverance by our Lord Jesus Christ,

10   who died for us, that at once – whether awake or sleeping – we should be alive with him. So encourage one another and fortify each other, as indeed you are doing.

But I do beg you, brothers, to acknowledge those who work so hard among you and act as your leaders in the Master, and advise you. Hold them in extra-special affection for their work. Be at peace among yourselves.

I appeal to you, brothers, give fair warning to the disorderly, encourage the fainthearted, stand by the

15   weak, be patient with all. See to it that none renders to any injury for injury, but always do the right thing by each other and everyone else. Always be cheerful, pray constantly, give thanks for everything; for this is God's

20   will in Christ for you. Do not still the Spirit, or scorn prophesies. Test everything: retain the good.[18] Refrain from anything that looks at all wrong.

Now may the God of peace himself sanctify you completely, and may you in your entirety, spirit, soul and body, be kept blameless till the coming of the Lord Jesus Christ. He who calls you is faithful, who indeed will accomplish this. Brothers pray for us also.

15 cf *Mt* 24:3.
16 See *Joel* 2:1–11.
17 An expression favoured by the Essenes, contrasting the Children of Light with the Children of Darkness (cf *Manual of Discipl.*).
18 A saying of Jesus cited in the Patristic literature was: "Become skilled money-changers, rejecting some things, but retaining what is good."

25   Convey our regards to all the brothers with a chaste kiss. I adjure you by the Lord to have this letter read to all the brothers. The loving-kindness of Lord Jesus Christ be with you.

To the Community at Thessalonica (2)

(Probably written from Corinth about AD 52)

1.1 Paul, Silvanus and Timotheus, to the community of Thessalonians in God our Father and the Lord Jesus Christ. May peace and prosperity be yours from God the Father and the Lord Jesus Christ.

We are bound invariably to thank God for you, brothers, as is only right, because your faith is so wonderfully increasing, and the love of each and all of you for one another is deepening; so that we ourselves boast of you in the communities of God, of your constancy and loyalty in all the persecutions and trials with which you have had to contend.

5 This is evidence of God's strict justice, in having treated you as worthy of the Kingdom of God, for which indeed you suffer. For that being so, it becomes just on God's part to repay affliction to those who afflict you, and to give to you who are afflicted relief with us when the Lord Jesus is revealed from heaven with his mighty angels with flaming fire inflicting retribution on those who do not acknowledge God and do not respond to the News of our Lord Jesus.[1] They shall pay the penalty of perpetual exclusion from the presence of the Master, and

10 the splendour of his majesty, when he comes at that time to be praised by his saints and admired by all who have believed because our testimony to you was believed. To this end we invariably pray for you, that our God may make you worthy of your vocation, and enable you to accomplish every praiseworthy object and devoted deed

---

1 cf the Essene *Damasc. Doc.* 2:4, "And power and might and great fury with flames of fire – all the angels of destruction – for those who turned aside from the Way and abhorred the statute."

which may serve to glorify the name of our Lord Jesus among you, and you in him, by the loving-kindness of our God and the Lord Jesus Christ.

2.1   Now I beg you, brothers, as regards the coming of our Lord Jesus Christ and our being gathered to him, not to take speedy leave of your senses or become agitated, either by a spirit intimation, or by a speech, or by any letter purporting to be from me, under the impression that the Day of the Lord has begun. Let no one deceive you in any way whatever; for it will not begin before the Defection has first taken place and the Lawless Man has been revealed, the Doomed One who opposes and elevates himself above everything regarded as a god or as an object of worship, so that he himself sits in God's
5   Temple claiming to be God.[2] Do you not recall that this is what I told you while I was still with you?

So now you know what is the retarding factor, that the Lawless One may be revealed at his proper time. Indeed the process[3] of lawlessness is already at work, only there is one who is a retarding factor until his removal. And then the Lawless One will be revealed, whom the Lord Jesus will consume with the breath of his mouth and annihilate with the radiance of his presence,[4] that one whose coming is attended, in the way Satan works, by
10   every kind of mendacious trickery practised on those who are perishing, because they have not welcomed the love of truth so as to be spared. For that reason God will send them a spirit of delusion so as to believe the lie, that all may be condemned who have not credited truth, but have taken pleasure in falsehood.

But I am bound invariably to thank God for you, brothers dear to the Master, because God has chosen you from the very beginning for deliverance, for the acquisition of the glory of our Lord Jesus Christ, by that consecration of spirit and attachment to truth to which
15   he called you by my News. So then, brothers stand fast, and keep a firm hold on the traditions[5] you have been

2 The Devil incarnate of apocalyptic thought. The Emperor Gaius Caligula (AD 40) tried to set up his statue as a god in the Temple at Jerusalem.
3 Lit "mystery".
4 cf *Isa* 11:4; *Mt* 24:27.
5 The doctrine handed on from teacher to disciple. See *I Cor* 11.2; *Rom* 6:17.

taught whether by my speech or correspondence.

May our Master himself, Jesus Christ, and God our Father, who has loved us and graciously granted us solid consolation and good hope, encourage and confirm your minds by every fair word and deed!

3.1   Finally, brothers, pray for me, that the word of the Lord may speed and be honoured as in your case, and that I may be delivered from inhuman and wicked men;[6] for faith is not found in everyone. But the Lord is faithful, and will establish you and shield you from harm. I have confidence in you in the Master, that you are following
5   and will continue to follow my injunctions. The Lord direct your minds to the love of God and the constancy of Christ!

But in the name of the Lord Jesus Christ, brothers, I bid you shun every brother who behaves as a shirker, and not in accordance with the tradition you have received from me. You are well aware that you ought to copy me; for I was no shirker among you, neither did I accept free board from anyone.[7] Rather with toil and hardship did I labour night and day so as not to be a burden to you in any way. Not that I have not the right; but that I personally should set you an example, so that you
10   should copy me. That is why when I was with you I gave you this order, "He who will not work, neither shall he eat." For I hear there are some among you behaving as shirkers, not busy but busybodies. I order and exhort such as these in the Lord Jesus Christ, that going quietly about their work they eat their own bread.

As for you, brothers, never hesitate to do the right thing; but if anyone pays no attention to what I say in this letter, mark that man, and have nothing to do with him,
15   that he may be ashamed. Yet do not treat him as an enemy, but warn him as a brother.

Now may the Lord of peace himself give you peace always in all circumstances![8] The Lord be with you all.

The greeting I subjoin in my own, Paul's, hand. It is

---

6 A Jewish morning supplication asks God for deliverance from arrogant and wicked men (*AJP* p 7).
7 Lit "Neither did I eat anyone's bread for nothing".
8 See the Aaronic Benediction, *Num* 6:26.

the mark of authenticity in every letter.[9] This is how I write. *The loving-kindness of the Lord Jesus Christ be with you all.*[10]

---

9 As is evident from these words, and an earlier reference in the letter, at least one forged letter in the name of Paul was in existence at this time, and had perhaps reached the Thessalonians. The practice was common and not considered so immoral in those days. The Nazarene 'Zealots for the Law' were no doubt responsible. These did all they could to turn Paul's converts against him, with considerable success, and did not scruple to pervert his teaching. See *Rom* 3:8.

10 The words italicised were added by Paul in his own handwriting. Most of Paul's letters were dictated.

To the Communities of Galatia

(Probably written from Antioch in the early Summer of AD 53[1])

1.1 Paul the envoy – not from any body of men or appointed by any man, but by Jesus Christ and God the Father who raised him from the dead – and all the brothers who are with me, to the communities of Galatia. May peace and prosperity be yours from God our Father and the Lord Jesus Christ, who gave himself for our sins to reclaim us from the present evil world in accordance with the will of our God and
5 Father, to whom be praise for evermore.[2] Amen.

I am amazed that you have so quickly turned your backs on the one who called you in Christ's mercy for some other version of the News. It is not really another, but there are certain people who are confusing you and want to alter the terms of the News of Christ. But even should I, or an angel from heaven, proclaim to you anything different to what I did proclaim to you, cursed be he! Having said that, I am going to repeat it. If anyone proclaims to you anything different to what you received, cursed be he!

10 Is it men I have to satisfy, or is it God? Or is it men I am trying to please? If I were still pleasing men I should be no servant of Christ. I must make it clear to you, brothers, that the News as proclaimed by me is no human contrivance, for I neither obtained it from anyone, nor was I taught it: it came through Jesus Christ's own revelation.

---

1 Some date the letter as late as AD 57, perhaps from Corinth. In favour of this view is the likeness to the letter to the Romans.
2 Paul constantly follows the practice of pious Jews in adding a doxology when speaking of the ways of God.

You have heard, of course, of my behaviour when I practised Judaism,[3] how I ruthlessly hounded down God's Community and ravaged it, and how I advanced in Judaism far beyond many students of my own age; for none was more keenly enthusiastic than I to master the

15   traditions of my ancestors. But when it pleased God, who separated me from my mother's womb and called me by his mercy, to reveal his Son to me that I should proclaim him to the Gentiles, I did not take immediate steps to consult any earthly authority, neither did I go up to Jerusalem to interview those who were envoys before me. Instead, I went away to Arabia, and returned again to Damascus. Not until three years had elapsed did I go up to Jerusalem to report to Cephas,[4] and I remained with him fifteen days. But I met none of the other envoys

20   except James the Master's brother.[5] These are the facts I am giving you. Before God, I am telling no lie!

After that I went to the regions of Syria and Cilicia, and remained unknown by sight to the Christian communities of Judea. They only heard that "he who formerly persecuted us now proclaims the conviction he once attacked", and they praised God for me.

2.1   After that, some fourteen years later, I again went up to Jerusalem with Barnabas, and also took Titus with me. I went there by a revelation and reported to them the terms of the News I proclaim to the Gentiles. This was privately to those of repute, in case I should strive or had been striving to no purpose. But there was no forcing of Titus, who accompanied me, to be circumcised, Greek though he was, despite the infiltrated false brothers who had crept in to spy out the liberty we enjoy in Christ Jesus

5   in order to enslave us. Not for an instant did we strike our colours, so that the true character of the News might be preserved to you.

As for those of repute – whatever they were makes no difference to me: God takes no one at face value – they imposed on me nothing additional. Quite the contrary. When they saw that I had been entrusted with the News

---

3 The Jewish way of life. Paul had followed the views and practices of the Pharisees. His beliefs remained Jewish.

4 The Hebrew form of the nickname Peter.

5 Paul's account of his movements should be compared with what is related in the *Acts*. James (Jacob) the next younger brother of Jesus, was at this time head of all believers in Jesus as Messiah. His Jewish piety was notorious.

for the Uncircumcised, as Peter for the Circumcised – for he who stimulated Peter to envoyship of the Circumcised stimulated me also in going to the Gentiles – and when they realised the privilege that had been granted me, then James, Cephas and John, the reputed 'Pillars', extended to myself and Barnabas the right hand of fellowship. We were to go to the Gentiles, they to the 10 Circumcised.[6] Oh yes, they did add one thing more, we were to remember the poor,[7] which personally I was only too ready to do.

So when Cephas came to Antioch I opposed him publicly, because he deserved censure. Before certain persons came from James he had eaten with Gentiles. But after their arrival he drew back and separated himself out of fear of those of the Circumcision. The other Jews played up to him, so that even Barnabas was carried away by their hypocrisy.

So when I saw that they were not acting in conformity with the true character of the News I said to Peter in front of them all, "If you, a born Jew, live like a Gentile, why 15 do you force the Gentiles to keep Jewish ways? We who are of Jewish race and not Gentile sinners,[8] knowing that no one is exonerated by following regulations but by faith in Jesus Christ, even we have trusted in Jesus Christ so as to be exonerated by faith in Christ and not by following regulations; for by following regulations "not a single human being will be exonerated".[9] But if, while seeking to be exonerated in Christ, we ourselves are found to be sinners, does that make Christ sin's agent? God forbid! So if I rebuild what I have demolished it is I who become a transgressor of my own accord. For in law I have died in the legal sense, so as to live in the divine 20 sense. I have shared Christ's crucifixion. I am alive, it is true, but strictly speaking it is not I who live, but Christ who lives in me. My present physical existence is by virtue of the life of God's Son, who loved me and gave himself for me. I am not going to be the one to refuse

6 Actually Paul had wanted Gentile believers to be reckoned as Israelites by faith. But this had been refused, unless they were full proselytes to Judaism. Paul would not accept this ruling.
7 The poor saints of Jerusalem.
8 As idolaters, living in violation of the Commandments.
9 cf *Ps* 143:2.

God's mercy. For if rectitude could be assured by law then Christ died in vain.

3.1   You senseless Galatians, who has cast a spell over you, you before whose gaze Jesus Christ was publicly displayed[10] as crucified? I only wish to know this from you, did you receive the Spirit by following regulations or by the response of faith? Are you so senseless, that having made a start spiritually you are now going to end up physically? Have you experienced so much to no 5   purpose? Does he who mediates the Spirit to you, and effects miracles among you, do it by following regulations or by the response of faith, just as Abraham "believed God, and it was accounted to him as rectitude"?[11]

Observe, then, that it is those with faith who are the children of Abraham. And the Scriptures, forseeing that God would exonerate the Gentiles by faith, proclaimed in advance the News to Abraham, "in you shall all the nations be blessed".[12] So it is those with faith who are 10   blessed along with believing Abraham. All those who follow regulations are under a curse, for it is stated, "Cursed is everyone who does not adhere to and observe all the precepts set down in the Code of Law".[13]

Thus it is evident that no one is exonerated before God by law, because "the just shall live *by faith*".[14] But the Law is not "by faith": it stipulates that "he who keeps the commandments shall live .by them".[15] Christ has released us from the law's curse by becoming a curse on our behalf, for it is stated "Cursed is everyone hanged on a tree",[16] so that Abraham's blessing might come to the Gentiles by Jesus Christ, that we should all receive the promise of the Spirit *by faith*.

15   Brothers, I speak in human terms; even in human practice a covenant once ratified cannot be set aside or amended. The undertakings were clearly given to Abra-

---

10 The word used signifies public placarding, but Paul probably had in mind the lifting up of the serpent in the wilderness. See *Num* 21:9 and cf *Jn* 3:14. He is referring to his own preaching.
11 *Gen* 15:6.
12 *Gen* 12:3.
13 *Deut* 27:26.
14 *Hab* 2:4.
15 *Lev* 18:5.
16 *Deut* 21:23.

ham "and to his seed".[17] It does not say "and to seeds", implying a number, but distinctly one, "and to your seed", that is to say "to Christ". So I say this, that the Law which came into force four hundred and thirty years later[18] cannot abrogate the covenant previously ratified by God so as to annul the promise; and God wanted to show his appreciation of Abraham by making a promise.

Why then was the Law given? It was introduced to deal with infringements until such time as the promised Seed should come, drawn up in due form by angels acting through a spokesman.[19] Since, however, a spokesman does not act for *one*, while God is ONE, does that mean that the Law is at variance with God's undertakings? God forbid! Certainly if a law could have been given capable of conferring life, then rectitude would have been by law. As it is, the Scripture[20] classes all together as sinners, that the promise by faith in Jesus Christ might be granted to those who believe.[21]

Before faith came we were under law's strict tutelage: we were classmates until the future should be revealed. Consequently, the Law was our disciplinarian till Christ came, so that we should be exonerated by faith. Now that faith has come we are no longer under a disciplinarian. You are all Sons of God by faith in Jesus Christ; for those who have been identified with Christ by immersion have assumed Christ's personality. It is impossible for there to be Jew or Greek, slave or freeman, male or female;[22] for in Jesus Christ you are all one and the same person. If you are *in* Christ you *are* "the Seed of Abraham", heirs in accordance with the promise.

4.1   What I am saying is this, that so long as the heir is under age, though he is actually master of the estate, his position hardly differs from that of a slave: he remains under supervisors and managers until the time fixed by his father. So it is with us. We too were under age, in

---

17 *Gen* 12:3.
18 The time of the sojourn of Israel in Egypt, *Exod* 12:40.
19 ie the angels, by whom in Jewish legend the Law was given, whose spokesman was the Angel of the Covenant.
20 *Ps* 143:2.
21 Paul's argument is challenged by *James' Epistle*.
22 Jewish daily prayer, thanking God for not making him a heathen, a slave, or a woman, in the order given here (*AJP* pp 5–6).

subjection to the elemental forces of the universe. Then, when the set time had arrived, God sent out his Son,
5   born of a woman, born under law,[23] that those under law might be redeemed, that we might receive adoption as sons. And because you are now sons, God has sent his Son's spirit into our hearts, crying, '*Abba*!' (Father!). Thus no longer is it a slave crying, but a son, and if a son, then by God's providence an heir also.

There was a time when not knowing God you were enslaved to those who in reality are no gods. But now acknowledging God, or rather being acknowledged by God, how comes it that you have turned back to the feeble and abject elemental forces? Do you intend to be
10   enslaved to them all over again? You have begun to observe special days and months, seasons and years. I begin to fear for you that I may have been wearing myself out for you to no purpose.

Do become as I am, that I in turn may be as you are, I do entreat you. I assure you that you have not wronged me. You well know how through physical infirmity I proclaimed the News to you originally. But the temptation afforded you by my physical condition did not induce you to mock or express disgust. Instead, you welcomed me as if I were God's messenger,[24] as if I was
15   Christ Jesus in person. What has become of the delight you exhibited? For I can testify that if need be you would have plucked out your eyes and given them to me. Have I become your enemy by being frank with you? They are paying court to you[25] for no good purpose: they really intend to ostracize you so that you should court them. It is good to be courted for a good purpose on all occasions, and not just when I am present with you, my children, for whom I travail once more until Christ is formed in
20   you. I only wish I could be with you at this moment, and change my tone, for I am quite distracted about you.

Tell me, you that want to be under law, do you never listen to the reading of the Law? For it is stated that Abraham had two sons, one by the slave-girl and one by

23 ie born in wedlock. cf *Rom* 1:3.
24 See *Acts* 14:12, where we learn how Paul was taken for Hermes (Mercury) messenger of the gods. In early Christian apologetics Jesus was likened to Mercury.
25 Those who came from James advocating the conversion of believing Gentiles to the faith of Israel, since they accepted the Messiah (Christ) as their king, and identified themselves with Israel.

the free-woman. But while the child of the slave girl was of physical origin, the child of the free-woman was born by promise. These are allegorical matters, for these women represent two covenants, the one is of Mount 25 Sinai bearing children for servitude. This is Hagar – for in Arabia *hajar* means Mount Sinai[26] – and corresponds to the present Jerusalem which is in servitude with her children. But the Jerusalem Above[27] is free, which is our mother Sarah,[28] for it is stated,

> *Rejoice, you barren one who does not bear!*
> *Cry out with joy, you who do not travail!*
> *For more are the children of the desolate*
> *Than of the woman who has a husband.*[29]

Now we, brothers, like Isaac, are children of promise. But just as then the child of physical origin persecuted 30 the child of spiritual origin, so it is now. Yet what does the Scripture say? "Cast out the slave-girl and her son, for the son of the slave-girl shall not share the inheritance with the son of the free-woman."[30] Consequently, brothers, we are not the children of the slave-girl, but of the free-woman, with the complete freedom Christ has given us. Stand firm, then, and refuse to be harnessed again to a yoke of bondage.

5.1   I, Paul, tell you plainly that if you become circumcised Christ is of no avail to you. And I declare to every circumcised person that he is obligated to observe the whole Law. You have become severed from Christ, those of you who would be exonerated by law: you have fallen 5 from grace. For it is spiritually, by faith, that we hold the expectation of rectitude; for in Christ Jesus it is neither circumcision nor uncircumcision that is efficacious, but faith stimulated by love.

You were running so well. Who brought you to a halt by making you lose confidence in the truth? That idea you have got never came from the one who called you. It 10 takes little leaven to leaven the mass. I personally am

---

26 The Sinai Peninsular called by the Arabs *el-Tijahah*.
27 The heavenly Jerusalem (Jerusalem Above). The Jewish mystics believed in the idea of 'as above so below'. See *Rev* 21:2.
28 In the text the name has been dropped, and perhaps also the author's explanation of the name which means 'noble'.
29 *Isa* 54:1.
30 *Gen* 21:9–10.

convinced of you in the Master that you will not change your minds. He who is confusing you must bear the blame, whoever he may be. And what of me, brothers? If I am still preaching circumcision, why am I still being persecuted? So much for the "abolition of the obstacle of the cross"![31] It would be a good thing if those who unsettle you over circumcision would cut themselves off as well!

Now you have been called to freedom, brothers. That does not mean freedom simply as an excuse for physical indulgence: it means that you are to serve one another through love. For the whole Law is summed up in this one precept, "You are to love your neighbour as your-

15 self".[32] But if you bite and devour each other, take care that you do not exterminate one another. I say, therefore, conduct yourselves spiritually, and do not allow your physical passions to have their way. For the physical nature has passions contrary to the spiritual nature, and the spiritual nature contrary to the physical, because these are in opposition to one another. So you are not free to do as you please. Yet if you are spiritually guided you are not under law.

Now the deeds of the physical nature are obvious: they

20 are adultery, impurity, sensuality, idolatry, sorcery, enmity, quarrelling, envy, passions, intrigues, dissensions, factions, malice, heavy drinking, revelling, and everything of the same description about which I have warned you, just as I am warning you now, that those who act in this way will not inherit the Kingdom of God. But the spiritual product is love, joy, peace, forbearance, kindliness, goodness, loyalty, gentleness, self-control. Against these no law is operative. Those who are in Christ Jesus have crucified the physical nature with its

25 passions and desires. If we are to live spiritually, let us also accept spiritual discipline. Let us not become self-assertive, defying one another, malicious to one another.

6.1 Brothers, if anyone has been detected in some fault, you who are spiritually-minded should correct him in a mild manner, having an eye on yourself in case you

---

31 Paul seems here to be borrowing a phrase from the propaganda of the Zealots for the Law. The idea of a crucified Messiah was repugnant to Jews (see *I Cor* 1:23). The death of Jesus had to be explained as an act of love and the means by which he entered into his glory.

32 *Lev* 19:18 (cf *Mt* 22:39–40; *Rom* 13:9–10).

should be tested. Bear one another's burdens, and thus carry out Christ's law.[33] But if anyone fancies himself to be somebody, when he is nothing of the kind, he suffers from self-delusion. Each must carefully examine his own work, and then he can have something to be proud of in

5   his own right instead of in another's; for each must shoulder his own load. But let him who has the Message imparted to him share all credit with his instructor.

Harbour no illusions. God is not to be hoodwinked. Whatever a man sows he will also reap. He who sows for his physical nature will reap decay as the physical consequences, while he who sows for the spiritual nature will reap eternal life as the spiritual consequences. Let us never grow weary of doing what is right; for by never

10   relaxing we shall reap in due course. So as opportunity is afforded us let us labour for the welfare of all, particularly of our kinsmen in faith.

Look how I have written to you in large characters with my own hand![34] Those who want to make a favourable impression in the physical sense press you to be circumcised, but only to evade persecution for Christ's cross. It is not as if these circumcised people were themselves observant. They only want you to be circumcised so that they can boast of your physical condition. For myself, God forbid that I should boast of anything but the cross of our Lord Jesus Christ, by which the world has been

15   crucified to me, and I to the world! It is neither circumcision nor uncircumcision that counts for anything, but a new creation. To all who toe this line, peace and mercy be upon them, and upon the Israel of God.[35]

From now on let no one deal me any more blows, for I carry the scars of Jesus on my body.[36]

The loving-kindness of the Lord Jesus Christ be with your spirit, brothers. Amen.

---

33 cf *Isa* 53:4; *Mt* 8:27.
34 As a mark of special esteem.
35 cf Jewish prayer, "May he bestow peace on us, and upon all Israel" (*AJP* pp 54, 76, etc). The 'Israel of God' or 'divine Israel' as distinguished from the physical Israel.
36 Probably with reference to the flogging Jesus underwent (*Mk* 15:15). Paul had been flogged.

To the Community at Corinth (1)[1]

(Written from Ephesus possibly in AD 55)

Excerpt One

I Cor

9.1   . . . Am I not a freeman?[2] Am I not an envoy? Have I not seen Jesus our Master? Are you not the product of my labour for the Master? If I am not regarded by others as an envoy, surely I am by you, for you are the confirmation of my envoyship for the Master.

Here, then, is my reply to those who cross-examine
5   me. Have we not the right to eat and drink? Have we not the right to take around with us a believing wife[3] like the other envoys do, and the Master's brothers,[4] and Cephas? Is it only I and Barnabas who have no right to give up our occupations? Whoever goes on military service at his own expense? Who plants a vineyard and does not partake of its fruit? Who herds a flock and does not eat the curds obtained from the flock? Am I speaking in human fashion, or does not the Law say the same thing? Surely it is stated in the Law of Moses, "You are not to muzzle the ox that treads out the corn".[5] Is God
10   concerned here for oxen, or speaking entirely for our benefit? For our benefit, surely, so that the ploughman

---

1 The existing two letters to the Corinthians are a combination of the original four. The first letter is referred to in *I Cor* 5:9, the second is largely represented by *I Cor.* The third is mentioned in *II Cor* 7:8, and the fourth corresponds to the greater part of *II Cor.* The original first letter dealt in part with the theme of association with immoral persons. As presented here *I Cor* 9:1–10:22 and *II Cor* 6:14–7:1 would belong to it.
2 As compared with a slave without rights.
3 Lit "a sister-wife".
4 Evidently the brothers of Jesus acted as missionaries.
5 *Deut* 25:4.

should have something to expect from his ploughing, and the thresher from his part of the work. If we have sown spiritual seed in you, is it too much to expect if we reap material things from you? If you grant others that right, should you not much more us, even if we have taken no advantage of that right, but have fended for ourselves entirely lest we should afford the slightest hindrance to the News of Christ.[6] Are you ignorant that those who perform priestly duties partake of the Temple dues, and that those who serve the altar share in what is offered at the altar?[7] In the same way the Master has laid down that those who proclaim the News should live off the News.[8]

15   Yet I have availed myself of none of these rights, and I have not mentioned them here with a view to getting anything for myself. I would sooner die first! Let no one take that as an empty boast. Granted that I do proclaim the News, there is nothing in that for me to boast of, for I am constrained to do it. Woe to me if I do not proclaim the News! Yet if I do it in a voluntary capacity I receive a reward. But if I am engaged to do it, it is my professional employment. What is the nature of my reward? It is that when I proclaim the News I can give it out free of charge by not exercising my rights.

But though I am in every sense a freeman, I have made
20   myself everyone's slave so as to win over far more. So I have been a Jew to Jews to win over Jews. I have been subject to law to those under law – not being under law myself – to win over those under law. I have been alien to law to those without law[9] – though not alien to God's law and legally bound to Christ – to win over those without law. I have been subject to limitations[10] to those with limitations, to win over those with limitations. To everyone I have been as they are, that at all events I should save some. And whatever I do it is for the News, that I may assure my share in it.

Are you ignorant that though all the runners race on the course only one receives the prize? So run as if you
25   meant to win. And every contestant exercises complete

6 Paul has particularly himself in mind.
7 cf *Lev* 2:3; 6:18.
8 cf *Lk* 10:7.
9 See below p 350, n 23.
10 Conscientious objection in matters of diet, etc.

self-mastery; but they do it for a perishable garland, we for an imperishable. That is how *I* run, in no uncertain fashion, and that is how *I* fight, with no threshing the air. I pummel my body and make it my slave, in case having preached to others I should fail to pass the test myself.

10.1   I would not have you ignorant, brothers, that our ancestors[11] were all under cover of the cloud and all passed through the sea, and all were immersed with the Mosaic immersion in the cloud and in the sea.[12] And they all partook of the same spiritual food[13] and drank the same spiritual drink; for they drank from that
5   accompanying rock,[14] the rock that was Christ. But God was not pleased with the majority of them, and they were laid low in the wilderness.

Now these things have become illustrations to us not to covet what is bad, as they did; not to be idolaters, as some of them were, as it is stated, "the people sat down to eat and drink and rose up to play",[15] not to indulge in immorality, as some of them did, and twenty-three thousand fell in one day; not to test the Lord, as some of
10   them did, and perished by snake bites; not to murmur, as some of them did, and perished by the destroyer.

Now these things happened to those people to furnish illustrations, and they were set down as a warning to us with whom the Consummation of the Ages has been reached.[16] So let him who stands have a care lest he fall. No superhuman temptation has come your way. God is faithful: he will never allow you to be tested beyond your strength, but along with the test he will provide a loop-hole also, to enable you to extricate yourself from it.

Consequently, dear friends, make good your escape
15   from idolatry. I am talking to men of sense. Consider carefully what I say. Is not the cup of blessing that we

---

11 Paul insisted that all Gentile converts were now Israelites, as being in and subject to the Messiah as Israel's king.

12 *Exod* 14:19–21, 31.

13 *Exod* 16:15, the manna.

14 *Num* 17:6; 20:8. In Jewish legend the rock was like a beehive, which rolled along beside the Israelites. When they camped it gave water as the people sang, "Spring up, O well" (*Num* 21:17).

15 *Exod* 32:6.

16 In reading the New Testament we must always have in mind that for Jesus and his followers, as for a great many Jews at this period, the end of the present world order was imminent, to be replaced by the new World Order of the Kingdom of God.

bless fellowship with Christ's blood? Is not the bread we break fellowship with Christ's body?[17] For we many are one loaf of bread, one body, since we all have a part of the one loaf of bread. Look at the physical Israel.[18] Are not those who partake of the sacrifices in fellowship with the altar of sacrifice? Of course I am not suggesting by this that an offering to an idol is anything, or that an idol is
20   anything. Of course not. What the Gentiles sacrifice they sacrifice to demons, and not to God, and I want you to have no fellowship with demons. You cannot drink the Lord's cup and the cup of demons. Neither can you share the Lord's table and the table of demons.[19] Are we to arouse the Lord's jealousy? Are we stronger than he?

Excerpt Two[20]

II Cor
6.14   . . . Do not be ill-matched[21] with unbelievers. For what has rectitude in common with lawlessness? Or what fellowship has light with darkness? What harmony has Christ with Beliar? Or what share has the faithful with the faithless? And what agreement has the temple of God with idols? For we are the temple of the Living God, as God has said,

> *'I will dwell with them and walk with them,*
> *And I will be their God, and they my people.'*[22]
> *'Therefore come out from among them,*
> *And be separate,' says the Lord.*
> *'Have no contact with the unclean.*[23]
> *And I will admit you within,*
> *And I will be a father to you,*
> *And you shall be my sons and daughters'*[24]
> *Says the Lord of hosts.*

17 Referring to the ceremonial blessing of bread and wine (Heb. *Kiddush*) at communal meals, especially on religious occasions.
18 Those who are Israelites by descent.
19 In the Graeco-Roman world the sacrificial meal was regarded as the table of the god (eg 'the table of the Lord Serapis'). The Jews regarded their communal meal as the table of the Lord. See below p 313, and cf the Mishnah, *Aboth* 3:4.
20 This excerpt may have followed the previous one almost directly.
21 Lit "yoked with another kind", relating to the Law of Diverse Kinds (*Deut* 22:9–11). A clean beast was not to be yoked with an unclean (see *Kilaim*, 8:2).
22 *Lev* 26:11–12.
23 *Isa* 52:11.
24 cf *Jer* 31:1, 9; *Isa* 43:6.

7.1   Having therefore these promises,[25] dear friends, let us cleanse ourselves from all physical and spiritual defilement, discharging our sacred duties[26] in the fear of the Lord. . .

25 As just quoted. But see also *Ezek* 37:21,23,28 (11:17, 20 in LXX), where, in *v* 17 of the Greek, *eisdechomai* ('admit within') is used.
26 As priests of God's temple.

To the Community at Corinth (2)[1]

(Written from Ephesus possibly in the Autumn of AD 55)

I Cor

1.1   Paul, by the will of God a chosen envoy of Jesus Christ, with brother Sosthenes, to the community of God at Corinth, consecrated in Jesus Christ as members of the holy assembly[2] in common with all who in every place invoke the name of our Lord Jesus Christ, their Master and ours. May peace and prosperity be yours from God our Father and the Lord Jesus Christ.

Invariably I thank God for you, for the way he has
5   favoured you in Christ Jesus, because he has so enriched you in every respect, both in speech and knowledge. Just as the testimony to Christ was so firmly established among you, so have you never lacked for any spiritual gifts while waiting for the revelation of our Lord Jesus Christ. God is faithful, who has chosen you for fellowship with his son Jesus Christ our Master.

10   Now in the name of our Lord Jesus Christ I urge you, brothers, all to hold together and not to have divisions among yourselves, but to accommodate yourselves to the selfsame outlook and viewpoint. For it has been conveyed to me about you, brothers, by Chloe's people, that quarrelling is going on among you. I mean this, that you are variously saying, "I side with Paul", or, "I go with Apollos", "I take Cephas' view", or, "I take Christ's". Has Christ been split up? Was Paul crucified on your behalf? Or were you immersed in the name of Paul? I am thankful I immersed none of you but Crispus[3] and

1 Commonly known as *I Corinthians*.
2 Answering to Heb *mikra kodesh* (holy convocation) as in *Exod* 12:16.
3 Former president of the synagogue at Corinth (*Acts* 18:8).

15   Gaius, so that no one can say you were immersed in my
name. Oh yes, I also immersed the household of
Stephanas. Otherwise I do not recall that I immersed
anyone else. For Christ did not send me out to immerse
but to proclaim the News; and not with clever words
either, in case Christ's cross should lose all its potency.
The message of the cross may be foolish to those who are
perishing, but to those who are being saved – to us – it is
the power of God; for it is stated,

> I will destroy the wisdom of the sages,
> And nullify the intellect of the intelligent.[4]

20   What becomes of the sage, the scribe, the scholar of
this world? Has not God made nonsense of the world's
wisdom?[5] For since in God's wisdom the world failed to
know God by wisdom, it pleased God to save those who
believe by the folly of preaching. For while the Jews
demand a sign, and the Greeks require wisdom, we
preach a crucified Christ,[6] an obstacle to Jews and nonsense to Gentiles. But to those who are chosen – Jews and
Greeks alike – a Christ who is the power of God and the

25   wisdom of God. For God's 'folly' is wiser than men, and
God's 'weakness' is stronger than men.

As regards the choice, take yourselves, brothers.
There are not many sages among you in the world's
sense, not many persons of consequence, not many
highborn. Instead, God has selected what is foolish in
the world to shame the wise, and what is weak to shame
the mighty, and what is of base origin and treated with
contempt has God chosen, and even what is non-
existent[7] to bring to an end the existing order, that not a

30   single human being should boast in God's presence. But
you are his offspring in Christ Jesus, who was begotten
to be wisdom to us from God, yes, and vindication,
consecration and ransom, so that, as it is stated, "Let him
who boasts do it in the Lord".[8]

2.1   So when I came to you, brothers, I did not come
disclosing to you the Divine Secret with imposing speech

---

4 *Isa* 29:14.
5 cf *Isa* 33:18; 44:25.
6 The reader must always understand 'Christ' as the Greek word for Messiah.
7 Possibly referring to the position of the slave, regarded literally in the
Graeco-Roman world as a 'non-entity'.
8 *Jer* 9:24.

or wisdom; for I was determined to be conscious of nothing while among you but of Jesus Christ, and of him as crucified. And so it was in weakness, and in fear, and in great trepidation, that I arrived among you; and my speech and proclamation was with no persuasive words of wisdom, but with spiritual and phenomenal
5 demonstration, so that your conviction should rest not on human wisdom but on divine power.

There is a wisdom which we employ with the initiated; but it is a wisdom that has nothing to do with this world, or with the transient forces governing this world.[9] It is the Hidden Wisdom of God contained in a Mystery,[10] which God formulated of old to be our glory before the Ages began, unknown to any of the forces governing this world; for had they known it they would never have crucified the Lord of Glory. But as it is stated,

> *What eye has never seen, nor ear heard,*
> *What never entered the mind of man,*
> *God has prepared for those who love him.*[11]

10 Yet God has revealed it to us by the Spirit; for the Spirit delves into everything, even into the profundities of God. For who among men knows a man's ideas except the human spirit which is in him? So too none can know God's ideas except the Divine Spirit. Now what we have received is not the spirit of the created world, but the Spirit that emanates from God, so that we may know what God graciously grants us to know.[12] Those are the things we speak of, not in the language that human wisdom provides, but in the fashion of spiritual instruction, bringing spiritually-equipped people into contact with spiritual realities. The materialist cannot entertain the ideas of the Divine Spirit: to him they are nonsense, and he cannot grasp them, because they have to be
15 discerned spiritually. But the spiritually-equipped person discerns all these things, though they are to be

9 The spirit-powers ruling the planet.
10 Paul here uses the language of the Mystery cults. The Jewish (Pharisee) mystics had two branches of Hidden Wisdom, the Lore of Creation (in *Gen* 1) and the Lore of the Chariot (in *Ezekiel*). Paul had been initiated into the former, as revealed in his letters. This dealt with the Heavenly Man as the image of God, the Messiah Above.
11 *Isa* 64:4.
12 *Deut* 29:29; Jewish *Amidah* prayer, *Bened.* 4, "Thou favourest man with knowledge" (*AJP* p 20).

discerned by no one unaided, "for who has ever known the mind of the Lord, that he should teach him?"[13] But we have Christ's mind.

3.1 It was impossible, however, brothers, for me to speak to you as spiritually-equipped people, only as physically-equipped, as infants in Christ. I had to feed you with milk rather than solid food, for you were not equal to it. Neither are you equal to it yet, for you are still at the physical stage.[14] As long as there is rivalry and wrangling among you, are you not physical and behaving in human fashion? Whenever someone comes out with "I take Paul's side", and another, "I am with Apollos", are 5 you not human? What then is Apollos, and what is Paul? Simply the agents, each as the Lord endowed him, by whom you believed. I did the planting, and Apollos did the watering, but God caused the growth. Consequently, neither the planter nor the waterer counts, only God the Grower. Both the planter and the waterer have the same standing, yet each will receive his individual reward according to his individual labour; for we are God's co-workers, and you are God's culture, God's construction.

10 By virtue of God's favour bestowed on me, I, like a skilled master-builder have laid the foundation, while another will build on it. Only let each take care in what way he builds on it. There can never be any other foundation laid than what has been laid,[15] the foundation that is Jesus Christ. But upon it it is open to anyone to erect an edifice of gold, silver, precious stones, wood, straw, or rush. The material in each case will be evident, for the Day will reveal it. Since fire will be the means of disclosure, the flame itself will prove what kind of material it is. If the material which anyone has used for 15 building survives, he will receive a reward. If anyone's material is burnt up, he will pay the penalty, though he will be saved himself, but barely, as if he had come through the flame.

Do you not realize that you are God's temple, and that the Divine Spirit resides in you? If anyone dishonours God's temple God will dishonour him; for God's temple

13 *Isa* 40:13.
14 Paul speaks as a Jewish adept in mysticism.
15 Christ (Messiah) as Foundation Stone. cf *I Pet* 2:4–6.

is holy, as you are meant to be.

Let no one delude himself. If any of you considers he is what passes for a wise man in this age, let him become a fool, so that he may become really wise; for this world's wisdom is folly to God, for it is stated, "He catches the

20 wise at their knavery",[16] and again, "The Lord knows how trivial are the arguments of the wise".[17]

4.1 So let no one boast of individuals. Everything is yours as it is, whether Paul, Apollos, Cephas, the whole created world, life and death, the present and future, all is yours, and you are Christ's, and Christ is God's. Consequently, we should be regarded merely as Christ's assistants, stewards of the Divine Mysteries, which implies the requirement in stewards that they should be found reliable. So it is of small concern to me whether I am examined by you or any human standard. I do not even examine myself. I am not aware of anything to my detriment; but that does not exonerate me. It is the

5 Master who will examine me. So do not judge prematurely, before the Master has come, who will bring dark secrets to light and reveal the heart's design; and then the praise that is appropriate will be accorded by God to each.

Now these things, brothers, I have applied figuratively to myself and Apollos for your benefit, that you may learn the truth by us "Not beyond what is ordained",[18] so that you may not get puffed up over one as compared with another. For who has singled you out? Or what do you possess that you have not received? And if you have received it, why do you boast as if you had not received it? Already you are glutted! Already you have grown rich! Already you have occupied the throne! And I only wish you had taken the throne, so that we could reign with you. As it seems to me, God has kept us envoys for the end of the show, like those doomed to death;[19] for we have become a spectacle for the universe,

10 for angels and men. We for Christ's sake are fools, while you in Christ are sensible people! We are weak, but you

16 *Job* 5:13.
17 *Ps* 94:11.
18 The source of this dictum is not known, but cf the saying of Paul's Jewish contemporary Johanan ben Zaccai, "If you have learnt much Divine Doctrine claim no merit for yourself, for to that end you were created" (*Aboth* 2:8).
19 Like condemned criminals in the arena.

are strong! You stand in high esteem, while we are in disgrace! To this very moment we hunger and thirst, we are ragged and knocked about, vagrant and toil-worn, labouring with our hands. When insulted we are polite, when persecuted we submit to it, when cursed we are conciliatory. Right up to now we are treated as the scum of the universe, the offscouring of everything.[20]

15 I am not writing this to shame you, but as dear children of mine I am reminding you. Should you have ten thousand guardians in Christ, you do not have that number of fathers. It is I, I in Christ, who have begotten you by the News. Copy me, therefore, I entreat you. That is why I have dispatched Timotheus to you, who is not only a dear child of mine but loyal to the Master, to recall to you the course I follow in Christ, which I commend everywhere to all the communities. There are some who are full of bluster under the impression that I shall not be visiting you. But if the Lord wills I shall be visiting you quite soon; and when I do I shall take cognizance not of the speech but of the spiritual power of

20 the blusterers. For the Kingdom of God consists not in speech but in spiritual power. Which do you prefer, that I visit you with a stick or in a mild and affectionate spirit?

5.1 I am reliably informed that there is immorality among you, immorality such as has no parallel among the Gentiles, that one should have his father's wife. And you are full of elation, instead of grieving, to the end that the person responsible should be removed from among you. I, however, absent as I am in body but present in spirit, have already – as if I were present – condemned the perpetrator of such a crime in the name of the Lord Jesus. Before the assembled company of yourselves and my spirit, invested with the authority of the Lord Jesus, the

5 sentence is that the person concerned be consigned to Satan for his physical destruction[21] that his spirit may be saved when the Day of the Lord comes.

There is no justification for your boasting. Are you not aware that "a little leaven leavens the whole lump"? Get rid of the old leaven that you may be a new lump, once

20 The metaphor is taken from the Athenian custom in the event of some dire calamity of throwing some of the human 'scum' of the city into the sea, to 'clean off' the guilt of the people.

21 The form of excommunication may have been akin to that of the Essenes. The expelled person was evidently expected to die.

more in the unleavened state, for our passover – Christ – has been sacrificed.[22] Consequently, let us observe the festival, not with the old leaven, nor with the leaven of vice and immorality, but with the unleavened bread of purity and sincerity.

10   In my letter[23] I wrote to you not to keep company with immoral characters,[24] not specifically the immoral of contemporary society, any more than with usurers, extortioners and idolaters, for in that case you would have to exclude yourselves completely from society. But I am writing to you now not to keep company at all with anyone bearing the name of brother if he is immoral, or a usurer, or idolater, or foul-mouthed, or a drunkard, or extortioner. You are not even to take meals with such people. Is it for me to judge those outside[25] when you do not judge those inside? Leave God to judge those outside, while you "put away the wicked from among you".[26]

6.1   Has any of you with a grievance against his fellow the temerity to bring his case before the evil-doers instead of before the saints? Or are you ignorant that the saints are to judge the world?[27] So if the world is to be judged by you, are you unqualified to deal with minor issues? Are you ignorant that we are to judge angels, let alone mundane matters? So if you have any mundane issues let those be appointed to try them who are the most

5   looked down on members of the community. I say this deliberately to shame you. Can it be possible that there is not a wise man among you competent to decide between one brother and another? But brother must go to law with brother, and before unbelievers too!

    It is already an admission of complete failure on your part that you have any causes between yourselves. Why not rather let yourselves be injured? Why not rather let yourselves be defrauded? Instead, you injure and defraud, and your own brothers too! Are you ignorant that evil-doers shall not inherit the Kingdom of God? Do

---

22 The passover sacrifice immediately preceded the Feast of Unleavened Bread. All the old leaven was destroyed before the festival.
23 Two probable excerpts from this letter are given above pp 297–301.
24 See p 9, n 15.
25 See p 13, n 28.
26 *Deut* 22:24.
27 When the Kingdom of God is constituted on earth. See *Mt* 19:28.

not delude yourselves. Neither the immoral, nor
10   idolaters, nor adulterers, nor homosexuals, nor thieves,
nor usurers, nor drunkards, nor the foul-mouthed, nor
extortioners, shall inherit the Kingdom of God. That is
what some of you were; but you have been cleansed, you
have been consecrated, you have been exonerated by the
name of our Lord Jesus Christ, and by the Spirit of God.

"I am free to do everything."[28] Yes, but everything is
not advantageous. I am free to do everything, provided I
do not fall into its power. "Food is for appetite, and
appetite for food", but God will do away with both the
one and the other. For the body is not for prostitution,
but for the Master, and the Master for the body. And the
God who raised up the Master will also by his power
raise us up.

Are you ignorant that your bodies are the organs of
Christ? Am I then to make the organs of Christ the
organs of a prostitute? God forbid! Or are you ignorant
that he who unites himself with a prostitute forms a
single body, for "the two" it is said, "shall become one
15   flesh"?[29] But he who unites himself with the Master
forms a single spirit. Shun prostitution. Any other kind
of sin a man may commit is independent of the body, but
the immoral man sins against his own body. Or are you
ignorant that your body is the temple of the holy Spirit
which is in you, which you have received from God, and
20   that you are not your own, having been acquired at a
high price? Then praise God with your body.

7.1   Now to turn to the matters on which you have written
me. It is preferable for a man not to have intercourse with
a woman.[30] But to avoid prostitution each should take
himself a wife, and each woman should have her own
husband. The husband should fulfil his obligations to his
wife, and similarly the wife to her husband. The wife has
not the control of her own body but the husband.
Similarly the husband has not the control of his own
5   body but the wife. Do not deprive one another, unless by
agreement for a time to devote yourselves to prayer.[31]

---

28 This quotation and the one that follows may possibly have been in the letter
from the Corinthians to which Paul is replying. See also below p 313.
29 *Gen* 2:24.
30 In view of the imminence of the Messianic Age.
31 *Test. XII Patr.* "There is a season for a man to embrace his wife, and a season
to abstain therefrom for his prayer." (*Test. Napht* 8:8).

But then renew your association, so that Satan should not tempt you through your unhealthy behaviour. I say this by way of accommodation, not of instruction. I would prefer everyone to be as I am. But each has his own gift from God, one in this way, another in that. Though I do say to the unmarried and to widows that it is preferable for them to remain like me. Yet if they cannot exercise self-control they should marry; for it is decidedly better to marry than to burn.

10   For those who are married, however, I stipulate – not indeed I but the Master – that the wife is to separate from her husband, and if she is separated she must remain unwed or be reconciled to her husband; and the husband is not to divorce his wife.[32] Beyond that, I say – not the Master – that if a brother has an unbelieving wife, and she is agreeable to living with him, he is not to divorce her. So with the wife who has an unbelieving husband, if he is agreeable to living with her, she is not to divorce her husband. For the unbelieving husband is consecrated by his wife, and the unbelieving wife is consecrated by the brother in faith. Otherwise your children would be

15   impure instead of holy as they are now. But if the unbelieving partner insists on separation, let them separate. In such cases neither a brother nor a sister is under duress; for God has decreed that you should be at peace. And you, wife, how can you tell whether you will not save your husband? Or you, husband, how can you tell whether you will not save your wife?

Otherwise, "to each as the Lord has assigned, for each as God has decreed".[33] So let him conduct himself, and so have I prescribed for all the communities.

Let anyone who was circumcised when he was called not undo the operation. If he was called in uncircumcision let him not be circumcised. Circumcision is of no consequence, neither is uncircumcision: it is the keeping

20   of God's commandments. Let each remain in the category in which he was called. Were you called as a slave, do not let it fret you; though if you have the opportunity to procure your freedom use it to the full. For the slave called by the Master is the Master's freedman. Similarly the freeman who is called is Christ's slave. You have

32 See *Mk* 10:8–9.
33 Source of quotation unknown to translator.

been acquired at a high price. Do not become slaves of men. Each as he was called, brothers, so let him continue before God.

25   Now as regards the unmarried I have no instructions from the Master, but I offer my opinion as one who has mercifully been permitted by the Lord to be continent. I consider, therefore, in view of the present stress that a man is best off if he is celibate. If you are united with a wife, do not seek to be free. If you are free of a wife, do not seek one; though if you should marry you have done nothing wrong. And if a girl should marry she has done nothing wrong either. But those who take this step face the cares of married life, which I would spare you.

Only I would urge this, brothers, time grows short. So from now on let those who have wives be as though they

30   had none, and those who mourn as though they did not mourn, and those who rejoice as though they did not rejoice, and those who acquire as though they did not possess, and those who are on friendly terms with society as though they were unsociable; for the existing order is passing away. I would have you care-free. The unmarried man is concerned with the Master's affairs, how he may please the Master; but the married man is concerned with social affairs, how he may please his wife, and he is torn two ways. So too the unmarried woman and girl is concerned with the Master's affairs, that she may be devoted physically and mentally; but the married woman is concerned with social affairs, how she

35   may please her husband. I am saying this in your own interest, not to hold you on a rein, but rather that not being pulled this way and that you may be more considerate and attentive to the Master.

However, if anyone feels he is being inconsiderate to his maiden, should she be passing her bloom, and therefore he owes it to her, let it be as he wishes: he does nothing wrong. Let them be married. But he who maintains a firm resolve, not having necessity, and is in full control of his own will, and has determined in his own mind to keep his maiden inviolate, will do well. So he who marries his maiden does well, but he who does not marry will do better still.

A wife is bound for her husband's entire lifetime; but should the husband go to his rest she is free to marry

40   whom she will, so long as he is in the Master. But in my

opinion she is happier to stay as she is, and there I think I have the Spirit of God.

8.1   Now as regards offerings to idols, we are aware that we all have knowledge. But knowledge puffs up while affection builds up. If anyone thinks he knows something, he still does not know it as well as he should: but if anyone is devoted to God he is given insight by him. For example, as regards food offered to idols, we are aware that an idol has no actual life, and that there is no God

5   other than the One. For even if there are so-called gods, whether of heaven or earth – since there are many 'gods' and many 'lords', for us there is still only One God, the Father, from whom all things derive, and to whom we belong,[34] and one Lord Jesus Christ, through whom all things come, and by whom we are. But this knowledge is not general. There are some who are so accustomed to the idea of idols that they eat such food as being actually offered to an idol, and their conscience being weak is defiled.

But food will not bring us near to God; for neither by not consuming are we retarded, nor by consuming are we advanced. But take care that your 'right' does not prove a hindrance to those whose conscience is weak.

10   For if anyone sees you who have knowledge sitting at table in an idol temple[35] will not he whose conscience is weak conclude from this that there is some benefit to be gained by eating what is offered to idols? So the weak one will be ruined by the very thing you know, that brother of yours for whom Christ died. Consequently, by sinning against your brothers and wounding their weak conscience you are sinning against Christ. For that reason, if food makes my brother stumble, then rather than be the cause of that I will never eat meat again.[36]

10.23   I am free to do everything, but everything is not advantageous. I am free to do everything, but not everything is beneficial. Let no one study his own interests,

25   but those of his fellow. Eat whatever is sold in the meat-market without making inquiries, for "the earth is the

---

34 Paul invariably distinguishes the Christ from God. See 11:3.

35 It was a pagan custom to send invitations to dine at the table of the god. See above p 300, n 19.

36 The argument is interrupted here by *I Cor* 9.1–10:22, which appears to belong to the previous letter mentioned in *I Cor* 5:9 (above pp 297–301) in conjunction with *II Cor* 6–7:1.

Lord's with all it contains".[37] And if any unbeliever gives you an invitation, and you feel like accepting, eat whatever is placed before you without making inquiries. But if someone says to you, "This is sacrificial food", then do not eat it, both for the sake of your informant and for conscience's sake. I say conscience, not yours but the other man's. But why should my freedom be governed

30   by another man's conscience? If I partake with pleasure, why should I be abused over what I am thankful for? The answer is, that whether you eat or drink, or whatever you do, do everything for the glory of God. Be free from offence both to Jews and Gentiles, and to God's Community, just as I accommodate myself to everyone in every way, not studying my own convenience but that of the multitude, that they may be saved. Copy me, as I copy Christ.

11.1   I do thank you for reminding yourselves of me in every way, and for maintaining the traditions as I transmitted them to you. But I want you to know that the head of every man is Christ, while the head of woman is man, and the head of Christ is God. Every man who prays or prophesies with covered head dishonours his head,

5   while every woman who prays or prophesies with unconcealed head dishonours her head; for it is just as if she were shaven. If the woman is not covered, let her also be shorn. If it is a shame for a woman to be shaven or shorn, let her be covered.[38] But it is not proper for a man to have his head concealed, being the image and glory of God;[39] but the woman is the glory of man. For man is not derived from woman, but woman from man;[40] and man was not created for the sake of woman, but woman for

10   the sake of man.[41] For this reason the woman ought to wear some head-covering[42] because of the angels. Beyond this, as relates to the Master, woman is not distinguished from man, nor man from woman. For just as the woman derives from man, so does the man owe

37 *Ps* 24:1.
38 Paul may be speaking of married women. For a wedded Jewess to go out bare-headed was to act like a prostitute.
39 *Gen* 50:26.
40 *Gen* 2:23.
41 *Gen* 2:18.
42 Lit "control over her head". Exposure to the gaze of angels during worship, when the heavens were opened, was no different to exposure to the gaze of men in the streets. And see *Gen* 6:1–2.

his being to woman; and equally they derive from God.

Judge for yourselves whether it is seemly for a woman to be uncovered when praying to God. Does not nature itself teach you that when a man has long tresses it is a
15 disgrace to him? But if a woman has long tresses it is her glory, for her tresses are given her as a natural drapery. If someone is inclined to be contentious on this issue, I can entertain no such practice, nor the communities of God.

But here is news I do not appreciate, that when you assemble it is not for the better but for the worse. I learn first of all that when you hold your meetings there are divisions among you, and to a certain extent I believe it. Obviously there must be some variations among you, that those who are particularly worthy among you may
20 be distinguished. But is not your coming together for the common purpose of eating the supper that is specifically the Master's? In partaking of this it is for each of you to have had his own supper beforehand. Yet one is famished and another is consumed with thirst. Have you no homes in which to eat and drink? Or do you mean to treat God's Community with contempt, and humiliate those who have no homes? What am I to say to you? Shall I commend you? This is something I cannot commend.

I indeed received from the Master what I have transmitted to you, that the Lord Jesus on the night he was betrayed took bread, and when he had given thanks broke it and said, "This signifies my body broken on
25 your behalf. Do this in commemoration of me."[43] In the same way he took the cup after the meal, saying, "This cup signifies the new covenant in my blood. Do this, as often as you drink it, in commemoration of me." So as often as you eat this bread and drink this cup you are making mention of the Master's death until he returns. Consequently, whoever eats the bread or drinks the cup unworthily will be held responsible for the Master's body and blood. So let a man examine himself, and after that eat the bread and drink the cup; for he who eats and drinks is eating and drinking a judgment on himself, not
30 discerning the body. That is why many of you are infirm and ailing, and a number have gone to their rest. If we have passed judgment on ourselves we shall not be judged; but if we are judged by the Master we are

43 *Lk* 22:19.

punished, so as not to be condemned with the world. Consequently, my brothers, when you assemble to eat this meal await your turn. But if anyone is famished let him eat at home, so that you do not come together for condemnation. As for other matters, I will settle these when I come.

12.1   Now about spiritual manifestations, brothers, I would not have you ignorant. You know the kind of Gentiles you were as regards dumb idols, misguided just as you were led. So I must inform you that no one speaking by the divine Spirit says, "Cursed be Jesus!" And no one is able to say, "Lord Jesus!" except by the holy Spirit.

5   But there are different kinds of gifts, though the same Spirit, and different kinds of function, though the same Master, and different kinds of motivation, though the same God, who motivates everything universally. And to each has been given that particular spiritual manifestation which was appropriate. For one has been given through the Spirit the faculty of wisdom, another according to the same Spirit the faculty of insight, and yet another the faculty of faith by the same Spirit. To another, still by the one Spirit, has been given gifts of

10   healing, to another the effecting of miracles, to another prophecy, to another the discerning of the nature of spirits, to yet another variety of tongues, to another interpretation of tongues. For all these manifestations one and the same Spirit is responsible, allocating specifically to each at will.

12.   For just as the body is a unity while possessing many organs, and all the organs of the body, though many, form a single body, so is Christ a unity. For by one Spirit we have all been immersed into one body, whether Jews or Gentiles, slaves or freemen,[44] and we have all been given a draught of the one Spirit. For the body is no

15   single organ, but many. If the foot should say, "I am not part of the body because I am not the hand", is it therefore any less a part of the body? Or if the ear should say, "I am not part of the body because I am not the eye", is it therefore any less a part of the body? If the entire body was eye where would be hearing? If the entire body was hearing where would be smelling? But we find that

---

44 In a morning prayer a Jew thanks God for not making him a heathen, a woman, or a slave. See *Gal* 3:48.

20 God has placed the organs in the body, every single one of them, exactly as he wanted. If it were entirely one organ, where would be the body? As it is, there are many organs but one body. The eye cannot say to the hand, "I do not require you". Nor can the head say to the feet, "I do not require you".

Much more are those organs of the body found to be requisite which are more delicate, and those which seem of less consequence are those to which we devote far more attention. It is our unattractive features that come in for beautifying treatment, for which our attractive features have no need. But God interrelates the body to 25 give added dignity to what is inferior, so that there may be no discrimination in the body, but that all the organs shall have the same concern for one another. So if one organ suffers, all the organs suffer with it, and if one organ is esteemed, all the organs rejoice with it.

Now you are Christ's body, and its respective organs, and God has placed these in the Community as follows: first envoys, second prophets, third teachers, next mediums, next those with gifts of healing, those with intuition, those who give guidance, and those with 30 varied tongues. Are all envoys? Are all prophets? Are all teachers? Are all mediums? Have all gifts of healing? Do all speak in tongues? Are all interpreters? Make the higher gifts your aim. Yet let me point out to you a still better course to pursue.

13.1 Though I speak the tongues of men and angels, and have not love, I have become a clanging gong or clashing cymbal. Even if I possess the power of prophecy and know all mysteries and secret lore, and have such faith that I can remove mountains,[45] if I have not love I am of no account. Even if I share out my possessions[46] and give my body to be burnt, if I have not love it avails me nothing.

5 Love is long-suffering and kind. Love is never jealous, self-assertive, blustering or inconsiderate. It never seeks its own ends, is never irritable, keeps no score of wrongs, never rejoices in injustice, but delights in truth.

Love is ever protective, ever trustful, ever hopeful, ever constant. Love never fails, but whether it is pro-

45 See *Mt* 17:20.
46 See *Mk* 10:21.

phesyings, they will come to an end, or whether it is tongues, they will cease, whether it is knowledge, it will come to an end. For we only know imperfectly, and

10   prophesy imperfectly. But when perfection is reached what is imperfect will come to an end. When I was a child, I talked like a child, I reasoned like a child, I argued like a child; but when I became a man I put an end to childish ways. So far we see indistinctly as in a mirror,[47] but then it will be face to face. So far I know imperfectly, but then I shall know as fully as I am known. At present faith, hope, and love, all three, continue; but the most enduring of them is love.

14.1   So pursue love, and make spiritual manifestations your aim, particularly the capacity to prophesy.[48] For he who speaks in a tongue addresses God, not his fellows, since no one can follow him. He is speaking mysterious things in spirit language.[49] But he who prophesies addresses his fellows for their benefit, encouragement and cheer. He who speaks in a tongue benefits himself,

5   while he who prophesies benefits the community. I wish you could all speak in tongues, but preferably that you could prophesy; for he who prophesies is greater than one who speaks in tongues, unless he can interpret so that the community is benefited.

Supposing, brothers, that I were to come to you speaking in tongues, how should I benefit you if I did not also speak by revelation, by knowledge, by prophecy, or by teaching? It would be like inanimate objects that emit a sound, such as a flute or harp. If no clear distinction of notes is rendered, how is it to be recognised what is being played on them? And if the trumpet sounds an uncertain call, who will prepare for battle? So with your tongues, if you do not utter plain speech how is it to be understood what you are saying? You will be talking to

10   the air. Still more, as there happen to be such a medley of sounds in the world, and nothing is soundless, should I not know the implication of a sound I shall be a barbarian to the speaker, and he will be a barbarian to me.

So with you, since you are ambitious for spiritual manifestations, aim at those which benefit the com-

---

47 Mirrors of burnished bronze, etc, as then used.
48 To prophesy was to give an inspired address, not specially to predict.
49 Speaking in tongues meant giving vent to sounds articulated as in speech, not necessarily belonging to any language used in human intercourse.

munity, that you may excel. Therefore let him who
speaks in a tongue pray for the ability to interpret. For if I
pray in a tongue, my spirit is engaged in prayer, but my
15   intelligence is not functioning. Is it not desirable, therefore, that I pray not only with the spirit, but also with the
intellect? Otherwise, if you only bless God in spirit, how
is one who is unlearned to make the "Amen" response at
the end of your thanksgiving, since he does not know
what you are saying? You are giving thanks fittingly, but
the other is not inspired by it. I thank God I speak in
tongues more than all of you, but in the community I
would rather speak five words with my intelligence so as
to instruct others than ten thousand words in a tongue.
20   Brothers, do not be mentally childish, though in evil be
as innocent as you please. But in mentality be adult. It is
stated in the Law,

> 'By those of alien tongues and lips will I address this people,
> Yet for all that they will not heed me', says the Lord.[50]

So tongues are a sign not to believers but to
unbelievers, while prophecy is not for unbelievers but
for believers. If, therefore, you hold a meeting of the
whole community, and all speak in tongues, and
unlearned people or unbelievers come in, will they not
say you are mad? But if all prophesy, and an unbeliever
or unlearned person enters, he will be convinced by all
he hears, he will be searched by all he hears, and the
25   secrets of his heart will be laid bare. And so, falling upon
his face, he will worship God, declaring, "Truly God is
with you!"

Is it not desirable then, brothers, that when you come
together each should have a psalm, an instruction, a
revelation, a tongue, or an interpretation, so that everything contributes to edification?

When someone speaks in a tongue, or perhaps two do
so, or three at most, and then in turn, there should be
one to interpret. If there should be no interpreter let the
speaker in a tongue keep silence in the community and
speak inwardly to God. And let two or three prophets
30   speak, and the others draw conclusions. But if a revelation comes to anyone seated there let the previous

---

50 *Isa* 28:11. Quoted from the Prophets, not the Law.

speaker keep silence; for you can all continue prophesying after the one with the revelation has finished, since
the spirits of the prophets remain under their control,[51]
that all may learn and all be encouraged. God is a God of
order, not of chaos.

As is the practice in all the communities of the saints let
the married women keep silence in the communities; for
they are not entitled to speak, being in a subordinate

35   position, as also says the Law.[52] If there is anything they
wish to learn let them consult their husbands at home,
for it is indecorous for married women to speak at
meetings.

Did the Message of God go out from you, or did it in
fact come to you? If anyone regards himself as a prophet
or medium let him acknowledge that what I am writing
to you is a commandment of the Master. If anyone is
ignorant, however, let him be ignorant. Consequently,
my brothers, be ambitious to prophesy, and do not

40   prevent speaking in tongues. But let everything be done
decently and in an orderly manner.

15.1   Now I would draw your attention, brothers, to the
News I proclaimed to you (which you accepted, on
which you have based yourselves, by means of which
you are being saved) in the very form in which I proclaimed it to you, if you have retained it, unless you
believed in a heedless manner. For I delivered to you as
basic what I had myself received: 'That Christ died for
our sins in accordance with the Scriptures; that he was
buried and raised up the third day in accordance with the

5   Scriptures; that he was seen by Cephas, then by the
twelve, after that on one occasion by more than five
hundred brothers (some of whom are gone to their rest);
after that he was seen by James,[53] then by all the
envoys.'[54] Last of all, as if by an untimely birth, he was
seen even by me; for I am the most insignificant of the
envoys, who does not deserve to be called an envoy,

---

51 A revelation took precedence over every other form of spirit message as a
direct communication by the holy Spirit, with the one who gave it out acting
only as a medium not in control of what he said.

52 *Gen* 3:16.

53 The brother of Jesus. In the Hebrew Gospel it was related that James had
refused to eat until he had seen the Son of Man risen from the dead. For the
text see Jerome, *Catal. Script. Eccl.* under *Jacobus*.

54 This section has been placed within single quotes as in the nature of a credo.

10 because I persecuted God's Community. But by God's mercy I am what I am, and his favour to me was not wasted, for I toiled harder than all of them, though not indeed I but God's favour that was with me. But whether it was myself or the others, this is what we proclaimed, and this is what you believed.

If then Christ was proclaimed as having been raised from the dead, how do some of you say that there is no resurrection of the dead? For if there is no resurrection of the dead, Christ cannot have been raised. And if Christ was not raised our proclamation was in vain and our

15 faith in vain, and we are exposed as false witnesses of God, since we have testified of God that he raised up Christ. This he cannot have done if the dead are not to be raised. For if the dead are not to be raised, neither can Christ have been raised. And if Christ has not been raised your faith is worthless: you are still in your sins. Then too, all who have gone to their rest in Christ have perished. If we are merely to have hope in Christ in this life we are to be pitied above all men.

20 But in fact Christ *has* been raised from the dead as the first fruits of those who have gone to their rest. For since by man came death,[55] so by man[56] also came resurrection from the dead. For as in Adam all die, so in Christ will all be brought to life, though each in his proper order, first Christ, followed at his coming by those who belong to Christ, then the remainder[57] when he has handed over the Kingdom to God, to the Father, after abolishing all

25 other government, authority and power. For he himself must rule until "he has put all enemies under his feet".[58] The final enemy to be abolished is death,[59] for *everything* is to be brought into subjection beneath his feet. But when it is said, "everything has been subjected",[60] it is obvious that this excludes the One who has made everything subject to him. When, then, everything is subjected to him, even the Son will be subject to the One who

55 *Gen* 3.
56 The Messiah as human, the Son of Man.
57 Gr. *telos*, here used not in the sense of 'the End' but the 'tail end' who are the vast majority. The order is processional, the general, his staff, and then the main body of men bringing up the rear. See *Rev* 20:4–6.
58 *Ps* 110:1.
59 See *Rev* 20:14.
60 See *Ps* 8:6.

has subjected everything to him, that God may reign supreme.

Otherwise, what are they doing who are immersed on behalf of the dead?[61] If the dead are not raised why be
30   immersed on their behalf? And why do we risk our lives all the time? "I am ready to die any day", you say. Yes, that is your boast, brothers, which I make good in Christ Jesus our Master. If, to borrow a human phrase, I have "fought with wild beasts at Ephesus",[62] how am I the gainer? If the dead are not raised, "Let us eat and drink, for to-morrow we die".[63] Oh no, do not delude yourselves! "Bad company ruins good character."[64] Sober up completely, and do not go to the bad; for some of you seem to ignore God's existence. I say this to shame you.

35   But someone may say, "How are the dead raised, and what kind of body do they have?" You dunce! Surely what you sow does not spring to life before it dies! And what you sow you do not sow in the bodily form that will emerge, but as bare grain, perhaps of wheat, or maybe of some other cereal. It is God who furnishes it with the body he wishes, each seed with its particular body. All flesh is not identical. There is the human, and besides that the flesh of animals, the flesh of birds, and the flesh
40   of fish. There are also celestial and terrestrial bodies. But the glory of the celestial is one thing, and that of the terrestrial is another. Apart from the glory of the sun, there is the glory of the moon, and of the stars, and star even differs from star in glory.

So is it with the resurrection of the dead. What is sown as perishable is raised imperishable. What is sown in humiliation is raised in honour. What is sown in weakness is raised in vitality. What is sown as a physical body is raised as a spiritual body. If there is such a thing as a physical body, there is also such a thing as a spiritual
45   body. Just as it is stated, "The first man (Adam) became a living soul",[65] so the last Adam became a vitalizing spirit. It was not the spiritual that came first but the physical, and after that the spiritual. The first man was "dust from

61 A Christian custom of substitutionary baptism for and on behalf of dear ones already dead.
62 Paul is using a figure of speech, not referring to a personal experience.
63 *Isa* 22:13.
64 From Menander, Athenian dramatist, 342–291 BC.
65 *Gen* 2:7.

the earth",[66] the second man was from heaven.[67] As is the nature of dust so are the creatures of dust; and as is the heavenly nature so are the heavenly beings. Just as we have worn the likeness of the dust nature, so shall we wear the likeness of the heavenly nature.

50   I tell you this, brothers, that flesh and blood cannot inherit the Kingdom of God, neither can the perishable inherit the imperishable. See, I will let you into a secret, we shall not all be laid to rest, but all of us will experience a change, in an instant, in the flicker of an eyelid, on the final trumpet note. For the trumpet will sound, and the dead will be raised up imperishable, and we shall experience a change. For this perishable nature must be invested with imperishability, and this mortal nature must be invested with immortality. And when this mortal nature has been invested with immorality, then the saying that is written will come true, "Death has been swallowed up in victory".[68]

55   *Where, O death, is your victory?*
Where, O grave, is your sting?[69]

The sting of death is sin, and the strength of sin is the Law. But thanks be to God, who has given us victory through our Lord Jesus Christ!

Consequently, dear brothers, be firm and immovable, always fully engaged in the Master's work, knowing that your toil for the Master is not in vain.

16.1   Now as regards the fund for the saints, follow the same arrangement as I have made with the communities in Galatia. The day after the Sabbath let each of you put by savings as he has prospered, so that collections do not have to be made when I come. Then when I come I will send whoever you designate by letter to convey your bounty to Jerusalem. If it is desirable that I should go too, they can travel with me.

---

66 *Ibid.*
67 The reader must apprehend Jewish occultism, one branch of which (*Maaseh Bereshith*) dealt with the creation of man in Genesis. According to the Jewish mystics God created the Heavenly Man as his image, the Archetype (Son of Man), in whose likeness Adam was formed. The Heavenly Man, the Messiah Above, was incarnated in Jesus as the Messiah Below, thus constituting him as the Second Adam, as Paul elaborated. See the *Book of Enoch*, and Paul's letters to the Asian communities, and those at Philippi and Colossae.
68 *Isa* 25:8.
69 *Hos* 13:14.

5   I propose to visit you when I pass through Macedonia
– for I intend to go through Macedonia – and perhaps I
may settle down with you, or at least spend the winter,
so that you can forward me on my further journey. I do
not want to see you merely in passing; for it is my hope, if
the Lord permits, to stay some time with you. I shall
remain at Ephesus at any rate until Pentecost, for a wide
and much frequented gateway has been opened to me,
10   and there is considerable opposition. Should Timotheus
come, be sure you put him at his ease, for he is as much
involved in the Master's work as I am. So let no one be
disrespectful to him. And forward him on his way in
peace that he may come to me, for I am expecting him
with the brothers.

Regarding Brother Apollos, I urged him strongly to
visit you with the brothers, but he was very much against
coming just now. However, he will come when
convenient.

Be alert, stand firm in the faith, be manly and sturdy! I
beg you, brothers, conduct all your affairs in a loving
15   spirit. You know how the house of Stephanas was the
firstfruits in Achaia, and how much it has devoted itself
to ministering to the saints. It is for you to submit
yourselves to people like these, and to all who collabor-
ate and work so hard. I rejoice at the arrival of Stephanas,
Fortunatus and Achaicus, which compensates for the
lack of your presence; for they relieve my mind and
yours. You should esteem such people.

20   The communities of Asia send you their regards.
Aquila and Prisca[70] send you their regards in the Master
together with the community at their house. All the
brothers send you their regards. Convey our regards to
one and all with a chaste kiss.

My personal regards in my own hand,

PAUL

If someone[71] does not love the Master, let him be
accursed.[72] *Maranatha!*[73]

The loving-kindness of the Lord Jesus be with you. My
love to you all in Christ Jesus.

70 The same as Priscilla. See above *Acts* 18:2.
71 Possibly a particular person is meant, who is never named. Alternatively
read 'anyone'.
72 "Accursed" (*anathema*). Possibly a copyist's error and we should read, "let
him be ardent again" (*anatherma*). cf *Mt* 24:12.
73 Aram. "Our Master, come" (*Marana tha*). cf *Rev* 22:20.

To the Community at Corinth (3)[1]

(Written from Ephesus possibly in the Spring of AD 56)

Commencement Lacking

II Cor
10.1   . . . Now I, Paul, personally entreat you by the mildness and moderation of Christ, I who am "humble when in your presence, but overbearing towards you when absent".[2] I pray that I do not have to be overbearing when I am present with the kind of persuasion I contemplate employing against those who reckon me as one who "moves on the material plane". In a material body I do move, but I do not fight with material weapons; for the weapons of my warfare are of no material character, but divine armaments for reducing strongholds,
   5 demolishing arguments, and every kind of high and mighty position taken up in opposition to God's assured knowledge, bringing every design into subjection to the authority of Christ, and being ever ready to punish any insubordination once your submission is complete.

Face the facts squarely. If a certain individual is convinced he is acting for Christ, let him consider this as well, that as he acts for Christ so do I. For even if I should seem to boast unduly of my authority, which the Master has given me to build you up, not to pull you down, I would not be ashamed, so long as it does not appear as if
  10 I am bent on intimidating you with my letters. For "his letters", says that individual, "are weighty and power-

1 Corresponding to *II Cor* 10–13. We have only the last part of this letter, but perhaps only a few introductory paragraphs are lost.
2 Here and elsewhere Paul appears to be quoting remarks adverse to himself which had been reported to him.

ful, but his physical appearance is insignificant and his speech is contemptible."[3]

Let that individual mark this, that what I am in word by letter when absent that am I also in deed when present. I would not dream of classing or comparing myself with those who indulge in self-commendation; for these measuring themselves by themselves and com-

15   paring themselves with themselves cease to be relative. I will not boast so disproportionately, but in terms of the extent of the line the God of measurement has measured out for me, reaching as far as to you. Clearly I am not overreaching myself where my line did not extend to you, for right the way to you I was first with the News of Christ.[4] I do not boast 'beyond measure' where others have laboured, but I trust, when your faith has expanded, to have my own line considerably prolonged by you, so as to allow me to proclaim the News to the regions beyond you, instead of boasting along another's line where the ground was already covered. "Let him who boasts boast in the Lord."[5] For it is not the man who commends himself who is approved, but he whom the Lord commends.

11.1   O that you would put up with a little of my 'folly', or at least put up with me! For I am jealous for you with a divine jealousy; for I have bespoken you as a chaste virgin for one husband, that I may give you to Christ. But I am afraid in case, as the Serpent beguiled Eve with his wiles, your minds should be corrupted from the simplicity and virtuousness to which Christ is entitled. For if someone who comes along can proclaim another Jesus whom I did not proclaim, or you can receive a different Spirit than you did receive, or a different News than you

5   accepted, you can well put up with me. For I reckon myself in no way way inferior to such 'super-envoys'. Even if I am uncultured in speech, I am not in knowledge, and managed to make everything clear to you.

Did I make a mistake in abasing myself that you might be exalted, by proclaiming the News to you free of

---

3 In early Christian tradition Paul is depicted as a rather ugly baldheaded man with a hooked nose and bow legs. He suffered from a complaint which evidently affected his speech, and he had poor eyesight.

4 The text is hard to translate as the author is playing on the idea of measurement in more than one sense.

5 Jer 9:24.

charge? I stripped other communities, taking payment to apply to your service. And when I was staying with you and went short, I was a dead weight to no one, for my shortage was fully made up by the brothers who came from Macedonia. In every way I kept myself – and shall

10 go on keeping myself – from being any burden to you. As Christ's truth is in me, I am not going to be denied this boast in the regions of Achaia! Why? Because I have no regard for you? God knows I have! But I make and am going on making this boast, that I may remove the pretext of those who want a pretext, that in what they can boast of they will be found to be my equals. Such people are false envoys, deceitful agents, masquerading as envoys of Christ. And no wonder, when Satan himself

15 masquerades as an angel of light! So it is hardly surprising if his ministers masquerade as ministers of religion, whose fate will correspond to their actions.

I say again, let no one take me for a fool. But if they must, then accept me as a fool, so that I may do a little boasting. What I am saying then, I am not saying sensibly, but as in folly, on this basis of boasting. Since many boast in human fashion, I too will boast; for sensible as

20 you are you gladly put up with fools. You even put up with it when somebody reduces you to cringing impotence, when somebody devours, grabs, makes a mat of you, and grinds your faces under his heel. I am speaking insultingly because I am so sick of it all.

In whatever way anyone may make sweeping claims – I am keeping up this fool talk – so can I. Are they Hebrews? So am I. Are they Israelites? So am I. Are they the seed of Abraham? So am I. Are they agents of Christ? Mad as it sounds, I am even more so. My labours have been harder, my terms of imprisonment longer, my floggings beyond all bounds, my risks of death more frequent. Five times I received from the Jews forty

25 strokes less one,[6] three times I have been beaten with Roman rods, once I was stoned,[7] three times shipwrecked, a night and a day consigned to the deep. Often have I taken the road, in peril of rivers, in peril of brigands, in peril from my own nation, in peril from Gentiles, in peril in town, in peril in the country, in peril

6 *Deut* 25:2–3. See JE.art. *Stripes.*
7 *Acts* 14:19.

at sea, in peril from false brothers, in toil and hardship, often sleepless, in hunger and thirst, often fasting, in cold and in nakedness. On top of all this there has been my daily concern, the care of all the communities. Who is ailing, and I do not share his ailment? Who is offended, and I do not share his indignation?

30   If I must boast, I will boast of my disabilities. He who is blessed for ever, the God and Father of our Lord Jesus, knows I am not lying. At Damascus the ethnarch of King Haretath picketed the city of the Damascenes to hem me in; but through a loophole I was let down the wall in a basket, and so escaped his clutches.[8]

12.1   If I must continue to boast, undesirable as that is, I will come to visions and revelations of the Master. I know a man in Christ, who fourteen years ago – whether in the physical or astral state, I do not know, God knows – was caught up as far as the third heaven.[9] I know that this man – whether in the physical state or otherwise, I do not know, God knows – was caught up into 'the Garden'[10] and heard ineffable words which no human is permitted

5   to utter. Of someone like this I will boast, but about myself I will not boast, only of my disabilities.

Even should I want to boast I should be no fool, for I state the truth. But I will refrain, in case anyone should think more of me than what he sees and hears. But with the transcendence of the revelàtions, in case I should be too elated, there was given me a spike in the flesh,[11] an emissary of Satan to prod me. On this score three times I entreated the Master to make it leave me. But he told me, "My favour is enough for you, for power is brought to full strength in weakness." Most gladly, therefore, will I rather boast of disabilities, that the power of Christ may

10   take up its quarters in me. So I am content with disabilities, assaults, physical punishments, persecutions and close confinements, for Christ's sake. For when I am weak then I am strong.

There, I have played the fool. You have driven me to it. For I ought to have had your championship; for in no

---

8 *Acts* 9:25.

9 Seven heavens were imagined, in layers one above the other.

10 'The Garden' (Paradise), the same as the third heaven, answering to the third degree of blessedness in Jewish occultism. See Talmud, *Chagigah*, 12a–b.

11 The cause of this twinge would appear to have been rheumatic.

way am I inferior to those super-envoys, even if I am of no consequence. Indeed, the marks of an envoy were produced among you persistently in signs, wonders and miracles. For in what were you outdone by the rest of the communities, except that I personally was no dead weight to you? Forgive me this injustice.

Observe, this is my third time of readiness to come to you. But I will be no dead weight to you; for I do not seek what is yours but *you*. For it is not the children who should provide for their parents but the parents for their 15 children. Most gladly will I spend and be spent to safeguard you. If I love you so dearly, should I not be loved as much? But there it is, I did not burden you. But "being naturally unscrupulous I took from you by guile," eh? Was it by anyone I have sent to you that I defrauded you? I begged Titus to visit you, and with him I sent our brother. Was it Titus who defrauded you? Have we not acted in the same spirit, followed in the same steps? Do not think from this that I am defending myself. I am speaking before God in Christ. Everything I 20 say, dear friends, is entirely for your benefit; for I fear much in case when I come I shall not find you in the frame of mind I would wish, nor you find me in the frame of mind you would wish. I fear in case there should be strife, rivalry, high-feeling, faction, recrimination, vilification, protestation and uproar, in case at my coming my God should humiliate me in front of you, and that I should break down over many who have fallen into sin, and have not repented of the impurity, immorality and licentiousness of which they have been guilty.

13.1   This is my third time of coming to you. "By the mouth of two or three witnesses every word shall be confirmed."[12] I have said previously, and being absent now I give warning as if present a second time,[13] to those who have fallen into sin and to all the others, that should I come once more I will not spare, since it is proof you require that Christ speaks by me. He at least is not weak, but powerful among you. For though he was crucified from weakness, he lives now by the power of God. And

---

12 *Deut* 19:15.

13 It is clear from the next letter that Paul had paid a short "distressing visit" to Corinth, and that the present letter was in lieu of a second visit. He therefore thinks of his readiness to come again as a third visit.

though we are weak in him, we too live with him by the
5   power of God. Test yourselves, examine yourselves,
whether *you* are in the faith. Or do you yourselves not
know that Jesus Christ is in you, whether by any chance
you are frauds? But I trust you will realise that I am no
fraud.

Now I pray God you may do no wrong in any way. Not
that I may be shown to be genuine, but that you may do
the right thing even did I appear a fraud. For I have no
power against the truth, only on behalf of truth. I am
happy whenever I am weak and you are strong. This too
10   I pray for, your perfection. That is why being absent I
write as I do, that when present I should not have to
employ severity, in accordance with the authority the
Master has given me to build up, not to pull down.

Finally, brothers, rejoice, put yourselves to rights, take
courage, be of the same mind, be at peace, and the God
of love and peace be with you. Convey my regards to one
and all with a chaste kiss. All the saints send you their
regards.

The loving-kindness of our Lord Jesus Christ, the love
of God, and the fellowship of the holy Spirit, be with you
all.

To the Community at Corinth (4)

(Probably written from Philippi in the summer of AD 56)

II Cor

1.1   Paul, by the will of God an envoy of Jesus Christ, with Brother Timotheus, to the community of God at Corinth and to all the saints resident throughout Achaia. May peace and prosperity be yours from God our Father and the Lord Jesus Christ.

Blessed be the God and Father of our Lord Jesus Christ, Father of mercies and God of all comfort, who comforts us in all our afflictions, that we may be enabled to comfort those who are in any affliction with the same

5   comfort we have received. Blessed be he, that just as a full share of Christ's suffering has come to me, so equally have I had my full share of comfort through Christ. And whether I am afflicted for your comfort and well-being, or comforted for your comfort, which is a stimulus to the endurance of the same sufferings that I suffer, my hope for you is constant, knowing that as we are fellows in suffering so are we in comfort also.

I would not have you ignorant, brothers, of the trying experience I have been through in Asia, how I was subjected to a weight so crushing in the extreme as to pass endurance, so that I had the gravest doubt whether I would survive. Rather for myself did I take it to be sentence of death, so that I should place no reliance on

10   myself but on God who raises the dead. It was he who shielded me from imminent death and shields me now, and whom I trust – with your co-operation in prayer on my behalf – to continue to shield me, so that thanksgiving to God on my account may be made by many persons for the kindness of so many towards me.

My pride, the testimony of my conscience, is this, that I have conducted myself in the world, not by means of any materialist philosophy but by divine mercy, in all innocence and utter sincerity, especially in my relations with you. I am consequently writing to you nothing but what you already well know or recognise, as indeed to some extent you have acknowledged, that I shall be your pride when the Day of our Lord Jesus comes, just as you will be mine.

15   It was from this confidence that I purposed visiting you previously, that you might have a second pleasure, both by my passing via yourselves on the way to Macedonia and visiting you again on my return from Macedonia, when you would forward me on my way to Judea. Was I merely proposing this casually? Or when I make proposals do I do so in the ordinary casual way, so that my "yes, yes" can equally mean "no, no"? As God is true, my word to you is never "yes-and-no"! For the Son of God, Jesus Christ, he who was proclaimed to you by us – by myself, Silvanus and Timotheus – did not come as a "yes-and-no". In him there came "yes", for every

20   promise of God is fulfilled in him who is the "Yes". That is why through him, we make the affirmation "Amen"[1] to God in praising him. It is God who has secured both us and you for Christ, who has had us duly signed and sealed, and has given us the advance payment of the Spirit in our hearts. I call God to witness for my life, that it is to spare you I have not come again to Corinth! Not that I claim any jurisdiction over your faith: I am but a contributor to your happiness. In faith you have your

2.1   own standing. But I made up my mind not to pay you another distressing visit, for if I distress you, who is going to cheer me except those I distress? So I wrote then and there,[2] in case by coming I should be grieved by those who should give me joy, being convinced of all of you that it is my happiness that is the concern of you all. I wrote to you in great trouble and anguish of mind, shedding many tears, not to grieve you, but because of the very deep affection you know I have for you.

5   If a certain individual has caused distress, he has not caused me distress, at least not to an extent that I have to

1 "So be it", in the expression "through our Lord Jesus Christ. Amen".
2 Namely the previous letter: the third letter, above p 325.

burden all of you with it. Let his censure by the majority suffice for that person, just as on the other hand it is for you to cheer and comfort him in case he should be completely overcome by the depth of his grief. Consequently, I entreat you to assure him of your affection. This was part of my object in writing, to ascertain your worth, whether you answer to all requirements. Whoever you forgive, so do I. Really, if anyone has to be forgiven, I am the one who has to be forgiven by you before Christ, in case Satan should catch me out; for I am not ignorant of his wiles.

Well, when I came to Troas in the interest of the News of Christ, and found a door opened to me by the Lord, I had no liberty of spirit because I did not find Brother Titus there. So taking leave of them I went off to Macedonia. Thanks be to God, who always leads me in triumph in Christ, and makes the perfume of the knowledge of him rise up through me in every place! For I am Christ's fragrance to God both among those who are being saved and among those who are perishing.[3] To the latter it is the odour of death leading to Death, while to the former it is the odour of life leading to Life. Who is adequate for such things? For I am not like the majority who water down God's message: I speak purely and plainly as from God, as standing in God's presence in Christ.

3.1 Have I begun to commend myself again? Or ought I like some to have procured letters of commendation to you or from you? Surely you are my letter, recorded on my heart, scrutinised and perused by all men. It is plain for all to see that you are Christ's letter composed on my behalf, recorded not in ink but in the Spirit of the Living God, not on tablets of stone but on tablets of the human heart.

Such is the confidence I have towards God through Christ. It is not that I am adequate in myself to deal with anything as of myself. My competence comes from God, who has qualified me to act as an administrator of a New Covenant, not in letter but in spirit; for the letter kills, but the Spirit vitalizes.[4]

---

3 As God's captive in Christ, Paul sees himself as a victim led along in the triumphal procession, and at the same time as the incense burnt in the victor's honour at various points on the route.

4 cf *Jer* 31:31–33.

Yet if the administration of death[5] in letters engraved on stones was glorious, so that the children of Israel could not look at Moses's face because of the transient shining of his face,[6] how much more shall the
10   administration of the Spirit be glorious? For if the administration of condemnation was glorious, much more glorious still shall be the administration of vindication. Even what did shine could hardly be said to shine in comparison with that surpassing glory. For if what was transient had a glory, much more glorious shall be that which is to endure.

So having an expectation like this I speak plainly, and not like Moses, who had to veil his face so that the children of Israel could not look at the conclusion of what was transient. Their perceptions were blinded; and down to this very day the same veil over the implication of the Old Covenant remains unremoved, since it is in
15   Christ that it is dispensed with. For till to-day, whenever Moses is read, the veil lies upon their mind. Yet whenever that mind "shall be turned to the Lord" the veil will be taken off.[7] "The Lord" means the Spirit, and where the Spirit of the Lord is there is freedom. So all of us, having our face unveiled to the glory of the Lord, reflecting as in a mirror the same image, are being transformed from glory to glory, as from the Lord who is Spirit.[8]

4.1   Having this administration, therefore, as mercy has been shown me, I am no shirker, but have renounced base subterfuges. I do not use cunning devices, nor water down God's Message, but by plain truth make contact with every human conscience in the sight of God. If my News is veiled at all, it is veiled to those who are perishing, where the god of this world has blinded the perception of the infidels, so that they should not see clearly the luminosity of the News of the glory of Christ,
5   who[9] is the image of God. For I do not proclaim myself but Christ Jesus as Master, and myself as your servant for

5 Because with Law came sin, and so death.
6 cf *Exod* 34:28–30.
7 *Exod* 34:34 (LXX).
8 Paul is conveying that the process of transformation continues, as we reflect more and more of the Spirit, until our final glorification at the resurrection of the dead, when we shall bear the full likeness of the heavenly, the pristine image of God, like Adam when first created (*Gen* 1:26).
9 Like Adam.

Jesus's sake, because it is the God who said, "Let light shine out of darkness", who has illumined my mind with the luminosity of the knowledge of God's glory on the face of Christ.

I have this treasure in an earthen vessel,[10] however, that the superabundance of the power may be of God, and not emanate from myself. I am harassed on every side, but not hemmed in; in great straits, but not devoid of resources; hard-pressed, but not abandoned; struck

10 down, but not destroyed,[11] always carrying around in my body the death-state of Jesus, that the life of Jesus may also be evident in my body. For always I who live am delivered up to death for Jesus's sake, that the life of Jesus may also be evident in my mortal frame. So then death is at work in me, but life in you.

Yet having the selfsame spirit of faith as is stated, "I have believed, therefore I have spoken",[12] I too believe, and therefore speak, knowing that he who raised up Jesus will also raise me up with Jesus, and set me beside

15 you. For all that has transpired is for your sake, that the mercy having been increased by the greater number participating in it[13] the thanksgiving also may be multiplied to the glory of God.

5.1 So I am no shirker; but if my exterior self is disabled my inner self is renewed. The momentary lightness of my affliction achieves for me correspondingly a lasting weight of glory. I pay no regard to the things that are seen, but to those that are unseen; for the things that are seen are temporary, while those that are unseen are permanent. For I know that when my earthly makeshift dwelling is demolished I possess a building from God, a dwelling that is not artificial, permanent in heaven. This is what I sigh for, longing to be under cover of my dwelling from heaven; for so sheltered I shall not be left out in the cold. Yes, that is what I – living in this hutment – sigh for, not wanting to be deprived of cover but to be under cover, so that what is mortal may be swallowed up by Life.

5 God, who has acquired me for this very end, has given

---

10 The physical body. cf *Jud* 7:16; *Jer* 32:14.
11 Paul is here using military terms.
12 *Ps* 116:10.
13 Paul refers to those who have been praying for his recovery from the serious illness mentioned in the previous letter.

me this down payment of the Spirit. So having every confidence, and knowing that while I am at home in the body I am absent from the Master – for I walk by faith and not by sight – I am both confident and content rather to be absent from the body and at home with the Master.

10 That is why I strive so eagerly, whether present or absent, to satisfy him; for we must all stand revealed before Christ's tribunal that each may be requited for his bodily actions, whatever he has done, either useful or worthless.

Sensible of the fear of the Lord, therefore, I persuade men, while my character stands fully revealed to God, and I trust also to your consciousness. I am not commending myself to you again, but furnishing you with grounds for boasting about me, so that you may have something to set against those who boast on the basis of outward appearance instead of the heart. Whether I have been 'raving', it has been for God, or in my senses, it has

15 been for you; for Christ's love deeply affects me. I have reached this conclusion, that as one died for all, all then were dead, and he died for all that those who live should live no longer for themselves but for him who died for them and rose again. From now on, therefore, we know no one in the physical sense. Even if we have known Christ in the physical sense,[14] we do so now no longer.

Consequently, if anyone is in Christ, he is a new creation. The old relationships have gone, replaced by the new. It is all God's doing, who through Christ has reconciled us to himself. And he has given us the administration of this reconciliation, the position being that in Christ God was reconciling the world to himself, not charging men's failings against them, and entrusting

20 us with the Message of reconciliation. Accordingly, we plead on Christ's behalf, as though God were entreating by us, we beg you on Christ's behalf, "Be reconciled to God", He made him who knew no sin to be as sin for us, that we might be guiltless with God by him.

6.1 As a fellow-worker, I also beg you not to receive the mercy of God to no purpose, for he says,

---

14 As the family and immediate followers of Jesus had done, and could thus claim more exact knowledge.

I have heard you at a time of receptiveness,
And aided you on a day of deliverance.[15]

Assuredly now is the "time of receptiveness", now is the "day of deliverance".

5 It is for me to create no difficulty of any kind, that no blame may attach to the administration. Rather in every way have I to commend myself as God's representative, by much patience, afflictions, suffering and anxiety; by lashes, imprisonment and mob violence; by toil, vigil and fasting; by impartiality, insight and perseverance; by kindness, spiritual fervour and unfeigned love; by honest speech and divine power; by the right and left hand weapons of right conduct; by honour and dishonour, ill-fame and good-fame; as a deceiver yet true; as an unknown yet well-known, as a dying man, yet very much alive; as disciplined yet not brought to death; as grieved yet ever rejoicing; as poor yet enriching many; as

10 possessing nothing yet owning everything.

Well, Corinthians, I have spoken frankly to you. I have bared my bosom. You have put no constraint on me, but you have put constraint on your own feelings. "Now it's your turn to pay *me* back", as one says to children. Now you too bare *your* bosoms.[16]

7.2 Make room for me. I have wronged no one. I have harmed no one. I have defrauded no one. I am not saying this censoriously; for as I have said before, "you are in my heart to die with and to live with".[17] I am filled with comfort. I am brim full of happiness despite all my troubles. For when I reached Macedonia I had no physical relief, but troubles on every side, "conflict without and terror within". But God, who comforts the cast down, comforted me by the arrival of Titus, and not only by his arrival but by the cheering report of you he brought, informing me of your longing for me, of your contrition, of your anxiety on my account, so that I was

5 made happier still.

Although I grieved you in the letter,[18] I have no regrets. Even if I had regrets, seeing that the letter in

---

15 *Isa* 49:8.
16 Omitting *II Cor* 6:14–7.1, as being part of an earlier letter. See p 246, n 1 and p 258, n 36. Quoted p 249.
17 Quoted perhaps from a part of the third letter, now missing.
18 The previous letter, above pp 268–272.

question had to cause you even an hour's distress, I am glad now, not that you were distressed, but because you were distressed into penitence, distressed indeed as God likes to see, so that you were in no way harmed by me.

10 For pain of the divine kind produces penitence leading to restoration, not to be regretted; but pain of the world's kind produces death. Take this very instance of grieving of the divine kind, how much concern it effected in you, instead of defensiveness, indignation, fear, complaint, passion and vindictiveness! In every way you have shown yourselves honourable in this affair. Therefore, though I wrote you as I did, it was not for the sake of the offender, not even for the sake of the victim, but that your concern for me might be plain to you in the sight of God.

That is why I have been cheered. And over and above my personal conversation I was made happier still by Titus's happiness, because all of you had set his mind at rest. So there has been no cause to retract anything I have boasted of to him about you. Rather, as I have spoken with complete truthfulness to you, so has the boast I

15 made to Titus been equally truthful. And his heart overflows towards you at the remembrance of the submissiveness of you all as you received him with fear and trepidation. I am happy to have complete confidence in you.

8.1 Now I would inform you, brothers, of the divine favour granted to the communities of Macedonia, how during a most testing trial the excess of their joy set against the extremity of their destitution enhanced the lavishness of their generosity, so that to the best of their capacity, I declare, and beyond their capacity, of their own accord and with many entreaties, they begged me for the favour and fellowship of joining in the service for

5 the saints.[19] It was not as I expected of them, but as they expected, that they gave first to the Master then to me by the will of God, so that I encouraged Titus that as he had begun so should he complete with you also the same expression of gratitude,[20] that just as you excel in every way, in faith, in speech, in knowledge, and zeal of every kind, and also in the affection you have for me, so should

19 The collection of funds for the poor saints of Judea.
20 For the gift of the Christian message.

you excel in this expression of gratitude also.

I am not saying this as an order, but because of the zeal of others and in proof of the genuineness of your affection. For you know the graciousness of our Lord Jesus Christ, how being rich he impoverished himself for your
10 sake, that you might be enriched by that poverty. But on this matter I do offer an opinion, for it is desirable that you should not only have initiated, but should maintain what you started a year ago. So now go on to complete what you initiated, that as is the keenness to keep it up so will be the effectiveness of what is done. For if the keenness is there, whatever one may do is acceptable: it is not as if one does nothing. For it is not a question of others having relief while you are in difficulties, but that in fairness at the present time your superfluity should compensate for their shortage, so that in turn their superfluity may make up for your shortage which will be
15 only right and proper, as it is stated, "He that had much had not too much, and he that had little did not go short".[21]

Thank God for putting the same concern on your behalf into the mind of Titus, so that he welcomed the proposal, and being so very admirable he visited you initially of his own accord. I have now sent with him the brother approved in the service of the News throughout the communities,[22] and not only so but elected by the communities as my travelling companion in this expression of gratitude administered and pressed forward by me for the honour of the Master. In this way provision
20 has been made that no one should find fault with me over this bounty which is administered by me; for I would be well-respected not only in the Lord's sight but also in the sight of men.[23] So I have sent with them my brother, whom I have proved to be admirable on so many occasions, and now more admirable than ever in the implicit confidence he places in you. So whether it is Titus, my associate and your fellow-worker, or my other brothers, envoys of the communities, they are a credit to Christ. Therefore furnish clear evidence in the sight of

21 *Exod* 16:18.
22 The unnamed brother has been thought by some to be Luke or Silas, but might be Tychicus or Trophimus. See above p 249.
23 cf *Prov* 3:4 (LXX); *Rom* 12:17.

the communities in demonstration of your affection and of my boast about you to them.

9.1   It is really quite superfluous for me to be writing to you about this service to the saints, for I am aware of your keenness which is what I boasted about you to the Macedonians. "Achaia", I said, "was all ready a year ago," and your enthusiasm has stimulated many. Yet I have dispatched the brothers in case my boast about you should have been an empty one in this respect, so that, as I have been saying you are ready, should it happen that Macedonians accompany me and find you are not ready, I, not to say you, would be ashamed in face of this

5   reality. I have considered it advisable, therefore, to propose to the brothers that they should visit you in advance and set in motion that previously announced goodwill-offering of yours, that the same being promptly forthcoming it will be like a goodwill-offering and not like an imposition.

There is this to add: "He that sows sparingly will reap sparingly, while he that sows liberally will reap liberally."[24] Let each follow his heart's dictate, not acting grudgingly or from necessity, for "the Lord loves a cheerful giver". [25] God is able to lavish every blessing upon you, so that always having sufficiency in every way you may be more than adequate for every good deed, just as it is stated,

> He has distributed his means;
> He has given to the poor;
> His beneficence endures for ever.[26]

10   He who supplies "seed to the sower, and bread for food"[27] will supply and multiply your produce and increase the fruits of your beneficence. So then, being enriched in every way for every act of generosity, whatever is done evokes by my agency thanksgiving to God. For the administration of this service not only makes up the shortage of the saints, but is further augmented by the volume of thanksgiving to God; for in appreciation of this ministration the saints praise God for

24 cf *Prov* 11:24 (LXX).
25 *Prov* 22:8 (LXX).
26 *Ps* 112:9 (LXX).
27 *Isa* 55:10 (LXX).

the strictness of your conformity with the Good News of Christ and the generosity of your fellowship with them and with all others. And their future wishes for you are expressed in prayer on your behalf because of God's 15 overwhelming kindness to you.[28] Thanks be to God for his incomparable gift!

Conclusion lacking[29]

28 In extending to Gentiles participation in the Messianic bliss.
29 The rest of *II Cor* is reproduced as the third letter to the community at Corinth (above pp 325–330). Probably little more than the concluding greeting is missing from this fourth letter.

To the Believers at Rome[1]
(Probably written from Corinth early in AD 57)

1.1 Paul, servant of Jesus Christ, a chosen envoy, assigned to the proclamation of God's News, which he had previously announced by his Prophets in the Sacred Writings, concerning his Son, Jesus Christ our Master, born in the physical sense of the line of David, but potently demonstrated to be God's Son in the sanctified spiritual sense by resurrection from the dead.[2] By

5 him I have obtained favour and envoyship to procure loyal submission to his authority on the part of all nations, among whom you likewise are summoned by Jesus Christ. To all God's dear ones in Rome, members of the Holy Assembly, may peace and prosperity be yours from God our Father and from the Lord Jesus Christ.

In the first place I thank my God through Jesus Christ for all of you that your faith is patent to the whole world. God is my witness, whom I serve devotedly in the cause of the News of his Son, that I never fail to make regular

10 reference to you in my prayers, requesting that somehow at long last, God willing, I may succeed in reaching you. For I do so long to see you, that I may impart to you some spiritual gift for your confirmation,[3] that is to say that I may find common encouragement with you through your and my mutual faith.[4]

---

1 In this letter, a kind of treatise, Paul does not address himself to the community (*ecclesia*) at Rome, which he had no part in creating, but to both Jewish and non-Jewish believers. He offers a reasoned statement of his faith and position, as uncertain whether they hold the same doctrines as himself.
2 See *Lk* 20:36.
3 Paul only reached Rome as a prisoner in AD 61.
4 Paul finds it hard to modify his own sense of authority, in face of the fact that envoys from Jerusalem had brought the Good News of the Messiah to Rome.

I do not want you to be in ignorance, brothers, that I have often proposed to visit you, though I have been prevented hitherto, in order that I may obtain some fruit of my labours among you as I have among other nations. I am indebted for such fruit both to Greeks and bar-
15 barians, to the cultured and the uncultured; so I am naturally eager to have the opportunity of proclaiming the News among you in Rome also. For I am not ashamed of the News: it is God's means of deliverance for all who believe, whether Jews or Gentiles. For by it God's justice is revealed by faith for faith, as it is stated, "By faith the just shall live".[5]

But God's wrath is revealed from heaven against all impiety and iniquity of men who wilfully suppress the truth, since they are well aware of the facts about God,
20 for God has made these plain to them. For ever since the creation of the world those unseen qualities of his, his immaterial nature, power and divinity, could be clearly perceived, apprehended through his works. So there is no excuse for them, when being acquainted with God they have neither praised nor thanked him as God, but have indulged in idle speculations and obscured their senseless minds. Professing to be wise they have behaved with utter folly, and have converted the glory of the imperishable God into the portrayal of the likeness of perishable men, birds, four-footed beasts and reptiles. Therefore, God has given them over to their hearts' desire for depravity, to the abuse of their bodies among
25 themselves, they who have exchanged God's truth for a lie, and worshipped and served the thing created instead of the Creator, blessed be he for ever. Amen.

Consequently God has given them over to their infamous passion; for their females have changed the normal function into the abnormal. The males, too, abandoning the normal function with females, inflamed with lust for one another, males for males, have engaged in indecency, duly receiving the reward appropriate to their irregularity between themselves. And just as they have not admitted God to a place in their consciousness, so God has given them over to a corrupt mind, to behave in unseemly fashion, perpetrating every kind of iniquity,

---

5 *Hab* 2:4. 'Shall live' now and in the Messianic Age.

obscenity, cupidity and depravity.[6] They are brim full of malice, murder, quarrelsomeness, knavery and
30   malignity, slanderers, libellers, anti-theistic, insolent, arrogant, brazen, contrivers of evil, defiant to parents, of low mentality, perfidious, lacking in affection, pitiless, the sort who well-knowing God's ordinance that those who are guilty of such behaviour deserve death, not only act in this way themselves, but applaud others who do so.

2.1   So there is no excuse for you, sir, whoever you may be, who sit in judgment; for in the very thing you judge others you condemn yourself, since you who judge act in the same way.

Now we know that God's sentence is a just one on those who have acted in this fashion. Do you reckon, therefore, you who judge those who have acted like this and yet do the same yourself, that you can escape God's sentence? Or do you affect to scorn the wealth of his consideration, forbearance and long-suffering, ignoring that God's consideration is designed to lead you to
5   repentance, preferring on account of your hard and impenitent heart to store up wrath for yourself in the Day of Wrath and disclosure of God's just doom. He it is who will "render to every man according to his deeds",[7] for those who by persistence in worthy actions seek glory, honour and immortality, it will be Eternal Life, while for those who are of a contentious nature and will not comply with the truth – but readily comply with falsehood – it will be wrath and anger. There will be affliction and anguish for every human being who engages in evil,
10   first for Jew then for Gentile[8]; but glory, honour and peace for all who do good, first for Jew then for Gentile; for there is no partiality on God's part.

As many as have sinned without law[9] shall perish without law, and as many as have sinned under law will be sentenced by law, on the day God judges the hidden things in men's lives by Jesus Christ, according to my presentation of the News. For it is not the hearers of law who are right with God, but the keepers of law who are

6 cf Tacit. *Annals*, XV.xliv, "The City of Rome, the common sewer into which everything infamous and abominable flows from all quarters of the world."
7 *Ps* 62:12.
8 Lit "Greek".
9 Paul has in mind the Law of Moses.

exonerated. When, therefore, such Gentiles as have no
law act instinctively as the Law requires, these having no
15   law are their own law. They thus display the operation of
that law which is written in their hearts, their conscience
endorsing such action, though in the meantime their
reasoning faculties may be engaged in a mutual conflict
of accusation and defence.[10]

Now you on the other hand are one who bears the
name of Jew. You rely on law and boast in God.[11] You are
acquainted with his will, and can make clear distinctions,[12] being instructed out of the Law. You are convinced that you are a guide to the blind, a light to those in
20   darkness, a tutor of the backward, a teacher of infants,
because in the Law you have the whole corpus of knowledge and truth.

Well then, you who teach others, do you never teach
yourself? You who proclaim "not to steal", do you steal?
You who say "not to commit adultery", do you commit
adultery? You who detest idols, do you rob temples? You
who boast in the Law, do you dishonour God by trans-
gressing the Law? Surely, as it is stated, "God's name is
profaned by you among the heathen".[13]

25   Circumcision is a definite advantage if you observe the
Law; but if you are a lawbreaker your circumcision is
converted into uncircumcision. So if the uncircumcised
person observes the moral principles of the Law, is not
his uncircumcision to be reckoned as circumcision? And
has not that uncircumcision which is by nature the right,
having carried out the Law, to judge you who in spite of
both code and circumcision are a lawbreaker? For he is no
Jew who is only one in appearance, nor is circumcision
simply what appears physically. The real Jew is he who is
one internally, and the real circumcision is that of the
heart, spiritual not literal, whose praise comes not from
men but from God.

3.1   What merit is there then in being a Jew? Or what
advantage does circumcision confer? Much in every

---

10 Without God's Law as guide the Gentile cannot always be clear as to what is
right and what is wrong.
11 In the Jew's daily affirmation, "Hear, O Israel, the Lord is our God, the Lord
is One".
12 Between good and evil, and between what is permitted and what is
prohibited.
13 *Mal* 1:11–12.

respect, primarily because the Jews were entrusted with the Oracles of God. What does it matter if some were untrustworthy? Does their untrustworthiness invalidate God's fidelity? God forbid! If only God be true, it matters not if every man be false, as it is stated,

> *That you should have your words vindicated,*
> *And prevail when you are arraigned.*[14]

5   But if our iniquity confirms God's rectitude, what are we to say, that God is unjust to vent his wrath? (I am speaking humanly.) God forbid! For in that case how can God judge the world? But if God's truth has more redounded to his praise by my untruth, why am I still adjudged a sinner? And why not as I am slanderously reported, and as some, whose condemnation is richly merited, allege that I say, "Let us do evil that good may come of it"?

What then? Do we Jews come off any better? Not at all. For we have already charged Jews and Gentiles alike with sinful behaviour, as it is stated,

> 10   *None is upright, not a single one.*
> *None gives heed: none seeks after God.*
> *All are defective, and worthless beside.*
> *None serves a useful purpose, not one.*
> *Their throat is a yawning tomb:*
> *They employ their tongues for deceit.*
> *The venom of asps is between their lips,*
> *Filling their mouth with bane and bitterness.*
> 15   *Their feet are swift to shed blood:*
> *Rack and ruin strew their path;*
> *And the way of peace they have not known.*
> *There is no fear of God before their eyes.*[15]

Now we know that whatever the Law states it declares to those who are governed by the Law, so that every mouth may be gagged and all the world become account-
20   able to God, since by following regulations "not a single human being will be exonerated"[16]; for through law comes acquaintance with sin.

But now, independent of law, the righteousness of

---

14 *Ps* 51:4.
15 Linking *Ps* 14:1–3; 5:9; 111:3; *Isa* 59:7–8; *Ps* 36:1.
16 *Ps* 142:2.

God has been made patent, attested both by the Law and the Prophets, that righteousness of God which is by faith in Jesus Christ, available to *all* who believe. (There is no distinction; for *all* have sinned and failed to reach God's standard.) These, by God's mercy, are freely exonerated through the discharge of liability by Christ Jesus, by their

25   reliance on his blood, whom God has appointed as an expiatory sacrifice in demonstration of his righteousness. In God's forbearance he overlooked the sins of past generations in view of the demonstration of his rectitude at the present time, so as to be both just himself, and the exonerator of whoever places his faith in Jesus.

Where then does boasting come in? It is excluded. By what law? Of regulations? No, by a law of faith; for we have reckoned that a man is exonerated by faith independent of legal regulations. For is he God of the Jews only, and not of the Gentiles? Surely of the Gentiles

30   also, if God is truly One. He exonerates the circumcised by their faith, and the uncircumcised by means of their acquired faith. Are we using faith to invalidate law? God forbid! Rather are we confirming law.[17]

4.1   What then are we to say of Abraham, our ancestor in the physical sense? If Abraham was exonerated by regulations he may well boast, though not to God. For what does the Scripture say, "Abraham relied on God, and it was credited to him as rectitude".[18] To one who carries out stipulations his reward is not reckoned as a

5   favour, but as a due. But to one who does not carry out stipulations, but relies on him who exonerates the ungodly, his faith is reckoned as rectitude, just as David speaks of the happiness of the man to whom rectitude is accounted independent of regulations:

Happy are they whose illegalities are forgiven,
And whose sins are covered over.
Happy is the man against whom the Lord counts not sin.[19]

Is that happiness reserved for the circumcised, or is it not also for the uncircumcised? Surely we have said, his

10   faith was credited to Abraham as rectitude. In what circumstances then was it credited, when he was in a

17 By propounding a law of faith.
18 *Gen* 15:6.
19 *Ps* 32:1–2.

state of circumcision or of uncircumcision? Not in a state of circumcision, surely, but in that of uncircumcision; for he received the mark of circumcision as a ratification of the rectitude arising from the faith he had while uncircumcised, so that he might be the father of all who believe coming from uncircumcision. At the same time he became the father of circumcision to those who – not on account of circumcision alone – follow in the steps of the faith of our father Abraham which he had when uncircumcised.

For it was not by law that the promise was made to Abraham, or to his seed, that he should be "heir of the world", but by rectitude deriving from faith. For if those based on law are heirs, faith is an empty thing and the promise is idle. The Law results in wrath, but where no law exists there can be no transgression either. Necessarily it is based on faith, so as to be a matter of favour, that the promise might be secured to *all* the seed, not only to that which is based on the Law, but also to that which is based on the faith of Abraham, who is our common ancestor, as it stated, "I have made you father of many nations".[20] Anticipating this, he relied on God the "Giver of life from the dead"[21] and the Namer of things as existing which as yet are non-existent. Against hope he relied on hope that he would be "father of many nations", as expressed in the words "so shall your seed be".[22] His faith never weakened with consciousness of the impotence of his own body – he was nearly a hundred years old at the time – and of Sarah's incapacity for motherhood. He did not challenge the promise of God incredulously, but fortified by faith he gave God credence, and was fully assured that what he had promised was practicable, and that he would carry it out. That is why it was "credited to him as rectitude".

Now it was not written in respect of Abraham alone that "it was credited to him", but also in respect of us to whom it would subsequently be credited, of those who trust in him who raised Jesus our Master from the dead, who was delivered up for our trespasses and raised up for our exoneration.

15

20

---

20 *Gen* 17:5.
21 Jewish *Amidah* prayer, *Bened.* 2 (*AJP*, p 45).
22 *Gen* 15:6.

5.1 So being exonerated on a basis of faith we enjoy peace with God through our Lord Jesus Christ, by whom we have secured admission to that state of favour in which we now stand, and boast in the prospect of God's esteem. And not only this, we even boast in afflictions, knowing that affliction fosters patience, patience fosters

5 experiment, experiment fosters expectation, and expectation never disappoints, because God's love has pervaded our minds by the holy Spirit which has been given us.

Moreover, Christ, when we were still helpless, died in due course for the ungodly. Now hardly for a devout man would anyone die, though possibly for a good man someone might dare to die. But God proves his own love for us, because Christ died for us while we were still sinners. Much more, therefore, being now exonerated by his blood, shall we be delivered from wrath through

10 him. If then, as enemies, we were reconciled to God by the death of his Son, much more, having become reconciled, shall we be delivered by his life. And not only this, we boast in God through our Lord Jesus Christ, by whose instrumentality we have obtained reconciliation.

Consequently, as by one man's agency sin entered the world, and by means of sin death, so death became the common lot of mankind, for all have sinned. For up to the time there was law sin was in the world, though sin was not charged as such while no law existed.[23] Nevertheless, death reigned from Adam down to Moses, even over those who technically had not sinned in a manner corresponding to the transgression of Adam, who pre-

15 figured him who was to come.[24] But the effect of the act of grace was very different to that of the transgression; for if by the transgression of one man the many died, far more has the mercy of God, and the free gift in mercy represented by the one man Jesus Christ, transcended this for the many. Other, indeed, was the effect of the gift to what happened by one person having sinned. The judgment for one transgression[25] brought condemna-

23 Here as elsewhere Paul does not regard law as having existed until the revelation of the Divine Law to Moses. That is why he speaks of the non-Jewish nations as being without law. The 1st cent. Jewish historian Josephus takes much the same position in his treatise *Against Apion*, where he argues that Gentile philosophers and lawgivers borrowed from the Jews.
24 As the Second Adam, the Son of Man.
25 See *Gen 3*.

tion, while the act of grace for many transgressions brought acquittal. Where, by the transgression of one, death reigned on account of the one, far more will those who have obtained the benefit of mercy, and the free gift of rectitude, reign in life on account of the one, Jesus Christ.

So then, as a single transgression led to condemnation for all mankind, so equally a single worthy action led to acquittal spelling life for all mankind. Just as by one man's disobedience the many were constituted sinners, so also by one man's obedience the many are constituted
20   righteous. Law came in additionally to magnify the transgression; but where sin abounded mercy abounded still more, that as sin reigned by death so should mercy reign through rectitude in Eternal Life by Jesus Christ our Master.

6.1   What are we to say then? Are we to continue in sin that mercy may be magnified? God forbid! We who have died so far as sin is concerned, how can we still live in it? Can you be ignorant that those who have become associated with Christ by immersion have become associated by it with his death? Through this association with him by immersion we are thus united with him in burial, so that as Christ was raised from the dead by means of the Father's glory, we too should conduct ourselves in new-
5   ness of life. For if we have become identified with the manner of his death, surely we should be with his resurrection also, knowing this, that our former self has been associated in crucifixion to dispose completely of the sinful body, that we should no longer be enslaved to sin; for the dead has met all the claims of sin upon him.

If we have died with Christ we believe that we shall also be associated with him in life, realising that Christ having risen from the dead cannot be put to death again:
10   death has no further power over him. As he died, he died permanently so far as sin was concerned, but as alive again, he lives to God. And so you no less can count yourselves dead so far as sin is concerned, but alive to God in Christ Jesus.

Therefore do not let sin rule your mortal body by obeying its lusts, nor offer your organs as instruments of iniquity where sin is concerned. Rather offer yourselves to God as alive from the dead, and your organs as instruments of rectitude to God. Sin shall not have dominion over you, for you are not under law but under mercy.

15   What then? Shall we sin because we are not under law but under mercy? God forbid! Do you not know that to whom you offer yourselves in obedience as slaves, to him you obey you are slaves, whether slaves of sin for death or of obedience for righteousness? But God be thanked that though you were slaves of sin you have since obeyed from the heart that model of teaching[26] which has been transmitted to you. Thus freed from sin, you have become enslaved to righteousness. (I am employing human terms because of the limitations of your physical nature.) For just as you offered your organs as slaves to uncleanness and lawlessness, for lawlessness, so have you now offered your organs as slaves to righteousness, for consecration.

20   When you were slaves of sin you were freemen as regards righteousness. What fruit had you then of those things of which you are now ashamed? For the end of those things is death. But now having been freed from sin and having become enslaved to God you have your fruit in consecration, the end of which is Eternal Life. For death is the pittance that sin pays, while God's bounty by Christ Jesus our Master is Eternal Life.

7.1   Can you be ignorant, brothers (for I am speaking to those familiar with law), that the Law is in control for as long as a man lives? For the wife subject to a husband is bound by law for the duration of her husband's life. But if the husband dies she ceases to be subject to marital control. It follows that if she becomes another man's during her husband's lifetime she will be pronounced an adulteress; but if her husband is dead she is free as far as the Law is concerned.

Consequently, my brothers, you too have been freed in law by death through the body of Christ, so as to be able to become another man's, his who was raised from
5   the dead, that we should be fruitful to God.[27] For when we stood in the physical relationship the sinful sensations induced by the Law actuated our organs to produce

26 Perhaps a manual of instruction on the lines of the *Didache* (*Teaching of the XII Apostles*). See also *Rom* 16:17.
27 Paul thinks of the physical Christ as one man, and the Christ after resurrection as another. The believer is now, as it were, the wife of the new spiritual husband to bear him spiritual offspring.

fruit for death. But now we are severed from the Law, that by which we were controlled being dead, so as to serve in a new way of the spirit and not in the old way of the letter.

What are we to say then? That the Law is sin? God forbid! But I should not have been acquainted with sin except through law; for I should not have known desire if the Law had not said, "You are not to covet". It was sin, seizing the opportunity through the commandment, that provoked in me every kind of desire; for apart from law sin was inert. I was alive once apart from law; but when the commandment came sin sprang to life, and I

10 died.[28] So I found the commandment which was intended for life tended to death; for sin seizing the opportunity through the commandment completely beguiled me, and through it slew me. Consequently the Law is indeed holy, and the commandment is holy, just and good.

Did then what is good become death to me? God forbid! But sin, that sin might be apparent through the good, brought about my death, that sin through the commandment might be exceedingly sinful. For we know that the Law is spiritual, but I on the other hand am

15 physical, the cat's-paw of sin. I do not perceive what I am about; for I find myself doing not what I wish to do, but doing instead what I detest.

So if I am doing what I do not wish to do, I grant that the Law is right. But there it is, it is not that I am doing whatever it is, but the indwelling sin in me. For I know that good does not reside in me, that is, in my physical nature.[29] The intention is there, but the capacity to carry out what is right is not; for I do not do the good I intend,

20 but the evil I do not intend. So if I do what I do not intend, it is no longer I who am doing it, but sin that dwells in me. I discover, therefore, the law, that whenever it is my intention to do the right the wrong asserts itself in me. In my inner self I delight in the Law of God,[30] but I perceive another law in my organs, warring against the law of my mind and making me prisoner to the law of sin which exists in my organs. So there it is, I

28 A Jewish child was not held responsible for his actions until after the age of twelve when he became *Barmitzvah* (Son of the Commandment).
29 cf Ps 38:3.
30 cf Ps 119:47, etc.

myself intellectually am bound to God's Law, but physically to sin's law. Miserable man that I am! Who will
25   rescue me from this body of death?[31] Thanks be to God,
through Jesus Christ our Master! So then mentally I do
indeed serve the Law of God, but with the flesh the law
of sin.

8.1   Thus there is no condemnation whatever for those
who are in Christ Jesus; for the law of the Spirit of Life in
Christ Jesus has freed me from the law of sin and death.
For the Law's powerlessness, due to its weakness
because of the physical factor, was remedied by God
sending his own Son in the likeness of sinful physical
nature. And as regards sin he passed sentence on sin in
Christ's physical being, so that the Law's claims should
be satisfied so far as we are concerned, we who do not
5   lead the physical but spiritual life. For those who are
physical are concerned with material matters. The
materialistic mentality spells death; the spiritual mentality spells life and peace. That is because the materialistic mentality is hostile to God; for it is not subordinated
to God's control, nor can it be. Those who have the
physical outlook cannot please God.

Now you do not have the physical but the spiritual
outlook, assuming that God's Spirit resides in you.
Naturally, if anyone does not possess the spirit of Christ
10   he does not belong to him. But if Christ is present in you
it means that the body is dead as a vehicle of sin, but the
spirit is alive as a vehicle of righteousness. And if the
Spirit that raised up Jesus from the dead resides in you,
then he that raised Christ Jesus from the dead will also
give life to your mortal bodies by very reason of his Spirit
indwelling in you.

So then, brothers, we are under no obligation to our
physical nature to live on the material plane; for if you
live on the material plane you will surely die. Whereas if
by the spiritual you put to death the practices of the body
you will live; for it is those who are led by the Spirit of
15   God who are the sons of God. You have not received a
servile spirit, to put you again in fear. It is a filial spirit

---

31 Or 'dead body'. Perhaps with reference to the crime of the Etruscan king
Mezentius, who bound living persons to dead bodies "hand to hand and
face to face" until they died a lingering ghastly death (Virgil, *Aeneid*, Bk VIII.
481–488).

you have received, whereby we cry "*Abba!*"[32] (Father!).

The Spirit joins its witness to our spirit that we are God's children. And if children then heirs, first heirs of God, and then joint-heirs with Christ. In that case we suffer together so as to be ennobled together also. I personally, count the sufferings of the present time as quite unworthy to be compared with the future glory that is to be revealed in us.

20   The eager longing of the Creation itself waits expectantly for the revelation of the Sons of God. For the Creation is subject to dissolution, not of its own choice, but through him who subjected it, yet in expectation that the Creation itself would be freed from servitude to decay to share the glorious freedom of the Children of God. We know indeed that the whole Creation groans and strains until now, and not it alone, but those who already enjoy the spiritual first-fruits – we ourselves – even they moan to themselves, waiting expectantly for the adoption, the redemption of their bodies.[33] For we are kept alive on hope. But hope that is in sight is not hope; for where one *sees*, where is there need for hope?

25   But if we hope for what we do not see, then we persist in our expectant waiting.

Likewise the Spirit comes to the assistance of our limitations; for we do not know how to express ourselves adequately in prayer. But the Spirit itself makes intercession with speechless moans, and God who searches the hearts knows what is the sense of the Spirit's utterances, that in God's way it is interceding for the saints. We know further, that for those who love God, for those called in accordance with his purpose, God makes everything turn out for the best. For, for those he had in view, he also planned in advance that they should come to resemble his Son, that thus he might be the

30   eldest of many brothers. And those he purposed in advance he duly called, and those he called he duly exonerated, and those he exonerated he will duly ennoble.

What then are we to say to all this? If God is for us, who is there against us? He who did not withhold his very

32 'Father' in Aramaic.
33 The language relates to the experience of an expectant mother.

own Son, but delivered him up for us all,[34] will he not also with him gladly give us everything else? Who dare accuse God's Elect? When God exonerates, who is there that can condemn? When Christ has died, still more has risen from the dead, is at God's right hand, and also 35 intercedes for us, who is to separate us from Christ's love? Can affliction, or confinement, or persecution, or famine, or destitution, or danger, or sword? As it is stated,

> For your sake we are killed the whole day long;
> We are reckoned as sheep for the slaughter.[35]

Yet in all these circumstances we are easy victors through him who has loved us. I am convinced that neither death nor life, neither angels nor ruling spirits, neither present nor future, neither powers above nor powers below, nor any other created being, will be able to sever us from the love of God which is in Christ Jesus our Master.

9.1 I am telling the truth in Christ, I am not lying, my conscience bearing me witness in the holy Spirit, when I say that I am in great grief and continual mental distress. For I could entreat that I personally was outcast from Christ for my brothers' sake, my kinsmen in the physical sense, who are Israelites, to whom belongs the Adoption,[36] and the Glory, and the Covenants, and the Law-5 giving, and the Service,[37] and the Promises, whose are the Patriarchs, and above all from whom in the physical sense came Christ, blessed be God for ever. Amen.

There is no question of God's word having failed; for it is not all who spring from Israel who are Israel, neither because they are the seed of Abraham are all of them his children. For "in Isaac shall your seed be called".[38] That is to say, not the children in the ordinary physical sense are the children of God, but the children of promise are reckoned as the seed.[39] For this is how the promise went: "About this time I will return, and Sarah will have a

34 cf the offering up of Isaac by Abraham (*Gen* 22:12), to which great spiritual significance was attached.
35 *Ps* 44:22.
36 ie as God's children.
37 Of God in the Temple. The passage relates to Jewish liturgy. cf *AJP*, p 149; "For the Law, for the Service, for the Prophets. . ."
38 *Gen* 21:12.
39 The argument is in line with Paul's view that 'those of faith', whether Jews or Gentiles, are the true Israel.

10   son".[40] And not only so, but when Rebecca had also conceived by one, namely our father Isaac, it was told her, "the elder shall serve the younger".[41] This was before the children were born, when they had done nothing either good or bad, in order that the purpose of God as regards choice should stand not on a basis of conduct but of calling, just as it is stated, "Jacob have I loved, but Esau I have hated".[42]

What are we to say then? That there is injustice on 15   God's part? God forbid! For he says to Moses, "I will show mercy to whom I would be merciful, and have compassion on whom I would be compassionate".[43] It follows that it is a matter not of what one wants, or what one tries to do, but of God's mercy; for the Scripture says to Pharaoh, "For this very reason I have raised you up, that through you I may display my power, and my name become known throughout the world".[44] It follows that he is merciful to whom he wishes, and whom he wishes he makes obdurate.

You will then say to me, "Why does he still blame anyone? For who is a match for his will?" If it comes to 20   that, who are you, sir, to answer God back? Is it for the model to say to the modeller, "Why did you make me like this?" Has not the potter in clay a perfect right to make out of the same lump one article as a thing of worth, another as a thing of no worth? Supposing that God, wishing to display his genius and demonstrate his ability, produced with immense pains crude articles prepared for destruction, in order to display the richness of his imagination on delicate articles which he had designed beforehand for distinction[45] – namely ourselves, whom he has called not from the Jews alone but 25   also from the Gentiles? He does indeed say in Hosea:

> *I will call them my people, who were not my people,*
> *And her beloved, who was not beloved.*

---

40 *Gen* 18:10.
41 *Gen* 25:23.
42 *Mal* 1:2–3.
43 *Exod* 33:19.
44 *Exod* 9:16.
45 The Greek conveys the full force of the metaphor because "crude articles" equally means "vessels of wrath" and "delicate articles" means also "vessels of mercy".

> *In the very place where it was said to them, 'You are not my*
>   *people',*
> *There shall they be called, 'Sons of the Living God'.*[46]

Isaiah also cries concerning Israel, "Though the number of the Children of Israel is as the sand of the sea, only a remnant will be saved. For the Lord will make a full and summary settlement on earth."[47] And as Isaiah said previously, "If the Lord of hosts had not left us some seed, we should have become as Sodom, we should have been like Gomorrah".[48]

30   What are we to say then? That the Gentiles who did not pursue righteousness have overtaken it, the righteousness that arises from faith, while Israel pursuing a law of righteousness has failed to attain it? That is so. Why? Because it was not by faith, but as by regulations. They stumbled at the stumbling-stone, as it is stated,

> *Lo, I place in Zion a stumbling-stone, a boulder to trip over;*
> *But he who believes in him will not come to grief.*[49]

10.1   It is indeed my fondest desire, brothers, and the burden of my petition to God, that they should be saved. I can testify that they have a deep passion for God, though without discernment. For failing to perceive God's righteousness, while busy with trying to establish their own, they did not subordinate themselves to God's righteousness. To all who believe, Christ is the end of

5   law as regards righteousness; for Moses writes concerning the righteousness that is by law that "that the man who acts up to it shall live by it".[50] But the righteousness that is by faith speaks thus: "Do not say to yourself, 'Who will ascend to heaven?' (that is, to bring Christ down) or, 'Who will descend into the abyss?'" (that is, to bring Christ up from the dead). What it declares is, "The word is very near you, in your mouth and in your mind"[51] (that is, the word of faith which we proclaim). For if you

46 *Hos* 2:23.
47 *Isa* 10:22 with 28:22.
48 *Isa* 1:9.
49 *Isa* 8:14 with 28:16 (LXX). "In him", or "In it", is an addition to the quotation, possibly taken from a collection of OT 'proofs' that Jesus was the Messiah.
50 *Lev* 18:5.
51 *Deut* 30:12–14.

will affirm "the word in your mouth" that Jesus is Master, and believe "in your mind" that God raised him
10 from the dead, you will be saved; for belief is by the mind for righteousness, and affirmation is by the mouth for salvation. The Scripture does indeed say, "Everyone who believes in him will never come to grief".[52] There is no distinction between Jew and Gentile: the same universal Lord is sufficient for all who invoke him, "for all who invoke the name of the Lord will be saved".[53] How then are they to invoke him in whom they have not believed? And how are they to believe what they have not heard? And how are they to hear without a preacher?
15 And how are they to preach unless they are sent? As it is stated, "How fair are the feet of those who bring good news!"[54]

But not all have responded to the news, for Isaiah says, "Lord, who has credited our report?"[55] So then faith comes by hearing, and hearing through the proclamation of Christ. But I say, have they not heard? Decidedly they have:

Their voice has resounded throughout the earth,
Their utterance to the utmost confines of the world.[56]

And I say, has Israel not known? First Moses says,

I will make you jealous over what is no nation;
Over a senseless nation I will anger you.[57]

20 While Isaiah takes the liberty of saying,

I have been found by those who did not seek me:
I have become evident to those who never asked for me.[58]

And of Israel he says, "All day long I have stretched out my hands to a refractory and contradictory people".[59]
11.1 I ask, therefore, has God rejected his people? God forbid! I myself am an Israelite, of the seed of Abraham, the tribe of Benjamin. God has not rejected his people

52 *Isa* 28:16.
53 *Joel* 2:32.
54 *Isa* 52:7.
55 *Isa* 53:1.
56 *Ps* 19:4.
57 *Deut* 32:21.
58 *Isa* 65:1.
59 *Isa* 65:2.

whom he knew of old. Or are you unaware of what the Scripture says in the person of Elijah, where he speaks to God about Israel, saying "Lord, they have killed your prophets, thrown down your altars, and I alone am left, and they seek my life"? But what does his Interlocutor say to him? "I have reserved for myself seven thousand

5   men, who have not bent the knee to Baal".[60] Just so at this present time by a merciful choice there is a remnant. If it is by mercy it is no longer by deeds, otherwise mercy would no longer be mercy.

What then, Israel has not found what it is seeking, but the chosen part has found it, while the rest were immobilised, exactly as it is stated, "God has given them a spirit of stupor, eyes that do not see, and ears that do not hear, to this very day".[61] And David says,

> Let their table become a snare and a trap,
> A hindrance and an obstacle to them.
10 > Let their eyes be dimmed that they see not,
> And their back be for ever bent.[62]

I ask, therefore, have they tripped in order that they should fall? God forbid! Rather that by their blunder salvation has come to the Gentiles to stir them to emulation. But if their blunder is the world's enrichment, and their discomfiture the Gentiles' enrichment, how much more their complete achievement? (I am speaking to you Gentiles.)

In so far, then, as I am an envoy to the Gentiles I make much of my office, if in that way I can provoke my own

15   kin to emulation, and save some of them. For if their loss has been the world's profit, what will their acquisition be but life from the dead? If the first-dough is holy, so is the whole lump,[63] and if the stem is holy, so are the branches.

Now if some of the branches have been pruned away, and you from a wild olive have now been grafted among them, sharing with them the sap-stream of the main olive stem, do not lord it over the branches. For if you do lord it, remember that it is not you who carry the stem, but the stem you. You will say then, "The branches have

60 *I Ki* 19:10, 18.
61 *Isa* 29:10 with *Deut* 29:4.
62 *Ps* 69:22–23.
63 cf *Num* 15:18–21; *Lev* 19:23–24.

20 been pruned away that I might be grafted in". Putting it fairly, they have been pruned away as lacking in confidence,[64] while you by confidence stand firm. So do not be arrogant, but fear. For if God did not spare the natural branches, neither will he spare you.

Mark, then, the kindness and severity of God, severity towards those branches which drooped, kindness to you, provided you continue to merit his kindness. Otherwise, you too will be cut out, while they, unless they continue to remain without trust, will be grafted back; for God can graft them in again. For if you were cut from an olive tree wild by nature, and grafted contrary to nature into a cultivated olive, how much more shall these which are the natural branches be grafted into their own olive tree?

25 I would not have you ignorant of this secret, brothers, in case you should "give yourselves airs",[65] that partial immobility has come to Israel until the full complement of Gentiles has come in; and so *all* Israel will be saved,[66] as it is stated,

> *The redeemer will come out of Zion:*
> *He will banish ungodliness from Jacob.*
> *For this is my covenant with them,*
> *When I take away their sins.*[67]

As regards the News they are out of favour for your sakes, but as regards the Choice they are dear to God for the Patriarchs' sake;[68] for God never goes back on his acts
30 of grace and his calling. Even as you once refused God obedience, but now have had mercy shown you in respect of their disobedience, so they also have now refused obedience in respect of the mercy shown to you, so that they may obtain mercy. For God has classed all together as disobedient that he may show mercy to all.

Oh, the infinite wealth of God's wisdom and knowledge! How inscrutable are his judgments and mysterious

---

64 "Confidence" may equally be read as "faith". But the metaphor calls for the former.
65 cf *Prov.* 3:7.
66 "All Israel has a share in the world to come" (*Sanhed.* 10:1).
67 *Isa* 59:20–21 with 27:9.
68 cf *Amidah* prayer, *Bened. I*, "Who bestowest loving-kindness and possessest all things; who rememberest the pious deeds of the Patriarchs, and in love will bring a redeemer to their children's children" (*AJP*, p 44).

his ways! Who has ever known the mind of the Lord, or
35   who has been his counsellor? Or who has first given to
him, that he must be repaid?[69] For from him, and
through him, and in him, are all things. To him be glory
for ever. Amen.

12.1   I exhort you[70] therefore, brothers, by God's tender
mercies, to offer your bodies as a holy living sacrifice
well-pleasing to God, which is your plain religious duty.
Do not accommodate yourselves to the age we live in,
but transform yourselves by a mental renovation, so that
you are competent to determine what is the good, well-
pleasing, and perfect will of God.

By virtue of the favour bestowed on me, I ask every
individual among you not to have a higher opinion of
himself than he should, but to think of himself modestly,
as God has allotted to each his share of worth. For just as
we have many organs in one body, and all the organs do
5   not perform the same function, so we are many persons
in one body in Christ, and that body as a unity has its
respective organs. Possessing, then, a variety of gifts
according to the favour granted us, let mutual regard be
unfeigned. If the gift is for prophecy, let it be exercised
with corresponding faithfulness. If it is for administration, let it be exercised in administration; if for teaching,
let it be for teaching, if for exhortation, let it be in
exhortation. He who has something to share, let him do
it generously. He who supervises, let him do it diligently. He who does a kindness, let him do it cheerfully.

Let love be unfeigned. Repudiate what is evil. Cleave
10   to what is good. In brotherly love be affectionate to one
another. In honour give precedence to one another. In
diligence do not be backward. In spiritual matters be
ardent. Be willing slaves to the Master, joyful in hope,
patient in affliction, persevering in prayer, sharing in
provision for the necessities of the saints, ready with
hospitality. Bless those who are so ready,[71] bless and do
15   not curse. Rejoice with those who rejoice. Weep with

---

69   cf *Ps* 145:3; *Isa* 40:13–14; *Job* 25:7, 41:11.

70   The paragraphs that follow are on similar lines to the *Didache* (*Teaching of the XII Apostles*), and may derive from an early Manual of Instruction. See above p 352, n 26.

71   The alternative rendering "those who persecute" is unsuitable in the context. The same word "ready" has just been used in association with hospitality.

those who weep. Be like-minded with one another. Do not be high and mighty, but consort with the humble. Do not give yourselves airs.[72] Never return evil for evil. Be well-respected in the sight of all men.[73] If possible, where it rests with you, be at peace with everyone. Do not avenge yourselves, dear friends, but give anger a wide berth, for it is stated, "Vengeance is mine, I will
20 requite, says the Lord".[74] Rather, "If your enemy is hungry, feed him, if he is thirsty, refresh him; for by so doing you will fill him with remorse".[75] Do not be overcome by evil, but overcome evil with good.

13.1   Let every individual be subject to the responsible authorities; for there is no authority except from God, and those who are constituted hold their appointment from God.[76] Whoever, therefore opposes the authority sets himself against the divine order, for those who resist it will duly receive punishment. Magistrates are not a terror to well-doers, but to evil-doers. If you would be free from fear of authority be of good behaviour, and you will earn its commendation; for the authority is God's administrator for your welfare. But if you do wrong, then be afraid, for he does not bear the sword without reason. In his capacity as God's administrator it is his official duty to inflict punishment on the evil-doer.

5   Of necessity you must be subject to the laws, not merely from considerations of punishment, but also of conscience, which applies equally to your payment of taxes. Those who levy them are God's officials regularly employed for this very purpose.[77] Render to everyone their dues, tribute to whoever is entitled to it, tax to whoever is entitled to it, respect to whoever is entitled to it, honour to whoever is entitled to it. Owe nothing to anyone except regard for one another; for he who shows another love has met all the requirements of law. "You-are not to commit adultery, you are not to murder, you

---

72 *Prov* 3:7 (LXX).
73 *Prov* 3:4 (LXX).
74 *Deut* 32:35.
75 *Prov* 25:21–22. Lit "will heap burning coals on his head".
76 Paul's teaching follows that of the Essenes. cf Jos. *Jewish War* II. espec. 140; the initiate swears "that he will always keep faith with all men, especially with the powers that be, since no ruler attains his office save by the will of God".
77 The teaching of Jesus did not agree with this, according to *Mt* 17:25–26; *Lk* 23:2.

are not to steal, you are not to covet",[78] and whatever other commandment there may be is summed up in this,

10   "You are to love your neighbour as yourself".[79] He who loves his neighbour will never do him an injury: so love is the sum total of law.

This further, because I know the time, that it is high time for you to awaken from sleep; for our deliverance is much nearer than when we believed. The night is far advanced. The day is at hand. Let us therefore lay aside what belongs to the darkness, and put on the habits of the light. Let us conduct ourselves with daytime decorum, not in revels and carousals, not in sexual intimacy and licentiousness, not in wrangling and rivalry. Rather, invest yourselves with the Lord Jesus Christ, and make no provision for the fulfilment of physical desires.

14.1   Associate with the man who is weak in faith, but not for controversial arguments. For one believes he may eat anything, while another of weaker calibre keeps to a vegetarian diet.[80] The man who eats must not be contemptuous of the one who does not. Neither must the man who does not eat condemn the one who does; for God has taken him into his service. Who are you to criticise another's retainer? To his own Master he stands or falls. And stand he will, for the Lord will see to it that he stands.

5   One man distinguishes one day above another, while someone else treats all days alike. Each must fully satisfy his own mind. He who observes a day observes it to the Lord, and he who eats every kind of food eats it to the Lord, because he thanks God for it. He who does not eat, his not eating is also to the Lord, for he too gives God thanks. None of us lives to himself, and none of us dies to himself. If we live, we live to the Lord, and if we die, we die to the Lord. Whether we live, or whether we die, we are the Lord's. That is why Christ died and came alive again, that he might have jurisdiction over both dead

10   and living. Why then do you condemn your brother, or why do you treat your brother with contempt? We must

---

78 *Exod* 22:13–17.
79 *Lev* 19:18, cf *Mt* 22:40.
80 This would relate to a mixed group of Jewish and non-Jewish believers, where the former would be vegetarians so as not to break the dietary laws. The position with holy days would be similar.

all stand at God's tribunal, for it is stated,

> 'As I live', says the Lord, 'every knee shall bend to me,
> And every tongue shall make full confession to God.'[81]

So then each of us must render an account of himself to God. Therefore let us no longer pass judgment on one another. Rather should you determine this, not to place any obstacle or impediment in your brother's way. I know and am convinced in the Lord Jesus that nothing is

15 impure in itself,[82] but if someone considers anything to be impure, for him it is so. And if your brother is distressed by the food you eat you are not behaving considerately. Do not by your food destroy one for whose sake Christ died. Do not let what is for your well-being be made a means of injury. For the Kingdom of God is not food and drink, but righteousness, peace, and joy in the holy Spirit. Whoever in such matters serves Christ is both well-pleasing to God and agreeable to men.

So then let us follow the ways of peace[83] and the things

20 that promote our mutual welfare. For a mere matter of food do not disrupt God's work. Everything is indeed clean; but it is a wrong thing for a man to be a means of offence by what he eats. The right course is neither to eat meat nor to drink wine, nor whatever else it may be that upsets your brother. As to the conviction you hold, hold it privately in the sight of God. Happy is the man who does not condemn himself by what he sanctions. But he who does discriminate stands condemned if he should eat, because it is not from conviction. For whatever is not done from conviction is sin.

15.1 It is the duty of those who are strong to bear the foibles of the weak, and not to gratify ourselves. It is for each of us to put his neighbour at ease so as to promote the general welfare. For even Christ did not please himself, as it is stated, "The reproaches which they cast on you fell on me".[84] Whatever, indeed, was set down was written entirely for our guidance, that through the sustaining power and encouragement of the Scriptures

5 we should have hope. May God who sustains and cheers

81 *Isa* 45:23.
82 cf *Mt* 15:11.
83 cf *Ps* 24:14.
84 *Ps* 69:9.

grant you to be likeminded with one another in accordance with Jesus Christ, that in complete unanimity, with one voice, you may praise God, the Father of our Lord Jesus Christ!

Therefore associate with one another for the glory of God, just as Christ associated himself with you. For I say that Christ became a representative of circumcision, as God's honour required, so as to make good his promise to the Patriarchs, and that the Gentiles should praise God for his mercy, as it is stated, "Therefore I will confess you among the Gentiles, and sing praises to your
10   name".[85] And again it says, "Rejoice, O Gentiles, with his people",[86] and further,

> Extol the Lord, all you Gentiles,
> And praise him, all you peoples.[87]

And again Isaiah says, "There shall be a root of Jesse, and one who arises to rule the Gentiles. In him shall the Gentiles hope."[88]

May the God of hope so fill you with joy and peace in believing, that you overflow with hope by virtue of the holy Spirit!

Naturally, I personally am completely convinced of you, my brothers, that you are the very soul of kindness, fully provided with all essential knowledge, and most
15   competent to admonish one another. But I have written to you more outspokenly than was warranted, simply to serve as a reminder to you, because of the favour God has granted me that I should be the ministrant of Christ Jesus for the Gentiles, carrying out the rite of God's News, that the offering up of the Gentiles might be acceptable when consecrated by the holy Spirit.[89] I hold, therefore, a privileged position in Christ Jesus in matters relating to God. I am not so audacious as to speak of anything which Christ has not effected by my agency, by virtue of signs and wonders, by virtue of the holy Spirit, to procure the obedience of the Gentiles in word and deed. So that from Jerusalem as far round as Illyricum[90] I

85 *Ps* 18:49.
86 *Deut* 32:43.
87 *Ps* 117:1.
88 *Isa* 11:1,10.
89 Paul is using the metaphor of a priest's functions.
90 District east of the Adriatic roughly the same as modern Albania.

20 have fully publicised the News of Christ. And thus have I most strenuously proclaimed the News, not where Christ's name was familiar, that I should not build on another's foundation, but rather as it is stated,

> *They shall see, to whom he was not reported,*
> *And those who have not heard shall consider.*[91]

That is why I have so frequently been prevented from visiting you. But now having nothing more that I may do in these regions, and having had a great longing these many years to visit you, whenever I travel to Spain I trust to have a sight of you in passing through, and to be forwarded by you on my way there after first making the most of my stay with you.[92]

25 Just now, however, I am setting out for Jerusalem to render the saints a service; for Macedonia and Achaia have been pleased to make a contribution of funds for the poor among the saints at Jerusalem.[93] It has pleased them to do so quite properly, since they are their debtors. For if the Gentiles have shared in their spiritual things, they are under obligation for their part to minister to them in material things. When, therefore, I have performed this service, and deposited this aid with them, I shall proceed via yourselves to Spain; and I know that when I come to you it will be with the full blessing of Christ.

30 Now I entreat you, brothers, by our Lord Jesus Christ, and by the bonds of spiritual affection, to aid me with your prayers to God on my behalf, that I may be protected from those in Judea who are disobedient, and that my mission to Jerusalem may be well received by the saints; so that coming on to you joyfully, God willing, I may take my rest in your company. The God of peace be with you all. Amen.

16.21 [94]My fellow-worker Timotheus sends you his regards, and so do my fellow-countrymen Lucius, Jason and

---

91 *Isa* 52:15.
92 Paul was never to get to Spain, and only reached Rome as a prisoner. See *Acts* 21–28.
93 See *Acts* 24:17.
94 Some regard *Rom* 16:1–20, which is placed here in the Greek, as a short personal note sent with Sister Phoebe as the bearer of the letter, serving both to introduce her and to convey Paul's personal greetings to a number of individuals. This passage is therefore transferred to the end of the letter.

Sosipater. (I, Tertius, who took down the letter, send you my regards in the Master.) My host Gaius sends you his regards, and so does the whole community. Erastus the city treasurer sends you his regards, as does Brother Quartus.

25   Now to him who can establish you in accordance with my presentation of the News and the proclamation of Jesus Christ in accordance with the revelation of the mystery for long ages kept secret, but now disclosed through the Prophetic Scriptures by order of the Eternal God, and made known to all nations to procure their loyal submission, to the only wise God be praise through Jesus Christ for ever and ever. Amen.

Covering Note

16.1   This is to commend to you Sister Phoebe, who is an administrator of the Cenchreae[95] community. Welcome her in the Master as befits saints, and assist her in whatever way she may require; for she has been of great assistance to many, including myself.

Give my regards to Prisca and Aquila, my fellow-workers in Christ Jesus, who have risked their necks on my behalf, and to whom not only I am grateful, but all
5   the communities among the Gentiles. Give my regards also to the community in their house. Then give my regards to my dear friend Epaenitus, Asia's first-fruits for Christ, also to Mary who has worked so hard for you. My regards to my fellow-countrymen and fellow-captives Andronicus and Junias, famed among the envoys, who also were in Christ before me.

My regards in the Master to my dear friend Amplias, also Urban our fellow-worker in Christ, and my dear
10   friend Stachys. My regards to Apelles approved in Christ, and also to the family of Aristobulus. Give my regards to my fellow-countryman Herodion, also those of the family of Narcissus who are in the Master, and those hard workers in the Master, Tryphena and Tryphosa.

My regards to dear Persis, who has worked so hard in the Master, also Rufus, chosen in the Master, and his mother, and therefore mine. My regards to Asyncritus,

---

95 Seaport on the east of the Gulf of Corinth. See *Acts* 18:18.

Phlegon, Hermes, Patrobas, Hermas, and the brothers
15   associated with them. My regards to Philologus and
Julia, Nereus and his sister, Olympas too, and all the
saints associated with them.

Convey my regards to one another with a chaste kiss.
All the communities of Christ send their regards.

Now I exhort you, brothers, to note those who create
doubts and difficulties in opposition to the teaching you
have learnt,[96] and keep away from them. Such as they do
not serve the Lord Christ, but their own appetites, and
by fair words and fine phrases seduce the minds of the
guileless. But your obedience has become common
knowledge. So I am quite happy about you, and only
want you to be wise where good is concerned, uncon-
20   taminated where evil is concerned.[97] The God of peace
will swiftly crush Satan under your heel.[98]

The loving-kindness of our Lord Jesus be with you all.

---

96 cf *Didache (Teaching of the XII Apostles)*, 4.
97 cf *Mt* 10:16.
98 The Old Serpent, *Gen* 3:15.

THE LETTERS OF PAUL OF TARSUS

Second Series

Letters From Rome

To the Community at Philippi
To the Communities of Asia
To the Community of Colossae
To Philemon
To Titus
To Timotheus (1)
To Timotheus (2)

Preface to Paul's Letters
(Second Series)

We are without the assistance of the *Acts* for knowledge of the close of Paul's life, and have to depend entirely on what can be gleaned from the second series of letters, those written from Rome. From these it is clear that, although confined under guard in a rented apartment while waiting for his case to be heard, Paul had full freedom of communication and the ministrations of his friends to solace him. He had initially every expectation that he would be set at liberty, and at one point was making plans for visits on his release. But he had enemies inside the Christian community as well as outside, who worked against him, and the first hearing of his case was indecisive.

The conditions of his imprisonment may then have been made more rigorous, and finally he appears to have recognised that his death was inevitable even if for a time postponed. Some scholars have held that he was freed and travelled again to Macedonia and Asia, and was later rearrested and brought back to Rome, and they would place his end in AD 66 or 67. The weight of evidence seems to the writer against this view, and it is accepted that Paul did not leave Rome and that his death was not later than the Spring of AD 64. The Great Fire of Rome for which the Christians were held responsible took place late in that year. The order and dating of the letters of this period has been governed by this hypothesis.

Scholars have also drawn attention to the differences of style and vocabulary in some of the letters compared with the earlier ones, and in those to *Titus* and *Timotheus* (1), to evidence of advanced Church government, thus throwing doubts on the Pauline authorship. Some would say that Pauline material has been worked up by other hands. The arguments for some posthumous editing are very strong, but not conclusive.

What is notable about the letters to Philippi and the Asian communities is their mystical passages, where Paul employs Jewish (Essene and Pharisee) occult doctrine to describe the nature of Christ and his relationship with the Church. Paul in his youth had been an adept in one branch of this doctrine, the *Mystery of the Creation* (in *Genesis*). Unfortunately these sources have largely been neglected by Christian exegetes and theologians, who thus have very largely failed to comprehend Paul's concepts. It is hoped that the present rectification will be of service.

The short letter to Philemon about his runaway slave Onesimus is delightful and appealing, and in those to Titus and Timotheus there is much to interest and inform about the organisation of the early Christian communities.

But chiefly with this whole series one has to read with the thought of the imprisoned author constantly in mind. Through what he writes we can see how he encourages himself with prayer, with vision, and with spiritual song. We can see how – even with his conviction of the imminent advent of Jesus to take his kingdom – he strives with counsel and clarification to leave behind what will keep believers on the right road until the Messianic Era dawns. Studied from this viewpoint there is indeed much to touch the emotions and impress the reader with the nobility of soul of a great sufferer and a very courageous and enterprising man.

To the Community at Philippi

(Probably written from Rome[1] about AD 61–2)

1.1   Paul and Timotheus, servants of Christ Jesus to all the saints in Christ Jesus living in Philippi, with their supervisors and administrators. May peace and prosperity be yours from God our Father and the Lord Jesus Christ.

Invariably I thank my God for every recollection of you whenever I pray for you. I offer my petition with joy for
5   the fellowship you have had with the News from the very beginning until now, being fully assured that he who promoted such well-doing on your part will maintain it to the Day of Jesus Christ.[2] It is indeed right that I should so think of you all, because I have you so much at heart, all of you having shared in the privilege I have of being in fetters and of defending and championing the News.

God is my witness how I long for you with all the yearning of Christ Jesus! And so it is my prayer that your love may bring you ever deeper insight and perception in
10   distinguishing points of difference,[3] that you may be unalloyed and untarnished till the Day of Christ, laden with the fruit of rectitude that comes through Jesus Christ, to the glory and praise of God.

Now I want to tell you, brothers, that my circumstances have rather tended to the advancement of the News; for my fetters have publicised Christ to the whole praetorium and everywhere else. The majority of the

1 Here Paul was under house-arrest awaiting the hearing of his appeal by the Emperor Nero (*Acts* 25:12; 28:16).
2 The day of Christ's return to earth at the beginning of the Messianic Age.
3 Relating to what is right and wrong. cf *Rom* 2:18.

brothers, having been fired with confidence in the Master by my fetters, have become much more venturesome,

15   giving out God's Message fearlessly. Some of course do it out of envy and rivalry,[4] but others proclaim Christ from goodwill. These do it out of regard, knowing that I am thus circumstanced for the defence of the News, while the former, who are not well-intentioned, announce Christ in a factious spirit trying deliberately to make trouble for me in my fettered state.

What does it matter? The main thing is that, whether in pretence or sincerity, Christ is proclaimed. For this I rejoice. But there is greater joy in store; for I know that this will be the salvation of me thanks to your prayers

20   and the supply of the spirit of Jesus Christ, with the earnest hope and expectation I have that I shall in no way be put to shame, but that freely and fully, now as always, Christ will be magnified in my person whether by life or death.

It is useful[5] to me to live, and an advantage to die. But if I am to live physically it means an effort on my part, and I hardly know which to choose. I am in a quandary between the two, having the longing to depart and be with Christ, for that would be so much better, yet on the other hand to remain in the flesh is more essential for

25   you. Finally convinced of this, I know I am to remain and be at the side of all of you for your advancement and joyfulness in faith, that your exultation in Christ Jesus may abound by me through my reappearance among you.

Only let your ordering of affairs be worthy of Christ's News, that whether I come and see you or remain absent I shall hear word of you that you are continuing to be of one spirit, single-mindedly contending for the faith of the News, and not the least alarmed by the tactics of your adversaries. This is a sure sign of defeat for them, but of deliverance for you, and this by God himself; for you have the privilege on Christ's account not only of believ-

30   ing in him[6] but of suffering for his sake. Yours is the same

4 The Christian community at Rome at this time was substantially composed of Jews (see *Romans*). Many members were naturally opposed to Paul's doctrine, especially his granting of Israelite status to non-Jews without obligation to observe the Mosaic laws (see *II Tim* 4:14–16)

5 By a scribal error *Christos* was substituted for *chrestos*. The mistake was easy since *Chrestos*, meaning useful, was a well-known proper name. The Roman historian Suetonius once referred to Christus as Chrestus.

6 "In him", ie "in God", believing in God on Christ's account.

kind of contest in which you have seen me engaged, and now learn that I am still engaging.

2.1   So if there is any encouragement in Christ you can give me, any consolation of affection, any fellowship of spirit, any deep concern and compassion, do fill me with the joy of it. So that in thus thinking alike, having the same affection, being kindred souls with a common viewpoint, there will be no trace of rivalry, no trace of self-importance, but only that humility of mind which regards others as superior to one's self, each studying not his own interests but those of his fellows.

5   Let your disposition, indeed, be that of Christ Jesus, who though he had godlike form, did not regard it as a prize to be equal to God,[7] but divested himself, taking the form of a servant. Appearing in human likeness, and disclosed in physical appearance as a man, he abased himself, and became subject to death, death by the cross.

10   That is why God has so exalted him, that at the name of Jesus every knee, heavenly, earthly and infernal, should bend, and every tongue acclaim Jesus Christ as lord, to the glory of God the Father.[8]

Therefore, dear friends, as invariably you have been obedient, not only when I have been present, but much more creditably now in my absence, earn your salvation with fear and trembling; for it is God who is prompting you both to want and to carry out what is well-pleasing.

15   Do everything without murmuring or argument, that you may be irreproachable and faultless, blameless children of God in the midst of a "perverse and crooked generation",[9] in which shine out like luminaries in a dark universe, radiating a message of Life,[10] my proud proof on the Day of Christ that I have neither striven nor toiled in vain. But even should I be poured out as the libation

---

7 Referring to the sin which Adam was tempted by Satan to commit, and which Lucifer in his former state had committed (*Gen* 3:5; *Isa* 14:12–14). Moses is said to have had a divine form, and as an infant to have received the crown from Pharaoh's head (Josephus, *Antiq* II 232–235). The Christ Above of the Jewish mystics had angelic likeness as a Son of God (*Dan* 4:25–28; *Job* 25–28; *Job* 1:6–7). He discarded his heavenly aspect at his incarnation, but once revealed it when he was transfigured (*Mk* 9:1–7).

8 The Spirit–Messiah, the heavenly Archetype, became incarnate in the human Jesus, according to Paul (*Rom* 1:3–4), thus creating the combination of Jesus and Messiah as Jesus-Christ.

9 *Deut* 32:5.

10 *Dan* 12:3.

and act of worship that your faith is called upon to make, I shall rejoice and congratulate you all, and similarly you will rejoice and congratulate me.[11]

Now I hope in the Lord Jesus to send Timotheus to you soon, that I myself may be heartened by knowing how
20   you fare. I have no one better qualified, one who is genuinely concerned with how you fare; for most study their own interests, not those of Christ Jesus. But you know the worth of Timotheus, how he has served with me in the News like a son with his father. Him, then, I hope to send as soon as ever I have a clear impression of my prospects, though I am convinced in the lord that I shall be in a position before long to come personally.
25   But I have considered it essential to send Brother Epaphroditus, my co-worker and campaigner and your envoy and minister to my needs,[12] because he misses you so, and frets because you had heard that he was ailing. Indeed he was ailing, almost at death's door. But God took pity on him, and not only on him but on me too, that I should not have one distress upon another. So I have sent him more expeditiously, that in seeing him again you may have joy, and I less sorrow. Give him, therefore, a joyful welcome in the Master, and hold such
30   as he in high regard, for in doing the Master's work he came so near death, jeopardising his life to make good your lack of opportunity to serve me.
3.1   Finally, brothers, rejoice in in the Master.

Here are the particular things I must mention to you, where indeed I do not falter while you are firm.[13]

Beware of the dogs! Beware of the cowardly workers! Beware of the Incision![14] It is we who are the Circumcision, we who are in service to God's Spirit and exult in Jesus Christ, and place no reliance on the physical,

---

11 Referring to the pagan practice of mutual congratulation at the close of the service in the temples when the ritual was ended, a ritual involving sacrifice and the pouring of a libation.

12 Epaphroditus was a Philippian who had been sent by his community to Rome with gifts and messages for Paul in prison there.

13 The tone of the letter changes abruptly at this point, and what follows was due to problems Paul had with the Jewish adherents of Jesus in Rome, on doctrinal grounds.

14 'Zealots for the Law' had been *incising* themselves into Paul's Gentile communities to cause them to become Jews. 'Dogs' refers to immoral non-Jews. At the entrance to Roman houses the legend *Cave Canem* (Beware of the Dog) was often to be read. Paul is warning against both licentious Gentiles and fanatical Jews.

though I could well do so. If anyone else thinks he can
5 rely on the physical, I even more so, circumcised as I was
on the eighth day, of the race of Israel, the tribe of
Benjamin, a Hebrew sprung from Hebrews, in obser-
vances a Pharisee, as regards zeal a persecutor of the
Community, as regards legal rectitude irreproachable.

But the very things that were an asset to me, these I
regard as a dead loss where Christ is concerned. Indeed,
I definitely regard everything as a dead loss because of
the excellence of the knowledge of Christ Jesus my lord,
for whom all is well lost and I regard it as so much
rubbish, that I may gain Christ, and be found in him, not
with my own rectitude which derives from law, but with
that which is through faith in Christ, the rectitude which
10 derives from God on a basis of faith. My concern is to
know him, and the power of his resurrection, to have
kinship with his sufferings, entering as closely as possible into the manner of his death, if by any means I may
attain the resurrection from the dead. There is no question of my having already obtained it, or of having
already been perfected. But I pursue, if I may but overtake, even as I was overtaken by Christ Jesus. Brothers, I
do not reckon myself to have overtaken as yet. But there
is this at least, forgetting what lies behind, and reaching
out to what lies ahead, I drive hard at the mark for the
15 prize of God's high calling in Christ Jesus.[15] Let those
who would be perfect be thus minded; but if you feel
differently God will surely make this plain to you. The
main thing is, to whatever extent we have forged ahead,
to keep on the same course.

Copy me, brothers, and pay close attention to those
who behave as I have set the example. For there are
many, as I have often told you, and now tell you even
with tears, who behave as enemies of Christ's cross,
whose end is destruction, whose god is their appetite,
and whose glory is in their shame, whose minds are on
20 earthly matters. But our form of government originates
in heaven, from which source we expect as deliverer the
Lord Jesus Christ, who will transform the body of our
humble state so that it corresponds to his glorious body
by the power which enables him to bring everything
under his control.

---

15 The allusion is to Greek foot races and their finishing post.

4.1   Therefore, dear and desired brothers, my joy and crown, stand fast in the Master, my dear ones. I beg Euodia and Syntyche to be of one mind in the Master. Yes, I also ask you, true Synsyge,[16] to bring these sisters in faith together, who aided me in the News with Clement and the other co-workers of mine, whose names are in the Book of Life.[17]

5   Rejoice in the Master always. I repeat, rejoice! Let your moderation be known to everyone. The Master is at hand. Have no anxiety, but always make your requests known to God by prayer and supplication with thanksgiving; and God's peace which towers above[18] all reasoning, will stand guard over your minds and thoughts in Christ Jesus.

Finally, brothers, whatever is honest, whatever is reputable, whatever is just, whatever is pure, whatever is likeable, whatever is elevated, if there is something virtuous or laudable, concentrate on such things. Practice all you have learnt and received and heard and seen in me, and the God of peace be with you.

10   I have rejoiced in the Master greatly that now at last your thought for me could find fresh expression, for indeed you had always thought that way but lacked opportunity. It is not out of considerations of want that I am saying this, for I have learnt to manage however I am situated. I have had experience of being in reduced circumstances and of having ample. I have been through the whole curriculum, to be replete and to be hungry, to have ample and to go short. I can cope with everything by him who strengthens me. You have none the less done a kindness in associating yourselves with my difficulties.

15   Let me tell you Philippians that in the early days of the News, when I left Macedonia, there was not a single community which associated itself with me in the matter of giving and gaining other than yourselves, so that even at Thessalonica you sent once and again a contribution for my needs. It is not that I am looking for gifts. What I am looking for is the yield that swells your credit account. I have indeed enough and to spare. I am fully

16 The name Synsyge means 'Yoke-fellow'. Paul asks him to act up to his name in reconciling two quarrelling ladies.
17 cf *Exod* 32:32.
18 Like a dominating and protective fortress.

supplied, having received from Epaphroditus what your means allowed, a sweet-smelling perfume, an acceptable sacrifice, well-pleasing to God. My God, in turn, will supply every need of yours in Christ Jesus out of his wealth in glory. To God our Father be praise for ever and ever. Amen.

20

Give my regards to every saint in Christ Jesus. The brothers who are with me send you their regards. All the saints send you their regards, particularly those of Caesar's household.

May the loving-kindness of the Lord Jesus Christ be with your spirit.

To the Communities in Asia

The Ephesian Copy
(Probably written from Rome in AD 61 or 62)

1.1   Paul, by the will of God an envoy of Christ Jesus, to the saints resident in [*Ephesus*][1] and to the faithful in Christ Jesus. May peace and prosperity be yours from God our Father and the Lord Jesus Christ.

Blessed be the God and Father of our Lord Jesus Christ, who has blessed us with every spiritual blessing in the heavenly spheres in Christ, just as in him God made choice of us in love[2] before the universe was founded, that we should be holy and blameless in his
5   presence. For he designated us in advance for adoption as his own through Jesus Christ, as it pleased his will, to the great renown of his loving-kindness with which he has favoured us in the Beloved. In Christ we have redemption by his blood, absolution from transgression, by virtue of the wealth of loving-kindness which God has lavished upon us, in having made known to us in all wisdom and understanding,[3] as it pleased him, the secret of his intention, which he purposed in Christ, for
10   that ultimate Government when he shall have brought everything under Christ's jurisdiction both in heaven and on earth. Yes, under him in whom we too have our allotted place, assigned to us in advance, according to

---

1 While in some MSS Ephesus is given as the destination, in others it is omitted. The letter is of a general character intended for communities in Asia not founded by Paul, of which he had information, probably through Epaphras (see the letter to Colossae). These may particularly have been Laodicea and Hierapolis.

2 Jewish *Ahabah* prayer, "Blessed art thou, O Lord, who hast chosen thy people Israel in love" (AJP p 46).

3 Jewish *Amidah* prayer (*Bened* IV), "Thou favourest man with knowledge" (AJP pp 39–40).

the plan of God, who makes everything work out in accordance with his design and intention; so that we should be to his great renown who [as Jews] set our hope in advance on Christ.[4] In him also you [Gentiles] after hearing the Message of Truth, the News of your salvation, and after believing in him, were sealed with the holy Spirit of promise which is the advance payment on our inheritance, the promise to redeem what was purchased, to God's great renown.

15   Consequently, I too, having heard of the faith you have in the Lord Jesus, which is common to all the saints, never cease giving thanks on your account, making mention of you in my prayers, that the God of our Lord Jesus Christ,[5] the Father of glory, may give you a spirit of wisdom and revelation to acquire knowledge of him. I pray that with your mental vision illumined you may know the nature of the hope of God's calling, what is the glorious wealth of his inheritance in the saints, and the surpassing extent of his power available to us who have believed. This was indicated by the operation of the

20   mighty force God employed with Christ in raising him from the dead and seating him at his right hand in the heavenly spheres high above every entity that has existence not only in this world but in that which is to come. He has indeed "put everything under his feet",[6] and over and above has given him headship of the Community, which is his Body, the full dimension of him who fills the entire universe.[7]

2.1   You [Gentiles] too were once dead in the trespasses and sins in which you lived in conformity with the Aeons of this world, the Archon[8] of the government of the lower atmosphere, the spirit of him who now animates

---

4 ie the Messiah. The whole passage relates to the ultimate Messianic Government of the Cosmos under the Son of Man.

5 See n 1. Early Christian faith carefully distinguished Christ from God (cf *Acts* 2:22, 7:55).

6 *Ps* 8:6.

7 It was believed by the Jewish mystics that the Heavenly Man (Son of Man), in whose likeness Adam was created, had reached from earth to heaven. Christ with the Church are here the Head and Body of this cosmic figure (see further n 16). *Maaseh Bereshith* (The Mystery of Creation), dealing with *Gen* 1–3, was one of the departments of Jewish mysticism in which Paul had been trained.

8 "Aeon", "Archon". Spirit powers subordinate to Beliar, the Evil Force controlling the existing world order. To understand Paul a knowledge of Pharisee and Essene occult teaching is indispensable.

the Children of Disobedience. We likewise [all we Jews] were once tarred with the same brush in the indulgence of our physical passions, fulfilling our physical desires and inclinations, and by nature Children of Wrath like the rest. But God being full of compassion because of the

5   great love he had for us even when were dead in trespasses, has brought us all back to life with Christ – it is by mercy that you have been spared – and has raised us up together, and seated us together in the heavenly spheres in Christ Jesus. For it is by mercy that you have been spared through faith, not in any way by your own efforts, nor by your own deeds – it is God's gift so that no

10   one should boast. We are entirely his handiwork, created in Christ Jesus for those good deeds with which God pre-arranged that we should be occupied.

So bear in mind that you were once Gentiles in the physical sense, who are termed the Uncircumcision by those termed in respect of an operation in the flesh the Circumcision, because at that time you were without benefit of Christ, aliens to the body politic of Israel, and strangers to the covenants of promise. But now in Christ Jesus you who were once far off have been brought near by the blood of Christ. For he is our peacemaker, who has united both Jew and Gentile, having abolished the

15   dividing partition-wall,[9] and having in his person neutralised the cause of enmity, the Law of command-ments set down in ordinances, so that the two should in him be welded into one new man. Thus he has reconciled both to God by one body through the cross, having in his own person killed the enmity, and by his coming proclaimed "peace to you the far off, and peace to the near",[10] because through him by one Spirit we both have access to the Father.

So now you are no longer strangers and foreigners, but fellow-citizens of the saints, parts of God's house, hav-

20   ing been built upon the foundation of the Envoys and Prophets with Christ Jesus himself as the coping-stone, where each block having been closely fitted together[11]

9 The allusion is to the balustrade in the Temple at Jerusalem which separated the Court of Israel from the Court of the Gentiles. Gentiles who trespassed into the Court of Israel did so on pain of death as warning notices proclaimed. The Gentile believer in Christ, according to Paul, has acquired Israelite status.

10 *Isa* 59:19.

11 In the Temple stones were fitted without mortar.

grows course upon course into a sacred fane in the Master, into which you too have been built as a spiritual abode of God.

3.1   To this end I, Paul, am the prisoner of Jesus for you Gentiles. You must surely have heard of the administration of God's mercy granted me for your benefit, how by revelation he acquainted me with the secret, as I have previously stated it above. From this you may gather

5   how well-versed I am in the Messianic Mystery, which in previous generations was never made known to mankind as now revealed under inspiration to God's holy envoys and prophets, the secret that by the News the Gentiles were to be joint-heirs, jointly incorporated [in Israel], and joint participants in the promise in Christ Jesus. Of this News I was made a minister, by the gift of God's mercy granted me in accordance with the operation of his power. To me, the least of all the saints, was this privilege given, that I should proclaim to the Gentiles the inexhaustible wealth of Christ, and publish the details of the secret kept hidden from the Aeons[12] by God

10   who created all things; so that the Wisdom of God in all its multitudinous aspects should now be made known through the Community to the Rulers and Authorities in the heavenly spheres, in accordance with the Plan of the Ages which God formed in Christ Jesus our Master. In him, by faith in him, we enter God's presence boldly and confidently. So I beg you not to take hardly my trials on your behalf, which are an honour to you.

15   To this end I bend my knees to the Father, from whom every order of being both in heaven and on earth derives its existence, that in accordance with the wealth of his glory he may grant you by his Spirit to be powerfully strengthened in the inner self, that the Christ may make his abode in your minds by faith, that being deep-rooted and well-grounded in love you may be able to grasp with all the saints what is the Breadth, the Length, the Depth and the Height, that you may know, what indeed surpasses knowledge, the love of Christ, that you may be filled with the immensity of God.

20   Now to him who is supremely powerful to do infinitely more than we can ask or think, in accordance

---

12 According to Paul it had not previously been disclosed that Gentiles, by faith, were to form an integral part of the New Israel, the redeemed People of God. Paul had been the recipient of this revelation.

with the power that operates in us, to him be glory in the
Community and in Christ Jesus to all generations for
ever and ever. Amen.

4.1   I entreat you therefore, I the Master's prisoner, to
behave in a manner worthy of the calling with which you
have been called, with all humility and gentleness, with
long-suffering, being patient with one another in love,
striving to keep unity of spirit by the binding force of
peace. There is one Body and Spirit, just as you were
5   called with one expectation of your calling, one Master,
one Faith, one Immersion, one God and Father of all, and
through all, and in all.

And to each one of us there has been granted some
favour corresponding to the extent of Christ's bounty, as
it is stated, "Having ascended on high he made captivity
captive, and bestowed gifts on men".[13] That he ascended
implies that he also descended into the lower regions of
10   the earth.[14] He who descended is the same as he who
ascended to the uppermost part of the heavens,[15] that he
might fill the universe. To some he gave gifts as envoys,
some as prophets, some as preachers, some as pastors
and teachers, for the training of the saints, for the work
of administration, and the development of the Body of
Christ, until we all reach unity of faith and knowledge of
the Son of God, the Perfect Man, the measure of the
stature of the full-grown Christ.[16] No longer should we
be infants, tossed on the waves and swept this way and
that by every wind of doctrine by the facile knavery of
15   men practised in the contrivance of deceit; but speaking
the truth in love we should grow up collectively to him,
Christ, who is the Head, from whom the whole Body –
closely joined together and knit by every connecting part
has its growth promoted for the Body's harmonious
development.

This then I say and solemnly declare in the Master,
that you are no longer to behave as the Gentiles behave
in the levity of their minds. They, having their intellect
dimmed, being alien to the divine life through their

---

13 *Ps* 68:18.
14 In the early Christian *Odes of Solomon* the descent of Christ to the under-
world is described as the Head going down to the Feet (*Ode* 23:14).
15 Seven heavens, in layers, were postulated.
16 Here the Body is to grow up to the Head, to the stature of the universe-
filling Man. See JE Art. *Adam Kadmon* (the Archetypal Man).

ignorance and the obtuseness of their minds, being lost
to decent feelings, have given themselves over to licentiousness, to indulge in every kind of impurity with

20   avidity. But you have not so learnt what Christ means –
that is, if you have attended to him and been instructed
by him, as the truth is in Jesus – namely, that you should
abandon what accords with the former mode of life of the
old degenerate personality with its treacherous lusts,
that you should have the temper of your minds
renovated, and put on the new personality fashioned
after God in rectitude and the sanctity of truth.

25   So abandoning falsehood "let each speak the truth to
his fellow."[17] "Be angry, yet sin not."[18] Let not the sun
go down on your anger, nor give the Devil his opportunity. Let him that stole steal no more. Instead let him toil,
putting his hand to worthy employment that he may
have something to give to any who are in need. Let no
foul language pass your lips, only what is good for some
constructive purpose, that it may give pleasure to the

30   listeners. And do not grieve God's holy Spirit by which
you have been sealed for the Day of Redemption. Put
aside all bitterness and passion, anger, vituperation and
abuse, and every kind of malice. Instead be kindly
disposed to one another, large-hearted, merciful to each

5.1   other as God has been merciful to you in Christ. Follow
God's example, then, as dear children, and behave with
affection, just as Christ loved you and offered himself for
you as "an offering and sacrifice of pleasing odour to
God". But let there be no mention among you of vice and
any kind of impurity or lechery, as befits saints, nor
obscenity, levity, or facetiousness, which are unbecom-
ing. Preferably let there be thanksgiving. You surely
know this, that no immoral person, nor impure, nor
rapacious (which means an idol-worshipper), shall have
any inheritance in the Kingdom of Christ and of God.

5   Let no one beguile you with empty words, for because
of this the wrath of God falls upon the Children of
Disobedience. Do not be of their company therefore; for
though once you belonged to darkness, now in the
Master you belong to the light. Behave like Children of

17 *Zech* 8:6.
18 *Ps* 37:8.

the Light[19] – the Light that has its fruits in every kind of
10   goodness, in uprightness and honesty – approving what
is acceptable to the Master. And have no fellowship with
the unfruitful works of darkness, but rather refute them,
though it is shameful to speak of the things such people
do in secret. For whatever is refuted has light thrown
upon it, since all visibility is due to light. This is why it is
stated,

> Rouse yourself, sleeper,
> And arise from the dead,
> And Christ shall shine on you![20]

15   Pay strict attention, therefore, to the way you behave,
as wise people, not unwise, using the time profitably, for
these are evil days. So do not be stupid, but compre-
hending, as to what are the Master's wishes. And do not
get drunk with wine, in which is sottishness, but be filled
spiritually, chanting psalms and hymns and spiritual
odes, singing and making melody in your hearts to the
20   Lord, above all invariably giving thanks to God the
Father in the name of our Lord Jesus Christ.

Be submissive to one another in the fear of Christ, the
wives to their husbands as to the Master; for man is the
head of woman as Christ is the head of the Community,
being as he is the preserver of the Body. But as the
Community is subject to Christ, so should wives be to
25   their husbands in every way. Husbands, love your
wives, even as Christ loved the Community and gave
himself for her sake, that he might consecrate her,
having been cleansed by the ritual bath of water,[21] so to
speak, that he might take the Community to himself, as a
bride to be proud of, not having a spot[22] or wrinkle, or
anything of the kind, as well as being chaste and unblemished. So ought husbands to cherish their wives as their
own bodies. He who cherishes his wife cherishes himself; for no one ever hated his own flesh, but cares for and
30   tends it, as indeed Christ does the Community, since we

---

19 A term used by the Jewish Essenes to denote the Elect.
20 Like the Essenes the early Christians used to sing hymns at dawn in praise
of the 'Sun of righteousness' (cf *Mal* 4:2). These lines may be from one such
hymn. See also *Jn* 1:1–17.
21 Baptism, under the figure of the ritual bath of purification taken by Jewish
women, here prior to the marriage ceremony, *kiddushin* (consecration).
22 cf *Cant* 4:7.

are members of his body. "For this cause a man shall leave father and mother, and unite with his wife, and the two shall be one flesh."[23] This is a great mystery: I am speaking here of the relationship between Christ and the Community. Just so you too, every one of you, should thus love his wife as himself; and the wife should respect her husband.

6.1   Children, obey your parents, for it is rightly said, "Honour your father and your mother",[24] which is the first commandment with a promise attached to it, namely, "that it may be well with you, and that you may live long on the earth". And you fathers, do not provoke your children, but bring them up in the discipline and admonition of the Lord.[25]

5   Slaves, obey those who in the physical sense are your masters with fear and trembling in singleness of mind as you obey Christ, not with service meant to catch the eye, like those who want to ingratiate themselves, but as slaves of Christ carrying out God's behests. Give service with real goodwill, as having the Lord in mind rather than men, knowing that each one, whether slave or freeman, has whatever good he may do treasured up by the Lord. And you masters, act in the same way towards your slaves, refraining from threats, knowing that both their and your Master is in heaven, and that with him there is no partiality.

10   Finally, make yourselves strong in the Lord and in the power of his might. Array yourselves in the full armour of God, so that you may stand up to the artfulness of the Adversary. For we are not contending with mortals but with angelic Rulers and Authorities, with the Overlords of the Dark State, the spirit forces of evil in the heavenly spheres.

Therefore take to yourselves the full armour of God that you may be able to withstand in the evil day, and having completely overcome, to go on standing. Stand, therefore, with your loins girded with truth,[26] clad in the

15   corselet of rectitude,[27] with your feet shod with the sureness of the News of peace.[28] To complete your

23 *Gen* 2:24.
24 *Exod* 20:12.
25 cf *Gen* 18:19.
26 cf *Isa* 11:5.
27 cf *Isa* 59:17.
28 cf *Isa* 52:7.

equipment, hold before you the shield of faith with which you will be able to extinguish the flaming darts of the Evil One, and take the helmet of preservation, and the sword of the Spirit – which means God's Word.

Pray at all times in the Spirit with every kind of petition and supplication for all the saints, being intent on this with all diligence and entreaty, and on my behalf that fluent speech may be given me boldly to make known 20 the Mystery on account of which I am an ambassador in chains,[29] that even so placed I may speak as boldly as it behoves me to speak.

But so that you too may know the state of my affairs, how I fare, Tychicus,[30] that dear brother and loyal minister in the Master, will inform you. I have dispatched him to you for this express purpose, that you may know my concerns and that he may cheer your hearts.

Peace be with the brothers, and affection with faith, from God the Father and the Lord Jesus Christ. May well-being be the portion of all who love our Lord Jesus Christ unfeignedly.

29 At this time Paul was in Rome as prisoner awaiting trial.
30 See *II Tim* 4:12.

To the Community at Colossae

(Place and Time of Writing as for the last Letter)

1.1   Paul, by the will of God an envoy of Jesus Christ, with brother Timotheus, to the saints and faithful brothers in Christ at Colossae. May peace and prosperity be yours from God our Father.

I thank God, the Father of our Lord Jesus Christ, and invariably pray for you, having heard of your faith in Christ Jesus and the affection you have for all the saints
5   on account of the hope held in heavenly reserve for you. This Hope you first heard expressed in the True Message of the News, which reached you, as it has reached everywhere else in the world, producing fruit and increasing – again as it has done among you – from the very day you heard it. You then became truly conscious of God's mercy as you learnt it from our dear fellow-servant Epaphras. He is a faithful minister of Christ on your behalf, who also has informed me of your spiritual affection.

Accordingly, I too, from the day I heard, have never ceased to pray for you, and to request that you may be filled with the knowledge of God's will in all wisdom and
10   spiritual comprehension, so as to behave in a manner worthy of the Master to his entire satisfaction by every good deed you do. You are thus producing fruit and increasing in the knowledge of God, endued by his glorious power with every capacity for much patience and long-suffering with joy.

I give thanks to the Father, who has qualified you to share the lot of the saints in Light, who has rescued us from the dominion of Darkness and transferred us to the Kingdom of his dear Son, by whom we obtain redemp-

15 tion, absolution from our sins. He[1] is the image of the Unseen God, the firstborn of all creation, that everything in heaven and earth might be founded on him, seen and unseen alike, whether angelic Thrones or Lordships or Rulers or Authorities. Everything was created through him and for him. He is the antecedent of everything, and on him everything was framed.[2] So also is he Head of the Body, the Community, that is to say, the fount and origin of it, the firstborn from the dead, that in every connexion he might take precedence. For it pleased God that by him

20 the whole should be governed, and through him – his making peace through the blood of his cross – to bring everything once more into harmony with the Divine self, whether on earth or in heaven.

You yourselves were formerly alienated and hostile in attitude when you were engaged in evil deeds; but now Christ has reconciled you to God by the death of his physical body, so as to present you before God chaste, blameless and irreproachable, assuming that you remain firm and unmoved in the Faith, and do not deviate from the Hope of the News which you have heard, which has been proclaimed to every creature under heaven, and of which I, Paul, was made a minister.

So I rejoice in my sufferings for your sake, and make good in my flesh the deficiencies of the Messianic Woes[3]

25 for the sake of Christ's Body, namely the Community, of which I was made a minister, in accordance with God's mandate granted me for you, to give effect to God's message, the secret kept hidden from all the ages and generations, but now published to his saints. To them God would make known what wealth of glory this secret holds for the Gentiles, namely Christ in you, the expectation of glory. He it is whom we proclaim, advising everyone and teaching everyone with all wisdom, that we may present everyone perfect in Christ.

This is what I toil for, striving with his energy who so

2.1 powerfully motivates me. Indeed, I wish you to know

---

1 As the Archetypal Man (cf *Gen* 1:26).
2 The belief was that the Archetypal Man (Son of Man), the Messiah (Christ) Above had been incarnated in Jesus as the Messiah Below, having in the Beginning served as the Expression (Word) of God on which the Universe was framed. The concept emanated from mystical Jewish teaching.
3 Known in Jewish teaching as the 'Pangs of Messiah' which would precede the birth of the Messianic Era.

what a severe trial I am undergoing on your account, and on account of those of Laodicea, and of as many others as have never seen me personally, that their minds may be encouraged, being confirmed in their love and in the solid wealth of absolute certainty in knowledge of God's secret, yes, of Christ himself, in whom are hidden all the treasures of wisdom and knowledge. I say this in case anyone should mislead you with specious arguments.

5 For even if I am absent physically I am nevertheless with you in spirit, observing with pleasure your good order and the solidarity of your faith in Christ.

As, therefore, you have accepted Christ Jesus as Master, behave in his way, base yourselves and build yourselves on him, and maintain yourselves in the Faith as you have been taught it, excelling in it with thanksgiving.

Take care that no one gets hold of you with philosophy and worthless craft belonging to human tradition, to the elemental forces of the world instead of to Christ; for it is in him that the immensity of the Divine Wisdom cor-

10 porately dwells, and it is in him – Head of all Rulers and Authorities – that you are made complete. It is in him too that you have been pared by a circumcision not man-made, by the stripping away of the physical body, by Christ's kind of circumcision, being buried with him by immersion. In him equally you have been raised up by faith in the might of God who raised him from the dead.

So you who were dead in transgressions, and in your physical uncircumcision, God has brought to life with him, having forgiven us all our transgressions. He not only cancelled the writ against us with its stipulations, which were adverse to us, but also took it away entirely,

15 nailing it to the cross. After having despoiled the angelic Rulers and Authorities, he paraded them in public by the cross.[4]

Let no one judge you, therefore, in matters of food and drink, or in such a matter as a Jewish festival, New Moon, or sabbath, which represent only a shadow of things to come, and of which Christ is the substance. Let no one arbitrarily influence you to fast and engage in the worship of angels,[5] inducing you to share his visions,

4 Like prisoners in a victor's procession. Paul takes the view that the Law had been drawn up by the angelic Powers. And see *Gal* 3:13, 19.
5 The heavenly hierarchy of the Jewish mystics.

being vainly puffed up by his physical mind and not holding to the Head, from whom the whole Body, connected and integrated by the joints and ligaments, grows in God's way.

20   If you have died with Christ to the Elemental Forces of the Cosmos, why, as though still living in the world, are you controlled by stipulations – "Do not handle! Do not taste! Do not touch!" – which imply that everything contaminates[6] by its use, in accordance with human commandments and doctrines? Such prescriptions, indeed, seem to have some sense in them in subordination of the will, fasting and asceticism, but they are not really efficacious against human indulgence.

3.1   If, therefore, you have been raised up with Christ, seek the things that are on high, where Christ is, seated at God's right hand. Set your minds on the things that are above, not on what is on earth; for you have died, and your life has been secreted with Christ in God. When Christ, who enshrines our life, is revealed, then you too will be revealed with him in glory.

5   So treat your organs on earth as dead for fornication, impurity, lust, unlawful desire, and rapacity (which means idol-worship), things that bring down the wrath of God. In such things you too once indulged when you led that kind of life. But now you must discard all alike, anger, rage, malice, abuse, foul language. Do not lie to one another, having divested yourselves of the former

10   man and his deeds, and having put on the new man, renovated in knowledge, in conformity with the likeness of God who created him, where there can be no question of Gentile[7] and Jew, circumcision and uncircumcision, Barbarian, Scythian, slave or freeman, but of Christ wholly and completely.

Put on, therefore, as God's Elect, saints and beloved ones, feelings of compassion, benevolence, humility, gentleness, long-suffering, bearing with one another and forgiving one another should any have a complaint against another. As the Lord has forgiven you, do you also forgive. And over and above these qualities put on love, which represents the band[8] that gives the finishing

---

6 Or "sends to perdition".
7 Paul commonly uses the word 'Greek', as here, to represent non-Jews.
8 ie the belt or girdle which completes the attire.

15   touch. And let Christ's peace direct your minds, the peace to which you were called as one Body. And be thankful. Let the Message of Christ dwell in you richly in all its wisdom, teaching and admonishing one another graciously by psalms, hymns and spiritual odes, singing to God in your hearts. And whatever you do, by word or deed, do it all in the name of the Lord Jesus, giving thanks to God the Father by him.

Wives, be submissive to your husbands as is befitting in the Master. Husbands, love your wives and do not

20   treat them harshly. Children, obey your parents in everything, for this is well-pleasing to the Lord.[9] Fathers, do not fret your children, in case they should be discouraged. Slaves, in everything obey those who in the physical sense are your masters, not with service that catches the eye like those who wish to ingratiate themselves, but in singleness of mind, fearing the Lord. Whatever you do, do it with real goodwill, as having the Lord in mind rather than men, knowing that you will receive from the Lord the recompense that is due. Serve

25   the Lord Christ; for he who does wrong will be paid back for his wrong-doing, and there is no partiality shown.

4.1   Masters, treat your slaves equitably and fairly, knowing that you too have a Master in heaven.

Apply yourselves constantly to prayer, being incited to it by thankfulness. At the same time pray for me, that God may give me opportunity to speak, to declare the secret of Christ on account of which I am fettered, that I

5   should disclose it as it behoves me to speak. Behave with circumspection towards those who are 'outside', using the time profitably. Invariably let your speech be gracious, flavoured with salt, that you may know how to answer all and sundry.

As to my affairs, Tychicus, that dear brother and loyal minister and fellow-servant in the Master, will fully inform you. I have dispatched him to you for this express purpose, that you may know how I fare and that he may cheer your hearts, and with him faithful and dear brother Onesimus,[10] who is one of yourselves. They will tell you of all that goes on here.[11]

10   My fellow-prisoner Aristarchus sends you his regards,

9 See *Exod* 20:12.
10 See the letter to *Philemon*.
11 ie in Rome, where Paul was a prisoner.

as does Barnabas's kinsman Mark (about whom you have been advised: welcome him should he visit you), and so does Jesus known as Justus. They belong to the Circumcision, and they alone have been my co-workers for the Kingdom of God: they have been a great comfort to me. Epaphras, one of yourselves, a servant of Christ Jesus, sends you his regards. Invariably he contends for you at prayer times that you may stand, sound and fully assured, by the whole will of God. I can testify that he has put up a great fight for you, and for those of Laodicea and Hierapolis. Dear Doctor Luke sends you his regards, and so does Demas.

15   Give my regards to the brothers at Laodicea, also to Nympha and the community in her house. When this letter has been read by you arrange also for it to be read in the Laodician community, and get their letter from Laodicea,[12] that you too may read it. And tell Archippus, "See to it that you carry out the ministry you have received in the Master!"

My regards in my own hand,
PAUL.
Remember my fetters![13] Wishing you every happiness.

---

12 Either the letter to the Asians known as the letter to the *Ephesians*, or another which has not been preserved.
13 ie in prayer.

To Philemon

(Written from Rome about AD 62)

1.1 Paul, prisoner of Christ Jesus, with brother
     Timotheus, to our dear friend and co-worker
     Philemon, to our sister Apphia, to our fellow-
     campaigner Archippus,[1] and to the community in
     your house. May peace and prosperity be yours from
     God our Father and the Lord Jesus Christ.

   Invariably I thank God, making mention of you in my
5 prayers, learning of the affection and loyalty you have
   for the Lord Jesus and for all the saints, whereby the
   fellowship of your faith may prove effective in securing
   knowledge of every good thing that is ours in Christ. I
   have indeed been given much happiness and encouragement by your affection, brother, because through you
   the hearts of the saints have been refreshed.

   Consequently, while regarding myself in Christ as
   quite at liberty to insist on the point, yet out of affecton I
   prefer to appeal to you, being such as I am, that old man
   Paul, and also at present a prisoner of Christ Jesus.

10 It is for a son of mine I appeal to you, one whom I have
   begotten in my bonds, Onesimus, who was previously
   worthless to you, but now is of very real worth both to
   you and me. I have sent him back to you, which means
   that I have parted with my own heart. I would much
   rather have kept him with me, so that he might have
   served me instead of you in the bonds of the News; but I
   did not wish to do anything without your assent, in case
   your kindness might seem an obligation instead of being
15 voluntary. Perhaps the reason he was parted from you
   for a while may be that you might have him wholly ever
   after, no longer as just a slave, but over and above a
   slave, as a dear brother, particularly to me, but how

---

1 Mentioned at the close of the letter to Colossae.

much more so to you with a physical tie as well as in the Master.

So if you regard me as a kinsman, receive him as you would myself. If he has wronged you, or owes you anything, put that down to my account. I, Paul, put this in my own handwriting, "I will make restitution in full". Need I say to you that actually you owe me your own

20   self? Well, brother, let me have some 'benefit'[2] out of you in the Master? Refresh my heart in Christ.

I am writing to you in full confidence of your compliance, knowing that you will do even more than I ask. At the same time prepare to have me also as your guest, for I anticipate that through your prayers I shall be granted to you.

My fellow-prisoner Epaphras[3] sends you his regards in Christ Jesus. So do my fellow-workers[4] Mark, Aristarchus, Demas and Luke.

25   The loving-kindness of our Lord Jesus Christ be with your spirit.

---

2 Playing on the name Onesimus, meaning 'beneficial'. Paul pleads most movingly on behalf of this runaway slave, who has become a Christian. Instead of being beneficial Onesimus had proved worthless to Philemon.
3 See above, *Col* 4:12.
4 All these individuals are referred to in the letter to *Colossae*.

To Titus

(Probably written from Rome in AD 62)

1.1   Paul, servant of God, and envoy of Jesus Christ for purposes of faith in God, and for the knowledge of the Truth, as it concerns devoutness in prospect of Eternal Life, which the never false God promised in the remote past and in due course revealed by his Message with the proclamation of which I have been entrusted by order of God our Saviour, to Titus my true son in our common faith. May peace and prosperity be yours from God the Father and Christ Jesus our deliverer.

5   I left you in Crete with good reason, to tie up what loose ends were left, and to ordain elders for each town as I directed you, assuming there is someone of blameless character, husband of one wife, having believing children, someone not open to the charge of profligacy
10 or disorderliness.[1] For there are many disorderly vaporisers and bamboozlers, particularly those from the Circumcision, people who must be muzzled, the kind who subvert whole households, teaching things they have no business to do from mercenary motives. One of themselves, an exponent of their own,[2] has said, "The Cretans, ever cheats, brute beasts and idle windbags".[3] That is a true description. For that very reason rebuke them sharply, that they may be sound in the Faith, paying no heed to Judaic myths and injunctions of men

1 The following passage, verses 7–9, appears to be an addition. "For the supervisor (ie bishop) should be irreproachable, as God's appointed steward, not domineering, not irritable, not a tippler, not a brawler, not mercenary, but open-handed, one who cares for goodness, is discreet, just, consecrated, disciplined, a close adherent of the trustworthy Message in terms of the Teaching, so that he may be able to exhort by sound instruction and confute opponents."
2 Epimenides, Cretan poet and philosopher.
3 The poem of Epimenides on *Oracles*, quoted by Callimachus, *Hymn to Zeus*, 8.

15   who have turned away from the truth. To the pure everything is pure, but to the polluted and unbelieving nothing is pure, because both their minds and consciences are warped. They profess to know God, but by their actions they disown him, being disgusting and mutinous, hopeless for any useful service.

2.1   It is for you to state what is consistent with sound teaching, to tell the older men to be sober, dignified, discreet sound in faith, in love, in constancy. Tell the older women similarly to maintain a condition suited to a reverent nature, not to be spiteful, not addicted to drink, givers of good advice, so that they may influence the young women to be devoted to husband and children, to be sensible, chaste, domesticated, decent, submissive to their husbands, that God's Message may not come into disrepute. In the same way exhort the young men to be temperate. In every connexion you yourself should set an example of good behaviour, by purity of teaching, plain sense, and sound principles that cannot be impugned, so that he who is against us may respect our

5   position, finding nothing detrimental to say about us.[4]

10   Slaves should be in subjection to their masters, giving entire satisfaction, not answering back, not pilfering, but giving proof of complete trustworthiness, that in every way they may be a credit to the teaching of God our Saviour. For God's mercy has manifested itself for the salvation of all men, instructing us that, abandoning impiety and wordly passions, we should live temperately, justly and devoutly in the present time, waiting for the blessed Hope and visible manifestation of the glory of the Great God, and of our Deliverer Jesus Christ, who gave himself for us to free us from all our iniquities and to purify for himself a special people eager

15   for good deeds.[5]

Declare these things, exhort and reprove, with every possible authority. Let no one treat you casually. Remind

3.1   them to be subject to rulers and authorities, to be law-abiding, ready for every useful service, in no way abusive, to be free from pugnacity, equable, always exhibiting a mild demeanour towards everyone. I myself was once lacking in sense, ungovernable, erratic, a slave to various passions and pleasures, spending my time in

4 cf *Acts* 28:22. It is clear that already the Christians were in bad odour.
5 cf *Ezek* 37:23: *Deut* 14:2.

resentment and jealousy, gloomy, hating others. But when the goodness and benevolence of God our Saviour became clear, not because of any righteous actions I had performed, but in accordance with his mercy, he saved me by the washing and the renovating power of the holy Spirit which he lavished upon me richly through Jesus Christ our Deliverer; so that being exonerated by that act of grace I became an heir in accordance with the expectation of Eternal Life.

10   This is a true saying, and I want you to be very positive about it, that "Those who have believed in God should be concerned to offer themselves for honest employment". This is a proper and helpful thing for men to do. But avoid foolish issues and genealogies, wrangles and legal quibbles;[6] for these are unhelpful and senseless. Have no more to do with the dissentient man after giving him a first and second warning, seeing that anyone like this has turned away and erred deliberately, and stands self-condemned.

When I despatch Artemas to you, or Tychicus,[7] do your utmost to come to me at Nicopolis, for I have decided to pass the winter there.[8] Afford the lawyer Zenas and also Apollos every facility for their journey, so that they are short of nothing. Our people must really learn to offer themselves for honest employment to meet essential needs, so that they are not unproductive.

15   All here send you their regards. My regards to those who truly esteem me.

Wishing you all every happiness.

6 When Paul was a prisoner in Rome there was conflict between his views and those especially of the Jewish members of the Christian Community there who had once formed the majority. See *II Tim* 4:14–17. Paul seems to be referring to such points of disagreement (cf *I Tim* 1:6–11).

7 Tychicus was bearer of the letters to Asia (Ephesians) and Colossae. It is suggested that the Nicopolis where Paul proposed to spend the winter, assuming he was released, was the one in Epirus on the western coast of Greece.

8 At the time of writing Paul anticipated that he would be released by the Roman government (see *Phil* 1:24–26 and especially *Philemon* 22). But in this he was thwarted by fate.

To Timotheus (1)
(Probably written from Rome in AD 63)

1.1   Paul, envoy of Christ Jesus by appointment of God our
Saviour and of Christ Jesus our Hope, to Timotheus
my true son in faith. May prosperity, mercy and peace
be yours from God the Father and Christ Jesus our
Master.

As I begged you when you were leaving for
Macedonia,[1] do stay on at Ephesus to impress on some
there not to teach different doctrine, not to concern
themselves with myths and interminable genealogies,
matters which raise issues rather than promote the
5   divine government which rests on faith. The essence of
the precept still is love,[2] love out of a pure heart, a clear
conscience, and unfeigned faith. From these some, having missed the mark, have gone off at a tangent into
senseless talk, wanting to be teachers of the Law, but
neither understanding what they are talking about, nor
what they are really driving at.[3]

We all know how valuable the Law is if it is consulted
legitimately. But we recognize none the less that the law
is not put there for the upright, but for the lawless and
refractory, the impious and the sinners, the ungodly and
profane, patricides and matricides, those guilty of
10   manslaughter, vicious persons, homosexuals, man-traf-
fickers, liars, perjurers, and whatever else there may be
that is opposed to sound teaching in conformity with the
News of the glory of the Blessed God with which I have
been entrusted.

---

1 Timotheus appears to have gone from Rome to Ephesus, and at Paul's
request to have remained there.
2 *Deut* 6:5.
3 The New Testament collection was the product of the Christian communities outside Israel, so that the views of the Judeo-Christian envoys and
members are very little represented. But see the Open Letters of *James* and
Judas (Jude).

I feel deeply grateful to the one who has empowered me, to Christ Jesus our Master, that he considered me sufficiently trustworthy to take into service, I who previously had been a slanderer, a persecutor, and a man of violence. But I obtained mercy because I acted unwittingly in unbelief. But our Master's loving-kindness, together with the faith and love that is in Christ Jesus, was more than adequate.

15   This is a true saying, and deserving of unqualified acceptance, that "Christ Jesus came into the world to save sinners". Of these I am foremost. But I obtained mercy for the very reason that by me Christ Jesus might exhibit his full forbearance as a general indication to those who would come to believe in him for Eternal Life. To the imperishable, invisible King of the Universe,[4] the Only God, be honour and glory for ever and ever. Amen.

This signal[5] I transmit to you, son Timotheus, in conformity with the prognostications about you, that in their terms you may set out to wage a gallant campaign, in possession of faith and a clear conscience, a campaign which some having declined have come to grief over the

20   Faith. Among these are Hymenaeus and Alexander,[6] whom I have consigned to Satan that they may be disciplined not to speak profanely.

2.1   In the first place, therefore, I require that petitions, prayers intercessions and thanksgivings be offered for everyone, for kings and all holding positions of authority, so that we may pass a quiet and tranquil life in all godliness and gravity. This is proper and well-pleasing in the sight of God our Saviour, who desires everyone to be saved and come to acknowledge the

5   Truth. There is One God, and one intermediary between God and mankind, the Man Christ Jesus, who gave himself as a ransom for all, as will be demonstrated in due course. To announce this I was made a herald and envoy – I am telling the truth, I am not lying – a faithful and true teacher of the Gentiles.

I therefore desire the men everywhere to offer prayer, raising holy hands free from passion and controversy. Similarly, their wives should dress themselves unob-

4 Paul is using the language of congregational Jewish prayer and praise.
5 ie the doxology just quoted. Here and in the words that follow, Paul is using the metaphor of a military expedition by sea.
6 Perhaps the same as Alexander the blacksmith (*II Tim* 4:14).

trusively, with modesty and moderation, not adorning
themselves with lace and gold or pearl embroidery or
10   expensive material, but with what is becoming for
women professing to be religious, with kind actions. Let
a wife learn passively with complete submissiveness. I
do not permit a wife to teach, nor to exercise a husband's
prerogative, but to be passive. For Adam was formed
first, and then Eve. And it was not Adam who was
beguiled; but the woman being completely beguiled fell
15   into transgression. Yet she shall be saved by child-
bearing,[7] provided that the couple remain faithful, affectionate and devoted, and also practise moderation.

3.1   This is a true saying, "If anyone aspires to be a
supervisor he desires honourable employment". The
supervisor ought therefore to be irreproachable,
husband of one wife, sober, temperate, mannerly,
hospitable, a good teacher, not truculent, nor pugnacious, but equable, pacific, free from avarice, managing
his own household wisely, keeping his children in order
5   with all gravity. For if anyone does not know how to
manage his own household, how is he to take charge of
God's community? He should not be a recent convert, in
case by becoming conceited he meets with the Devil's
fate. He ought also to be well-spoken of by those 'outside', in case he falls into disrepute and the Devil's snare.

Administrators likewise should be grave, not gossipers, not addicted to liberal potations, not money-
grubbers, holding the mystery of the Faith with a clear
10   conscience. They should also first be on probation: then
let them act as administrators when proved satisfactory.
Their wives too should be grave, never malicious, sober,
entirely reliable. Let administrators remain married to
one wife, managing their children and their own households well. For those who act well as administrators
acquire an influential status and great liberty of speech
for the Faith that is in Jesus Christ.

I am writing to you in this way, hoping to visit you
15   shortly, but in case I am delayed, that you may know
how life ought to be lived in the house of God, which is
the Community of the Living God, the prop and stay of

---

7 *Gen* 3:16.

the Truth. Admittedly it is a great thing, this Mystery of Devoutness which (in Christ)[8]

> *Was made visible physically,*
> *Vindicated spiritually,*
> *Seen by angels,*
> *Proclaimed to the Gentiles,*
> *Believed in in the world,*
> *Taken up again in glory.*[9]

4.1   Now the Spirit categorically declares, "In the latter times some will desert the Faith, paying attention to misleading spirits and pronouncements of demons, speaking falsely with intent to deceive",[10] having their own conscience seared, forbidding marriage, and requiring abstention from foods which God has created to be partaken of with thanksgiving by those who believe and fully understand the truth. For every provision of God is good, and by no means to be refused if it is accepted with

5   thanksgiving; for it is consecrated by the recitation of the grace to God.

If you put these things to the brothers you will be a worthy minister of Christ Jesus, primed in the principles of the Faith and in the right teaching you have consistently followed. But deprecate irreverent matters and old wives' tales. Train yourself for devoutness. "Physical training is of limited usefulness, but devoutness is of unlimited usefulness, providing assurance both for the present life and for that which is to come." This is a true

10   saying and deserving of unqualified acceptance. That is why we toil and strive, because we have fixed our hope on the Living God, who is the Saviour of all men, particularly of believers. Impress and teach these things.

Let no one despise your youth; but set an example to believers by speech, by behaviour, by faith, by purity. Devote yourself until I come to exposition, exhortation and instruction. Do not neglect the gift you have, which was bestowed on you by a prophetic intimation which

15   accompanied your ordination[11] by the elders. Exercise and develop these faculties, that your progress may be

---

8 The words "in Christ" are not in the text, but are required by the sense.
9 Possibly from an early hymn.
10 cf *Dan* 8:23–26; *Mt* 24:10–12.
11 Lit "laying on of hands".

marked by all. Keep a firm hold on yourself and on the doctrine. Be true to them; for by so doing you will save both yourself and those who listen to you.

5.1   Do not reprimand an elder, but appeal to him as if he were your father, and to the younger men as brothers, to the older women as your mother, and to the younger women chastely as sisters. Care for widows who are lone widows. But where a widow has children or grand-children let these first learn to discharge their filial duty and to make suitable return to the authors of their being,

5   for this is well-pleasing in God's sight. But the lone and solitary widow has her hope in God, and gives herself to prayers and petitions night and day. The fast-living woman, however, is dead in life. Impress these things on them, that they may be irreproachable. So if any man does not provide for his own relations, and especially his own family, he has disavowed the Faith and is worse than an unbeliever.

Do not let a widow be put on the register[12] at a lower age than sixty, a woman who has been the wife of one

10   husband, with testimonials to her kind actions, such as that she has brought up children, given hospitality to strangers, washed the feet of saints, relieved those in distress, or has been responsible for some other good deed.

But decline to register the younger widows; for when they become capricious towards Christ they want to marry, earning condemnation for disregarding the first claim on their allegiance. At the same time they learn to be idle, going the round of houses; and not only to be idle, but also gossipers and meddlers, talking about what is none of their business. I therefore prefer the younger women to marry, to have children, keep house, and give no kind of pretext to the ill-disposed to indulge in abuse,

15   for already some have gone off the road after Satan. Should any believers have widows to take care of, let them give them assistance and not burden the com-munity, so that lone widows may be provided for.

Let the elders who govern well be treated as deserving of twice as much consideration, particularly those who are occupied with speaking and instruction. The Scrip-ture truly says, "You are not to muzzle the ox that treads

12 So as to receive communal maintenance.

out the corn",[13] and "the workman deserves his wages".[14]

20 Do not admit an accusation against an elder unless it is supported by two or three witnesses. But publicly reprove those that do sin, that it may deter the others. I charge you before God and Christ Jesus and the elect angels[15] to maintain these principles without prejudice, doing nothing with bias. Do not ordain anyone hastily, nor become involved in the sins of others. Keep yourself unpolluted.

Do not be a water drinker any longer, but take a little wine for the sake of your stomach and your chronic 25 ailments. Some men's sins are patent, standing out for condemnation, but with others they are kept in the background. In the same way also their good deeds are patent; but even when they are not they cannot be concealed.

6.1 Let as many as are under the yoke as slaves regard their owners as deserving of every consideration, that the Name of God and the doctrine may not be brought into disrepute. But let not those who have owners who are believers be presumptuous towards them because they are brothers. Rather should they be meticulous in serving because those who are deriving the benefit of the useful service are believers and friends. Teach and advocate these things.

If anyone teaches anything different, and does not propound sound principles, those of our Lord Jesus Christ, and instruction that is consistent with godliness, he is befogged, knowing nothing clearly, crazy about 5 issues and fights over words, which give rise to antagonism, rivalry, slanders, evil suspicions, and violent altercations of men whose minds are warped and bereft of truth, imagining good business to be the same thing as godliness. But godliness plus contentment is the best possible business; for we have brought nothing into the world, neither is there anything we can take out of it. Having food and shelter let us be content with these.

Those who want to be rich expose themselves to temptations and pitfalls, and to many foolish and harm-

---

13 *Deut* 25:4.
14 See *Exod* 24:15 and cf *Lk* 10:7.
15 cf Jos *Jewish War* II 401, "I call your Sanctuary and God's holy angels . . . to witness".

ful cravings, which drag men down to ruin and perdi-

10   tion. The root of all the evils is avarice, and some having clutched at it have strayed from the Faith and racked themselves with many torments.

Do you, man of God, fly from these things. But pursue rectitude, devoutness, faith, love, constancy and gentleness. Fight the gallant contest of the Faith to the finish. Put up a real struggle for Eternal Life, to which you were called. Having made the noble confession before many witnesses, I charge you before God the Source of all life,[16] and before Christ Jesus who made the noble confession before Pontius Pilate,[17] to keep the injunction unsullied, unimpeachable, until the visible appearance

15   of our Lord Jesus Christ, which the blessed and sole Sovereign[18] will display in due course, the King of kings and Lord of lords, who alone is deathless, dwelling in unapproachable light, whom no man has seen, nor can see. To him be honour and everlasting might. Amen.

Impress on those who are rich in this present world not to be arrogant, nor to build their hopes on such an uncertain thing as riches, but on God who provides everything in profusion for our enjoyment. Impress on them to be beneficent, rich in kind actions, to be generous and public-spirited, storing up for themselves a useful fund for the future, so as to secure the Life worth living.

20   Guard what is committed to your care, Timotheus, avoiding the irreverent jargon and contradictions of the falsely termed "Knowledge",[19] which some professing have fallen into error regarding the Faith.

Wishing you every happiness.

---

16 cf *I Sam* 2:6 (LXX).
17 The only confession made by Jesus before Pilate, which the Gospels report, is that he was king of the Jews. The reference may be to some uncanonical source.
18 ie God Almighty.
19 Gr. *Gnosis* (Gnostic systems).

To Timotheus (2)
(Probably written from Rome in AD 63)

1.1   Paul, by the will of God an envoy of Christ Jesus in conformity with the promise of Life that is in Christ Jesus, to his dear son Timotheus. May prosperity, mercy and peace be yours from God the Father and Christ Jesus our Master.

I am grateful to God, whom I serve with a pure conscience as did my forebears, as I am unremitting in mentioning you to him in my petitions, longing night and day to see you, very mindful of your tears, that I may be filled with joy.

I cherish the recollection of your guileless faith, which first resided in your grandma Lois and your mother
5   Eunice, and I am sure does still in you. It is on this ground that I would urge you to fan the flame of the divine gift imparted to you when I ordained you; for God has not given us a spirit of timidity, but of resolution, devotion and correction. So do not be ashamed of the testimony of our Master, nor of me his prisoner, but bear your share of hardship for the News as God enables you. He has saved us and called us with a holy calling, not in accordance with our actions, but in accordance with his own purpose and mercy bestowed on us in Christ Jesus
10   before the Ages began, but now tangibly expressed through the visible appearance of Christ Jesus our Deliverer, who has put death out of action and brought Life and imperishability into operation by the News, of which I am appointed herald, envoy and teacher. It is on this ground that I suffer as I do. But I am not ashamed of it, for I know in whom I have put my trust, and am confident that he is able to keep secure what I have entrusted to him until that Day comes.

Hold fast the outline of sound principles you have heard from me by the faith and love that is in Christ

Jesus. Keep safe that noble deposit which by the holy
15   Spirit resides in us. You are well aware that all the Asiatic
believers[1] have turned from me, among them Phygelus
and Hermogenes. The Lord have compassion on the
household of Onesiphorus,[2] because he often heartened
me and was never ashamed of my chain; but on arrival at
Rome he made diligent inquiry for me and found out
where I was. The Lord grant him to find mercy[3] when the
Day comes. And the many ways in which he looked after
me in Ephesus you know better than anyone.

2.1   Be resolute therefore, my son, in the loving-kindness
that is in Christ Jesus, and what you have heard as from
me through many witnesses, commit to reliable persons,
who will be competent in turn to teach others. Bear your
share of hardship like a good soldier of Christ Jesus. No
one going off to war saddles himself with the respon-
sibilities of life, since he aims to satisfy his enlisting
5   officer. Also if anyone contends in the Games, he will not
be crowned if he does not adhere to the rules. The farmer
who has put in the labour ought to have first claim on the
produce. Note what I say. The Lord will grant you
complete understanding.

Always remember, Jesus Christ of the lineage of David
was raised from the dead in my presentation of the
News. For this I suffer hardship to the extent of
imprisonment, like a malefactor. But God's Message is
10   not fettered. Because of that I submit to everything for
the sake of the Elect, that they too may obtain the
salvation that is in Christ Jesus with eternal glory. It is a
true saying,

'If we have died with him, we shall also live with him;
If we are constant, we shall also reign with him;
If we disown him, so will he disown us;
If we are disloyal, he will still be faithful.'

Faithful, because he cannot deny himself. Remind them
of this, begging them most solemnly before God not to
battle over words, which gains nothing, and only dis-
15   concerts the listeners. Be at pains to prove yourself
competent to God, a workman who has no need to

1 ie those in the Province of Asia, such as at Ephesus.
2 The passage seems to convey that Onesiphorus had died.
3 Lit "The Lord grant him to find mercy from the Lord", a Hebraism. cf *Gen* 19:24.

be ashamed, having kept to the straight line with the Message of Truth.

But evade irreverent jargon. Those who employ it only further the progress of impiety, and their speech mortifies like a gangrene. Among them are Hymenaeus and Philetus, who have fallen into error regarding the Truth, saying that the resurrection has already taken place, and have overturned the faith of some.

At least God's solid foundation stays firm bearing this stamp on it, "The Lord knows those who are truly his",[4] and, "Let all who pronounce the name of the Lord stand

20   aside from iniquity".[5] But in a large establishment there are not only vessels of gold and silver, but also of wood and earthenware, the ones for best and the other for common use. Should anyone make himself pure from the latter, he will become a vessel for best use, cleansed, fit for the Owner's employment, in complete readiness for every useful service.

Fly from youthful passions, but pursue rectitude, faith, love and peace, with those who invoke the name of the Lord with a pure mind. Deprecate foolish and idle issues, knowing that they breed strife. The Master's servant ought not to wrangle, but to be pacific towards

25   all, instructive, forbearing, quietly correcting opponents, so that perhaps God may grant them a change of mind to realise the truth and be brought to their senses, being recovered by him from the Devil's clutches, who had taken possession of them for his own purposes.

3.1   You must know this, however, that in the Last Days hard times are in store; for men will be selfish, money-grubbing, brazen, arrogant, slanderous, defiant to parents, ungrateful, irreligious, lacking in affection, implacable, spiteful, uncontrolled, savage, disliking good, treacherous, headstrong, conceited, preferring

5   pleasure to piety, maintaining a semblance of devoutness but denying its efficacy. Turn away from all such people; for from them come those who gain an entrance into households and captivate immature females, piled high with peccadiloes, swayed by whims and fancies, always learning, but never really able to grasp the Truth.

---

4 *Num* 16:5 (LXX).
5 cf *Num* 16:26–27 (LXX).

In the same kind of way as Jannes and Jambres[6] opposed Moses, so do these men, warped in mind, unsound in the Faith, oppose the Truth. But they will make no further headway, for their folly will be patent to all, as indeed was that of those magicians.

10   But you have closely followed my teaching, my method, presentation, forbearance, devotion and constancy, the persecutions and sufferings I met with an Antioch, Iconium and Lystra, the various kinds of persecution I underwent, from all of which the Lord rescued me. And indeed all who desire to live dutifully in Christ Jesus must expect persecution. But wicked men and imposters will flourish as time goes by, deceiving and being deceived. You, however, adhere to the things you have learnt and been convinced of, seeing from whom

15   you learnt them, and that from infancy you have known the holy Scriptures, which have power to make you wise for salvation by faith that is in Christ Jesus. Each document is divinely inspired, and consequently advantageous for instruction, reproof, reclamation and moral discipline, so that the Man of God may be expert, fully equipped for every useful undertaking.

4.1   I charge you before God, and before Christ Jesus, who will judge the living and the dead, and in view of his visible appearing and reign, proclaim the Message, apply yourself to this in season and out of season. Reprove, censure, exhort, with all forbearance and diligence. For the time will come when they will not tolerate sound teaching, but following their own desires will load themselves with teachers who tickle the ear, and will turn a deaf ear to the Truth, turning instead to myths.

5   You, however, keep perfectly cool, endure hardships, do your duty as a standard-bearer of the News, fulfil the conditions of your service. For I am now on the eve of peace, and the time for my discharge is approaching. I have fought a gallant contest; I have completed the course; I have kept the Faith. There remains in store for me the crown to which I am entitled, which the Master, that honourable judge, will award me on that Day; and not me alone, but all who delightedly welcomed his personal presence.

10   Do your utmost to come to me quickly, for Demas,

6 The legendary court magicians of Pharaoh.

loving the present world, has deserted me and gone off to Thessalonica, Crescens has gone to Gaul, Titus to Dalmatia. Only Luke remains with me. Pick up Mark and bring him with you, for he is valuable to me in administrative work, and I have dispatched Tychicus to Ephesus. When you come bring the heavy jacket I left with Carpus at Troas, also the books, particularly the parchments. Alexander the blacksmith has shown himself very ill-disposed towards me. The Lord will requite

15 him in accordance with his actions.[7] Watch out for him yourself, for he is strongly opposed to our views. At the first hearing of my defence no one supported me: everyone deserted me. May it not be counted against them! But my master supported and strengthened me; so that through me the proclamation might ring out, and all the Gentiles might hear it; and I was "saved from the jaws of the lion".[8] The Lord will continue to rescue me from every evil agency and preserve me for his heavenly Kingdom. To him be glory for ever and ever. Amen.

Give my regards to Prisca and Aquila, and to the

20 household of Onesiphorus. Erastus is still at Corinth, while Trophimus I left ill at Miletus. Do your utmost to come to me before winter sets in.

Eubulus sends you his regards, so do Prudens, Linus, Claudia, and all the brothers.

The Lord Jesus be with your spirit. Wishing you every happiness.

---

7 cf *Ps* 28:4; *II Sam* 3:39.
8 cf *Ps* 22:1. Paul is using a Jewish stock phrase for the power of tryannical rulers, in this case the Emperor Nero. See Jos. *Antiq* XVIII 228–229. Paul has evidently been remanded, but no longer now expected his freedom.

HOMILY ON THE HIGH PRIESTHOOD OF CHRIST

For Jewish Readers
(*Hebrews*)

Preface to the Homily to the Hebrews

There has been much speculation as to the authorship and destination of this document. Eastern tradition ascribed the work to Paul; but it has long been recognised from the language, style and character of the book that it cannot have been written by him, though the author's viewpoint is in many respects Pauline. Among suggested writers the most probable is Apollos, Paul's esteemed fellow-worker. He is described in the *Acts* as an Alexandrian Jew, a learned man, well-versed in the Scriptures, fully in keeping with the character of the work. He is at home in the Greek language, which he employs with considerable literary skill, and with delight in shades of meaning and plays on words. For his Old Testament quotations he employs the Alexandrian text of the Greek version, and he was evidently well-acquainted with the works of Philo, the Alexandrian Jewish philosopher of the first century AD.·

The *Homily* is directed to a particular community of Jewish followers of Jesus, who knew personally both the author and Timotheus, Paul's devoted assistant. This is important, as it indicates – assuming that these touches have not been introduced to lend colour to Pauline authorship – that these believers were located in some city of Greece or Asia Minor where there was a considerable Jewish population. The most likely is Ephesus, where both Apollos and Timotheus worked.

The document furnishes three other notable pieces of information, that the believers in question had suffered some persecution, that Timotheus had been imprisoned but was now released, and that the author was probably writing from Italy. With the evidence that the Temple at Jerusalem was still standing, this suggests a date of composition around AD 65–67; but of course it could be later.

To the Hebrews

1.1   At various times and in varied fashions God spoke of old to our fathers by the prophets; but at the close of these times he has spoken to us by a Son, whom he appointed heir to everything.[1] By him also he instituted the Aeons.[2] He, being the reflection of God's glory and the exact expression of his nature,[3] bringing everything into being by the exercise[4] of God's power, when he had effected an expiation for sins, sat down at the right hand of the Majesty in the heavenly heights. In this respect he is superior to the angels, in so far as he has obtained a

5   more exalted status than theirs. For to which of the angels did God ever say, "You are my son, to-day I have begotten you"?[5] Or again, "I will be a father to him, and he shall be a son to me".[6] Or again, when he introduces the Firstborn to his world estate, he says, "And let all God's angels pay him homage".[7]

Now as regards the angels, God says,

Who employs spirits as his messengers,
And fiery flames as his agents.[8]

1 cf Gen. 1:28. In this book we are in the realm of Jewish mysticism where much was made of man being created in the image of God. An Archetypal (Heavenly) Man was conceived, equated with the Messiah Above (the Son of Man). See *Book of Enoch*. In Jewish-Christian teaching this Man had incarnated in Jesus at his baptism.
2 Or "Ages".
3 *Gen* 1:26.
4 Lit "expression" (cf *Prov* 8)
5 *Ps* 2:7 (LXX).
6 *II Sam* 7:14 (LXX).
7 *Deut* 32:43 (LXX).
8 *Ps* 104:4.

But as regards the Son,

> *Your Throne, O God, is of eternal duration:*
> *A Sceptre of Justice[9] is the sceptre of your kingdom.*
> *You have loved rectitude and hated injustice;*
> *Therefore God – yes, your God – has anointed you*
> *With coronation oil in the presence of your peers.[10]*

10   And also,

> *You in the beginning, Lord, founded the earth,*
> *And the heavens are your handiwork.*
> *They will perish, but you will endure.*
> *They will all grow old like a garment,*
> *And like a robe you will fold them away.*
> *But you will be ever the same,*
> *And your years will never cease.[11]*

And to which of the angels did God ever say,

> *Be seated at my right hand,*
> *Till I make your foes your footstool.[12]*

Are they not all ministering spirits sent out for the service of those who are to obtain salvation?

2.1   That is why we ought to pay much closer attention to the things we have heard, so that we never let them slip. For if the Message spoken by angels[13] held good, and every failure or neglect brought just retribution, how are we to escape punishment if we should prove negligent of so great a salvation, which, originating with the Master's own declaration, was confirmed to us by those who heard him, and corroborated by God by signs and wonders, and by a variety of phenomena and distributions of holy Spirit at his discretion?

5   Now it was not to angels that God made subject that future state of affairs of which we are speaking; for in one place a certain writer has expressed it thus:

> *What is Man, that you are mindful of him?*
> *Or the Son of Man, that you take account of him?*
> *You made him only slightly inferior to angels:*

---

9 Messiah as Throne and Sceptre.
10 *Ps* 45:6–7.
11 *Ps* 102:25–27.
12 *Ps* 110:1.
13 The Law at Sinai given, according to Jewish legend, through the medium of angels. See *Gal* 3:19.

You crowned him with dignity and honour.
You set him over the work of your hands,
And made everything subject to him.[14]

By this "making everything subject to him" he left nothing outside his control. As it is, we do not see as yet that everything has been made subject to him. But as regards being made "only slightly inferior to angels" we do see Jesus by experiencing death having been "crowned with dignity and honour", that thus in God's

10   mercy he should taste death for all mankind. For it seemed fitting to God, for whom and by whom everything exists, in raising many sons to dignity, to perfect by sufferings the one responsible for their salvation. He indeed who sanctifies and those who are sanctified have all one parentage, for which reason he is not ashamed to call them brothers, saying,

I will declare your Name to my brothers,
I will praise you before the Community.[15]

And again, "I will put my trust in him".[16] And again, "Here am I with the children God has given me".[17]

Since, therefore, the children have human nature, so did he[18] share it equally with them; so that by death he might put out of commission him who wields the power

15   of death, namely the Devil, and release all those inhibited throughout their lives by fear of death. For where was the point of lending a helping hand to angels? It was the descendants of Abraham that needed a helping hand. Consequently it was essential for him to become in every respect like his brothers, that he might be a compassionate and trustworthy High Priest in matters relating to God, to propitiate for the people's sins; for having experienced temptation himself he is able to aid those who are tempted.

3.1   Wherefore, holy brothers, comrades of the heavenly calling, take note of Jesus the Representative and High Priest of our confession, how faithful he was to him who appointed him, as was Moses "in all his house".[19] But

14 *Ps* 8:4–6.
15 *Ps* 22:22.
16 *Isa* 12:2.
17 *Isa* 8:18.
18 As the heavenly Son of Man incarnate in Jesus.
19 *Num* 12:7.

Jesus was thought worthy of greater dignity than Moses, in so far as he who has constructed the house derives more honour from it; for every house must be constructed by someone, though it is God who has constructed all things.

5   Now Moses indeed was faithful in all God's house as a privileged retainer, in proof of the things that were to be declared; but Christ was faithful as a son over his own house, the house which we represent, if we hold tenaciously to our confidence and pride in our Hope. So, as the holy Spirit says,

To-day, should you hear his voice,
Harden not your hearts as in the provocation,
At the time of testing in the wilderness,
Where your fathers tested me experimentally,
And saw my activities for forty years.
10   *So I was grieved with that generation,*
And said, They are ever astray at heart.
Never have they really known my ways.
As I swore then in my anger,
Never shall they enter my rest.[20]

Take care, then, brothers, lest there should be in any one of you an evil disloyal heart to make you revolt from the Living God. Rather exhort each other daily, while it can still be called 'to-day', in case any of you should be hardened by sin's subversive power. For we have become Christ's comrades, provided that we adhere steadfastly to the end to the fundamental basis of that
15   association, in that it is said,

To-day, should you hear his voice,
Harden not your hearts as in the provocation.

For some having heard did provoke, though not all those who came out of Egypt under Moses. With whom, then, was it God was grieved for forty years? Was it not with those who had sinned, whose bodies fell in the wilderness?[21] And to whom did he swear they should not enter his rest, if not to those who were disobedient? So we see that they were prevented from entering by disaffection.
4.1   Let us be deeply concerned, therefore, lest while a

20 *Ps* 95:7–11.
21 *Ps* 106:26.

promise of entering God's rest is left open any of you may seem to have missed it. For we too, just like them, have been the recipients of Good News; but in their case the Message heard was of no avail because it did not come to grips with faith in the hearers. It is we who have believed who will enter God's rest, as he said, "As I swore then in my anger, never shall *they* enter my rest", even though it is from labours that had been completed from the creation of the world. For in one place he speaks of the seventh day as follows, "And God rested the
5   seventh day from all his labours".[22] And again in this passage, "Never shall they enter my rest". Since, therefore, it is left open for some to enter it, and those who were first given the Good News did not enter because of disobedience, God again fixes a time, namely 'today', saying after a considerable interval through David, as quoted,

> *To-day, should you hear his voice,*
> *Harden not your hearts as in the provocation.*

Had Joshua[23] given the people rest, God would not here be speaking about another day later on. So a
10   sabbath-keeping is left open for God's people. He who enters God's rest has himself rested from his own labours as God did from his. Let us therefore do our utmost to enter that rest, in case anyone should fall by the very same factor of disobedience. For God's Message is keen and eager, sharper than any double-edged dagger, piercing to the very juncture between soul and spirit, joints and marrow, and able to detect the feelings and intents of the heart. There is no created thing unnoticed by him, for everything is naked and exposed to the sight of him with whom we have to deal.

Having, therefore, a great High Priest who has passed through the heavens,[24] Jesus the Son of God, let us hold
15   fast to our confession. For we do not have a High Priest who cannot sympathise with our failings, having – though without sin[25] – been tempted similarly in every respect. Let us therefore confidently approach the Mercy

---

22 *Gen* 2:2.
23 Gr. "Jesus".
24 The Seven Heavens of the Jewish Mystics.
25 The Logos (Word) has "no participation in sin" (Philo, *De Profug*. 20). The Logos is also called by Philo "High Priest".

5.1

Seat,[26] that we may obtain mercy and find favour so as to receive adequate aid. For every High Priest, being selected from men, appointed on behalf of men for divine duties to present offerings and sacrifices for sins, is capable of friendly sympathy for the ignorant and erring, since he himself is prone to failings, and for that very reason is obliged to bring offerings for sins[27] for himself, as well as for the people. And no one assumes this dignity on his own: he is called to office by God, as Aaron

5   was. Thus even Christ did not raise himself to the dignity of High Priest: it was he who said to him, "You are my son: to-day I have begotten you".[28] And God also said elsewhere, "You are a priest for ever after the order of Melchizedek".[29]

Christ, in the days of his physical existence,[30] having offered petitions, and indeed supplications, with loud sobbing and tears to him who could save him from death,[31] was heard because of his piety. Though he was a son, he learnt obedience by what he suffered. And being perfected, he became for all who obey him the means of

10   their eternal salvation, having been appointed by God as High Priest after the order of Melchizedek.[32]

We are minded to say a great deal on this subject that is hard to explain since you have become dull of hearing. For when by this time you should be teachers, you again need someone to teach you the most elementary principles of the Divine Oracles. Yes, you have become in need of milk, not of solid food. For everyone who is at the milk-feeding stage is lacking in moral judgment; for he is a babe. Solid food is for grown-ups, for those who from long practice have had their faculties trained to distinguish good from evil.

6.1   So leaving the subject of first Christian principles let us bring ourselves to maturity, not re-laying a foundation of repentance of our dead deeds, of faith in God, of instruc-

---

26 *Exod* 25:17.

27 See *Lev* 4:3; 16:5–6.

28 *Ps* 2:7. According to Jewish-Christian sources these were the words heard by Jesus at his baptism. It was at this moment that the Messiah Above, the heavenly Son of Man, entered into him.

29 *Ps* 110:4.

30 As the Son of Man incarnate.

31 In the Garden of Gethsemane (cf *Lk* 22:44).

32 According to Philo, "the Logos is shadowed forth by Melchizedek" (See Philo, *Alleg. Interp.* III 82).

tion about immersions, ordinations, resurrection from the dead and eternal judgment. This is what we must do, God permitting. For it is impossible for those who have once been enlightened, who have experienced the heavenly gift, and become sharers of the holy Spirit, and

5 have truly experienced divine utterance[33] – the powers indeed of the world to come – and then have fallen away, to make a fresh start with repentance; for they have re-crucified the Son of God for their part, and held him up to scorn. For soil that absorbs the rain which falls frequently upon it, and bears vegetation suited to the use of those by whom indeed it is cultivated, will enjoy God's bless-ing. But if it produces thorns and thistles it is worthless and the next thing to a curse, and will end up in burning.

We are convinced, however, that the better fate carry-ing salvation with it will be yours, dear friends, even if

10 we do speak in this way. God is not unjust. There has been no forgetfulness of your work on his part, nor of the love you have shown for his Name in ministering to the saints, and maintaining this ministry. And it is our desire that the same zeal should be exhibited by each of you, so as to make absolutely sure of the Hope to the very end, so that you do not become sluggish, but imitators of those who by faith and perseverance are entitled to the prom-ises. For when God made a promise to Abraham he swore by himself, since he could swear by no one greater,[34] saying, "Assuredly, I will bless you and

15 increase you".[35] And so, having persevered, Abraham gained the promise. For men swear by what is greater, and for them the oath in ratification marks the conclusion of every controversy.[36] In this instance God, being desirous of showing the heirs of the promise more positively the unalterability of his purpose, negotiated by oath; so that by two unalterable facts,[37] impossible for God to falsify, we who have fled for refuge[38] might have strong incentive to grasp the Hope extended to us. To this we cling as a safe and secure anchor for the soul,

33 Speaking with tongues, or prophetic speech.
34 cf Philo, *De Legg. Alleg.* III:72. "Having well confirmed his promise even by an oath . . . for you see that God swears not by another – for nothing is superior to himself – but by himself, who is the best of all."
35 *Gen* 27:16–17.
36 cf *Exod* 22:11.
37 The promise and the oath.
38 See *I Ki* 1:50.

20   passing in behind the curtain,[39] where Jesus, appointed permanent High Priest after the order of Melchizedek, has entered in advance on our behalf.

7.1   Now this Melchizedek, king of Salem, priest of the Most High God, was he who met Abraham on his return from the slaughter of the kings and blessed him, to whom Abraham allocated a tenth of everything.[40] He is in the first place, by translation of his name, "king of righteousness", and in the second place king of Salem, which means "king of peace", without father, without mother, without ancestry, having neither beginning of days nor end of life.[41] Being therefore a representation of the Son of God, he remains priest in perpetuity.

Observe, then, what an important person he was to whom Abraham – the Patriarch – gave a tenth of the
5   spoils. Those truly of the sons of Levi, who possess the priesthood, are entitled in accordance with the Law to tithe the people, namely their brothers, although sprung from the loins of Abraham. But this man, not of that line, has tithed Abraham and blessed the holder of the promises. And beyond all argument it is the inferior who is blessed by the superior. Again, in the one instance it is men subject to death who receive tithes, while in the other,[42] it is on record that he still lives on. As one might put it, through Abraham even Levi, who receives tithes,
10   has been tithed, for he was still in his father's loins[43] when Melchizedek met Abraham.

If, therefore, perfection had been by means of the Levitical pristhood, for by that priesthood the people were given their legislation, why was it still required that a different priest should arise after the order of Melchizedek instead of carrying on after the order of Aaron?[44] For, the priesthood being altered, of necessity an alteration of law is involved. For he to whom these matters relate belonged to a different tribe, no member of which was devoted to the service of the altar. For it is

---

39 cf *Lev* 16:15.
40 See *Gen* 14:18–20.
41 Scripture makes no mention of Melchizedek's parentage, ancestry, birth or death.
42 ie in the case of Melchizedek.
43 Levi being Abraham's great-grandson not yet born.
44 It is to be noted that the Maccabean Levitical kings, first with John Hyrcanus, had used the Melchizedek title, calling themselves 'priests of the Most High God'.

evident that our Master sprang from Judah, concerning
15 which tribe Moses said nothing about priesthood. And
what is of greater consequence, it is quite clear that a
different priest is to arise after the order of Melchizedek,
who is made priest not in terms of an evanescent commandment but by virtue of an indestructible life. For the
testimony runs, "You are a priest *for ever* after the order
of Melchizedek".

There has been a definite setting aside of the previous
commandment on account of its limitations and
unsatisfactory character. For the Law perfected nothing,
though it paved the way for a better prospect by which
we draw near to God. And in so far as the change was not
20 made without an oath-taking – for those other priests
were installed without an oath-taking, but he with an
oath-taking by him who swore to him, "The Lord has
sworn, and will not revoke his word: you are a priest for
ever" – to that extent Jesus had surety of a better
covenant.

Now those others who are made priests are numerous,
being prevented by death from continuing in office. But
he, because he continues for ever, retains the priesthood
25 in unbroken tenure. Consequently he is able to save
absolutely those who approach God through him, since
he is always alive to intercede on their behalf.

This was the kind of High Priest we required, one who
is consecrated, guileless, undefiled, distinct from sinners, higher than the heavens, one who does not have
daily necessity like other High Priests first to offer sacrifice for his own sins and then for the sins of the people;
for this he did once and for all when he offered up
himself. The Law indeed appoints men with failings as
High Priests; but the terms of the oath-taking subsequent
to the Law appoints a Son who has been permanently
perfected.

8.1 To summarize what has been said, we have a High
Priest of this sort, who has taken his seat at the right
hand of the throne of the Majesty in the heavens, a
ministrant of the sacred rites and of the True Tabernacle,
which the Lord and not man erected.

Now every High Priest is appointed to present offerings and sacrifices, so it was necessary that this one too
should have something to offer. If indeed he were on
earth he would not be a priest at all, there being already

those who present the offerings in accordance with the
5   Law. These serve as a token and shadow of the heavenly
reality, as Moses was directed when about to carry out
the construction of the Tabernacle. "See", God said,
"that you make everything after the pattern shown you
on the mountain."[45]

But now Jesus has obtained a more important
ministration in so far as he is the negotiator of a better
covenant, instituted by God on the basis of better promises. For if that first covenant had been entirely satisfactory, no occasion would have been sought for a second.
But expressing dissatisfaction God says,

> 'Lo, the time will come,' says the Lord,
> 'When I will contract a new covenant
> With the house of Israel and the house of Judah,
> Not like the covenant I made with their fathers
> On the day I took them by the hand
> To lead them out of the land of Egypt:
> For they did not adhere to my covenant.
> So I left them to themselves', says the Lord.
> 10   'But this is the covenant with the house of Israel
> I will make after those days', says the Lord.
> 'I will put my laws into their minds,
> And on their hearts I will inscribe them.
> Yes, I will be their God,
> And they shall be my people.
> And they shall teach no more each his fellow,
> And each his brother, saying "Know the Lord";
> For they all shall know me
> From the least to the greatest of them;
> For I will be merciful to their iniquities,
> And their sins I will remember no more.'[46]

By saying "a *new* covenant", he has rendered the
previous one antiquated; and what is antiquated and
decrepit is on the verge of extinction.
9.1   Yet, indeed, even the previous covenant had its
regulations for worship connected with an earthly Sanctuary. For there was an outer Tabernacle erected in
which was both the lampstand and the table with its

45 *Exod* 25:40.
46 *Jer* 31:31–34.

display of loaves. This was called the Holy Place. And beyond the inner curtain was a Tabernacle called the Most Holy Place, which had the golden censer and the Ark of the Covenant entirely overlaid with gold, in which was the jar containing manna, and Aaron's rod 5 that budded, and the tablets of the Covenant. Above the Ark, overshadowing the Propitiatory were the glorious Cherubim, about which one cannot now speak precisely.

But while these comprised the furnishings, it is only into the outer Tabernacle that the priests enter regularly in the performance of their duties. Into the inner Tabernacle only the High Priest enters once a year, not without blood, which he offers up for his own and the people's sins of ignorance. By this the holy Spirit has indicated that the way into the Most Holy is not yet opened up so long as the outer Tabernacle, which served as an illustration down to the present era, still retains its function. In accordance with this both offering and sacrifices are presented which are incapable, so far as the conscience is concerned, of perfecting the worshippers 10 simply by meat-offerings and drink-offerings and various lustrations, material regulations imposed until the Era of Revision.

But Christ having come as High Priest of the good things in store, he has entered once and for all into the sacred precincts Above, through the better and more perfect Tabernacle that is not artificial – that is to say, not of this created world[47] and not with blood of goats and calves, but with his own blood, procuring permanent redemption.

For if the blood of goats and bulls, and the ashes of a heifer sprinkled on those who have incurred defilement, restores the ritual purity of the flesh, how much more shall the blood of Christ, who by his eternal spirit offered himself unblemished to God, purify our consciences from dead deeds to serve the Living God? 15 Consequently he is the negotiator of a New Covenant; so that from a death having occurred in discharge of liability for violations of the previous covenant those who have been called may obtain the promise of the eternal inheritance. For where there is a covenant there

47 It was believed that the earthly Santuary and also the city of Jerusalem had heavenly counterparts. See *Gal* 4:26; *Rev* 21:2. Similarly Jesus as the earthly Messiah had his counterpart in the heavenly Messiah (the Son of Man).

must be provision of a death on the contractor's part. A covenant is ratified over corpses, otherwise it has no validity while the contractor lives. For this reason neither was the previous covenant inaugurated without blood; for when all the commandments of the Law had been recited by Moses to all the people, he took the blood of calves and goats, with water, scarlet wool and hyssop, and sprinkled both the book itself and all the people

20   saying, "This is the blood of the covenant which God has enjoined on you".[48] And both the Tabernacle and all the utensils of the ritual he similarly sprinkled with blood. Indeed, according to the Law, practically everything is purified by blood, and without effusion of blood there is no absolution.

Of necessity, therefore, the representations of the heavenly realities[49] were purified by such means, but the heavenly realities themselves with better sacrifices than these. For Christ has entered into no artificial Sanctuary, a copy of the true, but into heaven itself, there to appear

25   in God's presence on our behalf. Neither has he entered that he may offer himself frequently, as the High Priest annually enters the sacred precincts with other blood;[50] for then he would have needed to suffer many times since the foundation of the world. As it is, he has appeared only once at the Consummation of the Ages to put away sin by his self-sacrifice. And in so far as it is determined that men shall die but once, and after that follows judgment, so Christ also, being offered once to take away the sins of many,[51] will show himself a second time without sin to those who await him for their salvation.[52]

10.1   For the Law being a shadow of the good things in store, not the very image of the actualities, the High Priests can never with those sacrifices which they offer annually perfect for all time those who approach God. If they could, would not the sacrifices have ceased to be offered? For the worshippers, no longer having any consciousness of sins, would have been purified once

48 *Exod* 24:8.
49 See above, n 47.
50 *Lev* 16:17.
51 cf *Isa* 53:12.
52 On the annual Day of Atonement the people eagerly awaited the safe return of the High Priest.

and for all. But in these sacrifices there is an annual reminder of sins; for it is impossible for the blood of bulls 5 and goats to take away sins. Consequently when Christ enters the world he says,

> *Sacrifice and offering you have not desired:*
> *A body you have prepared for me.*
> *Holocausts and sin-offerings you have not welcomed.*
> *Then said I, lo, I have come –*
> *In the roll of the book it is written of me –*
> *To carry out your will, O Lord.*[53]

Besides saying, "Sacrifices and offerings, holocausts and sin-offerings, you have neither desired nor welcomed" – these being offered in accordance with the Law – he goes on to say, "Lo, I have come to carry out your will". He 10 abolishes the former to establish the latter. By this "will" we are consecrated through the offering of the body of Jesus Christ once and for all.

Moreover, every priest daily *stands* while officiating, and frequently offers the same sacrifices, which can never do away with sins. But this priest, having offered a single sacrifice for sins for all time, *sat down* "at the right hand of God",[54] waiting thereafter for "his enemies to be made his footstool". For by one offering he has perfected 15 for all time those who are consecrated. The holy Spirit is also our witness, for after having said, "This is the covenant I will make with them after those days", the Lord says, "I will put my laws in their hearts, and on their minds I will write them, and their sins and iniquities I will remember no more". Where, then, there is absolution from these an offering for sins is no longer required.

Having therefore, brothers, confidence by the blood of Jesus to use the entrance into the sacred precincts which 20 he has inaugurated for us, a way through the curtain fresh and vital, namely the way of his flesh, and having a supreme priest over the House of God, let us approach God with sincere minds and absolute faith, with hearts sprinkled from a bad conscience and our bodies washed with pure water. Let us adhere inflexibly to the confession of our Hope; for he who has promised is faithful.

53 Ps 40:6–8.
54 Ps 110:1. The author may be thinking of the fact that in the Temple only the king was permitted to be seated. Talmud, *Sot.* fol. 41a.

And let us vie with one another in intensifying our
25   love and worthy actions, not neglecting assembling
together, as is the custom with some, but encouraging
one another, all the more as you see the Day approaching. For if we deliberately persist in sinning after receiving knowledge of the truth, no longer is there left a
sacrifice for those sins, nothing but a dread foreboding of
judgment and of an eager flame ready to devour the
adversaries.[55] Anyone who has spurned the Law of
Moses is put to death without mercy on the testimony of
two or three witnesses. Of how much more terrible a
penalty do you think him deserving who has treated the
Son of God with contempt, and has held the blood of the
covenant by which he was sanctified as something vile,
30   and has mocked the Spirit of mercy? We do indeed know
him who has said, "Vengeance is mine. I will requite",[56]
and also, "The Lord will judge his people".[57] It is a
terrible thing to fall into the hands of the Living God.

Recall those early days in which when you were
illumined you endured a great bout of sufferings, partly
as being yourselves the butt of insults and attacks, and
partly as having fellowship with those who had been so
treated. For you had sympathy with the prisoners, and
you accepted with equanimity the seizure of your property, knowing yourselves to have a better and perma-
35   nent possession. Do not cast away your confidence,
then, which will have a substantial reward; for you will
need all your constancy, so that when you have carried
out the will of God you may obtain the promise.

> For only a very little longer,
> And the Coming One will come, and not delay.
> But my upright one shall live by faith.
> Yet should he draw back,
> My soul shall have no pleasure in him.[58]

But we are not of those who draw back to our destruction, but those with faith to gain our souls.

11.1   Now faith is the solid ground of our expectations, the
proof of unseen actualities. By this faith the Ancients had
testimony borne to them. By it we apprehend that the

55 cf *Zeph.* 1:15–16.
56 *Deut* 32:35.
57 *Deut* 32:36.
58 *Hab* 2:3–4 (LXX), where, however, line 3 follows line 5.

Aeons were instituted by the Divine utterance, so that what is seen did not proceed from any visible causes.

In faith Abel offered to God a greater sacrifice than Cain, by which testimony was borne to him as righteous, God himself testifying about his offerings; and by that faith, though dead, he still speaks.

5   In faith Enoch was translated without experiencing death, and was not to be found because God had translated him. But before he was translated it is on record that he pleased God. Now without faith it is not possible to please God, for he who approaches God must have faith in his existence, and that he rewards those who seek him out.

In faith Noah, deliberating about what was as yet unseen, and being prudent, constructed an ark to save his family, by which he passed judgment on the world, and became heir of that rectitude which rests on faith.

In faith Abraham obeyed, when called to set out for a region which he was destined to receive as an inheritance, and started out with no idea of where he was going. In faith he took up residence in the promised land, as in a foreign country, living in tents, as did Isaac

10   and Jacob the co-heirs of the same promise. He waited for the city with foundations whose architect and builder is God. In faith also, when past the prime of life, he received the capacity to beget children, because he held him to be faithful who had promised. And so there was begotten of one man, as good as dead, "as the very stars of heaven for multitude, and countless as the sands on the seashore".[59]

All these died in faith without having obtained the promises, but viewing them from afar, and hailing them, and confessing that they were 'strangers and sojourners on earth'.[60] People who speak like this make it clear that

15   they are in quest of a homeland; for if indeed their minds were on that land from which they emigrated opportunity was theirs to return. As it is, they are reaching out for a better, namely a heavenly one. Therefore God is not ashamed to be called *their* God, for he has a city in readiness for them.

In faith Abraham when he was tested yielded up Isaac;

59 *Gen* 22:17.
60 *Gen* 23:4.

and he who had received the promises offered up the only son of whom he had been told, "By Isaac shall offspring be given you".[61] He reckoned that God could even raise the dead, from whence indeed, figuratively speaking, he received Isaac back.

20   In faith Isaac also blessed Jacob and Esau in respect of what was to come. In faith Jacob when dying blessed each of the sons of Joseph, and bowed upon the head of his staff. In faith Joseph approaching his end made mention of the exodus of the children of Israel, and gave injunctions about his bones.

In faith Moses when born was hidden for three months by his parents, because they saw he was a fine child and were not afraid of the king's edict.

In faith Moses when grown up refused to be called the
25   son of Pharaoh's daughter, preferring to endure adversity with God's people than to enjoy the temporary pleasures of sin. He deemed the reproach of Christ greater wealth than the treasures of Egypt, fearless of the king's anger; for he was resolute in having the Invisible King in mind. In faith he kept the Passover and the daubing of blood,[62] that the destroyer of the first-born should not touch the Israelites. In faith they crossed the Red Sea as on dry land; but when the Egyptians attempted it they were engulfed.

30   In faith the walls of Jericho fell after being encircled for seven days. In faith Rahab did not perish with the disobedient, because she received the spies peaceably.

And why should I continue? Time would fail me to tell of Gideon, Barak, Samson, Jephthah, of David too and Samuel, and the Prophets, who by faith conquered kingdoms, executed justice, won promises, stopped the mouths of lions, deprived fire of its power, escaped the devouring sword, from being weak were made strong, became mighty in battle and hurled back the ranks of the
35   foe. Women by resurrection had their dead restored. Others had their limbs broken with clubs, refusing to accept release, so as to gain a better rising. Others were subjected to horse-play and flogging, and yet others to chains and imprisonment. They were stoned, burnt alive, tortured, sawn in two, and put to death by the

61 *Gen* 21:12.
62 On the lintels and doorposts. *Exod* 12:22.

sword. They went about in skeepskins and goatskins, in dire want, oppressed and ill-treated, men of whom the world was unworthy. They roamed over deserts and mountains, and lay in caves and holes in the ground. Yet all these, standing on record for their faith, did not secure the promise, God having had our best interest in view, that they should not be perfected without us.

12.1   This being the case, with such a dense throng of witnesses ranged about us, we too must throw aside every hampering conceit and closely-clinging sin. Let us run with grim determination our appointed course, keeping Jesus the starter and finisher of faith's race fixedly in view, who for the sake of the bliss in store for him bore the cross, having scorned the shame, and has now taken his seat on the right hand of the throne of God. For think, if you can, of any who have had to endure such concerted opposition of sinners against themselves,[63] in case you get distressed and your hearts fail you. You have not resisted till you bled struggling 5   against sin, and you have completely forgotten the exhortation which appeals to you in filial terms:

> *Son, make not light of the Lord's discipline,*
> *Nor be indifferent when reproved by him.*
> *For the Lord disciplines him whom he loves,*
> *And corrects every son he receives.*[64]

Submit to discipline, since God treats you as sons; for where is the son whom his father does not discipline? But if you are without the discipline of which all have their share, then you are bastards and not sons.

Since, then, we have had those who were fathers of our physical being as disciplinarians, and we had a wholesome respect for them, shall we not much rather submit ourselves to the Father of our spirits, and live? 10   For they indeed disciplined us for a brief period at their discretion, but he for our lasting good, that we may take after him in holiness. No discipline seems pleasant at the time: it is painful. But afterwards it repays those who are trained by it with the tranquil fruit of rectitude.

So tense the listless hands and the limp knees, and make firm straight tracks with your feet,[65] that the

63 cf *Acts* 4:25–27.
64 *Prov* 3:11–12.
65 cf *Job* 4:3–4.

lagging step may not turn off the road, but rather recover ground. Follow peace with everyone, and that consecra-
15   tion without which no one will see the Lord, keeping a sharp look-out in case anyone is falling away from God's mercy, lest any bitter root springing up should cause inflammation and many be poisoned by it,[66] in case anyone should be immoral or unprincipled like Esau, who sold his birthright for a single meal. You know how when he wanted later to inherit the blessing he was rejected; for he discovered there was no opportunity left for his change of mind, though he tried tearfully to find it.

But you have not approached one who must grope,[67] nor to what is ablaze with fire, nor to murk, nor gloom, nor storm, nor trumpet-blast, nor to a Voice speaking,[68] which those who heard refused to have another word
20   addressed to them;[69] for they could not bear what had been commanded, "If even a beast touches the mountain it shall be stoned".[70] Indeed, so awful was the spectacle that Moses said, "I am terrified and trembling".[71]

Instead you have approached Mount Zion, and the city of the Living God (heavenly Jerusalem), myriads of angels, the solemn assembly and gathering of the First-born who are registered in heaven, God the judge of all, spirits of the just who have been perfected, Jesus the negotiator of a fresh covenant, and the spattered blood
25   that speaks to better purpose than Abel's. Beware of disregarding the Speaker; for if they did not escape who refused to listen to him who conferred with them on earth, how much more we who turn our backs on Him who confers with us from heaven? His voice then shook the earth, but now God has promised, saying, "Once more I will shake not the earth alone, but heaven also".[72] And this "once more" indicates a replacement of what is shaken, as with things that are made, that what is unshaken may undure. Therefore, because we are obtaining an unshaken Kingdom, let us feel the gratitude

---

66 cf *Deut* 29:18.
67 Like blind Isaac, *Gen* 27:21 (LXX).
68 cf *Deut* 4:11–12.
69 cf *Exod* 20:19.
70 *Exod* 19:12–13.
71 Perhaps taken from an apocryphal work.
72 *Hag* 2:6.

that will cause us to serve God acceptably with reverence and awe; for our God is an all-consuming fire.[73]

13.1   Let brotherly affection continue. Never neglect hospitality, for by giving it some have unwittingly entertained angels.[74] Remember those who are in bonds, as if you were bound with them, and those who are ill-treated, as having bodies yourselves.

Marriage is entirely honourable, and the undefiled marriage-bed; but God will judge the immoral and adulterous.

5   Let your nature be free from avarice. Be content with what you have, for God has said, "I will never fail you nor desert you".[75] So that we may confidently say, "The Lord is my helper: I will not fear. What can man do to me?"[76]

Remember your leaders, those who have declared God's Message to you. Copy their faith, closely observing the outcome of their manner of life.

Jesus Christ is the same nowadays and always, so do not be misled by varied and novel doctrines. It is well for the mind to be confirmed by loving-kindness, not by food, from which those who have argued about it have
10   never gained any benefit. We have an altar off which those who serve the Tabernacle have no right to eat; for in the case of those beasts whose blood is brought into the sacred precincts by the High Priest for sin, their carcases are to be burnt outside the camp.[77] Therefore Jesus too, that he might sanctify the people by his own blood, suffered outside the gate.[78] So let us go to him "outside the camp", bearing his reproach;[79] for here we have no permanent city, we are seeking one that is to
15   come.[80] Through him, therefore, let us continually offer to God "the sacrifice of thanksgiving",[81] namely, "the fruit of our lips",[82] confessing his Name.[83] But never

---

73 *Deut* 4:24.
74 cf *Gen* 19:1–2.
75 *Josh* 1:5.
76 *Ps* 118:6.
77 *Exod* 29:14.
78 Of the city of Jerusalem.
79 Like the scapegoat, *Lev* 16:10.
80 ie the New Jerusalem.
81 *Lev* 7:12.
82 *Hos* 14:2.
83 *I Ki* 8:33.

neglect social service and fellowship, for with such sacrifices God is well-pleased.

Obey your leaders and give way to them, for they keep watch over your souls as those who must render an account, that they may do so with joy and not with sighing, for that would be detrimental to you.

Pray for us, for we trust that we have a good conscience, being anxious to live worthily in every way. But I particularly appeal to you for prayer that I may be restored to you sooner.

20   Now may the God of peace, who brought back from the dead that great shepherd of the sheep, our Lord Jesus, with the blood of a lasting covenant, equip you with every virtue to do his will, performing by you through Jesus Christ what is well-pleasing in his sight, to whom be glory for ever. Amen.

Postcript

I beg you, brothers, bear with this message of exhortation, for indeed only to a slight extent have I given you orders. Let me add the news that Brother Timotheus has been released. If he comes soon I will see you with him.

Give my regards to all your leaders and all the saints. The Italians send you their regards.

25   Wishing you all every happiness.

FOUR OPEN LETTERS

PETER
Open Letter to Gentile Converts in Asia
I Peter

JAMES
Open Letter to the Twelve Tribes

JUDAS (Jude)
Open Letter to Gentile Communities

'PETER' (2)
Open Letter to Gentile Converts in Asia
II Peter

Preface to the Four Open Letters

It was customary for the central Jewish Religious Authority in Jerusalem to address open or encyclical letters to the Jewish communities in other lands, advising on matters both religious and secular. The letters in this Group, attributed to Peter, James and Jude, are Christian specimens of the same class of correspondence. The Christian Jewish Authority, consisting of the envoys and elders at Jerusalem, regarded itself and was for a considerable time regarded as standing in the same relationship to the Christian communities elsewhere as the Sanhedrin at Jerusalem to the Jews of the Dispersion. As with the Essenes, representatives of communities were expected to make reports, particularly at Pentecost.

The first head of the Nazorean Council was James the Just, the brother of Jesus next in age, with Peter acting as a kind of vice-president. After the martyrdom of James about AD 62, and at the beginning of the Jewish war with Rome, the Nazoreans left Jerusalem for the region of Pella, east of the Jordan. There Simon son of Cleophas, or Klopas, a name easily confused with that of Peter (Simon Kephas), a first cousin of Jesus, was elected president, and the Christian Sanhedrin, including other surviving relatives of Jesus known as 'the Heirs', ruled the Community down to the beginning of the second century. Among them we learn of James and Sokker, grandchildren of Jude, a younger brother of Jesus.

Appreciation of the existence of this Christian Jewish Authority is essential, not only for an understanding of these letters, but also of much else in the literary heritage of primitive Christianity. Only now is it beginning to be recognised how substantial was its contribution.

The letter of Peter (*I Peter*) has been placed first as there is a fair possibility that it was written by the apostle from Rome (under the designation Babylon). It approximates more closely than the others to the type of letter written by Paul, and it has been held that the author was familiar at least with Paul's letter to the

Roman believers (*Romans*) and his letter to Asian communities (*Ephesians*) written from Rome. The writer calls upon believers from the Gentiles to be of good behaviour under conditions of severe trial, and to give no offence to the authorities. The letter was composed in Greek though no doubt dictated in Aramaic to Silvanus (Silas). The curious commendation of the amanuensis may mean that Peter, ignorant of Greek, was expressing his confidence that what he had said had in fact been set down.

There is a great deal less confidence in the authenticity of the letter of James, due to the good Greek in which it is written and to the lack of early references to the letter. It may be, however, that an early work, one of the earliest in the New Testament, was later discovered and made the groundwork of the present document. As evidence in favour of the letter's general antiquity much is made of the Judaic tone and the absence of a developed Christology. The document is related in spirit to the Jewish 'Wisdom' books in the Apocrypha. The author demands practical proof of faith in the performance of worthy and charitable actions, not merely an assertion of possessing it. Some would see in this an attack on Paul or Pauline teaching.

A difficulty in the way of accepting the work as genuine would be removed if it is allowed to have emanated from Jewish-Christian circles in the name of the James who was the grandson of Jude, to whom reference has been made. Tradition tells that he with his brother Sokker (perhaps Judas Sokker) gained their living as farmers, and there are numerous allusions to land and farm in the letter.

Rural similies also occur in the short letter of Judas (Jude), who describes himself as "brother of James". Here again the writer could have been one of the brothers of Jesus, or a grandson of that Jude. The letter attacks antinomian licentiousness in the Gentile-Christian communities, and the author draws freely on Jewish apocryphal books to make his points. These works were highly venerated in Essene and kindred circles.

The fourth letter, claiming to be a second letter by Peter, is certainly pseudepigraphic. Both the external and even more the internal evidence is against the book's genuineness as the work of the Apostle. The writer has assumed Peter's identity in order to reinforce the message of Jude, which to some extent he has attempted to copy. His manner of referring to Christ, his acceptance of Paul's letters as Scripture, his allusions to the envoys, and his response to those who through the passage of time had become sceptical about the Second Advent, all reveal his late date. It has been held that the author was acquainted with the *Antiquities* of Josephus dating from the close of the first century AD, and as the letter was also subsequent to that of Jude, its composition prior to the beginning of the second century is improbable. At this date the real Peter had been dead for almost half a century.

Open Letter to Gentile Converts in Asia

Peter

1.1   Peter, envoy of Jesus Christ, to the elect strangers[1] of the Pontic, Galatian, Cappadocian, Asian and Bithynian areas of the Dispersion, elected in accordance with the prescience of God the Father, by spiritual consecration, to give obedience[2] and to be sprinkled with the blood of Jesus Christ. May abundant peace and prosperity be yours.

     Blessed be the God and Father of our Lord Jesus, who in his great loving-kindness has given us a new birth into a bright and joyous hope by the resurrection of Jesus Christ from the dead, into an imperishable, pure and fadeless inheritance that has been kept safely in heaven

5   for you, who by the power of God are being safeguarded by faith for a salvation ready to be revealed in the Last Time. In this you rejoice, even though for a brief space now, as needs must be, you are saddened by various trials; that the testing of your faith, so much more precious than gold that perishes, yet is tested by fire, may result in praise, esteem and honour at the revelation of Jesus Christ.

     Him you love, never having set eyes on him, but believing in him, still without seeing him, you yet rejoice with unutterable and exalted joy, anticipating the final

10   outcome of your faith, the salvation of your souls. Prophets who have prophesied of the mercy that would be yours have studied and investigated the theme of this salvation, seeking to know the exact, or at least the

---

1 "Elect strangers" may be a Christian equivalent of the Hebrew *Ger-zedek* ('pious stranger'), technically a Gentile convert to Judaism. Believers of Gentile origin are indicated here.
2 ie to the proclamation of the One God and his Message.

approximate date, which the spirit of Christ in them was indicating when it testified in advance to the sufferings that would befall Christ and the glory to follow. To them it was revealed that it was not for themselves, but for you, they were giving out those things which have now been reported to you by those who have conveyed the News to you with holy Spirit sent from heaven, things that angels long to pry into.

Brace your minds therefore, remain calm and collected, expectant of the favour to be granted you at the revelation of Jesus Christ. As obedient children, do not model yourselves on your former lusts in your
15   ignorance, but as the One who has called you is holy, so be holy in all your behaviour, since it is stated, "You shall be holy, for I am holy".[3] And as you address yourselves to a Father who judges quite impartially in accordance with each individual's work, spend the remainder of the time of your sojourning reverentially, knowing that it was with no perishable materials, silver or gold, you were ransomed from your erroneous way of life handed down by your ancestors, but with the precious blood of
20   Christ, as of a lamb without spot or blemish.[4] He was indeed foreordained before the foundation of the world, but only revealed at the end of the Ages for you who by him trust in God, who raised him from the dead and bestowed honour upon him, so that your faith and hope should be in God.

With your souls purified for sincere brotherly affection by obedience to the truth, love one another devotedly from the heart as those born anew not from a perishable life-germ but an imperishable, through the Message of the Living and Everlasting God. For,

All flesh is grass,
And all its glory as the flower of grass.
The grass withers, and the flower droops;
25   *But the word of the Lord endures for ever.*[5]

It is that word which has been conveyed to you by the Good News.
2.1   Laying aside, therefore, everything base and deceitful,

3 *Lev* 11:44.
4 cf *Lev* 22:18–20.
5 *Isa* 11:6–8.

insincerities, jealousies and malicious gossiping, be eager like newborn babes for the pure and wholesome milk, once you have experienced how excellent the Master is, that you may grow to salvation by it. Coming to him, that precious stone,[6] rejected indeed by men, but
5   chosen and prized where God is concerned, be built yourselves as precious stones into a spiritual dwelling, as a holy priesthood to offer up spiritual sacrifices through Jesus Christ acceptable to God, since it is contained in the Scripture,

> *See, I lay in Zion a chosen stone, a prized corner stone.*
> *Whoever trusts in him will never come to grief.*[7]

The honour, then, is for you who believe, but for the unbelieving, "the stone which the builders rejected is made the coping-stone"[8] and "a stumbling stone and boulder to trip over".[9] They stumbled at the Message, being disobedient, as indeed was ordained. But you are "a chosen race, a royal priesthood, a holy nation,[10] a people for God's ownership",[11] that you may recite the merits of him[12] who has called you from darkness into
10   his marvellous light, who once were "no people", but now are God's people, who once "had not obtained mercy", but now have received mercy.[13]

Dear friends, I appeal to you as strangers and sojourners to refrain from those physical lusts which are at war with the soul. Conduct yourselves honourably among the Gentiles, so that, remarking your good behaviour in the very connexion in which they speak against you as evil-doers,[14] they may praise God on the Day of Visitation.

Give your obedience for the Master's sake to every human institution, whether it is to the emperor as paramount, or to governors as sent by him for the punishment of evil-doers and the commendation of well-
15   doers; for so is the will of God, that you should silence

6 Lit "living stone".
7 *Isa* 28:16.
8 *Ps* 118:22.
9 *Isa* 8:14.
10 *Exod* 19:6.
11 *Exod* 19:5.
12 *Isa* 43:21 (LXX).
13 *Hos* 2:23.
14 The Christians were accused of immoral actions in their secret meetings.

the ignorant assertions of foolish men by well-doing. Give your obedience as freemen, or rather as slaves of God, not using your freedom as a pretext for depravity. Honour all, love the brotherhood, honour the emperor.

Domestic servants, be respectfully submissive to your masters, not only to those who are kind and considerate, but also to those who are wilful. For it is acceptable to God if for conscience's sake a man bears pain, suffering
20   unjustly. But what virtue is it if you take it quietly when you are struck for your faults? But if you take it quietly when you suffer for well-doing, that is acceptable to God. To this indeed you were called, for Christ himself suffered on your behalf, leaving you a copy, that you should follow in his tracks. He committed no sin, nor did he employ deceit, when abused he did not return abuse,[15] when suffering he uttered no threats, but left matters to him who judges justly. He himself in his own body carried our sins to the gibbet, that "being taken from the earth" as regards sins we should live in rec-
25   titude; by "whose bruise you have been healed".[16] For you were "as sheep that have strayed", but now you have returned to the shepherd and guardian of your souls.

3.1   You wives, likewise, be submissive to your husbands, so that if any refuse acceptance of the Message they may be won over by the conduct of their wives with never a word said, having remarked the respectful virtuousness of your conduct. Of such women let not the adornment be the external one of braided hair, golden necklaces, or embroidered dresses, but the hidden one of the human heart in the imperishable beauty of a reposeful and gentle spirit, which is of great worth in the sight of God.
5   It was thus the saintly women of old adorned themselves, who fixed there hope on God, being submissive to their husbands, as Sarah obeyed Abraham, calling him "master".[17] It is her daughters you are while you go quietly about your good work and do not get nervously flustered.[18] You husbands too, cohabit with your wives understandingly, giving due satisfaction to the woman's

15 This is not correct of the Jesus of the Fourth Gospel. cf *Jn* 8:44. But this Gospel was not yet written.
16 The references are to *Isa* 53. The continual reference to the conduct of slaves in the text shows how many converts came from this class.
17 *Gen* 18:12.
18 *Prov* 3:25, though in a different connection.

requirements as the weaker vessel, as also being joint-heirs to the privilege of Life, that your prayers may not be obstructed.

The main thing is that all of you should be united, in sympathy with one another, affectionately disposed, kind-hearted, humble-minded, not returning evil for evil, or insult for insult, but on the contrary blessing, because for this you were called, that you should inherit a blessing.

10   *For he who desires a pleasant life*
     And to see peaceful days,
     Let him keep his tongue from evil
     And his lips from speaking guile;
     Let him avoid evil and do good;
     Let him seek peace and pursue it.
     For the Lord's eyes are on the upright,
     And his ears are attentive to their prayer.
     But the Lord's face is against the evil-doers.[19]

And who is there who will harm you if you are zealous for what is good? But if you should suffer for righteousness's sake you are indeed fortunate! But "do not be afraid of the dread of them, neither be dismayed, and sanctify the Lord God in your hearts",[20] being ever ready to answer those who question you about the Hope that is yours, though mildly and respectfully with a good conscience, so that those who impugn your good conduct as Christians may be ashamed of what they say against you. It is indeed better, if that is God's will, to suffer for well-doing than for evil-doing; because Christ himself died for sins once and for all, the just for the unjust, to bring us to God, being put to death in the flesh but revived in the spirit, in which also Enoch[21] went and preached to the spirits in prison who formerly were disobedient, while God's forbearance in Noah's time awaited the completion of the Ark, in which a few, namely eight persons, were preserved by water. A counterpart of that water, the rite of immersion, not the

---

19 *Ps* 34:12–16.
20 *Isa* 8:12–13.
21 It has been credibly suggested that the name 'Enoch' has been omitted by a scribal slip because of the immediately preceding Greek uncials (without word division) reading ENOKAI ('in which also'). See *Enoch* 13–15, for his transactions with the errant angels.

removal of physical dirt but the request to God for a clear conscience, now preserves you also by the resurrection of Jesus Christ, who is at God's right hand, having passed into heaven, angels, authorities and powers having been made subject to him.

4.1   Christ, then, having suffered physically, arm yourselves with the like attitude (for the physical sufferer has ceased to sin) so as to spend the remainder of your physical existence no longer controlled by human passions but by the will of God. It is enough to have devoted the time that has gone by to Gentile pursuits, when you indulged in various forms of licentiousness, sexual lusts, drinking bouts, revels, carousals and disorderly idolatries. They find it extraordinary that you do not join with them in the same excess of debauchery, and slander

5   you. But they must render an account to him who stands ready to judge the living and the dead. That is why the News was proclaimed to the dead also, that they may be judged as men are judged physically, but live as God lives spiritually.

The climax approaches. Be temperate and sober, therefore, so as to attend to your prayers. Above all assiduously cultivate love among yourselves, for love atones for a multitude of sins.[22] Be ungrudging in your

10   hospitality to one another. As each has been endowed, administer your particular gifts among yourselves as good stewards of God's varied favours. When one preaches, let it be with all the power at God's command, that in every connexion, through Jesus Christ, God may be glorified, to whom belongs the glory and dominion for ever. Amen.

Do not be amazed, dear friends, at the fiery experience that has come to test you, as though something strange had happened to you. Rather rejoice that to some extent you share Christ's sufferings, so that at the revelation of his glory you may also rejoice exceedingly. If you are calumniated for Christ's sake, how fortunate you are, for the Spirit of glory and of God rests upon you!

15   But let none of you suffer as a murderer, or as a thief, or as an evil-doer, or an interfering busybody. But if it is as a Christian, let him not be ashamed, let him praise God on that account, because it is the proper course for

22 *Prov* 10:12.

the Judgment to begin with the household of God. And if it begins with us, how will it end for those who have disobeyed God's News? "If the righteous shall scarcely be saved, where will the ungodly and the sinner come in?"[23] Wherefore let those who suffer for well-doing, in accordance with the will of God, commit their souls to a faithful Creator.

5.1 I beg the elders among you, therefore, I who am a fellow-elder and witness of Christ's sufferings, a sharer too in the glory that is about to be revealed, shepherd God's flock that is among you, not compulsorily but voluntarily, not self-interestedly but disinterestedly, not as domineering over your charges but as being examples to your flock. Then when the Head Shepherd appears you will obtain the evergreen wreath of honour.

5 Similarly, you younger men, subordinate yourselves to the older ones. Always wear humility's apron[24] with one another, for "God sets himself against the arrogant, but bestows favour on the humble."[25]

Humble yourselves, therefore, under the mighty hand of God, that you may be exalted in due course, casting all your care upon him because he cares for you. Be sober, be alert! Your adversary the Devil is on the prowl like a roaring lion seeking prey. Resist him, steadfast in faith, knowing that the very same experiences are being faced

10 by your fraternity elsewhere in the world. But the God of all mercy, who has called you to his eternal glory in Christ, after you have suffered a while, will himself condition, establish and strengthen you. To him be dominion for ever. Amen.

I have written to you thus very briefly by Silvanus,[26] a reliable brother as I hold, urging and affirming that this is the true grace of God. Stand in that.

Your elect sister-community in Babylon[27] sends you regards, as also does my son Mark. Convey my regards to one another with an affectionate kiss.

Peace be with all of you who are in Christ.

---

23 *Prov* 11:31 (LXX).
24 Humility is likened to the menial's apron.
25 *Prov* 3:34.
26 The same as Silas, companion of Paul. The 'reliability' is assumed to be in the capacity of faithful translator and amanuensis, since Peter's native tongue was Aramaic. But it is possible that the term 'reliable' is employed in the doctrinal sense.
27 A Jewish apocalyptic designation of Rome. See *Rev* 17:5; 18:2.

Open Letter to the Twelve Tribes

James

1.1   James, servant of God and the Lord Jesus Christ, sends
greetings to the Twelve Tribes of the Dispersion.

Count it a most favourable occurrence, brothers, when
you meet with various trying experiences, recognising
that the testing of your faith gives rise to constancy. But
let constancy fulfil its complete function, so that you may
5   be whole and hale, deficient in nothing. If any of you
lacks wisdom, let him ask God, who gives to all bounti-
fully and unstintingly, and it will be granted him. Only
let him ask in faith with no misgiving, for the doubter is
like a wave of the sea, driven by the wind and tossed
hither and thither. Let not such a man, an indecisive
character, vacillating in all his ways, expect to receive
anything from the Lord.

Let the lowly brother rejoice when his circumstances
10   are improved, but the well-to-do brother when his are
reduced, for like the flower of grass he will pass away.[1]
Once the sun has risen with its scorching rays it withers
the grass, its flower drops, and its pleasant aspect is
destroyed. Just so will the rich man shrivel in his tracks.

Happy is the man who holds out under temptation.
For having been tested he will receive the award of Life,
which God has promised to those who love him. Let no
one say when he is tempted, "I am being tempted by
God"; for God is incapable of being tempted by evil and
himself tempts no one. But each is tempted when beck-
15   oned and enticed by his own desires. Then, when desire
is embraced[2] it begets sin, and sin once accomplished
brings forth death. Do not delude yourselves, dear

---

1 cf *Ps* 90:3–7; *Isa* 40:6–8.
2 The simile relates to a harlot's enticements.

brothers. From Above comes every noble legacy and perfect gift, descending from the Supreme Luminary, which knows neither rising nor setting nor waxing and waning.[3] Of set purpose he begot us by the Message of Truth, so as to be in the nature of first-fruits of its creative activities.

20 You are aware of this, dear brothers. But let everyone be quick to listen, reluctant to speak, slow to be angry; for a man's anger does not serve the ends of divine justice. So weeding out every foul weed and rank growth in our moral nature, let us gently receive the implanted word that is able to save our lives.

Act on the Message, and do not merely listen to it, deluding yourselves. Whoever hears the Message, but fails to act on it, is like a man who observes his natural appearance in a mirror. He takes stock of himself, but when he goes away he immediately forgets what he is 25 like. But he who has looked into the untarnished law of liberty,[4] and stayed to gaze, being no forgetful listener but an active doer, will be blessed in what he does. If anyone deems himself devout, not curbing his tongue but gulling his own mind, his devoutness is worthless. Pure and unalloyed devoutness in God's view is to care for the orphan and widow in their affliction and to keep himself unsullied by the world.

2.1 Brothers, hold the faith of our Lord Jesus Christ with no partialities in your esteem. If a man with a gold ring, splendidly dressed, enters your synagogue, and there also comes in a poor man meanly dressed, but you show regard for the one wearing fine clothes and say, "Please sit here where you'll be comfortable", while you say to the poor man, "You can stand", or, "sit on the floor at my feet", are you not making distinctions among yourselves and letting wrong considerations weigh with you?

5 Hearken, my dear brothers, has not God chosen the poor by this world's standards, but rich in faith and heirs of the Kingdom he has promised to those who love him? But you have insulted the poor. Do not the rich oppress you and drag you into court? Do they not profane that fair name by which you are called? If you will but carry out that prince of laws in the Scripture, "You are to love

3 Referring respectively to sun and moon.
4 The writer would seem to allude to the New Covenant code as in the Sermon on the Mount, interpreting the Law of Release, *Deut* 15:1–15.

your neighbour as yourself",[5] you will do well. But if you exhibit partiality you commit a sin, and are convicted by 10 the Law as transgressors; for whoever may keep the whole Law, yet fail in one particular, becomes guilty in respect of all the rest. For he who said, "Do not commit adultery", also said, "Do not murder". So if you do not commit adultery, yet commit murder,[6] you have become a transgressor of the Law. So speak and so act, as those who will be judged by the law of liberty; for there will be judgment without mercy for him who has shown no mercy, while mercy will override judgment.

Of what avail is it, brothers, for someone to say he has faith, when he has no deeds to show for it? Can faith save 15 him? If a brother or sister is destitute, lacking even daily food, and one of you says to them, "Go in peace. Mind you keep warm and take enough nourishment", but you give them no physical necessities for the purpose, what avails it? So with faith. Unless deeds spring from it it is dead in isolation.

One may put it this way. You have faith, you say, while I have deeds. Show me your faith independent of deeds, and I will show you my faith by my deeds. You believe there is one God, you say. It is well that you do 20 believe it. But so do the demons, and they shudder. Can you not realise, you dunce, that faith without deeds is unproductive? Was not our father Abraham vindicated by his deeds when he offered his son Isaac upon the altar? Can you not see how faith assisted his deeds, and by his deeds his faith was perfected? And so the Scripture was fulfilled which states, "Abraham believed God, and it was credited to him as rectitude",[7] and he was called "the friend of God".[8] You see, then, that a man is 25 vindicated by his deeds, and not simply by faith. Was not Rahab the harlot likewise vindicated by her deeds, when she entertained the messengers and got them out another way?[9] For as the body without the spirit is dead, so is faith without deeds.

3.1   Do not be all-inclusive teachers, brothers, knowing that we shall receive greater condemnation; for by

5 *Lev* 19:18.
6 *Exod* 20:13–14. Murder here is metaphorical, cf *Mt* 5:21–22.
7 *Gen* 15:6.
8 *Isa* 41:8.
9 ie from Jericho. See *Josh* 6.

attempting many things we fail in all. If a man makes no mistakes in a subject, he is an expert,[10] capable also of curbing his whole body. Look how we put bits in the mouths of horses to make them obey us, and so we steer their whole bodies. Look too at the ships. Large as they are and driven along by stiff breezes, they are steered by a tiny rudder wherever the whim of the helmsman

5   directs. Just so the tongue is an insignificant organ, but it boasts great things. Look how small a spark sets so mighty a forest ablaze! The very rule of misrule the tongue establishes among our organs: it is the soiler of the whole body and the inflamer of the process of generation,[11] being inflamed itself by Gehenna.[12] Every species of beast and bird, reptile and marine creature, has been tamed by the human species. But the tongue no one can tame: it is an ungovernable evil, saturated with

10   deadly poison. With it we bless the Lord our Father, and equally with it we curse men made in the image of God. Out of the same mouth proceed blessing and cursing. This should not be, my brothers. Does a fountain gush fresh and brackish water from the same vent? Can a fig tree, my brothers, yield olives, or a vine figs? No more can salt water yield fresh.

Who among you claims wisdom and sagacity? Let him display his accomplishments by worthy conduct, with the moderation of wisdom. But if you have bitter jealousy and rivalry in your minds, do not boast and lie

15   where truth is concerned. That wisdom never came from Above: it is earthly, materialistic and diabolical. For where bitter jealousy and rivalry exist, there will be found anarchy and every ugly business. But the wisdom from Above is first of all impartial, then peaceable, reasonable, persuasive, laden with mercy and beneficial fruits, free from favouritism and insincerity. For those who make peace the fruit of righteousness will be sown in peace.

4.1   What is the cause of your bellicose and pugnacious propensities? Is it not the animal instincts that war in your organs? You desire, but fail to acquire. Your covet and envy, but you cannot secure. You battle and fight,

---

10 Lit "a perfect man".
11 James the Just was a practising ascetic.
12 ie Hell fire.

but you do not possess by refusing to ask. You ask and then do not obtain, because you ask wrongly so that you can pander to your animal instincts. You adulterous creatures! Are you aware that the world's intimacy means God's hostility? Whoever, therefore, wants to be a friend of the world renders himself an enemy of God.
5 Or do you imagine that the Scripture states to no purpose, "With *jealousy* does he desire the spirit which he has caused to dwell in us"?[13] Yet he bestows even greater loving-kindness, which is why it says, "God sets himself against the arrogant, but bestows loving-kindness on the humble".[14] Submit yourselves to God therefore, but oppose the Devil and he will fly from you.

> *Draw near to God*
>   *and he will draw near to you.*
> *Cleanse your hands, you sinners,*
>   *and purify your hearts, you double-minded.*
> *Afflict your souls,*
>   *yes, mourn and weep.*
> *Let your laughter be turned to grief,*
>   *and your joy to sorrow.*
> 10 *Abase yourselves before the Lord,*
>   *and he will raise uou up.*[15]

Do not rail at one another, brothers. He who rails at his brother and condemns his brother rails at the Law and condemns the Law. But if you condemn the Law, you are no observer of the Law, but a judge of it. There is but one Lawgiver and judge, who has power to preserve and destroy. Who are you, then, to judge your neighbour?

Come then, you who declare, "To-day or to-morrow we will journey to this or that city, stay a year there, trade and make a profit", you who have no say in to-morrow's events. For what is your life? You are but a mist that is
15 visible for a while and then vanishes. Instead of this you ought to say, "If the Lord wills, we shall be alive and do so-and-so". As it is you take pride in your boastings, and all such pride is wicked.
5.1 Come then, you rich, shed copious tears for the miseries that are coming upon you. Your riches have rotted

13 Not in the OT. Perhaps from an apocryphal source regarded by the author as inspired.
14 *Prov* 3:34.
15 Possibly from a liturgical source for the Day of Atonement.

and your clothes have become motheaten. Your gold and silver are rusted over, and their rust will be evidence against you, and will eat into your flesh as a fire you have stored up for yourselves for the Last Days. See how the pay of the labourers who have reaped your meadows cries out, which you have kept back, and the plaints of the harvesters have reached the ears of the Lord of hosts.

5   You have grazed and gambolled upon the land, you have fattened yourselves up for a Day of Slaughter. You have condemned, you have murdered the upright. He does not resist you.[16]

Have patience then, brothers, till the coming of the Lord.[17] See how the farmer waits for the precious fruit of the earth, being patient until it can receive the early and late rains. So have patience yourselves, fortify your minds, for the coming of the Lord is at hand. Do not complain against one another, brothers, lest you are judged. Lo, the Judge stands at the door!

10   Take the prophets, brothers, who have spoken in the name of the Lord, as an example of suffering and fortitude. See how we eulogise those who have endured. You have heard of the constancy of Job, and you know its happy ending, how the Lord is full of compassion and tender mercy.[18] And above all, brothers, do not swear, either by heaven or earth, or with any other oath. Let your "Yes" mean yes, and your "No" mean no, lest you incur condemnation.[19]

Is any of you depressed? Let him pray. Is anyone cheerful? Let him sing psalms. Is any of you ailing? Let him summon the elders of the community, and let them pray for him after anointing him with oil in the name of

15   the Lord. And the request in faith shall save the sick, and the Lord will raise him up.[20] If he has committed sins they will be forgiven him. Confess your sins to one another, therefore, and pray for one another, that you may be cured. The heartfelt petition of an upright man is very efficacious. Elijah was a human being exactly like ourselves, and he prayed earnestly that it might not rain, and no rain fell on the land for three years and six

16 On this passage cf *Wisd* 2:6–20; cf also *Isa* 53:7; *Acts* 7:52.
17 See *Ps* 96:13; *Isa* 40:10–11; *Zech* 14:1–5.
18 See *Job* 42:10; cf *Num* 14:18.
19 In accordance with Essene practice. See p 65, n 21 (*Mt.* 6:37).
20 Like the Essenes, the early Christians practised healing and exorcism.

months. Then he prayed again, and the heavens gave rain and the earth yielded its fruit.

Brothers, if any of you should stray from the Truth, 20 and someone corrects him, be sure that he who turns a transgressor from the error of his ways will save his own soul and atone for a multitude of sins.[21]

21 cf *Ps* 32:1–2.

Open Letter to Gentile Communities

Judas

1.1   Judas, servant of Jesus Christ and brother of James, to the members of the communities dear to God the Father and kept by Jesus Christ.

While making every endeavour, dear friends, to write you on the theme of our common salvation, I have found myself obliged to write urging you to contend for the faith once and for all delivered to the saints. For certain people have managed to creep in, ungodly persons set down of old for judgment, converting the mercy of our God into licentiousness and disowning the Sole Sovereign and our Lord Jesus Christ.

5   I would remind you, therefore, though you once knew all this, how the Lord having saved the people from the land of Egypt afterwards destroyed those who did not believe. The angels too, who did not keep to their own province, but forsook their native habitat,[1] he has kept in close confinement[2] in subterranean gloom for the Judgment of the Great Day, even as Sodom and Gomorrah and the towns in their proximity, having after the same manner as these taken to obscene ways and indulgence in unnatural vice, are presented as an example, suffering the penalty of perpetual burning.

Notwithstanding this, these dreamers similarly defile the flesh, defy disciplines, and speak slightingly of dignities. Yet even the Archangel Michael, when, at odds with the Devil, he argued about the body of Moses, did not care to make an abusive attack on him, but said, "The

10   Lord rebuke you!"[3] But these people speak slightingly of

---

1 *Gen* 6:2; *Enoch* 12:2, "the Watchers of the heaven who have abandoned the high heaven . . . and have defiled themselves with women".
2 Or "enduring fetters" (*Enoch* 14:5).
3 *Assumpt. Moses*, cf *Zech* 3:2.

such things as they know nothing about, while in such things as instinctively they are familiar with, like brute beasts, in these they corrupt themselves. Woe to them! They have travelled the road of Cain, and plunged greedily for gain into the vice of Balaam, and perished in the mutiny of Korah.[4] These are the hidden snags sharing the entertainment of your love-feasts, feeding themselves fearlessly, empty clouds carried away by winds, trees, that are autumn-blasted and barren, dead twice over, torn up by the roots, raging breakers of the sea foaming with their own shame, wandering stars for whom is reserved the blackness of darkness for ever.[5]

Concerning these men Enoch, the seventh from Adam, prophesied saying, "Lo, the Lord comes with

15　myriads of his holy ones to execute judgment upon all, and to convict all the ungodly of all the their ungodly deeds for which they have been responsible, and of all the harsh things ungodly sinners have spoken against him".[6] These men are complainers, bewailers of their lot, followers of their impulses, with mouths that speak fulsomely,[7] flattering people for some expected benefit.

20　You however, dear friends, recall the words spoken in advance by the envoys of our Lord Jesus Christ, when they told you, "In the Last Times deceivers will come, followers of their ungodly impulses".[8] These are the separatists, unspiritual materialists. You however, dear friends, develop yourselves in your most sacred faith, praying by the holy Spirit, retaining God's regard, awaiting the mercy of our Lord Jesus Christ for Eternal Life. Take pity on some, of course, and save them with eager resolution, snatching them from the blaze.[9] Take pity on others too, but save them with repugnance, loathing even the tunic soiled by the flesh.

Now to him who is able to keep you steady, and enable you to stand proudly blameless in the presence of his

25　glory, to the Only God our Saviour, be glory, majesty, might and dominion, through Jesus Christ our Master, from all eternity, now, and to all eternity. Amen.

4 The sequence 'travelled-plunged greedily-perished' bears some resemblance to the fate of the Gadarene swine, *Mt* 8:22.
5 cf *Enoch* 18:14, 16.
6 *Enoch* 1:9.
7 cf *Assumpt. Moses* 6:6–9.
8 *Mt* 24:24; *Acts* 20:29–31.
9 *Amos* 4:11; *Zech* 3:2.

Open Letter to Gentile Converts in Asia

'Peter' (2)

1.1   Simeon Peter, servant and envoy of Jesus Christ, to those[1] who by the beneficence of our God and of our Saviour Jesus Christ have obtained a faith equal in privilege to ours. May abundant peace and prosperity be yours in the knowledge of God and of Jesus our Master.

Since God's divine power has granted us everything useful for life and piety through knowledge of him who has called us to his own nobility and virtue, by which those precious and marvellous promises have been given us, that, having by them escaped the corruption the world is heir to by passion, you may become sharers
5   of the divine nature; for that very reason, having additionally brought to bear the utmost diligence, join virtue to your faith, knowledge to virtue, self-control to knowledge, constancy to self-control, piety to constancy, brotherly affection to piety, and love to brotherly affection. For where these qualities exist and abound they assure that you are neither uncultivated nor unfruitful where the knowledge of our Lord Jesus Christ is concerned. But in that man's case where these are not present, he is blind, being short-sighted, obtaining absolutely nothing[2] from his cleansing from his sins in the not so distant past.
10   Preferably therefore, brothers, use every endeavour to make your calling and choice certain, for by practising these qualities you will never come to grief. And thus an ample entrance will be afforded you into the Lasting Kingdom of our Lord and Saviour Jesus Christ.

---

1 Gentile converts who did not observe the Law of Moses.
2 Lit "a blur" or "blank" in accordance with the metaphor.

I therefore intend always to remind you of these things, though you know them and are firmly established in the revealed truth. But I think it right, so long as I remain in this mortal frame, to keep you wide awake by reminder, knowing that the laying aside of my frame will come very soon now, as our Lord Jesus Christ

15   has shown me. I will further endeavour to enable you after my departure to keep these things constantly in mind.

For we have not followed cleverly contrived fables when we acquainted you with the power and presence of our Lord Jesus Christ, but were eye-witnesses of his majesty; for he received from God the Father honour and glory when from the Supernal Glory language such as this was addressed to him, "You are my dear son, with whom I am well-satisfied".[3] These were the very words we ourselves heard addressed to him from heaven when we were with him on the holy mount. And we possess the even more definite Prophetic Message to which you will do well to pay attention, a Message that is like a lamp shining in a dismal place until daylight streams in and

20   the morning star rises in your hearts. But this you must realize first of all, that no prophecy of Scripture is to be interpreted individually, for prophecy never came at human bidding: men spoke from God under compulsion of the holy Spirit.

2.1   Nevertheless there were false prophets among the people, just as there will be false teachers among you, who will introduce subversive principles, disowning even the Sovereign Lord who bought them, and bringing on themselves swift destruction. Many will follow them in their immoral courses, with the result that the True Way will be maligned. Yes, in their rapacity these false teachers will cheat you with their fabricated messages. But not for long will their judgment dawdle, or their destruction drowse.

God did not spare angels who had sinned, but hurling them down to Tartarus consigned them to caverns of

5   darkness, there to await judgment. He did not spare the ancient world, but saved Noah, eighth preacher of righteousness,[4] bringing a Deluge upon the world of

---

3 cf *Mt* 17:5.
4 Eighth in succession to Seth. cf *Gen* 5.

impious men. The cities of Sodom and Gomorrah also he sentenced to be burnt to ashes, making them a warning of what was in store for the impious, but rescued virtuous Lot utterly prostrated by the licentious behaviour of these immoral people. For that virtuous man by what he saw and heard while living among them tortured his pure soul day after day with their lawless behaviour. If the Lord did these things he surely knows how to rescue the pious from temptation, and to keep the

10   wicked under restraint for the Day of Judgment, particularly those who in their vile lust go in for unnatural vice and despise discipline. Daring, presumptuous, they are not the least overawed by dignities, speaking slightingly of them. Whereas angels who are greater in might and power than such dignities make no abusive attack on them before the Lord. These men, however, like natural brute beasts made for capture and destruction, speaking slightingly, as they do, of such things as they know nothing about, will surely perish in their corruption, suffering injury as the reward for inflicting injury.

These are the people who deem wantonness in the daytime a special pleasure: blots and disgraces, luxuriating in their seductive wiles, even when feasting with you, with eyes full of adultery that never rest a moment from sin, enticing unstable souls, with a mind fully trained in gaining their ends. Offspring of execration!

15   They have gone astray, abandoning the straight road, following in the steps of Balaam son of Beor, who loved the fees of iniquity, but was reproved for his transgressions: a dumb beast of burden speaking with a human voice checked the prophet's aberration.

They are springs without water, tempest-driven spray, for whom the blackness of darkness is reserved. With their high-flown nonsensical talk they entice with their base physical passions those who have only just escaped from those who live in error. They promise them liberty, while they themselves are the slaves of corruption; for a man is enslaved by whatever he gives way to.

20   For if, escaping from the world's pollutions by knowledge of the Lord and Saviour Jesus Christ, they are vanquished by being again enmeshed by them,[5] their last state is worse than the first.[6] Far better for them

5 A metaphor taken from the *retiarii*, gladiators armed with net and trident.
6 cf *Mt* 12:45.

never to have known the way of righteousness, than knowing it to have gone back on the sacred injunction delivered to them. They only confirm what the true proverb says, "The dog has returned to his vomit, and the washed sow to her wallowing in the mire".[7]

3.1   . The letter I am writing to you now, dear friends, is my second, and my intention with these letters is to stimulate your clear thinking by reminder, that the words spoken beforehand by the holy Prophets, and the injunction of the Lord and Saviour by your envoys, may be brought back to you.

In the first place you must realise this, that in the Last Days there will surely come scoffers, following their own desires and saying, "What has become of the promise of his advent, for since the fathers fell asleep everything goes on exactly as it has done since the beginning of

5   Creation?"[8] They choose to ignore the fact that the sky and the earth, formed by the Word of God out of water and by water,[9] had been a long time in existence, yet the world of those days perished, inundated with water by these agencies.[10] By the very same Word the present sky and earth have been stocked with fire, kept for the Day of Judgment and the destruction of ungodly mortals.

There is this too that must not escape your notice, dear friends, that a single day with the Lord is as a thousand years, and a thousand years as a single day.[11] The Lord is not dilatory in fulfilling his promise as some reckon dilatoriness: he is forbearing to you, not wanting any to perish, but all to come to repentance.

10   Nevertheless the Day of the Lord will come like a thief, when the sky will vanish with a roar, the elements will be disintegrated with intense heat, and of the earth and its occupants there will be left no trace. Since in this manner all these are to be disintegrated, what pure-living and devout persons ought you to be while eagerly expecting the Day of the Lord, in which the sky will go up in flames and the elements melt away with intense heat? Yet in accordance with God's promise we expect a New Sky and a New Earth[12] wherein righteousness dwells.

7 cf *Prov* 26:11, and see *Mt* 7:6.
8 Evidential of the late date of this letter, which could not be by Peter.
9 *Gen* 1:6–10.
10 See *Gen* 7:11.
11 cf *Ps* 90:4.
12 cf *Isa* 65:17.

Consequently, dear friends, because we expect these things let us be anxious to be found by him[13] in peace,
15 spotless and unblemished, and regard the forbearance of our Master as our salvation. Our dear brother Paul, according to the wisdom given him, has also written you to the same effect,[14] as indeed is true of all his letters where he speaks of these matters, letters in which there are certain things by no means easy to understand, which the unskilled and unstable twist to their own ruination as they do the rest of the Scriptures.[15]

Being forewarned then, dear friends, be on your guard, so that you are not deprived of that firm support[16] by being led away by the error of unprincipled persons. Grow, then, in the favour and knowledge of our Lord and Saviour Jesus Christ, to whom be praise both now and for time eternal.[17]

---

13 "Him" ie Christ.
14 In his letter to the Asian Communities (*Ephesians*), cf *Eph* 3:2–4; 4:30; 5:6–8.
15 Another evidence of the late date of this letter. By this time evidently Paul's letters had been collected and were held to rank as Scripture.
16 ie 'of the Scriptures'.
17 Lit "to the Day of Eternity". A doxology relating to Christ is a further evidence of late date, as is also the expression "Our Lord and Saviour Jesus Christ".

THE WRITINGS OF JOHN

The Discourses of the Logos
Gospel according to John

On the Theme of Life
I John

To The Elect Lady and Her Children
II John

To Gaius
III John

The Revelation of Jesus Christ

The Discourses of the Logos
Preface to John

What are known as the Johannine writings in the New Testament consist of a *Gospel*, a *Tract*, two *Letters*, and a Book of *Visions*. They are a puzzling collection, especially the *Gospel*. The first is anonymous, but is stated to contain the reminiscences of someone described as the 'Dear Disciple' of Jesus. The tract (*I John*) is also anonymous, but appears to be by the same writer as the two letters (*II* and *III John*), the author of which calls himself 'the Elder' or 'Presbyter'. It is only the book of visions (*Revelation*) that is actually stated to have been recorded by a person of the name of John. On linguistic grounds alone it is almost certain that this John was not identical with the Elder, or with the author of the Gospel in its present form; yet the *Revelation* is not wholly unrelated to the other documents.

What is said in the *Gospel* about Jesus, and the sentiments in it expressed by him, have made this work the most treasured document in the New Testament for orthodox Christians, and helped to give rise to the belief that the 'Dear Disciple' was in fact one of the Twelve Apostles, namely John the son of Zebedee. The evidences which exist, however, are totally against this view. We shall, of course, be examining these evidences, both in the *Gospel* and in surviving traditions and sources. But one point may be represented immediately. John the son of Zebedee was a rough uncouth Galilean fisherman, whereas the *Gospel* is from a source or sources highly literate and intellectual.

The investigation of the Johannine problem calls for a fully open and uncommitted mind, capacity for research, and literary and linguistic equipment.

A large part of the *Gospel* consists of discourses of Jesus. Where these run to some length they are dealt with in the Greek manner, where the audience (in this case the Jews or the disciples) interject questions or comments, which keep the discourse going. When we compare these discourses and other statements with Jesus's manner of speech in the other *Gospels* it is very clear that it is not the same man speaking.

The Jesus of the Synoptic *Gospels* speaks in a Jewish manner, both in theme and construction, as may be noted in the Sermon on the Mount. The Jesus of John's *Gospel*, however, largely speaks in a quite different idiom, and as a non-Jew, and often in a pretentious alien manner. He speaks of the Law given to Moses as "*your* Law", instead of "*our* Law", and declares that "all who came before me were thieves and robbers". He even refers to God after himself, in saying, "I and my Father are one".

It is evident that such material has been composed for Jesus by a Greek Christian, and by comparison of the language and style there is a strong case for claiming that he was the author of the *First Epistle of John* (John the Elder). This John was still living around AD 140 in the region of Asia Minor, and is referred by Papias of Hierapolis as one in a position to relate things said and done by Jesus. This date is obviously too late for any immediate disciple of Jesus to have still been living. To whose recollections, then, did this John have access?

The answer is that a direct disciple of Jesus is known to have been living at Ephesus down to the beginning of the second century, where John the Elder could have had contact with him. This disciple was also called John. Eusebius in his *Ecclesiastical History* reports that at Ephesus were to be found the tombs of both Johns. His information came from a letter written by Polycrates bishop of Ephesus to Victor of Rome. Polycrates had made this important statement:

> "Moreover, John that rested on the bosom of our Lord, who was a priest that wore the sacerdotal plate, witness and teacher, he, also, rests at Ephesus."

The 'Dear Disciple' is disclosed as a Jewish priest, and this is wholly consistent with what is said in the Fourth *Gospel*. He betrays his priestly office in the reminiscences which form part of the text. He makes exact referencs to Jewish ritual and Temple worship, and when he speaks of the priests not going into Pilate's praetorium to avoid defilement. He himself will not enter the tomb in which Jesus had been laid until he knows there is no corpse there. He is of a distinguished Jewish sacerdotal family and was personally known to the High Priest. He has a house in Jerusalem, and after the crucifixion gave hospitality there to the mother of Jesus. Naturally he knows the topography of Jerusalem well, and he also introduces and explains Aramaic words. It is to be inferred that it was John the Priest's house, with the large upper room, that was the scene of the Passover Supper, where the 'Dear Disciple' as master of the house had the seat of honour next to that of Jesus, leaning on the breast of the Messiah, as related in the *Gospel*. There were thus fourteen persons present.

Tradition records that the 'Dear Disciple' lived finally at Ephesus to extreme old age (cf *Jn* 21:22–23), and was eventually persuaded to dictate his recollections of Jesus. These would appear to have been drawn upon in the Fourth *Gospel*, taking the form of a series of signs which establish that Jesus was the Messiah, introduced by the formula, "After this", or "After these events", a design which is preserved down to 7:1 and is then abandoned until 19:38. Early patristic quotations, and even fragments of an unknown Gospel (*Egerton Papyrus I*), reveal a form of certain sayings in the Fourth *Gospel* much closer in style and character to what we find in the Synoptics. It is also now known that certain passages are reflective of the Essene Dead Sea Scrolls, and the story of the woman taken in adultery (*Jn* 8) was also to be found in the *Gospel of the Hebrews*.

We thus face the evidence that John's *Gospel* as we have it is a composite document. Its basis is the memoirs of John the Priest, who is encountered initially as a disciple of John the Baptist, an Essene link. The fact that John the Priest was an advanced student of Jewish mysticism may help to explain the attraction of his work for the Greek Elder. The *Gospel* contains in the narrative portions a great deal that is characteristic of the author of the *Revelation*, while the *Revelation*, in the Messages to the Seven Communities, and some other passages, contains material which is typical of the author of a large part of the present Gospel. See the Prefaces to the *Letters* and the *Revelation*.

The second work, which has so largely been imposed on and has superseded the other, is a dialogue document in the Greek Platonic tradition. It is in two parts. The first is a discourse of Jesus to the Jews, and the second a discourse to the apostles. The first part has been chopped up, and most unskilfully inserted at different points, often months apart and quite inappropriately, and out of the dialogue's natural order. The second part, also to some extent in disarray, occupies *Jn* 13–17, section 6 of the present translation. Scholars have long recognised, even when regarding the *Gospel* as a unity, that there have been a number of displacements. These can only be represented tentatively, and those which the present editor has proposed do not in all cases coincide with the proposals of others. The changes can be followed by the student by means of the footnotes.

It may well be that in the heading of *I John*, a tract which it has been held was meant to introduce the Gospel, we have the actual title of the dialogue document, namely "On the Theme (or Message) of Life", in Greek *Peri tou Logou tes Zoes*, or in the briefer form of the Latin Vulgate, *De Verbo Vitae*. In the discourses of Jesus in the Gospel he largely speaks in the manner the author of *I John* writes.

The author of the *Gospel*, as we now have it, clearly in two footnotes (*Jn* 19:35 and 21:24) distinguishes himself from the 'Dear Disciple' of whose reminiscences he has availed himself. These footnotes are in the characteristic style of the Elder who is the author of *I John* (cf *Jn* 21:24 with *I Jn* 12). The last chapter of the *Gospel* also confirms the tradition that the 'Dear Disciple' lived to a very great age.

The Prologue to the Fourth *Gospel* is of some service both in locating and dating the book in its present form. This Prologue is an antiphonal chant or hymn, which could well be the very same that is mentioned by Pliny the Younger in his letter to the Emperor Trajan about the Christians (*c* AD 112) sent when he was Governor of Bithynia. The 'Dear Disciple' is said to have died in Trajan's reign and to have been buried at Ephesus. These links with Asia Minor are reinforced by the prominence given to the Apostle Philip in the *Gospel*. He is stated to have been buried at Hierapolis. Andrew and Thomas also, who are specially mentioned in the *Gospel*, are quoted in apostolic sources used by Papias of Hierapolis. The traditions would therefore appear to be authentic which make Asia Minor the region of publication of the Fourth *Gospel*; and since Trajan became emperor in AD 98 the book in its present form may approximately be dated about the end of the first decade of the second century.
century.

It was the Emperor Domitian, the predecessor of Trajan, a great persecutor of the Christians, who banished the 'Dear Disciple' to the island of Patmos, where the *Revelation* was received. This was a Roman punishment of eminent persons. Incidentally it was Domitian who insisted on being addressed as 'Our Lord and God' (see Suetonius, *Dom* 8), words put into the mouth of Thomas with reference to Jesus (*Jn* 20:28).

Finally, to make it very clear that John the son of Zebedee was not the 'Dear Disciple', we have the statement in *Luke* that Peter and John the son of Zebedee were the two whom Jesus sent to the master of the house where Jesus would eat the passover. Also the 'Dear Disciple' is distinguished from the fisherman John in the story in *Jn* 21 (see verses 2 and 7).

The closing chapter of the Fourth *Gospel* conveys further that the 'Dear Disciple' would live to a great age, which was true of

John the Priest. Peter is represented as somewhat jealous of "this man", which he had no cause to be if the son of Zebedee was concerned. Peter and the two sons of Zebedee were on equal intimacy with Jesus, sharing specially in his experiences. It is the eminent 'outsider' from Jerusalem, whose influence on Jesus Peter resents.

Much more could be said, and further elucidation will be found both in the text and notes.

The Good News of Jesus Christ

John's Version

Prologue[1]

1.1 'In the Beginning was the Word.[2]
    And the Word was with God.
So the Word was divine.
    It was in the Beginning with God.
By it everything had being.
    And without it nothing had being.[3]
What had being by it was Life.
    And Life was the Light of men.
5 And the Light shines in the Darkness.
    And the Darkness could not suppress it.'

There was a man sent from God called John. He came as a witness, to testify about the Light, that all might believe through him. He was not himself the Light, but came that he should testify about the Light.

'This was the true Light.
    It illumines all who enter the world.
10 He was in the world [and the world had being by
                          him].[4]
    But the world did not recognise him.

---

1 The Prologue consists of a hymn interspersed with brief remarks. It is antiphonal, the alternate lines being chanted as a response. Our work was published in Asia Minor early in the 2nd century, and this hymn could well be the one mentioned by Pliny the Younger, when as Governor of Bithynia (c AD 112) he wrote about the Christians to the Emperor Trajan that "they met on a certain fixed day before it was light and sang an antiphonal chant to Christ, as to a god".
2 The *Logos*, the Expressed Concept. And see Philo Judaeus.
3 cf *Prov* 8:22–31.
4 Possibly an interpolation.

He came to his own domains.
> *And his own did not receive him.'*

On those who did receive him, those who believed in him,[5] he conferred the privilege of becoming children of God, who owed their being not to race, nor to physical intention, nor to human design, but to God.

'The Word took bodily form and dwelt with us.
> *And we beheld his glory.*
Glory as of the Father's Only-begotten.
> *Full of loving-kindness and truth.'*

15   John testified of him and proclaimed – these were his very words – "He who comes after me ranks before me; for he is my superior".

'For of his bounty we have all received.
> *Yes, mercy added to mercy.*
For the Law was given by Moses.
> *Loving-kindness and Truth came by Jesus Christ.'*

No one has ever seen God.[6] God's Only-Begotten, who is in the Father's bosom, he has portrayed him.[7]

5 cf *Jn* 12:36.
6 cf *I Jn* 4:12.
7 cf *Gen* 1:26. Christ as Second Adam.

i

Here is John's testimony when the Jews of Jerusalem sent priests and Levites to him to ask him, "Who are you?" He admitted without the slightest hesitation, he clearly admitted, "I am not the Messiah".
20   Then they asked him, "What then? Are you Elijah?"
"I am not", he said.
"Are you the Prophet?"[1]
"No", he replied.
Then they said to him, "Who are you, then, that we may give an answer to those who sent us? What do you say of yourself?"
He said, "I am a voice crying in the wilderness, 'Level the Lord's road,'[2] as announced by the prophet Isaiah."

1 The expected Prophet like Moses.
2 *Isa* 40:3.

25 "They asked him further, "Why then are you immersing if you are not the Messiah, nor Elijah, nor the Prophet?"

"I am immersing in water," John replied. "But there stands among you one whom you do not know, my successor, whose sandal-strap I am not worthy to unlace."[b]

On the following day John saw Jesus approaching him and said, "See, the Lamb of God who takes away the sin

30 of the world! It is he of whom I said, 'After me will come a man who ranks above me; for he is my superior.' I did not know him, only that he would be revealed to Israel. That is why I came immersing in water."

John testified further, "I saw the Spirit flutter down like a dove from heaven and settle on him. I did not know him. I only knew that he who sent me to immerse in water told me, 'The one on whom you see the Spirit descend and settle is he who will immerse in holy Spirit.' I did see it, and have testified that he is the Son of God."

35 The next day John was again standing with two of his disciples, and seeing Jesus go by, he said, "There goes the Lamb of God!" His two disciples heard his exclamation and followed Jesus. Jesus turned and observing them following him said to them, "What is it you want?"

"To know where you are staying, Rabbi,"[c] they told him.

"Come and see", he said.[d]

So they went along and saw where he was staying and

40 remained with him the rest of the day. One of the two who was beside John and heard what he said was Andrew brother of Simon Peter. First thing in the morning he found his brother Simon and said to him, "We have found the Messiah!"[e]

He brought him to Jesus. When Jesus saw him he said

---

a Those who were sent belonged to the Pharisees.
b These things took place at Bethany-beyond-Jordan[3] where John was imersing.
c Translated this means 'Teacher'.
d It was about 4 o'clock (lit 10th hour).
e Translated this means 'Anointed One' (*Christos*).

---

3 Probably meaning 'Place of a boat'. An alternative reading is Beth-abara (Place of the crossing, ie ford).

to him, "You are Simon son of John, are you not? You shall be called Kepha."*f*

On the following day Jesus wished to leave for Galilee, and found Philip. "Follow me!" Jesus told him.*g*

45   Philip in turn found Nathaniel, and said to hm, "We have found him of whom Moses wrote in the Law, and the Prophets also, Jesus son of Joseph from Nazareth!"

"Whatever good can come out of Nazareth?" replied Nathaniel.

Philip said to him, "Come and see."

Jesus saw Nathaniel coming towards him, and said to him, "Here is a true Israelite in whom there is no guile."

"Have we met before?" Nathaniel inquired.

Jesus replied, "I saw you before Philip called you, when you were under the fig tree."[4]

"Rabbi", said Nathaniel, "you *are* the Son of God, you *are* the King of Israel!"[5]

50   Jesus said to him, "Do you believe this because I told you I saw you beneath the fig tree? You shall see much more than that. I tell you for a positive fact,[6] you shall see the sky wide open and the angels of God ascending and descending on the Son of Man."[7]

2.1   The next day but one there was a wedding at Cana of Galilee, and the mother of Jesus was there. Jesus had also been invited to the wedding with his disciples. When they ran short of wine the mother of Jesus said to him, "They have no wine".

"What do you want with me, Madam?" Jesus said to her, "My time has not yet come."

5   "Do whatever he tells you", his mother said to the servants.

Now there were six stone water-jars standing there in accordance with Jewish requirements for purification, each holding from seventeen to twenty-five gallons.

"Fill the jars with water", Jesus instructed the servants.

f   Meaning 'Rock' (*Petros*).
g   Philip was from Bethsaida, the same town as Andrew and Peter.

---

4   cf *Zech* 3:8–10, "I will bring forth my servant the Branch . . . In that day, says the Lord of hosts, you shall call every man his neighbour under the vine and under the fig tree."
5   cf *I Chron.* 28:6; *Ps* 2:6–7.
6   "Positive fact" representing the double "Amen" in the text.
7   cf Jacob's dream, *Gen* 28:12.

So they filled them to the brim.

Then he said to them, "Now ladle it out, and serve it to the chairman of the banquet."

So they served it.

When the chairman of the banquet tasted the water that had become wine, and had no knowledge of its source, though the servants who had drawn the water 10 knew, the chairman called across to the bridegroom, "Most people put out the best wine first, and the inferior when everyone is drunk. You have saved up the best wine till now."

Jesus performed this, the very first of his signs, in Cana of Galilee, and revealed his quality: and his disciples believed in him.

ii

After this Jesus went down to Capernaum, he, and his mother, and his brothers, and his disciples, but they did not stay there very long.

The Jewish Passover was approaching, and Jesus went up to Jerusalem. In the Temple he found the dealers in oxen, sheep and doves, and the money-changers sitting. 15 And when he had made a lash of twisted rushes he drove them all from the sacred enclosure, sheep and oxen as well, and sent the money-changers' coins flying and overturned their tables, while he told the dove-sellers, "Take these out of here. Do not make a mart of my Father's house."[a][1]

The Jews wanted an explanation, and said to him, "What sign have you to show us for acting like this?"

Jesus replied, "Demolish this temple, and in three days I will raise it up".

20   "This Temple has been under construction for forty-six years",[2] said the Jews, "and are you going to raise it up in three days?"[b]

a   His disciples remembered how it was stated, "Zeal for your House shall consume me" (*Ps* 69:9).
b   But he spoke of the temple of his body. When, therefore, he had risen from the dead his disciples remembered that he had said this, and they believed the Scripture (*Hos* 6:1–2) and the saying Jesus had spoken.

---

1 In the other Gospels the Cleansing of the Temple is placed more probably in Passion Week.
2 Herod the Great is held to have begun the reconstruction of the Temple around 20 BC.

While he was in Jerusalem for the Passover, for the festival, many believed in him when they saw the signs he performed.[c]

3.1   There was one man who belonged to the Pharisees, called Nicodemus, a member of the Jewish government. This man came to Jesus at night, and said to him, "Rabbi, we know that you are a teacher come from God[3] for no one can perform such signs as you do unless God is with him."

Jesus replied, "I tell you for a positive fact, unless one is born from Above[4] one cannot see the Kingdom of God".

Nicodemus said to him, "How can a man be born when he is old? Surely he cannot enter his mother's womb a second time and be born?"

5   Jesus answered, "I tell you for a positive fact, unless one is born of water and spirit one cannot enter the Kingdom of God. What is born physically is physical, and what is born spiritually is spiritual. Do not be surprised at my telling you that you have to be born from Above. The wind[5] blows where it will. You hear the sound of it, but you do not know where it comes from or where it is going. So is everyone who is born of the Spirit".

"How can this be?" Nicodemus inquired.

10   "You are a teacher in Israel,[6] and do not know this?" said Jesus. "I tell you for a positive fact, we discourse of what we know, and testify to what we have seen; but you do not accept our testimony. If I tell you mundane things, and you are incredulous, how will you credit it if I tell you heavenly things? And no one has ascended to heaven but he who has descended from heaven, the Son of Man. And just as Moses elevated the serpent in the

15   wilderness,[7] so must the Son of Man be elevated, that all

---

c   But Jesus did not trust himself to them since he knew all men, and had no need for anyone to speak on a man's behalf because he himself was well aware of that person's character.

---

3   cf *Mk* 12:14 and parallels.
4   This may equally be understood as 'born again'.
5   The same Greek word means both wind and spirit.
6   A Jewish coloquialism.
7   See *Num* 21:8–9.

who believe in him may have Eternal Life."*a*8

a For God loved the world so dearly as to give his Only-begotten Son, so that all who believe in him should not perish but have Eternal Life. God did not send his Son into the world to condemn the world, but that the world might be saved by him. Whoever believes in him will not be condemned, but whoever does not believe in him has been condemned already, because he has not believed in God's Only-begotten Son. The condemnation consists in this, that Light has entered the world, but men held darkness dearer than light, for their deeds were evil. For everyone who does wrong hates the light, and does not come to the light, that his deeds may not be reproved. But whoever does right comes to the light, that it may be evident that his deeds are godly.[9]

---

8 While much that was in his documentary source (the Memoirs of John the Priest) has been adapted by the Greek author to bring the text into line with his ideas, as here, some passages, largely by way of commentary, stand out as his distinctive contribution. Wherever possible attention has been drawn to these, as in this instance, and some have been placed below the main body of the text and in slightly smaller type. See preface to the book. The present passage is *Jn* 3:16–21.

9 Lit "done in God".

iii

After these events Jesus went with his disciples into Judea, and spent some time there immersing people. John also was immersing at Aenon,[1] close to Salim, because there was an ample water supply, and the people came and were immersed, for John had not yet been thrown into prison.

25　　When an argument started between the disciples of John and the Jews[2] about purification, they came to John and said to him, "Rabbi, he who was with you beyond Jordan, of whom you have testified, is immersing, and everyone is flocking to him."

John replied, "No one can receive anything unless Heaven has given it him. You can testify yourselves that I said, 'I am not the Messiah, but am sent ahead of him.' It is the bridegroom who has the bride. But the grooms-man, who stands and listens to him, rejoices greatly at the bridegroom's voice. That joy of mine is now realised.

1 Ain-nun, situated south-east of the modern Nablus.
2 The disciples of John were also Jews by religion. We should understand 'Judeans', compared with other areas like Galilee.

30   He must grow greater and I grow less."[a]

4.1   When then the Master learnt that the Pharisees had heard, "Jesus is making and immersing more disciples than John",[b] he left Judea and returned to Galilee.

Now he was obliged to pass through Samaria. In so
5   doing he came to a Samaritan town called Shechem,[3] close to the plot of ground which Jacob gave his son Joseph. Jacob's well was there. Jesus, exhausted from the journey, had just sat down on the well's rim,[c] when a Samaritan woman came to draw water.

Jesus said to her, "Please give me a drink."[d]

The Samaritan woman answered, "How can you, a Jew, ask a drink from me, a Samaritan woman?"[e]

10   "If you only knew God's gift," Jesus replied, "and who it is who is saying to you, 'Give me a drink', you would have asked him, and he would have given you living water."[4]

"Sir", she said, "you have nothing to draw with, and the well is deep. How will you obtain this living water? Are you greater than our father Jacob, who gave us this well, and drank from it himself, and his sons too, and his cattle?"

Jesus answered, "Whoever drinks this water will grow thirsty again, but he who drinks the water I will give him will never thirst any more; for the water I will give him will become a spring of water welling up inside him in Eternal Life."

15   "Sir", said the woman, "give me this water, so that I

---

a He who comes from Above is superior to all. He who is earthly remains earthly, and speaks in an earthly way. He who comes from heaven is superior to all. As he has seen and heard so he testifies, but no one accepts his testimony. Whoever does accept his testimony has confirmed that god is True; for he whom God has sent speaks the words of God, because God does not give him the Spirit stintingly. The Father loves the Son, and has placed everything in his hands. He who believes in the Son will have Eternal Life, while he who disobeys the Son will never see Life: God's wrath will abide on him (*Jn* 3:31–36).

b Though Jesus himself did not immerse, it was his disciples.

c It was about midday.

d His disciples had gone off to the town to buy food.

e Jews do not associate with Samaritans.

---

3 Following the correct reading of the Old Syriac. The Greek reads Sychar.
4 'Living water' also means 'flowing water' (cf *Jer* 2:13, etc.).

shall never thirst, nor have to come here to draw."

"Go and call your husband", he said to her, "and come back here."

"I have no husband", the woman replied.

Jesus said to her, "You rightly say, 'I have no husband', for you have had five husbands, and the man you have now is not your husband. There you have spoken the truth."

20   "I see you are a prophet, sir", said the woman. "Our fathers worshipped on this mountain.[5] But your people say that at Jerusalem is the place where we ought to worship."

"Believe me, madam", Jesus told her, "the time is coming when they will worship the Father neither on this mountain nor in Jerusalem. Your people worship One whom they do not know, while our people worship One whom they do know.[f] Yes, the time is coming, indeed it is here already, when all true worshippers wll worship the Father spiritually and sincerely,[g] for these are the kind of worshippers the Father seeks."

25   The woman said to him, "I know that Messiah will come.[h] When he is here he will tell us all about it."

Jesus replied, "I who speak to you am he."

At this juncture his disciples returned, and were dumbfounded to find him talking with a woman.[i]

Abandoning her water-pot the woman then sped away to the town, and said to the men, "You must come and see someone who told me everything I had done. Could he possibly be the Messiah?"

30   So they left the town and went out to him.

In the meantime his disciples had been begging Jesus, "Rabbi, do eat."

"I have food to eat that you do not know of", he told them.

---

f For salvation comes from the Jews.

g God is Spirit, and those who worship him must do so spiritually and sincerely.

h The one called Christ (ie in Greek. Ed.).

i At any rate no one said, "What are you inquiring about?" or "Why are you talking to her?"[7]

---

5 Mt. Gerizim, where stood the rival Samaritan temple.

7 It was not considered proper for a Rabbi to converse with a woman if he was by himself.

"Can someone have brought him food?" the disciples asked one another.

Jesus said to them, "Food to me means to do the will of
35   him who sent me and to complete his work. Do you not say, 'Another four months and harvest time will be here'? Look, I tell you! Raise your eyes and see for yourselves how white is the land for harvesting!⁶ The reaper can already see his reward in view, and gather his crop for Eternal Life, so that the sower may rejoice equally with the reaper. Herein the saying is verified, 'It is one thing to sow, and another to reap.' I have sent you to reap where you have done no work. Others have done the work, and you have had the benefit of it."

Many of the Samaritans of that town believed in him through the woman's statement, "He told me every-
40   thing I have done." So when the Samaritans reached him they begged him to stay with them. And he did spend two days there; and many more believed in him through his discourse, and they told the woman, "Our belief is no longer due to what you told us. We have heard him ourselves and are convinced that he really is the world's saviour."

When the two days had ended Jesus left there for Galilee, though he himself testified that a prophet is of
45   no repute in his own country. Consequently when he reached Galilee the Galileans only welcomed him because of everything they had seen him do at Jerusalem during the festival.ʲ

So he came once more to Cana of Galilee, where he had turned the water into wine.

Now there was an imperial officer whose son was ill at Capernaum. When he heard that Jesus had returned to Galilee from Judea, he went to him and begged him to come down and cure his son;⁹ for he lay at death's door. Jesus, however, said to him, "Nothing will make you believe unless you see signs and wonders."

"Do come down, sir," urged the officer, "before my child dies."

50   "Go home", Jesus replied. "Your son will live."

j   They too had been at the festival.⁸

---

6 Referring to the approaching Samaritans.
8 ie the Passover.
9 Other *Gospels* speak of a centurion's servant. See *Mt* 8:5–13; *Lk* 7:1–10.

The man believed what Jesus had told him and went away. He was well on the way home when his servants met him with the news that his son was alive. He asked them at what time he had shown improvement.

"Yesterday at one o'clock the fever left him", they replied.

The father knew then that it was the very time Jesus had told him, "Your son will live", and he believed together with his whole household.

This then is the second sign Jesus performed, after he came from Judea to Galilee.

iv[1]

6.1   After these events Jesus crossed the Sea of Galilee.[a] A large crowd followed him because they saw the signs he performed on the sick.

Jesus climbed the mountain and sat down there with his disciples. The Jewish festival of Passover was approaching.[2]

5   When Jesus raised his eyes and saw a large crowd coming to him, he said to Philip, "Where are we to buy bread for these people to eat?"[b]

Philip replied, "Two hundred dinars' worth of bread will hardly give each of them a piece."

One of his disciples, Andrew, Simon Peter's brother, said to him, "There is a lad here with five barley loaves and two small fish. But what good are they to so many?"

10   Jesus said, "Get the men seated."[c]

So the men sat down to the number of about five thousand.

Then Jesus broke the loaves, and when he had given thanks he distributed portions to those who were seated, and also as much as they wanted of the small fishes.

a   That is the Sea of Tiberias.
b   He said this to test him, for he knew perfectly well what he intended to do.
c   There was plenty of grass on the spot.

1 Transposing *Jn* 6 to follow *Jn* 4, as required by the sequence of events. See below p 493.
2 This is the second Passover to be mentioned. There would seem to have been several intervening incidents in Galilee which have been omitted.

When they were satisfied, he said to his disciples, "Gather up the fragments that are left so that nothing is lost."

So they gathered them up, and filled twelve baskets with the fragments of the five barley loaves left over from what they had eaten.

Then the people on seeing the sign he had performed said, "This is surely the Prophet who was to come into the world!"[3]

15   As soon as Jesus realised that they were intending to carry him off to make him king,[4] he again withdrew to the mountain, but alone.

When evening came his disciples went down to the sea, and going on board ship crossed over the sea to Capernaum. By this time it was dark, and still Jesus had not joined them, while the sea had become rough with a strong wind blowing. When, however, they had rowed some three or four miles, they saw Jesus walking on the sea and approaching the ship, and they were terrified.

20   But he said to them, "It is I. Don't be alarmed!"

Then they readily took him on board, and at once the ship reached the shore for which they had been making.

The next day the crowd standing on the far side of the sea realised that only one boat had been there, and that Jesus had not gone on board with his disciples, but that they had left on their own. Boats from Tiberias, however, put in close to the spot where they had eaten the bread after the Master had given thanks. So when the crowd was aware that neither Jesus nor his disciples were there any longer they took these boats and made for

25   Capernaum in quest of Jesus. Having found him on the other side of the sea, they said to him, "Rabbi, how did you get here?"

Jesus replied, "I tell you for a positive fact, you do not seek me because you have seen signs, but because you ate the bread and were satisfied. Do not labour for the food that perishes, but for the food that endures in

---

3 *Deut* 18:15.

4 While Jesus was aware that as Messiah he was king of the Jews, he refused to claim this kingship until he went to Jerusalem for the last time, because he would be violating the Roman law of sovereignty, the punishment for which was death. His teaching work would have promptly terminated. So he employed the disguise of the term 'Son of Man'.

Eternal Life, which the Son of Man will give you; for this the Father, God, has confirmed."[5]

··

"What must we do to carry out the works of God?"[6] they asked him.

"The work of God simply means this", Jesus replied, "that you believe in him God has sent."

30 "What sign do you perform", they said, "that we may see it and believe in you? What miracle do you work? Our fathers ate the manna in the wilderness, as it is stated, 'He gave them bread from heaven to eat.'"[7]

Jesus said to them, "I tell you for a positive fact, Moses did not give you the bread from heaven, but my Father will give you the real bread from heaven. God's bread is that which comes down from heaven and gives life to the world."

"Sir", they urged, "never fail to give us that bread."

35 "I am the bread of life", Jesus told them. "Whoever comes to me will never hunger, and whoever believes in me will never thirst any more. But as I have said to you, though you have seen you still do not believe.[8] Everyone whom the Father gives me will come to me, and none who comes to me will I ever reject; for I have come down from heaven not to carry out my own will, but the will of him who has sent me. The will of him who has sent me is this, that I must lose no part of whatever he has given

40 me, but must raise it up on the Last Day. For the will of my Father is that whoever sees the Son and believes in him shall have Eternal Life, and I must raise him up on the Last Day."

The Jews[9] murmured about him, because he said, "I am the bread that has come down from heaven", and said, "Isn't he Jesus the son of Joseph, whose father and

5 The last part of the sentence appears to have been added to link with what follows, where both the style of speech and the sentiments are quite unlike the Jesus of the Synoptic *Gospels*. The Greek Elder's material is indicated by a dotted rule.

6 The reference to the "works of God" comes in abruptly, and is followed by dialogue on the theme of "the bread from heaven", introduced here because of the feeding of the 5,000. We note that Jesus says "Moses did not give *you*" when he should have said *us*, being himself a Jew.

7 *Ps* 78 (LXX).

8 Jesus had not exactly said this before, unless in a missing dialogue passage. But cf 4:48.

9 The writer speaks as a non-Jew. By Jews he does not mean Judeans, for the scene is laid in Galilee. See n *e* p 492.

mother we know? How then can he say, 'I have come down from heaven'?"

Jesus said to them, "Do not mutter to one another. No one can come to me unless the Father who has sent me

45   draws him, and I must raise him up on the Last Day. It is stated in the prophets, 'And they will all be taught by God.'[10] Whoever has listened to the Father and learnt will come to me.[d]

"I tell you for a positive fact, whoever believes in me will have Eternal Life. I am the bread of life. Your[11] fathers ate the manna in the wilderness and died. The bread that comes down from heaven is otherwise, that

50   anyone may eat of it and not die. I am the living bread that has come down from heaven. If anyone eats of this bread he will live for ever. And the bread I will give for the life of the world is my flesh."

The Jews then disputed with one another saying, "How can he give us his flesh to eat?"

So Jesus said to them, "I tell you for a positive fact, if you do not eat the flesh of the Son of Man and drink his blood you will not have life in yourselves.[12] Whoever chews my flesh and drinks my blood will have Eternal

55   Life, and I must raise him up on the Last Day; for my flesh is true food and my blood is true drink. Whoever chews my flesh and drinks my blood continues in me.[13] Just as the Living Father has sent me, and I live through the Father, so he who chews me will likewise live through me. This is the bread that has come down from heaven, not the kind the fathers ate and died. He who chews this bread will live for ever."[e]

60   Many of his disciples when they heard this said, "This is intolerable![14] How can one listen to such talk?"

Conscious that his disciples were murmuring about it, Jesus said to them, "So this offends you, does it? Supposing you were to see the Son of Man ascend to where he

---

d Not that anyone has seen the Father, except him who is from God: he has seen the Father.

e Jesus said all this in the synagogue, while teaching in Capernaum.

---

10 *Isa* 54:13.

11 Again Jesus is made to speak as a non-Jew.

12 The writer takes a pagan position relating to the Mystery Cults.

13 cf I *Jn* 2:24.

14 "Intolerable", lit "a stiff, or harsh, saying". The writer may be attacking those who opposed his Christology. (cf I *Jn* 2:19; II *Jn* 10; III *Jn* 8–10).

was before? The Spirit is the life-giving agency: the physical counts for nothing. The words I have addressed to you are Spirit, and they are Life. But there are some of

65 you who do not believe.*ᶠ* That is why I said to you that no one can come to me unless it is granted him by my Father."

As a consequence many of his disciples parted company, and no longer associated with him.

Jesus then said to the twelve, "Don't you also want to go?"

Simon Peter answered, "Sir, to whom shall we go? You have the Message[15] of Eternal Life, and we have believed and are convinced that you are the Holy One of God."

70 "Have I not chosen you, the twelve?" Jesus said to them, "Yet even of you one is a traitor."[16,ᵍ]

....

f For Jesus knew from the very first who they were who did not believe, and who it was would betray him.

g He was speaking of Judas son of Simon Iscariot.[17] For it was he, one of the twelve, who was to betray him.*

---

*   Here John the Priest's record is resumed. Ed.

15 "Message" lit "words".

16 Gr *diabolos*, a false accuser.

17 Probably the same as Simon the Zealot (Qananean), listed as one of the twelve envoys. Iscariot probably means 'One of the *Sicarii*' (dagger-men, assassins). cf Jos. *Jewish War*, II. 254–256.

V[1]

5.1 After these events there was a Jewish festival,[2] and Jesus went up to Jerusalem.

Now at Jerusalem there is a bathing pool by the Sheep Gate,[3] which in Hebrew goes by the name of Bethzatha.[4] It has five porticoes. In these there were always lying a host of invalids, blind people, lame, and people with

5 withered limbs, waiting for the water to bubble.*ᵃ* There

a For an angel of the Lord descended into the pool from time to time, and agitated the water. Whoever then got in first was cured of whatever complaint he was suffering from.

---

1 *Jn* 5 is placed here after 6, which gives a better sequence of events. *Jn* 7 follows awkwardly after 6, since in the latter Jesus is already in Galilee. The reason is given in *Jn* 5:16.

2 Either the Passover referred to at the beginning of the previous section, or perhaps the feast of Pentecost following it.

3 Or 'Market'.

4 Probably Aram. 'Place of Alkaline Salt'.

was one man there who had been an invalid for thirty-eight years. When Jesus saw him lying there, and learnt that he had already been lying there a long time, he said to him, "Do you wish to be cured?"

"Sir", the invalid replied, "I have no one to put me into the pool when the water is agitated, and while I am getting there someone else steps down before me."

Jesus said to him, "Rise, pick up your mattress, and walk!"

10   At once the man was cured, and took up his mattress and walked. That day was the sabbath. So the Jews said to the man who had been cured, "It is the sabbath, and it is not permitted for you to carry your mattress."

But he answered, "He who cured me told me, 'Pick up your mattress and walk.'"[5]

They asked him, "Who was it told you to pick it up and walk?"

The man who was cured did not know who it was.[b] Later, however, Jesus encountered him in the Temple, and said to him, "See, you are cured now. Sin no more, or worse may befall you."

15   The man went away and told the Jews it was Jesus who had cured him. It was for this reason that the Jews persecuted Jesus, because he did such things on the sabbath.[6]

....

"My Father is still at work", Jesus replied, "so I am working too."

For this, then, the Jews in addition sought to kill him, because not only did he violate the sabbath, but also claimed God as his father, putting himself on a level with God.[7]

Therefore he answered and said to them, "I tell you for a positive fact, the Son can do nothing on his own

b For Jesus had moved off because of the crowd in the place.

---

5 cf *Mk* 2:9.

6 From about here until the end of Section v we have another block of material characteristic of the Greek Elder. It would seem to be placed here because of the reference to curing on the sabbath, though other themes are introduced.

7 The author seems unaware that Adam, King Solomon, and the Children of Israel, are termed 'Son of God' in the Scriptures, without any suggestion of their deity. But he writes as a Greek. The real Jesus spoke humbly (*Mk* 10:17–18).

account, only what he sees the Father do. What he does
20 the Son copies; for the Father loves the Son, and shows
him whatever he does. And he will show him how to do
greater miracles than this, that you may marvel. For just
as the Father raises the dead and revives them, so will the
Son revive whom he will. Neither does the Father judge
anyone: he has entrusted all judgment to the Son, that all
may honour the Son as they honour the Father. Whoever
does not honour the Son does not honour the Father who
has sent him.

"I tell you for a positive fact, whoever hears my
message and believes in him who has sent me will have
Eternal Life, and will not come to judgment: he has
passed from death to life.

25   "I tell you for a positive fact, the time is coming, indeed
it is already here, when the dead will hear the voice of the
Son of God,[8] and those who hear it will live. For just as
the Father has life in himself, so has he granted the Son to
have life in himself, and has given him authority to
execute judgment, because he is the Son of Man. Do not
wonder at this, for the time is coming when those who
are entombed will hear his voice and come forth, those
who have done good to the Resurrection of Life, and
those who have done evil to the Resurrection of Judg-
30 ment.[9] I can do nothing on my own. As I hear I judge,
and my judgment is just, because I am not serving my
own interests but the interests of him who has sent me.

"If I were to testify on my own behalf my testimony
would not be valid. There is someone else who testifies
of me, and I know that the testimony he gives of me is
valid. You sent to John, and he testified truly. It is not
that I require human testimony: I am only saying this
35 that you may be saved. He was a burning and shining
light, and you were delighted for a time to bask in his
light. But I have more important testimony than John's.
The miracles which the Father has granted me to perform, the miracles I do, these testify of me that the Father
has sent me. And he who sent me, the Father himself,
has testified of me. You have never heard his voice, or
seen his form, and his Message has no lodgment in you,
because you do not believe in him whom he has sent.

8 Jesus only referred to himself as Son of Man, never Son of God, except in
  this Gospel, by John the Elder.
9 cf *Dan* 12:2 and *Rev* 20.

You pore over the Scriptures, because you think they will give you Eternal Life; and it is they which testify of me.

40   Yet you do not want to come to me that you may have life.

"I do not require human praise, but I do know you, that you have not the love of God in you. I have come in my Father's name, and you do not receive me. If another should come in his own name you will receive him. How can you believe, you who receive praise from one another, but do not seek the praise that comes from the

45   Only God? Do not think I will complain of you to the Father. Moses, the one on whom you have pinned your hopes, is the one who will complain of you. Had you believed Moses you would have believed me, for he wrote of me. But if you do not believe his writings, why should you believe my words?

7.19   [10]"Did not Moses give you the Law? Yet none of you keeps the Law. Why do you seek to kill me?"

The crowd responded, "You are demon-possessed! Who seeks to kill you?"

Jesus said to them, "I have performed one miracle and you are all amazed. Surely Moses gave you circumcision,[c] and you circumcise a man on the sabbath! If a man can receive circumcision on the sabbath that the Law of Moses may not be broken, why are you so enraged with me because I have made a man whole on the Sabbath? Do not judge by appearance. Judge justly."

· ·

c Not that it derives from Moses; it derives from the Patriarchs.

---

10 Transposing *Jn* 7:19–24 to follow *Jn* 5:47, completing the Greek Elder's additions to Section v. There has been some tampering with Section vi, but no block of material has been included.

vi

7.1   After these events Jesus toured Galilee.[a] Now the Jewish festival of Tabernacles[1] was approaching. So his brothers said to him, "Cross into Judea, that your disciples there too may see the miracles you perform. For no one does anything in secret if he seeks to be in the public eye. If you perform these miracles show yourself to the world."[b]

a He would not tour Judea because the Jews sought to kill him.
b For neither did his brothers believe in him.

---

1 The autumn harvest festival, when the people lived in booths.

6   Jesus replied, "My time has not arrived yet, but any time is your time. The world cannot hate you, but it does hate me, because I testify of it that its deeds are evil. You go up for the festival. I am not going up yet for this festival, because my time has not yet come."

10   Having said this he stayed on in Galilee. But after his brothers had gone up for the festival he too went up, not openly but secretly.

The Jews looked for him at the festival and inquired, "Where is he?" And there was a great deal of murmuring about him among the crowds, some saying, "He is a good man", while others said, "No, he is leading the people astray."[c]

The festival was already half over when Jesus went up

15   to the Temple and taught there. The Jews were amazed and said, "How has he acquired book-learning without having studied?"

Jesus replied, "My teaching is not my own, but his who sent me. Whoever wishes to do his will will know whether the teaching is God's or whether I am stating my own views. Whoever gives his own views seeks his personal glory, but he who seeks the glory of him who has sent him is sincere, and there is no falseness in him."

7.25   [2]Then some of the Jerusalemites said, "Isn't he the man they seek to kill? Yet here he is speaking freely, and they say nothing to him. Unless, of course, the rulers have recognised that he is the Messiah. Yet we know where this man comes from, while when the Messiah comes no one will know where he comes from."

Jesus therefore proclaimed in the Temple as he taught, "You know me, and you know where I come from. And I have not come of my own accord. He who has sent me is indeed trustworthy, whom you do not know. I know him, because I am from him, and he sent me."

30   At this they sought to seize him, yet no one laid hands on him because his time had not yet come.[3]

c No one, of course, spoke openly about him for fear of the Jews.

---

2 *Jn* 7:25 here follows 7:18. See n 10, p 496.

3 From here until the end of *Jn* 12 the text is in considerable disorder owing to the unskilful insertions of the Dialogue material. The sequence of events as this may have appeared in the Elder's source has been seriously dislocated, while the Discourse of Jesus to the Jews (already begun above pp 494–496) has had its continuity destroyed. The corrections of order which have been attempted by the editor and translator are to be regarded as purely conjectural. At this point *Jn* 8:12–20 has been inserted between *Jn* 7:30 and 31.

8.12   Jesus now addressed them again saying, "I am the light of the world. Whoever follows me will not walk in the dark, but have the light of life."

The Pharisees said to him, "You are testifying on your own behalf. Your testimony is not valid."

Jesus replied, "Though I testify on my own behalf my testimony is valid, for I know where I came from and where I am going. But you do not know where I came

15   from nor where I am going. You judge by human standards, while I judge no one. But if I were to judge, my judgment would be valid because I am not alone. There is myself and him who has sent me. And in your Law[4] it is stated that the testimony of two persons is valid. There is myself who am testifying on my own behalf, and there is the Father who has sent me who testifies on my behalf."

"Where is your father?" they said to him.

Jesus replied, "You neither know me nor my Father. Had you known me you would have known my Father also."

20   He said these things in the treasury,[5] as he taught in
7.30   the Temple. And no one seized him because his time had not yet come.[6] Many of the people believed in him, and said, "When the Messiah comes will he exhibit more signs than this man does?"

The Pharisees heard what the people were murmuring about him, so the head priests and Pharisees sent officers to arrest him.[7]

7.37   On the last day, the principal day[8] of the festival, Jesus stood and proclaimed, "If anyone thirsts let him come to me and drink. 'He who believes in me,' as the Scripture says, 'from his interior streams of living water shall flow.' "[d9]

40   Some of the people when they heard these words said,

---

d He said this with reference to the Spirit which those who believed in him were to receive. For as yet there was no Spirit, because Jesus was not yet glorified.

---

4 Expressions like "*your* Law" are always indications of the work of the Greek Elder posing as Jesus.
5 Where offerings were placed by worshippers in trumpet-shaped chests.
6 Here follows *Jn* 7:31–2.
7 Omitting here *Jn* 7:33–6, transferred to follow 12:32, below p 511.
8 Called 'The Great Hosanna'.
9 Slightly varying *Isa* 28:16–17.

"This is surely the Prophet." Others said, "He is the Messiah." But the first replied, "The Messiah will not come from Galilee. Doesn't the Scripture say that the Messiah will come from the line of David, and from David's village of Bethlehem?"

So there was a conflict of opinion among the people on his account. Some were for seizing him, but no one laid hands on him.

45 The officers then returned to the head priests and Pharisees, who asked them, "Why have you not brought him?"

The officers answered, "No man ever spoke like this."

"Have you too been led astray?" said the Pharisees. "Have any of the rulers of the Pharisees believed in him? But these people who do not know the Law are accursed."[10]

50 Nicodemus,[e] who was one of them, said to them, "Does our Law condemn a man without first hearing what he has to say and knowing what he is doing?"

"Do you too come from Galilee?" they answered, "Look for yourself, and you will find that the Prophet will not come from Galilee."[11]

e The one who came to Jesus in the first instance.

---

10 The ignorant were scorned as boors (*amme-haaretz*).
11 Alternatively, "that no prophet will come from Galilee".

vii

7.53 [1][Then everyone went to his own house, but Jesus
8.1 wentto the Mount of Olives. At daybreak he was once more in the Temple, and all the people came to him, and he seated himself and taught them.

Then the scribes and Pharisees brought a woman caught committing adultery, and placed her before him saying, "Teacher, this woman was caught in the very act
5 of adultery. Now Moses in the Law commanded that such should be stoned.[2] But what do you say?"

They said this to tempt him, so that they could have grounds for charging him.[3] Jesus, however, bent down

---

1 The passage within square brackets is in a different style and omitted in some MSS. In others it is placed elsewhere, including in one group after *Lk* 21:37.
2 cf *Lev* 20:10; *Deut* 22:22.
3 cf *Mt* 19:3; *Lk* 20:19–20.

and drew on the ground with his finger. When they repeated their question he straightened up and said to them, "Let whichever of you is sinless be the first to throw a stone at her." And again he bent down and scrawled on the ground.

When they heard this, one by one they slunk away, beginning with the older men; and he was left alone with the woman in front of him.

10   Then Jesus raised himself and said to her, "Madam, where are they? Has no one condemned you?"

"No one, sir", she said.

Jesus told her, "Neither do I condemn you. Go, and do not sin again in future."]

8.31   [4]Then said Jesus to the Jews who believed in him, "If you adhere to my message you will indeed be my disciples, and will come to know the truth, and the truth will liberate you."

"We are Abraham's offspring", they replied, "and were never in slavery to anyone. Why do you say, 'You will be freemen'?"

Jesus answered, "I tell you for a positive fact, whoever
35   commits sin is a slave. But the slave is not a permanent member of the household, while the son is.[5] So if the Son makes you makes you free, you will really be freemen. I know you are Abraham's offspring, yet you seek to kill me because my message finds no place in you. I speak from personal experience of the Father, while you do only what you have heard from *your* father."

"Abraham is our father", they said to him.

"If you were children of Abraham", Jesus told them,
40   "you would do Abraham's deeds. Yet here you seek to kill me, a man who has told you the truth which I have heard from God. Abraham did not do that. You do the deeds of your father."

4 When the interpolation is removed it is clear that Jesus had not left the Temple. He was presumably still teaching on the last day of the festival of Tabernacles. From *Jn* 7:31,39 it is shown that many believed in him at this time, which was why the head priests and Pharisees intervened. It seems best therefore to resume the Dialogue at 8:31. The Dialogue material 8:12–20 has already been restored to its probable position after 7:30 (above p 498). The passages 8:21–30 and 7:33–36 seem to belong to another part of the material found in *Jn* 12.

5 cf *Heb* 3:5–6. This homily (*Hebrews*) may have been directed to the community at Ephesus, and therefore might have been known to our author resident there. It represents an earlier stage in the development of the Logos doctrine.

"We were not born illegitimately", they protested. "We have One Father, God!"[6]

Jesus told them, "If God were your Father you would love me; for I emanated and came from God. I did not come of my own accord: he sent me. How is it you do not recognise my voice? It is because you cannot heed my message. You have the Devil for a father, and would carry out your father's behests. He was a manslayer from the very first, and could never abide the truth; for truth is alien to him. When he utters a lie he speaks his own

45   language; for he is a liar and the father of lies. But because I speak the truth you do not believe me. Whoever belongs to God heeds the words of God. The very fact that you do not heed me proves that you do not belong to God."

The Jews replied, "Are we not justified in saying you are a Samaritan[7] and demon-possessed?"

Jesus answered, "I am not demon-possessed. I honour

50   my Father, and you dishonour me. I do not seek my own glory. There is One who seeks and decides that.

"I tell you for a positive fact, whoever holds fast to my message will never experience death."

The Jews said, "Now we are certain you are demon-possessed. Abraham died, and so did the Prophets, yet you say, 'Whoever holds fast to my message will never experience death.' Are you superior to our father Abraham who died, and to the Prophets who died? Who do you claim to be?"

Jesus answered, "If I glorify myself, my glory amounts to nothing. It is my Father who glorifies me, whom you

55   say is your God. Yet you are not acquainted with him, while I know him. Were I to say I do not know him, I should be like you, a liar. But I do know him, and hold fast to his message. Your father Abraham rejoiced that he would see my day:[8] he has seen it and is glad."

The Jews said to him, "You are not yet fifty, and Abraham has seen you!"[9]

Jesus told them, "I tell you for a positive fact, I existed before Abraham was born."

---

6 cf *Mal.* 2:10.
7 Implying 'idolatrous-heretic' a term of abuse.
8 cf *Heb* 6:12–7:10.
9 Alternatively, "and you have seen Abraham?"

Then they picked up stones to throw at him. But Jesus hid himself, and left the Temple.

viii

9.1   As Jesus went on his way he saw a man blind from birth, and his disciples asked him, "Rabbi, who sinned, he or his parents, that he was born blind?"

Jesus replied, "Neither he nor his parents sinned. He was born blind that he might afford an illustration of God's work. While daylight lasts we must do the work of him who has sent me. The night will come when no one

5   can work. While I am in the world I illumine the world."

Having said this, he spat on the ground and made clay with the saliva, and dabbed the clay on the man's eye,[1] and said to him "Go and wash in the Pool of Siloam."[a][2]

So he went away and washed, and returned with his sight.

His neighbours, and those who had known him previously when he was a beggar, said, "Isn't he the man who used to sit and beg?"

Others said, "Yes, that's the man."

Others said, "No, it isn't. But he's like him."

"It *is* me", the man said.

10   "How then were your eyes opened?" they asked him.

"The man called Jesus made clay and anointed my eyes", he replied, "and told me, 'Go to Siloam and wash.' So when I had gone there and washed I found I could see."

"Where is he?" they inquired.

"I don't know", he said.

They brought the former blind man to the Pharisees.[b]

15   The Pharisees in turn asked him how he had obtained his sight. He told them, "He put clay on my eyes, and I washed, and now I can see."

"This man is not from God", said some of the Pharisees, "for he does not observe the sabbath."

a   To be translated 'Sent' (Heb *Shiloah* Ed.).

b   For it had been the sabbath, the day that Jesus made clay and opened his eyes.

1 cf *Mt* 20:34.

2 At the south-east corner of the city.

But others said, "How can a man who is a sinner perform such signs?"

So there was a conflict of opinion between them.

Then they addressed the blind man again, "What do you say of him for having opened you eyes?"

"He is a prophet", he said.

But the Jews refused to credit that he had been blind and had gained his sight until they had called the man's parents and asked them, "Is this your son, whom you say was born blind? How then does he now see?"

20 "We know this is our son", his parents replied, "and that he was born blind. But we do not know how he can now see, and we have not the least idea who has opened his eyes. Ask him. He is grown up and can speak for himself."[c]

Then they recalled the man who had been blind and said to him, "Give God the praise. We know this man is a sinner."

25 He replied, "Whether he is a sinner I do not know. But one thing I do know, that I was blind and now I can see."

They said to him, "What did he do to you? How did he open your eyes?"

"I have already told you that", he answered, "and you took no notice. Why do you want to hear it again? Surely you are not wanting to become his disciple?"

Then they hurled abuse at him and said, "You are his disciple. We are Moses's disciples. We know that God spoke to Moses; but him – we don't know where he is from."

30 The man replied, "That's what is so surprising, that you don't know where he is from; yet he has opened my eyes. We know that God does not listen to sinners,[4] but he does listen to whoever is God-fearing and carries out

---

c They spoke thus because they were afraid of the Jews. For the Jews had already agreed that if anyone confessed Christ he should be expelled from the synagogue.[3] That is why his parents said, "He is grown up. Ask him yourselves."

---

3 Nothing is known of any attempt to exclude Jews from the synagogue for accepting Jesus as Messiah before about AD 80. Even then the method was indirect, by including in the prayers a general curse on heretics (*minim*) which naturally they could not recite. There was no formal ban until very much later. The word *aposynagogos* occurs only in this Gospel (9:22; 12:42; 16:2).

4 A Jewish writer would not have made such a statement.

his will. It is quite unheard of that anyone should open the eyes of one blind from birth. If he were not from God, he could never do it."

"You dare to teach us, you misbegotten bastard!" they cried, and ejected him forthwith.

35   Jesus heard that they had ejected him, and when he had found him said to him, "Do you believe in the Son of Man?"

He answered, "Who is he, sir, for me to believe in him?"

Jesus told him, "You have not only seen him, but he is talking to you now."

"I do believe, sir," he said, and prostrated himself before him.

Then Jesus said, "I came into this world as a judgment, that those who do not see should see, and those who do see should become blind."

40   Some of the Pharisees who were there with him heard this, said to him, "Surely we are not blind?"

Jesus told them, "If you were blind, you would be free from sin; but since you say, 'We see', your sin remains."

10.6   ⁵Jesus addressed this saying to them; but they failed to grasp his meaning.

So Jesus spoke again, "I tell you for a positive fact, I am the door for the sheep. All those who came before me are thieves and robbers; but the sheep have not listened to them. I am the door. Whoever enters by me will be safe,

10   and will come in and go out, and find pasture. The thief only comes to steal and kill and destroy. I have come that they may have life, and ever more life.

10.1   "I tell you for a positive fact, whoever does not use the gate to the sheep-pen, but gets in another way, is a thief and a robber, while he who uses the gate is the shepherd of the sheep. The doorkeeper lets him in, and the sheep not only listen to his voice, but he calls his own sheep by name, and leads them out. When his own sheep are all outside, he walks in front of them, and the sheep follow him because they know his voice. They will not follow

5   anyone else, but run from him, because they do not recognise the voices of strangers.

10.11   "I am the good shepherd. The good shepherd will give his life for the sheep. But the hireling, not being the

---

5 Placing *Jn* 10:6–10 before 1–5.

shepherd, with sheep that are not his own, when he sees the woolf coming abandons the sheep and runs away, leaving the wolf to ravage and scatter them, because the hireling has no concern for the sheep.

15 "I am the good shepherd, and know my own sheep, and they know me, just as the Father knows me and I know the Father, and I give my life for the sheep. There are other sheep I have, which do not belong to this pen.[6] I must bring them in also, and they will listen to my voice, and there shall be one flock with one shepherd.

"That is why the Father loves me, because I give my life, that I may take it back. No one takes it from me: I give it of my own accord. I have the right to give it, and the right to take it back.[7] This instructon I have received from my Father."

20 There was a further conflict of opinion among the Jews over these words. Many of them said, "He is demon-possessed and mad. Why do you pay any attention to him?"

Others said, "These are not the ravings of a demoniac. Can a demon open the eyes of the blind?"

The Feast of Dedication[8] now took place in Jerusalem. It was winter, and Jesus was strolling in the Temple, in Solomon's Portico. The Jews surrounded him, and said to him, "How long are you going to keep us in suspense? If you are the Messiah, tell us plainly."

....

25 [9]Jesus replied, "I have told you, and you do not believe. The miracles I perform in my Father's name testify of me. But you do not believe because you do not belong to my sheep. My sheep listen to my voice, and I know them, and they follow me. And I will give them Eternal Life, and they will never perish, and no one shall wrest them from my hand. My Father, who has given me every-

---

6 Section viii has so much been taken over by the Greek Elder that comparatively little of John the Priest's material remains. The reference here to Gentile conversions, initiated by Paul, is a case in point. cf *Mt* 10:5.

7 Here Jesus claims the power to raise himself from the dead (and see 11:25). Earlier teaching claimed that it was God who raised Jesus.

8 Commemorating the rededication of the Temple by Judas Maccabaeus (165 BC). The festival (*Chanukah*) falls in December.

9 This section *Jn* 10:25–39 is so characteristic of the Greek Elder and so out of keeping with the sentiments of the Jesus of the Synoptic *Gospels* that it has been placed within dotted rules. No Jew could speak in this manner.

thing, is stronger, and no one can wrest anything from
30   my Father's hand. I and the Father are one."

Once again the Jews picked up stones to stone him.

Jesus said, "I have shown you from the Father many
notable miracles. For which of them are you going to
stone me?"

The Jews answered, "We are not going to stone you for
a notable miracle, but for blasphemy, because you who
are a man make yourself God."

"Is it not stated in your Law," Jesus replied, "'I said,
35   you are gods'?[10] If he called them gods to whom God's
Message came, and there is no evading the Scripture,[11]
how can you say to him whom the Father consecrated
and sent into the world, 'You blaspheme', because I said,
'I am God's Son'? If I do not perform my Father's
miracles, do not believe me. But if I do, even if you do not
believe me, believe the miracles, that you may realise
and recognise that the Father is in me and I am in the
Father."

Then once more they attempted to seize him, but he
escaped their clutches.

....

40   He went away again to the farther side of the Jordan, to
the place where John had been immersing originally,
and stayed there. Many came to him and declared, "John
performed no sign, but everything John said of this man
was true." And many there believed in him.

10 *Ps* 82:6.
11 The quotation from the OT is from *Ps* 82:6, which is not in the Law (the Five
Books of Moses), but in the Writings.

ix[1]

11.1   Now a certain man was ill, Lazarus of Bethany, the
village of Mary and her sister Martha.[a2] So the sisters sent
to Jesus to say, "Master, your dear friend is ill."

a It was the Mary who anointed the Master with perfume, and wiped
his feet with her hair (see *Jn* 12:3. Ed.), whose brother Lazarus was
ill.

1 The whole of this section in its present form is attributable to John the Elder.
But it appears to be based on some recollection of John the Priest. The
Lazarus story, unknown to the Synoptic *Gospels,* seems designed as a
curtain-raiser to the resurrection of Jesus himself.
2 See *Lk* 10:38–39.

When Jesus heard this he said, "This illness is not fatal, but for the glory of God, that the Son of God may be glorified by it."[b]

6 After hearing that Lazarus was ill he remained where he was for a further two days. Only when these had expired did he say to his disciples, "Let us return to Judea."

"Rabbi", his disciples protested, "the Judeans only recently attempted to stone you, and yet you are going back there?"

Jesus answered, "Are there not twelve hours in the day? Provided one walks in the daytime one will not

10 stumble, because one sees the light of this world. But if one walks at night, one will stumble, because one has not the benefit of the light."

After saying this he paused, and then declared, "Our friend Lazarus has fallen asleep, but I am going to awaken him."

The disciples said to him, "Master, if he has fallen asleep he will be all right."[c]

15 Then Jesus told them plainly, "Lazarus is dead. And for your sakes I am glad we were not there, that you may believe. Nevertheless let us go to him."

Thomas, called Twin, said to his fellow-disciples, "Let us go too that we may die with him."

When Jesus arrived he found that Lazarus had already been four days in the tomb.[d] Many of the Jews had come to condole with Martha and Mary for the loss of their

20 brother. As soon, therefore, as Martha heard that Jesus was coming she went out to meet him, while Mary remained seated indoors.[4]

"If only you had been here, Master", Martha greeted Jesus, "my brother would not have died. But even now, I know that whatever you ask God he will grant it you."

"Your brother will rise again", Jesus told her.

---

b Jesus had a high regard for Martha and her sister and for Lazaraus.
c Jesus was referring to his death, but they imagined he was speaking of normal sleep.
d Bethany was close to Jerusalem, only about two miles[3] away.

3·Gr 'about fifteen stadia'.
4 In accordance with custom the chief mourners remained indoors seated on the floor or on low stools during the days of mourning.

"I know he will rise again in the Resurrection on the Last Day", Martha replied.

25   "I am Resurrection and Life", Jesus told her. "Whoever believes in me will live even if he has died, and everyone who lives[5] and believes in me will never die at all. Do you believe this?"

"Yes, Master", she said. "I fully believe that you are the Messiah, the Son of God, who was to come into the world."

When she had said this she went off and quietly called her sister Mary and said, "The Teacher is here and asking for you."

29   As soon as she heard that, she rose quickly and went to him.[e] Then the Jews who were in the house with her to console her, seeing her get up quickly and go out, followed her, thinking she was going to the tomb to weep there. Mary, however, directly she came to the place where Jesus was, fell at his feet when she saw him, and said to him, "If only you had been here, Master, my brother would not have died."

When Jesus saw her weeping, and the Jews who accompanied her weeping, he groaned inwardly and was much upset.

"Where have you put him?" he asked.

"Come and see, sir", they said.

35   Jesus wept.

"See how fond of him he was", said the Jews, though some said, "Could not he, who opened the eyes of the blind, have done something so that he would not have died?"

Still groaning, Jesus came to the tomb.[f] "Roll aside the boulder!"[6] he ordered.

The deceased's sister Martha protested to him, "Master, by this time he will be putrefying. It is the fourth day."[7]

---

e   Jesus had not yet entered the village, but was still at the spot where Martha had met him.

f   It was a cave with a boulder across it.

---

5 ie until the Last Day of the present world order.

6 This was a huge stone cut to the shape of a solid wheel, which ran in a groove across the entrance to the tomb to close it. The tomb, of course, was above ground, part of a natural or artificial cave.

7 Jesus was in his own tomb less than two days.

40   Jesus said to her, "Did I not tell you that if you would believe you would behold God's glory?"

Then they rolled aside the boulder.

Jesus raised his eyes heavenwards and said, "I thank thee, Father, for having heard me. I know that thou dost always hear me, but I have said this because of the people standing by, that they may believe thou hast sent me."

Having spoken thus, he called out loudly, "Lazarus, come forth!"

The dead man emerged with his feet and hands strapped with bandages, and his face bound round with a cloth.

Jesus said to them, "Unbind him, and let him go free."

45   Many of the Jews who were visiting Mary and saw what he had done believed in him. But some of them went to the Pharisees and told them what Jesus had done. So the head priests and Pharisees convened the Sanhedrin and said, "What are we going to do, for this man performs many signs? If we leave him alone everyone will believe in him, and the Romans will come and take away both our place[8] and our nation."

One of their number, Caiaphas, who was the reigning
50   high priest,[9] said to them, "It does not seem to have occurred to you that it is in your own interest that one man should die for the people rather than the whole nation perish."[g]

So that day they decided to kill him.

Jesus, therefore, no longer moved about openly among the Judeans, but retired to the country close to the wilderness, to a town called Ephraim, and there stayed with his disciples.

g He did not say this of his own accord, but as the reigning high priest he prophesied that Jesus would died for the nation, and not for the nation only, but also that the widely scattered children of God should be gathered in one body.

---

8 Possibly meaning the Temple. And see Jos *Antiq* XX.123.
9 Lit "being high priest that year." *Eniautos* can mean a term of years. The office was one of annual appointment.

x

55   Now the Jewish Passover was approaching, and many went up from the country to Jerusalem prior to the

Passover to undergo purification. They looked out for Jesus, and remarked to one another as they stood in the Temple, "What do you think, that he will not attend the festival?"[a]

12.1   Six days before the Passover, however, Jesus came to Bethany.[b] So they gave a dinner for him there. Martha waited at table, while Lazarus was one of those who dined with them. Mary then took a pound of genuine most expensive spikenard, and anointed the feet of Jesus, and then wiped his feet with her hair. The whole house was filled with the perfume of the ointment.

5   Then Judas Iscariot[c] said, "Why wasn't this ointment sold for three hundred dinars and the money given to the poor?"[d]

Jesus said, "Leave her alone, for she had actually kept it for the day of my burial. You have the poor with you always, but you will not always have me."

A considerable number of Jews got to know he was there, and came not simply on account of Jesus, but also to see Lazarus whom he had raised from the dead.[e]

12   The next day the vast crowd attending the festival, having learnt that Jesus was coming to Jerusalem, took palm-branches and went out to meet him shouting, "Hosanna! Blessed is he who comes in the name of the Lord.[1] Blessed be the king of Israel."

Finding a young ass, Jesus rode on it, as it is stated,

15   "Never fear, daughter of Zion! See, your king is coming, riding on an ass's colt!"[f2]

---

a For the head priests and Pharisees had given orders that anyone who knew where he was should disclose it, so that they could arrest him.

b Where Lazarus lived, whom Jesus had raised from the dead.

c One of his disciples, who was about to betray him.

d He said this not because he was concerned about the poor, but because he was a thief and had the alms-bag, and pilfered what was put in it.

e The head priests had decided to kill Lazarus as well, because due to him many of the Jews went away and believed in Jesus.

f His disciples did not realise the significance of these things at first; but when Jesus was glorified then they recalled how this had been stated of him. Moreover, the people who had been with him when he called Lazarus from the tomb gave their testimony. This indeed was why the crowd met him, because they heard that he had performed this sign.

---

1 *Ps* 118:25–26.
2 *Zech* 9:9.

The Pharisees thereupon said to one another, "See for yourselves how helpless you are! Look, the whole world has gone after him!"

20   In fact among those going up to worship at the festival were some Greeks. These came to Philip of Bethsaida in Galilee with the request, "Sir, we should like to meet Jesus."

Philip went and told Andrew, and then Andrew and Philip told Jesus.

Jesus answered, "The time has come for the Son of Man to be glorified!

"I tell you for a positive fact, unless the grain of wheat falls into the ground and dies it will remain solitary; but if
25   it dies it will yield much fruit. Whoever loves his life will forfeit it, but whoever hates his life in this world will preserve it for Life Eternal. If anyone would serve me, let him follow me, and where I am there will my servant be also.[3] If anyone will serve me the Father will honour him.

"Just now my soul is deeply troubled. What am I to say? 'Father, save me from this hour'? No, that is why I have come to this hour. Father, glorify thy name."[4]

Then there came a voice from heaven, "I have glorified it, and will further glorify it."

The people who stood there and heard it said that it had thundered.[5] Others said, "An angel spoke to him."
30   Jesus answered, "This voice did not come for my sake, but for yours. Now is the judgment of this world! Now shall the ruler of this world be cast out![6] While I, when I am lifted from the earth will draw all men to me."[g]

....

7.33   [7]Then Jesus said, "For a brief space I shall be with you, and then I go to him who has sent me. You will seek me, but you will not find me,[8] and where I shall be you cannot come."

g He said this to indicate the kind of death he was going to die.

---

3 cf *Lk* 9:23–24.
4 Reminiscent of the account of Jesus in the Garden of Gethsemane (cf *Mk* 14:33–36). The companions of Jesus then were Peter, James and John, as at the time of the Transfiguration, when also there was a voice from heaven (*Mk* 9:7).
5 The same word in Greek is used for 'voice' and 'sound'.
6 The inimical angel-power (Belial). cf *Rev.* 12:9.
7 Inserting here *Jn* 7:33–36 as required by 12:9.
8 Perhaps on the basis of these words the apocryphal *Acts of Pilate* makes the Jews scour the country for Jesus after his resurrection.

35   "Where is he going to that we shall not find him?" the Jews asked themselves. "Surely he is not going to the Dispersion among the Greeks to teach the Greeks? What does he mean when he says, 'You will seek me, but will not find me, and where I shall be you cannot come'?"

8.21   ⁹Jesus repeated, "I am going away, and you will seek me, and you will die in your sins. Where I am going you cannot come."

The Jews then said, "Is he going to kill himself, that he says, 'Where I am going you cannot come.'?"

"You are from below", he replied, "while I am from Above. You are of this world, while I am not of this world. I told you you will die in your sins; for unless you believe that I am he you will die in your sins."

25   "Who are you?" they asked him.

Jesus replied, "When you have lifted up the Son of Man, then you will realise that I am he. Of my own accord I can do nothing, but as the Father has taught me so I speak. And he who has sent me is with me. He has not left me on my own, for I always do what pleases him."

The people responded, "We have heard out of the Law that the Messiah will remain for ever. Why then do you say, the Son of Man must be lifted up? Who is this Son of Man?"

Jesus answered, "First comes what I have yet to say to you. I have a great deal to say and judge of you. He who has sent me is indeed true, and I tell the world only what I have heard from him."ʰ

30   When he said this many believed in him.

12.44   ¹⁰Jesus then cried, "Whoever believes in me, does not believe in me, but in him who has sent me. And he who sees me, sees him who has sent me. I have come as a light to the world, that everyone who believes in me should not remain in darkness. And if anyone hears my words and does not keep them, I will not judge him; for I did not

---

h They did not realise that he was speaking to them of the Father.

---

9 Inserting here *Jn* 8:21–30, but transposing verses 26 and 29 and placing 12:34 between them as the sense requires, As the text of 12:32–38 stands in the Greek the people refer to Jesus having spoken of lifting up the Son of Man, when he had not said "Son of Man", only "I, when I am lifted from the earth".

10 Resuming at *Jn* 12:44–50.

come to judge the world, but to save the world. Whoever disregards me, and does not accept my words, has that which judges him. The Message I proclaim, that is what will judge him on the Last Day. For I do not speak of my own accord: it is the Father himself, who has sent me, who has given me his instructions what I am to say, and
50   what I am to declare. And I know that his instruction means Eternal Life. What I say, then, is exactly what the Father has told me to say."

12.35   [11]Then Jesus told them, "The light will not be with you much longer. Walk while you have the light, lest darkness overtake you. He that walks in darkness does not know where he is going. While you have the light, believe in the light, that you may become sons of light."[12]

When Jesus had said this, he went away and was hidden from them. But though he had performed many signs in their presence they did not believe in him, that the saying of the prophet Isaiah might come true, "Lord, who has believed our report, and to whom is the arm of the Lord revealed?"[i][13]

i The reason they were unable to believe was because Isaiah said further, "He has blinded their eyes, and hardened their minds, lest they should see with their eyes, and understand with their minds, and return; and I must heal them."[14] Isaiah said this because he saw his glory, and spoke of him. As a matter of fact, however, even among the rulers many believed in him. But they did not openly admit it on account of the Pharisees, in case they should be excommunicated; for they had a higher regard for human praise than for God's praise.

---

11 Continuing with 12:35–43.
12 The Essenes contrasted themselves as 'Sons of Light' with the 'Sons of Darkness'.
13 *Isa* 53:1.
14 *Isa* 6:9–10.

xi[1]

13.1   Now before the Passover festival, Jesus, knowing that the time had come for him to pass over from this world to the Father, having cared for his own who were in the world, he cared for them to the last.

At supper time, the Devil having already instigated

1 The greater part of this section is the work of the Greek Elder, as will be evident to the reader, but there is a substream attributable to John the Jewish Priest.

Simon's son Judas Iscariot to betray him, Jesus, knowing the Father had given everything into his keeping, and that he came from God and was going to God, rose from table, and after disrobing took a towel and tied it round

5   him. Then he poured water into the basin, and proceeded to wash the disciples' feet, and to dry them with the towel that was round him.

He came to Simon Peter. "Master", he protested, "are *you* going to wash my feet?"

"What I am doing", Jesus replied, "you do not understand now, but you will presently."

"Never shall you wash my feet", cried Peter.

"If I do not wash you", Jesus answered, "you are none of mine."

"In that case", Simon Peter said to him, "do not wash just my feet, Master, but my hands and head as well."

10   "He who has newly bathed", said Jesus, "only needs his feet washed to be completely clean. And you disciples are clean, though not all for you."[a]

When he had washed their feet and resumed his garments Jesus sat down and said to them, "Do you realize what I have done for you? You call me Teacher and Master, and you speak correctly, for so I am. If I then, the Teacher and Master, have washed your feet,

15   you ought to wash each other's feet. I have set you an example, that you should do as I have done for you.

"I tell you for a positive fact, the servant is not superior to his master, nor the messenger to him who has sent him. If you know this, happy are you if you act upon it. I am not saying this to all of you – I know those I have chosen – but that the Scripture should be fulfilled, 'He who has enjoyed my hospitality has lifted his heel against me.'[2] I am telling you this before it happens, so that when it comes to pass you may believe that I am he.

20   "I tell you for a positive fact, he who receives whoever I send receives me,[3] and he who receives me receives him who has sent me."

When he had said this, Jesus was deeply moved and

a He knew who would betray him. That is why he said, "Not all of you are clean".

---

2 *Ps* 41:9.
3 cf *Mt* 10:40.

testified, "I tell you for a positive fact, one of you will betray me."

The disciples looked at each other uncertain to whom he was referring.

One of his disciples of whom Jesus was fond was reclining on his bosom.[4] So Simon Peter leaned over to him and said, "Ask him who he means."

25 Leaning back against the breast of Jesus he said to him, "Who is it, Master?"

Jesus replied, "It is one for whom I dip the morsel and offer it to him."[5]

Then dipping the morsel he tendered it to Judas Iscariot son of Simon; and with the morsel Satan entered him.

Jesus then said to him, "What you have to do, do quickly."[b]

30 On receiving the morsel Judas immediately went out. It was night.

When he had gone, Jesus said, "Now the Son of Man is glorified, and God is glorified in him. God will both glorify him in himself, and glorify him immediately.

"My dear children, I shall be with you only a while longer. You will look for me, but as I told the Jews, so I say to you now, 'Where I am going you cannot come.' I give you a fresh instruction, to love one another. As I 35 have loved you, so must you love one another. By this, your love for one another, everyone will recognize that you are my disciples."

"Where are you going, Master?" Simon inquired.

Jesus replied, "Where I am going you cannot follow me now, but you will follow me later."

"Why can't I follow you now, Master?" said Peter. "I will give my life for you."

"So you will give your life for me?" Jesus replied. "I tell

b No one seated there knew why he said this to him. Some, however, imagined, since Judas had the alms-bag, that Jesus was telling him, "Buy what we need for the festival", or that he should give something to the poor.

---

4 John the Priest speaks modestly. He was the fourteenth male present, as master of the house seated in the place next in honour to Jesus. The diners lay at the table on couches with their feet outward and their shoulder propped against their neighbour.

5 The dipping and eating of bitter herbs was part of the service for Passover eve.

you for a positive fact, the cock will not have crowed before you deny me three times over.

14.1   [6]"Do not let your minds be troubled. Have faith in God, and have faith in me too. There are many apartments in my Father's house. Had it not been so I would certainly have told you, for I go to prepare accommodation for you. And if I go and prepare accommodation for you, I will come back and take you to myself, that where I am you may be also. And to where I am going you know the way."

5   Thomas said to him, "Master, we don't know where you are going, so how can we know the way?"

Jesus said to him, "I myself am Way and Truth and Life. No one reaches the Father except by me. If you knew me, you would also perceive my Father. From now on you do know him, and have seen him."[7]

Philip said to him, "Show us the Father, Master, and we shall be content."

Jesus replied, "Have I been with you all so long, yet you have not recognized me, Philip? He who has seen me has seen the Father. Why then do you say, 'Show us

10   the Father'? Do you not believe that I am in the Father, and that the Father is in me? The words I speak to you I do not speak of my own accord: the Father who dwells in me performs his own miracles. Believe me, that I am in the Father, and the Father is in me. But if not, believe because of the miracles themselves.

"I tell you for a positive fact, he who believes in me will perform the same miracles as myself, and even greater miracles will he perform, because I am going to the Father. I will do indeed whatever you ask in my name, that the Father may be glorified in the Son. If you ask anything in my name I will do it.

15   "If you care for me, carry out my instructions; and I will beg the Father to give you another Adviser to be with you permanently, namely the Spirit of Truth, whom the

6 Throughout the Discourse material that follows there appear to be several cases of misplacement. But since no narrative intervenes no rectification has been attempted except in one instance (see p 517 and notes).

7 In *Genesis* it is said that Adam was made in the image of God. Some Jewish mystics therefore conceived that there must be a Heavenly Man (Son of Man) in whose image Adam was created, who represented the image of God; and that this Archetypal Man would act as the Messiah Above, the heavenly counterpart of the Messiah below. See *Bk of Enoch*, and *Dan* 7:13–14.

world cannot receive, because it neither perceives him nor knows him. But you will know him, because he will dwell with you and be with you.[8] I will not leave you forsaken; I will come to you. Very soon the world will see me no longer, but you will see me, because I am alive;

20 and you will live. When that time comes you will realize that I am in the Father, and you are in me, and I am in you. He who possesses my instructions and keeps them, he is the man who cares for me. He who cares for me will be loved by my Father. I too will love him, and manifest myself to him."

Judas, not Iscariot, said to him, "Why are you going to manifest yourself to us and not to the world?"

Jesus answered, "If anyone cares for me he will heed my message, and my Father will love him; and we will come to him and make our abode with him. He who does not care for me will not heed my words; yet the message you are hearing is not mine but the Father's who has sent me.

15.1   [9]"I am the true vine, and my Father is the cultivator. Every branch of mine that does not bear fruit he removes, and every one that bears fruit he prunes that it may bear finer fruit. You are already sound fruit through the message I have proclaimed to you. Continue in me and I will continue in you. Just as the branch cannot bear fruit of its own accord unless it continues in the vine, so cannot you unless you continue in me.

5   "I am the vine, while you are the branches. He who continues in me, and I in him, will bear much fruit, because apart from me you are powerless. If anyone does not continue in me he is cast off – as a branch is – and withers, and men gather such branches and throw them on the fire to be burnt. If you continue in me, and my words remain in you, you shall ask what you will and it shall be done for you. By this is my Father glorified, by your bearing much fruit and being disciples of mine. As my Father has loved me, so have I loved you. Retain my

10   affection. If you obey my instructions you will retain my affection, just as I have obeyed the Father's instructions and retain his affection.

"I have spoken to you thus that I may have joy in you,

---

8 Or 'in you'.

9 Omitting here *Jn* 14:25–31, and transferring these verses to their proper place following 16:31.

and that your joy may be complete. It is my instructon that you love one another as I have loved you. No one has a love greater than that man's who will lay down his life for his friends. You are my friends if you carry out
15　what I have enjoined on you. I call you servants no longer; for the servant does not know what his master is about. I have addressed you as friends, because I have acquainted you with everything I have heard from my Father. It is not you who have chosen me: it is I who have chosen you and placed you so that you may proceed to bear fruit, and that your fruit may endure, so that whatever you ask the Father in my name he will grant you.

"This is what I have enjoined upon you, that you love one another. If the world hates you, you know that it hated me before it hated you. If you belonged to the world the world would be fond of its own. But because you do not belong to the world, since I have chosen you out of the world, therefore the world will hate you,
20　Remember what I have said to you, 'The servant is not superior to his master.'[10] If they have persecuted me, they will also persecute you. If they have not heeded my Message, neither will they heed yours. They will do all this to you on my account, because they do not know him who has sent me. If I had not come and spoken to them no sin would have been theirs; but now they have both seen and hated me and my Father also, since the
25　saying had to be fulfilled that is stated in their Law, 'They hated me without cause.'[11] When the Adviser comes, whom I will send you from the Father, the Spirit of Truth that emanates from the Father, he will testify of me, and you too shall testify because you have been with me from the first.

16.1　"I have spoken to you thus that you may not be thrown off your balance. They will excommunicate you. The time will even come when anyone who kills you will think he is performing a sacred duty. They will do this because they have neither acknowledged the Father nor myself. I have told you this, however, so that when the time comes you will recall that I said it to you. I did not
5　speak of this to you before, because I was with you. But

---

10 See *Jn* 13:16.
11 See *Ps* 35:19; 69:4, not in the Law. Again the Elder makes Jesus speak as an alien.

now I am going to him who sent me, [and none of you asks me, 'Where are you going?']¹² and because I have spoken to you thus your hearts are filled with grief. I am telling you the truth, however, that it is to your advantage that I depart. For unless I go the Adviser will never come to you. But if I go, I will send him to you. And when he comes he will convict the world in respect of all sin, justice and judgment; sin, because they do not believe in

10   me; justice, because I am going to the Father and you will see me no more; and judgment, because the ruler of this world¹³ will be judged.

"I have a great deal more to tell you, but you cannot receive it now. When he comes, however, the Spirit of Truth, he will initiate you into the full truth. He will not speak for himself, but say exactly what he hears, and convey to you what comes.¹⁴ He will glorify me, because he will receive what is mine and convey it to you.

15   Whatever the Father possesses is mine. That is why I say, he will receive what is mine and convey it to you.

"Soon you will no longer see me, but soon after you will behold¹⁵ me."

Some of his disciples asked the others, "What does he mean when he tells us, 'Soon you will no longer see me, but soon after you will behold me,' [and, 'I am going to the Father']?"¹⁶

The others replied, "We have no idea. What does he mean when he says, 'Soon'?"

Jesus knew that they wanted to ask him, and said to them, "You are questioning one another, are you not, about what I said; 'Soon you will no longer see me, but

20   soon after you will behold me'? I tell you for a positive fact, you will weep and wail, while the world will rejoice. You will mourn, but your mourning will be turned into joy. A woman is dismayed when she is about to give birth, because her time has come. But once the babe is born she no longer remembers her pangs in her joy that a

---

12 Either a gloss, or indicating a displacement, since Peter had already asked this very question (*Jn* 13:36).
13 Satan (Beliar). The Gnostics however made Jehovah, the God of the Jews, act as Demiurge. Jesus revealed the Unknown Father.
14 ie mediumistically. Alternatively, 'what is coming'.
15 Gr *Opsesthe*, suggesting an appearance of an abnormal kind.
16 Perhaps a gloss. While these words had been used just before (*Jn* 16:10), they had also been used some time back at 14:12. But the Greek Elder makes Jesus speak very repetitiously.

man-child is born into the world. So you too will grieve
sorely now. But I will appear to you, and your hearts will
rejoice, and no one will be able to take your joy from you.
When that time comes you will not need to ask me for
anything. I tell you for a positive fact, whatever you ask
the Father he will grant you for my sake. So far you have
asked nothing in my name. Ask, and you shall receive,
that your joy may be complete.

25   "I have spoken to you enigmatically thus far. The time
will come when I shall no longer speak to you enigmatically, but will inform you about the Father plainly. When
that time comes you will ask in my name, and I will not
say to you, 'I will ask the Father on your behalf.' The
Father himself will love you, because you have loved me
and believed that I came from the Father. I came from the
Father and entered the world. Now I am leaving the
world again and going to the Father."

His disciples said to him, "There, now you are speak-
30 ing plainly and not enigmatically. Now we know that
you know everything and need no one to question you.
This makes us believe that you come from God."

Jesus replied, "So you do believe now? The time will
indeed come, in fact it has come, when you will disperse
each to his own home[17] and leave me completely alone.
But I shall not be completely alone; for the Father will be
with me. I have told you this so that you may be at peace
where I am concerned. In the world you will have
affliction, but take courage, I have overcome the world.

14.25   [18]"I have spoken to you thus while I am with you. But
the Adviser, the holy Spirit, whom the Father will send
in my name, will give you full instructions[19] and remind
you of everything I have told you. I leave you peace. I
give you my own peace. I do not give it as the world gives
it. Do not be distressed or dismayed. You have heard me
say, 'I am going away, but I will come to you.' If you
cared for me you would surely be glad that I am going to
the Father, for the Father is superior to myself. I have
told you now before it happens so that when it happens
you may believe.

30   "I shall not speak to you much more. The ruler of the

17 cf *Mt* 26:31,56.
18 Inserting here 14:25–31, see p 517, n 9.
19 Lit "will teach you everything".

world is coming, and in me he will get nothing, except that the world will know that I love the Father, and as the Father has given me commandment so I act. Rise, let us be going!"[20]

17.1   When Jesus had spoken thus, he lifted his eyes to heaven and said, "Father, the time has come. Glorify thy Son, that thy Son may glorify thee, just as thou gavest him authority over all flesh, so that to all whom thou hast given him he should grant Eternal Life. Eternal Life consists in knowing thee, the only True God, and him whom thou hast sent, Jesus Christ. I have glorified thee on earth by completing the work thou gavest me to do.

5   So now glorify me in thy dwelling place, Father, with the glory I had with thee before the world existed.

"I have revealed thy name to the men thou gavest me out of the world. Thine they were, and thou gavest them to me; and they have heeded thy Message. They know now that everything thou hast given me comes from thee; for the words thou gavest me I have given them, and they have accepted and clearly understood that I have come from thee, and have believed that thou hast sent me. I ask on their behalf – I do not ask on behalf of the world, but for those thou hast given me – for they are

10   thine, and all that is mine is thine, and I am glorified in them. I shall no longer be in the world, but they will be in the world, while I come to thee.

"Holy Father, keep in thy name those thou hast given me, that they may be one as we are. While I have been with them I have kept in thy name those whom thou hast given me, and guarded them, and not one of them is lost except the doomed one,[21] that the Scripture should be fulfilled.[22]

"But now I am coming to thee. So I am saying this in the world, that they may experience the full measure of my happiness. I have given them thy Message, and the world has hated them, because they are not of the world

15   any more than I am of the world. I do not ask that thou shouldst take them out of the world, but that thou wouldst keep them from harm.[23] Consecrate them by the

---

20 cf *Mk* 14:42; *Mt* 26:46. From *Jn* 12:27–28 it is evident that the Elder was familiar with the story of the Agony in the Garden, but in the interests of the Discourse he has omitted it.
21 Lit "Son of Perdition".
22 cf *Ps* 109:7–8.
23 cf *Mt* 6:13.

Truth. Thy Message is Truth. Just as thou didst send me into the world, so have I sent them into the world; and on their behalf I have consecrated myself, that they too may be consecrated by Truth.

20   "Neither do I ask on behalf of these alone, but also on behalf of those who will believe in me through their report, that they all may be one, as thou, Father, art in me and I in thee, that they also may be one in us, that the world may believe thou hast sent me. So the glory thou hast given me I have given them, that they may be one as we are one, that the world may know that thou hast sent me, and that thou hast loved them as thou hast loved me.

"Father, I desire that what thou hast given me, even these, may be with me where I shall be, that they may see my glory which thou hast given me; for thou didst love me before the foundation of the world.

25   "Righteous Father, though the world has not known thee, I have known thee, and these have known that thou hast sent me. And I have made known thy name to them, and will make it known, so that the love with which thou hast loved me may be in them, as I am in them."

xii[1]

18.1   When Jesus had spoken thus, he passed over the brook Kidron with his disciples, where there was an orchard into which he and his disciples entered.[a]

Judas, therefore, having obtained a cohort and officers from the head priests and Pharisees, went there with lanterns and torches and weapons.

Then Jesus, who knew everything that was to befall him, came out and said to them, "Who are you looking for?"

5   "Jesus the Nazarene", they replied.

"I am he", he told them.

Judas himself, who betrayed him, was standing there with them. As Jesus said, "I am he", he stepped back and fell prostrate.

---

a Judas, who betrayed him, was familiar with the spot, because Jesus often resorted there with his disciples.

---

1 Much of John the Priest's material remains in this section, but it has been overworked by the Greek Elder in line with his doctrine.

Then Jesus asked them again, "Who are you looking for?"

When they said, "Jesus the Nazarene", Jesus replied, "I have told you I am he. So if it is only myself you want let these others go away."[b]

10   At this juncture Simon Peter, who carried a sword, drew it and struck the high priest's servant,[c] severing his ear.

"Return your sword to its sheath", Jesus told Peter, "Shall I not drink the cup the Father has given me?"[2]

The cohort with its tribune and the Jewish officials then laid hold of Jesus, bound him, and conducted him

15   to Annas[3] in the first instance.[d] Simon Peter and another disciple[4] followed Jesus. Now that disciple was a relative[5] of the high priest, and accompanied Jesus into the yard of the high priest's palace, but Peter was standing at the entrance outside. The other disciple, therefore, the relative of the high priest, went out and spoke to the woman doorkeeper and secured Peter's admission.

The woman then said to Peter, "Aren't you one of the man's disciples?"

"No, I'm not", he said.

The servants and officers had lit a charcoal brazier, because it was cold, and stood warming themselves. So Peter stood with them, and warmed himself too.

Meanwhile, the high priest had been interrogating Jesus about his disciples and about his teaching.

20   Jesus answered, "I have spoken quite openly to the world. I have invariably taught in the synagogue and in the Temple,[6] where all the Jews congregate,[7] and have

---

b That the saying he uttered, "I have lost none of those thou hast given me", should come true. (See above *Jn* 17:12. Ed.).

c The servant's name was Malchus.

d He was father-in-law of Caiaphas, who was the reigning high priest. It was Caiaphas who had counselled the Jews, "It is advisable that one man should die for the people."

---

2 Another indication of the writer's knowledge of the Agony in the Garden. See *Lk* 22:42.

3 Annas son of Seth, appointed high priest by Quirinius in AD 7.

4 The 'Dear Disciple', John the Priest, a modest self-reference.

5 Reading *gnotos* instead of *gnostos*, 'acquaintance'. From what immediately follows it is quite clear that the disciple was not John the son of Zebedee.

6 cf *Mt* 26:55.

7 The real Jesus would not have to tell this to the high priest of the Temple of all people. We are again with the Greek Elder.

said nothing secretly. Why do you ask me? Ask those who have listened to what I said to them. They know what I said."

When he said this, one of the officers who was standing by struck Jesus and said, "Is that the way to answer the high priest?"[8]

Jesus replied, "If I have spoken wrongly, tell me what was wrong; but if rightly, why do you strike me?"

25 Then Annas sent him bound to the high priest Caiaphas. Simon Peter was still standing and warming himself.

Then they said to him, "Aren't you one of his disciples?"

He denied it and said, "No, I'm not."

One of the high priest's servants[e] said, "Didn't I see you in the orchard with him?"

Once more Peter denied, and immediately a cock crowed.[9]

From Caiaphas they conducted Jesus to the praetorium. It was now early morning. But they did not enter the praetorium so as not to be defiled, and thus prevented from eating the passover. Pilate therefore went out to them and said, "What charge do you bring against this man?"

30 "Had he not been a criminal", they replied, "we should not have handed him over to you."

"In that case", said Pilate, "take him yourselves and sentence him in accordance with your law."

The Jews answered, "We have no power to execute anyone."[f][10]

Pilate then went into the praetorium and summoned Jesus, and said to him, "Are you the king of the Jews?"

[11]Jesus replied, "Are you asking this of your own

---

e He was a kinsman of the one whose ear Peter had severed.
f That the saying should come true by which he had indicated the kind of death he would die.[12]

---

8 Again the real Jesus would not have expressed himself so rudely to a high official who was now an old man, even if he did dislike him.

9 See *Jn* 13:38.

10 According to Jewish tradition the Sanhedrin was deprived by the Romans of power to try capital cases about AD 30, forty years before the destruction of the Temple.

11 What follows is the creation of the Greek Elder.

12 *Jn* 12:32–33.

accord, or did others suggest it to you about me?"

35   "Am I a Jew?" said Pilate. "Your own people and the head priests have handed you over to me. What have you done?"

Jesus replied, "My kingdom is not of this world. Had my kingdom been of this world my supporters would have struggled to prevent my being handed over to the Jews. My kingdom, however, is not from that source."

"You *are* a king then?" Pilate said to him.

Jesus replied, "As you say, I am a king. The reason I was born and came into the world was to testify to the truth. All who own the truth listen to my voice."

"What does truth mean?" Pilate said to him.

When he had said this he went out again to the Jews and told them, "I can find nothing whatever against him. But you have a practice that at the Passover I should release one person to you. Do you wish me to release the king of the Jews to you?"

40   They shouted back, "Not this man, Bar-Abbas!"[g]

19.1   Pilate then had Jesus flogged, and the soldiers plaited a victor's wreath out of thorns and set it on his head, and draped round him a crimson cloak, and saluted him with, "Hail, king of the Jews!", and struck him.

Once more Pilate went out, and said to them, "I am going to bring him out to you, that you may know that I find nothing whatever against him."[13]

5   Then Jesus came out, wearing the thorn wreath and the crimson cloak, and Pilate announced, "Here he is!"

When they saw him, the head priests and their supporters shouted, "Crucify him, crucify him!"

Pilate said to them, "Crucify him yourselves, for I find nothing against him."

The Jews replied, "We have a law, and in accordance with that law he ought to die, because he claimed to be God's son."[14]

When Pilate heard this he was even more alarmed, and went back into the praetorium and said to Jesus, "Where do you come from?"

But Jesus gave him no reply.

---

g Bar-Abbas was a brigand.

---

13 Pilate acts here entirely out of character. See Josephus, *Antiq.*, and especially Philo, *Embassy to Gaius* 302–303.

14 There was no such law. King Solomon was called God's son.

10   Pilate then said to him, "Have you nothing to say to me? Do you not know that I have power to release you and power to crucify you?"

Jesus replied, "You could have no power over me at all unless it was given you from Above. Consequently he who handed me over to you is more to blame than you are."

Because of this Pilate endeavoured to release him. But the Jews shouted, "If you release him, you are no friend of Caesar's. Whoever claims to be king is in opposition to Caesar."[15]

When Pilate heard these expressions he brought Jesus out and seated himself on the tribunal in the place called the Tiled Court, but in Hebrew *Gabbatha*,[h][16] and said to the Jews, "Here is your king!"

15   "Off with him, off with him! Crucify him!" they shouted.

Pilate said to them, "'Am I to crucify your king?"

The head priests responded, "We have no king but Caesar."

Then Pilate handed him over to them to be crucified.[18]

So they took Jesus, and carrying his own cross he went out to what was called Skull Place, that is to say, in Hebrew, *Golgotha*. There they crucified him, and along with him two others on either side, with Jesus in the middle. Pilate also wrote a notice and posted it up on the cross, to this effect, "Jesus the Nazarene, King of the Jews".

20   Many Jews read the notice, because the place where Jesus was crucified was close to the city, and it was written in Hebrew, Latin and Greek.

So the Jewish head priests said to Pilate, "Do not put 'King of the Jews', but 'He said I am King of the Jews' ".

Pilate replied, "What I have written I have written."

And when the soldiers crucified Jesus they took his

h It was the preparation day of the Passover, about six o'clock in the morning.[17]

---

15 By accepting that he was Messiah, king of the Jews, Jesus had committed high treason against Caesar in Roman law. Pilate had to condemn Jesus.
16 Aram. *Gabbatha* (the Platform).
17 Roman reckoning. The first hour (Jewish reckoning).
18 Jews did not execute by crucifixion. It was a Roman practice.

clothes and divided them into four lots, one lot for each soldier, leaving the tunic over. Now the tunic was seam-less throughout, woven in one piece. So they said to one another. "Don't let us tear it, but draw lots and see who gets it."[i]

25   Standing by the cross of Jesus were his mother, and his mother's sister, Mary the wife of Clopas, and Mary of Magdala. Then Jesus, noticing his mother and the dis-ciple of whom he was fond standing there, said to his mother, "Madam, this is your son." Then he said to his disciple, "This is your mother." From that time the disciple took her into his own home.

After this Jesus, conscious that all was now over, said, "I am thirsty."[j]

There was a jar full of vinegar placed there. So they saturated a sponge with vinegar, fixed it on a spike,[19]

30   and put it to his mouth. When he had received the vinegar he said, "It is all over", and bowing his head yielded up his spirit.

Then the Jews,[k] that the bodies should not remain on the cross on the sabbath,[l] requested Pilate that their legs might be broken and the corpses removed.

So the soldiers went and broke the legs of the first, and of the other man crucified with him. But when they came to Jesus, as they saw he was already dead, they did not break his legs; but one of the soldiers with his lance pierced his side, and there came out blood and water.[m]

---

i That the Scripture should come true, "They divided my garments among them, and for my clothing they cast lots" (*Ps* 22:18). This is exactly what the soldiers did.

j That the Scripture should be accomplished (*Ps* 69:21).

k As it was the Preparation Day.

l That sabbath was a High Day.

m He who saw it has stated this,[20] and his statement is completely reliable, and he knows he is telling the truth, that you too may believe. This happened that the Scripture should come true. "Not a bone of his shall be fractured" (*Ps* 34:20, LXX), and still another Scripture says, "They shall look at him whom they have pierced" (*Zech* 12:10).

---

19 Reading *hysso* for *hyssopo* (hyssop). The scribal error was probably due to the fact that in the Greek the word immediately following without a break begins with 'p'.

20 Here the Greek John the Elder clearly distinguishes himself from the 'Dear Disciple', the Jewish John the Priest.

xiii

38   [1]After these events, Joseph of Arimathea[a] sought Pilate's leave to remove the body of Jesus, and Pilate committed it to him. So he went and removed the body. Nicodemus[b] also went, carrying a compound of myrrh and aloes weighing about seventy-five pounds.[2] Then
40   they took the body of Jesus, and wrapped it in swathes of linen with the spices.[c]

Now in the locality where Jesus was crucified there was an orchard, and in the orchard a new tomb in which no one had ever been laid previously. There then they laid Jesus.[d]

20.1   On the day after the sabbath Mary of Magdala came very early to the tomb while it was still dark, and saw that the boulder had been moved from the tomb.[3] So she ran to Simon Peter and the other disciple of whom Jesus was fond, and told them, "They have removed the Master from the tomb, and we[4] don't know where they have put him."

So Peter and the other disciple set out and came to the tomb. They both ran together; but the other disciple out-
5   distanced Peter[5] and reached the tomb first, and stooping down saw the linen wrappings lying there. He did not go in however.[6] Then following him came Simon Peter, and entered the tomb. There he saw both the wrappings and also the cloth that had covered Jesus's head, not lying with the wrappings, but apart, folded up by itself. Then the other disciple, who had reached the tomb first, also went in, and saw for himself and
10   believed.[e] Then the disciples returned home.

a   He was a disciple of Jesus, but kept the fact secret for fear fear of the Jews.
b   The one who first of all came to Jesus by night.
c   As is the Jewish custom.
d   On account of the Jewish Preparation Day, because it was close by.
e   For so far they had not understood the Scripture that he must rise from the dead.

---

1   "After these events." This division of the text is regularly employed up to *Jn* 7:1 (section vi), and resumed here.
2   Gr. 'one hundred litras'.
3   Rolled back in its groove.
4   Other women were there (*Mk* 16:1–8).
5   Being much younger.
6   Being a priest, who would incur defilement from a corpse.

Meanwhile Mary stood outside the tomb close by, weeping. As she wept she peered into the tomb and saw two angels there, one at the head and one at the feet where the body of Jesus had lain.

"Madam", they said to her, "why are you crying?"

"Because they have taken away my Master", she replied, "and I don't know where they have laid him."

When she had said this she turned round, and saw Jesus standing there, though she did not realise it was Jesus.

15   Jesus said to her, "Madam, why are you crying? Who are you looking for?"

Thinking he was the gardener, she said to him, "Sir, if you have moved him, tell me where you have put him and I will take him away."

Jesus said to her, "Mary!"

She turned and said to him in Hebrew, "*Rabboni!*"[f]

"Do not detain me",[7] Jesus said to her, "for I have not yet ascended to my Father. Go to my brothers, and tell them I am ascending to my Father and your Father, to my God and your God."

Mary of Magdala went and informed the disciples, "I have seen the Master", and gave them his message.

The evening of that day, the day after the sabbath, when the doors had been bolted where the disciples were for fear of the Jews.[8] Jesus came and stood before

20   them, and said, "Peace be with you." So saying he showed his hands and side.

The disciples were delighted to see the Master.[9]

Again he said to them, "Peace be with you. As the Father has sent me, so am I sending you."

With this he expelled a deep breath, and said to them, "Receive the holy Spirit! Those whose sins you forgive will be forgiven, and those whom you condemn will be condemned."

Thomas, however, one of the twelve, who was called

f   That is to say, "Teacher!"

7   Or, "Do not cling to me".

8   According to the uncanonical *Gospel of Peter* the disciples were in hiding because they were being sought in the belief that they were intending to set fire to the Temple.

9   *Matthew* (28:16) makes the disciples return from Jerusalem to Galilee without having seen Jesus.

25   Twin, was not with them when Jesus came. So the other disciples told him, "We have seen the Master."

But he replied, "Unless I see the scar of the nails in his hands, and insert my finger in the nail scars, and insert my hand into his side, I shall not believe it."

Eight days later the disciples were again indoors, and this time Thomas was with them. When the doors were bolted Jesus came and stood before them, and said "Peace be with you."

Then he said to Thomas, "Bring your finger here where my hands are, and bring your hand and insert it into my side, and do not be incredulous but believing."

Thomas answered, "My Lord and my God!"[10]

Jesus said to him, "You have believed because you have seen me. Happy are they who have believed without seeing!"

30   Many other signs did Jesus perform in the presence of his disciples, which have not been recorded in this book. But these have been recorded that you may believe that Jesus is the Messiah, the Son of God, and by believing have Life on his account.

10 The Elder may have put this expression into the mouth of Thomas in response to the fact that the Emperor Domitian near the close of the 1st century AD had insisted on having himself addressed as "Our Lord and God", Suetonius, *Domit* 13.

xiv

21.1   After these events Jesus revealed himself again to the disciples at the Sea of Tiberias. He appeared in this way. Simon Peter, Thomas called Twin, Nathaniel from Cana of Galilee, the sons of Zebedee, and two other disciples, were together.[1] Simon Peter said to them, "I am going fishing."[2]

"Very well", they told him, "we will come with you."

So they went on board the boat; but that night they caught nothing. When morning came there was Jesus standing on the shore.[a]

a The disciples did not actually know it was the Master.

1 One of these two disciples of his will have been John the Priest, the 'Dear Disciple', clearly in the context not one of the sons of Zebedee.

2 The *Gospel of Peter* also makes some of the disciples go to the sea with Peter, but the extant fragment breaks off at this point.

5   Jesus then hailed them, "Have you anything to eat there, lads?"

"No", they replied.

"Cast your net on the right side of the ship", he told them, "and you will find fish."

So they cast the net, and now they could hardly haul it in for the quantity of fish.

At this, the disciple of whom Jesus was fond said to Peter, "It is the Master!"[3]

As soon as Simon Peter heard it was the Master, he tied his smock round him[b] and leapt into the sea. But the other disciples came to shore in the dinghy[c] dragging the net full of fish.

As they landed they saw a charcoal fire burning and a small fish with bread being baked.

10   "Bring some of the small fish you have just caught", Jesus said to them.

So Peter went aboard and drew the net to land full of large fish, a hundred and fifty-three of them; yet in spite of there being so many the net was not broken.

"Come and breakfast", said Jesus.

None of the disciples had the temerity to ask him, "Who are you?" knowing it was the Master.

Jesus came and took the bread and distributed it to them, and the fish as well.[d]

15   When they had breakfasted, Jesus said to Simon Peter, "Simon son of John, do you love me more than these others?"

"Of course, Master", he replied, "You know I am devoted to you."

"Tend my lambs", he told him.

Again he asked him for the second time, "Simon son of John, do you love me?"

"Of course, Master", he replied. "You know I am devoted to you."

"Shepherd my sheep", he told him.

---

b   He was naked.
c   They were not far from the shore, only about a hundred yards.
d   This was now the third occasion on which Jesus had appeared to the disciples after rising from the dead.

---

3   As the Synoptic tradition indicates, there had been an intimation by Jesus that he would rendezvous with his disciples in Galilee.

For the third time he asked him, "Simon son of John, are you devoted to me?"

Peter was vexed that he asked him a third time, "Are you devoted to me?" and said to him, "You know everything, Master. You must know I am devoted to you."

"Tend my sheep", Jesus said to him. "I tell you for a positive fact, when you were young, you fastened your girdle and went wherever you wished. But when you are old, you will stretch out your hands, and someone else will fasten you and convey you where you will not wish."[e]

Having said this, he added, "Follow me."

20   Turning round, Peter noticed that the disciple of whom Jesus was fond had been following.[f] Seeing him, Peter said to Jesus, "What about him, Master?"

Jesus replied, "Supposing I wish him to remain until I come, what concern is that of yours? You follow me."[g]

---

e He said this in indication of the kind of death by which he would glorify God.[4]

f The one who reclined on his breast at the supper, and said, "Master, who is it who will betray you?"

g Thus the saying got about among the brothers that that disciple would not die, though Jesus never told him he would not die, he only said, "Supposing I wish him to remain until I come, what concern is that of yours?" He is the disciple who testified to these matters and recorded them, and we know that his testimony is trustworthy.[5] There is also much else that Jesus did, which if every item were to be recorded I very much doubt if the world itself could find room for the books that would have to be written.

---

4 According to tradition the Romans crucified Peter head downwards.

5 John the Elder seems here clearly to distinguish himself from John the Priest, the 'Dear Disciple', whose memoirs he has been using as the basis for his own contributions. cf *III Jn* 12. Tradition makes John the Priest live to a very great age. Hence the idea that got around that he would survive until the Second Advent of Jesus.

Preface to the Letters of John the Elder

Three letters of John, the Elder not the Priest, are extant. The authenticity of these is not in doubt. Strictly speaking, however, the first is not a letter at all, but a tract or homily. In the present version it is suggested that the opening sentence is really the title and description. The word *peri* ('concerning', or 'on the subject of'), is constantly used in Greek descriptive titles; and certainly *The Theme of Life* is the subject of this document, Life as appearing in Christ and Life as possessed by him. The same thinking, and indeed language, is frequently represented in the Elder's expansion of John the Priest's reminiscences. Some have held that the tract was intended to commend the expanded Gospel.

The second and third letters are real letters, the former written to an unnamed community of believers, "the Elect Lady and her Children", and the latter to Gaius, possibly an influential member of the same community. The letters reveal the clash of personalities as well as the conflict of beliefs that was taking place in the communities of Asia Minor in the first quarter of the second century.

In defence of his particular Christology, very different to that of the earlier disciples, the Elder speaks his mind bluntly, and fully in keeping with the tales told of his uncompromising nature. That very same voice speaks through the lips of Jesus in the Discourses in the Fourth *Gospel* and in the Messages to the Seven Communities inserted in the *Revelation*. It is consistent and unmistakable. Yet with friends it can be surprisingly sweet and tender.

Especially in the tract, or first letter, there are so many allusions to the *Gospel* as we have it that it would disturb the reading too much to list them. But the reader will now be able to recognise them. As we have seen with the *Gospel*, and so here also, the author has so united his own work with the records of the 'Dear Disciple' that he can speak of 'we' who have seen and touched Jesus. We do not know whether there was a personal relationship between the assertive young Elder and the aged John the Priest, but it seems probable from the traditions that the former had gained the latter's confidence, and took full advantage of his favourable position.

Letter of John (1)
On The Theme of Life[1]

1.1 He who was from of old, whom we have heard, whom we have seen with our own eyes, whom we have inspected, and whom our hands have touched.

Not only was Life made visible, but we have seen it, and solemnly affirm this, and proclaim to you that Eternal Life which was with the Father and was made visible to us.

Him whom we have seen and heard we proclaim to you also, that you too may have fellowship with us. And the fellowship, is with the Father and with his Son Jesus Christ; and we are writing this to you that your[2] joy may be complete

5   It is the very same Message we have heard from him which we are conveying to you, that "God is Light, and there is no trace of darkness in him". If we say, "We have fellowship with him", and walk in the dark, we lie, and are not keeping to the truth. But if we walk in the light we have fellowship with one another, and the blood of his

10   Son cleanses us from all iniquity. If we say, "We have not sinned", we make him a liar, and his word is not in us.

2.1   I am writing this to you, dear children, that you may not sin; but should anyone sin we have an intercessor with the Father, Jesus Christ the Just. He is a propitiator where our sins are concerned, and not only ours but those of the whole world. We are conscious that we know him in this way if we obey his instructions. He who says, "I know him", but does not obey his instructions is

5   a liar, and truth is not in him. Whoever obeys him, in him truly the love of God is accomplished. In this way we are conscious that we are in him. He who says he continues

---

1 These words are here regarded as the title of the tract, "Life" being personified and manifested in Jesus Christ. Alternatively read, "On the Word of Life". See prefaces to John's *Gospel* and these letters.
2 Alternatively, with some MSS, read "our".

in him ought himself to behave as he behaved.

Dear friends, it is no new instruction I am sending you, but the old one which you have heard from the very first. The old instruction is the Message you have heard. Yet I *am* sending you a new instruction, something that holds good for him and for you, that the darkness is passing away, and the True Light already shines. He who claims to be in the light and hates his brother is still in the 10 darkness. He who loves his brother continues in the light, and in it there is no pitfall. But he who hates his brother is in darkness, and walks in the dark, and does not know where he is going, because the darkness has blinded his eyes.

I am writing to you, dear children, because your sins are forgiven for his sake. I am writing to you, fathers, because you have known him who is from of old. I am writing to you, youths, because you have overcome the Evil One.

I have written to you, children, because you have known the Father. I have written to you, fathers, because you have known him who is from of old. I have written to you, youths, because you are strong and the word of God remains in you, and you have overcome the Evil 15 One. Do not love the world, nor what is in the world. If anyone loves the world, there is no love of the Father in him. For everything that is in the world, desire of the flesh, desire of the eyes, and the hollow sham of life in general, belongs not to the Father, but to the world. And the world with its desire is passing away, while he who does the will of God will endure for ever.

Children, it is the Last Hour. And as you have heard, "Antichrist will come", well, there are plenty of Antichrists in existence now, by which fact we know it is the Last Hour. They went out from us, but they did not belong to us.[3] Had they belonged to us, they would surely have remained with us. They went out, indeed, 20 to, make it clear that all do not belong to us. You, however, are consecrated by the Holy One. You do know, all of you. I have not written to you because you do not know the truth, but because you do know it, and

3 At this period, when the faithful believed that the Second Advent of Christ must be imminent, many new doctrines were flourishing, such as Docetism and Gnosticism, claiming that there had been no actual physical incarnation.

because no lie has any connexion with the truth.

Who but he is a liar, who denies that Jesus is the Christ? He is the Antichrist, he who denies the Father and the Son. Whoever denies the Son cannot have the Father either. He who confesses the Son has the Father also. As for you, let what you have heard from the beginning continue in you. Should what you have heard from the beginning continue in you, then you will
25 continue both in the Son and in the Father. And this is the promise he has made us, the promise of Eternal Life.

I have written this to you regarding those who would deceive you. As for you, the consecration you have received from him will continue in you, and there will be no need for anyone to teach you, since his consecration will teach you about everything; and this will be truth and no lie. So as it has taught you, continue in him.
3.1 And now, dear children, continue in him, so that whenever he shall appear we may meet him confidently on his arrival, and not shrink from him in shame. If you are aware that he is just, you must know that everyone who does justice is born of him. Look what love it is the Father has bestowed on us, that we should be called Children of God. And that is what we are. That is why the world does not recognise us, because it did not know him. Yes, dear friends, we are Children of God now, though it is not yet evident what we shall be. We only know that when he appears we shall be like him, for we shall behold him as he is. And everyone who has this expectation purifies himself, as he is pure.

Whoever commits sin commits lawlessness. Sin,
5 indeed, *is* lawlessness. And you know that he appeared to take away sin, and in him there is no sin. Whoever continues in him does not sin, while whoever sins has neither seen him nor known him.

Do not deceive yourselves, dear children. He who executes justice is just, as he is just. He who commits sin belongs to the Devil; for the Devil has continued to sin from the beginning. To this end the Son of God appeared, that he might undo the Devil's works.

Whoever is born of God does not commit sin, because his seed remains in him; and he cannot sin, for he is
10 begotten of God. This is what differentiates the Children of God from the Children of the Devil. Whoever does not do justice does not belong to God, neither does he who

does not love his neighbour. For the very declaration you have heard from the beginning is that we should love one another, and not be like Cain, who belonged to the Evil One, and slew his brother. And why did he slay him? Because his own deeds were evil, while those of his brother were good.

Do not be in the least surprised, brothers, if the world hates you. We know indeed that we have passed from Death to Life, because we love the brothers. He who does not love his brother continues in Death. Whoever hates his brother is a manslayer, and you know that no manslayer has any continuance of Eternal Life in him. We have known what love is from the fact that the Son of God[4] laid down his life for us. We too ought to lay down our lives for our brothers. But he who has worldly means, and observes his brother in need, and withholds his compassion from him, how does the love of God continue in him?

Let us not love, dear children, merely in speech and word, but in deed and reality. In this way we shall know that we belong to the Truth, and shall relieve our minds in his presence should our minds accuse us; for God is greater than our minds and knows everything. Should our minds not accuse us, dear friends, we shall have confidence towards God, and whatever we ask for we shall obtain from him, because we obey his commandments and do what is pleasing in his sight. And it is his commandment that we should believe in his Son Jesus Christ, and that we should love one another as Christ enjoined on us. Whoever obeys his instructions continues in him, and he in him who obeys. And the way we recognise that he continues in us is by his spirit which he has given us.

4.1   Do not credit every spirit, dear friends. Examine the spirits to find out whether they are from God, because many false prophets are abroad in the world. You will recognise the spirit from God in this way: every spirit which confesses that Jesus Christ has come in the flesh is from God, while every spirit which does not admit the physical existence[5] of Jesus is not from God. And this is the spirit of Antichrist, which you have heard wll come.

4 The text simply reads "he".
5 Lit "come in the flesh".

Now you, dear children, belong to God, and have overcome the Antichrists[6]; for he who is in you is greater
5   than he who is in the world. They belong to the world. That is why they speak in a worldly way and the world listens to them. We belong to God. He who knows God will listen to us, while he who does not belong to God will not listen to us. This is how we shall discern the spirit of truth and the spirit of error.[7]

Love one another, dear friends, because love is from God, and everyone who does love is born of God and knows God. He who does not love does not know God; for God is Love. God's love has been made evident to us in this way, that God sent his only begotten Son into the
10   world that we might have Life through him. This is where love comes in, not in our having loved God, but in his having loved us, and having sent his Son as propitiator where our sins were concerned.

If God so loved us, dear friends, we too ought to love one another. No one has ever yet seen God,[8] but if we love one another God continues in us, and his love is perfected in us. This is how we know that we are continuing in him and he in us, because he has given us some of his own Spirit, and we have seen and testified that the Father has sent the Son as saviour of the world.
15   Whoever confesses that Jesus is the Son of God, God continues in him and he in God. We ourselves have known and have believed the love which God has for us.

God is Love, and he who continues in love continues in God, and God continues in him. It is in this way that love is perfected where we are concerned, so that we should have confidence on the Day of Judgment; because as he is so are we in the world. There is no such thing as fear in love. Rather does complete love expel fear. For fear causes timorousness: he who is afraid is not perfect in his love. We love, because God loved us in the
20   first place. If anyone says, "I love God", yet hates his brother, he is a liar. For he who does not love his brother whom he has seen, cannot love God whom he has not seen. Indeed, we have this very commandment from

6 The author opposes those who denied that Jesus Christ had existed physically. He only seemed to be a man and to suffer. The text reads "them", but the Antichrists are meant.
7 Or, "detect the true spirit and the false spirit."
8 cf *Jn* 14:9.

him,[9] that he who loves God must love his brother also.

5.1   Whoever believes that Jesus is the Christ is begotten of God, and whoever loves him who begot loves him who is begotten of him. It is when we do love God and keep his commandments that we realise that we love the Children of God. Love of God consists in our obeying his commandments. And his commandments are not burdensome, for whatever is begotten of God overcomes the world. The victory that overcomes the world lies in our

5   faith. Who is it overcomes the world but he who believes that Jesus is Son of God? He it is, Jesus Christ, who has gone through water and blood,[10] not only water, but water and blood.

Now it is the Spirit that affirms this, because the Spirit is Truth. For there are three that give their testimony, the Spirit, the water, and the blood, and the three are in complete accord. If we accept the evidence of men, the testimony of God is greater, because it is indeed the

10   testimony of God that he has given regarding his Son. He who believes in the Son of God has the evidence in himself. He who does not believe God has made him a liar, because he has not credited the testimony which God has given regarding his Son. The evidence consists in this, that God has given us Eternal Life, and that this Life is in his Son. He who possesses the Son possesses Life. He who does not possess the Son of God does not possess Life.

I have written this to you – those who believe in the name of the Son of God – that you may be aware that you do possess Eternal Life. The confidence we have, then, where God is concerned, is this, that if we ask anything which is in accordance with his will he will listen to us.

15   And if we know that he listens to our requests, we know equally that we shall obtain whatever it may be we have asked him for.

If anyone sees his brother committing a sin that is not deadly, he shall ask, and God will grant him life. This applies to those who commit sins which are not deadly. There is such a thing as a deadly sin.[11] I am not suggest-

9 See *Deut* 6:5; *Lev* 19:18; *Mt* 22:37–39.
10 The baptism of water and that of blood (*Mk* 10:38; *Lk* 12:50), the crucifixion. The Fourth *Gospel* stresses that water and blood came out when the side of Jesus was pierced (*Jn* 19:34).
11 What the author would think of as deadly sins are listed in *Rev* 21:8.

ing that he should pray in respect of that. Every iniquity is of course sin, but there is such a thing as sin that is not deadly.

We know that whoever is born of God does not sin, since he who was begotten of God keeps him, and the Evil One does not get hold of him. We know that we belong to God, while the whole world is in the clutches of 20 the Evil One. We know too that the Son of God has come and has given us insight so that we should know the True One.[12] And in his Son Jesus Christ we are in the True One. He is the True God and Eternal Life. Guard yourselves from idols, dear children.

12 cf *Jn* 17:3. There could be a hint of Marcionism here, the doctrine that the world was created by a secondary God, rather than the Unknown Father revealed by Jesus, the Old Testament God of the Jews.

Letter of John (2)
To the Elect Lady and her Children

1.1   The Elder, to the Elect Lady and her children, whom I
truly love for the Truth's sake, and not only I but all
indeed who have known the Truth, which continues
in us and will be with us for ever. There will be loving-
kindness, mercy and peace with us from God the
Father, and from Jesus Christ the Son of the Father, in
truth and in love.

I was extremely happy to find children of yours follow-
5   ing the truth, as we were commanded by the Father. So
now I put it to you, Lady, not as sending you a new
injunction, but one we have had from the beginning,
that we should love one another. And the love consists in
this, in our living in accordance with his commandments. In order that you may follow it, this is what the
injunction to love one another[1] means, as you have
heard from the beginning.

For many deceivers are abroad in the world, those who
do not admit Jesus Christ as having come in the flesh.[2]
Here is 'the Deceiver' and the 'Antichrist'! Be on your
guard, so that we do not lose what we have laboured for,
but receive a full reward. Whoever goes beyond, and
does not remain within Christ's teaching, will not possess God. It is he who remains within the teaching who
10   will possess the Father and the Son. If anyone comes to
you and does not bring this teaching, do not receive him
into your homes, do not even bid him welcome; for he
who bids him welcome shares in his evil deeds.

---

1 'To love one another' is implied, but the words are not in the text.
2 cf the Elder's first letter.

Having so much to say to you, I do not want to do it with paper and ink, I am hoping instead to come and see you, and speak to you personally, that your[3] joy may be complete.

The children of your Elect Sister send you their regards.

3 Or "our".

Letter of John (3)
To Gaius

1.1   The Elder, to dear Gaius,[1] for whom I have a genuine affection.

First and foremost, dear friend, I trust you are well and prosperous, as prosperous as your soul is. You may be sure I was extremely happy when brothers came and testified to your sincerity, as you follow the True Faith. There is no greater satisfaction for me than to hear that my children are following the True Faith.

5   You are doing a creditable thing, dear friend, whatever you may do for the brothers and to some extent for strangers. They have given evidence of your affection before the community, and you will do well to forward them on their way in a manner worthy of God; for they have set out for his Name's sake taking nothing from the Gentiles. We ought, therefore, to sponsor such as they, that we may be co-workers with the Truth.

I have written something to the community.[2] But Diotrephes who fancies himself as their leader, finds no

10   room for us. Consequently, if I do come, I shall raise the matter of his behaviour, fooling me with worthless words. And not content with that, he will not entertain the brothers either, and those who wish to do so he prevents, and expels them from the community.

Do not copy the bad example, dear friend, but the good. The well-doer belongs to God. The evil-doer has not seen God. Everyone speaks highly of Demetrius,[3] and so does Truth itself. And we too pay our tribute, and you know that our testimony is trustworthy.[4]

---

1 Evidently a person of some means and influence, probably belonging to the community addressed in the previous letter.

2 Possibly referring to the previous letter (*Jn* II).

3 Perhaps the bearer of these letters.

4 cf *Jn* 21:24, and above p 532, n 4.

I have a great deal to say to you, but I will not do it with ink and pen. I hope however to see you shortly, and then we will have a personal talk.

Peace be with you. The friends send you their regards. Give the friends individual greetings from us.

Preface to the Revelation

The *Revelation* belongs to a class of Jewish visionary writings which had developed in the period of the Hasmonean dynasty (160–166 BC), and flourished for some centuries after, especially among the eclectic bodies in Judaism, whose members were largely responsible for their composition. This literature drew much of its imagery and apparatus from Babylonian and Persian religious concepts and pictorial presentations. The Jewish mystics borrowed and extended the range of symbols, adapting their significance to their own monotheistic and messianic faith. They also employed them to provide a dramatic commentary on past and present events, and a prophetic forecast of the future.

Through dreams and visions and homilies put into the mouths of ancient patriarchs and seers, the ways of God were justified to generations of his people experiencing suffering and calamity. The seer is often transported to heaven and from that celestial region he sees the march of events on earth from the divine viewpoint. There is judgment on Israel for its sins, but after the judgment there will be deliverance for the faithful, the destruction of the wicked and the oppressor, and finally the Messianic Era, the Biblical concept of the Golden Age. It is important to appreciate that the authors of these books never deal with the remote future: they are concerned with contemporary conditions and what lies almost immediately ahead. Where they furnish a review of the past it is to build up their case, and to satisfy the historic requirements of the period in which the individual lived whose name the actual writer has borrowed, Enoch, Abraham, Moses, etc.

The apocalyptic books represent a particular art form in which the initiated among the saints were instructed. They were trained in the eschatological interpretation of the Scriptures (their hidden references to the Last Times), and in the science of symbol and cipher, by which the full meaning of the images, numbers and colours used could be understood. Lacking a great deal of that equipment we cannot now determine the significance of all the allusions; but by studying many examples of the literature which are extant, we can sufficiently master the method to obtain a considerable part of the sense, that is if we do not impose on it our own suppositions.

The *Revelation* (or *Apocalypse*) *of Jesus Christ* is such an excellent specimen of the literature that it can only have been written by an expert, one moreover who was intimately acquainted with the Temple and its ministries, and conversant with the eschatological interpretation of the *Song of Moses* (*Deut* 32). The writer thinks in Hebrew, and the sounds of certain Hebrew words enter into the visions. He writes however in a not very literary Greek. If the name of John, given in the book as the seer and recorder, belongs to the original work and is not a pseudonym, he may be identified with John the Priest, the 'Dear Disciple' of Jesus, who, according to tradition, settled in Ephesus after having suffered the Roman punishment of banishment to an island, in this case Patmos, off the coast of Asia Minor, in the time of the Emperor Domitian. John is said to have seen the visions around AD 95–96, when the Christians were refusing to acknowledge the Emperor's deity.

The tradition may well be correct, since it comes from sources sufficiently near in time and locality, and it receives strong support from the contents of the book itself. If the author was indeed the 'Dear Disciple' of Jesus we learn more from the work about himself and his background. He first appears in the Fourth *Gospel* as a disciple of the prophetic preacher of the Last Times, John the Baptist, so that his association with the Jewish mystical and prophetic groups, such as the Essenes, is likely enough. The Fourth *Gospel* also suggests that he was of a priestly family, as was stated of him by Polycrates, Bishop of Ephesus, a century later. Certainly it is improbable that anyone not a priest could be so intimate with matters concerning the Temple of Jerusalem as the author of the *Revelation*.

The work now is not entirely in its original form. Both the beginning and the end have been altered and are in some confusion. There are also some interpolations in the body of the document. As it stands the visions are set within a framework of a letter addressed to seven Christian communities in Asia Minor, each of which is given a separate message. These messages and some other passages and phrases have quite a different character, tone and doctrinal viewpoint, reminding us forcibly of the Fourth *Gospel*'s Dialogue material. It is likely that the additions and changes were the work of John the Elder, who also lived and died at Ephesus, and who took over for his own purposes the recollections of John the Priest.

In the present version square brackets and dotted rules are

used to distinguish many of these elements. The whole question of authorship, however, is too complex for any final judgment and there is room for the view that a non-Christian apocalyptic source has been partly utilised.

As to the structure, the series of visions is in two parts, the first dealing with the judgments on Israel, and the second with the judgments on the Nations (especially Rome); and there is an intentional parallelism between them. In Book I the earthly scene is the Land of Israel; in Book II it is the Roman Empire. Yet the story is continuous, commencing with events preceding the Jewish War with Rome (AD 67–70) and culminating in the anticipated destruction of the Empire, the coming of the Messianic Era, and the Last Judgment.

It is possible to identify many of the allusions from contemporary records and other apocalyptic writings. To assist the reader the notes to this book and references to other books have been somewhat enlarged, and cross headings have been inserted. It is hoped that these will make the *Revelation* less mysterious. But it would be missing the whole purpose of the book if it was imagined to be simply history and prophecy presented through images and symbols. Its greatness lies in the fact that it exhibits human affairs as seen by the Eternal Presence on the Throne. Through inspired literary creation it asks and answers the question, "Shall not the Judge of all the Earth do right?"

The Revelation of Jesus Christ

Prologue

1.1   The Revelation of Jesus Christ, which God gave him to
show to his servants what must shortly transpire. So he
made it known by communicating it through his angel to
his servant John, who in turn gave out God's Message
and the testimony of Jesus Christ so far as he saw.

Happy is he who reads and those who hear the terms
of the prophecy, and who heed the matters recorded in
it; for the time is at hand!

"I am the Alpha and the Omega", says the Lord God,
who Is and Was and Shall be,[1] the Almighty.[2]

....

[John, to the Seven Communities in Asia. May peace
and prosperity[3] be yours from him who Is and Was and
Shall be, and from the seven spirits which are before his

5   throne, and from Jesus Christ the trustworthy witness,
the first-born from the dead, and the ruler of earthly
kings.

To him who loved us and has freed us from our sins by
his blood, and has given us kingship as priests to God his
Father,[4] to him be glory and dominion for ever. Amen.

He will indeed come with clouds, and every eye will
behold him, including those who pierced him,[5] and all
the tribes of the earth will mourn because of him. Even
so. Amen.]

---

1 cf *Targ. Pal.* at *Deut* 32:39.
2 Transferring 1:8 to its proper position after verse 3.
3 cf *III Jn* 2.
4 cf *Exod* 19:6; *I Pet* 2:5.
5 *Zech* 12:10 and see *Dan* 7:13; *Mt* 26:64.

Vision of the Angel-Messiah

I, John, your brother and associate in the persecution, and in the kingship and constancy in Jesus, was on the island called Patmos for the sake of God's Message and
10   the testimony of Jesus. I became estatic on the Lord's day, and heard behind me a loud voice like a trumpet horn[6] saying, "Set down in a book what you see[7] [and dispatch it to the seven communities, to Ephesus, Smyrna, Pergamum, Thyatira, Sardis, Philadelphia and Laodicea]".

I turned to face the voice that addressed me; and when I had turned round I saw seven golden lampstands, and in front of the lampstands a human figure clad in an ankle-length robe, clasped at the breast with a golden girdle. His head and hair were white as wool, white as
15   snow, and his eyes like a fiery flame. His feet were like burnished bronze, as if heated white hot in a furnace, and his voice was like the booming of many waters. In his right hand he held seven stars, and from his mouth projected a sharp two-edged sword. His whole aspect was like the sun in full blaze.[8]

When I saw him I fell at his feet as though dead. But he laid his right hand upon me and said, "Do not be afraid. I am the First and the Last, and the Living One. I was dead, but now I am alive for evermore, and hold the keys of Death and Hades.[9] Write, therefore, what you see, what is happening now, and what will transpire after-
20   wards. [As to the implication[10] of the seven stars which you see in my right hand and of the seven golden lampstands, the seven stars are representatives of the seven communities, and the seven lampstands are the seven communities themselves.][11]

....

6 The *shofar* (ram's horn trumpet), cf *Ezek* 3:12.
7 cf *Tobit* 12:20 (the Apocrypha).
8 The vision is of the Messianic Son of Man in heaven. According to the early Jewish followers of Jesus, "Messiah was created, like one of the archangels, yet greater." The description take its rise from *Dan* 7:9 and that of the high priest Simon son of Onias in *Ecclus* 1:5–11, and developed in *Enoch* 47:3–7. The Christians believed the heavenly Son of Man had incarnated in Jesus at his baptism.
9 Jewish *Sheol*.
10 Gr *mysterion*.
11 Here and occupying chs 2–3 we have an interpolation by John the Elder in his characteristic language and ideas.

Messages to the Seven Communities

2.1 "To the representative of the community at Ephesus write as follows:

"Thus says he who holds the seven stars in his right hand, he who walks among the seven golden lampstands, 'I know your works, your labour and your constancy, and that you cannot stand the wicked, and have tested those who call themselves envoys, when they are not, and have found them to be liars. You have shown constancy, and have borne much for my name, and have not grown weary. I have against you, however,

5 that you have forsaken your former love. Recall, then, the state from which you have fallen, and repent, and be as you used to be. Otherwise, if you do not repent, I will come and remove your lampstand from its position. It is at least creditable that you detest the deeds of the Nicolaitans[12] as I do.'"

Let the discerning take note of what the Spirit says to the communities; *I will grant the victor the right to eat from the Tree of Life[13] which is in the Garden of God.*

"To the representative of the community at Smyrna write as follows:

"Thus says the First and the Last, who was dead and revived, 'I know your affliction and poverty, yet you are rich, and I know the impudence[14] of those who claim to be Jews,[15] when they are not, but are a synagogue of

10 Satan. Do not be afraid of what you are to suffer. The Devil is going to throw some of you into prison, that you may be tested, and you will experience persecution for ten days. Be loyal, even unto death, and I will give you the award[16] of Life.'

"Let the discerning take note of what the Spirit says to the communities, *The Victor shall not be harmed by the Second Death.*[17]

"To the representative of the community at Pergamum write as follows:

12 Believed to be a semi-Gnostic sect.
13 *Test. Levi*, 18:11.
14 Lit "blasphemy".
15 This may allude to the false envoys (2:2), or to non-Jewish Christians seeking to avoid persecution by claiming to be Jews, since at this time Judaism was a licenced religion by the Romans and Christianity was not.
16 Lit "the garland" (victor's wreath).
17 After the Resurrection of Judgment. See *Targ. Pal.* on *Deut* 33:6.

"Thus says he who has the sharp two-edged sword, 'I know where you live, where Satan's seat is,[18] and that you hold fast to my name, and did not deny my Faith even at the time when Antipas my loyal witness was slain among you, there where Satan dwells. But I have a few things against you, that you have there adherents of the teaching of Balaam, who instructed Balak to lay a trap for the children of Israel, to make them eat food dedi-

15 cated to idols, and to indulge in sexual vice. So do you likewise have adherents of the teaching of the Nicolaitans. Repent, then, or else I will come swiftly and fight them with the sword of my mouth.'

"Let the discerning take note of what the Spirit says to the communities, *I will give the victor the hidden manna.*[19] *I will also give him a white pebble with a mystic name*[20] *graven on it known only to him who receives it.*

"To the representative of the community at Thyatira write as follows:

"Thus says the Son of God, who has eyes like a fiery flame and feet like burnished bronze, 'I know your works, and your love, your faith, service and constancy,

20 and that your latest works excel the former. Yet I have against you that you let that Jezebel of a woman, who calls herself a prophetess, not only teach, but beguile my servants into indulgence in immorality and eating food dedicated to idols. I have given her time to repent, but she has no intention of repenting of her immorality. I will indeed send her to bed, and send those who have committed adultery with her great affliction, unless they repent of their deeds; and I will slay her children by Death. And all the communities shall know that I am he who investigates minds and motives,[21] and I will requite each of you in accordance with your deeds.

"'To you, then, I say, and to the rest at Thyatira who have not accepted this teaching, and have not known what they call "the profundities of Satan", I will lay upon you no additional burden to what you already carry.

25 Hold fast till I come.'

"*I will give the victor, and he who takes care of my interests to the end, authority over the nations, and he shall herd them with*

18 Centre of Emperor worship.
19 cf *Apoc Baruch*, 29:8.
20 cf *Rev* 3:12; 19:12; *Isa* 62:2; 65:15.
21 Lit "examines kidneys and heart" (*Jer* 11:20).

an iron-shod staff, and as earthenware jars they shall be crushed,[22] as I have received authority from my Father; and I will give him the Morning Star."

Let the discerning take note of what the Spirit says to the communities.

3.1 "To the representative of the community at Sardis write as follows:

"Thus says he who has the seven spirits of God and the seven stars, 'I know your works, that you have a name for being alive, but are really dead. Rouse yourself, and rally what remains, that is on the verge of extinction, for I have not found your affairs satisfactory in the sight of my God. Recall, therefore, what you have seen and heard,[23] heed it and repent. If you fail to rouse yourself I will come like a thief, and you will not know at what time I shall come upon you.[24] Yet you have a few persons at Sardis who have not soiled their garments, and they shall walk with me in white, because they are worthy.'

5 *"The victor shall be clad in white garments, and I will not erase his name from the Book of Life, but own his name in the presence of my Father and in the presence of his angels."*[25]

Let the discerning take note of what the Spirit says to the communities.

"To the representative of the community at Philadelphia write as follows:

"Thus says the holy one and true, who has the key of David, who opens and none shall close, and closes and none shall open, 'I know your works, that you have a little strength and have kept my Message, and have not denied my name. I have indeed set before you an open door, which none shall be able to close. Lo, I will make them members of Satan's synagogue who claim to be Jews, when they are not, but lie. Yes, I will make them come and grovel at your feet, and know that I have loved

10 you. Because you have kept my Message with constancy, I too will keep you from the hour of trial that is about to come upon the whole world,[26] to try the

---

22 cf *Ps* 2:8–9.
23 cf *I Jn* 1:1.
24 cf *Lk* 12:39.
25 cf *Lk* 12:8.
26 The Second Advent was held to be imminent, when the nations would be judged prior to the Millennium.

inhabitants of the earth. I shall come very soon. Hold on to what you have, that no one may take your award.'

"*I will make the victor a pillar in the Temple of my God, and he shall never go outside it again. And I will engrave on him the name of my God, and the name of the City of my God, New Jerusalem, which will descend from heaven from my God, and my own new name.*"

Let the discerning take note of what the Spirit says to the communities.

"To the representative of the community at Laodicea write as follows:

"Thus says the Amen,[27] the trustworthy and reliable

15   witness, the beginning of God's creation,[28] 'I know your works, that you are neither frigid nor fervent. So because you are tepid instead of frigid or fervent, I am going to spit you out of mouth, because you say, "I am rich and prosperous, and in need of nothing", and do not realise that you are wretched and pitiable, poor, blind and naked. I recommend you to buy from me gold refined in the furnace, that you may be truly rich, and white robes, that you may be clothed, that the shame of your nakedness is no longer exposed; and eye-salve to anoint your eyes, that you may see. Those whom I care for I reprove

20   and discipline. Strive, therefore, to make amends. Lo, I stand at the door and knock. Whoever hears my voice and opens the door, I will come in to him and dine with him, and he with me.'

"*I will give the victor the right to sit beside me on my throne, just as I was victorious and have sat beside my Father on his throne.*"

Let the discerning take note of what the Spirit says to the communities.[29]

....

Book I

Vision of the Court of God

4.1   After this I saw, and, lo, a door stood open in heaven, and the first voice I had heard speaking to me, that was

---

27 See *II Cor* 1:20.

28 Clearly John the Elder himself believed that the heavenly Christ was a created being, as did the early Christians.

29 John the Elder's substantial addition ends here. The change of style in the writing can immediately be noticed.

like a trumpet horn, said, "Ascend here,[1] and I will show you what will happen hereafter."

At once I was in ecstasy, and there in heaven was placed a throne, and upon the throne a Presence was seated. And he who sat there presented to the gaze the brilliance of jasper and the fiery glow of the sardius, while an irridescence of emerald hue encircled the throne. Surrounding the throne were twenty-four other thrones, and upon these were seated twenty-four Elders clothed in white raiment with golden wreaths upon their 5 heads; and from the throne proceeded lightning flashes, voices, and peals of thunder.[2]

Seven flaring torches flared before the throne (which are the seven spirits of God), and also before the throne lay a glassy sea like crystal. At the base of the throne on all sides of it were four Living-Creatures,[3] studded with eyes in front and at the back. The first Living-Creatures resembled a lion, the scond a calf, the third had a human face, and the fourth resembled a flying eagle. These four Living-Creatures, each one of them possessing six wings studded with eyes all over and underneath, never pause day and night from saying,

Holy, holy, holy, is the Lord God Almighty,[4]
Who Was, and Is, and Shall be.

And whensoever the Living-Creatures render praise, honour and thanksgiving to him who sits on the throne, 10 to him who lives for ever and ever, the twenty-four Elders prostrate themselves before the throne, and worship him who lives for ever and ever,[5] and lay their wreaths before the throne, saying,

Worthy art thou, O Lord our God,
To receive praise, honour, and might;
For thou hast created all things,
And by thy will they existed and were created.

---

1 In Heb. *'Ale-hena'*, onomatopoeic.
2 The heavenly Temple where God is seated in state. The Elders correspond to the twenty-four courses of priests, Levites and laymen, of the earthly Temple. On God's glory see *Ezek* 1:28.
3 cf *Ezek* 1.
4 cf *Isa* 6:2. On the doxologies see AJP, p 39.
5 In the Temple priests and people prostrated themselves when the ineffable Name of God was pronounced by the high priest.

A Lamb receives the Sealed Book of Prophecy

5.1   Now I saw in the right hand of him who sat on the throne a small scroll with writing on both sides, secured with seven seals.[6] I also saw a stalwart angel proclaiming in a loud voice, "Who is worthy to open the scroll and break its seven seals?"

But no one in heaven, nor on earth, nor beneath the earth, was able to open the scroll or to look at it. I wept a great deal because no one worthy was found either to

5   open the scroll or to look at it. But one of the Elders said to me, "Do not weep. See, the Lion of the tribe of Judah, the Stock of David, has prevailed to open the scroll with its seven seals."

Then I saw standing in front of the throne and the four Living-Creatures, and in front of the Elders, a Lamb, as though it had been butchered. It had seven horns and seven eyes (which are the seven spirits of God dispatched to every part of the world). And it came and took the scroll from the right hand of him who sat upon the throne. When it had taken the scroll, the four Living-Creatures and the twenty-four Elders prostrated themselves before the Lamb, each holding a lyre and golden bowls full of incense (which represent the prayers of the saints). And they sang a new song, saying,

Worthy art thou to take the scroll,
And to open up its seals;
For being slain, thou didst buy
With thy blood for God
Those of all tribes and tongues,
Of peoples and of nations,
10   *And for our God hast made them*
Kings and priests to reign on earth.[7]

Then I saw, and heard the voice of many angels round the throne, and the Living-Creatures, and the Elders, numbering myriads and thousands of thousands, crying aloud:

Worthy is the butchered Lamb,
To receive power and wealth,
And wisdom and strength,
And honour and glory and praise.

6 cf *Ezek* 2:10.
7 This is the NT teaching about the faithful. Heaven is never their home: they reign over a redeemed Earth.

And every created thing in heaven, and on earth, and beneath the earth, I heard saying,

To him who sitteth on the throne,
[And to the Lamb]
Be praise and honour and glory,
And dominion for ever and ever.

And the four Living-Creatures said, "Amen". And the Elders prostrated themselves and worshipped.

The Lamb breaks the Seals

6.1   Then I saw that the Lamb had opened one of the seven seals. And I heard one of the four Living-Creatures say like a clap of thunder, "Come!"

I looked, and there was a white horse, and its rider carried a bow, and a victor's wreath was given him, and away he rode conquering and to conquer.

And when he had opened the second seal I heard the second Living-Creature say, "Come!"

And there came out another horse, fiery red this time. Its rider was permitted to take peace from the earth, so that men should slaughter one another; and to him was given a great scimitar.

5   And when he had opened the third seal I heard the third Living-Creature say, "Come!"

I looked, and there was a black horse, and its rider had a pair of scales in his hand. And I heard among the four Living-Creatures what sounded like a voice saying, "A quart of wheat for a denar, and three quarts of barley for a denar; but do not harm the oil and the wine."[8]

And when he had opened the fourth seal I heard the voice of the fourth Living-Creature say, "Come!"

I looked, and there was a livid horse. The name of its rider was Death, and Hades attended him.

To these four was given power over a quarter of the earth, to slay with the sword, with famine, and with pestilence, and by the wild beasts of the earth.[9]

And when he had opened the fifth seal I saw below the altar the souls of those butchered for the word of God

---

8 Famine prices are to rule, but wine and oil used in the Temple services are to be spared. cf Jos. *Jewish War*, V. 565.
9 *Ezek* 14:21. Prayer was regularly recited by the Jews asking God to "keep from us the enemy, Pestilence, Sword, Famine and Death". These are the four horses and their riders.

10   and the testimony which they bore. They were crying
aloud, "How long will it be, holy and true Sovereign
Lord, before thou dost judge and avenge our blood on
those who dwell on earth?"[10]

Then there was given to each of them a white robe,[11]
and they were told to remain quiet for a while longer
until the number of their fellow-servants and brothers
should be completed, who were about to be slain as they
had been.

When he opened the sixth seal I saw that a great earthquake resulted; and the sun grew black as goat's hair
cloth, and the full moon turned blood red, while the stars
of heaven fell to earth[12] like unripe figs shed from a fig
tree when shaken by a tempest. The very heavens
rebounded like a scroll rolling up,[13] and every mountain

15   and island was dislodged from its place. The kings of the
earth, the statesmen and generals, the rich and the
powerful, and every slave and freeman, hid themselves
in dens and mountain clefts,[14] and cried to the mountains and cliffs, "Topple over us, and hide us from the
presence of him who sits on the throne [and from the
wrath of the Lamb], for the terrible day of their wrath has
come, and who will be able to endure it?"

Preservation of Loyal Israel

7.1   After this I saw four angels standing at the four corners
of the earth, restraining the four winds of the earth so
that no wind should blow on land and sea, nor on any
tree.

Then I saw another angel mount up from the sunrise
holding the seal of the Living God. And he cried aloud to
the four angels charged with harming the land and sea,
"Do not harm the land, nor the sea, nor the trees, before

---

10 cf *Deut* 32:43. Jewish legend told of the blood of Zechariah son of Jehoiada,
murdered in the Court of the Priests, crying out for vengeance, and being
appeased by the slaughter of priests and Israelites by Nebuzaradan.
Christian legend transferred the circumstances to the slaughter of
Zechariah father of John the Baptist, with the Roman general Titus as
avenger of his blood.

11 Jewish candidates for the priesthood, if found without blemish, were given
white robes, and if rejected black robes.

12 cf *Joel* 2:10.

13 *Isa* 34:4.

14 *Isa* 2:19.

we have marked the servants of God on their foreheads."[15]

I heard the number of those who were marked: it was a hundred and forty-four thousand out of all the tribes of Israel.

5   From the tribe of Judah twelve thousand were marked;[16]
From the tribe of Reuben twelve thousand;
From the tribe of Gad twelve thousand;
From the tribe of Asher twelve thousand;
From the tribe of Manasseh twelve thousand;
From the tribe of Simeon twelve thousand;
From the tribe of Levi twelve thousand;
From the tribe of Issachar twelve thousand;
From the tribe of Zebulon twelve thousand;
From the tribe of Joseph twelve thousand;
From the tribe of Benjamin twelve thousand.

The Redeemed of the Gentiles

After this I saw, and there was a vast concourse, impossible to count, from every nation, tribe, people and tongue, standing before the throne [and before the Lamb], clad in white robes with palm branches in their
10   hands. And they cried aloud saying, "Hosanna[17] to our God who sits upon the throne [and to the Lamb]."

Then all the angels where they stood before the throne, and the Elders, and the four Living-Creatures, prostrated themselves before the throne and worshipped God saying, "Amen. Blessing, glory, wisdom, thanksgiving, honour, power and might, be to our God for ever and ever."

Then one of the Elders put the question to me, "Who are these who are arrayed in white robes, and where do they come from?"

"You know that, sir", I replied.

Then he told me, "These are they who have come out of the Great Persecution, and have washed their robes

---

15 Before the judgment begins the saints are marked with the cruciform Hebrew letter *tau* (*Ezek.* 9:4) that they may escape injury, as the Israelites did in Egypt when the angel of death passed through Egypt.

16 Judah heads the list as the royal tribe. Dan is omitted as the tribe given over to idolatry (*Test. Dan* 5:4).

17 Lit "salvation". The seer beholds the Elect of the Gentiles (*Mt* 24:31). They appear before God as the Jews appeared before him in the earthly Temple at the Feast of Tabernacles (the feast of ingathering), bearing palm branches and singing their Hosannas.

15   and made them white in the blood of the Lamb. That is why they are before the throne of God, and minister to him day and night in his Temple. And he who sits upon the throne will dwell with them. They shall neither hunger nor thirst any more, nor shall the sun scorch them, nor any heat;[18] for the Lamb who is before the throne will tend them, and guide them to well-springs of Waters of Life, and God will wipe away all tears from their eyes."

Vision of the Seven Angels with War Horns

8.1   And when he had opened the seventh seal there was silence in heaven for about half an hour.[19]

Then I saw the seven angels who stood before God;[20] and they were given seven war horns. And another angel came and stood at the altar with a golden censer, and a large quantity of incense was given him so that he should offer the prayers of all the saints at the golden altar before the throne. And the smoke of the incense bearing the prayers of the saints ascended before God

5   from the angel's hand. Then the angel took the censer and filled it with fire from the altar and cast it upon the earth, and there were thunders, and voices, and lightnings, and an earthquake.

Then the seven angels with the seven war horns prepared to sound an alarm.[21]

The first angel sounded, and a hail of fire mingled with blood rained upon the earth. A third of the land was burnt up, a third of the trees were burnt up, and a third of

---

18 Possibly alluding to the Neronian persecution of AD 64, when many Christians were turned into flaming torches. On the language see *Isa* 49:38 and *Deut* 32:24.

19 In the Temple, when the incense was offered, the people retired from the court and prostrated themselves in silent prayer and adoration.

20 These are the seven archangels (*Enoch* 20).

21 "For these things they sound the alarm in every place, for blasting, mildew, locusts, caterpillars, evil beasts, and the sword" (*Taanith* 6). For the judgments on Israel, which follow, the seer has drawn upon the eschatological interpretation of the *Song of Moses* (*Deut* 32) in the Palestinean *Targum*. All the evils of the four Beasts of Daniel's vision (7), Babylon, Medo-Persia, Greece and Syria, are combined for the seer in the sufferings of the Jews before and during their war with the Romans (AD 67–71).

the vegetation was burnt up.[22]

The second angel sounded, and something like a great flaming mountain was hurled into the sea. A third of the sea turned to blood, a third of the animate creatures in the sea died, and a third of the shipping was disabled.[23]

10   The third angel sounded, and a great meteor blazing like a torch fell from heaven and landed on a third of the river and wells of water. The meteor was called Wormwood; and a third of the waters turned to wormwood, and many people died of the waters that were made bitter.[24]

The fourth angel sounded, and a third of the sun was eclipsed, and a third of the moon, and a third of the stars; so that a third of them was blotted out, and the day lost a third of its visibility and the night likewise.[25]

Then I saw and heard a lone eagle flying in midheaven screaming "Alas,[26] alas, alas, for the inhabitants of the earth, because of the remaining blasts of the horns of the three angels who are about to sound!"[27]

9.1   Then the fifth angel sounded, and I saw that a meteor from heaven had fallen to earth. To it was given the key of the vent of the Abyss, and it opened the vent of the Abyss, and smoke ascended from the vent. Out of the smoke swarmed locusts on to the earth, and they were given the kind of power that scorpions of the earth possess. They were told that they must not harm the grass, nor any vegetation, nor any tree, only those

---

22 All the blasts signify judgment on the land of Israel. They are couched in visionary and prophetic language, yet reflect conditions in Israel during the Roman war. The first blast suggests the punitive expedition of Cestius Gallus which signalized the outbreak of hostilities. "He overran the countryside, sacking everything in his path and burning the surrounding villages' (Jos. *Jewish War* II 504–5).

23 cf the battle of Joppas, when the Jewish ships were wrecked and broken on the rocks, and many sailors committed suicide "so that a wide area of sea was red with their blood" (*Jewish War* III 426). Also the battle of the Sea of Galilee: "One could see the whole lake red with blood and covered with corpses" (*Jewish War* III 529).

24 In the war there was poisoning of wells and fountains. Josephus says also that in the terrific heat-wave in the summer of 67 many died of thirst. See *Jewish War* III 312–313).

25 Perhaps alluding to the murder by the Zealots of many of the aristocracy and eminent citizens of Jerusalem (*Jewish War* IV 138–142).

26 In Hebrew *Oye*, onomatopoeic, sounding *oee*.

27 The previous judgments have preceded the advance of the Roman armies on Jerusalem. The eagle may symbolise the opening of the second phase, the coming of the war to the capital, scene of the final judgment.

human beings who did not have the divine seal on their
5   foreheads. They were not to kill them, only to torment
them for five months. The kind of torment they were to
inflict was to be like that of a scorpion when it stings a
man.

In those days men will seek death, but will not find it;
they will long to die, but death will elude them.

The appearance of the locusts[28] was like horses
accoutred for battle. On their heads were golden crests,
and their features were like human features. They had
manes like women's tresses, and their teeth were
leonine. They had scaly fronts like steel breastplates, and
the whirr of their wings was like cavalry charging into
10   battle. They had tails like scorpions equipped with
stings, and it was in their tails that their power lay to hurt
men for five months. They had a king over them, the
angel of the Abyss, whose name in Hebrew is *Abaddon*,
but in Greek he is called Apollyon.

One calamity is over, but there are still two calamities to follow

Then the sixth angel sounded, and issuing from the
golden altar that was before God I heard a solitary voice
saying to the sixth angel with the war horn, "Free the
four angels chained beside the great river Euphrates!"[29]
15   So the four angels were freed, who had been reserved
for this very hour and day and month and year, to slay
the third of men. The host of horsemen numbered twice
a myriad myriad.[30] I heard the number of them.

In the vision this is how I saw the horses and their
riders.[31] They had breastplates of fiery hue, smoke-blue

28 The fifth blast sets in motion a swarm of demonic locusts. This reflects the
locust army of *Joel* 2, the "incursion of the *shedim*" of *Apoc. Baruch* 27:9, and
the combined forces of *Targ. Pal.* on *Deut* 32. From the description of the
locusts the seer has in mind the Roman army. The troops wear helmets with
horsehair tails (like women's tresses), and are clad in mail. cf Jos. *Jewish
War*, III 93–97. The army had quickfirers for discharging arrows, called
'scorpions'.

29 In the Syriac *Appocalypse of Ezra* the four angels are four kings. See below
n 31.

30 For the symbolic number of 200,000,000 cf *Ps* 68:17.

31 An invading host from the East was part of current apocalyptic expectation,
with the Parthians specially in view. Historically, four allies joined the
Romans in the attack on Israel, Antiochus of Commagene, Agrippa II,
Soemus of Emesa, and the Arab Malchus, by furnishing cavalry and archers
(Jos. *Jewish War*, III 4:64–69). The Parthian king Volosges offered to supply
the Romans with 40,000 mounted archers (Tacit. *Hist*. IV:51; Suet. *Vespas*. 6).

and sulphur-yellow. The heads of the horses were leonine, and from their mouths belched fire and smoke and sulphur. By these three plagues the third of men were slain, by the fire, the smoke and the sulphur, which belched from their mouths. The power of the horses lay in their mouths and in their tails; for their tails were like serpents, possessing heads, and it is with these they inflict injury.[32]

20   Yet the rest of men, who were not killed by these plagues, did not repent of the works of their hands, but continued to worship demons, and idols of gold and silver, bronze and stone and wood, which can neither see, nor hear, nor move. Nor did they repent of their murders, their sorceries, their immorality, and their robberies.[33]

Vision of the Angel with the Small Scroll

10.1   Then I saw another mighty angel descend from heaven, clad in cloud and with a rainbow on his head. His face was like the sun, and his legs like pillars of fire, and in his hand he held a small open scroll. He set his right foot on the sea and his left foot on the land, and cried aloud as though a lion were roaring.[34]

When he cried the seven thunders responded, and when they did so I was about to set down what they said. But there came a voice from heaven saying, "Seal up what the seven thunders have said, and do not write it down."

5   Then the angel I had seen take his stand upon the sea and the land raised his right hand to heaven and swore by him who lives for ever and ever, who created heaven and all that is in it, and earth and all that is it, and the sea and all that is in it, that there will be no further interval, but that in the days when the seventh angel shall sound his horn God's mystery will be at an end, as he declared to his servants the Prophets.[35]

Then the voice from heaven which I had heard addressed me again and said, "Go and take the small scroll that

---

32 The Parthians twisted their horses' tails to points and the archers could shoot backwards over the tails. Symbolic creatures with serpent-headed tails are featured in ancient murals.

33 cf *Deut* 32:37–38 and Jos. *Jewish War*, IV 9:56–60.

34 cf *Dan* 10:15–6.

35 cf *Dan* 10:5–6; *Deut* 32:39–43.

lies open in the hand of the angel standing on sea and land".

So I went to the angel and said to him, "Give me the small scroll".

"Take it and digest it", he replied. "It will make your stomach bitter, though in your mouth it will be sweet as honey."[36]

10   So I took the small scroll from the angel's hand and digested it; and it was sweet as honey in my mouth, but when I had eaten it my stomach was made bitter. And I was told, "You must prophesy further concerning many peoples, nations, tongues and kings".

The Two Witnesses

11.1   There was now given me a cane like a measuring-rod[37] with the order, "Rise, and measure the Temple of God, and the altar, and compute those who worship there; but exclude the court outside the Temple, and do not measure that, since it is given to the Gentiles, and they will tread the Holy City under foot for forty-two months.[38] But I will cause my two witnesses to prophesy for twelve hundred and sixty days clothed in sackcloth. (These are the two olive trees and the two lampstands
5   which stand before the Lord of the earth.)[39] If anyone purposes to harm them fire will issue from their mouths and devour their enemies; so if anyone should seek to harm them that is how he will be killed. They have the power to shut heaven, so that no rain will fall in the period when they are prophesying, and they have power over water, to turn it into blood, and to smite the earth with every kind of plague as often as they wish.

"When they have concluded their testimony, the Beast who rises from the Abyss will make war on them, and overcome them and kill them, and leave their corpses

---

36 *Ezek* 2:9–3:3.

37 cf *Ezek* 40:3; Jos. *Jewish War*, VI 5:11–12. The court outside the Temple proper was known as the Court of the Gentiles. No Gentile could pass beyond this court on pain of death.

38 *Dan* 12:7.

39 Though the judgments on Israel are now far advanced, a final opportunity of repentance and relief is given if they will heed the two faithful witnesses, the Law and the Prophets (*Mt* 22:40; *Lk* 16:31), symbolised by Moses and Elijah (*Mt* 17:3), as shown by the powers given them. cf *Zech* 4 on the two olive trees.

lying on the square of the Great City[40] which in the spiritual sense is called Sodom and Egypt,[41] where also their lord was crucified. And some of the people, tribes, tongues and nations will observe their corpses during three and a half days, and will not permit their corpses to

10 be interred. And those who dwell on earth will rejoice over them and make merry, and send gifts to one another, because those two prophets tormented those who dwell on earth."

But after the three days the breath of life from God entered them, and they stood on their feet;[42] and great fear seized those who saw them. Then they heard a loud voice from heaven saying to them, "Ascend here!" And they ascended to heaven in a cloud while their enemies watched them. That very hour there was a great earthquake, and the tenth part of the city collapsed. Seven thousand people were killed in the earthquake, while the rest were frightened and offered praise to the God of heaven.

The second calamity is over. The third calamity will follow speedily

15 Then the seventh angel sounded, and loud voices in heaven proclaimed, "The dominion of the world has become the dominion of our Lord and his Anointed, and he shall reign for ever and ever."

And the twenty-four Elders who were seated before God on their thrones prostrated themselves and worshipped God, saying, "We give thanks unto thee, Lord God Almighty, who Wast and Art, because thou hast taken to thee thy great powers and hast reigned. The heathen raged;[43] but thy wrath has come, and the time for the dead to be judged, and for reward to be given to thy servants the Prophets, and to the Saints, and to those both high and low who revere thy Name, the time to

---

40 The seer may have in mind the high priests Ananus and Jesus murdered in Jerusalem, whose bodies were cast out without burial (Jos. *Jewish War*, IV v:315–317).

41 "I believe that, had the Romans delayed to punish those reprobates, either the earth would have opened and swallowed up the city, or it . . . would have tasted anew the thunderbolt of Sodom" (*Jewish War*, V. viii. 566).

42 cf *Ezek* 37:9; *Hos* 6:2.

43 cf *Ps* 2:1; 46:5–6.

destroy those who destroy the earth."[44]

Then the Temple of God in heaven was opened, and the Ark of his Covenant was revealed in his Temple.[45] And there were lightning flashes, and voices, and peals of thunder, and an earthquake, and heavy hail.

Book Two

Vision of the Woman and the Dragon[1]

12.1   Now there appeared in heaven a great sign, a Woman clothed with the sun, with the moon beneath her feet, and upon her head a wreath of twelve stars. She was with child, and cried out in her pangs straining to be delivered.

Another sign also appeared in heaven. This took the form of a great fiery Dragon with seven heads and ten horns, whose tail carried away a third of the stars of heaven and flung them to earth. The Dragon stood before the Woman who was about to give birth, so that when her child was born he could devour it.

5   She bore a son, a male child, who is to herd all nations with an iron-shod staff;[2] but the child was snatched away to God and to his throne.[3] The Woman fled to the

---

44 The judgments on Israel are now ended, and those upon the Gentiles are about to commence. From this moment the sovereignty of God over the world is specifically exercised, where before only his sovereignty over his own people was apparent.

45 To mark the new development the curtains of the Holy of Holies of the heavenly Temple are drawn aside disclosing the Ark of God's Covenant. God's people are in his care. In the synagogues still the Ark containing the sacred scrolls of Scripture is opened at the most solemn moments in the service.

---

1 This vision introduces the events recorded in Book II. The Woman and the Dragon in the astrological sense are constellations symbolising the Good and Evil Powers, while terrestrially they are Loyal Israel (cf *Gen* 37:9), mother of the Messiah, and the tyrant adversary embodied in the Roman Empire.

2 *Ps* 2:9.

3 According to a Jewish legend the Messiah was spirited away at birth, and there is a similar legend about the infant John the Baptist. A version of the latter legend says that his mother fled with him to a mountain which opened to receive them into safety when Herod's soldiers were killing the babes in Bethlehem believing John was the Messiah designate.

wilderness, where she has a place prepared for her by God, for her to be cared for there for twelve hundred and sixty days.[4]

Then war broke out in heaven. Michael[5] and his angels fought the Dragon, and the Dragon and his angels fought, but did not prevail, neither was a trace of them left any longer in heaven. The great Dragon was flung out, the primeval Serpent, called Devil and Satan, deceiver of the whole world. Yes, he was flung to earth, and his angels along with him.

10   Then I heard a loud voice in heaven say, "Now indeed the salvation, power and dominion of our God, and the authority of his Anointed, has become effective; for the accuser of our brothers, who accused them before God day and night, has been flung out. They overcame him by the blood of the Lamb, and the declaration of their testimony, and did not cling to life till death should claim them. Rejoice, therefore, O heavens, and all who dwell there! But alas for land and sea; for the Devil has come down to you in a great rage, knowing that his time is short."

When the Dragon found himself flung to earth, he pursued the Woman who had given birth to the male child. But the Woman was given the two wings of the great eagle,[6] so that she might wing her way to the wilderness, to her place there, where she is to be cared for for a time, times, and a half, from the presence of the Serpent.

15   Then the Serpent spouted water after the Woman like a river to carry her away with a flood. But the earth aided the Woman and the earth gaped and swallowed the river which the Dragon spouted from his mouth.[7] So the Dragon was enraged against the Woman, and went off to make war with the remainder of her offspring, who keep the commandments of God and hold the testimony of

4 Historically, the Emperor Vespasian, after the fall of Jerusalem, tried to seize those who were of Davidic descent, but the family of Jesus had made good their escape to the wilderness beyond Jordan.
5 Guardian angel of Israel, *Dan* 10:4, 21.
6 cf *Exod* 19:4.
7 An allusion, perhaps, to the Jordan being in flood when the Nazarenes were escaping to the wilderness. A dragon was thought to lurk in the river sucking up the water when the river was low and spouting it out when it was in spate. Josephus tells of Jewish refugees unable to escape the Romans because of the flooded Jordan.

Jesus; and he stood on the sand of the sea.[8]

Vision of the Two Beasts

13.1   Now I saw a Beast with ten horns and seven heads rise out of the sea. On his horns were ten crowns, and on his head blasphemous titles. The Beast I saw was like a leopard, with the feet of a bear, and the jaws of a lion. And the Dragon conferred on him his own power and throne, and great authority. One of his heads was as if wounded to death, but his death stroke had been healed.[9] The whole earth was in awe of the Beast. They worshipped the Beast too, saying.

> *Who is like the Beast?*
> *Who can contend with him?*[10]

5   He was permitted to use boastful and blasphemous language, and allowed to do so for forty-two months. And he opened his mouth in profanity against God, maligning his Name and his dwelling-place, everything of a heavenly nature. He was also permitted to make war with the Saints and to overcome them, and was given authority over every race, and people, tongue and nation. And all who dwell on earth will worship him,[11] everyone whose name has not been written from the foundation of the world in the Book of Life [of the butchered Lamb].

10   Let the discerning take note. *If anyone is destined for captivity, to captivity he will go. If anyone is destined to death by the sword, by the sword must he be slain.*[12] Here is where the constancy and loyalty of the Saints is required.

Then I saw another Beast rise out of the land.[13] He had two horns like a lamb, but he spoke like a dragon. He

8 ie the Mediterranean.
9 The heads are Roman emperors. The one wounded to death is Nero. The stroke was healed because the Imperial regime continued under a new dynasty, the Flavian.
10 A blasphemous parody of *Exod* 15:11. cf Agrippa's speech: 'Almost every nation under the sun does homage to the Roman arms" (Jos. *Jewish War*, II 16:380).
11 The religious cult of Rome and the Emperor was maintained throughout the Empire.
12 cf *Jer* 15:2. Exile or death were the penalties for violation of the imperial majesty.
13 The two Beasts appear in Jewish legend as Leviathan (the Beast from the Sea) and Behemoth (the Beast from the Land). See *Enoch*, 60:6–10; *Apoc Baruch*, 29:4.

exercises all the authority of the first Beast in his presence, and he causes the earth and all who dwell in it to worship the first Beast whose death stroke was healed. He also performs great signs, making fire from heaven fall to earth in the sight of men, and so deceives those who dwell on earth by the signs he is permitted to perform in the presence of the Beast, telling those who dwell on earth to make an image of the Beast who had the

15   dagger thrust and yet lived.[14] He was also permitted to animate the image of the Beast, so that the image of the Beast could speak, and he causes such as refuse to worship the image of the Beast to be slain. He further causes all, both high and low, rich and poor, free and slave to receive a stamp on their right hand or forehead,[15] so that none should be able to buy or sell unless he had the stamp either of the name of the Beast or of the number of his name.

This is where wisdom is required. Let him who has the wit to do so compute the numerical value of the Beast; for it is calculated in man's way. His number is 616.[16]

The Elect on Zion

14.1   Then I saw, and there on Mount Zion stood the Lamb, and with him a hundred and forty-four thousand who had [his name and] the Name of the Father written on their foreheads.

And I heard a sound from heaven like the booming of many waters and like a peal of heavy thunder. The sound I heard was also like that of harpers playing their harps. They were singing a new song before the throne, and before the four Living-Creatures, and the Elders; but none but the hundred and forty thousand redeemed

14 The emperor's statue was a sacred object, and Domitian, since he was a god, insisted that he be addressed as "Our Lord and God Domitian."

15 cf *Deut* 6:8. All, of whatever rank or occupation, must use the Imperial stamp in transactions.

16 Many MSS read 666, but the more difficult number is more probable. Greek and Hebrew letters have a numerical value. The Roman imperial stamp was in Greek, and the solution of the figure will depend on when the seer is writing. From tradition and the details given this would seem to be the end of the reign of Domitian, who was assassinated in AD 96. See Euseb. *Eccl Hist* III 17–18. From known examples the Imperial stamp for AD 95–96 would read ΙΔ ΚΑΙΣΑΡΟΣ (14th year of Caesar's reign). This adds up to 616 (14+20+1+10+200+1+100+70+200). Domitian was known as 'the bald Nero' and the addition of the letter 'N' (Nero) =50, would bring the total to 666. See further *Sibyl Orac* V 39–40.

from the earth could learn the song. [There are they who have not been defiled with women: they are celibate.] These are they who attend the Lamb wherever he goes: they are the redeemed out of mankind, the firstlings

5   belonging to God[17] [and the Lamb], and in their mouth no falsehood was found: they are faultless.

Final Warning to the Gentiles

Now I saw another angel flying in mid-heaven with a firm and final ultimatum to deliver to those who dwell on earth, to every nation, tribe, tongue and people, in these terms, "Revere God, and offer praise to him, for the time of his judgment has come. Worship him, therefore, who made heaven and earth, the sea and the springs of water."

Another, a second angel followed behind crying, "Great Babylon has fallen, has fallen,[18] she who made all nations drink the strong wine of her immorality."

Yet another, a third angel, followed these, proclaiming loudly, "Whoever worships the Beast and his image, and

10   receives his stamp on forehead or hand,[19] shall surely drink the strong wine of God which is undiluted in the goblet of his wrath,[20] and shall be tortured by fire and sulphur in the presence of the holy angels [and in the presence of the Lamb]. The smoke of their torment will ascend for ever and ever. Those who worship the Beast and his image, and whoever receives his stamp, will have no respite day and night."

Here is where the constancy of the Saints is required, those who keep God's commandments and are loyal to Jesus.

Then I heard a voice from heaven saying, "Write this down. Happy are the dead who die in the Master[21] from now on!"

"Even so", the Spirit agrees, "that they may rest from their labours, for their deeds accompany them."

---

17 *Exod* 13:12. With much of this section there has been interference with the text by John the Priest.
18 The fiat against Rome has gone forth. cf *Isa* 21:9.
19 ie brainworkers and manual workers.
20 cf *Jer* 25:12–17.
21 Or "in the Lord" meaning God as distinct from the Messiah. See 11:15.

Vision of the Two Harvests[22]

Then I looked, and there was a white cloud, and seated on the cloud a manlike figure[23] with a golden garland on 15 his head and a sharp sickle in his hand. And another angel emerged from the Temple calling loudly to him who was seated on the cloud, "Use your sickle and reap, for the time to reap has come. Earth's harvest is fully ripe."

So he who sat on the cloud brought down his sickle upon the earth and the earth was reaped.

Now another angel emerged from the Temple in heaven, and he too had a sharp sickle. Another angel, with power over fire, emerged from the altar and shouted to the one with the sharp sickle, "Use your sharp sickle, and gather the clusters of earth's vineyard, for its grapes are fully ripe."

So the angel brought down his sickle, and gathered earth's vintage, and cast it into the great winepress of the 20 wrath of God. And the winepress was trodden outside the city, and blood gushed from the winepress to the height of the horses' bridles one thousand six hundred stadia away.[24]

The Saints from the Gentiles approve God's Judgment

15.1 Now I saw another great and amazing sign in heaven, seven angels with the seven last plagues; for by these plagues the wrath of God will be accomplished.

I also saw what looked like a glassy sea veined with fire, and those who had come off victors from the Beast, and his image, and the number of his name, were standing by the glassy sea holding harps of God. They sing the song of Moses,[25] the servant of God [and the

---

22 The harvests of Mercy and Condemnation. The first is a corn harvest gathering the saints, while the second is a vintage harvest for crushing applying to sinners.

23 Lit "Son of Man".

24 About 200 miles. cf *Isa* 63:5 and *Enoch* 100:1–3: "Brothers will fall in death . . . until it streams with their blood like a river . . . And the horses will walk up to the breast in the blood of sinners."

25 "The song of Moses", ie *Deut* 32 with *Exod* 15:1–18. Believers who have remained loyal in Domitian's persecution stand on the brink of the Red Sea of fire and sink the triumph song.

song of the Lamb], as follows:

> *Great and marvellous are thy works,*
> *Lord God Almighty.*
> *Just and true are thy ways,*
> *O everlasting King.*[26]
> *Who shall not fear thee, O Lord,*
> *And glorify thy name?*
> *For thou alone art holy.*
> *For all nations shall come*
> *And worship before thee;*[27]
> *For thy judgments are revealed.*

Vision of the Seven Angels with Golden Bowls

5   After this I saw that the shrine of the Tabernacle of Testimony in heaven had been opened, and the seven angels with the seven plagues emerged from the shrine robed in pure shining white linen, clasped at the breast with golden girdles. Then one of the four Living-Creatures handed the seven angels seven golden bowls filled with the wrath of God, who lives for ever and ever.[28] And the Temple was filled with smoke from the glory of God and his might,[29] and none might enter the Temple until the seven plagues of the seven angels had been accomplished.

16.1   Then I heard a loud voice from the Temple telling the seven angels, "Go, and empty the seven bowls of the wrath of God on to the earth!"[30]

So the first angel went and emptied his bowl on the land, and an evil and malignant ulcer broke out on the men who had the stamp of the Beast, and who worshipped his image.

The second angel emptied his bowl into the sea, and it

---

26 cf *Targ Onkel* at *Deut* 32:4: "Ascribe ye greatness unto our God, the Mighty One whose works are perfect, for all his ways are justice . . . just and true is he".

27 cf *Exod* 15:11 and *Ps* 86:8–10.

28 Again there comes a solemn moment before the judgments on the nations begin. The bowls symbol is used appropriately in accordance with *Ps* 79:6–7.

29 *Isa* 6:4.

30 The judgments intensify those inflicted on Israel, and are reminiscent of the Plagues of Egypt (cf *I Pet* 4:17). They are still future, but the seer may have had in mind the great eruption of Vesuvius (cf *Sibyl Orac* IV 130–136), and the plague "such as was scarcely ever known before" (Suet. *Titus*, 8).

turned like the blood of a corpse, and everything in the sea that had the breath of life died.

The third angel emptied his bowl on the rivers and springs of water, and they turned to blood.

5 Then I heard the angel of the waters say, "Just art thou who Art and Wast, the Holy One, that thou has judged thus; for they have shed the blood of saints and prophets, and thou hast given them blood to drink as they deserve."

And I heard the altar say, "Even so, Lord God Almighty. True and just are thy judgments."

The fourth angel emptied his bowl on the sun, and it was permitted to scorch men with fire. And men were scorched with a burning heat, and blasphemed the Name of God who had control over these plagues; yet they did not repent so as to offer him praise.

10 The fifth angel emptied his bowl on the seat of the Beast, and his realm was plunged into darkness. And they gnawed their tongues in agony, and blasphemed the God of heaven because of their agony, and because of their ulcers; yet they did not repent of their deeds.

The sixth angel emptied his bowl on the great river Euphrates, and its stream was dried up, that the way of the Kings of the East might be prepared.[31]

The Dragon gathers his Forces

Now I saw issue from the mouth of the Dragon, and the mouth of the Beast, and the mouth of the False Prophet, three foul spirits like frogs. These are the spirits of wonder-working demons, on a mission to the kings of the entire world, to gather them together for the battle of the Great Day of God Almighty.[32] And they gathered them together to the place called in Hebrew ARMAGEDDON.[33]

31 The eastern forces come this time as enemies, not as allies, of Rome. "Then shall come to the west the strife of war stirred up, and the exiled man of Rome (Nero redivivus), lifting up a mighty sword, crossing the Euphrates with many tens of thousands" (*Sibyl Orac* IV 137–139).

32 cf *I Ki* 22:19–23 for the source of the thought of the foul spirits enticing the kings to battle.

33 Probably an adaptation of the Hebrew 'Rama-Gad-Yavan' (Rama of Gad of the Greeks) as a contemporary name of the ancient Ramoth-Gilead (*I Ki* 22:20). Gad-Yavan occurs as a place name in the Mishnah (*Zab* 1:5). cf Arimathea for the Hebrew *Ramathaim*. In the OT story one of the kings concerned is Jehoshaphat (the Lord is Judge), with which the seer may be linking *Joel* 3:9–17, calling all nations to the Valley of Jehoshaphat, "for there will I sit to judge all the heathen round about".

15　　　*I will surely come like a thief. Happy is he who is on the alert
and retains his garments,*[34] *lest he go about naked and they see
his shame.*

Then the seventh angel emptied his bowl in the air.
And a loud voice issued from the Temple, from the
throne, saying, "It is done!" Then came lightning
flashes, voices, and peals of thunder, and a great earthquake such as there had never been since man was on the
earth, so prolonged and so violent a quake. The Great
City was split into three parts, and the cities of the
Gentiles fell, and Great Babylon was remembered before
God to be given the goblet of the strong wine of his
20　wrath. Every island vanished, mountains disappeared
from existence, and a fiery hail, the stones weighing
about a talent,[35] rained on men from heaven. And men
blasphemed God because of the plague of hail, for the
plague was indeed terrible.

Vision of the Woman on the Scarlet Beast

17.1　　　One of the angels with the seven bowls now came and
spoke to me and said, "Come, and I will show you the
judgment of the Great Harlot who sits on many waters,[36]
with whom the kings of the earth have committed
immorality, and the inhabitants of the earth have
become intoxicated with the wine of her immorality."

He conveyed me in spirit to the desert; and there I saw
a Woman seated on a Scarlet Beast studded with blasphemous titles, and which had seven heads and ten
horns. The Woman was arrayed in purple and scarlet
decked out with gold, precious stones and pearls. In her
right hand she held a golden goblet filled with abomin-
5　ations and the foulness of her immorality.[37] On her
forehead there was written the significant title, GREAT
BABYLON, MOTHER OF HARLOTS AND EARTH'S
ABOMINATIONS.

I saw the woman intoxicated with the blood of the

---

34 In the Temple the captain of the guard went the rounds at night, and if any
of the watch was found dozing at his post he set fire to his garments with his
torch (*Midd* 1:2).

35 This was the weight of the stones thrown by the Roman engines (Jos. *Jewish
War*, III 6:167). The enemy now receives his own with interest.

36 See *Jer* 51:12–13. Here the woman is Rome. "Then shall the world be ruled
under a woman's hand, and obey her in all things" (*Sibyl Orac* Bk III 75).

37 The image may have been taken from a representation on a coin, or mural
decoration of the time.

Saints, and the blood of the martyrs of Jesus, and I marvelled greatly at the sight of her.

The angel said to me, "Why are you amazed? I will tell you the significance of the Woman, and of the Beast with seven heads and ten horns that carries her. The Beast you have seen was, and is not, and is about to rise out of the Abyss and go to destruction.[38] Those who dwell on earth will be amazed, whose names have not been written from the foundation of the world in the Book of Life, when they see that the Beast was, and is not, yet still is.[39]

This is where the intelligent mind is required. The seven heads are seven hills[40] on which the Woman is
10   seated. And there are seven kings[41]: five have fallen, one is, and the other has not yet come; but when he does come he will only continue for a short time. The Beast which was, and is not, he is himself the eighth, and is of the seven, and will go to destruction. The ten horns you have seen are ten kings, who have not yet received their kingdoms, but will receive royal authority with the Beast for one hour. They will be united in their resolve to offer their royal authority to the Beast. They will fight with the Lamb, but the Lamb will overcome them, for he is supreme lord and king, and those who are on his side are called, chosen, and loyal.
15   "The waters you have seen," he told me, "where the Harlot is seated, and peoples and masses, nations and tongues. Both the ten horns you have seen, and the Beast, will hate the Harlot, and make her naked and solitary, and devour her flesh, and burn her with fire;[42] for God has put it into their minds to execute his will, and to be united in their resolve to offer their royal power to

---

38 The Beast is the Imperial power which supports Rome, and in particular Nero, "who was, is not, yet still is". He was believed to have escaped and expected to return. He is "about to rise from the Abyss".

39 "Was, and is not, yet still is." While the words have a special meaning, they are also the deliberate perversion of "Who Is, and Was, and Shall be", used of God.

40 The seven hills of Rome.

41 The kings are the emperors Gaius (first to order his statue to be worshipped), Claudius, Nero, Vespasian, and Titus. The one 'who is' is Domitian, and the one to come for a brief time is Nerva (reigned AD 96–98). The eighth who is of the seven will be the returned Nero.

42 Nero-Antichrist, now anti-Rome, with his ten allies, "the Kings of the East", will attack and destroy Rome.

the Beast until God's pronouncements are accomplished. And the Woman you have seen is that Great City which exercises sovereignty over the kings of the earth."

The Doom of Rome

18.1   After this I saw another angel with great authority descend from heaven, and the earth was illumined by his glory. With stentorian voice he cried, "GREAT BABYLON HAS FALLEN, HAS FALLEN, and has become the habitation of demons, and the haunt of every foul spirit, and the haunt of every foul and hateful bird;[43] for all nations have drunk the strong wine of her immorality, the kings of the earth have committed immorality with her, and the merchants of the earth have grown rich through her insatiable desires."

Then I heard another voice from heaven say, "Leave her, my people, lest you participate in her sins, and 5 partake of her plagues, for her sins have piled up to heaven, and God has remembered her iniquities.[44] Treat her as she has treated you, and doubly so, in accordance with her deeds.[45] In the very goblet she mixed for others, mix double for her. To the extent that she has glorified herself and waxed wanton, by so much render to her anguish and sorrow. For she says to herself, 'I sit a queen, and am no widow. Sorrow I shall never know.' Therefore in a single day her plagues shall come, death and sorrow, and famine,[46] and by fire she shall be consumed; for mighty is the Lord God who judges her.[47] "The kings of the earth, who have committed immorality and been wanton with her, shall mourn and lament over her when they see the smoke of her conflagration, 10 keeping their distance from fear of her torment, and

43 cf *Isa* 13:19–22; 24:14.
44 cf *Jer* 50:8; 51:9.
45 *Jer* 50:15; *Ps* 137:8.
46 *Isa* 42:8–9.
47 With the general picture may be compard *Sibyl Orac* IV 159–179: "And from heaven a great star shall fall on the dread ocean and burn up the deep sea, with Babylon itself and the land of Italy, the cause that many of the Hebrews perished, holy and faithful, and the people of truth . . . Woe to thee, thou city of the Latin land, all unclean, thou maenad circled with vipers, thou shalt sit a widow on thy hills . . . Thou saidst, 'I am alone, and none shall depoil me.' Yet now shall God who lives for ever destroy both thee and thine . . . Abide thou alone, thou lawless city, wrapt in burning fire."

saying, 'Alas, alas, for that great city Babylon, that mighty city! In a single hour your judgment has come!'

"The merchants of the earth shall mourn and lament over her;[48] for now there are none to buy their cargoes, cargoes of gold and silver, precious stones and pearls, fine linen and purple, silk and scarlet, loads of aromatic wood and articles of ivory, articles of rare woods, bronze, iron and marble, cinnamon and spices of the orient, incense, myrrh and frankincense, wine and olive oil, wheat and fine flour, sheep and cattle, horses and chariots, and bodies and souls of men.

"The luscious fruits your soul craved for are gone from you. All your fads and fancies are gone from you, and never shall you indulge them more.

15   "The traders in these things, who have been enriched by her, shall anchor at a distance from fear of her torment, mourning and lamenting, and saying, 'Alas, alas, for that great city, which was arrayed in fine linen, purple, and scarlet, and decked out with gold, precious stones and pearls! All that wealth is gone, gone in a single hour!'

"And every navigator and voyager, the sailors and seafarers, standing at a distance will cry as they watch the smoke of her conflagration, 'Where is the like of this great city?' Throwing dust on their heads, they will mourn and lament, crying, 'Alas, alas, for that great city, by whose ample means all with ships at sea were enriched! All is gone, gone in a single hour!'

20   "But rejoice over her, O heaven, and you Saints, Envoys and Prophets; for God has executed your judgment on her."

Then a strong angel lifted a stone like a huge millstone, and flung it into the sea, exclaiming, "Thus with violence shall that great city Babylon be thrown down, and never rise again![49] Never again shall the music of harpists, musicians, flautists, and trumpeters, be heard in you![50] Never again shall craftsmen of any craft be found in you! Never again shall the sound of a mill be heard in you! Never again shall the light of a lamp shine in you! Never again shall be heard in you the voice of bridegroom and

---

48 cf the prophecy against Tyre, *Ezek* 27.
49 cf *Jer* 51:63–64.
50 cf *Ezek* 26:13–14.

bride! Your merchants were the princes of the earth; for all nations were bewitched by your spells. But in her was found the blood of Prophets and Saints and all who were butchered on earth."

The Paeans of Praise in Heaven

19.1   After this I heard the sound as of a mighty throng in heaven saying,

> *Hallelujah!*[51]
> *Salvation, glory, and power,*
> *Be unto our God;*
> *For true and just are his judgments.*
> *He hath judged the Great Harlot,*
> *Who corrupted the earth with her vice;*
> *And hath avenged at her hands*
> *The blood of his servants.*[52]

Once more they said, "Hallelujah! Her smoke shall ascend for ever."

Then the twenty-four Elders and the four Living-Creatures prostrated themselves and worshipped God who sits on the throne, saying, "Amen. Hallelujah!"

5   While a voice issuing from the throne said, "O sing unto our God, all ye his servants, ye who revere him, both high and low."[53]

Then I heard the sound of a vast concourse, like the booming of many waters, and like peals of heavy thunder, saying,

> *Hallelujah!*
> *For the Lord God Almighty reigneth,*
> *Let us be glad and rejoice,*[54]
> *And render praise to him;*
> *For the Lamb's wedding-day is here,*
> *And his spouse hath made herself ready.*

She was permitted to be robed in pure shining white linen.[55] (The fine linen represents the state of righteous-

---

51 See the opening of the festal Hallel Psalms (*Ps* 113–118), which were sung in the Temple by the choir.

52 cf *Targ Pal* at *Deut* 32:41: "Rejoice ye nations, and ye people of the house of Israel; for he hath avenged the blood of his servants which was shed". Again the seer looks to the *Song of Moses*.

53 cf *Ps* 113:1; 115:11.

54 cf *Ps* 118:24.

55 The robes of priests in the Temple in a state of ritual purity.

ness of the Saints.)

Then he said to me, "Write this down. Happy are those who are invited to the wedding-banquet of the Lamb. These are God's very words", he added.

10   At this I prostrated myself at his feet and worshipped him. But he said to me, "Forbear! I am only the fellow-servant of you and your brothers who have the testimony of Jesus. Worship God." (The testimony of Jesus means the spirit of prophecy.)

The Battle with the Beast

Now I saw heaven open, and there was a White Horse whose rider is faithful and true, and who judges and fights with justice. His eyes were like a fiery flame, and on his head were many crowns with a title engraved on them which no one but himself understands. He was clad in a robe spattered with blood,[56] and bore the name "The Word of God".

Behind him on white horses followed the heavenly
15   hosts, clad in pure white linen, while from his mouth there projected a sharp two-edged sword with which to smite the nations. He shall herd them with an iron-shod staff;[57] and it is he who shall tread the winepress of the wrath of God Almighty.[58] On his robe and upon his thigh he bears the title, "Supreme King and Lord".

Then I saw an angel standing in the sun, and he shouted loudly to all the birds that fly in midheaven, "Come, flock to the great feast of God, and devour the flesh of kings, and the flesh of captains, and the flesh of warriors, and the flesh of horses and their riders, and the flesh of men in general, free and slave, high and low."[59]

Now I saw the Beast, and the kings of the earth, and their armies, assembled to do battle with the rider on the
20   horse and his hosts. And the Beast was captured, and with him the False Prophet who performed signs in his presence by which those who had received the stamp of the Beast and worshipped his image had been deceived. Both of them were flung alive into the Lake of Fire

56 cf *Isa* 63:1–4.
57 *Ps* 2:9.
58 *Isa* 63:3.
59 cf *Ezek* 39:17–20.

burning with sulphur,[60] while the rest were slain by the sword of the rider on the horse, which projected from his mouth; and all the birds were glutted with their flesh.[61]

The Millennium and Fate of the Dragon

20.1   Then I saw an angel descend from heaven with the key of the Abyss and a heavy chain in his hand. And he seized the Dragon, the primeval Serpent, who is the Devil and Satan, and bound him for a thousand years, hurled him into the Abyss, and locked and sealed him up; so that he should deceive the nations no more till the thousand years were ended. Thereafter he has to be freed for a brief period.

I also saw thrones and those who were seated on them, to whom judgment was referred, together with the souls of those beheaded for the testimony of Jesus and for the sake of God's Message. These had not worshipped the Beast or his image, did not receive his stamp on their forehead; and they lived and reigned with
5   the Messiah for a thousand years. The rest of the dead, however, did not come to life until the thousand years were ended.

This constitutes the First Resurrection. Happy and blessed is he who shares in the First Resurrection. Over such as these the Second Death has no power. They will be priests of God and the Messiah, and will reign with him a thousand years.

When the thousand years have ended Satan will be freed from his prison, and will go out to deceive the nations that are in the four corners of the earth, Gog and Magog, and assemble them for battle, the number of whom is as the sand of the sea. Across the breadth of the earth they came up, and encircled the encampment of the Saints and the Beloved City.[62] But fire fell from
10   heaven and devoured them, and their deceiver the Devil was flung into the Lake of Fire and sulphur where the

---

60 cf *Apoc Bar* 40:1–3: "The last leader of that time will be left alive, when the multitude of his hosts will be put to the sword, and be bound; and they will take him up to Mt Zion, and my Messiah will convict him of all his impieties . . . Afterwards he will put him to death, and protect the rest of my people . . . And his (Messiah's) principate will stand for ever, until the world of corruption is at an end, and until the times aforesaid are fulfilled."
61 cf *Sibyl Orac* Bk IV 697–698: "The very earth shall drink the blood of the slain, and the beasts shall be glutted with their flesh."
62 cf on this passage *Ezek* 38–39; *Joel* 3; *Zech* 14.

Beast and the False Prophet already were; and they will be tormented day and night for ever and ever.

The Last Judgment and Final Age

Now I saw a great White Throne and him who sat on it, from whose presence earth and heaven fled and were lost to view. And I saw the dead, high and low, standing before the throne and the books were opened.[63] Another book was also opened, the Book of Life, and the dead were judged according to their deeds by what was recorded in the books. The sea presented the dead who were in it, and Death and Hades presented the dead who were in them, and they were judged each one according to their deeds. Then Death and Hades were flung into the Lake of Fire. This, the Lake of Fire, is the Second Death, and whoever was not found inscribed in the Book of Life was flung into the Lake of Fire.

15

21.1 Now I saw a new heaven and a new earth.[64] The previous heaven and earth had passed away, and the sea existed no longer. I also saw the City, the New Jerusalem, descending from heaven from God in all her glory, like a bride adorned for her husband.[65]

I also heard a loud voice from the throne say, "Behold, God's dwelling-place is with men, and he will dwell among them.[66] And they shall be his people, and God himself will be with them and wipe all tears from their eyes, and there shall be no more death. Neither shall there be sorrow, nor mourning, nor grief any more. The old conditions have passed away."[67]

5

Then he who sat on the throne said, "Lo, I make everything anew." He said also, "Write this down, for these words are trustworthy and true."

[Then he said to me, "It is done. I am the Alpha and Omega, the Beginning and the End. To the thirsty I will give freely of the spring of the Water of Life. The victor shall inherit all this, and I will be his God, and he shall be

---

63 *Dan* 7:10.
64 cf *Isa* 65:17; *Enoch* 45:4–5, 91:16; and *Targ Jer* at *Deut* 32:1.
65 cf *Isa* 61:10 and *Test Dan* 5:12–13: "And the saints shall rest in Eden, and in the New Jerusalem will the righteous rejoice, and it shall be unto the glory of God for ever. And no longer shall Jerusalem endure desolation, nor Israel be led captive; for the Lord shall be in the midst of it."
66 cf *Ezek* 48:35.
67 *Isa* 43:18–19.

my son. But the cowardly, the disloyal, the vicious, the murderous, the immoral, sorcerers, idolaters, and all liars, shall have their portion (which is the Second Death) in the Lake that burns with fire and sulphur."][68]

Vision of the New Jerusalem[69]

Now there came one of the seven angels who had the seven bowls filled with the seven last plagues, and said to me, "Come, and I will show you the Bride, the Lamb's wife."

10   He conveyed me in spirit to the summit of a huge and lofty mountain,[70] and showed me the Holy City, the new Jerusalem, which had descended from heaven from God, possessing the glory of God. The brightness of it was like some precious stone, like polished jasper. It had an immense and high wall, with twelve gates, and at the gates were twelve angels, while engraved on the gates were names, those of the twelve tribes of Israel.[71] On the east were three gates, on the north were three gates, on the south were three gates, and on the west were three gates. The wall of the city had twelve foundation-stones, and on these were the twelve names of the twelve envoys of the Lamb.

15   Now he who spoke to me had a golden measuring-reed,[72] so that he could measure the City, with its gates and wall. The City lay foursquare, the length and breadth of it being the same. His measurement of the City with the reed came out at twelve thousand stadia. The length, the breadth and the height of it were identical. Its wall measured a hundred and forty-four cubits, man's standard of measurement (which was the angel's standard).[73] The wall was constructed of jasper, and the City itself of pure gold like clear glass. The foundations of the City's wall were adorned with all kinds of precious stones;[74] the first foundation-stone with jasper, the second with sapphire, the third with chalcedony, the

20   fourth with emerald, the fifth with onyx, the sixth with

68 We have here an interpolation by John the Elder.
69 It has been considered that this section should immediately follow 21:2.
70 *Isa* 2:2; *Ezek* 40:2. Jewish legend has it that the mountains Tabor, Carmel, and Zion, will be piled on one another, and Jerusalem set on top of them.
71 *Ezek* 40:3.
72 See *Ezek* 48:30ff.
73 Symbolic multiples of twelve.
74 *Isa* 44:11–12.

sardius, the seventh with chrysolite, the eighth with beryl, the ninth with topaz, the tenth with chrysoprase, the eleventh with jacinth, and the twelfth with amethyst. The twelve gates were twelve pearls, each gate a single pearl; and the streets of the city were of pure gold plate like transparent glass.

25   I saw no Temple in it; for the Lord God Almighty is its Temple [and the Lamb]. The City requires neither sun nor moon to shine on it; for the glory of God illumines it[75] [and its lamp is theLamb]. The nations shall walk in the light of it and the kings of the earth will bring their splendour into it.[76] The gates of it shall never be shut from day to day[77] (for there will be no night there). They will admit the glory and pride of the nations into it, but there shall never enter it anything profane,[78] or anything that causes idolatry[79] or deceit, only those who are inscribed in the Book of Life [of the Lamb].[80]

22.1   Then he showed me the river of the Water of Life clear as crystal flowing from the throne of God[81] [and the Lamb] down the middle of the street of the City. And on either side of the river grew the Tree of Life bearing twelve kinds of fruit, yielding its fruit for each month respectively, while the leaves of the tree were for the healing of the nations. There will be no more anything accursed. The throne of God [and of the Lamb] will be in the City, and his servants will minister to him, and behold his face, and his name shall be on their foreheads.

5   There will be night no more, neither will they have need of the light of lamp or light of the sun; for the Lord God will shine upon them, and they shall reign for ever and ever.

    And he said to me, "This information is trustworthy and true. The Lord God of the holy Prophets sent his angel to show his servants what is about to take place." [Behold, I am coming very soon. Blessed be he who notes what is said in the predictions of this book.]

---

75 *Isa* 60:19–20.
76 *Isa* 60:3.
77 *Isa* 60:11.
78 *Isa* 52:1.
79 Lit "abomination".
80 Only those ordained to enter shall go into the New Jerusalem (*Baba Bathra*, fol. 75b).
81 On this passage see *Ezek* 47:1–12.

Epilogue

I, John, heard and saw all this, and when I had seen and heard it I prostrated myself at the feet of the angel who had shown me these things. But he said to me, "Forbear. I am only the fellow-servant of yourself and your brothers the Prophets, and of those who heed the prophetic message of this book. Worship God."

10   And he[82] said to me, "Do not seal up the words of the prophecy of this book; for the time is at hand. He that is unjust, let him stay unjust; and he who is vile, let him stay vile; and he that is righteous, let him stay righteous and he who is holy, let him stay holy. [I shall come very soon. My reward is with me to give to each what his actions have merited.][83]

....

15   "I am the Alpha and Omega, the First and the Last, the Beginning and the End. Happy are those who wash their robes that they may have a claim upon the Tree of Life and enter by the gates into the City. Outside are the dogs, the sorcerers, the immoral, murderers, idolaters, and all who love and practise what is false.

"I, Jesus, have sent my angel to testify these things to you for the communities. I am the stock and scion of David, the bright Morning Star."

Both the Spirit and the Bride say, "Come!" Let the hearer too say, "Come!" Let him who is thirsty come. Let whoever wishes take the Water of Life freely.

I testify to all who hear the prophetic words of this book that if anyone shall add to them, God will add to him the plagues set down in this book.[84] And if anyone subtracts from the words of the book of this prophecy, God will subtract from him his share in the Tree of Life, and in the Holy City, the matters recorded in this book.

20   He who testifies to these things says, "*I shall come very soon.*"

Amen. Come, Lord Jesus!

The loving-kindness of the Lord Jesus Christ be with the Saints.[85]

82 The speaker is again the Angel of Jesus.
83 Either the whole Epilogue, or from this point, would appear to be the work of John the Elder.
84 cf Jos. *Against Apion*, 1:8, referring to the Old Testament: "No one has been so bold as either to add anything to them or take anything from them".
85 The work in its present form is framed in a letter (1:4).

CHRONOLOGY OF NEW TESTAMENT TIMES

Death of Herod the Great. Archelaus becomes ruler of Judea, and Herod Antipas tetrarch of Galilee and Perea	4 BC
Jewish Sabbatical Year	5–6 AD
Archelaus deposed. Judea united to Roman Province of Syria. Quirinius legate of Syria, and Coponius procurator of Judea	6
Roman tax Census taken. Ananus son of Seth made high priest	6–7
Jewish Sabbatical Year	12–13
Death of Augustus Caesar. Accession of Tiberius	14
Jewish Sabbatical Year	19–20
Roman Census Year	20–21
Joseph Caiaphas made high priest	25
Pontius Pilate procurator of Judea in succession to Valerius Gratus	26
Jewish Sabbatical Year	26–27
Activities of John the Baptist	(c)30–34
Jewish Sabbatical Year	33–34
Jesus baptised by John (?)	34
Roman Census Year. Initial activities of Jesus. Arrest of John the Baptist	34–35
Execution of John by Herod Antipas	35
War between Herod and the Nabataeans (winter)	35–36
Crucifixion of Jesus by Pilate (spring)	36
Nazarene Community at Jerusalem formed (summer)	
L. Vitellius, legate of Syria visits Jerusalem, deposes Caiaphas as high priest and appoints Jonathan son of Annas against him	
Attack on Nazarenes by Saul of Tarsus. Many seek refuge in Batanea and Auranitis (winter)	

	AD
Death of the Emperor Tiberius, succeeded by Gaius Caligula (March)	37
Damascus leased by the Emperor Gaius to Aretas IV, king of the Nabateans	
Saul of Tarsus, now a Nazorean, leaves Damascus for Nabatean Arabia	
Nazarene influence extended by refugees. Groups formed include one at Syrian Antioch, where disciples first called Christians	37–38
Central Nazarene Authority created at Jerusalem under Jacob (James) brother of Jesus	38
P. Petronius appointed legate of Syria by Gaius	39
Saul returns to Damascus, escapes arrest, and visits Jerusalem. He is sent to Tarsus	
The Emperor Gaius designs to have his statue placed in the Temple at Jerusalem	
The Jews protest about the statue to Petronius, while in Rome King Agrippa seeks to dissuade the Emperor	40
Jewish Sabbatical Year	40–41
The Emperor Gaius assassinated, succeeded by Claudius (Jan. 41)	
Herod Agrippa made king of Judea	
Saul is brought to Antioch by the Nazarene Cypriot Barnabas	
Martyrdom of James son of Zebedee	43
Agrippa imprisons Peter, but his escape is contrived (spring)	44
Death of King Agrippa	
Cassius Longinus legate of Syria	45
Great famine in Israel	46
Tiberius Alexander procurator of Judea	
Jewish Sabbatical Year	47–48
First missionary journey of Saul (Paul) and Barnabas	
Roman Census Year	48–49
Tiberius Alexander acts against the Nazarenes and Zealots. Jacob and Simon, sons of Judas of Galilee, crucified	
Nazarenes launch missionary campaign in many parts of the Roman Empire	
Controversy at Antioch on status of Gentile believers in Jesus, followed by Nazarene Council meeting at Jerusalem on this issue	49–50

	AD
Messianic propaganda spread by Jewish Zealots in many parts of the Roman Empire. Claudius expels foreign Jews from Rome and warns the Alexandrians	
Paul's second missionary journey begins. First Christian propaganda documents in Greek (not in New Testament) initiated about this time	50
Disorders in Galilee and Judea, and Romans attack Jewish Zealots to prevent a rebellion	51–52
Paul at Athens and Corinth	
Paul returns to Antioch after keeping Pentecost at Jerusalem. In early summer he begins his third missionary journey	53
Jewish Sabbatical Year	54–55
Death of Claudius and accession of Nero (Oct.)	54
The Zealots and Prophets active in Judea, and Nazarene militants campaign against Paul in some of the communities created by him	
Jewish *Sicarii* (dagger-men) in Jerusalem. They assassinate the high priest Jonathan son of Annas	55
Anti-Roman hostility expands in Israel, with faction and class-war. Some of the Sadducean hierarchy start to rob the poor and patriotic priests of their share of the tithes	55–58
Paul reports to Nazarene Council at Jerusalem bringing gifts from the Gentile Christian communities (spring)	58
Paul is held prisoner by the Romans after being attacked in the Temple. Sent to Caesarea to appear before the procurator Felix. He is remanded in custody	
Ananias deposed as high priest by Agrippa II. Replaced by Ishmael son of Pheabi	59
Porcius Festus procurator of Judea. Paul is sent to Rome, having appealed to Caesar	60
Paul eventually reaches Rome as a prisoner	61
Agrippa gives the high priesthood to Joseph Cabi	
Jewish Sabbatical Year	61–62
Ananus, son of Annas now high priest	62
Jacob (James), brother of Jesus, executed by Ananus after death of Festus	

	AD
Albinus becomes procurator of Judea, and Ananus is deposed as high priest by Agrippa	
First hearing of Paul's appeal in Rome	
Second hearing and condemnation	63–64
Great Fire of Rome. Many Christians executed	64
Martyrdom of Peter (date uncertain)	
Rebuilt Temple at Jerusalem finally completed	65
Simeon son of Cleophas, cousin of Jesus, becomes leader of the Nazarenes	
The Jews are goaded into revolt against the Romans	
Nazarenes remove their government from Jerusalem to Transjordan	
Jewish War with Rome begins	66
Death of Emperor Nero	68
Vespasian becomes Emperor. His son Titus captures Jerusalem	70
Death of Vespasian. Accession of Titus	79
Death of Titus. Accession of Domitian	81
Period of production of written *Gospels* commences	
Emperor Domitian persecutes the Christians	85–95
Domitian assassinated. Accession of Nerva	96
Death of Nerva. Accession of Trajan	98
Martyrdom of Simeon son of Cleophas	(c) 100

Note: Dating of Christian events is approximate

Bibliography of Antique Sources Employed

The Old Testament and Apocrypha

Where the references are to the Greek Version this is indicated by the Roman numerals LXX (the Septuagint).

The New Testament

Manuscripts in Greek, Latin, Syriac and Hebrew. The Latin is commonly known as the Vulgate. The chief Greek codices are Sinaiticus and Alexandrinus, while others employed are:

Codex D (Bezae) on *Luke-Acts*
Curetonian Syriac on *Luke*
(Sin. Syr.) Sinaitic Syriac on
   Luke
Old Hebrew (Du Tillet)
   version of *Matthew*
Old Latin versions of *Matthew*
   and *Luke*

The Targums Aramaic Paraphrases of the Pentateuch

Targum of Jerusalem
Targum of Onkelos
Targum of Palestine (or of
   Jonathan ben Uzziel)

Apocalyptic and Pseudepigraphic Writings

Ahikar, Book of
Apocalypse of Baruch
Apocalypse of Ezra
Assumption of Moses

Enoch, Book of
Psalms of Solomon
Sibylline Oracles
Testaments of the XII Patriarchs:
   Testament of Levi
   Testament of Judah
   Testament of Dan
   Testament of Naphtali
   Testament of God
   Testament of Joseph
   Testament of Benjamin

Books of the Essenes

Including:
Commentary on Habakkuk
(DD) *Damascus Document*
Manual of Discipline

Classics: Roman, Greek and Jewish Authors[1]

Aratus, *Phenomena*
Callimachus, *Hymn to Zeus*
Claudius, *Letter to the*
   Alexandrians
Cleanthes, *Hymn to Zeus*
Dio Cassius, *History*
Epimenides
Horace, *Odes*
Josephus,
   Against Apion
   Antiquities of the Jews
   Jewish War
Menander
Philo Judaeus, *Works*
Pliny, *Natural History*
Pliny the Younger,
   Letter to Trajan
Plutarch, *Lives*
Suetonius, *Lives of the Caesars*
Tacitus,
   Annals
   History
Virgil, *Aeneid*

1 Special appreciation is expressed to the Loeb Classical Library.

Early Christian Literature

Abgar, Letter of
Acts of Barnabas
Acts of Paul and Thekla
Acts of Pilate
Didache: Teaching of the
   XII Apostles
Eusebius, *Ecclesiastical History*
Gospel according to the Hebrews
Gospel of the Nativity of Mary
Gospel of Peter
Jerome, *Letter to Augustine*
Julius Africanus, *Letter to*
   Aristides
Odes of Solomon
Papias, *Exposition of the*
   Dominical Oracles
Prochorus, *Acts of John*

Rabbinical Literature
(The *Mishnah*[2])

Berachoth
Kilaim
Shekalim
Taanith
Nazir
Sanhedrin
Aboth
Middoth
Zabim

Rabbinical Literature
(The *Talmud*[3])

Shabbath
Megilah

2 The Jewish ('Oral Law') as compiled by Rabbi Judah the Patriarch at the close
   of the second century AD. The order of the various tractates is followed here.
3 The Talmud consists of the Mishnah with the Gemara (Rabbinical discus-
   sions on the Mishnah). TJ before the name of a tractate refers to the
   Palestinean rescension (*Talmud Jerushalmi*), compiled towards the end of the
   fourth century AD. All other references are to the Babylonian rescension
   (*Talmud Babli*) about a century later.

(TJ) *Taanith*
Chagigah
Sotah
Gittin
Baba Kama
Baba Bathra
Sanhedrin
Aboda Zara
Arachin

Special Sources

Midrashim (various)
(AJP) *Authorised (Jewish)*
   Prayer Book (Singer)
(JE) *Jewish Encyclopaedia.*
Archaeological discoveries.
Linguistic studies
The Passover Plot
The Pentecost Revolution